Heretics and Scholars
in the
High Middle Ages

1000–1200

Other books by Heinrich Fichtenau in English translation:

Living in the Tenth Century: Mentalities and Social Orders
The Carolingian Empire: The Age of Charlemagne

Heinrich Fichtenau

Heretics and Scholars in the High Middle Ages

1000–1200

Translated by
Denise A. Kaiser

The Pennsylvania State University Press
University Park, Pennsylvania

This English translation of *Ketzer und Professoren: Häresie und Vernunftglaube im Hochmittelalter* was made possible through the kind support of the Austrian Bundesministerium für Wissenschaft und Verkehr and the Bundesministerium für Auswärtige Angelegenheiten. Thanks are due the Institut für Österreichische Geschichtsforschung in Vienna for making this support possible.

Published with the support of the Austrian Cultural Institute, New York.

Library of Congress Cataloging-in-Publication Data

Fichtenau, Heinrich.
    [Ketzer und Professoren. English]
    Heretics and scholars in the high Middle Ages, 1000–1200 /
Heinrich Fichtenau ; translated by Denise A. Kaiser.
       p.   cm.
    Includes bibliographical references and index.
    ISBN 0–271–01765–1 (alk. paper)
    1. Heresies, Christian—History—Middle Ages, 600–1500.
    2. Rationalism—History.   3. Europe—Church history—600–1500.   I. Title.
    BT1319.F5313   1998
    272'.6—dc21
                                                97-33622
                                                CIP

First published in Germany as *Ketzer und Professoren: Häresie und Vernunftglaube im Hochmittelalter*. © C. H. Beck´sche Verlagsbuchhandlung (Oscar Beck), München 1992

English translation © 1998 The Pennsylvania State University
All rights reserved
Printed in the United States of America
Published by The Pennsylvania State University Press,
University Park, PA 16802-1003

Contents

Translator's Note

This English translation of *Ketzer und Professoren: Häresie und Vernunft-glaube im Hochmittelalter,* by Heinrich Fichtenau (Munich: C. H. Beck, 1992), has enjoyed the support of many individuals and institutions. First and foremost of those deserving thanks is Professor Fichtenau himself. While preparing the translation, I was privileged to be able to turn to him *ad libitum* for sympathetic and valuable advice. He has taken an intimate interest in almost all aspects of the English version: graciously reviewing and suggesting modifications to the text, refining passages to clarify his views for an English-speaking audience, and updating footnotes and bibliographical references. On occasion, he has even favored this medievalist with brief notes summarizing the reasoning behind particular passages and statements.

An engaging and scholarly author is, however, but the first, though essential, party to the preparation of an academic book. Penn State Press and Mr. Peter Potter are to be thanked for recognizing the value of this work and undertaking its publication. As a laudable service to its readers, the press has decided to preserve the scholarly apparatus. It should be noted that the title gracing this book was the product of a thoughtful exchange between the press and Professor Fichtenau. Thanks are due the Austrian Bundesministerium für Wissenschaft und Verkehr and the Bundesministerium für Auswärtige Angelegenheiten for their support which made possible this translation. Thanks are also due the Austrian Cultural Institute and Peter Mikl, Attaché for Science and the Arts, in New York City, for lending their support to this project.

In keeping with the German text, I have striven to produce a translation absorbing to the academic adept, yet accessible to the academic novice. Should either type of reader find the English version wanting, then the blame must be placed on me and my rhetorical inadequacies. Most illustrative of this guiding principle is the treatment of foreign-language citations. A number of Latin terms and phrases appear in the German version of the book. Since they are germane to the text, they are retained here and supplemented by English definitions, which I have based upon either the German translation offered by Professor Fichtenau (in parentheses) or the Latin original (square brackets). In the original text of this book, longer passages drawn from Latin or other non-English works were translated into German; in preparing the English text, I have either drawn upon that German version or, if the quotation occurs in a readily available English translation, used an excerpt and amended the note accordingly. Non-English quotations reproduced in the notes have been retained and translated, again either by myself (square brackets) or Professor Fichtenau (parentheses). For biblical citations, I have consulted the English Revised Standard Version and the Vulgate.

Fortune has in many respects smiled upon this undertaking. Its agents were the individuals mentioned above, and the members of my family and circle of friends. On a personal note, I wish to express my gratitude to my husband, Dr. Greg Dworkin, and my mother, Mrs. Hedy Kaiser, who have yet again sustained me during the performance of an exacting and exciting project.

Introduction

 "Do not engage in research if you wish not to go astray!" This pessimistic piece of advice was directed at theologians by a preacher whose master, Gilbert of Poitiers, had been brought up on charges of heresy.[1] Superfluous knowledge had always been viewed with skepticism, particularly by monks. As Jerome wrote, the monk was charged with grieving for himself and the world, not, however, with being a scholar.[2] That this remark was not to be taken literally is evident alone from the fact that Jerome himself founded a form of scholarly biblical exegesis. To be sure, anything beyond that and the study of patristic writings was deemed pointless by rigorists.[3] Whoever took an innovative tack might have voiced the same complaint about such individuals as had William of Conches: "They prefer to remain ignorant rather than consult others, and when they know that someone is engaging in research, they shout that he is a heretic."[4]

The medieval worldview was never as uniform as it might appear from the modern perspective, and the struggle over fundamental issues was never fiercer than in the eleventh and twelfth centuries. Under contention were the methods associated with scholarship: Was one to abide by the tried-and-true system, or was one to ascend to new heights, drawing upon the expertise of the Greek philosophers and possibly coming to doubt propositions passed down since time immemorial? "It is namely through doubt that we come to engage in research [and] through research that we come upon the truth."[5] It was common knowledge long before Montaigne and the sixteenth century that philosophizing means doubting or at least begins with doubt. This might have been sufferable in those instances where small intellectual groups of masters and their students were involved. It was more troubling when doubts about the religious doctrines of the church and particularly the function of the clergy seized the sorts of individuals who in earlier times would not have been expected to entertain such thoughts. Around 1000 various regions of the West were visited by heresies, which seemed to fade temporarily after 1051 and then came to light with growing force in the twelfth century. In the course of that very century, a sort of antichurch evolved, the Cathars, who had their own bishops, dioceses, and cloisters. This group's doctrine was a myth that accorded with contemporary feelings about life and its attendant problems.

It is up to the historian to describe the past and to venture an explanation. The simpler such explanations are, however, the less the historian puts his faith in them. Indeed, the phenomena involved here are quite often complex and proceed from a variety of different causes, even if the sources do not sufficiently document all of them. At the close of our century we can better understand some aspects of that long bygone age than could our predecessors. Yet, there is much that must remain unresolved or can only be surmised.

Why do we hear almost nothing about heretics over the course of so many generations and then so much after 1000? This cannot be due to a merely incidental silence on the part of the sources. A better explanation would be that in history there are relatively stable epochs and then those marked by sudden change, indeed unforeseen innovations. What is usually termed a quantum leap in physics and a mutation in biology has—to a limited degree—its parallel in history. In the eleventh century, as compared with the tenth century, many trends quickly gathered momentum.[6] There were developments of a far-reaching nature, and this was new as well, at least inasmuch as ideas that would previously have cropped up only in isolated and scattered instances gained broad exposure. Change affected quite distinct spheres of human existence, people's internal attitudes and their external conduct.

Of concern first of all is the role played by popular religiosity. We know that baptizing the inhabitants of the West was just the first step in the area's so-called Christianization. In a hodgepodge with Christian ideas, archaic notions continued to have an impact, and local saints' cults often influenced the daily religious life of laypeople more strongly than did faith in God. Now there were countervailing tendencies, a yearning among many for something fundamental and universal. As a consequence, these Christians were often alienated from the local cults and even the local clergy; they gained a clear view of the clergy's failure to attend to the pastoral needs of the common people—sometimes there was no one at all to attend to those needs, as in the growing settlements outside town walls (*suburbia*), or just a solitary priest.

Changes in the social framework may have promoted the new attitude, but they scarcely produced it—neither urban life nor the existence of craftspeople can seriously be credited with having caused heretical movements. Much the same holds true for the abuses by the lower clergy. Those were hardly any worse in the eleventh century than they had been in the ninth or tenth. Nevertheless, what was formerly tolerated now evoked protest. One might ask whether some individuals had not in fact experienced a change in attitude toward the established conditions. Was giving expression to crises triggered by developmental factors involved in this change?

The question should not spur historians to dabble in a field unfamiliar to them, that of human psychology. All the same, adolescent psychology does provide us with a clear-cut picture of personality crises, which normally have a positive value for the individual. With the disappearance of their "basic trust," maturing individuals analyze and criticize the world around them for no immediate reason, and they withdraw as much as possible from their environment, discovering their inner lives. What is for some but a passing developmental phase remains for others a decades-long feature of their lives. Some achieve a respite by acting out, while the majority endure the crisis period in silence. Even today there are few autobiographical accounts of this experience, and in the High Middle Ages they were far and away the exception. We do possess an eleventh-century account of the crisis of faith suffered by the young monk Otloh of St. Emmeram, and in the twelfth century the nun Elizabeth of Sch"nau was driven to the brink of suicide by doubts about Christ's nature.[7]

Monks and nuns were better equipped to extricate themselves from such difficulties than were laypeople. Many of the latter saw only the dark side of the world, in which the devil, rather than God, seemed to hold sway. To this very day such notions recur in times of trouble. During World War II, this author heard it said in the Ukraine: "There is no God, but the devil does exist." (Boga nema, a čort jest.)

If God confined his activity to the heavenly spheres and the earth was entrusted to the devil, was the latter perhaps the earth's creator? Count Raymond VI of Toulouse used to say, "It goes to show that the devil created the world, for nothing works out the way I want."[8]

Only a mighty lord could talk in that way. The "common" people of Provence would have been content just to cease feeling like the victims of oppression by both worldly and otherworldly powers. The Cathars residing there recounted that the apostles had implored Christ to grant them immunity from fearing anyone ever again. Christ responded that servants could not receive a greater boon than their lord.[9] The notion that the world was a vale of tears was a familiar one to Catholics as well; it was left to the Cathars to experience and describe it as hell.

Did these heretics lack that equanimity of spirit which along with a simple trust in God lends itself to overcoming adversity? An observation made by Tertullian as far back as the late second century bears recalling in this context: It was heretics and (pagan) philosophers in particular who wondered whence the evil in this world had come.[10] "Whence evil?" [Unde malum?]—this question was also posed by Christians who were not heretics, and with greater urgency among the common populace than among intellectuals, who readily drew solace from the scholarly and rather abstract determination that evil does not truly possess the quality of being. After the Bulgarian kingdom was conquered, devastated, and largely stripped of its inhabitants in the tenth century, this problem gained such currency there that it was viewed as the reason people were deserting the church. At the time a priest named Cosmas, who is our main source on the Bogomils, wrote, "We hear many of our [people] say, 'Why does God allow mankind to be attacked by the devil?'" Cosmas responded that it was necessary in order to distinguish the servants of God from those of the devil.[11] Not all Christians found such talk enlightening. Many remained members of the sect that the priest Bogomil had founded back in the days of the Bulgarian czardom.

The sectarians renounced the clergy, and of the things associated with Christian practice, they were able to look only to the Bible for guidance. That text spoke less about the devil than about abstract forms of evil: the desertion of Yahweh in the Old Testament, coldheartedness toward one's neighbor in the New. Hence, the heretics revamped the Bible with the help of the allegorical form of textual interpretation inherited from late antiquity—in general, however, by dispensing with almost the entire Old Testament. The Mosaic Law seemed to have been crafted by the evil enemy rather than by God. Above all, however, the sect adopted and further elaborated upon a myth that imparted new and exciting material about Satan to the Slavic peasantry: He was a son of God or perhaps even a god himself, but at any rate the creator of the world, thus apparently accounting for its evil nature. "Some [Bogomils] term him a fallen angel," Cosmas further recounted of their notions of Satan; "others make him the 'dishonest steward.'"[12] Biblical analogies were incorporated into the myth; since it was transmitted orally, no one was disturbed by the existence of disparate variations on the central theme. The first attempts to codify the elements of the myth were the work of Cathars in the West.

The form of the free mythic narrative was not confined to works addressing the problem of evil; it might also be used to transport the reader to more luminous heights, where it approximated rational ideas. Due to Plato and the "Platonisms" of subsequent centuries, a less spontaneous sort of myth, tinged with philosophy, gained currency during the Middle Ages. This myth was more compatible with traditional Christianity because it did not revamp that system of beliefs, but could be passed down in tandem as the perspective of noble pagans. However, the intellectual constructs of this myth assumed astounding potency during a revival of philosophy in the twelfth century. Plato's subdued creative imagery came to be augmented by his nonmythical propositions.[13]

In the model developed by Middle Platonism and Neoplatonism, the cosmos was conceived of as a descending hierarchy, ranging from the pure intellect of God down to humans. The operative entities in the cosmos were simultaneously philosophical concepts and real efficacious powers. In the twelfth century, scholars with a poetic bent followed up on these ideas; they devoted themselves to natural philosophy and expressed themselves in a semimythical form, letting the goddess "Nature" [Natura] voice ideas that might perhaps have been dangerous to express in prose. At the school in Chartres, people addressed questions about the macrocosm and about man, who was viewed as a microcosm. This was still a far cry from science in the modern sense; these authors mistrusted sensory experience and believed that they could "think up" the structure of the cosmos.

In addition to Plato, Aristotle as well had an impact on the West, initially due not to his scientific writings, but rather to his work as a logician. His dialectic, already taught at schools in a rudimentary fashion before this time, became a discipline students found inspiring. It involved expressing one's proposition rationally and lucidly and engaging in a contest of opinions. These were organized in the Scholastic manner according to thesis and antithesis; observing the rules of the discipline, the master would render his *sententia* (opinion or sentence) and solve the problem—at least in a formal sense. The method was applied to theology in an attempt at least to delineate, even if not to solve, the mysteries of the faith.

Such goings-on at the new advanced schools greatly distressed some pious Christians, particularly those who were monks. They had been taught in the monastery to block out the profane world and its thinking; this involved a process of edification geared to cultivating a personality devoted to God, for all else represented idle curiosity. In the monastic milieu there existed a mode of biblical exegesis that was not confined to textual explication. Monks probed beneath the words of the Bible for deeper levels of a hidden meaning that digressed from rational knowledge. The allegorized Holy Scriptures were a world unto themselves, apprehended better with the heart than with the mind.

That is what one learned in the monastery, but the monastic schools were deteriorating; in France above all, they were superseded by cathedral schools and independent circles of masters and students. The young men who thronged to these groups were not closely watched novices. They wore the garb of clerics, yet were often marked by intellectual bohemianism. In this milieu, the rudimentary curriculum of the "liberal arts" was superseded by specialized training in the subjects of grammar, logic, theology, jurisprudence, and medicine. People studied for years on end, and some belatedly or never found their way back into a settled way of life.

Together with a new formalism, new notions concerning content entered into the thinking at the new schools, and these ideas were bolstered by the authority of great philosophers and their commentators. If a new "rational" and systematic Christian theology did now emerge, it was one that progressed along a very narrow path under the distrustful eyes of conservatives, above all those who professed Benedictine monasticism, especially Cistercians under the leadership of Bernard of Clairvaux. Even *magistri* [masters] were fond of accusing their academic colleagues of heresy—not always an entirely misguided move, nevertheless one that very often had the effect of bringing theses warranting debate into the purview of ecclesiastical courts.

The only way an individual could become a "heretic" in the canonical and strict sense of the word was to persist in his or her errors after having been reported to the authorities, tried by a court, and exhorted to accept the correct doctrine; a heresy consisted of the teachings of such a convicted heretic and those of his or her adherents. Hence, the ecclesiastical authorities could not save themselves the bother of a legal proceeding by simply branding an individual a Manichaean or Sabellian. When even learned individuals engaged in that sort of activity, it became all the more evident that the old concepts had lost their meaning. Sometimes, the decision to hold an ecclesiastical proceeding was reached only reluctantly, when subtle theses that could be judged only by specialists were involved. If the defendant recanted, as many a person was compelled to do even repeatedly, then everyone was spared further unpleasantness. Educated theologians were not burned at the stake in those days, but rather condemned to silence and consigned to a monastery. It never even came to that in certain serious cases. For example, Joachim of Fiore was never pronounced a heretic, because he would routinely swear that he would undertake to amend offending portions of his work. He even received confirmation from Pope Honorius III that he was to be regarded a *vir catholicus* [Catholic].[14]

The figure of the scholarly heretic, whom the fathers of the church had encountered in earlier centuries, existed now again side by side with the proponents of popular heresies; there was, however, a great difference between the previous and present periods: Unlike their predecessors, the masters wrote for a specialized audience and did not act as missionaries on behalf of their theses. For that reason, they were exposed less than heretical popular preachers to the danger of suffering "summary judgment" at the hands of a mob. Every such incidence of rough justice was lamented by the clergy; for laypeople, watching heretics burn at the stake may have been a sort of public entertainment.

Death by fire was an ancient folk punishment for witches and sorcerers, who were thereby prevented from rising again from the grave and occasioning evil. The first time heretics were burned at the stake in conjunction with legal proceedings was at the order of Emperor Frederick II in 1224. Mass burnings were instituted during the Albigensian Crusade as part of the effort to eradicate Catharism. As a rule, such episodes involved believers who chose to die rather than recant.

The court of popular opinion did not for the most part need to examine the beliefs of an individual in order to render its verdict. The extent to which the populace could be guided by appearances is illustrated by a case from the mid-eleventh century. In France at that time people were murdered as heretics because their pale complexions implied that they were fasting inordinately.[15] The advocates of the ecclesiastical reform movement broadened the crime of heresy to comprise the most diverse offenses,[16] and in this way they mobilized the faithful particularly against simony, the purchase of ecclesiastical offices that involved ordination. In Italy during the thirteenth century the concept of heresy was extended even to encompass cursing, breaking a vow, engaging in usury, fortune-telling, and so forth.[17] This had the effect of turning average citizens into actual or potential heretics, and they were likely to get used to this state of affairs.

The speculative theologians of the twelfth century were also used to engaging in intellectual experimentation at the margins of orthodoxy and hence to continually inviting suspicions of heresy. This was an era marked by the tumultuous development of "reasoned-out" propositions, an era marked also by competition between "schools" seeking to outdo one another. Abelard's knowledge of his colleagues and of himself came through when he wrote: "The heretic is not the product of ignorance, but of pride, whenever an individual undertakes to make a name for himself by means of some novelty or oddity that he defends against all in order to appear to be the greatest of all."[18] And his adversary Bernard of Clairvaux seconded him: "Heretics have always aspired to achieve fame on the strength of their singular knowledge."[19] Coming up with something new was viewed as a dubious enterprise by medieval traditionalists; young academics and those theologians making inroads into the unknown thought otherwise. William of Conches defended himself against the charge of heresy with a comment celebrated ever since: Something was heretical, not because it had hitherto not been written down, but rather because it was contrary to the faith.[20]

The present book does not purport to delineate the affinity between academic theology and heresy, but rather to investigate "nonconformist" tendencies that exhibit a new attitude. It is difficult enough to comprehend the tenth century at least in terms of the principal cultural phenomena; performing such an undertaking for the next two centuries would be well-nigh impossible. This period is so rich in new phenomena and in sources recounting them that it is necessary to single out what appears especially characteristic of the era. Two such phenomena typifying this age are heresy and early Scholasticism, involving as they did an alteration in the way some people apprehended the earthly and unearthly spheres and, on the other hand, a radical attempt by some to come up with new bases for their intellectual life. The close of the twelfth century did not bring this endeavor to a close, but rather to a pause. In 1200 the king of France laid the groundwork for the establishment of the University of Paris,[21] thus initiating the institutionalization of the advanced schools. The crusade against heretics decimated the Cathars in southern France, and a terrible fate also befell certain theologians educated in Paris: In 1210 ten priests who had studied with a particular master were burned at the stake in Paris.[22] It was also believed at this time that a ban should be placed on Aristotle's scientific works. In spite of some serious disputes, there was soon a new resurgence in scholarship—a resurgence based on the foundation laid in the twelfth century and yet different from anything dreamt by that foregoing age.

"Heresiology" and the history of early Scholasticism are two topics of such scope that one is precluded from compressing them into a single comprehensive study. However, it is the intent of this work to provide a sketch of only the main lineaments of bygone points of view as a background against which the thought and actions of individuals living during that epoch will be thrown into relief. Moreover, it is not the purpose of this book to communicate a contemporary message, or at least none beyond the observation that, even during diverse epochs, human nature does not change.

My thanks to Penn State Press and Mr. Peter J. Potter for undertaking the publication of this book. I wish to thank my friend Prof. Patrick J. Geary for his sound counsel. Dr. Denise A. Kaiser has translated the German text with empathy and understanding, reviewed many of the references, and corrected the occasional minor error. Through her I have gained a more thorough knowledge of my work and for that as well she has my warm gratitude.

Part One
The Heresies

1

Western Heretics in the Eleventh Century

In the waning days of the Christian Roman Empire and into the Byzantine era, theologians and those in wider scholarly circles as well wrestled with religious doctrines, above all those concerning the Trinity and the Incarnation. Apologist works, like those by Saint Augustine, preserved the memory of these struggles among Latin speakers. During this period, hardly any truly heretical movements were still to be found in France; rather, there were occasional theological disputes and eccentric saints. In the days of Saint Boniface, for example, a certain Aldebert made his appearance as an itinerant preacher to the peasants and even attained the office of bishop. In 744 he was deposed for his unorthodox behavior; he was said to have distributed some of his hair and nail clippings to people as "relics."

The situation appears to have changed around the year 1000. The notion that people at the time knelt in prayer in churches, awaiting the coming of the Antichrist or the Second Coming of Christ, is a romantic legend. Admittedly, two chroniclers, considering it an extraordinary time, did refer to the "millennium," and they embellished their narratives accordingly. Writing in the twelfth century, Sigebert of Gembloux dated an earthquake, a comet, and a "snake in the sky" to that epoch-making year.[1] In the fourth decade of the eleventh century Rodulfus Glaber in Cluny collected all the information he could find about heresies—and even fictitious material—for his description of the millennial year since Christ's birth or, alternatively, since the Passion. Since Rodulfus aimed to edify and not to write history, it is not easy for historians to separate the wheat from the chaff here.

Rodulfus's tale, that Sardinia was full of heretics who had "corrupted" a portion of the inhabitants of Spain but had been "exterminated," was apparently fictitious. "All this accords with the prophecy [!] of St. John, who said that the Devil would be freed after the thousand years."[2] In any case, other than this account there is no further evidence for heretics in Sardinia and Spain at that time.

What Rodulfus related in the same context about a "heresy found in Italy" should be taken more seriously. In those days a man named Vilgard living in Ravenna immersed himself in the study of grammar, just as had always been "the custom of these Italians who neglect all other arts to concentrate upon this one." His knowledge made him arrogant and foolish. One night demons disguised as the poets Virgil, Horace, and Juvenal appeared before him and thanked him for the high esteem in which he held them; in the future he would share their fame. Deranged by this experience, "he began arrogantly (*turgide*) to preach against the holy faith, asserting that the sayings of the poets should be believed in everything. In the end he was found to be a heretic and condemned by Peter, the bishop of that city. Many throughout Italy at this time were found to be tainted with this perverse doctrine, and they too perished, by the sword or by fire."[3]

Did the enthusiasm of a classical philologist suffice to brand him a heretic? For the most part, the account has been noted with reservation. "Why Vilgard was the first heretic to be burned or beheaded in the Middle Ages remains . . . shrouded in mystery."[4] Some aspects of the account certainly do not make sense, including the vague statement at the end, that there was a whole sect of such madmen and that they were put to death. As for Vilgard himself, strictly speaking we are told only that he was condemned by the church; everything else might be an embellishment, much like the concluding remark about heretics in Sardinia and Spain. The earliest evidence for the existence of heretics (holding unknown beliefs) in northern Italy dates to the years before 1046 in Verona.[5] They may have already existed at the time Rodulfus wrote this chapter, sometime before 1030, but we know nothing of their condemnation. The reference to Archbishop Peter may be a further embellishment; he may have been well known because he held his office for forty-four years, though only until 971.

Grammar was one of the *artes*, or "seven liberal arts," and at the introductory level it already incorporated readings from classical literature. Vilgard may have been active at a monastic or a cathedral school; there is little likelihood that schools supported by towns existed at this time.[6] Opinions had always differed about reading the pagan classics. Rigorists considered them harmful, many others found them useful, and some praised them effusively, above all during the so-called Carolingian Renaissance. In those days a priest from Mainz declared that Cicero, Virgil, and other writers had ascended to heaven after Christ freed them from Limbo.[7] Even if Vilgard espoused similar beliefs, they still did not make him a heretic. When the priests put to the stake in Paris in 1210 asserted "that God had spoken through Ovid just in the same way as through Augustine,"[8] that was more troubling, though it became heretical only within the context of their overall doctrine.

If one took such assertions a step further, however, the classical authors attained the stature of theological authorities, like the fathers of the church or even the Bible. Plato's *Timaeus* was explicated as if it were a sacred text and extolled as a prophecy of the Christian Trinity. The veneration of Virgil also has a long history. In the fourth century excerpts from Virgil's works were collected into pastiches, or *centones*, forming a Christian text. However, of prime importance was Virgil's fourth *Eclogue*, which as far back as the days of Constantine the Great was interpreted as presaging the Virgin Birth and Kingdom of Christ. Augustine had affirmed the eclogue's Christological meaning, and thence it was clear to all that Virgil must have been inspired by the Holy Spirit: These lines were meant to be interpreted in a Christian sense. If Virgil had not expressed himself more clearly, that was due to his circumspection.[9] The first to reserve judgment on this matter was Peter Abelard, who noted that the poet may not have been conscious of the inspiration the Sibyl or even he himself received from the Holy Spirit.[10]

Since late classical times people had enjoyed scrutinizing their literary heritage for profound moral or religious inner meanings. The amorous escapades of gods who were no longer venerated thus again merited study. The same Abelard could write: "What was formerly viewed as fable and superficially regarded as serving [Christians] no purpose later revealed itself as full of mysteries. Now it is more acceptable, since it contributes much to the body of [Christian] learning."[11]

The Bible had always been examined for allegorical meanings, and in the process exegetes continually discovered new edifying interpretations. Should not the Christian philologist be able to make similar contributions to religious devotion by explicating the classics? Fulgentius of Ruspe, an adherent of Saint Augustine, wrote an allegorical commentary on the *Aeneid*, and others followed in his footsteps. Thus, Virgil's opening words "Arma virumque cano" were taken to signify the power and wisdom of Christ, who was prefigured by the hero Aeneas.[12] When Bernard Silvestris wrote a commentary on the first six books of the *Aeneid* in the twelfth century, he did so in the conviction—already held by Macrobius—that Virgil was as much a great philosopher as a great poet. Did the master Vilgard in Ravenna attempt to use a similar approach? If so, because of the narrow-mindedness of his superiors it did not work out well for him. It is possible, however, that he went further than the other commentators on Virgil. That is no reason to describe him as unchristian, as some historians have done.

Rodulfus Glaber recounted a second story, this one from France, about the existence of heretics around the year 1000. It takes place on the plains of Champagne, in a hamlet called Vertus not far from Châlons-sur-Marne.[13] Later on, this region was marked by heresy again and again; without intending to draw any conclusions, we should note that 184 Cathars were burned at the stake in 1239 in the mountain town of Mont-Aimé, only four kilometers from Vertus.[14] A synod is said to have been held in Châlons in 1012 because of heretics.[15] The bishop of Châlons was again occupied with the problem of heretics during 1043–48.

Rodulfus's account involves the bishop of Châlons as well, a "learned" old man named Gebuin who was the diocesan bishop for Vertus. (This probably refers to Gebuin I [d. 998], bishop for many years, rather than to Gebuin II [d. 1004].[16] Support for the earlier date may be garnered from the warning made by Abbot Abbo of Fleury in 995 or 996 to his kings, Hugh Capet and Robert II, to banish the "ignominy of heresy" from the land.)[17]

According to Rodulfus, a man named Leutard fell asleep while tilling the fields near Vertus and dreamed of bees attacking and stinging him and "ordering him to do things impossible for humankind." Upon awakening he went home and threw out his wife—"justifying the separation by pretended reference to evangelical precept." Leutard then went into the village church and smashed the crucifix bearing the figure of the Savior. When confronted by the villagers, Leutard asserted that he had acted in accordance with a miraculous revelation from God. At first, he was taken for a madman, but people soon thronged to him, since among other things he preached to them that it was unnecessary to pay tithes (to the church)—certainly welcome news to the peasants. As for his other beliefs, Rodulfus unfortunately reported only that Leutard had said that some utterances of the prophets had been useful, others unreliable. In the presence of Bishop Gebuin, Leutard cited passages from the Holy Scriptures in his own defense—a practice he wished "he had not learnt"; of course, he was unsuccessful. Gebuin brought the community back into the fold, and Leutard, abandoned and "defeated," jumped into a well. This is one of the few known instances of suicide in the early Middle Ages.[18]

The business about the bees can probably be disregarded as an embellishment by the author, even though it should be noted that bees were considered symbolic of chastity because of the way they propagated— which would fit in with Leutard's hostility to marriage.[19] In a passage by Gregory of Tours, we read how a man was driven insane by a swarm of flies sent by the devil. The man became a soothsayer, healer, and deceiver of the people, who took him for the returned Christ.[20]

Leutard is depicted as a man of the people (*plebeius*); even if he worked in the fields, he was not necessarily a peasant. Artisans, shepherds, and others also had fields, which they cultivated for supplemental support. According to Rodulfus, Leutard wished to appear learned (*doctor*), voiced opinions about the prophets, and cited scriptural passages, all without the requisite training. Laymen from the lower classes could not as a rule read, and it is even less likely that they would be familiar with the books of the Old Testament prophets. Leutard perhaps only repeated what he had heard from others, including a few biblical quotations handed down orally—if so, then he was neither the "lone wolf" nor "heresiarch" scholarly research has repeatedly made him out to be. It is quite possible that he was an adherent of a sectarian movement that remained otherwise hidden from view by drawing less attention to itself than did Leutard.

It is a pity that we know so little about Leutard's teachings and are thus unable to place him with certainty within a broader context. Yet, it is noteworthy that according to Cosmas the Priest, the Bogomils in the East often repudiated the prophets entirely; elsewhere, the sixteen books of the prophets were revered, while the prophecies found in the books of the Kings were rejected.[21] The issue could not be sidestepped altogether, above all in light of the recurring allusions in the New Testament to the fulfillment of the prophets' words. Incidentally, this question was to remain problematic for later, western Cathars influenced by the Bogomils. In an "exposé" of Cathar teachings the master Bonaccursus noted: "Some hold that the prophets' utterances are revelations from God; others, however, believe that they proceed from the devil."[22]

The crucifix was not the actual focus of worship in a village church; the local saint was foremost in people's minds. Leutard did not attack the saint, not verbally or by destroying his or her image, which most probably stood in the church. The destruction of the crucifix can hardly be viewed as symbolic of Leutard's dissatisfaction with the inefficacy of his prayers; it must be seen in a broader context. Several explanations suggest themselves in this case. First, Claudius, bishop of Turin (d. 827), opposed the worship of saints, their images, and relics, and he banned the display of crucifixes in the churches within his diocese. Such were the painful aftershocks of the "iconoclastic controversy," which had convulsed the East in the eighth century. No connection can be found, however, between that episode and the actions of Leutard of Vertus. Second, the cross itself might have aroused antipathy as an instrument of torture, just as Goethe later termed it. Cosmas tells us that the Bogomils said: "If someone kills the king's son with a piece of wood, is it likely that the king would then consider the piece of wood worthy of veneration?"[23] Later on in the early twelfth century, the heretic Peter of Bruis stridently opposed the veneration of the cross; he ultimately set fire to a pile of crosses, and the outraged bystanders tossed him into the flames. In that case we see a total revolt against a piety based on material objects and against the clergy; perhaps Bogomil teachings were partially behind it.[24]

Last, opposition to the cross may be seen against a background of Docetism: Christ had not suffered on the cross, and possessed only the semblance of a body, since all matter was either evil in and of itself or derived from the devil. The Bogomils held such views, which also served as the premise underlying their line of argument against the cross as well as their hostility to marriage.[25] Admittedly, Leutard did not refer to any such beliefs, citing instead the Gospels as the basis for his repudiation of his wife. Refusing to pay tithes to the church may to be sure also be associated with the anticlericalism characteristic of the Bogomils, yet asceticism and anticlericalism were not confined to Bogomils. Moreover, we lack definitive proof for Leutard's opposition to the clergy, and we must not equate such opposition to the clergy with rejection of the priesthood.[26] All the same, it is safe to say that Leutard could hardly have come up with this heresy "on his own," and if the heresy was borrowed from others, they were most likely Bogomils.

But how could people from the Balkans have wound up in a tiny village in Champagne? That is hard to imagine, so there must have been intermediaries, widely traveled individuals who dealt with Leutard for business reasons. Sheep rearing flourished on the dry, high plateau of northern Champagne;[27] and evidence indicates cloth production and international trade in cloth in this area at a later period. International trade followed old trade routes, some dating back to Roman times. One stretched from Auxerre and Troyes to Châlons-sur-Marne and beyond to Rheims and Amiens.[28] We know that later on the bishop of Châlons again dealt with heretics. As for the famous fairs of Champagne, some trace their rise to the tenth century,[29] though the standard work in the field favors the eleventh century.[30] Yet, Leutard was not necessarily a sheep raiser, nor was he necessarily introduced to Bible study by a foreign merchant. In this case, we can only speculate and nothing more.

Gebuin, bishop of Châlons, dealt with Leutard, and it was one of his successors, Roger I, who addressed the issue of heresy at the abovementioned synod, about which we have very little information.[31] This occurred in October 1012, and Bishop Gerard of Cambrai and Arras may have been referring to these heretics in a letter written at a later date—not before 1025—to a colleague named "R," perhaps Roger of Châlons: "As you know, dear brother, we have informed you that such people [heretics] reside in your diocese, and we have proved this by means of solid evidence. Because they feared punishment, they hypocritically asserted their orthodoxy, and you did not convict them, and let them go free, as if they were innocent."[32] The lack of a conviction, the bishop continued, confused simple souls and caused them to be led astray (by the heretics). The heretics had carried on missionary work in Gerard's diocese; however, after their vehement denials he persuaded them to make partial confessions. He recounted some of their religious doctrines "and other things the following passages from this little book demonstrate [*quae huius libelli sequentia indicant*]." In fact, Gerard's report of a synod he held in Arras at the beginning of 1025 to combat these heretics follows in the printed texts and the twelfth-century manuscript that is their source.

Some scholars believe that the letter was associated with the report purely by accident, and that it pertains to heretics found in Liège during Bishop Reginard's tenure.[33] This is not impossible, even though Reginard probably first assumed his office during the course of 1025. Indeed, the letter then need not have been written immediately after or in connection with the synod in Arras, but later on, after the events in Liège. Thus, it would have nothing to do with Châlons or with the synod of 1012. The objection has also been raised that there is no documentary evidence for the existence of heretics in Liège before the twelfth century.[34] The following item may be cited in support of their presence.

Between 1010 and 1027 E[gbert], a schoolmaster in Liège, wrote a didactic poem entitled *Fecunda ratis*, which included a nineteen-verse description "of the evil French" (*de malis Francigenis*). As a subject of the Holy Roman Empire, Egbert did not like the French and wrote: "From the West, whence storms arise, there recently came an evil heresy. The French people are hostile to God; they curse (swear oaths) on their spears and daggers, on the bowels and soul of Christ—it is a wonder that they have not been struck by lightning or swallowed up by the earth. In their savagery they are also two-faced, murderers when enraged; they are driven by an evil error and obvious madness. Do not admit them as guests, but bolt the doors lest such people should creep in during the night and bring you, your wife, or your son to ruin [by means of their teaching?]. For who knows what the devil has put into their heads? . . . Whoever wishes, can believe them; I believe absolutely nothing they say."[35] Thus, the writer knew nothing about heretics in Liège, but feared

that people from France might come to pose a threat to the city. It seemed
necessary to give his students and their families a timely warning.

The threat to Liège came from the West, which most probably meant the
area around Arras, the northernmost part of France, in the period before
the synod of 1025, which would dispel the specter of heresy. This fits with
the likely dating of the work's dedication to a Bishop "Aboldus" (Adal-
bold of Utrecht, 1010–27) to the period 1018–22.[36] Egbert of Liège held the
French in low esteem, and in that respect he was not unique. People were
influenced by the political tensions between the French king and imperial
authority, embodied from afar and almost exclusively by the imperial
bishops. One of them, the bishop of Cambrai, oversaw a diocese that was
partially in French territory: the area around Arras, to which Gerard seems
to have paid particular attention. If the work currently under discussion
had been meant for Roger I, bishop of Châlons, then we would better
understand its tone. Concealed beneath the formal civility lies the charge
of professional incompetence. Previous admonitions to attend to the
heretics in his diocese were of no avail, and the investigation came to
naught—now they reaped the fruits of this conduct: The heretics in
Roger's city sent out messengers to proselytize in Arras.

The imperial bishop's vigilant concern for his flock in France stands in
favorable contrast to this negligence. In spite of their vehement denials
Gerard induced partial confessions from the heretics and gave them
thorough instruction at the synod until they—presumably—saw the
error of their ways and recanted. Drawing upon the sum of his theological
erudition, he wrote down his instructions in the form of a polished treatise
and forwarded this little book to his colleague for use against the heretics
in that diocese.[37] Whether the recipient was pleased by the gift remains
unknown.

The synod in Arras was held in 1025, and its timing may not have been
accidental either, but related to the change of ruler at that time. Bishop
Gerard was a native of the region around Liège and served as chaplain to
Henry II, even though he had belonged to the cathedral school and
chapter at Rheims, where his kinsman was archbishop.[38] In 1012 King
Henry entrusted the diocese straddling the border to his chaplain, perhaps
trusting also in Gerard's connections in the area. From an ecclesiastical point
of view, the bishop of Cambrai was subordinate to the metropolitan at
Rheims, who served the king of France. Thus, Rheims did not object to the
fact that Gerard was still only a deacon and had yet to receive higher
orders. After he had in 1012, the above-mentioned synod was supposedly
held in Châlons. In theory Gerard may already by that time have passed
along information to his fellow bishop that would redound to his own
favor. In 1022 heretics close to the king of France were burned at the stake

in Orléans; we shall hear more about them below. In response to the unstable conditions of the times, the northern French bishops assembled in 1023 to agree upon a Peace of God. In fear for his secular prerogatives as count and loath to be drawn into the French sphere of influence, Gerard of Cambrai declined to attend.[39] He might have acted differently had he been able to foresee that his sole patron, the emperor, would die a few months later (July 13, 1024).

Gerard of Cambrai could expect little from the newly elected Salian king, Conrad II. Most of the nobles in Lorraine viewed Conrad with reserve at best and enmity at worst. In 1024–25 William V, duke of Aquitaine, in league with nobles from lower Lorraine, sought to promote the son of the count of Anjou as a rival candidate for king. This could only portend an invasion by the king of France into lower Lorraine. Gerard of Cambrai sent gifts to the king in order to ward off the danger to Cambrai, the first imperial city on the invasion route.[40]

Should we be surprised that under such circumstances the bishop of Cambrai found the time to hold a synod and probably to compose the report as well? Or should we discern in both actions the secondary goal at least of appearing to be an exemplary defender of the faith in the eyes of the French king, thrown off balance by the affair in Orléans? There was no immediate threat to Cambrai in the period after Christmas, since at that time wars were not waged in winter. Either the heretics in Arras first came to light then, or they now presented the occasion for an ostentatious display—nothing, after all, happened to the heretics, since the bishop was satisfied with a formal declaration of their piety and sent them home "with his blessing."[41] He had treated them with as much leniency as had his colleague "R." Was that because they had not committed the most grievous errors, or because these people were needed for some reason? Both were probably the case.

Whatever Bishop Gerard may have said at the synod, it was directed less at the heretics—who after all, according to his own testimony, did not understand Latin—than at the clergymen in attendance and probably also at his friends among the bishops of northern France. The expanded, written version, to which were appended many learned references, made for "a kind of exposé of orthodox doctrine."[42] In addition to the theological grandiloquence, we find a rhetorical device of the following ilk: "There would still be so much more to say, if only the time were available; but since the day draws to a close, that reminds us all to go home."[43] This is a classical *topos*, one form of *conclusio*. However, what follows immediately thereupon is not the conclusion to the work, but a hymn to the Eucharist in liturgical-hymnic style, consisting of short, rhyming cola like those characteristic of sacred plainsong. He had pulled out all the stops here, certainly not for the benefit of people who would need to have this sort of thing translated for them.

Who were the heretics in Arras? According to Gerard's letter, they came from Bishop "R"'s city, thus probably from Châlons, but according to the record of the synod, they came "from the region of Italy."[44] That need not be seen as a contradiction and already provides us with a clue to the heretics' walk of life. The earliest evidence for merchants from Italy in northern France dates from 1074;[45] the defendants also asserted that they earned their living through manual labor[46]—that could scarcely refer to merchants. Were they peasants, they would have been bound to the soil. Thus, above all we must weigh the possibility that they plied craftsmen's trades. Many French churches were under construction at the dawn of the new millennium, including the ones in Châlons and Arras.[47] The most diversely skilled craftsmen were needed for the adornment of houses of worship, for unlike those today they were furnished with tapestries; thus, the talents of weavers and dyers were also engaged. Just as the Italians were famous for their artistic taste all over Europe during the Middle Ages, so were they known for their technical expertise; they set the fashion in cloth dying up until the introduction of American dyewoods. Last, a craft—like the tentmaking practiced by Saint Paul—was the best source of income (and camouflage) for wandering missionaries. Whoever longed to return to the early days of the church might seek to imitate the apostles in this respect as well. A century later, when weavers were the targets of malicious derision, they rebutted that they earned their living through manual labor in accordance with the law-abiding conduct of the early Christians and the apostles.[48]

When asked who had established their way of life (*disciplina*), the heretics of Arras responded that they had "listened to a man from Italy named Gundulf. They had received instruction from him in the tenets of the Gospels and apostles, and would accept no other text except this one, which they would observe by word and act."[49] Gundulf himself did not appear; he had run his "school" somewhere far away and apparently presented his students with a written list of precepts for them to take on their travels far and wide. Disillusioned by the innumerable and poorly substantiated church precepts, simple people may very well have asked Gundulf for a synopsis of his teaching that contained its most important and essential aspects. Gundulf spared them from studying the Gospels and the Epistles, something they were not capable of doing, even if one or two of them could read a little. They surely lacked the command of Latin required to tackle the Holy Scriptures; as of yet we know of no translations of the Bible into a Romance language that date from this period.

The heretics justified themselves by asserting that the law (*lex*) and the regimen of their lives, which they had accepted from their "master," did not controvert the Gospels: One was to flee the world, tame the flesh of worldly desire, support oneself through manual labor, harm no one, and show charity to all "who are gripped with zeal for our *propositum*."[50] This last term means more than "purpose" or "intention," denoting rather the will to adopt the—in most cases monastic—ways of a community, or else the monastic life itself.[51] And in fact, the points enumerated here prescribe a way of life approximating monasticism, as the precursor to a "third order" for pious laypeople. One thing Saint Francis would not have sanctioned, however, was the notion that the precept to love thy neighbor applies only to the members of one's own community.

The question of how much credence should be lent to Gerard's account already arises here. He could not stray too far from the truth, because the treatise was read by the participants in the synod. In his favor, also, is the fact that he did not refer to the traditional system of heresy derived from the late classical period and did not attempt to classify the people in Arras according to one of these former movements;[52] on the contrary, he stated that this was a "new" heresy. However, the bishop may perhaps be reproached for thinking through the theological implications of the heretics' way of life, thereby effecting its "dogmatization."

Gundulf established a congregation and sent it on its way, provided with biblical precepts and prohibitions. It is unlikely that those included the order to stay away from the "established" church, though that would have been self-evident. These individuals were mainly concerned with observing a Christian way of life; they attributed less importance to the sacraments of the church, a stance they shared with the broad cross section of laypeople. It is possible the heretics of Arras believed that whoever observed a Christian way of life had no need for grace through the church, since he was assured entry into heaven.

In Gerard's treatise this belief is developed into a theological doctrine of justification. "You are attempting to establish the doctrine of a false justice that you favor over divine grace to such an extent that you ascribe all to your own merits."[53] It would have been easy for Gerard to label this attitude Pelagianism, that is, the denial of an essential necessity for divine grace. He did not do so, in all likelihood because he realized upon interrogating the heretics that they had no doctrinal system. There is no mention of central concepts like original sin, salvation, or the Trinity. The bishop often had to come up with the technical term himself in order to proceed with his summary of their religious dogma.

Some of the things Gerard ascertained were expressions of popular beliefs; he had probably heard these things before. How can the Eucharist be the Body of Christ, when again and again the Body is distributed and consumed by so many people living at various times and places? What purpose does infant baptism serve, given that it is often performed by sinful priests and in the knowledge that the baptismal promises will only be broken again and again? Why should a church be considered a holy place, when it consists but of stones and mortar and a person can pray just as well at home? Is not the man who has committed a grave sin damned forever, and how can the performance of penance release him from that sin?[54]

Objections to the Eucharist did play a role in the theological debate, yet one certainly should not conclude from this that the heretics of Arras "had upon analysis accepted a realistic doctrine of the Holy Communion" and "that they were up-to-date on the status of the discussion."[55] These people lacked a command of the basic terms needed to comprehend a discussion of theology. At work here was an unrefined, sensory-based imagination; and it represented popular belief, while its antithesis, spiritualism, was more at home in monastic and ascetic circles. Yet, the heretics of Arras were held to have embraced spiritualism as well.

"You believe that nothing of a material nature should occur in church, as the water and the chrism in the mystery of baptism are [material]," an argument cited by Gerard[56] that does not appear among the heretics' objections to infant baptism. The bishop had already explained in detail why baptism was performed using "material water."[57] It is not clear if he intended thereby to counter the heretics' views or to prove his erudition. Had he taken these concepts to their "logical conclusion" so that he could then disprove them? For example, Gerard addressed in detail the subject of sacerdotal ordination, and perhaps that is why he asserted that the heretics wished to convey the gift of the Holy Spirit by means of wicked magic spells at crossroads and in groves, "in the manner of a mystery of consecration."[58] Perhaps, in the manner of the apostles, they recited prayers over the neophytes, but they hardly practiced "baptism of the Holy Spirit," something we shall return to later. The only known use of concrete symbols among the heretics of Arras concerns the washing of feet;[59] the bishop considered it incompatible with spiritualism because it involved "material water." The heretics would surely have realized this inconsistency themselves had they rejected all material things as unclean.

We do not doubt the group's strict sexual asceticism. Twice—once in the letter to "R" and once in his treatise—the bishop laid stress on the heretics' false belief that no married person may enter the kingdom of heaven.[60] This is not from the Bible, but according to a report by a Greek author, this tenet reflects the Bogomil viewpoint.[61] Elsewhere Gerard spoke of the false belief that *legitimae* [lawful] marriages, that is, those celebrated in church, were to be avoided.[62] This was a popular view at a time when marriage was in transition and evolving from a purely family matter into a church sacrament. The total rejection of marriage may have constituted one of the religious tenets held by the people of Arras. It does not have to be derived from the Bogomils; wandering craftsmen had no household and may have wished to make a virtue of necessity. It could just as well have been the case that—as in monastic life—virginity for men was regarded as an ideal. Admittedly, that would hardly explain the severity of the rejection.

The unworthiness of the clergy is mentioned only peripherally, in connection with infant baptism. The accused did not wish to annoy the clergy, and in any case anticlericalism was hardly of prime importance to their way of thought; they also lacked the aggressive manner of a Leutard of Vertus. They did not smash the crucifix, but rather attested that it had no "potency" in and of itself, other than through its formation by human hands, and was therefore not worthy of veneration.[63] It did not matter where one was buried, since cemeteries were not hallowed ground.[64] Such ideas were indicative of skepticism, but hardly part of a systematic religious doctrine. One cannot assert that for the heretics of Arras there existed an absolute dichotomy between the spirit and matter:[65] They would perhaps not have even understood this tenet.

Thus, it appears difficult to place the heretics of Arras in a Gnostic-dualistic context. Rather, they can be seen as precursors of a "Bible-based Christianity," modeled on the apostles, that reached its peak in the twelfth century. Let us return to Châlons-sur-Marne.

Between 1043 and 1048 Bishop Roger II of Châlons wrote to Wazo, bishop of Liège, [66] that in one part of his diocese there were peasants who adhered to the perverse beliefs of the Manichaeans, committed obscene acts at secret meetings, and purportedly conveyed the Holy Spirit through the superstitious imposition of hands. Roger traced these mistaken beliefs back to Mani, the father of Manichaeism. The heretics "force whomever they can to join their band; they detest marriage and not only abstain from eating meat, but believe that each time an animal is slaughtered, a sin is committed," on the basis of the Old Testament commandment prohibiting murder. Once converted by these heretics, simple people were transformed into orators surpassing the Catholics in ability. The bishop sought his colleague's valuable advice on whether he should surrender these people to the sword of secular authority. In his response,[67] Wazo expounded at length on the fifth commandment, which does not pertain to the slaughter of animals, and he recommended the excommunication, but not the surrender, of the sinners.

As commendable as this advice was, we are thereby deprived of more detailed knowledge of the views held by this group. The only thing it held in common with the people of Arras was the rejection of marriage. On the one hand, just as in Leutard's case, peasants were said to be involved, and again it is not out of the question that they came up with their beliefs on their own. On the other hand, Bishop Roger asserted that the peasants had referred to Mani as the founder of their sect and considered him the Holy Spirit, something about which they were without doubt very closely "questioned." This leaves us with the baptism of the Holy Spirit by imposition of hands, the prohibition against slaughtering animals and the resulting vegetarianism, and an indication that they accepted the Old Testament. The last point distinguishes them from Bogomils,[68] to whom misogamy and vegetarianism could be ascribed. The earliest evidence for the baptism of the Holy Spirit among the Bogomils dates to around the middle of the century in western Anatolia,[69] probably as a rite of initiation; of course, it may have been practiced there even earlier. On the other hand, the Acts of the Apostles refer several times to an imposition of hands in association with the Holy Spirit,[70] so the introduction of this practice—without recourse to the Catholic liturgy—would strike "biblical scholars" as reasonable. It later assumed a central role for the Cathars.

Here, in fact, we seem to encounter the very spiritualism we hesitated to ascribe to the heretics of Arras. Baptism of the Holy Spirit avoids the use of matter and thus may be associated with asceticism in food as well as with an "abhorrence" of marriage. This was not Manichaeism; as Roger's correspondent correctly noted with reference to Augustine,[71] Manichaeism encompasses the view that plants also possess living spirits or souls. It is conceivable that the influence of the Bogomils stretched westward through Italy, where there were heretics (of the Eastern type?) at that time.[72]

Châlons was under the jurisdiction of the archbishop of Rheims, and heretics were excommunicated in 1049 at a provincial synod there attended by the well-traveled Pope Leo IX.[73] It is probably safe to assume that the bishop of Châlons took Wazo's advice, but sought a solemn setting for the condemnation. The case was probably investigated in greater detail, since, contrary to the views of the two correspondents, it concerned "new heretics." Their way of thought closely resembled that of the theologian Berengar of Tours, whose doctrine about Holy Communion caused quite a stir at that time.[74]

We hear nothing more about the heretics of Champagne, and in general the ensuing years are marked by a great paucity of sources concerning heresy. It was not until 1144/45 that the clergy of Liège reported to Pope Lucius II about a heresy that had originated at a "Mons Guimari" in France and spread into various regions, among them areas within the diocese of Liège. They were probably referring to Mont-Aimé, later the center of Cathar activity and perhaps of the sect's bishopric,[75] right near Vertus, where Leutard had lived.

We must now leave this region swarming with heretics and turn our attention to southern France, where the ground was being tilled for what would prove to be a rich harvest for the Cathars in the twelfth century. Let us first, however, take a close look at an incident that occurred in far-off Goslar in 1051, two years after the synod in Rheims. Goslar was a royal residence with a chapter of canons, and a second chapter was founded by Agnes of Poitou, wife of Henry III; in particular, the imperial monastery of Saints Simon and Jude was founded in 1047, and the cathedral church was consecrated in 1050. All this construction was made easier by the abundance of silver the royal mint obtained by mining near Goslar. It does not take a great stretch of imagination to surmise that craftsmen from various lands, perhaps including some from western France, the empress's native land, would meet at this residence. In addition, merchants would be on hand to provide those items the court household and religious facilities needed from other countries.

The imperial couple celebrated Christmas 1051 at Goslar; also present was Godfrey II, the Bearded, who had once been the duke of Upper Lorraine, was then deposed and taken into custody for participating in a revolt, and was now again at liberty. He figures in this account by the annalist Lampert of Hersfeld: "Here [in Goslar] heretics were captured by Duke Godfrey and hanged."[76] Herman of Reichenau supplemented the information by reporting the involvement of "a Manichaean sect" "that was prohibited from eating meat."[77] They were convicted by a royal council in the presence of the emperor, who issued the order for their execution.[78]

We learn something more about the case from the letter by Wazo of Liège cited above:[79] The bishop of Châlons should not behave like those Frenchmen who declare people to be heretics because they have pale complexions, and kill them. The late Bishop Wazo would never have agreed to the course of action taken in Goslar: Sectarians of this bent (like those discovered in Châlons, *quidam huiusmodi erroris sectatores* [certain followers of this kind of error]) would have been hanged only after a long discussion of their errors and their excommunication. The only ground Anselm of Liège himself can offer for their execution was their refusal to comply with an order from the bishop to kill a chicken.

As the point of departure for his explanation, Anselm used the above-mentioned letter from Roger II of Châlons about the "Manichaeans" in his diocese who condemned eating meat and the slaughter of animals. If the heretics were ordered to perform this kind of slaughter at court, it was certainly not to put their obedience to the test—they were suspected of being Manichaeans, which they were not. Having himself subscribed to this religion for some years, Augustine depicted its animism thus: Animals and plants possess souls and can be murdered.[80] It is unclear, even improbable, that the heretics of Goslar thought likewise; no doubt they were actually concerned about keeping the fifth commandment. It is no more likely that they knew about the third-century Persian nobleman who founded Manichaeism than that the people of Châlons did. Modern scholars have spoken of a Western "neo-Manichaeism" in the very medieval conviction that the fragments of heretical views that have come down to us can be fleshed out with the overall Manichaean conception of the world, including "cosmological dualism," transmigration of the soul, etc. This is certainly not the case. The basic premises of Eastern thought that are ultimately traceable back to Manichaeism or parallel ideas traveled over many intermediate routes to the West; some had already arrived before Catharism.

Where did the heretics of Goslar come from? For a century historians have looked to Lorraine as their homeland, owing to the involvement of Duke Godfrey.[81] However, he had not entered his duchy since the revolt in 1047 and had not brought the heretics along with him; rather, they were found in Goslar. That he of all people was entrusted with the matter leads to the supposition, however, that the people came from the West and that he probably spoke their language and was more familiar than others with their circumstances. That the emperor allowed him to act was a good portent for a future return to power. By 1054 Godfrey rejoined the upper ranks of the imperial nobility through his marriage to the widow of Boniface of Canossa, margrave of Tuscia (Tuscany).

We still have to deal with the West: In 1027 or 1028 William V, duke of Aquitaine and father of the future empress Agnes, conferred with bishops and abbots in Charroux (south of Poitiers) concerning how "to exterminate the heresy spread among the people by the Manichaeans."[82] According to the details of the story, Manichaeans had come to light in Aquitaine and were advising people to disavow the following: baptism, the sign of the cross, the church and the Savior, the veneration of saints, and legitimate marriages, as well as eating meat. They had alienated many simple people from the faith. "All the Aquitainian princes were also present, whom he [the duke] called upon to make peace and to revere the Catholic Church."[83] Public doubt would prove to be fertile ground for heretical movements in the next century as well.

The teachings listed are characteristic of Bogomilism, as described by Cosmas the Priest and, at the beginning of the twelfth century, by Euthymios Zigabenos. They are not characteristic of Bogomilism alone; people fabricated some of these things time and time again or could even "extract" them from patristic works—in particular, Augustine's writings against Manichaeism. It is out of the question that "simple people" (*simplices, vulgus*) could engage in the latter, thus leaving us with the possibility or even the probability that we are dealing with an importation from the East. The heresy in Aquitaine was not "exterminated" by force, a step the clergy was certainly not yet ready to take. Thus, it is hardly surprising that in 1056 an ecclesiastical assembly threatened with excommunication all those who afforded protection or other assistance to the heretics. In addition, we learn from the annalist Adémar of Chabannes that heretics were discovered in Toulouse and "annihilated" (*destructi*); in various parts of the West, he continued, messengers of the Antichrist came forward (at that time).[84] Holographs of Adémar's chronicle exist; he concluded his work right after 1028. The entry about the heretics of Toulouse is found in an eleventh-century copy of the chronicle, in the middle of the account concerning the events of 1022 in Orléans. This is probably an interpolation made somewhat later, which means we are not justified in presuming that in Toulouse heresy can be traced back to the 1020s without a break. All the same, we see here the inception of something that would occupy an ecclesiastical assembly anew in 1119 and, from then on, constitute the chief problem facing the ecclesiastical and secular authorities in southern France.

It appears that in Lower Lorraine people possessed only hazy information about the events in France—this in spite of the fact that at that time the emperor was in league with Aquitaine and the count of Anjou against the king of France. Yet, around 1050 Theodoin, bishop of Liège, admonished King Henry I of France to take measures against heretics. In his warning, he named Bruno, bishop of Angers, and Berengar of Tours, whom we will discuss later on in detail.[85] Berengar was an educated theologian who revived the ninth-century "Eucharist controversy" and was as a result, from 1050 on, condemned many times. This was not associated with the heretics in Aquitaine, but Theodoin drew a connection between them: Bruno and Berengar considered the Body of Christ "a shadow and a semblance" and opposed legitimate marriages and infant baptism,[86] errors against which Theodoin marshaled the authority of the fathers of the church. We are reminded of Gerard, bishop of Cambrai, who was just as fond of showing off his knowledge to the French.

If heretical beliefs from the East were present in Aquitaine, then it is probable that they came via Italy. An account in fact exists that may be placed in this context: "The sons of the devil, the princes of darkness, reign and rule everywhere. Italy was not accustomed to 'nurse' heresies—nowadays we hear that in some parts of the country the kindling for heresies is present in great measure. . . . Unfortunate Greece never could exist without this kind of thing. Verona, the noblest city in Italy, becomes fecund with them. Ravenna is radiant and Venice happy, for they never sanctioned tolerating God's enemies."[87] Thus wrote a Venetian named Gerard, who had studied in France and then as a cleric entered into the service of Saint Stephen, the first king of Hungary. He advanced as far as bishop of Csanád (Marosvár, Transylvania) and was killed by pagans in 1046. The text containing the observations cited above must have been written shortly before his death.[88]

Gerard suffered from "heresies" in his diocese. Among other things, people demanded that the money they had paid the clergy to recite requiem masses be returned; the heretics apparently denied that these masses had any effect on the salvation of the departed. This would be in line with Bogomil beliefs.[89] The suspected connection is bolstered by Gerard's comment in the same passage that "almost unanimously they all deny the resurrection of the flesh" and by his reference to the helping hand the heretics received from the "Methodians," in other words, the Slavic church. Such things had attracted the bishop's attention, which of course does not prove that the group in Verona must also have been Bogomil. However, this possibility should not be dismissed.

Verona was linked to Venice by close trading relationships, and for a long time the Veronese penny served as the common currency in Venice. In the late twelfth century there was a congregation of Cathars in Verona who felt so safe that they held an assembly there in 1184, while the pope and emperor sojourned in the city to consult about measures against the heretics.[90] Until 1015 Gerard had been a monk and abbot at San Giorgio (Maggiore) in Venice; he had been born into a respected Venetian family, and he would have remained in contact. In short, he could have known what was going on in Verona and what the town fathers apparently did not wish to know. It is quite possible that yet other Italian cities harbored congregations of heretics of which Gerard had no knowledge. During this period of burgeoning urban development, most townspeople had concerns other than preserving orthodoxy.

Up to this point we have focused on the heresies of *hoi polloi*, who were not always taken quite seriously at that time. However, there were at least two other instances of heresy in the eleventh century that involved members of the upper classes. One instance above all must have caused a sensation, for it involved court clerics, including the confessor to the queen of France. The affair was so embarrassing that Helgald of Fleury, biographer of King Robert the Pious, did not even report it. However, we possess accounts by the annalists Rodulfus Glaber and Adémar of Chabannes, a description by the monk Andreas of Fleury, a letter to Spain from a monk named John, and above all a detailed report in a cartulary from the monastery of Saint-Père in Chartres,[91] which contains other historical material as well. Of prime importance to this case was Aréfast, a Norman who later entered Saint-Père;[92] did he give an account of the affair to a monk named Paul who compiled the cartulary? It is not very likely, because the cartulary was not written until the 1080s; if transmitted orally by some other route, the nature of the story would have altered dramatically over the course of more than sixty years. We probably have before us a record written right after 1022 and incorporated by Paul into his work. It appears after an entry about a gift made by Aréfast in 1026 at the latest.[93]

Another possible source of information may have been Everard, sacristan at the cathedral of Chartres; he became a monk at Saint-Père in 1024. It was he, not the absent bishop, who instructed Aréfast on playing his role as *agent provocateur*. As the bishop's confidant, Everard may have attended the synod against the heretics in Orléans. The aforementioned report, which may have been based on the acts of the synod, was perhaps intended for Fulbert, bishop of Chartres. The monk Paul apparently "improved on" the original version of this report by embellishing it with gruesome details and incorporated it into his cartulary. The matter-of-fact and knowledgeable report suddenly veers off into an excursus (*digressio*) on the magical machinations of the heretics.

The proceedings against the group were apparently part of a political intrigue.[94] Around 1010 Leutrich, archbishop of Sens (near Orléans), had elevated his candidate Thierry (Theodoric) to bishop of Orléans with the backing of the royal couple. Fulbert, bishop of Chartres, on behalf of his own, unsuccessful candidate, raised a protest against the rigged election. In 1021 the tables turned, and without perceptible protest Thierry returned back to Sens; from there he planned to travel on to Rome, but died beforehand in 1023. An opposition candidate named Odalric took Thierry's place in Orléans. He was the lord of Pithiviers Castle (located between Orléans and Paris) and held a demesne near Chartres. Bishop Fulbert—either before or following violent clashes with Thierry in Orléans—had ordained Odalric as a priest, and he—not the duly responsible archbishop of Sens—also consecrated him bishop. This all occurred in the same year that a temporary resolution was reached on the issue of royal jurisdiction over Champagne: King Robert had been forced to enfeoff one of the great feudal princes, Count Eudo II of Blois, with central and western Champagne, which had just become vacant. It seems that the time was ripe at this juncture to eradicate heresy and to replace the cathedral chapter, too, upon the heels of the bishop. For Fulbert of Chartres this was a triumph; for the royal couple, Archbishop Leutrich, and the royal party in Orléans, a bitter defeat. Only after the death of Bishop Fulbert (1028) did Archbishop Leutrich get his satisfaction: The man he elevated to bishop in Chartres expelled Aréfast and Everard, the surviving main protagonists in the unearthing of the heretics, from the monastery of Saint-Père.

Now, finally, let us turn to the account in the cartulary. Aréfast had a cleric in his household named Herbert, whom he sent to Orléans to study. There, his teachers were two respected clergymen, Stephen and Lisoius. He passed on their teachings to Aréfast, who in turn informed Count Richard II of Normandy, his feudal lord, with the request that King Robert the Pious be alerted. Robert summoned Aréfast and Herbert to Orléans; on the way, they stopped off in Chartres to confer with Bishop Fulbert. The bishop, however, had just departed for Rome, so the above-mentioned cathedral sacristan, Everard, assumed the responsibility of preparing Aréfast, the Norman *miles* (knight), to act as a spy in Orléans. Once there, he took part in the religious instruction, and we possess detailed information about what transpired and later served as the charges.

Then, as agreed, the royal couple came to Orléans, accompanied by eminent clergymen, and conducted the purge over Christmas 1022. The spiritual aspect of the incident was dealt with on December 28 in the cathedral. Aréfast and his people came out in chains, as if they were the accused. With Norman cunning Aréfast pretended to be a layman confused by the clergymen and requested that they be examined by the synod concerning the things they told him. Stephen and Lisoius persisted in their beliefs, and of the remaining defendants only two, a priest and a nun, recanted. According to another source, ten canons at Orléans cathedral made up the "hard core."[95] After they were driven from the cathedral, secular jurisdiction could take its course. Queen Constance set things in motion by knocking out one of Stephen's—her confessor's—eyes with a staff. This seemingly impulsive act of revenge may have been a well-calculated gesture performed for the benefit of the crowd waiting outside of the church, as a way of disassociating herself from a heretic who had once been her spiritual advisor. If Stephen and Lisoius willingly taught the Norman knight Aréfast about their unorthodox beliefs, they would have done likewise with the queen—and what about with the king? At stake was the reputation of Robert "the Pious." Hence, the heretics were also condemned to death by burning, something totally unheard of at the time. Marked for execution, they were taken outside of the city to a "tent" built of wood and there burned to death.

This is the earliest auto-da-fé in the West for which we have solid evidence. It must have made an extraordinary impression upon people, so much so that a document was even dated by the event.[96] Hardly anyone was stirred by the sight of thieves consigned to the gallows, something that was part and parcel of secular life, so to speak. A burning stirred the popular imagination more powerfully, just because of its similarity to the popular punishment for witchcraft. Rodulfus Glaber depicted how the condemned had boasted about their resolution, but then screamed pitiably that the devil had led them astray. An attempt was made to pull them from the flames, but the heretics' bodies had crumbled into dust.[97]

The incident in Orléans may also have prompted Rodulfus Glaber to mention other heretics who perished "by the sword or by fire" in Italy at the close of the story about Vilgard.[98] Annalists like Rodulfus shared the common belief that these flames represented but a foretaste of the flames of hell awaiting the evildoers.[99] Later on, it was felt that burning still left time for repentance at the very last minute and for arriving at the correct belief, which would offer protection against the punishments of hell. Such considerations were certainly far from the pious king's mind; he wished to send a signal about his own orthodoxy.

The dénouement of the story, so to speak, involved the exhumation of a corpse and the investigation of other suspicious occurrences. According to the testimony of his colleagues, Deodatus, at one time the cantor of the cathedral and dead already for three years, had belonged to the sect; he was now hastily reburied outside of the cemetery, in an out-of-the-way place.[100] The persecutions suffered by the monk and annalist Odorannus in Sens have also been viewed in this conjunction: Ambushed by "false brothers," he only barely escaped death; he fled to the monastery of Saint-Denis.[101] Odorannus attributed the persecution to his opposition to an anthropomorphic concept of God, which, in very general terms, would fit in with the ideas of the sect in Orléans. After two years, however, Odorannus was summoned back to his monastery with all due respect, which surely argues against his having belonged to that circle. All the same, the public atmosphere seems to have become highly charged, which under certain circumstances could prove dangerous to anyone espousing unusual doctrines. In any case, Rodulfus's observations at the conclusion of his report about the incident at Orléans are improbable: "Later, wherever adherents of this perverse sect were discovered, they were everywhere destroyed by the same avenging punishment (i.e., burning)."[102] He had already made the same assertion about the heretics in Italy, of which there were hardly any.

King Robert's biographer took pains to depict the king's fearless efforts on behalf of orthodoxy: The ruler threatened Leutrich, archbishop of Sens, with deposition, because "he did not think well of the Lord [Christ]." Thereupon, Leutrich kept quiet about the "perverse" tenets, though they thrived out in the world (among laypeople).[103] The issue here apparently involved determining whether an individual merited communion, and it was rooted in the belief that if an unworthy person took communion,

Christ in the wafer suffered pain. This had nothing to do with the heretics of Orléans. Furthermore, Bishop Adalbero of Laon also appears to have come under suspicion of heresy on the basis of an allusion in his poem "On Faith," dedicated to King Robert.[104]

The climate after 1022 of "sniffing out heretics" is expressed in a letter sent from Fleury by a monk named John to the bishop of Vich, who was the abbot of two monasteries in Spain.[105] He depicted the events in Orléans, adding this warning: "Search through your diocese and through your monasteries lest someone under the guise of piety become obdurate in this offense, God forfend!"

The scandal in Orléans was a serious setback to efforts by the king of France to emphasize his "most Christian" stature. Partial to monks, he had few friends among the higher secular clergy, and Adalbero of Laon told the bitter truth in another poem dedicated to King Robert. So much transpires in a topsy-turvy way, the poem relates: Uneducated men are elevated to bishop; scholars are barred from participating in the condemnation of a great heresy; even the king does not avail himself of their counsel—surely a reference to the synod of Orléans.[106]

So few bishops participated in the synod that the question was raised whether it even qualified as an ecclesiastical assembly: In attendance were two archbishops and three bishops,[107] namely, Bishop Ulrich of Orléans, the bishop of Paris, and the bishop of Beauvais, who, according to the account in the cartulary, led the cross-examination. Later, around 1037, Rodulfus Glaber provided little concrete information about the synod, although he might have heard about it from Ulrich of Orléans, whom he once met. He instead supplied a general theological excursus against heretics. As for the origin of the heretics of Orléans, his account is not plausible: A wandering woman stopped off in Orléans and infected people, including educated clergymen from the best families, with the "poison of her wickedness."[108] Because of their association with Eve and the snake, women were viewed with suspicion by monks, particularly as advisors (and wandering pilgrims—or prostitutes).

A similar spirit informs the report by the monk Adémar of Chabannes, that the heresy was fabricated by a peasant; according to an interpolation in one version, he came "from Périgord"[109] (the present-day départements of Dordogne and Lot-et-Garonne). The amplification that the peasant practiced magic served further to debase the intellectual niveau of the sect. Besides this notion, we see the quite common supposition that a heresy requires a foreign heresiarch who has "brought in" the heresy like a disease. Since the devil was at any rate involved,[110] people could find it conceivable that educated lords were misled by such people.

Apart from and in conjunction with "Manichaeism," the practice of devilish arts, particularly those pertaining also to sexual practices, was part of the common conception of every heresy. This is hardly surprising, given the pronouncements of the early churchmen, who like the rhetoricians only rarely eschewed the defamation of an enemy. Thus, we read in Adémar's chronicle that the clergymen in Orléans worshiped the devil first in the form of an Ethiopian, then in the form of the Angel of Light (Lucifer), in return for which he paid them a great deal of money. It would be criminal to recount the things they practiced in secret; in public, they pretended to be Christians. The peasant, their ringleader, had in his possession some powder made from the ashes of murdered boys and used it to change people into Manichaeans.[111] Not knowing anything else about the sect's doctrines, Adémar availed himself of the most interesting tidbits culled from the general portrayal of heresy.

The canons' doctrines were carefully recorded in the cartulary of Saint-Père in Chartres, but Paul, the monk who copied this record, apparently found that they lacked an important ingredient, which he supplied in a *digressio*. There he depicted in detail a black mass celebrated by the canons in Orléans, an orgy involving women and the very devil himself. The children resulting from such unions were killed and burned into ashes—the resulting magic powder (see above) turned a person into a heretic for life. "May Christians be on their guard against such shameful behavior!"[112]

These accounts could be dismissed as monkish fantasies if only some historians had not lent them credence. People have always practiced magic and indulged in sexual excess, but such activities are not in the least congruous with the canons' pronouncements, which we are about to consider. Whoever thought in such a primitive manner would hardly have known what to make of the sect's doctrines. Orgies, burning the children resulting from such unions, the preparation of a magic "bread" from their ashes, which was consumed "as a kind of sacrament"—all of this can be found in connection with the heretics of Soissons (1114) in the autobiography of Guibert, abbot of Nogent.[113] Popular if just because of its gruesomeness, the story circulated among the monastic clergy; Adémar— and he was certainly not the first—used it as an interlude ("preachers' tale") in a sermon.[114] The narrative always ends with the remark that whoever even once savors such magical charms is possessed by heresy (or doubt) forever.

Establishing whether it is possible to identify literary precedents for this tale or whether we are dealing here with a product of a popular "oral history" is not all that important. The story might also be imported from Byzantium, where at that time Michael Psellos wrote a *Dialogue on the Efficacy of Demons* linking them to orgies and the murder of children.[115] In any case the tale is a very old one, for, according to Tertullian, pagan Romans already ascribed it to the Christians, whose Holy Communion struck them as a *sacramentum infanticidii* [sacrament of infanticide] in conjunction with a *convivium incesti* [feast of unchastity].[116]

We are thus dealing with a widely disseminated tale marked by a polemical twist against the enemies of one's own religion. It is hence unlikely that the canons of Orléans had experimented with magic or with drugs.[117] Most scholars agree that they actually embodied a form of "Gnostic Christianity" made up of "Illuminati" who in their personal experience found the traditional expression of the Christian religion and church bloodless. While contemporaneous sources list various aspects of their propositions, the context of their tenets becomes plain in the cartulary. We shall return to that account at the conclusion of our discussion.

The monk Andreas of Fleury probably witnessed the synod.[118] In his view the defendants were lying when they said that they believed in the Trinity and the Incarnation of Christ. On the other hand, they acknowledged their skepticism concerning the existence of the church, baptism, penance, and the ordination of priests and bishops; they considered the blessing of marriages by the church to be unnecessary. In support they referred to the Holy Spirit: Infants to be baptized do not possess the Holy Spirit anymore than unworthy priests do. However, the clergymen of Orléans surely believed that they possessed the Holy Spirit. A problematic statement follows, which we will need to discuss further: "They boasted that they had a mother like unto the mother of God."[119]

As we have already heard, shortly after 1022 a monk named John of Fleury wrote to the bishop of Vich in Spain concerning the things he had heard about the people of Orléans:[120] They denied baptism, the Eucharist, and the forgiveness of sins, and despised marriage. They abstained from eating meat and lard "as if those things were unclean." It is not clear if the closing words were an embellishment by the writer of the letter, who in the monastery was after all subject to similar, if not quite that extensive, rules established by Saint Benedict. Canons ate meat and were not supposed to assume monastic duties.

An echo of the affair also registered in Auxerre, in the form of an account by the admittedly none-too-reliable Rodulfus Glaber. The heretics had declared that everything found in the Old and New Testaments about the Trinity was nonsense; lacking a creator, heaven and earth have always existed. Like the Epicureans, the heretics believed that vices went unpunished.[121] According to Rodulfus, they considered charitable and righteous works unnecessary effort, not, as we know them to be, the pledge for eternal reward. The heretics said that they possessed sufficient proof for the truth of their doctrines.

Rodulfus Glaber did not know very much about these doctrines, as becomes evident in his theological excursus aimed at proving their falsehood. In it he discussed God and the world in general, expressing Christian beliefs that could very well have been, and in fact perhaps were, written by someone else. The most concrete example is his rebuttal of the tenet that "heaven and earth, as we see them," were not created and were eternal. We find nothing of the sort in the cartulary, which speaks of God, the Creator. Are we to believe that the clergy in Orléans had been influenced by John Scotus (Eriugena)?[122] It is not very likely. However, it is totally unlikely that Bogomilism was operative here:[123] There is no mention of any opposition to an evil principle, nor is matter equated with evil. Just as Augustine polemicized against the Manichaeans, so did he against the concept of the eternity of the world.[124] This may be something Rodulfus gleaned from his readings and included to prove his erudition.

Up to now, we have skirted the best source on the sect's doctrines, the cartulary of the monastery of Saint-Père in Chartres. It has been held in low regard, on the one hand because of the approximately sixty-year interval between the events and the redaction of the collection, and on the other because of the "fantasized depiction," above all the devilish orgies and murder of children. If we extract this excursus as a widely disseminated tale, then the contrast between the excursus and the matter-of-fact, objective account found in the main portion becomes thoroughly evident. Both cannot have been written by the selfsame author, and it is easy to suppose that we are looking at a later revision of a contemporaneous and valuable text. The canons' responses betray their theological training, little of which would have survived over many decades of oral transmission. While the other sources emphasize the negative aspects of the heresy, here we can see clearly what was at issue for the canons of Orléans.

Of prime importance is a personal religious experience, a "doctrine transmitted by the Holy Spirit," revealed only to one pure in mind or spirit.[125] "The eyes of his pure spirit" are opened up "to the light of true belief" through a laying-on of hands by several sectarians; he is purified of all sin and filled with the gifts of the Holy Spirit. The Holy Spirit, so they said, reveals to him all the profundities of the Holy Scriptures and their true divinity. Satiated (spiritually) with heavenly sustenance, the initiate sees visions of angels; if he wishes, in the visions he is transported to other spheres. He lacks nothing, for God will always be by his side: God, in whom all the treasures of wisdom and all riches have their existence.

Visionaries were not necessarily heretics. They became heretics when they attributed absolute validity to their personal vision and regarded as worthless the church's means for attaining grace. That the canons of Orléans felt they possessed the Holy Spirit and the true interpretation of the Bible might have been sufferable had they not claimed to monopolize both, so to speak. They may not have done this out of presumption, but rather in consequence of an extreme spiritualism. This spiritualism reduced the sacraments to the one that did not involve a material substrate, not baptismal water or bread and wine: namely, the laying-on of hands. This spiritualism could not subscribe to Christ's Incarnation, even by means of a Virgin Birth, or to the Passion of Christ, the passion of a god whose essence was after all spirit. When questioned about both of these things, the canons answered skeptically: "We were not there, and we cannot believe that it is true." On the Virgin Birth: "What nature denies deviates always from [the will of] the Creator." And last, on the role of the Second Person of the Trinity in the creation: "You can tell such things to people who know about worldly things and believe the tales of men made of flesh, tales written on animal skins. We, however, have a law inscribed by the Holy Spirit in the innermost part of man, and we know nothing but what we have learned from God, the author [*conditor*] of all things. You lecture us in vain; the things you say are superfluous and lead away from the deity. Already we see our king, who reigns in heaven, who bears us upward in his hand to immortal triumph, and who bestows the joys of heaven upon us."[126]

Faith is not based on hearsay or on readings from the Holy Scriptures, but on the inner revelation to a Pentecostal congregation, which is how the clergymen in Orléans saw themselves. They studied the Bible and extracted its deepest secrets; but its texts served only to bolster their essential beliefs. Therein lies a distinction between this system and the Gnosticism of the late classical period, which we should not overlook. Deciphering the secret meaning of biblical passages, or allegorization, appears to be of secondary importance here; the meaning was supposed to spring from the fundamental spiritual experience. Whoever possessed the Holy Spirit dissociated himself thereby from the average person and was predisposed to mysticism. This mysticism could be associated with visions, as, for example, in the case of Hildegard of Bingen in the twelfth century. Seen from this perspective, the heretics of Orléans were early harbingers of the mysticism that started evolving only later.

Some have contended that the laying-on of hands was of Bogomil derivation,[127] but the earliest evidence we have for the laying-on of hands in the East dates from the second half of the eleventh century, although it may have been practiced there earlier. The laying-on of hands is employed in various ways in the church liturgy, and it is found in the Bible, particularly in passages concerning the Holy Spirit. The heretics asserted that the laying-on of hands in the ordination of priests and bishops was invalid because those who conferred it, unlike the members of the sect, did not possess the Holy Spirit. Evidence for a striking resemblance here to Bogomil thought, hitherto unnoted, comes from a text by Euthymios Zigabenos (around 1100). According to Andreas of Fleury, the clergymen of Orléans maintained that they possessed something like unto the Mother of God.[128] Zigabenos wrote: "They explained that each of them [the Bogomils] deserves the title Mother of God, for the Holy Spirit dwells in each of them, and therefore each of them gives birth to the Word."[129]

It must remain unresolved here whether we are dealing with a case of parallel beliefs arising spontaneously in two places or with an adoption from the East—by whatever route. On the other hand, their knowledge and occasional adoption of ideas enunciated by Augustine is demonstrable. At one point he had said that there is an outer world of things perceived by the senses and, on the other hand, an inner vision (*mentus intuitus*); in addition, there is belief, which arises from neither: for example, the belief in the Virgin Birth of Christ, a corporeal event that we would have been able to perceive with our senses had we been present at the time (*si tunc adessemus*).[130] We recall that when questioned about their beliefs concerning the Virgin Birth, Passion, and Reincarnation, the heretics responded: "We were not there, and we cannot believe that it is true."[131] That sounds like a quotation from Augustine and may denote that the sectarians did not esteem either tangible reality or belief in the literal meaning of the Revelation, but that they derived their religion solely from divine illumination, the inner vision. Whatever had not been "envisioned" need not be believed.

Was this skepticism or the deliverance from skepticism? In this case we can only speculate that these people, or at least some of them, had lost their faith in the mysteries, sacraments, and authority of the church and that they now attained something they regarded as a higher form of Christianity. It was supposed to be an advanced form of religiosity, an anticipation of the Beatific Vision in paradise.

Whoever progressed that far could no longer be weighed down by sin. Andreas of Fleury reported the heretics believed that after having committed a mortal sin no one could return to the state of grace by any means. According to the cartulary, the laying-on of hands was said to deliver an individual from the "stain of sin,"[132] which may be a reference to a rite of initiation, the entry into that state of grace the established church was not able to convey. In any case, the people of Orléans considered themselves innocent saints, hence their feeling of self-confidence as well. These ideas also may be found in Augustine's works, where many passages speak of a mystical Beatific Vision attainable in this life.[133] According to his *Confessiones*, the spiritual person needs "no one any longer to instruct him; he recognizes God's will by means of divine illumination." The Holy

Spirit dispenses his gifts among the *spirituales* [spiritual ones]: wisdom comprehensible only to the perfects (*perfecti*) above all; additionally, knowledge of temporal things, healing power, prophecy, etc.[134] People have thought that the canons of Orléans became heretics because of their overly enthusiastic reading of Saint Augustine's works against the Manichaeans; it is more likely that they read his principal works. All in all, it is unlikely that the canons derived their doctrines from books. What they hoped to find in them was confirmation of their experiences. In the eleventh century much was written about the Holy Spirit, in the course of which the issue of inspiration by the Holy Spirit was addressed.[135] Around 1200 the students of Amalric of Bena went so far as to teach that the Holy Spirit was incarnate in spiritual people and revealed himself in them, so that each of them could call himself Christ and Holy Spirit.[136]

Whenever faith takes a back seat to illumination, miracles are also no longer needed: "What nature denies deviates always from the Creator."[137] We will see what part the idea of nature played in these centuries—it was always a matter of God's will being personified by nature. Miracles violated the laws ordained by God himself, and in the days of early Scholasticism thinkers limited God's power to absolute necessity. In addition to the wording that something was "contrary to nature," Abelard came up with the more felicitous phrasing that God's actions in this instance exist "beyond nature" (*supra naturam*).[138] The clergymen of Orléans were not the only ones to have trouble with this topic, above all with the human nature of Christ and the real presence of Body and Blood in the Holy Communion; it is here, however, that their heresy is most manifest. This probably also accounts for the tone of irritation in their answer and the biting reference to the "animal skins," the parchment of the Holy Scriptures.

These people were certainly spiritualists, but it is possible that they did not revive the docetic notion that, as God, Christ could only have possessed a semblance of a body. It has been remarked that it is not clear whether in Orléans the difficulty lay in acknowledging the humanity of Christ or, contrariwise, the divinity of Christ.[139] If we are to believe the cartulary, the heretics denied the Passion, the "real" entombment, and the Resurrection of Christ. In viewing the divine as incompatible with the biblical account, they were probably more extreme than Docetes. Whereas in other cases the Bible served as the mainstay for heretical movements, it played a very limited role here. The Bible could not be disregarded entirely: The passage closes with a reference to the heavenly king, who will exalt the sectarians into his kingdom. Admittedly, we should not dismiss the possibility that their words were rendered in such a way as to conform with traditional modes of thought.

When we compare the incident in Orléans with the one in Arras, it becomes evident—contrary to the opinion of some—that the two are completely incongruous. The craftsmen of Arras formed a devout association possessing a (written) "rule" made up of passages from the Bible; in Bishop Gerard's report they appear to be submissive and educable laymen. The intellectuals of Orléans were full of imperturbable self-confidence and lectured the bishop cross-examining them. They had that quality in common with the bishop of Cambrai and Arras—as well as a command of the "scholarly literature." However, they interpreted it differently, at least in one case that we should mention briefly here.

Bishop Gerard discussed the function of the church building in his report: It is called *ecclesia* [church] because it contains the assembled people (Greek: *ekklesía*).[140] The statement can be traced back to Augustine and Varro. Gerard adopted the term *ecclesia*, derived from the people belonging to the church, while the people of Orléans rejected that usage: The (spiritual) idea of a church could not be applied to a (concrete) structure.[141] In this connection, by the way, they could have referred to another passage by Augustine in which he termed the assembled people in truth (*vere*) the church.[142] This illustration was preserved in the theological disputes of the twelfth century, as when Gerhoh of Reichersberg informed the pope that Abelard's students maintained that the human Christ could be called God only by association, as, for example, the name of the container is substituted for the contents, or the church building for the people assembled in it.[143]

The issue seems to be of minor importance, but we have to appreciate what it must have meant to the members of the cathedral chapter at Orléans to disparage the site of their daily liturgical observance in this way. The clergymen no longer believed in the materially delimited institution to which they had once dedicated their lives. The tension between the sad reality of their existence and the emphatic uplift provided by a mysticism not bound to any religious community must have been very great. The canons of Orléans suffered a terrible death, but it released them from the hopeless mess of their lives.

According to the testimony of Andreas of Fleury, only members of the clergy were involved in Orléans. We now turn to a heresy that likewise exhibits learned characteristics but was sustained by distinguished laymen. These events occurred sometime between 1027 and 1034, and for a long time it was assumed they transpired at Monteforte, a castle in the diocese of Asti. In fact, however, the castle was in Monforte d'Alba, southeast of Turin.[144] Due to Saracen incursions, the diocese of Alba was merged with the diocese of Asti in 969, then later reestablished after the

Saracens abandoned their footholds in the maritime Alps. According to Landulf, the prime source of information concerning the heresy,[145] it was "a castle above the town named Mons Fortis," but this native of Milan did not know the region. It contains only hills, and one of them would have been fortified as a stronghold against the Saracens or other disturbers of the peace—a minor territory at whose center resided free inhabitants subject to the judicial authority of a count. This is thoroughly consistent with the description of the inhabitants as "many of that people's (the Lombards') nobles," given by Rodulfus Glaber[146]—as always, not very well informed—and with the presence of a countess in Monforte. She was the seigneur and leader of the commune; its inhabitants are said to have united in opposition to attempts by the archbishop of Milan to obtain absolute control over Monforte,[147] but this is not substantiated by any source on Monforte.

Landulf wrote in the twelfth century, but his report contains concrete information and lists the questions, posed during the cross-examination, in the format of a record for a heresy trial. He may have consulted such records at the archbishop's court in Milan.[148] Unlike the report in the cartulary from Saint-Père in Chartres, the value of Landulf's account has gone unquestioned. No horror stories here, but we can rely on Rodulfus Glaber for that: He contended that in Monforte they had worshiped idols "as had the pagans," and celebrated the Holy Communion in an unseemly way jointly with Jews—we lack further "details." Instead, there follows the story of a mortally ill knight who was visited by a lady from the heretics' castle; a band of evil spirits "with black clothes and very sinister faces" accompanied her. Then the devil himself explained to the knight that Conrad (the Salian Conrad II) had attained the imperial crown (1027) with his help.[149] (As great as Cluny's esteem for Henry II had been, so little was its enthusiasm for his successor.) Out of the entire report at most one item of information appears useful, that it did not pertain to "Manichaeans" but—as indicated by the rubric—to a heresy "fabricated" (or "found") in Italy. Incidentally, Landulf also said that at issue was a recently (*nuper*) emerged and previously unheard-of (*inaudita*) heresy.

The description of the sect's discovery is less dramatic than in the case of Orléans. Landulf tells us that Aribert, archbishop of Milan, had undertaken a circuit of pastoral visitations that included a stop in Turin. There, he heard about the heresy and summoned one of its adherents from Monforte to come tell him openly all about it. The man was named Gerard, and it has been suspected that he was the count of Monforte, who had entered a monastery in 1014.[150] In any event, in the account he bears no title indicating a rank and therefore may just have been a spokesman for the free individuals who took up residence in the village fortress. He must have possessed some religious education. Was he educated at the "external school" of a monastery or by a religious advisor, by, for example, the parish priest of the fortress? Just as little was heard about laypeople in Orléans, so was little prominence given to clergymen in this instance. According to Gerard's testimony, individuals drawn from the higher ranks of society lived communally, called themselves "brothers," treated their wives like mothers and sisters, were vegetarians, always fasted, and prayed "constantly." Praying day and night in shifts [a "prayer chain"] had been attempted at one time in Carolingian monasteries; in Monforte it was at the least practiced by the sect's elders (*maiores*). Property was held in common, in fact, "in common with all people," whatever that was supposed to mean.

We have here—apart from the sect's membership—an early example of a lay religious community of the sort we will encounter in the last decade of the eleventh century in southern Germany.[151] There, "entire villages (*villae*)" were devoted to the communal life with all property held in common in the manner of the primitive church, men and women guided by secular clergymen or monks, defamed by those bearing them ill will, but protected by Pope Urban II. In the case of Monforte, however, spiritual care was in the hands of the *maiores*, who prayed a great deal and perhaps led Bible classes; presumably, the daily readings from the Old and New Testaments we hear about were held communally. No doubt not everyone could read, and not everyone had use of his or her own copy of the Holy Scriptures.

The "elders" do not appear to have performed any other religious functions. The archbishop sought to determine the identities of the individuals behind the heretics by posing the sly question, To whom did they make confession? And he received an answer that people have puzzled over: They had a *pontifex* (pontiff), though he was not tonsured, and besides him there were no others and no (church) office (*ministerium*).[152] This did not refer to the pope in Rome, but to someone who "daily visits our brothers scattered all over the whole world" and forgives them their sins. Some have thought of him as an itinerant bishop, but the very omnipresence of the figure alone indicates that he was the Holy Spirit; the term "brothers" did not necessarily refer to members of the local sect in Monforte, but to good Christians everywhere. Thus, it fits that there was no answer to the question, What part of the world did the doctrine come from then? No one knew. Its starting point must have been the Bible group in Monforte.

The Holy Spirit and the Holy Scriptures uniquely interpreted were of prime importance to the thinking of the people in Monforte. Christ was born of Mary, in other words, of the Holy Scriptures; the Holy Spirit was humble knowledge of the Bible. We will speak of this shortly. These propositions were enough for the archbishop; he took "all of them he could find" into custody, including the countess, and brought them to Milan. There they were not held in strict confinement, for the peasants crowded around to catch sight of them. The heretics instructed them on the basis of "misleading fragments torn out of the Holy Scriptures."

The rest of the story is quickly told. Contrary to the archbishop's wishes the city magistrates issued an ultimatum: The heretics were to choose between veneration of a crucifix and the stake. A few chose the crucifix and recited the credo, "but many, covering their faces with their hands, strode into the flames."

Such was the heroic strength of their convictions and at the same time the fulfillment of a ritualistic precept. At the inquiry Gerard had said the following: "If we are tortured by evil people and as a result die, we will rejoice; if, however, we die a natural death, our nearest one [nearest relative?] kills us before we breathe our last."

This peculiar tenet remains unexplained. It may be interpreted as an expression of "spiritualism," but that would be quite the generalization. Some researchers have pointed out that the Cathars practiced a voluntary form of starvation, the *endura*—though much later and only rarely documented.[153] Since the Bible played such a prominent role in their thinking, actual passages from the Bible may have prompted this practice. In general, martyrs were held in higher esteem than saints who died natural deaths (as "confessors"), and perhaps being killed put one on an equal footing with a martyr. In the Revelation to John all those who were beheaded for their testimony to Jesus are lauded for their holiness, and they ruled together with Christ for a thousand years; the rest of the dead joined them only after the thousand years had passed (Rev. 20:4–5). Be that as it may, the heretics viewed a torturous death with equanimity, even joy. As for Gerard, the spokesman sent to appear before the archbishop, Landulf described him thus: "He was completely prepared for martyrdom and was eager to end his life with the most severe torments."

As for the actual theological teachings of the sect, they were preserved only in fragments and copied down without any attempt to comprehend them; thus, some may have been altered or at least vulgarized. Each individual proposition can be analyzed, but we should not expect them to amount to a doctrine.

Gerard listed the Persons of the Trinity and explained: "What I have termed the 'Father' is the eternal God, who is all things from the beginning[154] and in whom all things exist." This sounds somewhat pantheistic and leaves open the question about the creation out of nothingness. Some have noted analogies to the works of John Scotus (Eriugena),[155] but without explaining how the commune at Monforte could have gotten its hands on this very learned but at the time little-known author.

"What I have called the Son is the spirit of man beloved by God." In the Gospel According to Matthew, a voice from a cloud says, "That is my beloved Son" (Matt. 17:5, Transfiguration of Jesus); Christ himself often referred to himself as the "Son of Man." In this case, however, we are dealing with the spirit (*animus*); the disregard for the body seems to be an outgrowth of spiritualism and appears gleaned from the writings of John Scotus (Eriugena) or Augustine.[156] Works by the latter author were more likely to have been available in Monforte; after all, they had the Old as well as the New Testaments, probably in two or more volumes, as well as a collection of church laws (*canones*), which Gerard cited during his testimony. The same may be true for Gerard's next elucidation: "What I have called the Holy Spirit is the understanding [*intellectus*] of sacred sciences, by which all things are governed with the gift of discernment [*discrete*]." Like the concept of *animus hominis* [spirit of man], the concept of *intellectus* may also have been derived from Neoplatonism, transmitted possibly in Augustine's works.

In response to a question about Jesus, son of the Virgin and "Word of the Father," Gerard said: "He is a Spirit, who was born to the Virgin Mary according to the senses [*sensualiter*];[157] that means [*videlicet*] he was born of the Holy Scriptures." Only according to ordinary understanding is Christ the son of the Virgin Mary, but in the higher allegorical sense the Holy Scriptures are his mother. One would be hard-pressed to produce parallel passages for this doctrine, which seems to have been unique to the people of Monforte. It must be the result of a line of reasoning that equated Logos [word] at the beginning of the Gospel According to John with the "word" in the sense of the word of God, the Holy Scriptures. This word is preexistent in God the Father; it comes to mankind in Christ; and even the Holy Spirit—according to the last sentence of Gerard's theological explanation—is to be understood by means of the word. "The Holy Spirit is an understanding of the Holy Scriptures based on veneration."

Thus, we have here ideas that propound to unravel the secret of the Trinity by involving the Holy Scriptures. The issue is placed in a different context and linked with the message of God to mankind. Pursuing this idea further, it becomes evident that the word emanates from God into the souls of humans; thus, they are inspired just like in Orléans. However, we are probably dealing with, if anything, a fragmentary line of thought, intuitive and unsystematic. In any event, what he heard did not make the archbishop indignant, but "dumfounded."

Just as in Orléans, there is no tenet addressing evil. Therefore, the people from Monforte were also not Cathars, although it has been asserted that they were. What is more, they read the Old Testament in Monforte, while Bogomils and Cathars condemned it entirely or to some extent as reflecting the rule of the evil principle. Any reference to dualism in this case is out of the question; were they to have thought through or integrated their doctrines into a theological system, these individuals would hardly have come up with dualism.

Comparing the heretics of Monforte to those in Arras, we find in both cases laypeople who regulated their lives according to biblical precepts and wished to form a strong community. In Arras they were satisfied with the basic precepts written down by Gundulf; the people of Monforte were "Bible exegetes" who had developed the rudiments of a unique theology. In Arras they accepted with resignation the instruction imparted by the bishop, while the free peasants of Monforte and their countess could no longer find their way back into the fold, no more than the clerics of Orléans.

Orléans (1022), Arras (1025), and Monforte (ca. 1030) are three relatively well-documented incidents, and the amount of information we possess is head and shoulders above what chroniclers customarily supplied in their reports; in Goslar (1051) no one took the trouble to prepare an official record, or it has not been handed down to us, not even in excerpts. We have no such good fortune in the second half of the century, and there are almost no short accounts either. The one that is in any event the best comes from a Cluniac monastery in Nevers, for the year 1075: "In this year the heretic Belinus was killed, and his companions were also consigned to death."[158] In Nevers the road from Tours reaches and spans the curve in the Loire River; the city is an ancient episcopal seat. From 1066 to 1097 a church dedicated to Saint Stephen rose up in the city's suburb, and in 1076 the Church of Christ the Savior was consecrated. Were the heretics artisans engaged in the building trades, merchants, or neither? We also know nothing about their teachings. The name Belinus must have been derived from the place-name Belin or the surrounding area, the Belinois (arrondissement Bordeaux, approximately two hundred kilometers from Nevers as the crow flies).

A much less valuable source, a letter from Theodoin, bishop of Liège, to King Henry I of France,[159] contains an account of heresy. In 1049 or 1050 this imperial bishop instructed the king to beware of heresies in France: The Scholastic Berengar in Tours and Bruno, bishop of Angers, asserted that the host was only a phantom and not the body of Christ; they opposed legitimate (church) marriages and infant baptism. Berengar's teaching about the Eucharist will concern us later. The church doctrine on marriage was at that time in the process of being formulated, and many considered marriage a family matter, with or without the blessing of the church. Infant baptism, given the child's inability to recite the declaration of faith, was perceived as scandalous and not merely in heretical circles. In any case, the letter cannot be reckoned among the reliable sources on heresy.

Furthermore, a letter addressed to the clergy of Sisteron (in upper Provence) from Pope Nicholas II in 1060 is of very questionable value:[160] The newly consecrated bishop should not ordain any married individuals, cripples, or Africans (*Afros*)—the latter because some of them were Manichaeans, and others had been rebaptized. As Jeffrey Burton Russell discerned, this is a copy of warnings issued by Pope Gregory II. People in Rome chose to believe that Saracens were still to be found in the maritime Alps. They certainly knew nothing about Saracen beliefs, so they retained an image dating back to the eighth century.

In the search for heretical views in the second half of the eleventh century, reference has also been made to a polemical tract written around 1085: the *Liber contra Wolfelmum* by Manegold of Lautenbach. The work attacks "philosophers," progressive contemporaries of Manegold who were influenced by classical literature. In order to categorize them, he called them by the names Mani, Arius, and Origen; he listed some mistaken ideas they held, which cannot be traced back entirely to the fathers of the church. Were they actually false doctrines held by heretics in Manegold's own times?[161] Surely not. First of all, the passage addresses the transmigration of souls. This is an ancient idea, but the earliest evidence for its currency among heretics (Bogomils) dates to the twelfth century. Second, equating the soul with human blood comes up; it is another ancient notion, the earliest evidence for which as a heresy dates to around 1300 among Cathars. Third, he deals with ideas concerning the body as the prison of the soul that are not new and that are encountered elsewhere, above all in works by Plotinus and his followers, and were picked up by the Cathars. Finally, Manegold concluded in another work that the Old Testament had only limited worth in the age of the new covenant—quite a moderate conclusion in light of the enmity the Bogomils and Cathars bore against the God of the Old Testament and all, or at least the greater part, of its books.

Had Manegold known contemporaries who advocated any of the first three doctrines, born polemicist that he was, he probably would have gone into more detail about their heresies. His purpose in writing was to open the eyes of "modern philosophers" to the dangers of ancient philosophy. Manegold traced back to Empedocles the equation of soul and blood, for example, and other items to Pythagoras and Plato. His source was Macrobius's *Somnium Scipionis*, which contained the opinions of eighteen ancient philosophers on the soul. It concludes with the question, how could anyone enter heaven if the soul is blood?[162]

Thus, for this period we discover very little pertaining to true heretics, which has led some to conclude that heresy in the West was "extinguished for half a century."[163] On the other hand, we encounter the epithet "heretic" quite often, which is also evidenced by reading Manegold. Even more than in other epochs, in the second half of the century people loved to stamp their theological or political enemies as "heretics." The charge was leveled time and time again during the debates of the so-called Investiture Contest. Reformers labeled Archbishop Wibert of Ravenna, who would later crown Henry IV emperor, a "heresiarch" in the wake of his elevation to antipope as Clement III (1080).[164] The concept of simony was also applied in a way that spawned such accusations: Laymen were to have nothing to do with ecclesiastical offices; simony was a false interpretation of the works of the Holy Spirit, ergo, a heresy. For example, this is what Gregory VII meant when he wrote Countess Adela of Flanders that the Archdeacon Hubert of Thérouanne had succumbed to heresy; and, therefore, no one should give credence to his words. According to the Gregorian interpretation, he was a simoniac, and despite that, he soon succeeded in becoming a bishop.[165] For the most part, people were more moderate in their thinking, and around the very end of the twelfth century, there is an example of a puristic heretic receiving a lecture on the distinction between the personal sinfulness of an ecclesiastical office-holder and his inviolable office.[166]

Contrariwise, the Gregorian view of *simoniaca haeresis* [the heresy of simony] might be considered heretical by the anti-Gregorians, that is, by the conservatives among the imperial clergy; one supporter of the Gregorian view paid dearly for this at the stake. We know only his name—in the garbled form of "Ramihrdus"—from a chronicle of Saint Andrew's in Cambrai.[167] The bishop there heard that this man was preaching unorthodox tenets in a village (Férin, near Lambres, south of Douai?).[168] The bishop examined him before a clerical assembly, but found nothing objectionable in the man's testimony. Yet, when "Ramihrdus" was asked to receive the Eucharist as proof that he spoke truly, he refused on the grounds that he would not accept the sacrament from the hand of the bishop or the hands of the abbots or priests, because they were either simoniacs or greedy. Thereupon, he was declared a heresiarch (*heresiarcha*, leader of a heresy); some men, including a few in the bishop's service (*ministeriales*), placed him in a hut and consigned both the man and the structure to flames. Many of his followers preserved his remains, and even in 1135 the chronicler wrote: "To this day many members of his sect are found in a few suburbs (*oppida*), and people who work in the weaving trade are known by his name."

The incident had repercussions: Pope Gregory VII wrote to the bishop of Paris that he had heard that the people of Cambrai had burned a man for rejecting the divine service ministered by simoniac and married priests;[169] due to the cruelty of the act the perpetrators were to be excommunicated. Gerard II, the elected bishop of Cambrai to whom the message was really addressed, had to defend himself, before a synod of French churchmen called by Gregory, against the charges of simony and burning a man to death.[170]

Like Bishop Gerard I, Gerard II also had trouble with people from the French portion of his diocese; like the heretics of Arras, the followers of "Ramihrdus" were also laypeople, and it is unlikely that individual was himself a cleric. As we have noted, almost forty years later his name was a term for weavers, and he and his followers were probably also craftsmen. Later on, weaving would be the "classical" craft for heretics.

The activities of "Ramihrdus" can be placed in the context of church reform "from the bottom up," for which the Patarenes in Milan are the best known instance. A discussion of that movement is not within the scope of this book. Suffice it to say, they wished to bring about a reform of the higher clergy by boycotting their celebration of the sacraments; there was nothing heretical about this in the eleventh century, though in this instance the papacy also must have hesitated before lending support to the Patarenes.

The events in Milan and other northern Italian cities seem to have reverberated in the French portion of Flanders. In 1076 Bishop Benzo of Alba, a supporter of Henry IV and propagandist in the Investiture Contest, was driven out of his diocese by Patarenes; the same thing might have occurred in 1077 to Bishop Gerard of Cambrai had he not been willing to grant privileges to the rebellious populace.[171] In such a tense situation, in conjunction with the nationalistic clashes within the diocese, the actions against the "heretics" take on a different complexion. A bishop loyal to the king would consider it necessary to make an example of the Gregorian vanguard. "Ramihrdus" was sacrificed to make a political point.

New to the second half of the eleventh century were, on the one hand, the intensity of religious feeling within wide circles of the lay population and, on the other hand, the fact that there existed within the clergy a faction receptive to this frame of mind. Whoever rejected the clergy on account of its worldliness no longer had to withdraw into a very circumscribed group that quickly became "illegal." Monks too became allies in the daily battle against the powers that be and delivered sermons to the

general populace, something previously unheard of for monks. At stake
now was not merely the reform of religious communities, but also the
proper order of the world.

North of the Alps, the abbey of Hirsau in the Black Forest was a leader
in this movement, soon reforming other monasteries. In the *Book on
Preserving the Unity of the Church*[172] the monks of Hirsau are accused of
undermining both the kingdom and the papacy's cause; a "civil war"
(*intestinum bellum*) rages among the monks, who are "split into many
sects." Above all, the book contends, monks should remain in their
monasteries, but they force themselves out into the world and dispatch
the "bearers of their words" in every direction: They preach that "the
church of God, the justice of God, and the holy priesthood are found only
in them and their followers." In addition, they say "that they are heavenly
[*caelestes*] and spiritual Christians [*spirituales*] and the sons of God." Elsewhere, we find complaints about the wanderers (*girovagi*), who, under the
guise of monks, roam all over, sowing discord. In the next sentence we
read that laypeople were disseminating the monstrous (excessive) papal
decree against married clergymen.[173] Wandering monks and laypeople
involved in ecclesiastical affairs were working hand in hand to achieve the
goals of reform.

If a layperson desired to base his way of life on the monastic-ascetic
model, he now met with rejection only from one clerical party, while from
another he drew succor and advice. We have already referred briefly to
certain communities of laypeople found in southern Germany.[174] According to Bernold of St. Blasien, in many villages communal life flourished
among both the clergy and the laity, who pledged themselves and their
possessions to this way of life. They did not wear a habit, but "were equal
in merit to the secular clergy and to monks." Their communal life took
place under the supervision of and in service to the regular clergy. The
account goes on to say that certain people became jealous of these
brothers, although it was clear to all that they lived in the manner of the
primitive church. "Innumerable" men and women entered convents or
monasteries; even in the villages there likewise lived "innumerable virgins who had consecrated themselves to God, and married people who
lived like monastics [*religiose*]" and obeyed monks. The communities
flourished above all throughout Swabia; here "whole villages" dedicated
themselves to living devoutly and "competed with each other over the
sanctity of their morals."

Abbot William of Hirsau had introduced into his monasteries the
institution of lay brothers based on the Italian model. In addition, groups
of laypeople appear increasingly to have been admitted into the network
of religious communities, working for and also no doubt residing in them.

Yet, there were also other settlements that lived "entirely" (*ex integro*) according to religious precepts; Bernold wrote that a priest cared for the inhabitants' souls. While he may have overestimated the extent of the phenomenon, it was no fabrication. The schism in the church between "good" and "bad," between saints and the justifiably excommunicated, left a very strong impression upon common people and increased people's insecurity to such an extent that they awaited God's direct intervention. In times like these, it was a good idea to be devout, particularly in light of the omens Bernold described: blood seen flowing out of the Host, and toads and fish seen falling (out of a tornado?) from the sky. "Many people, even monks, interpreted this as an omen of events to come within the empire."[175]

Bernold's account is a unique depiction of the way people thought in a southern Germany torn apart by war and religious factionalism. The situation was similar in Italy, though better in France, where an "Investiture Contest" had just been avoided. Popular religious ferment in the face of bad conditions found a new outlet in the Peace of God movement; it was steered away from home in the People's Crusade led by Peter the Hermit (of Amiens), or found repose in the lay brotherhood within the Cistercian order. Admittedly, all this only partially explains the almost total lack of accounts concerning heretics in the late eleventh century. We can establish the facts; we should not, however, explain them away with a handful of generalizations.

All the same, we can surmise one thing: Lay heretics of the eleventh century were concerned less with dogmatic matters than with the inner stability provided by a rule of conduct. Now there were exemplary figures among the clergy, zealous ascetics and preachers who offered this support. One no longer needed to become a heretic in order to practice the apostolic life, free of institutional constraints. There were even monks who had freed themselves from the constraint of physical *stabilitas* [remaining in the same monastery for life] and pointed out the path to sanctity.

2

The Twelfth Century: Non-Cathars

 The first half of the twelfth century was marked by the appearance of major preachers exercising great influence over churchgoers. Men like Norbert of Xanten and Bernard of Clairvaux come to mind; the Premonstratensians and Cistercians followed in their footsteps. Gifted as speakers and often active in ecclesiastical politics, they remained within the orthodox fold. Arnold of Brescia was also orthodox, but political forces gained the upper hand in his case, and he met with an unfortunate end because of his demand that the clergy practice poverty and be free of sin. Last, we find a group of individuals who championed "populist" causes. They not only inveighed against the clergy, but also disseminated among the people novel doctrines that were influenced by popular thought. If "still" and more or less anonymous groups of sectarians were the norm in the eleventh century, then now there were "loud" followers of masters whose names they bore: "Tanchelmistae, Petrobrusiani, Heinriciani, Eunitae, Arnaldistae" [Tanchelmists, Petrobrusians, Henricians, Eonists, Arnoldists].[1] Mobilized by the agents of church reform, the laity had gained free rein; the changing living conditions in the cities, for example, or, to be more exact, in the suburbs, were also a contributing factor. To be sure, there was also concurrently "stillness" in rural areas, a phenomenon to which the sources only rarely make mention.

The sermons were delivered mainly by itinerant preachers, hence under circumstances quite unlike the quiet, enclosed existence characteristic of traditional monks above all, who were not customarily permitted to preach. For the most part, the sermons eluded ecclesiastical supervision, were delivered out of doors altogether or in a church, as a form of popular entertainment against which intervention would have been difficult. The bishop was supposed to preach in cities, but he often only preached to clerical and educated audiences that understood Latin. There were the priests and their exhortations every Sunday, at least in those places where things were well administered. That being the situation, people knew ahead of time what the parish priest would say; it was quite different with an itinerant preacher, whose very appearance seemed to announce his sanctity. People pursued him, accompanied him on his travels, and they expected him to perform miracles. The possession of such power over people led some of these individuals down ever stranger paths.

First on our list is Tanchelm, who claimed a following in Flanders, Zealand, and Brabant. Purporting to be a monk, he was among those espousing the view that unworthy priests could not perform valid sacraments. This was the basic premise held by the Patarenes, and Tanchelm also shared their conviction that the clergy of the country was corrupt. As a consequence, he advised the faithful to go on a sort of strike and suspend the payment of tithes. That message was incendiary enough; it was stoked by the extraordinary oratorical gift of this man, who had suffered a personal disappointment at the hands of the Catholic Church: In 1112 he and a priest named Everwacher were dispatched to Rome in the service of Count Robert II of Flanders. They were charged with convincing Pope Paschal II to incorporate Zealand into a French diocese—thereby depriving the imperial bishop of Utrecht of part of his bishopric. The mission was unsuccessful, and the clergymen of Utrecht did everything they could to make the life of this enemy of the diocese miserable. The prime source of information on Tanchelm is a letter from the clergy of Utrecht to the archbishop of Cologne asking him to take Tanchelm into custody and not to set him free under any circumstances.[2] We see once again how politics in this borderland were a factor in the depiction of a heretic found there, for we are not at all sure that all the peculiarities the Utrechters imputed to Tanchelm reflected the truth.

"He asserted that the church existed only in him and his followers. The church . . . this man wants to ascribe just to the 'Tanchelmists' alone!" This Donatist premise perforce led to the idea of a "church of the pure," yet Tanchelm did not attempt to invest himself or his followers with church offices—except for one parish whose tithes went to support Everwacher, the priest who had accompanied him to Rome. Furthermore, he had "the audacity to call himself God": Christ was God because he "possessed the Holy Spirit, and he [Tanchelm] was not of lower rank, . . . because he had received the fullness of the Holy Spirit." The final assertion may have been one of Tanchelm's propositions; but that is scarcely true of the first one, assuming one is not predisposed to see pantheism at work here.

That the man did not lack imagination is evident from the religious spectacles he staged with his adherents. At his order a statue of the Virgin Mary was supposedly fetched from a church, and he held it by the hand to signify his engagement to Mary. He told the people to give him wedding gifts—whereupon women bestowed their jewelry on him. Thus, what we see here was a dubious, though psychologically effective, type of the collection. Tanchelm needed money because he traveled like a prince: Under the leadership of a blacksmith, twelve men representing the twelve apostles and allegedly a woman representing the Virgin Mary accompanied Tanchelm. The party acted both as a bodyguard and as a religious confraternity. In Utrecht they were referred to as a "guild," in other words, as one of those craft or trade associations providing mutual assistance and also serving political purposes. The reference to a blacksmith points to the close relationship later found so often between the practical arts and a heretical movement.

Subsequently, around 1155, the story underwent embellishment. It was said that approximately three thousand armed men accompanied Tanchelm so that no one, neither count nor duke, could oppose him; he paraded around in clothes embroidered with gold and braided his hair with gold. Tanchelm's adherents drank his bath water or carried it off as a relic.[3] A second version of the same account introduces the subject of orgies,[4] which had already been warily alluded to—"it is said"—in the letter from the clergy in Utrecht. The purpose of all this was to discredit the adherents of the sect after Tanchelm's murder by a priest.

That incident took place in 1115; four years later Bishop Burchard of Cambrai founded a collegiate church in Antwerp dedicated to eradicating the "Tanchelmist" heresy. This move did not achieve its goal, and it took the Premonstratensian Norbert of Xanten to deal with the sect (1124). Besides, the former group was made up of canons, while Norbert's newly established reform order practiced strict asceticism. People wanted to see saints, and there they were.

Fantastic stories about Tanchelm's appearance and his doctrines continued to circulate, transfiguring him into a sort of Antichrist. A trace of this can even be found in Abelard's *Theologia "Scholarium,"* where it is truly unexpected:[5] Tanchelm had himself proclaimed the Son of God and, "as it is said," had the people he had led astray build him a temple.

This man was a reformer who carried away the crowd with the power of his preaching and mobilized it against the local clergy; his sermons may have contained heretical material, but that was not the focus of his efforts. The mobs he craved were found in the small, rapidly up-and-coming urban settlements. These were gaining in social and political importance, without the ecclesiastical authorities taking any notice of what was afoot. For instance, in Tanchelm's day Antwerp comprised a single parish with one parish priest subject to the bishop of Cambrai. As the city grew in wealth, there arose a network of affiliated churches whose prebendaries were not priests for the most part and who might be married; they resided in their own homes and let others attend to the celebration of the mass.[6] This was like adding fuel to an already highly incendiary political situation, for at the time Tanchelm journeyed to Rome, the conflict between Henry V and Pope Paschal II had reached a dramatic climax. In addition, it was a period of communal movements; although we cannot assert that in Tanchelm's case we are dealing with an "urban" heresy, still the idea of freedom for townspeople was already in the air. The natural adversary of sectarianism was the local bishop; in places where there was no bishop, due to a vacancy (as in Utrecht) or due to the small size of the town (as in Antwerp), things could take quite a free course. Tanchelm was imprisoned in Cologne, yet he was released without having been tried for heresy; a trial would probably have been difficult to hold and might have sparked uprisings in the city.

Tanchelm must have possessed a certain amount of intelligence; otherwise he could not have been sent to Pope Paschal II in Rome. He inveighed against the clergy, but left churches and monasteries in peace. Things were different with Eon of Stella from Loudeac in Brittany. He was a member of the minor nobility,[7] "illiteratus et idiota" [unlettered and uneducated], and was a leader of a robber band rather than a reformer. In this case, public sentiment against the clergy seems to have sought, not sanctity, but a splendid lordliness that claimed to have been legitimized spiritually. Surrounded by members of his family and friends, he gallivanted about with droves of people, who saw in him the "Lord of Lords"; his extensive entourage lent him weight and gained him entrée to churches and monasteries, which were ransacked. "A splendid glory seemed to envelop him, and a regal extravagance; his attendants did not work, dressed in magnificent clothes, ate expensive foods, and did all this with the greatest merriment." Those who sought to seize him were corrupted by this false splendor—it was obvious to the chronicler that the devil had a hand in it.

Devilish arts also appeared to account for the robbers' being "borne through various provinces with wondrous speed" and staying hidden for a time in difficult terrain, then sallying forth again by surprise. Forces were sent against Eon in vain, for they did not find him. The archbishop of Rheims later found it easy, however, to have him captured—it appears that when the prelate's troops came upon the scene, it was not the devil, but the Bretons, who cut off the aid they had provided up until then in this game of hide-and-seek. The inner circle of his followers was taken along with Eon; he had given them new, important-sounding names: "Wisdom," "Knowledge," "Insight," and so forth. Another source recounts that they bore the names of angels, apostles, archbishops, and bishops[8]—as in a carnival play. In any event, William of Newburgh found an informant who reported that he himself had heard the man called "Insight" threaten revenge (on the sheriff) and invoke the earth to open up, even as he was on his way to the stake. The others too stood their ground and defended their new names until death. "Such was the power of the error, once it had affixed itself to someone's heart."

Since ancient times people had believed that a name was the key to the essence of a thing or else to a person; some monks and many popes adopted a new name as if they wished to become a "new person" in a new sphere of existence. Eon himself, it was said, had construed his personal role from his name: He had applied the liturgical formula "Per eum qui venturus est iudicare vivos et mortuos, et saeculum per ignem" (Through him who is still to come to judge the living and the dead, and the world, by fire), to his own name, perceiving "Eon" in the "eum"—as pronounced by a Breton, they possibly did sound alike. Eon was thus the son of God. This may have been meant as a joke by clergymen poking fun at an uneducated layman, but it is also recounted by Otto of Freising,[9] a reputable historian who took this report seriously.

In 1148 Eon again had his big chance, when at the Council of Rheims he repeated the liturgical formula, asserting that he was the "Eon" that was still to come to judge the living and the dead, and the world, through fire. William of Newburgh also reported that Eon held a staff in the shape of the letter Y. When asked what it signified, he replied, "This is something very secret. As long as the two ends point upward, like now, God possesses two-thirds of the universe and entrusts me with one-third. When I turn the two upper ends toward the ground and point the single part upward, I entrust God with only one-third [of the world]." At this, the prelates at the council properly had a laugh at his expense.

If we take the incident seriously nonetheless, we see that it is not without internal consistency. Eon is the Christ of the Parousia and as such part of the Trinity; he is entitled (probably just for that reason) to rule one-third of the world. In his hand he carries a sort of divining rod, a magical implement; the dipping of the rod held a hidden meaning. Did it herald the Last Judgment, at which Christ will pass judgment with even greater might?

Otto of Freising explained that Eon did not merit the appellation "heretic," for he had been so peasantlike and uneducated. He might have been right, for without access to the Holy Scriptures one could undertake neither the apostolic life nor the interpretation of doctrine. Eon probably heard the Latin phrase during a recitation of the liturgy, thought he detected his name in the phrase, and made it the basis for his self-portrayal. Eon was ridiculed as unlettered, and in spite of the damage he inflicted on his country's church, the pope and the prelates at the council were inclined to be clement. As a result, Eon was able to spend his last days in the dungeon of Abbot Suger of Saint-Denis, who was at the time serving as a sort of royal administrator. Oddly enough, Eon had not been burned to death along with his followers right after he was taken prisoner. He may have had the support of his family or even a portion of his countrymen, who were not well-disposed toward the clergy.

Tanchelm and Eon of Stella belong to two different generations, but we have reviewed them in succession because of the "populist" streak characterizing their rise, given the anticlerical tenor of the times. We now turn to a type of itinerant preacher that should have met with more success and through whom we can already trace a sort of spiritual lineage. By this, we mean Peter of Bruis and Henry the Monk. Of the same generation, their rise and doctrines entirely warranted serious consideration; men like Peter the Venerable and Bernard of Clairvaux thought it imperative to oppose them. They are linked to Tanchelm in some respects, but to Eon of Stella in none except their anticlericalism.

Peter of Bruis was a priest from the Dauphiné,[10] probably the parish priest of Bruys, near Rosans (arrondissement Gap, Hautes-Alpes). Around 1112 or 1113 he seems to have embarked upon the itinerant life of a heretic preacher, one that he would maintain for twenty years, until the close of 1132 or beginning of 1133. In large part our knowledge of him stems from a polemical work by Peter the Venerable, the prominent abbot of Cluny, entitled *Against the Petrobrusians*.[11] This source appears to be free of biased fabrications, though perhaps a rudimentary doctrine has been "thought through" here and there, as in the case of the heretics of Arras. One of the canons issued by the Synod of Toulouse (1119) may also have been directed against Peter of Bruis.[12] This crude man's modus operandi is marked by a tendency to use force. In the tract mentioned above, Peter the Venerable leveled a charge against both Peter of Bruis and Henry the Monk that probably applied only to the former man: Priests had been whipped, imprisoned, or forcibly compelled to marry. He had preached that the crucifix was not to be venerated, but instead, "in revenge for the suffering and death" of the Lord, to be "disgraced with every outrage, chopped up with swords, burned in a fire."[13] People should not build any churches and should tear down the ones already built, for a person could

pray just as well at an inn as at church. The simple folk dwelling at the foot
of the Alps would go for such forceful talk.

Still, we must not imagine that Peter of Bruis was just some uncouth
mountain dweller. Peter the Venerable reasoned with him and his followers to consider the many ecclesiastical authorities (*auctoritates*, citations
from the canon of ecclesiastical works) that supported the recitation of the
Psalms. Priests, "which you were after all yourselves," were after all most
particularly given to reciting these hymns. With regard to the doctrine of
the Eucharist, Peter had even formulated, on his own, the view that the
transubstantiation of the bread and wine into the Body and Blood of
Christ was an occurrence that could never again be repeated.[14] As for the
custom of baptizing infant children, which was controversial among the
populace, he introduced—and was apparently the first to do so—the
practice of rebaptism, on the assumption that the first one was invalid.
Both Peter the Venerable and Abelard documented such baptisms; Abelard
added that they were coerced.[15] Thus, there was no real presence in the
Eucharist, though there was perhaps a baptism that was considered
sacramental, probably in the form of a baptism with water.[16] Prayers or
offers on behalf of the dead had no effect—the explanation for this
assertion lies in the belief that there is no purgatory, that the dead already
dwell in either heaven or hell.

The question arises whether there was a system at the root of these
beliefs or whether they represent the denial of selected established doctrines. The paucity of tenets may give the impression that the latter is the
case; we do not know how Peter of Bruis thought about many essential
aspects of orthodoxy, and we also cannot discern any positive precepts.
Was Peter the Venerable so poorly informed, or had he included everything that was known? The amount of detail in his tract suggests the latter.
Scholars have endeavored to come up with a positive compilation of
Peter's precepts by characterizing them as indicative of "spiritualism":
There should be no physical church building, no crucifixes, no transubstantiation of bread and wine. But then, what about baptism with water?
Spiritualism is usually linked with asceticism; in this case, priests were
forced to marry, and the sectarians roasted meat on Good Friday.

There is even less reason for suspecting "dualism," for we hear nothing
about the conflict between a good and an evil god, a world of light and a
world of darkness. Peter the Venerable did not consider the "Petrobrusians" to be Manichaeans; in his opinion, they were a "new" sect, though
he had dealt with Manichaeism in some detail.[17] It is striking how high
feelings ran, particularly in reference to church buildings and the crucifix.
Up until now, we have encountered such fervor—apart from Eon of
Stella—only in Leutard of Vertus; the heretics of Arras may have termed

the crucifix worthless, but did not smash it into pieces. In addition, Peter of Bruis rejected the Old Testament, in contrast to the heretics of Orléans or those of Arras[18]—the latter relied on a compendium of passages from the New Testament, while the Old Testament lay outside of their scope. On the other hand, Leutard of Vertus was hostile to the crucifix and partially rejected the Old Testament texts. As we have already stated, both stances seem to be Bogomil.

James Fearns correctly discerned that in spite of these beliefs Peter of Bruis was no Bogomil. His conjecture that individual Bogomil tenets infiltrated a little-developed Western heresy is probably correct. Incidentally, in formulating his own doctrine, Henry the Monk, the spiritual heir to Peter of Bruis, apparently again dropped the opposition to both the crucifix and the Old Testament, since neither is mentioned any further.[19]

It is instructive to read how Peter was said to have died: He set fire to a mountain of crucifixes, and the outraged onlookers tossed him into the flames. His adherents, found in the Dauphiné and in portions of southwestern France up to the Pyrenees, later joined with those of Henry the Monk. Some historians viewed Peter of Bruis as a proto-Waldensian or as a precursor of Protestantism. However, even in retrospect, we cannot fit him into any group, just as his contemporaries were unable to pigeonhole him. As for the individual Bogomil tenets held by this man, they seem to be harbingers of Catharism, which would come to light in the West a few years later.

Henry the Monk,[20] often mistakenly called "Henry of Lausanne," was not a student of Peter of Bruis, but he was the "heir to his wickedness," according to Peter the Venerable; we are not certain whether the two preachers ever met. There is solid evidence also for Henry's presence in northern France, in Le Mans (1116), where he supposedly arrived from Lausanne—only later, if at all, did he visit the area exposed to the heresy of Peter of Bruis. Numerous sources, Bernard of Clairvaux among them, attest that Henry was a renegade monk.[21] On the other hand, he did not know what a *professio* (public taking of monastic vows) was and thus could scarcely have been a monk.[22] Saint Bernard considered Henry *litteratus* [lettered], yet in Le Mans, Henry refused to read an indictment against him; when it was read to him, his response was limited to a single Latin word in protest. It may be that he had a "passive" command of Latin, while his "active" command of the language and his knowledge of the Psalms were weak. All this argues against Henry's having come from a Cluniac monastery. He asserted that he had been consecrated as a deacon, but there is no way to confirm that. His doctrines bespeak a broader interest in theology than do those handed down from Peter of Bruis. Henry cut a striking figure in public, and that was probably the

intended effect, capturing all the fervor of an ascetic man of God. He chose
to make his entry into Le Mans on Ash Wednesday, at the beginning of
Lent. Like Jesus Christ, the chronicler wrote, Henry sent two of his
followers to precede him; they carried poles affixed with iron crucifixes
and were greeted in the suburbs "like messengers from the Lord of the
universe." Henry was dressed like a penitent, with bare feet, even in the
winter, and a long unkempt beard, an imposing, still youthful man. He
took up residence with the people in the suburbs, eating his meager meals
with them, and he was an outstanding orator, appealing to his listeners'
consciences in "a terrifying voice." He was considered a prophet, for he
told people their sins by reading their faces. The bishop of Le Mans,
Hildebert of Lavardin, a poet and scholar, trusted him; before setting out
for Rome, he gave Henry permission to preach in the city.

By this act, the chronicler wrote, the bishop delivered a Trojan horse into
the city. Many clerics turned to Henry and sat at his feet when he called for
a boycott of the (propertied) clergy. However, he went much further than
invoking the weapon of the Patarenes: The clergymen's houses were to be
destroyed, their possessions dispersed, and they themselves stoned. The
civil authorities were able to avert this with effort; all the same, clergymen
were beaten and pelted with dirt when they wished to negotiate with
Henry. One of the clergymen was called "William, who does not drink
water,"[23] an epithet that shows how much tension there was between the
clergy and townspeople even before Henry arrived on the scene.

In addition to the old agenda of the Patarenes, Henry also had a social
one: The prostitutes of the city were to renounce their trade and enter into
the state of matrimony. As long as the count protected the clergy of Le
Mans from riots, there was no impediment to a short-lived success in this
area. The prostitutes cut off their hair, removed their costly garments, and
threw everything into a bonfire. Many young men married these women,
and were able to do so because Henry provided the financial portion of
their marriage settlements. Since they were not supported for life, the
young men moved away from the city, and their wives again turned to
prostitution.

When Bishop Hildebert returned home, Henry withdrew to a fortification while the townspeople prepared a very unfriendly reception for their
pastor. The bishop was soon rid of his problem: A fire devastated a large
part of the suburbs of Le Mans. People saw it as a judgment from God, and
the tide turned. Hildebert examined Henry's knowledge and found it
lacking. We have no information that he was tested concerning his
faith—even though the clergy of Le Mans had asserted in a public letter
that Henry disputed the divinity of Christ and other doctrines of the
faith.[24] Trying Henry for heresy was certainly not in the bishop's best

interests, so he had Henry the Monk expelled from his city and was able to devote himself to rebuilding the suburbs.

Henry was later active in Poitiers and in Bordeaux, was captured in 1135, and was forced to recant and vow to enter the monastery of Cîteaux. He was soon set free, and in 1139 he surfaced in Toulouse. Bernard of Clairvaux visited Toulouse that spring and sought to hold a public debate with him, but Henry dodged the discussion. From then on, we find nothing more about him in trustworthy sources. Transcriptions of his sermons had been made and circulated among the "Henricians." Peter the Venerable saw one such codex, but was not entirely convinced that Henry had been its author.[25] Propositions concerning his teachings are found in a work by a monk named William;[26] they elucidate his conduct toward the clergy of Le Mans and on this point resemble more the views of the Patarenes than those of Peter of Bruis: Unworthy priests did not possess the power to bind and loosen, which is why people should confess to laypeople, and they could not transubstantiate bread and wine into the Body and Blood of Christ. Clerics should be poor and not assume any prebends. Furthermore, Henry—like others—opposed infant baptism, which should not lead us to conclude that he denied original sin.[27] The consent of the two parties sufficed to contract a marriage. Henry rejected the building of churches, even though he preached in them and did not have any destroyed at Le Mans.

Was Henry a heretic? The clergy of Le Mans labeled him one, just as he accused those clergymen of heresy. The dispute revolved around the efficacy of sacraments celebrated by unworthy priests and the entanglement of such individuals in worldly affairs. Henry's views probably placed him at the fringes of the church, and bishops found his position questionable, yet did not mount an all-out attack. They wanted to silence him, but not put him to the stake.

Was this man a Cathar? Certainly not, even if he had no respect for the Old Testament. This answer is supported by his affirmation of marriage and the baptism of adults with water. No one called him a Manichaean. His manner was loud and noisy, in contrast to those "still" paths traversed by Catharism as it spread, secretly forming groups and engaging in indoctrination. As far as we know, that heresy had its first stirrings a few years before Henry's last appearance. However, just like those sectarians, he probably benefited from the dynamics of urban life and struggles for political power, as well as from the atmosphere of instability.

The extraordinary success of these major preachers was made possible by a strong yearning for religious fervor; since the second half of the eleventh century, "revived" individuals could be found in sections of the laity. In those cases where they were not clustered around established religious centers, they depended upon the ministration of itinerant preachers, who now also included monks. These ministers could act as mouthpieces for popular views and complaints about the clergy and its religious functions, as well as about misunderstood religious dogma. In 1119 Pope Calixtus II held a synod in Toulouse, and a "canon concerning heretics" is preserved among its records.[28] It was perhaps directed against the adherents of Peter of Bruis, but certainly not just them. Twenty years later, it was found necessary to incorporate this canon into the records of the Second Lateran Council.[29] It reads: "Whosoever under the guise of piety condemns the Eucharist, infant baptism, the priesthood, and religious ordination, as well as legitimate matrimony, we shall banish from the church of God as a heretic." Around 1122, in the region of Sedan, two priests and two laymen were discovered who rejected the real presence in the Eucharist and infant baptism.[30] We recall that as early as 1048–50 Bishop Theodoin of Liège complained to the king of France that in his realm there were heresies concerning the real presence of Christ in the Eucharist, legitimate (ecclesiastical) matrimony, and infant baptism.[31] With Henry the Monk we also encounter marriage based solely on consent and the rejection of infant baptism—this places him within a social context marked by a line of popular thought that could be transmuted into heresy. Henry challenged the necessity for infant baptism on the basis of his view that unbaptized infants could also be saved, because it would be unjust for God to damn someone for a sin committed by another. At the hands of Henry's opponent, William, who was armed with theological arguments, this proposition became a rejection of the doctrine of original sin, because it was attributed only to the first two humans.[32]

We encounter doubt again and again on another point, the efficacy of prayer and of masses for the dead. Were the dead not judged immediately upon death, since they were consigned to either heaven or hell? Gerard I, bishop of Cambrai, felt it necessary to instruct the heretics of Arras about purgatory, and Gerard of Csanád complained about people who demanded the return of their offerings on behalf of unfortunate souls. Bogomils and Cathars denied that prayers for the dead were of any value. Peter of Bruis was as opposed to such prayers and offerings on behalf of the dead as he was to the Eucharist and infant baptism. In 1135 some men "clad in religious attire" appeared in Liège; they called prayers for the dead purposeless and rejected "legitimate" marriages as well as infant baptism. They were alleged to hold their wives in common, which may have been a malicious fabrication or may reflect confusion over their opposition to church marriages. The populace wanted to stone these men, but several were able to escape; three were captured, of whom two recanted and one was burned at the stake.[33] Some have surmised that

Bogomilism was at work here, but that is not at all certain. Not much later, a community adhering to the aforementioned beliefs existed alongside and in competition with the first definitely identifiable groups of Cathars.

Around 1144 Everwin, provost of the Premonstratensian monastery of Steinfeld, in the Eifel region, wrote Bernard of Clairvaux concerning some heretics found near Cologne,[34] and he described their teachings in detail— they were undoubtedly Cathars, and we will hear about them again later. He continued: "In our region there are still other heretics, completely distinct from the first ones; both groups were discovered as a result of their disunity and falling out with one another."[35] The members of the second group condemned all the sacraments, except for the baptism of adults, thus denying the Eucharist and sacramental marriage, and they furthermore did not believe in purgatory or the efficacy of prayer for the dead. Priests did possess moral authority, like the scribes in the Old Testament, but not the power to ordain: That power had completely disappeared since the time of the apostles due to the clergy's worldly way of life. Therefore, the clergy also could not administer the sacrament of baptism; Christ himself did that. They held views about infant baptism not in keeping with the Gospels, Everwin reported. The marriage bond was considered indissoluble, but only virgins should be admitted to that state. The sins of the righteous were forgiven solely on the basis of contrition, and penance was not necessary. As for the customs and rites of the church, they adopted only those found in the days of Christ and the apostles; all else was superstition.

Thus, it becomes quite clear that we are not dealing with a fundamental anticlericalism rooted in a dualistic outlook on the world. Obedience to ecclesiastical authority was based on Christ's words: "practice . . . whatever they tell you" (Matt. 23:3). As for all else, one must adhere to the Gospels and draw from them a rule of conduct; Everwin had noted the relevant passages. Diverse elements converge here: a "reforming spirit" that strips priests of the power to consecrate and administer the rest of the sacraments because of their way of life and, in that spirit's wake, application of this debasement to the whole clergy, along with recourse to the written word. The very factors that had created difficulties for this way of thinking were now conveniently rendered irrelevant. Either they were not mentioned in the Gospels, like infant baptism and purgatory, or the clergy could not make them real, like the Eucharist.

Everwin himself had participated in the cross-examinations and did not offer anything beyond a matter-of-fact, firsthand account in his communication to Bernard. What probably made the strongest impression on him was the assertion, made by some members of this group who had abjured the heresy, that it was very widespread: "They told us that these [sectarians] had a very large number [of believers], who were scattered all over, and that they had [among them] many of our secular clergy [*clericis*] and monks."[36] Even if the first part was at the very least an exaggeration, it illustrates how much more of a threat a "still" form of heresy was to the ecclesiastical authorities than the vociferous popular movements dependent on charismatic figures who preached repentance.

By the middle of the century, the charismatic style had already run its course. For some time, the last in the line of its practitioners was Arnold of Brescia, who was executed in 1155. However, he was not the typical preacher of repentance, above all because of the predominantly political nature of his activities as part of a Roman communal movement that was late to get off the ground; we need not go into that here. In addition, he was for a time a student of Abelard in Paris, therefore far surpassing someone like Peter of Bruis or Henry the Monk in terms of his education. For all that, he was never formally accused of heresy. His grasps for power and possession of the church, indeed expulsion of the pope from Rome, made him a disciplinary case; disobedience could be construed as heresy only in the very broadest sense of the word. Arnold was hardly a heretic. Otto of Freising, who always expressed himself with care, remarked, "He is said to have held unreasonable views with regard to the sacrament of the altar and infant baptism [*non sane dicitur sensisse*]."[37] The meaning of this remains unclear; in the minds of contemporaries, at any rate, the portrayal fit such a man beyond the pale.

Arnold had disciples, who were, if anything, to be found among the poor students in Paris,[38] and they should not be taken to have been members of a sect in Italy. His name was known far and wide, and whoever championed the apostolic poverty of the clergy was quickly reckoned an "Arnoldist." According to Otto Morena, there were those in northern Italy who "in derision" (*derisorie*) were called "sons of Arnold."[39] Such individuals did not take on concrete forms of a sect.

Arnold and the "Arnoldists" were descendants of the Patarenes, who had acted as the mouthpieces for displeasure at the secularization of the clergy. Whoever believed that unworthy bishops were not able to administer a valid consecration and that those they had consecrated were not able to celebrate valid sacraments soon came to view the teachings of that clergy and of the church altogether with opprobrium. In league with like-minded individuals, such people might seek to infer the "real" Christianity of the Gospels, or, alternatively, they could listen to doctrines disseminated by venerable men—be they wandering hermits, pilgrims, pious merchants. Imparted was a myth from the East that offered a plausible explanation for the evil in this world; those who advocated this myth were called Cathars, which later became *Ketzer* [heretics] in German.

For a while the Cathars qualified simply as *the* heretics, for there were few others besides them. We shall talk about these non-Cathar groups in the following paragraphs. Of course, we will not always be able to draw a firm line between the sects and orthodox fringe groups.

We have already heard about the heretics near Cologne from the account by Everwin of Steinfeld in 1144. Not long after, there was a community elsewhere in the Rhineland that was distinguishable from the Cathars solely on the basis of its precepts concerning marriage: Only virgins could enter into marriage, they were permitted to have just one child, and from then on they were to abstain from intercourse. Supervision was even provided to ensure the preservation of chastity. At all times, two men or two women were to share a bed "in order to guard each other." This is found in an account by Ekbert of Schönau,[40] brother of the visionary Elizabeth of Schönau (d. 1184), friend of Rainald of Dassel, and an opponent of the Cathars from the time he had been a canon in Bonn. He called the group "the followers of Hartwin" and did not list any further unique beliefs. They were rigorists who had searched through the Bible for a new mode of life but who also cited John Chrysostom in support of their rejection of remarriage. It is doubtful that they were heretics, and it is certain that they were not Cathars, which is how Ekbert seemed to classify them.

In any case, Everwin of Steinfeld reported that the group of non-Cathars in Cologne made virginity of both partners a prerequisite for marriage; this group was doubtlessly heretical on account of other teachings.[41] Perhaps that is why Hartwin's followers were justly termed perpetuators of that sect in Cologne.[42] The manner mentioned for supervising sexual relations presupposed above all, however, a communal way of life. This may reflect the influence of, or at least the power of the example set by, the houses of Cathars. In any case, something new was at work here, something that left behind few tracks.

Some sources do provide reports about the appearance of heretical groups, but are silent concerning their beliefs. This reflected a general uncertainty about how to fit the sects involved into the system of heresies handed down from the early church. Thus, we find written in one instance: "Some say that they are Manichaeans, others call them Montanists, some Arians, Pope Alexander [III, 1159–81] labeled them Patarenes [*Pateriuos*]."[43] This pertained to heretics from Flanders, whose ranks were said to include people from all social strata, even the nobility and clergy; they had no leader—we do not know if they were Cathars ("Manichaeans") or the continuators of a reform group ("Patarenes"). At that time people in Flanders knew all about the Cathars. Alexander III may have been correct in his assessment; he probably detected above all the anticlericalism in their testimony.

Whoever no longer trusted the clergy very often became an exegete in the hopes of discovering thereby a new course for his way of life. The New Testament and the Epistles usually sufficed in this search. Those who wished to be very thorough, if they were in the position to procure and study voluminous tomes, could also consult the Old Testament; in an urban setting Jewish scholars may have provided assistance in this undertaking. Moreover, by studying the Old Testament one became acquainted with a God-fearing, strictly regulated way of life.

There had always been Judaizers and individual converts to Judaism, but the first clear evidence for a sect's deciding to live according to Jewish—as well as Christian—law without undergoing such conversions dates to 1184 in northern Italy. These people were termed Passagini,[44] a word of unknown etymology. They practiced circumcision, obeyed the dietary laws, and observed the Sabbath; they did not believe in the divine nature of Christ, rejected the Eucharist, sacramental baptism, and the veneration of icons, saints, and relics: God alone was to be venerated. The sect was limited to northern Italy for good reason. A life based on Mosaic Law and on biblical authorities could thrive only in close proximity to individuals well versed in all these things. Nothing is known concerning the persecution of these groups; other targets and problems occupied the residents of the northern Italian cities. The Cathars already in their midst were also, for the most part, left in peace.

At issue in those instances were the urban middle classes; a different way of life was open to simple craftsmen in the suburbs and to the rural populace, similar to the way of life we have already seen was widespread in Swabia before the turn of the century:[45] communal prayer and work with humility, plain dress, and abstention from theological speculation. In northern Italy there were rural communities consisting of such devout individuals,[46] and there were the Humiliati, who primarily belonged to the artisan classes but were certainly not members of the "lowest social classes" struggling against exploitation by the cloth industry.[47] They were not itinerant, but lived with their families; from 1179 on there is evidence for houses of Humiliati in Milan, too, run like monasteries and shared by men and women. The Humiliati did not abstain from marriage, but rather from riches and luxury, quarrels, telling lies, and also swearing oaths, in accordance with the Gospels. This proved troublesome, for the oath was an essential legal remedy recognized by ecclesiastical and secular authorities alike. The Humiliati's desire to preach to their fellow believers presented another difficulty. Preaching of this sort was forbidden by the Third Lateran Council in 1179, and in 1184 Pope Lucius III excommunicated the Humiliati, along with the Cathars, Waldensians, and others. It was not until the beginning of the pontificate of Innocent III (1198) that a pope sought out a new policy toward the fringe groups, not least because they represented a valuable counterweight to the spreading Cathar heresy. Scholastically trained theologian that he was, Innocent cast about for a practicable *distinctio*: the distinction between true heresy and fringe groups, the distinction between an absolutely necessary oath and an unnecessary one, and between preaching about questions of faith and preaching about a moral life. The former kind of preaching remained prohibited for nonclergymen; the latter now became permissible—a fundamentally important ruling. This opened the door for the Humiliati to obtain a set of regulations in 1201 by which they were henceforth divided into three groups: clergymen (canons and canonesses), laypeople observing a monastic way of life, and laypeople living with their families. Bishops were instructed to allow the Humiliati to preach, though the Humiliati had to receive permission each time. In this manner, the way would be smoothed for the new order, yet church discipline would be safeguarded—an excellent solution in theory, if not always feasible in practice.

In the thirteenth century the Waldensians gained much greater importance than the Humiliati; a general reincorporation into orthodoxy would not prove to be their lot. They had much in common with the Humiliati, including their demand for permission to preach. However, they were itinerant preachers and thus represented an unstable element. People were predisposed to view them as followers of Henry the Monk,[48] and because of their way of life, contemporaries often took them to be a group related to the Cathars. Both views are incorrect. They wished to live according to the Gospels and remain within the church, with the condition that the Gospels be granted priority over church regulations. The Waldensians represented a disciplinary case that first developed into a doctrinal heresy in the thirteenth century.

Most often, the founder of the group is identified as Peter Waldes, though the earliest evidence for this name dates to the fourteenth century. "Waldes" is a toponym meaning "from Waadtland" (Pays de Vaud, western Switzerland). He was a well-to-do married merchant, residing in Lyon, who had a grammarian translate the Gospels, Psalter, and a collection of sentences into the vernacular. In essence, this was nothing new; around the same time a priest in Liège translated the Acts of the Apostles and the legend of Saint Agnes.[49] We hear that, in addition to the Bible and the "sentences of the (church) fathers," the legend of Saint Alexius made an impression upon Waldes: It concerns the son of a rich man who quit his parents' house and then came back in order to live there unrecognized and in poverty as a beggar. After giving away his possessions, Waldes abandoned his trade and family (around 1173), and wandered about preaching the Gospels. Thus, he led the apostolic life, like some already before him, but it was not for long. In accordance with canonical regulations, the archbishop of Lyon prohibited this layman from preaching.

"Go and teach all peoples!" and "God is to be obeyed more than men"—these two passages determined Waldes' future lot, as well as that of the Waldensians over the centuries up to the present day; as is well known, of all the sects that arose in the Middle Ages, it is the only one that has adherents even today. During the two centuries preceding Waldes' appearance, we also find isolated incidents of laymen preaching, but they were usually told that the biblical call to preach was not to be taken that literally; otherwise, feeble-minded old men, old women, and deaf mutes would have to preach.[50] Waldes appealed to the pope and in 1179 probably traveled with a companion to Rome, where the Third Lateran Council was being held. A member of the English delegation, Walter Map, later depicted with pleasure how the two were made to look ridiculous during the interrogation about their beliefs.[51] According to another account written much later, Alexander III granted the Waldensians permission to preach, admittedly only "at the request" of the duly responsible clergy. This was a subtle way of denying permission.

The Cathars were already very widespread in those years, and the Waldensians, their natural competitors, preached against them with zeal. Once again, in 1180, Waldes attempted to persuade a papal legate attending the Synod of Lyon of the merits of his case by means of a thoroughly orthodox confession of faith, but the archbishop of Lyon would not relent. It was possible that the door might be opened to something that not just the clergy found offensive: that, in accordance with the call to preach, women—presumably even reformed prostitutes—would exercise the right to preach as well. Over the course of the following two years, Waldes and his followers went into exile. Now there were Waldensians in Provence, as in Alsace, Piedmont, and Lombardy.[52]

With that, they took the first step on their future path, a path leading to a split from the church. The Waldensians still desired, and for a long time continued to desire, to be Catholic, but the lack of priests to celebrate the Eucharist and administer the sacraments could only lead to the development of alternative practices; in addition, they were akin to groups not bound to any religious community or to sectarian groups, even if the Waldensians attacked them. They themselves were now members of the "underground," at a time when there was no Innocent III yet to consolidate them, like the Humiliati and others, into the official church again. One might say that Waldes was born a generation too early. When it came to Francis and his adherents, successful efforts were made to avoid these mistakes. There were also other reasons why the Franciscan movement fared better than the Waldensians: In cases of conflict, Waldes gave precedence to the Holy Scriptures interpreted literally, whereas Francis of Assisi gave precedence to the orders of the Roman Church.

3

The Twelfth Century: Bogomils and Cathars

 "In the days of the orthodox czar Peter there lived in Bulgaria a priest named Bogomil . . . , who was the first to disseminate the heresy in the land of Bulgaria." Thus begins Cosmas's tract against the Bogomils.[1] At the time he wrote, the Bulgarian czardom had already crumbled under the blows of invaders: First came a Russian army, then a Byzantine force led by Emperor John Tzimisces; following the emperor's death, the population revolted, and a splinter Bulgarian empire was temporarily restored in Macedonia. At the time he wrote this work, Cosmas probably resided in the eastern portion of the country, which had remained under Byzantine rule. It was around then, thus during turbulent times, that "Kosmas presbyter" [Cosmas the Priest] composed this work in Old Slavonic. As a presbyter he was more than a village priest; the Greek word conveys a higher status than the Slavonic one.

It was necessary to write the polemical work in the Slavonic language, since people would scarcely have been able to understand it otherwise. The Slavic peasantry was only superficially subjugated by the Bulgarians and Greeks, and people lived out their lives in ignorance and piety within the smallest orbits; the higher clergy was remote, as was whatever still passed for secular authority. It is within this context that we must view Bogomilism, marked by undercurrents of hate and despair in a semiravaged land.

Was Bogomil an actual person? Some researchers have labeled him a literary fiction,[2] although we ought to give credence to Cosmas. The heresiarch's name provides additional evidence: People were convinced that a person's name revealed his or her essence, yet in this instance exactly the opposite was true; Cosmas wrote with regret that instead of being Bogomil (which roughly means "worthy of God's mercy"),[3] he was in no way worthy of God's mercy. On behalf of those faithful who were literate, still more numerous in the Balkans than in the West, and of the priests above all, the poor and ignorant village clerics, Cosmas wanted to draw a distinction between the religious agitators and the—as yet—orthodox majority. It would take the next two hundred years for Bogomilism to become the "official religion" in Bosnia.

According to Cosmas the sect came into existence during the rule of the Bulgarian czar Peter (927–69), and this information corresponds with two references to "Manichaeans" found in Byzantine sources.[4] The second source intermixes elements of Bogomilism with tenets held by the Paulicians, a martial sect not at all oriented toward asceticism, whose ties to the Bogomil sect remain questionable. Common to both sects was an anticlericalism that also smacked of "nationalism": The higher clergy thought in terms of the Greek language and the patriarchy of Constantinople. These clergymen were labeled Pharisees, drunkards, and sluggards. They seem to have had little interest in ministering to their flocks or, what was more difficult, to the apostates. Even Cosmas remarked: "We should let these people [the Bogomils] proceed on their way to damnation; it is easier to convert an animal than a heretic."[5] Such sentiments, which Cosmas would have heard often enough, show that those who criticized the clergy did not err entirely.

The Bogomils kept the public peace as well: They attended church "out of fear of people"; they kissed the crucifix and icons. They were "like sheep," "gentle, humble, quiet," observed fasts, did not engage in idle conversation, did not indulge in any loud laughter and vulgar jokes. "They avoid drawing attention to themselves and do all this outwardly only, so that no one can distinguish them from true Christians."[6] Among themselves, again according to Cosmas, their hate for the ruling class came to the surface: "They instruct their adherents not to submit to the authorities; they hate the rich, they hate the emperors, ridicule their superiors, complain about the lords; they believe that God hates those who work for the emperor above all, and they advise all their followers not to perform statutory labor for their lords."[7]

It is possible to interpret these words so that they appear to be a platform for casting off the yoke of domination.[8] Yet, such a revolt never took place. Constantinople first took notice of the sect's existence around 1110, long after crusaders had clashed with the Bogomils in Macedonia in 1096.[9] The sectarians' strength continued to lie in their ability to conform outwardly to society. Thus, their teachings continued to exercise influence under the most diverse political conditions up until the end of the fourteenth century. The last traces of Bogomilism did not disappear until the seventeenth century, after many years of Turkish domination.

The proponents of Bogomilism, some of whom were former clergymen, preached to the faithful about humility and subservience to the authorities. They thus sought to blunt people's profound dissatisfaction with their rulers and with their harsh lives, conducted under precarious circumstances, though at the price of an "inward exile." The Bogomil was not a do-gooder; he thought rather to escape from this world. Performing service for one's master did not help achieve this goal; such work was not a form of asceticism, but purposeless. Nonetheless, only a few Bogomils abandoned the peasant life to become itinerant preachers fed and sheltered by their listeners: "They wander from house to house and devour what belongs to others."[10] In this wise the sectarians were not compelled to drop their disguise, for it was common to come across itinerant monks living on modest alms, often going on a pilgrimage[11] or feigning to be on one. Such individuals may have reached the West more often than we think. They wore clerical garb, the rough and dark cloak of a monk; Cosmas reproached these itinerant preachers for "wearing our garments."[12] Thus, at this juncture there was already a Bogomil intelligentsia, although even later on it never became as entrenched as the *perfecti* [perfects] were among the Cathars. Priests were also to be found in the ranks of the Bogomils; while they belonged to the sect, they still continued to perform their duties, "perhaps out of fear of the secular powers that be."[13]

Certain passages in Cosmas's work appear to refer to these latter individuals. How else could one explain his reproach of the "wealthy" for not lending the books they owned to the "poor" who asked to read and copy them.[14] The wealthy acted in that way because book owners were held in higher esteem when they quoted passages unknown to the populace.[15] Cosmas was referring here to the Old and New Testaments as well as to texts in support of their doctrine concerning the Bible; he called for the destruction of any text stating that the word of God was not to be made accessible to one's brethren.[16] This last sentence may refer to Bogomil works asserting that the Old Testament and patristic works were to be repudiated.

According to Cosmas, the Bogomils had two ways of winning people over to their community: by being humble and fasting, on the one hand, and—probably in reference to the intelligentsia—by restricting access to the Gospels and explicating it in a godless manner, on the other.[17] "Whatever the heretics read, they distort."[18] In other words, they were skilled at manipulating biblical passages to prove that the Bogomil myth was correct.

The main tenet of this myth was that the devil had created the world and that as a result everything connected with the creation was "unclean" and to be renounced. The devil also bore the name of Mammon,[19] a word found in the Gospels to denote "property" in a negative sense. Baptized infants were called "the children of Mammon" or "the children of the wealthy," "for Mammon is wealth"; the Bogomils would turn away from such children and spit while holding their noses, as if they were in the presence of something indecent.[20] The issue whether the devil was a god, in the sense of "radical dualism," or a wayward son of God had not yet aroused any strong feelings; at least Cosmas made no reference to it. Indeed, it was not his aim to proffer a theology of Bogomilism—it was probably systematized only later on—and he provided only fragmentary information about their beliefs: The devil, not God, performed miracles; the devil also effected Christ's miracles in order to confuse people. Or, as the upper class believed, miracles were biblical allegories depicted as actual happenings by the Evangelists.[21] They had to renounce the Old Testament, of course, which depicted the world as the creation of the good God; any veneration of the Virgin Mary was rejected as well, as were the sacraments, the reliquaries and icons of the saints, and above all the crucifix. It was not possible that Christ willingly suffered death for man's redemption, and the crucifix "is, if anything, an enemy of God" and to be scorned. Cosmas continued: "Demons fear Christ's crucifix, and the heretics cut it into pieces and make tools from it," which thus made them worse than the demons.[22]

This fervid renunciation of all established beliefs was delimited by the practical realities of the lives conducted by the Bogomils. "If the devil created the whole visible world," asked Cosmas, "why do you then eat bread and drink water?"[23] Apparently, they nourished themselves in the simple manner of monks; we hear nothing further about a life-threatening form of asceticism. Of course, it was a strenuous undertaking to observe the hours for prayer; the upper class of clerics and semiclerics were probably the only ones subject to their observance. The following, some-what puzzling remark by Cosmas could scarcely refer to the peasants, who spent their days working in the fields: "They prayed behind closed doors four times during the day and four times at night, in addition to reciting the five [canonical] hours with their doors open."[24] Since in orthodox circles the clergy were required to observe the canonical hours, the Bogomils could sometimes keep their doors open without anyone being scandalized.

The Bogomils did not recognize a priesthood in the usual sense, and they renounced the conferment of the power to ordain, renouncing likewise the belief that the liturgy dated back to the Apostolic Age: They credited John Chrysostom (patriarch of Constantinople, 398–404) with composing the liturgy.[25] Only a relatively well-educated person could have made such a remark to Cosmas; it is quite rare to encounter "historical" criticism among heretics. Another noteworthy item recounted by Cosmas—and only by him—was that Bogomil women could hear confession and forgive sins.[26] This practice is not encountered again until the late Middle Ages in the case of a branch of Waldensians.

We know little about the eleventh-century Bogomils. At the beginning of the twelfth century the Byzantine Empire became conscious of their existence, and the Byzantines had the habit of putting everything into writing. In 1110 (or 1118) Emperor Alexios Comnenos ordered the theologian Euthymios Zigabenos to write a tract about the heresies of the day. In Byzantine fashion it bore the title *Dogmatic Panoply*.[27] It was based on the testimony of a monk named Basileios, who played a key role among the Bogomils, and of other members of the sect in Constantinople. To what extent Bogomils in the Balkans held the same views is difficult to say. A letter written in the eleventh century by the monk Euthymios of the Peribleptos monastery already pointed out regional differences between groups, noting that people in northwestern Anatolia did not think in exactly the same way as those in southern Anatolia. Unfortunately, this letter does not otherwise provide us with much new information.[28]

Since Cosmas's time, some new usages had been introduced into the liturgy, above all a "baptism of the Holy Spirit." All those present, men and women, would lay their hands on the head of the sectarian, who thereby became a full member—a "master" or "apostle"—of the sect. An individual thereby joined the ranks of the "clerics," thus receiving the dark cloak characteristic of Eastern monasticism.[29] This rite was a sacramental act of consecration, a form of ordination performed by the congregation. The baptism of the Holy Spirit presumably dates back to the middle of the eleventh century and was used first by the Bogomils residing in northwestern Anatolia.[30] The liturgical act was accompanied by prayers, and the Gospels were placed upon the head of the person receiving the ordination. Incidentally, this would be for the second time, since the individual would previously have had the book containing the Gospels placed on his head in a sort of initiation rite. The prior ceremony marked the beginning of a probationary period, whereas the subsequent one prompted the Holy Spirit to take up residence in the candidate: From now on he was a perfect and could no longer commit a sin. The dichotomy between "believers" (*credentes*) and "perfects" (*perfecti*) would later become a hallmark of Catharism.

Only afterward was the Bogomil allowed to pray, to recite the only prayer that was in fact allowed, namely, the Lord's Prayer. Obeying the

Gospels literally (Matt. 6:9), the Bogomils restricted their devotions to reciting the Lord's Prayer, a practice that may have contributed somewhat to the limited development of Bogomil spirituality. But even in this respect, it might have worked out differently: The Messalians, a sect dating to the fourth and fifth centuries, strove for a mystical union with the Holy Spirit by chanting the Lord's Prayer over and over again.[31] Such continuous prayer was not customary among Bogomils, for, as noted above, they performed their obsecrations at fixed times. In any case, the Holy Spirit resided continuously in the "apostles," the upper class, and it was thus possible for them to be called "God-bearing" (*theotokos*), analogous to the God-bearing Virgin Mary of orthodoxy.[32]

In principle the members of the quasi-clerical upper class were all on an equal footing, though, of course, there may have been some notion of precedence based on an individual's personality or seniority according to his date of baptism. Also, we cannot speak of a single church in the twelfth century, but of many "churches" grouped locally or regionally. These churches may have used a separate act of consecration to install "elders," from whose ranks bishops would later be drawn. The first elder we know of was Simon "of Drugunthia" (probably located in Thrace);[33] Nicetas, his immediate successor, traveled from Constantinople to the West and participated in a Cathar synod (1167) that we have yet to discuss. From that point on, determining the validity of a consecration was an issue that would haunt the Bogomils and Cathars, much as it had already preoccupied the orthodox. In Cosmas's day the Bogomils had denied that the established church embodied the "apostolic succession," the succession of consecration beginning with the apostles,[34] but they had not yet claimed it for their community. Now they appropriated this principle for themselves, and at the same time, again along the lines of the Orthodox Church, they set up a form of hierarchy. They now had bishops (apostles, teachers), and, later on, deacons as well. However, just as the churches—and in 1167 there were five located in the area stretching from Constantinople to Dalmatia—lacked a centralized hierarchical leadership, so they also lacked a completely standardized doctrine.[35]

Little seems to have changed in the upper class's way of life in the intervening period since Cosmas had written his account. There were now prohibitions against eating meat and drinking wine, but Cosmas had already mentioned that the Bogomils ate bread and drank water. As for the prohibition against wine, it was deemed necessary to invent a special legend: The devil had planted a grape vine in the middle of paradise; it was this vine that was the tree of knowledge, and a grape, not the apple, figures in the rest of the story.[36]

More significantly, the evil principle was now concretized in a mythical story. Previously, it apparently sufficed to know that the devil had created the world—a negation of the belief that the creation was good, not really one facet of a myth. This myth began to evolve with the further elucidation of the relationship between the evil principle and the good God. Either there were two coexistent deities of equal rank ("radical dualism"), or God had besides Christ an older (or, alternatively, younger) son, the devil, who had rebelled against his Father ("moderate dualism"). Scholars have overemphasized the dichotomy between the two forms of dualism and engaged in protracted disputes about their origin and spread; what we do know is that the actions taken by Bishop Nicetas when he came to the West were in conformance with radical dualism. While tensions and rivalries of various kinds did exist among the Bogomil churches, it is nevertheless unwarranted to characterize them as a schism between the radical dualism of "Drugunthia" and the moderate dualism of other groups.[37] People in Constantinople appear to have given more thought to theological matters than those living elsewhere did, and Nicetas seems to have raised the dichotomy to a point of contention in the West. Mythical thinking admits of any number of possibilities, a fact that may strike a theologian as outrageous. Thus, for example, at one point some speculated that there was a diabolical trinity,[38] and they did not thereby meet with any difficulties.

Of crucial importance to the average Bogomil was the knowledge that Satan was the "ruler of this world" (John 14:30 and 16:11).[39] It was here that the stories came into play: The Father had designated God's older son to succeed him as ruler of his realm, but the son rebelled against his father, was deposed, and established his own sphere of dominion, the material creation, which he imbued with the souls of angels. The younger son, Christ, descended to earth to show these souls how to escape from their imprisonment in bodies that the devil had fashioned for them; Christ himself was a spirit without a body, passed through Mary in that form, and did not suffer on the cross, which would have been a human and not a divine thing to do. Others said that Christ, "the Word," was the Archangel Michael (analogous to the fallen archangel Satanael), the one who had bound Satan in hell and freed the souls of men.[40]

That Christ possessed the spiritual semblance of a body has been part and parcel of heterodox Christology from as far back as the second century. This "Docetism" was rediscovered time and time again, whenever matter was regarded as unclean or evil. Byzantine theologians were the first to incorporate this doctrine into Bogomilism and, most likely, a new interpretation of original sin as well: The original sin consisted in the fall of the angels who turned away from God and toward Satan. All humans suffer in consequence, and their personal sin consists in having a positive attitude toward the world and its temptations. Put succinctly, sinlessness consists in abstention from worldly things,[41] in conjunction with an infusion of the Holy Spirit. All humans are sinners except those who have received the baptism of the Holy Spirit and practice asceticism. There was a certain attraction to reducing moral existence in this way to a question of good or evil.

The subsequent paths taken by Bogomilism are not part of our story here. On the other hand, its influence on the West is of importance. What we label Catharism is a Western outgrowth of this sect. After much debate most agree that from around 1140 on there were Cathars in the West; this conclusion holds up if we discount individual Bogomil doctrines that may have made their way to the West even earlier. We have already heard about one questionable incident, that of the heretic Leutard of Vertus.[42] Also worthy of note is a group of heretics whom we have not yet touched upon; according to an account by Guibert of Nogent, they resided in the region around Soissons shortly before 1114.[43] It was said that in Bucy-le-Long, a village near Soissons, these people, above all the peasant (*rusticus*) Clement and his brother Everard, asserted that the course God willed for the son of the Virgin was a figment of the imagination (*fantasma*). They abhorred the Eucharist and described the priest's mouth as the maw of hell, rejecting likewise marriage and procreation. They boasted that they observed the apostolic life and read (!) only the Acts of the Apostles.

The veracity of this story is, however, undercut by Guibert's referring in the same context to the widely disseminated tale of orgies and the immolation of children.[44] In addition he wrote: "If one rereads the list of heresies compiled by Augustine, one realizes that this one is most like that of the Manichaeans." This comment led Guibert's editor, E.-R. Labande, to dismiss the entire passage as derivative, even though the sentence in whole or at least in most part refers to the immolation of children. Labande's application of the word *fantasma* to Christ's semblance of a body is misleading.[45] That is not what Guibert of Nogent wrote.

Since Guibert had interrogated one of the heretics at the order of the bishop, he had no need for supplementary material out of Augustine and was merely following the time-honored custom of classifying the group according the old list of heresies. Guibert was also not examining the heretic about his Christological theories, but instead about the oft-renounced infant baptism. The heretic responded cunningly, for the answer appeared to be orthodox: "He who believes and is baptized will be saved" (Mark 16:16). Guibert grasped the deeper meaning of the verse to the heretic, that belief takes precedence over baptism, but yet another meaning might have lain hidden in the biblical text: What sort of baptism were they possibly thinking of, given that they viewed the mouth of the priest as the yawning abyss of hell? Was it perhaps a "baptism of the Holy Spirit"?

In his autobiography Guibert denounced Count John of Soissons (died around 1115) for loving heretics and commending the Jewish faith without observing it. John had maintained that many wise men had told him that all men should hold their wives in common and that it would not be a sin. Furthermore, the count made remarks about Christ that even the Jews would not dare to make. Guibert was the author of a tract entitled *On the Incarnation Against the Jews*, which he himself said was aimed at the count.[46] In this work he disputed the arguments used by the Jews to disprove the Virgin Birth and responded to the question "whether God made his creation good or evil."[47] This issue is not in any way indicative of Jewish doctrine, any more than the remark (attributed to the count) that followed: "People believe that God is omnipotent, but surely he was not omnipotent."[48]

John of Soissons participated in church life in the conventional fashion, yet had his own ideas about religion and listened to what Jews and heretics had to tell him. It was highly unlikely that the Jews would have told him that libertinism was no sin—had he heard that from the heretics? The Cathars believed that worldly people were subject to the devil, so they could marry whomever and however they wished; the path to bliss, on the other hand, lay through the baptism of the Holy Spirit. Of course, it remains entirely doubtful whether there is some link here with Bogomil-Cathar thought. The same holds true for John's views on Christology and the Virgin Birth, and finally his skepticism about the goodness of creation. Anyone could harbor doubts about God's omnipotence as well. The use of the past tense "was," however, seems to indicate that the reference was to omnipotence in the creation—who then wielded the rest of the power?

Such questions must be left unanswered; it is striking, nonetheless, how closely the beliefs held by this group and its sympathizer, Count John, approximated certain modes of thought characteristic of the Bogomils and Cathars. Yet, the sect's appearance certainly cannot be attributed solely to a single putative mission from the East. It would seem that the way the sect thought about some things resembled what many people were thinking and what only a few, like Count John, dared put into words.

We possess almost no information concerning a mission to the West. Nevertheless, it is extremely unlikely that Catharism in the West represented a "spontaneous" movement "parallel" to Bogomilism in the East, and that no missionaries, in the guise of itinerant hermits, pilgrims, merchants, or craftsmen, formed a link between them. The earliest group of Cathars was found in Cologne from 1144 on, and based on a letter written by Hildegard of Bingen, they may even have been in existence as early as March 1140.[49] In those days the civil war between the Hohen-staufen and the Welfs was drawing to a close, and the crusade led by Conrad III and Louis VII would soon serve to deflect internal tensions outward. Bogomilism was thriving in Byzantium: Soon after 1140 it spread into Bosnia,[50] while in the central portion of the Byzantine Empire the sect was subject to persecution, particularly in the wake of Emperor Manuel I's accession to the throne in 1143. The first burnings of Bogomils had already occurred during the reign of his predecessor, Alexios I; but now even the patriarch of Constantinople fell under their spell and had to be deposed in 1147. Later the emperor himself was said to be a sympa-thizer, which certainly could not have been true.[51] And Bishop Nicetas, the one who traveled to the West in 1167 in order to "reform" the Cathars, was a later product of the Bogomil church in Constantinople.

Even before Nicetas's appearance, then, the Cathars in the West knew that they were part of an ancient tradition, or even a succession. The Cathars living in Cologne in 1144, to whom we now turn our attention, told Everwin of Steinfeld that a great many Cathars were to be found all over the world, living secretly in Greece and in other countries ever since the time of the martyrs.[52] We made mention above of a letter Everwin wrote to Bernard of Clairvaux recounting the existence of two unrelated, mutually opposed sectarian groups in Cologne; there we discussed one of the groups—the one that was not Cathar.[53] In the entry for 1143, the annals for the monastery of Brauweiler, near Cologne, report that the sectarians were indicted and that in Bonn three heretics were burned to death.[54] The heretics in Cologne were treated more leniently, for they were either subjected to an ordeal by water or allowed to flee. It is possible that they were adherents of the non-Cathar group, while the heretics encoun-tered in Bonn were obdurate defenders of their faith who may well have been Cathars. Some years later, when he was a canon in Bonn, Ekbert of Schönau came in contact with the resident Cathars, who wished to convert him.[55]

According to Everwin's account, the Cathars in Cologne asserted that the Church was embodied by them alone. "We and our forefathers, appointed as apostles, have continued to enjoy Christ's grace and will continue to do so until the end of the world." "And they are those heretics, who call themselves apostles and have their own bishop (*papa*)." They comprised "listeners" (*auditores*) and "believers" (*credentes*), supervised by the "elect" (*electi*). Women were also admitted into the ranks of the believers and the elect, just as the apostles took their wives with them on their wanderings. The believers were drawn from the ranks of the listen-ers through the laying-on of hands, and they were permitted to attend the prayers (of the elect) and were required to complete a probationary period, after which they received baptism "in fire and spirit," thereby joining the elect. Once they became members of the elect, they were permitted to baptize others and "consecrate Christ's Body and Blood" at meals. That was effected by reciting the Lord's Prayer.

In this regard Everwin must have misunderstood his sources. The Bogomils, as well the Cathars, did not subscribe to the real presence of Christ in bread and wine. The elect (later termed the perfect, *perfectus*) celebrated a memorial service, which involved blessing and distributing the bread and wine, analogous to the "popular" eulogia found in the liturgy of the Catholic Church.[56] As for the Cathar hierarchy in Cologne, it further resembled the Bogomil hierarchy in Constantinople in that the episcopal leader of the regional or local church bore the title *papa(s)*, thus strictly speaking "pope," just as Nicetas had in 1167. There could no more be a "pope" among the Cathars than there could be among the Bogomils.[57]

The apostolic life (of the elect) entailed complete poverty and itinerancy, fasting, prayer, and working "day and night" in order to earn one's keep. We may add that itinerancy and work were most compatible with the craft and merchant trades, but least compatible with the seasonal work of the agricultural proletariat. As for fasting, milk and dairy products were as forbidden as meat. "They condemn marriage, but I could not discover the reason why." The key lies in the precept to avoid all nourishment arising *ex coitu* [as a result of sexual intercourse]: Everything having to do with sex was unclean to the highest degree; it goes without saying, the Cathar women also lived chastely ("so they say," a leery Everwin added).

Everwin's sources did not initiate him into their actual doctrines. We learn nothing about the devil's creation of the world, Christ's semblance of a body, and the emancipation of souls from their imprisonment in the body. "As for their sacraments, they keep them hidden," wrote Everwin, unaware that the heretics' sole sacrament was the baptism of the Holy Spirit, concerning which he was in fact informed. The lack of information about the doctrine's main elements should not deceive us into doubting whether the group espoused Catharism. The sectarians' customs and organization match those of the Cathars to such an extent that we are on firm ground here. For example, besides the bishop there was an "associate" (*cum socio suo*), who corresponds exactly to the *filius major* of the later Bogomils and Cathars. This term pertains to the bishop's deputy and heir apparent, first found within the Bulgarian church around 1190.[58]

It also fell to the bishop and his deputy to defend their doctrines in the presence of the archbishop of Cologne and the members of the upper nobility at a gathering of clergymen and laymen. In their defense they cited the words of Christ and the apostles, but to no avail. Thereupon, they requested permission to consult with their *magistri* [masters], most likely brothers who were particularly knowledgeable about the Bible, but the proceeding never went that far. A mob "stole" the heretics "without our wanting them to," and burned them to death. Everwin praised the patience, even serenity, with which the heretics embraced their torture-some end.

The heresy in Cologne was not eradicated by this action; not long afterward Ekbert of Schönau would recount new information about its adherents. The group in Cologne and Bonn was also by no means the only one in the West, for in 1144 or 1145 there were reports of Cathars from Champagne arriving in Liège. The clergy there sounded the alarm in a letter to Pope Lucius II:[59] A heresy had spread from the village "Mons Guimari" in France, and according to the testimony of its adherents, "all the cities of the French and our own [Roman-German] empire have to a great extent been infected with the poison of the error." "Mons Guimari" is most likely Mont-Aimé, the mountain stronghold that would later purportedly shelter the Cathar bishop and was the site of a mass execution of Cathars in 1239; we have already spoken of this locale, because the village of Vertus, where the heretic Leutard lived, lay in the immediate vicinity.[60] While the estimated number of adherents is naturally an exag-geration, nevertheless the entire story was not woven out of thin air. Like Champagne, the cities on the Rhine and the Maas were centers of commerce. While we cannot attest that the heretics were merchants, still they must have been seasoned travelers and probably not entirely without financial means. One converted heretic from Liège was sent to Pope Lucius, while the others were required to undertake pilgrimages to various shrines. Those who could not be converted, on the other hand, were burned to death by "the people."

The letter stated that in Liège, much as in Cologne, there were "listen-ers" and "believers" (*credentes*), and that the upper class there was termed the "Christians," a label later applied to the Cathar "perfects." There is only an indirect reference to a bishop, occurring in a passage about "priests" and "other prelates as among us." This last remark was certainly a misunderstanding. The heretics opposed the (Catholic) sacraments, swearing oaths, and marriage, and they believed that one could receive the Holy Spirit only after performing good works. There was disagree-ment among the Cathars concerning the problem of justification by merit.[61] In order to stay under cover, the heretics participated in the sacraments of the church.

Around the same time, Catharism made its appearance in southwestern France (in Périgord, Dordogne, Lot-et-Garonne). In response, an other-wise unknown monk named Heribert sent out a letter of warning to "all Christians."[62] He scarcely understood the essence of the sect's beliefs. Yet, he was surely referring to Cathars, if only on the basis of the remark that, instead of taking communion, the sectarians ate "a morsel of bread" and knelt in prayer "a hundred times a day." (We will have more to say about Cathar ritualism later on.) Relevant from a social-historical perspective is his remark that noblemen as well as clergymen, monks as well as nuns, went abroad as preachers. If a priest tarried in a place and celebrated the mass, he did not recite the words from the canon, and he concealed the host at the altar or in the missal. The Cathars could be shackled with iron chains and guarded closely in an upside-down wine barrel—nonetheless, the next morning the prisoners would be at large and the barrel full of wine. "They also do many other miraculous things." That they had the devil's help was obvious to everyone. Furthermore: "No one is so boorish that within eight days in their company he would not become so knowledgeable about the Bible that he would never be vanquished by either word or deed."

The letter shows how a mind molded chiefly by popular perception viewed heterodoxy. Heribert opened his description with the comment that the sectarians did not eat meat and drank very little wine. Their unusual customs came second; he was astounded by their firmly rooted knowledge of the Bible and their ability to attract even people of some standing. Their opposition to the mass was crucial, for it proved that they had been sent, not by God, but by the devil, who helped them perform magic. Thus, it was fitting that they be subject to the punishment for sorcerers, death by fire.

The clergy's standard protest, that they had not wanted things to go that far, was probably for the most part sincere. Most of the clerics knew too that so zealous a faith would not be met with the same punishment as murder. However, mob justice served as a complement to the ecclesiastical proceedings, and following the conclusion of the scholarly cross-examination, the outraged populace got its due.

Over the course of seven years there were reports of Cathars in Bonn, Cologne, Liège, Champagne, and Périgord. If one were to draw a line connecting these points, it would stretch approximately one thousand kilometers from northeastern to southwestern Europe. The phenomenon had assumed continental proportions, and it was high time for the clergy to take countermeasures. Not much could be expected of the papacy, but there was one intellectual powerhouse of European stature: Bernard of Clairvaux. In 1147 he went to southern France to combat Catharism, much as he had already confronted Henry the Monk and his adherents. Bernard discovered, however, that it was easier to launch a crusade—as he had recently done—than to vanquish the Cathars. He discerned the difference between the two types of heretics, the "loud" ones, who debated in public, and the ones who worked in a still manner; he nevertheless misunderstood both in thinking that all heretics were concerned with gaining renown by means of their unique knowledge.[63] It was not Bernard's style to rebut one biblical quote with another and to wrestle stubbornly to uproot a firmly held doctrine. "Responding to each point would be an interminable and completely worthless endeavor. . . . They are not convinced by rational arguments, because they do not grasp them; nor are they reformed by quotes from authorities whom they renounce; nor do they submit to persuasion, for they are crazy." The well-constructed tripartite oratorical sentence closes with this effective *conclusio*: "Experience teaches us: They would rather die than convert."[64]

Bernard, the man of genius, had no empathy for the dry, bizarre manner of these people. All the same he did not just complain about them, but also tried to study them: how they fasted, earned their living through manual work, deceived no one, and participated outwardly in the life of the church. To his horror he established that the heretics also included priests, who had abandoned their parish congregations and, bearded and untonsured, now lived among weavers.[65] Bernard did not suspect them of dishonorable motives, even though he was scandalized that the men and women of the Cathar upper class lived communally. From him we learn for the first time which profession the sectarians favored, something we shall discuss later.

In 1148 the ecclesiastical assembly held in Rheims ridiculed Eon of Stella; however, it pronounced an excommunication "against the heresiarchs and their adherents in Gascony, Provence, and elsewhere" and placed an interdict "over their estates."[66] Heretics had been excommunicated in Rheims as early as 1049, but the use of the interdict—exclusion from sacramental life—was something new. Good as well as evil people living in a place were affected by the exclusion, the devout more than the irreligious, the Catholics even more than the sectarians; the premise underlying an interdict was that the Catholic population would put pressure on the dissidents in order to have the punishment lifted. The fact that such a measure was taken indicates the extent to which Catharism must have claimed adherents among the population in certain areas. Among them were probably noblemen "on whose estates" the heretics had found refuge. Heribert the Monk reported in his letter that laymen, even noblemen, abandoned their possessions because of the sect.[67] Bernard had already complained that noblemen shielded the Cathars.[68]

This was true for southern France. In northern France, the situation would only rarely have been thus, for there the movement preferred to remain underground. A second synod held in Rheims in 1157 opposed the "sects of Manichaeans" (Cathars), who confuse the simple people "and use very reprobate weavers who often flee from one place to another and change their names to entrap wenches burdened by sin."[69] That the heretics stayed on the move and used different names indicates that the ecclesiastical and secular authorities were on the lookout for them. Again, we hear that the Cathars practiced the profession of weaving. According to Ekbert of Schönau, they bore the appellation "weaver" (*texerant*) after their customary craft.[70]

We have already related how the Cathars in Bonn attempted to convert Ekbert, brother of the visionary Elizabeth of Schönau, while he was still cathedral canon there.[71] Later, in 1163, when he was a monk at the monastery of Schönau, Ekbert witnessed the burning of five Cathars, including a girl who showed particular courage. This experience moved him to become the first to undertake a "scholarly" study of Catharism. His thirteen "sermons against the errors of the Cathars"[72] contain many valuable observations and a comparison of Catharism to Manichaeism, which he believed was the source for Catharism. This assumption has led scholars to question whether he modified some of his material for the sake of consistency. After he had become the abbot of his monastery, Ekbert again had dealings with the Cathars, in 1167, this time in Mainz, where some forty Cathars were not burned to death, but merely driven out of the city.

The sectarians had in the meantime advanced as far as England. A group consisting of approximately thirty individuals, men and women, and led by a certain Gerard landed there around 1162. They met with little success, for they were allegedly able to convert only one old woman; afterward they were prosecuted and driven off the island.[73] The Anglo-Norman state did not provide a fertile ground for "dissenters." Although one might surmise that they came from Henry II's powerful domain on the mainland, it is nonetheless assumed that the envoys hailed from either Flanders or the Rhineland. It is more likely that they originated in Flanders, since it was from there, about the same time, that five Cathars came to Cologne, the same ones who were later burned to death.[74] The presence of Cathars in Flanders is further substantiated by an incident involving a prebend attached to a parish located within the present-day city limits of Brussels: A cleric holding this benefice was deposed for being a Cathar, and he fought the action repeatedly in court; the dispute lasted through the 1150s and 1160s.[75]

Even though heretics were depicted as boorish and uneducated time after time, clergymen were nevertheless won over by their teaching or at least gave some thought to Cathar tenets. We see this occurring with even such a figure as Hildegard of Bingen, at the very time when Ekbert of Schönau wrote against the heresy in 1163. God does not cause everything to occur and does not order anything to grow; or, since olden times Christ has not appeared, in other words, has not become human—such ideas may very well have come under discussion at Hildegard's cloister.[76] And it was from this milieu that she set off on a journey down the Rhine, including a stop in Cologne, and conducted a widespread correspondence.

In 1163 an ecclesiastical assembly in Tours presided over by Alexander III attacked the Cathars, above all those in Gascony and the area around Toulouse; in 1179 the Third Lateran Council reiterated these place-names. Albi and Carcassonne are identified elsewhere as the focal points for heresy in the south of France, and numerous accounts from the last third of the twelfth century report the presence of Cathars in northern France as well.[77] With reference to this time period, however, it is more important briefly to discuss the sect's expansion into northern Italy.

Since 1159 northern Italy had been in terrible straits. The papal election held that year resulted in a schism between Victor IV, supported by Frederick Barbarossa, and Alexander III, an important figure whom broad portions of Europe acknowledged as pope, yet who had to flee to France. In 1162 the emperor had Milan destroyed; it was not until 1167 that the residents could return—with Cathar preachers in their midst, appearing in public.[78] The decade-long struggle between the two supreme powers meant that only the local town authorities now were able to carry out their duties, and rarely did those duties include combating heresy. What was the use of a bishop's bringing charges against heretics if the town officials had no intention of punishing them! Thus, a golden age for sectarians existed in Italy down to the thirteenth century, at which point the country became a refuge for persecuted Cathars from southwestern France. During that period, it is true, imperial edicts were issued against heretics, but the cities rarely thought to enforce them; the Ghibellines and Cathars shared a common interest in repelling papal claims to power. At the end of the twelfth century, the Cathars allegedly considered taking control of the papal city of Orvieto and defending the heavily fortified mountain town in the bishop's absence. Threatened with exile, the Catholics residing in the town appealed to the pope for an overseer, who was murdered in 1199.[79] He lies enshrined in the Orvieto cathedral.

Catharism had taken root in the city soon after 1150 in the person of a certain Ormanninus from Parma. Around 1170 two preachers came to Orvieto from Florence, followed at the end of the century by a missionary from Viterbo. That we possess so little information concerning Catharism in these cities during its early days can be laid to the haphazard survival of sources. We do possess detailed information for the region around Milan, where northern French Cathars successfully proselytized the population in the terrible times after their forced resettlement. Their first converts were a gravedigger named Mark, a weaver, and a smith from the village of Concorezzo, near Milan. Mark became the deacon of the Italian Cathars, then their bishop.[80] Furthermore, according to the account by Gerard of Csanád, the first (Bogomil) community in Verona was probably in existence around 1045.[81] Individuals traveling through northern Italy on their way from the East or northern Italians converted by such individuals may have acted as conduits for the early Catharism found in the lands along the Rhine and in Champagne. No evidence exists on the matter.

Nicetas, Bogomil bishop of Constantinople, visited Mark, the deacon in Concorezzo, before 1167 and ordained him bishop. Nicetas may have taken the usual sea route from Constantinople to Venice and finally traveled by river to Verona. Mark and Nicetas then journeyed together to southern France, where—most probably in 1167[82]—a "council" of Cathar bishops was held at Saint-Félix de Caraman, near Toulouse. Some preparation would have been necessary to organize such a meeting. It would have been impossible for Nicetas to have met Mark in the village of Concorezzo by chance; hence we may assume that there must have been some kind of communication network linking the central figures in the sect. The intermediaries may have been inconspicuous "listeners" to the sect's doctrine, perhaps merchants who would have been well informed for professional reasons. Nicetas's tales about the "seven churches" of the Bogomils (cf. Apoc. 1:4) directed the Cathars' attention to theological and organizational issues; Nazarius, a successor to Mark of Concorezzo, traveled to Bulgaria several times around the end of the century.[83] During the schism that erupted before 1190, the adherents of the bishop of Concorezzo were also termed Bulgari.[84]

The link to the East contributed greatly to the internal rifts within Italian Catharism. Nicetas had introduced the Cathars in the West to the dogmatism of Constantinople. Soon after his return to his homeland and Bishop Mark's death, however, a delegation of Bulgarian Bogomils appeared from "abroad" bearing terrible news: Nicetas's predecessor had been caught in a sexually compromising situation. This rendered Nicetas's ordination invalid, and, consequently, those of Mark and his successor were invalid as well.[85] What strikes us as extreme fastidiousness was in fact just a weapon in the armory of church politics, one that had already been used by Italian Catholics one hundred years earlier. There was a dichotomy between two schools of theology stemming above all from the conflict between Byzantium and the new (second) Bulgarian empire, which had recently freed itself from Byzantine rule (1186). As long as the principle that succession depended on valid ordinations was adhered to, there was no solution to the rivalry between the churches. In place of

Mark's single bishopric there were, by the end of the century, six. The bishops either procured their ordination from various churches in the East, or they dispensed with that sort of legitimatization and contented themselves with election by the congregation. Much as Italy recognized no overall political power but a multitude of powers—marked by feuds and alliances—so, too, the Italian Cathars had split into parties and cliques. It can be argued whether political, individual, or dogmatic factors were paramount in the formation of parties. In any case, the absence of persecution also contributed to the unpleasant situation, which must have scared away some of the "listeners." This provides at least a partial explanation for the considerably worse overall performance by Catharism in Italy than in southern France.

It was necessary to describe in broad outline the spread of early Catharism in Germany, France, and Italy as a prerequisite to a comprehensive doctrinal review, which, of course, cannot be colored by regional and other differences. These differences are already found in the designations for the sect, which did not have a generally accepted name. This can also be attributed to the fact that the actual "church" consisted only of the upper class, in the form of sinless "good people" (*boni homines*), as opposed to sinners—believers as well as nonbelievers. It has been proposed that the heretics themselves used the term "Cathars," in other words, the pure ones (Greek: *katharoi*). More likely, as reported by Ekbert of Schönau, that was what they were called in Germany "by the common people," in other words, in the vernacular; in that case, the name must be derived from a German word that sounds similar. It would also have been odd indeed for the leaders of the oldest communities in the German-speaking areas to select as their name a Greek word not used by the Bogomils. On the other hand, Ekbert certainly knew this word in association with church history: In the third century, the sectarian Novatianists called themselves Katharoi, and a branch of the Manichaeans viewed themselves as *katharistae* (the purifying ones). Ekbert was familiar with these terms from Saint Augustine's apologetical works. The scholarly term gained acceptance in later tracts.

Today, we refer to them for the most part as the Cathars and by that do not mean just the upper class. We also occasionally come across the expression "Albigensian," though it in fact denotes only the Cathars from the diocese of Albi in southern France. Yet, we find the term already applied broadly in medieval works. It is better, nonetheless, not to use the term, since it has recently acquired a technical meaning, besides its very general one, as the theological tendency to radical dualism. Using it can only lead to confusion. Additional old terms are "Patarenes" (used in Italy

outside of the areas where the former Pataria from Milan had wielded
influence), "Popelicani," "Piphles," "Arians," and "weavers" (*texerants*), a
designation derived from their widely practiced occupation.[86] The controversies surrounding each of these names are not resolved, but need not
concern us here. The Cathars would hardly have been satisfied with these
terms: Already in Ekbert's day they called themselves "the church of God"
and considered themselves the apostles' successors.[87] In their view, the
Catholics were the heretics.[88]

For centuries there had not been such a fundamental rejection of the
established church.[89] To be sure, Tanchelm's adherents supposedly asserted that they alone were "the church," yet they did not have an
organization to rival that of the church; Tanchelm and his twelve apostles
did not qualify as a hierarchy. The Cathars not only organized themselves,
they also developed an—albeit rudimentary—historical consciousness.
Everwin of Steinfeld had already been told in Cologne that the community dated back to the age of the martyrs,[90] which, strictly speaking,
includes the Apostolic Age. A thirteenth-century Cathar ritual book explains the *consolamentum*, the baptism of the Holy Spirit, in this manner:
"The church of God has administered this holy baptism, conveying the
Holy Spirit, from the age of the apostles down to the present day; it has
been handed down from perfects (*boni homines*) to perfects until today and
will continue to be so until the end of the world."[91]

The Roman Church was completely discounted not merely in its established form, but also in terms of its historical underpinnings. Peter had
never been in Rome, his relics were fakes; the anti-Christian Roman
Empire, marked by its persecution of Christians, had been transferred by
Constantine the Great to Pope Silvester I together with his insignia; the
Roman papacy had perpetuated this ungodly empire. At the end of time
the true church would triumph over the "church of the evil" (*ecclesia
malignantium*).[92]

The Catholic Church embraces all those who have been baptized, saints
as well as sinners, the evil as well as the good. The Cathar Church,
however, consisted of those believers who were supposed to be sinless
vessels of the Holy Spirit. The elitist nature of the "perfects" as an upper
class and their saintly way of life had Donatist roots. They were "good
people," "Christians," in contrast with the sinful, unbaptized mass of
believers. This lower class was not permitted to call God Father and, as a
result, could not recite the Lord's Prayer. The upshot was that they could
not pray.

Did the nature of the upper class represent a fundamental break with
prevailing ideas? The common people were more amenable to such
thinking because as a rule Christians were accustomed to turning to

saints, not to God, the supreme judge. The Catholic saints were present in their relics. The Cathars, on the other hand, had living saints in their midst, and they would ask to be blessed anytime they encountered one of them; the perfect would give his blessing while the believer was on his knees or at least made a deep bow. This was called the *melioramentum*,[93] an "amelioration" brought about through prayer, much as Catholics expected saints to intercede with God. Like much else the Cathars did, the *melioramentum* also became ritualized and complex; still, its underlying assumption survived, as did the aspiration among the members of the lower classes to become such a perfect oneself at the end of one's life. That step represented a change in status, analogous to the way Catholic laymen sometimes entered a monastery at the end of their lives. In France many perfects resided in communal homes similar to monasteries and wore dark robes resembling the Bogomil monk's cloak. In appearance and function, the Cathar perfects corresponded to the Catholic clergy and were marked by a certain emphasis on a monklike manner still characteristic of the Eastern Church today.

Even among the apostles there had been questions of precedence, and in his monasteries Saint Benedict had ranked the monks according to the date of their profession. Among the Cathars in France the *ancia* (the "elder") corresponded to the abbot; he could preside over a convent, exercised liturgical functions, and preached. By the term *archicatharus* Ekbert of Schönau probably meant the *ancia*.[94] He could have deputies, other perfects who ranked below him in seniority, that is, in the date of their baptism of the Holy Spirit.[95] This sufficed for the organization of smaller groups; but if they grew, they would need further officeholders. The officials were, first, the deacon, who traveled about a larger district, led rituals of penance, and conferred baptisms of the Holy Spirit; second, the bishop, elected by the community and ordained by means of a new baptism of the Holy Spirit;[96] and third, his two deputies, the "elder son" and the "younger son" (*filius maior, filius minor*). Concomitant with the new baptism, the bishop assumed the *ordo*, that is, the status and dignity of his office, yet he had no distinctive official attire and no fundamentally new duties. He was itinerant, preaching and performing the liturgy just as before, more the first among equals than a commander. Bishops arrived at the council at Saint-Félix de Caraman "with their council,"[97] probably the elders of their district. In the Roman Church, much as in the secular sphere, the organization was based on the cities and their territories, and, thus, the bishop was "bishop of (name of city)" (*episcopus civitatis N.*). For the Cathars, things were different; although one spoke of the bishop of Albi, he had his residence in Lombers, and the bishop of Toulouse lived in Lavaur; that is, they lived in rural communities. They were more secure there than in proximity to the Catholic upper clergy and the secular authorities. Since the bishop was mostly itinerant, it hardly mattered where his residence was located.

While the text concerning the council at Saint-Félix does not mention the bishops' "elder and younger sons," these positions may nonetheless have already existed by then. For instance, Everwin of Steinfeld had spoken of the "bishop with his associate."[98] In the thirteenth century it became established practice for the "elder son" to be ordained, in other words, to receive a second baptism of the Holy Spirit, either by the bishop before his death or by the "younger son" afterward. At that point the "younger son" advanced to "elder son." While this was reasonable in theory, it did not always work out in practice.

As long as each region could be covered by a single bishop, there was no need for a fixed system of dioceses like that of the Roman Church. In southern France, however, that was already not the case, and a dispute arose between the Cathar bishops of Albi and Toulouse over the boundaries of their missions. It was in hopes of settling this dispute that the council at Saint-Félix was convened in 1167. Due to his stature as bishop of Constantinople and his great skill, Nicetas resolved the point of contention. As already noted, he came championing a hitherto unknown "pure doctrine" of radical dualism and consequently set himself up as a sort of "eldest one" among the attending bishops: His ordinations were valid, and those of the bishops had to be repeated; thus, Nicetas had precedence (*prioratus*) over them. This was an important position, one he apparently attained through his say-so alone. The question has even been raised whether he was a fraud, for we know nothing about him otherwise and very little about the bishopric of Constantinople. Perhaps his personal prestige was as important to him as the new doctrine.

If one of the perfects committed a minor sin, it could be included in the confession that the perfects had to recite jointly as part of a penitential ceremony: In the presence of a deacon they threw themselves upon the ground, and one of them recited a long vernacular formula taken from the Lyon ritual book. In grave instances the action taken depended—analogous to Catholic penitential practices of the time—on whether the sin had been committed openly. "Hidden" sins were expiated by means of a rigid fast, open ones by the loss of seniority (*prioratus*). In either event, a new baptism of the Holy Spirit was necessary. The bishop or, as the case may be, the "son" was stripped of his duties.[99]

The problem of invalid ordinations, which had convulsed the Catholic Church in the eleventh century, was from early on a source of concern for the Cathars as well. At Saint-Félix their bishops received a new baptism of the Holy Spirit from "dominus papa Niquinta," the senior bishop Nicetas,[100] because, when they had received their former baptisms, they had not subscribed to the true faith of radical dualism. After Nicetas had departed for home, it was discovered that he had committed a grave sin, and, consequently, the baptisms he had performed were invalid as well. On that account Mark, bishop of Concorezzo, wished to travel to the East in order to have himself baptized yet again.[101] A new baptism was also necessary if, for example, a perfect ate meat. One could not be more rigorous than that.

The baptism of the Holy Spirit was conveyed by the community of perfects, who, letting the eldest individual or the bishop go first, all laid their hands on the head of the candidate. There was no clear distinction between baptism of the Holy Spirit and ordination as bishop; in the latter case, too, it was the role of the community to convey the Holy Spirit, and the ordination was nevertheless rendered invalid by a single sin on the part of a participant. Catholics argued that only bishops, as successors to the apostles, could convey the Holy Spirit, although priests and deacons also possessed the Holy Spirit and held orders.[102] The Cathars evidenced scant interest in canon law and took no steps to work out the problem through laborious disputations—as done by the Roman Church.

The rite of baptism of the Holy Spirit included placing a copy of the Gospels on the head of the candidate and reciting the Lord's Prayer; later on, certain Cathars came to view the latter as the actual constitutive act. The believers looked on in silence, hoping that they themselves would someday be received in the same manner. In the meantime, however, it was preferable not to assume the onerous responsibilities incumbent on the perfects. People often postponed receiving the baptism of the Holy Spirit until the end of their lives, risking the possibility that they might die unbaptized. In order to mitigate this risk, they would enter into an agreement (convenenza): The believer declared his intent to be baptized, and a perfect declared his willingness to convey the baptism of the Holy Spirit to the believer even if the believer were no longer in possession of his faculties at the end of his life. The following was recounted of Count Raymond VI of Toulouse: "Up until today [the beginning of the thirteenth century] he has been accompanied by heretics in plain clothes in order to be under their care at the end of his life. For he believes that by means of the baptism of the Holy Spirit he . . . can be saved without any repentance."[103]

The liturgical forms for the baptism of the Holy Spirit and for other ceremonies were transcribed in a ritual book that has survived in two redactions from the thirteenth century. Some of its passages are identical to portions of the Bogomil liturgy as formulated in Asia Minor around 1050.[104] Of course, any conclusions based on this fact would be purely speculative. The ritual book retains little of the plainness and simplicity of the apostolic life, replete as it is with complex liturgical practices.[105] During the course of the thirteenth century this ritualism grew to grotesque proportions. According to an Italian tract, the following ritual was to be observed before the morning meal (and no doubt before the evening meal as well): Kneeling three times, the cook of the convent went to see the eldest person and recited some short prayers. After that, fourteen Lord's Prayers, three short prayers, another four Lord's Prayers, and three short prayers were recited, and then came the blessing of the bread by the elder.[106]

In other instances as well, prayer by the perfects consisted in the endless repetition of the Lord's Prayer; according to one calculation the "Lord's Prayer was recited as often as 250 times a day."[107] That might represent a record, to be sure, but one not inconceivable in those days. In 1201 Innocent III sanctioned the Humiliati's vow to observe each of the seven canonical hours with seven Lord's Prayers.[108] The Cathars prayed in Latin, but their sermons were delivered in the vernacular. They normally performed their devotions fifteen times a day, including during the night. The Lord's Prayer was explained and handed down in a sort of initiation ceremony that ushered in a probationary period prior to the bestowal of the baptism of the Holy Spirit. As early as the twelfth century, the Bogomils practiced such ceremonies, which involved placing a book containing the text of the Gospel of Saint John on the initiate's head in the belief that the text would enter the individual and purify him or her. In 1163 Ekbert of Schönau, without knowing what the "small book" contained, witnessed the Cathars celebrating this rite.[109] He interpreted the rite as a baptism, a view adopted by some scholars today.

Before meals or at other times too, perfects and believers could join together in celebrating the liturgical act of "breaking bread" or "blessing the bread," a practice that, as we have already noted, resembled the so-called eulogiae of the Middle Ages. From the Cathar point of view, it was impossible for this act to represent a transubstantiation of material bread into the transfigured body of Christ; if anything, it was a memorial rite. By the words "Hoc est" [This is], Christ meant his own body, or he was speaking allegorically: The bread is "Christ's law, which was given to all," one of the interpretations mentioned by Augustine[110]—not that he intended, however, to destroy faith in the real presence.

This line of thought was congruent with that portion of the Lord's Prayer called the "petition for bread," which contained a Greek word (*epiúsios*) rendered in Luke 11:3 as *quotidianus* (daily), but in Matt. 6:11 as *supersubstantialis* (exalted above all being [or every substance]). Both meanings are plausible from a philological point of view. The Cathars chose the latter meaning, but they were not the only ones: Saint Bernard of Clairvaux reproved Abelard for instructing that the latter version be recited at his monastery, the Paraclete, whereupon Abelard for his part accused Bernard of being a liturgical innovator.[111] The word *supersubstantialis* conformed to the Cathar view that the Lord's Prayer was the angels' hymn of praise taught by Christ to humans.[112] What was earthly, material bread to the angels? The blessed bread probably meant a great deal to the unbaptized common people, however, for in later times they took it home with them and preserved the bread like relics. For them, participation in the perfects' meals replaced participation in the celebration of the Catholic mass, and they gave heed to homiletic exhortations to improve their lives. But despite their endeavors, before receiving the baptism of the Holy Spirit they remained sinners denied salvation. Thus, one might have easily concluded that laypeople were not subject to any moral code, and that the baptism of the Holy Spirit at the end of one's life opened the door to saintliness at one fell swoop.

Peter of Vaux-de-Cernay could thus write the following about the "believers" at the beginning of the thirteenth century: "They devoted themselves to usury, acts of brigandage, murder, and the temptations of the flesh; they committed perjury and indulged in every wickedness. They believed they would be saved without making restitution to the person who was robbed, without confession and penance, so long as they managed to recite the Lord's Prayer and receive the imposition of hands from their masters before death."[113] This was surely an oversimplification, and the repeated assertions that the Cathar believers behaved immorally should similarly be viewed with caution. The practice of postponing conversion to the end of one's life was more characteristic of Eastern than Roman ecclesiastical thought, since the Roman Church provided for continuous, attendant supervision of its adherents' morals. From that perspective, it was a sign of inexcusable weakness to rely upon a final conversion.

Peter of Vaux-de-Cernay also overlooked the perfects' understandable desire to train other perfects, an admittedly protracted task carried out in secret. Ekbert of Schönau remarked that it took fifteen years for the sectarians to initiate sympathizers fully into their teachings, "or so they say."[114] Caution and lengthy observation of the candidate were certainly called for in cases where the baptism of the Holy Spirit was to be administered, not to someone about to die, but instead to a believer who would from that point on assume the difficult life of a perfect.

Scholars routinely refer to the perfects as *perfecti* [those who have been made perfect], but Ekbert, Alan of Lille, and others derive the term from the "perfect" [complete] initiation into the sect's secrets.[115] Ekbert asserted that the Rhenish Cathars themselves went by the name *perfecti*; they probably did so because of Christ's words: "If you would be perfect, go, sell what you possess and give to the poor" (Matt. 19:21), which closed with the call to follow the Lord. The term survived, alongside other designations referring to their mode of dress (*indutus, vestitus*), as well as the terms already noted above, "Christian" or "good person."

What may appear to be elitist arrogance, and may very well have been so to some extent, nevertheless has a doctrinal basis: Since the perfect is the vessel of the Holy Spirit, by definition he can only be a good person and a Christian. Orthodox monks and hermits tended to view their particular modes of existence as not just the best, but as the only truly Christian ones, and this may have influenced the Cathars.[116] "O you holy Cathars, you who cannot sin"—in such wise Ekbert addressed the perfects.[117] Unfortunately, the ironic undertone was justified; there were at all events individual cases where perfects were not all that they appeared to be to the believers. The most notorious case concerns Garattus, who was elected Lombard bishop around 1180 and wanted to travel to Bulgaria for his ordination: He was discovered with a woman. In the ensuing scandal the Cathars in northern Italy split up into six dioceses and two doctrinal branches.[118]

The perfects' holiness consisted of an inner attitude assessable only by external criteria: dietary and sexual asceticism, prayer, humble behavior, and inconspicuous itinerant preaching. Was there a Cathar spirituality? We know very little about that subject. If there was such a thing, it was not at any rate put into writing. The life of the perfects was difficult, for their holiness did not find expression in the silent contemplation of divine secrets, but rather in the magical aura of asceticism. Every man, even someone who engaged in warfare, was said to be safe from his enemies in the company of a perfect.[119] As late as the fourteenth century, in the sect's waning days, someone testified before an inquisition that ever since the perfects had been driven from the village of Sabartés, the land had been subject to bad weather.[120] Should a perfect commit a sin, the consequences were felt not just on earth: "If a perfect committed a grave sin . . . all whom he had baptized lost the Holy Spirit and had to be rebaptized. Indeed, even the [dead] ones who were saved fell down from heaven in consequence of the sin of their baptizer [*consolatoris*]."[121]

For centuries the church had struggled to Christianize popular religiosity, and by no means with complete success. Likewise, the fundamentalism and rigorism of the Cathars did not suffice to transform popular thought. For the most part Catharism lacked that element of intellectualism that was at least present at the higher echelons of Catholicism. One became a perfect without undergoing a test of faith, for what mattered was how one lived from that point on: The candidate swore to abstain from certain foods—cheese, milk, eggs, meat—and likewise from sexual intercourse.[122] The focus was placed on extremely concrete precepts, rather than on hard-to-grasp demands like one's love of God and the "edification" of a new personality.

Like the Bogomils, the Cathars virtually equated moral and physical purity; sin and uncleanliness were closely related concepts, both of which betokened the devil, their originator. Anything related to sexual intercourse represented the height of uncleanliness, even in the case of animals. This is what led to the prohibitions on certain foods. Count Raymond VI of Toulouse purportedly went so far as to maintain that the Cistercians would not be able to enter heaven, because they kept sheep, which engaged in sexual relations with each other.[123] Even if this were a malicious jest by the chronicler, it still exemplifies what course such an obsession with cleanliness could take. We hear how in later days a perfect traveled with his own dishes and rinsed his plate five or even nine times before every meal,[124] yet additional evidence for this practically compulsive mode of thought.

The perfects considered themselves members of an elite group elevated above the common crowd; they were the adoptive sons of God (based on Rom. 8:15), whom they were allowed to call Father. They lived like the apostles, as either itinerant preachers or residents of a single place, and not like mendicants, but wage earners; we will return to this later. Christ had sent his disciples out into the world in pairs, and the perfects, too, often appeared in pairs. Thus, they could keep an eye on each other, according to Ekbert, even to the extent of sleeping in pairs.[125] In the days before they were persecuted, the perfects were recognizable by their dark clothing and full beards, which dramatically accentuated their complexions, made pale by fasting. "[W]hat bearded barbarism!" exclaimed one chronicler at the end of the twelfth century.[126] Some of their vernacular sermons are extant,[127] and they are replete with quotes from the Bible. While this method of composition was not unknown to Catholic writers either, what is significant is how the heretics employed the quotations. In the case of Bernard of Clairvaux, the biblical passages underlying his speech do not diminish the eloquent flow of his Latin words. Bernard's sermons stir the listener, while the Cathars' sermons are meant rather to indoctrinate. It made quite a difference whether one spoke Latin—bolstered by classical rhetoric and that of the church fathers—or expressed oneself in the plain, as yet inelegant vernacular.

In addition to male perfects there were also female *perfectae*. At the beginning there must have been mixed convents, for Bernard of Clairvaux lashed out against the practice of men and women living communally: It would be easier, he said, to bring a dead man back to life than to preserve one's chastity in a place where men and women met constantly, sat side by side at meals, worked together, and slept near one another. Even if everything worked out all right, there would be the lingering suspicion of scandal (scandalum).[128] Later on, the Cathars maintained separate convents, although some of the female perfects continued to live with their families. They rarely figure prominently as preachers, and their participation in theological discussions seems to have been considered inappropriate as well. Even Countess Esclarmonde of Foix, head of the female convent of Pamiers, had to forbear when told during such a discussion: "Go, milady, spin wool on your distaff, it is not for you to speak before a gathering such as this."[129] Day-to-day life was of course different; we have a description of how "one woman wove, a second one spun wool, and yet a third preached that the devil had made all of creation."[130] In the Cathar convents people plied a trade, and yet again we come across textile production.

Did the female perfects enjoy a freer and higher status than did Catholic nuns? Some of the latter were also quite free. There were still "house nuns" living with their families. In some places, entering a monastery did not mean real seclusion from the world. Furthermore, there were wandering female pilgrims, not always of the best character, perhaps comparable to the "wenches" in whose company, according to Bernard of Clairvaux, the Cathars moved about (muliercularum circumductio); the Cathars justified themselves by saying that it was not forbidden in the Gospels.[131] By the time they came under persecution, we hear nothing about such liberties. Women were not permitted to hold any church offices (bishop, elder or younger "son," or deacon), but could participate in administering the baptism of the Holy Spirit. Their participation in baptisms later became more limited, and in the thirteenth century their baptisms were valid only as the last resort;[132] in other cases, the candidates for baptism had to be women.

We hear nothing about freedom and self-determination for women. A woman lived either with her family or under her spouse's protection and domination or cloistered in a convent. The theory that women made up a significant portion of the aristocratic adherents of Catharism in southern France has crumbled in the face of statistical review; rather, they were, if anything, underrepresented.[133] It was certainly easier, however, for the wives and mothers of noblemen to profess their Catharism openly than it was for the noblemen themselves, if only because the latter were invested with ecclesiastical fiefs, rights of patronage, etc. When a conflict arose— over the usurpation of ecclesiastical rights, for example—some people preferred to espouse Catharism. Catholic convents now lost the purpose they had served for the nobility, that of taking in surplus daughters, and families turned to women's convents run by the sect. The opening volley in the struggle by Diego of Osma and Dominic against the Cathars was their founding, in 1206, of a cloister for women, Prouille, which resembled a Cathar convent in every respect, including the performance of textile work. It received twelve noble daughters who had reembraced Catholicism.

Men often died at a younger age than women, particularly during times of war. In those cases where their widows were prevented from inheriting landed property as long as there were surviving male heirs, the widows posed a familiar problem, analogous to the one posed by daughters for whom there was no requisite dowry. Esclarmonde of Foix, the same woman who was unwilling to be silent in men's company, was widowed shortly after 1200, and she returned to her brother; he established a Cathar convent for her and other women in Pamiers (Ariège, north of Foix), which would later be the site of an inquisitorial tribunal. Count Raymond Roger also installed his former wife, Philippa, and his aunt there. It was a family convent analogous to Catholic proprietary monasteries.[134] In such convents three generations of women might live together; there were instances in which girls as young as ten or even seven years old received the baptism of the Holy Spirit. As in the case of Catholic convents, a "perfect" could be fetched back from the convent and marked for marriage.[135] The number of women attached to a convent was usually small, and the same was true for men's convents; there were often less than twelve members, and two dozen was quite the exception.[136] The earliest evidence for such figures dates from the thirteenth century.

Diego of Osma, the catalyst behind the Dominican order, is said to have founded the women's cloister of Prouille, located between Fanjeaux and Montréal, to receive the daughters of nobles who "due to their poverty" were accustomed to handing them over to the heretics to be raised.[137] Just as among Catholics, the only way for Cathars to sidestep the cost of a dowry was to dedicate their daughters to the religious life. The cloister or convent would in turn normally receive a donation as compensation, or it was entirely dependent on the donor, as in the case of a family convent. While Catholic nuns devoted themselves more to praying than to working— caring for the convent's garden, embroidering vestments, etc.—the perfects in the Cathar houses, both women and men, earned their keep through professional textile work.

Of prime importance were linen and cloth weaving; dye craft and the cloth trade, or trade in general, formed related activities. The Cathars practiced other professions as well, from that of notary to the unprestigious one of gravedigger (Mark of Concorezzo). In the late twelfth century people from around Modena were familiar with "the mills of the Patarenes," by whom they meant the Cathars.[138] That Saint Paul had been a tentmaker (Acts 18:3) was hardly why they were predominantly in the textile crafts; rather, that can be laid to practical considerations. Whoever led the apostolic life had to be on the move in order to spread the faith to all. While that would not have been possible with agriculture, it was with the industries of that time and with trade. Such occupations as butcher, tanner, or shoemaker, which involved contact with warm-blooded animals or, alternatively, their remains, were out of the question. Given that the evil god had made the world out of mud, being a bricklayer or potter meant sullying oneself with such matter. Coal mining was unclean, stonemasonry or blacksmithing was noisy and unclean; besides, that sort of work required physical strength beyond what could be expected from a vegetarian given to fasting. Of course, supply and demand also influenced the choice of a profession; at that time there was a growing demand for specialized weaving, since it was the earliest form of industrial production.

Spinning, on the other hand, continued to be purely manual work and, furthermore, a task appropriate for women. One scholar has described this activity as the "bottleneck in textile production" and has credited the female perfects with contributing to its elimination.[139] In any event, it was more efficient for the perfects to stick to the weaving loom and to leave it to families working out of their homes to spin the wool. A Cathar convent was not a "closed cottage industry"; rather, it depended upon the work of others; in this case they probably turned first to "believers." Another network of relationships benefiting the mission arose through the sale (or exchange) of the finished cloth either locally or through itinerant trade.

Textile production did not in general garner respect. In the thirteenth century, and probably even before then, it was considered one of the *inhonesta mercimonia* [disreputable trades], one of the occupations that no priest should practice.[140] After they were subjected to malicious scorn, the weavers of Kornelimünster and Looz asserted in protest that there were occupations much more despicable than theirs in Christendom, since they led honest lives. Only those things which led to sin were to be despised, and a poor weaver in the countryside was to be preferred to a judge in town who oppressed widows and orphans.[141] At that time, in 1135, the issue was not Cathars per se, but the environment in which heresy and social unrest could flourish.

Soon afterward, the term *texerant* was applied to Cathars in France, proving not only that they were identified with this craft, but also that people transferred their scorn for the craft to the heretics.[142] The word *textrina*, weavers' workshops, took on the secondary meaning of "basement hovel." Already in his day Ekbert of Schönau said the heretics banded together "in cellars and weavers' workshops and similar underground dwellings."[143] While such behavior underscored the poverty-stricken as well as the conspiratorial nature of the gatherings, the choice of their location may also have been rooted in technical considerations: Looms weighed a great deal and made a great deal of noise, and the best place for them was in a cellar, away from customary domiciles. There people could work "day and night" and gather together.

"We are the Poor of Christ," said the Cathars whom Everwin of Steinfeld knew in Cologne. "We have no home, no fields, no movable possessions of any kind, just as Christ had no possessions and bid his disciples to have none. You, however, we hear tell, amass house upon house, field upon field"; for even monks had communal property, although they had no personal possessions.[144] The weavers in Kornelimünster, just mentioned above, were laborers who worked for merchants. The situation in Cologne in 1143 may have been similar, although at around the same time the Cathars in Périgord did not accept any wages.[145] Cathars in general probably did not ascribe to this rigorist point of view. Where it had predominated, Cathars in any event soon adopted the view taken by the Catholic monastic clergy on this point: The community was permitted to accept and administer contributions, whereas each individual perfect remained poor. We have already heard about the *convenenza*, a contract guaranteeing that a person would receive the baptism of the Holy Spirit in exchange for the transfer or promise of property. Whenever a sick individual was about to be baptized, he was asked prior to the celebration of the liturgical ceremony if he owed the (Cathar) church anything; only if the answer was no could he be received among the perfects. "If one nevertheless prays to God on behalf of a deceitful and disloyal person, this prayer will not be granted";[146] in other words, the baptism was invalid. Whoever explained that he was truly unable to pay would be baptized regardless.

Particularly in the sect's early days such oblations did not consist of money, but of movable possessions and landed property. "They [the Cathars] began to make their homes in the small market towns and small cities; they owned fields and vineyards," wrote William of Puylaurens.[147] One of the accusations leveled by the Waldensians as part of their anti-Cathar propaganda was that the Cathars (i.e., their church) were not poor. They were also reproached for being closely associated with commerce. Around 1184 the Waldensian Durand of Huesca observed that nowhere in the New Testament does one find that the apostles were traders "and that they went to markets because of earthly matters of trade, in order to amass money there, which is what you [Cathars] do."[148]

In the twelfth century the view began to gain ground that merchants constituted a separate class, and wherever those merchants were Cathar "believers," people kept an especially close eye on their activities. However, in their roles as the heads of convents or as bishops, for example, the perfects also had to manage financial matters. If an individual did not want to debase himself to the low status held by the laborers in Kornelimünster, he could follow the cloth trade, which was associated with textile production. And a part of trade was going on trips, and in certain areas part of going on trips meant enjoying the protection of the landed aristocracy; the nobles felt that the protection they lent merited the collection of "protection money," and they indeed levied fees against prominent Cathars.[149] During the persecution later on, it was clear that money was one means of survival, for with money one could emigrate to Italy. The Waldensians distanced themselves from the merchant class because it was associated with lying, fraud, and the swearing of oaths. Broad sections of the population felt much the same, until in 1199 Pope Innocent III canonized the merchant Homobonus [good man] from Cremona, who had died only recently (1197). This was a prescient act and one not necessarily taken with an eye to the heretics. Merchants spread Homobonus's cult, and known as "heiliger Gutmann" [Saint Goodman], he became the patron saint of the tailors' guild in Basel, tailoring being one of the crafts linked professionally to the cloth trade. It is highly unlikely that the name Homobonus was connected to the Cathars; they were not the only ones sometimes to be termed "good people."

Besides craftspeople and merchants, some clerics also converted to Catharism. Everwin of Schönau had already heard from his sources that the doctrine of the Cathars was preached around the world "and that they claimed many of our [secular] clergy and monks."[150] Soon afterward (before 1147), a monk from Périgord named Heribert reported that the Cathars in his region included not just laypeople, "but also clerics, priests, monks, and nuns."[151] While some probably retained their religious office, others mingled with the Cathars and apparently did not hold any special rank. They may have been the *magistri* [masters] mentioned by some sources. One of the masters, Bonaccursus in Milan, switched sides in the late twelfth century and authored a confession attacking the sect.[152] In 1207 a Cathar "doctor" under the alias of Theodoric (Thierry) took part in a disputation with Catholics in Servian (Hérault)—he was actually a former canon, William from Nevers.[153] The reverse also occurred: In 1181 two Cathars recanted in Le Puy and became canons; one had been the Cathar bishop of Toulouse, yet neither knew how to speak Latin.[154]

Along with the established church itself, the Cathars renounced its educational program and corpus of ecclesiastical writing as a superstructure resting on an unchristian foundation. Throughout the whole history of the sect, there is no evidence for the existence of a single school analogous to the cathedral and monastic schools. Only in the thirteenth century did the Cathars even begin to understand that their dispute with Catholicism necessitated a "weapons parity": Being able to cite ever so many biblical quotations was no substitute for knowing the Latin language and Scholastic modes of thought. Conversely, not until the advent of the "modernity" espoused by Saint Dominic was the Scholastic form of disputation supplanted by something more straightforward. To prove his position, Saint Dominic presented a transcription of quotations (*auctoritates*, surely from the New Testament in this case) to one of the heretics for consideration. Another source links the text to an arbitration panel held in Montréal (1207), which was presented with written evidence by both sides. The arbiters were laymen, and they refused to reach a verdict.[155] Thus, this attempt at overcoming intellectual and language barriers came to naught.

It was not until the thirteenth century that the Cathars developed a modest body of "literature" in Latin, initially composed of written compilations of propositions and supporting quotations to aid in disputations. During the course of internal disputes among the Cathars after 1230, a certain John of Lugio in Italy wrote the sect's first "weighty work," consisting of 160 parchment sheets but extant only in fragments.[156] This body of material is neither quantitatively nor qualitatively comparable to the flood of works penned above all by the Dominican order and at the University of Paris.

Cathar theology dispenses almost entirely with the driving force of history: Church history does not unfold, and thus the progression from the old to the new covenant is meaningless. In just six chapters, one thirteenth-century treatise delineated the differences between the Old and New Testaments and the way each conceptualizes God: The God of the Old Testament is evil and mendacious—he breaks his promises and commits fornication;[157] it was not God, but the Prince of Evil Spirits, who handed down the Mosaic Law.[158] Even so, the New Testament harks back to the Old in many passages, and time and time again the New Testament is deemed the fulfillment of prophetic utterances in the Old. The Cathars could escape this dilemma either by contending that these prophecies were never really uttered and interpreting them allegorically or by acknowledging that at least some things in the Old Testament were derived from God. The Psalms and Proverbs were rather generally accepted, and the Psalms were also the easiest to interpret allegorically. Some Cathars—for example, a group from Desenzano—also acknowledged the Prophets and the Book of Job.[159]

The voluminous books of the Kings, however, did not have to be taken into account. There was a practical as well as an ideological aspect to trimming the canon: Catharism was a religion without libraries, one that held the written word at something of a distance. The itinerant Cathar carried his knowledge of the Bible with him like a treasure, but even someone living in the Middle Ages did not have unlimited powers of memorization. If he were able to recite portions of the Gospels by heart, that was already quite a bit. Later, and especially in the urban milieu of northern Italy, this attitude toward the written word underwent some change, but there was just no substitute for monastic and cathedral schools.

Catharism, above all early Catharism, was not a product of biblical exegesis; biblical exegesis was instead relegated to a secondary role, that of testifying to the accuracy of their beliefs concerning the creation myth and ascetic life. This endeavor could admit of contradictions and faulty reasoning, for only a few scholars might be discomfited thereby. More important than all the texts in the world were one's personal experiences in life and the conclusion those experiences led one to draw: The world is evil. Whatever the Cathars asserted about theology, cosmogony and cosmology, psychology and ethics, was entwined with this basic principle. The simpler these propositions were, the more they made sense to the believers.

Thus they believed as follows: Since the world is evil, its creator can only have been the devil. God is omnipotent in the sense that the heavenly lights and pure spirits, including those of humans, emanated from him. At the end of time, they will return to the new heaven and the new earth, to the heavenly Jerusalem. At present, however, human souls are imprisoned in matter, suffering an antithetical, material creation because of the devil, who is an evil son of God or the antithesis of God. The devil was the lord of the darkness that in the beginning covered the (then desolate and barren) earth; alternatively, it was God who created the world, but the devil divided the elements and saw to all the rest described in Genesis. He also possesses dominion over the world. "God does nothing in this world; he does not create the blossoms or the fruits, does not cause conception or birth. . . . In sum, he does nothing in this world."[160] It rests with each person to abnegate this world; Christ, an angel, has pointed out the way to us and taught us the right prayer. The baptism of the Holy Spirit restores the link to the world above, releasing people from the power of evil. There is no need for an extramundane hell, since this world is itself hell.[161] Should a person not achieve *stabilitas* [steadfastness] in God, then his soul must continue to wander from body to body.

"L'esperit pausat en carcer" (The spirit abides in a prison)—that is how it is phrased in the vernacular ritual book. Durand of Huesca wrote around 1220/22 that, according to the Cathars, bodies are the dungeons and fetters in which the sons and daughters of God are imprisoned by the devil, and God wants to get them back. From this Durand drew the edifying conclusion that anyone who puts Cathars to death is doing them a service and thereby pleasing the Lord.[162] This extremely pessimistic worldview was expressed best by Psalm 136, the lament of the Jews in the Babylonian exile,[163] which became a lamentation for life in a world perceived as alien and evil.

The original sin did not proceed from Adam and Eve, but beforehand from those angels who revolted against God and were banished from heaven. Those spiritual beings have been sentenced to live on earth; the sin committed by the first two human beings has been visited upon the whole human race inasmuch as Adam and Eve, with the devil's constant aid, set in motion the succession of human generations. Only after receiving the baptism of the Holy Spirit can one perform penance, and the perfects are penitents for themselves and all mankind.[164]

Christ had showed humans that penance and a return to the immaterial world were feasible; he was a former angel who due to his merits was embraced by God as an adoptive son. Thus, Christ did not redeem mankind by means of a sacrificial act, but instead by means of the right doctrine.[165] Although much about Cathar theology is fantastic, its matter-of-fact streak becomes particularly evident here: It affirms a myth instead of a mystery. The Trinity, too, is not a mystery to the Cathars.[166] The angels and spirits remaining in heaven are, just like Christ, emanations of God. Through the baptism of the Holy Spirit the imprisoned soul finds "its own" spirit, with which it will be reunited in heaven. There was never a virgin birth; Christ's body was a semblance of a body, and, consequently, Christ was not resurrected. Since none of these views was defined as dogma, they could be interpreted in various ways. Mary is an angel; alternatively, she was regarded allegorically as "the Church." In addition to the Christ hailing from the realm of light, there is an evil Christ, born in Bethlehem and subsequently crucified. It was this other Christ who ate and drank, and whose relationship with Mary Magdalene sparked comment— the good Christ meanwhile "neither truly took meat nor was ever in this world, except in a spiritual manner within Paul's body."[167]

Revealed here is an exegesis that is almost experimental in nature. By some means or another, it was necessary to adapt the material in the Bible to the predetermined principles of the Cathar worldview; moreover, there was no authoritative body to halt speculation. The speculative element may have been just the thing to strike a chord in contemporary thinking. While the Cathars took a new approach to the Bible, the early Scholastics gave a new twist to Christian exegesis as well as to philosophy and theology. As much as they differed in method and niveau, neither group had much use for miracles. The Cathars asserted that Christ did not perform any material miracles; passages in the Gospels pertaining to miracles were to be interpreted allegorically. Material miracles were perforce the devil's work.[168]

In order to present a fairly systematic compendium of Cathar doctrines, it was necessary in this chapter to overstep the chronological bounds of the twelfth century. It was also necessary to be somewhat selective and not overly punctilious about presenting the entire range of viewpoints espoused by Cathars. Our account was not meant to be exhaustive, and it is perhaps not very important that it be so. The numerous doctrinal differences in northern Italy appear to be related to efforts made by individual churches to differentiate themselves and to possess the "true doctrine." Here we were more interested in showing how they thought than in showing what the outcome of that process was in each particular instance. For that reason we will look at the myths and allegorization of the Cathars in a broader context.

4

Some Theories
About Heresy

When it comes to the study of history, nonprofessionals for the most part find the factual events much more engaging than scholarly theories about them; for that reason, the general reader may choose to skip this chapter. However, the urge to dig beneath the surface for the essence and roots of phenomena is found not just among historians. From the outset people have attempted to place heretics within broader contexts and have in the process come up with the most diverse opinions. No account of heresy may disregard all this material.

The extensive corpus of Graeco-Latin patristic literature seems replete with answers to questions about the more immediate origins of heresy. It contains accounts of many struggles, often quite personal ones, with schools of thought like Manichaeism and with the Gnosticism or Neoplatonism found among some groups. In a spiritual atmosphere marked by extreme vitality, thinkers proposed or repudiated ideas that worked their way into Christianity, either openly or covertly, irrespective of their orthodoxy or even heterodoxy. Whatever heretics may have espoused in the High Middle Ages had been thought of before or had antecedents. Thus, the question arises whether the beliefs we have before us were handed down over time or were discovered independently in the form of parallel ideas arising spontaneously in more than one time and place.

Around 1223 the very erudite and equally garrulous monk Caesarius of Heisterbach wrote that the Cathars had adopted "some points from the Manichaean dogma and some of the errors which Origen is said to have written against Periarchon, and very many which they had fashioned out of their own heads."[1] Here, by differentiating between borrowed and original material, and delineating in turn two different sorts of borrowed material, Caesarius rose above the common tendency to equate the Cathars with the Manichaeans. Caesarius properly identified Origen (born around 185), the greatest thinker produced by the Christian academy in Alexandria, with his most important work, *On First Principles*. This work promotes the doctrine that souls preexist in heaven prior to their conjunction with or exile into human bodies, and that they can be completely restored to their original, God-given state without undergoing the eternity of hell. In recent decades some scholars have surmised that the heresies had "Origenist" roots—for example, Jean Duvernoy, in the case of the Cathars, and Huguette Taviani, in the case of the heretics of Monforte.[2] To prove this conjecture one would have to perform the arduous undertaking of tracing the intermediate steps in the transmission of this philosophy from the third century onward. Duvernoy proposed that the connection was provided by the monks who participated in the disputes about Origenism around the end of the fourth century and into the fifth and were subsequently condemned by Justinian in 553. Other scholars, Taviani among them, looked to a heresy found in Spain in the fourth century, Priscillianism, which may have been influenced by Origenism and could have served as the link to Catharism, when defined broadly enough to include Monforte.

These speculations, which can be neither proved nor disproved, serve to "ennoble" Catharism: It did not originate somewhere in the Balkans, but in Alexandria, that stronghold of classical learning. Still, there is something to be said for the reference to Origen. He was the first to practice the allegorical interpretation of the Holy Scriptures systematically; without recourse to this exegetical technique, it would have been difficult for the Bogomils and Cathars to find a common denominator between their assertions and those of the Gospels. Furthermore, Origen was influenced by Platonism, and at his peak Plato had evoked the image of souls being drawn out of the bright splendor of the realm of the intellect and into the darkness of matter. Such ideas were within the reach of educated individuals able to extract them from classical literature. Origen was one of those individuals and perhaps the most important one for many centuries, but he did not "invent" the myth about the preexistence and fall of the souls.[3]

It is also possible to abandon the search for historical continuity all together and to take a purely phenomenological approach to Catharism vis-à-vis a variety of late classical beliefs. That is exactly what Hans Söderberg did in an estimable book bearing the subtitle *Études sur le gnosticisme de la basse antiquité, et du Moyen Âge* [Studies in the Gnosticism of late antiquity and the Middle Ages]. By means of comparative study, Söderberg discerned "a phenomenological concordance" among the ideas held by the Paulicians, Bogomils, and—for the most part—Cathars, which he interpreted as continuity.[4] In his words, these groups shared "a Gnostic frame of mind." Of course, this term embraces a whole assortment of viewpoints and hence "accommodates" various phenomena. On the other hand, Söderberg ascribed to these sects "a certain autonomy" in doctrinal matters. From the historian's perspective, at any rate, there is no link between gnosis and the Paulicians, and only a very tenuous connection between the Paulicians and the Bogomils. Söderberg, on phenomenological grounds, nevertheless affirmed "the existence of an unbroken chain of tradition linking medieval Gnosticism to Gnosticism in late antiquity."[5] However, the approximation between the two outlooks is more likely psychological in nature: The view that the world was impure and ruled by evil archons bespeaks a type of human existence, a feeling about life, that could give rise to doctrinal similarities. Moreover, Gnostic thinking was passed down by Christian apologists writing in the first centuries after Christ. While they found this doctrinal tradition inimical, some traces of Gnosticism can nevertheless still be seen in their way of thought.

Söderberg referred to the "heresy of the Cathars or neo-Manichaeans,"[6] thus placing himself—and he was in no way alone in this—squarely within a medieval tradition we have already encountered. Ekbert of Schönau, who subscribed to this tradition himself, appended to his sermons against the Cathars a collection of extracts from Saint Augustine's works against the Manichaeans; he did so in order to prove that Manichaeism was "the dregs of all sects."[7] Saint Augustine had himself belonged to this religious community between the years 374 and 383, but then vehemently distanced himself from Manichaeism, without, however, being able to purge Manichaean influences from his mode of thought. At stake was the great cosmological spectacle of "two distinct and mutually opposed realms, each equally eternal, namely, the realm of light and the realm of darkness"—that is how the Manichaeans described it, according to Augustine, who himself wrote about the dichotomy between the realm of God (or, rather, city of God) and the earthly realm.

According to Söderberg, Manichaeism differs from gnosis—or, more strictly speaking, from the other types of Gnosticism—in its dualism.[8] It is important to note that the Gnostics were often reflective in style, while the Manichaeans were active missionaries to the point of martyrdom. In late antiquity only the Manichaeans were condemned as enemies of the state. Diocletian, who persecuted the Christians, attacked the Manichaeans just as severely as did Justinian I, the most Christian emperor. Were it not for the Manichaeans, many Cathars would not have later been burned to death, for in the battle against heresy one followed the precedents set by the old imperial law, and on that basis the authorities could dispatch the heretics with clearer consciences than if they had engaged in a mob lynching.

As portrayed by Augustine, the Manichaeans regarded earthly phenomena as a contest between the principles of good and evil. The good god bestowed souls and spirits upon people, trees, plants, etc.; the prince of darkness imprisoned them in bodies and created five elements inimical to man: smoke, fire, darkness, water, and wind. The good god thereupon created five good elements out of his own substance: air, light, heavenly fire and water, and the good wind. Good and evil were commingled in all living creatures, which contain both a good and an evil nature. The good nature of a fruit is released when the fruit is eaten, but chopping down trees is tantamount to committing murder, for trees harbor souls. Killing animals was likewise prohibited: Their souls take flight, leaving behind unclean flesh, and princes of darkness arrive to punish the animals' murderers.

Thus, it becomes evident why in 1051 the sectarians in Goslar were put to a test to determine whether they would kill a chicken.[9] After they hesitated, it seemed clear that they were Manichaeans. What these people actually had in mind, however, was in all likelihood the fifth commandment, with its poorly defined prohibition against killing.

The Manichaeans taught that Christ did not in reality assume a physical form; baptism with water was to be renounced; humans did not exercise free will; and two souls, one good and one evil, resided in each person. Whenever people came across beliefs analogous to these or to similar propositions, they were quick to conclude that Manichaeism must be at work. For many—even modern scholars—conclusive proof seemed to lie in the similarity between the Manichaean hierarchy and that of the Bogomils and Cathars: The former had the "elect" (*electi*), who were prohibited from marrying, and married "listeners" (*auditores*); above them in rank were twelve "apostles," or "masters," and at the very top stood Mani himself, who embodied the Holy Spirit. According to Everwin of Steinfeld, the Cathars in Cologne also referred to the elect and to the listeners and their wives, and termed themselves apostles.[10]

In actuality, this material may have been gleaned from Augustine's works by either Everwin or the Cathars in Cologne. The adherents of gnosis and of Montanism were also divided into two groups, a lower class and the initiates (*psychikoi* and *pneumatikoi*),[11] and this sort of division was to be expected with any secret doctrine. In addition, it was natural that among the Manichaeans only the elect, not the listeners, were full members of the community, an arrangement we find again among the Cathars. According to Saint Augustine the elect would lay their hands upon the listeners kneeling before them, a practice Antoine Dondaine linked to the Cathar baptism of the Holy Spirit.[12] We encounter this gesture far and wide across Christendom and in the Old Testament, where it is already imbued with various meanings. Time and time again people returned to this fount of ritual, and outside influences did not necessarily come to bear on each observance of this rite. In addition, the Christian rite of ordination may very well also have served as a model for the Bogomils and Cathars.

No documentary evidence is available substantiating a historical continuity from Manichaeism to the Bogomils or Cathars. What has been cited as proof is very questionable. For example, Alberic of Trois-Fontaines (died after 1251) wrote that a Manichaean—Donatist?—bishop from Africa had once lived in exile in Champagne and converted the head of a band of robbers and his henchmen to heresy.[13] Even such a figure as Gerbert of Aurillac, later Pope Silvester II, was mistakenly suspected of harboring Manichaean sympathies, and in 991, when he was the archbishop-elect of Rheims, he was required to swear an "anti-Manichaean confession of faith." The text of this confession itself, however, had been drafted around 500 in response to the Priscillianism then in currency; it was actually that heresy which the Gallic clergy feared at the time. This confession of faith constituted the first canon of a collection of church statutes, which anyone ever needing the text of a solemn confession of faith might have consulted, whether in 991 or afterward.[14]

Dondaine discerned a close kinship between the operational aspects of Manichaean and Cathar doctrines, but he left open the question whether they were dependent from a historical viewpoint. Immediately before the outbreak of World War II, the discovery of some Cathar texts, the *Liber de duobus principiis* [Book of the two principles] above all, reopened the debate. Dondaine believed that on the basis of the newly discovered texts one was obligated to speak of Catharism as "neo-Manichaeism." Heinrich Sproemberg, a historian in the former German Democratic Republic, subsequently reached the same conclusion on the basis of a step-by-step review of the social undercurrents.[15] Dmitri Obolensky took this theory one step further in his book about the Bogomils and postulated that there had been a neo-Manichaean movement spanning the ninth through fourteenth centuries. In 1966 the sociologist Armand Abel reached a similar conclusion and lumped together Manichaeism, Paulicianism, Bogomilism, and Catharism as "Manichaean religions." Common to them all were cosmological dualism, contempt for matter, and the belief in a savior; they were also marked by a "religious hierarchy."[16]

When an idea is rehashed again and again, it often comes to encompass so much that its meaning is diluted. When Steven Runciman wrote his book *The Medieval Manichee,* he clearly felt that late classical Manichaeism and medieval "Christian Dualism . . . were two distinct and separate religions."[17] However, Runciman believed that the medieval sects had, strictly speaking, more in common with Mani's system than with Christianity; he noted that indeed all dualists were considered Manichaeans in the Middle Ages. We can understand why historians like to trace medieval points of view back into antiquity. Conversely, thinkers given to differentiating ideas would greet all such generalizations with suspicion. The same applies to the concept of "Christian Dualism," propounded even before Runciman. Again, we must refer to Dondaine, who wished to forge as close a link as possible between Bogomilism and the Western heresies. In his view, during the eleventh century Christian dualism consisted of Bogomilism on the one hand and of a sort of Western "catharisme primitif" [primitive Catharism] on the other; that is, it was a single entity, not two separate constructs. In Dondaine's view, the oft-used label "Manichaean" served as a tool for writers to abridge their accounts of the sectarians' beliefs; they could omit particular Manichaean features. Thus, Dondaine maintained, it is legitimate to assume that a single type of belief marked by regional variations was at work here.[18]

Dondaine was ahead of his times methodologically; as early as 1952 he analyzed the individual elements recounted by the sources in a quantitative manner and displayed the results in tabular form. Information pertaining to the Bogomils appeared in one column, that pertaining to the eleventh-century "Cathars" in the other. Gaps in the information were filled with material from other sources. The result was a foregone conclusion: Both Bogomilism and Catharism were forms of Christian dualism (neo-Manichaeism).

One example will suffice to show just how much can be read into the gaps. Rodulfus Glaber asserted that the heretics of Orléans believed that heaven and earth were eternal. According to Dondaine's interpretation, this was "a motif that must have been inspired by an inclination to radical dualism."[19] However, it is also possible that Rodulfus had gleaned this idea from the works of Aristotle or the Stoics, or in reading about Epicureanism, perhaps even from Augustine (*De civitate Dei,* XI, 4); he may also have misunderstood his source. Dondaine knew that in the original source they were referring to "God the founder of all things," but he was able to back his way out of this corner through his interpretation of the words "The Holy Spirit will teach you to recognize the true divinity." Dondaine hypothesized that they must thus have also recognized the existence of a "false divinity, in other words, the demon."[20]

At least Dondaine exercised some caution when he made these assertions, but that caution was thrown to the wind by subsequent writers who so amplified his ideas that the sect experienced an apotheosis. Duvernoy's volume *La religion des Cathares* [The religion of the Cathars] opens with this sentence: "Catharism was one of mankind's most widespread religions, holding sway over souls from Asia Minor to the Atlantic, from the tenth to the fifteenth century at the very least, for Catharism must be seen as intertwined with the Bogomilism of the Slavs and Byzantines."

In order not to sow any confusion, one should avoid using either term, Eastern Catharism or Western Bogomilism. There is no evidence for Catharism per se before 1140, and one would do well not to fold into Catharism all the heresies of the eleventh and early twelfth centuries. If we adhere to this narrow use of terminology, the question arises, What was the relationship between these Western heresies and Bogomilism? The documentary evidence for Bogomilism predates that for Western heresies, and there is no firm evidence for Western influences on the East at that time. Did Bogomilism therefore exert influence on the West already before 1140?

We have seen that in his later works Dondaine replied to this question in the affirmative. In doing so, he broke with Raffaello Morghen, who believed that the Western sectarians in the eleventh century constituted an evangelical movement seeking to reform the church from within,[21] one totally independent of Bogomilism. Russell primarily advocated Morghen's thesis in his book on church reform and "dissent," which he defined as the deviation from official teachings and moral guidance of the church. Robert Moore also shared this view and considered Morghen's thesis "generally accepted."[22] That is not quite accurate. What is broadly accepted is the fact that no one has been able to unearth any concrete evidence of Bogomil influence on the doctrines held by the Western sectarians in the eleventh and early twelfth centuries; Morghen's contention regarding the content of that doctrine, that they just subscribed to a simple "evangelism," has not, however, found general acceptance. Many scholars consider it possible or even likely that there were individual, unverifiable instances of Eastern thought filtering into the West. Moore himself admitted that it may have occurred, "though it is as difficult to prove as to disprove."[23] Malcolm Lambert and Arno Borst took similar positions in works published in 1977 and 1988, respectively. Lambert has in the meantime revised his opinion and deleted the descriptions of Eastern heresies from the second edition of his book (1992).[24]

At the fore of heresies known to have arisen in France in the eleventh century stands Leutard from Vertus, and his violent destruction of Christ's crucifix is reminiscent of similar actions taken by the Bogomils.[25] A further parallel may be found in the actions taken by Peter of Bruis more than one hundred years later, which lack any discernible relation to Leutard's heresy. As already noted above,[26] Peter had a bonfire made of shattered crucifixes, into which he was tossed by the outraged bystanders. Fearns recognized that Peter and the Bogomils were united in their "bitter hatred and premeditated acts of violence against the crucifix," and also that Cosmas and the Petrobrusians offered similar rationales for such actions. "This striking congruity in their positions, down to the very fine points of their reasoning, strongly suggests that the Petrobrusians, like the Cathars later on, acquired their contempt for the crucifix from the Bogomils."[27]

Besides this emotional attitude toward the crucifix, the heretics held other, less striking beliefs more amenable to rational explanation. For example, they opposed infant baptism, a practice not found in the New Testament; even Tertullian, in a work entitled *On Baptism*, had renounced it. The Bogomils—much like the Petrobrusians—pointed out that children lacked faith. Peter of Bruis, however, sanctioned adult baptism, whereas the Bogomils in general renounced all sacraments dependent upon matter. Fearns rightly called attention to this distinction between them, and enumerated eight more heretical groups in the West who renounced infant baptism—but not baptism altogether.[28] This shows us that the only way to evaluate a particular heretical viewpoint in a meaningful way is to place it correctly in the context of the group's overall mode of thought.

In the same way, we must be cautious about any line of argument deduced from the sources' silence on this or that doctrine. The testimony of the sources is for the most part very meager and unorganized, in other cases so general that an omission could mean essentially anything— insofar as the heretics revealed any information at all. Thus, we can assume that if the heretics had expressed any dualistic ideas, Bishop Gerard of Cambrai would have included them in his long exposition about the Synod of Arras (1025), and the same thing is probably true for the descriptions of the Synod of Orléans. Conversely, we cannot take the terse reports about the French heretics in the eleventh century as proof that they did not espouse certain doctrines. Only those who, like Jean Musy,[29] believe that the heretics in the West at this time possessed a unified doctrinal system are able to do so.

Finally, we must not overlook the spiritual and social atmosphere in which heresy evolved. We find it inconceivable that the clerics at court in Orléans were "deceived by a peasant who claimed he could perform miracles," as Adémar of Chabannes asserted.[30] Rodulfus Glaber referred to a woman from Italy in a similar context: "being possessed of the devil, [she] seduced whom she could, not just lay folk and fools but even many who passed as the most learned amongst the clergy."[31] From a historical point of view this could never happen. It is also unlikely that these educated men would look to the Bogomils for advice. The Bogomils were not the only group characterized by Docetism or the laying on of hands as an initiation rite,[32] and their lifestyle was a monkish one, with the attendant celibacy and vegetarianism. Benedict of Nursia, who can hardly be charged with having harbored "dualistic" sympathies, also exhibited this turn of mind. The monk John, our source for these two practices, deemed them important even though other ideas were more integral to the teachings of the heretics in Orléans. Evidence that the Bogomils practiced the laying on of hands stems only from a later date, although of course the rite may have been practiced as early as 1022 nonetheless. Paul had already attacked Docetism, and this mode of thought resurfaced subsequently again and again; it was certainly one of the basic concepts underlying Bogomil thought. It would have been perfectly natural for the clergymen in Orléans to have learned about Docetism from the fathers of the church, particularly Augustine. Their docetic beliefs were not expressions of dualism, but related rather to spiritualism; at least, they nowhere speak of the evil principle.

Educated individuals were more likely to have derived their ideas from books, while the uneducated had recourse only to oral instruction. Works written by the Bogomils played no discernible role in the West at that time. Still, there were probably people originally from Bogomil regions who may very well have imported this heresy into western areas. Cosmas referred to clerics who made pilgrimages to Jerusalem, Rome, "or to other cities."[33] One party of Balkan clergymen harbored anti-Byzantine sentiments and probably felt a closer affinity to Saint Peter than to Saint Andrew in Constantinople. Since some clergymen with Bogomil sympathies were outwardly orthodox, it is quite possible that pious travelers of that ilk surfaced in Italy and journeyed on to southern France to visit the shrines there. In Calabria the hermit Nilus was considered a Bulgarian, Frank, or Armenian; in Rome an Armenian, Simeon of Polirone, was taken for a heretic, and the people clamored for his death by stoning or fire.[34]

We have already discussed the possibility that a group of Bogomils lived in Verona (before 1046).[35] There allegedly is evidence for the existence of a "colony of Bulgarians" in the diocese of Turin in 1047,[36] but we should view that contention with caution. In a letter he sent from Constantinople to Phrygia around 1050, Euthymios of the Peribleptos monastery wrote that the Bogomils were dispersed throughout not just the Byzantine Empire but all of Christendom.[37] As might be expected, this is an exaggeration, yet the author of this letter may in fact have possessed information concerning the presence of Bogomils in the West.

The Cathars in Cologne in 1144 declared that their faith dated back to the age of the martyrs in Greece "and in some other countries."[38] This group cannot have been insignificant in size, for it required the ministrations of both a bishop and his deputy (*socius*); this conclusion is bolstered by the account of their dispute with the other, non-Cathar group of heretics given by Everwin of Steinfeld. He repeated the sectarians' assertion that they were found all over the world and, to be sure, "in very great numbers." The two groups may have merged in 1163, with the result that the non-Cathars became "believers" and the Cathars constituted the "perfects."[39] This theory has not been proved beyond a doubt, however. Unfortunately, the account does not tell us the Cathars' place of origin; perhaps they came from Italy or Champagne, where Cathars had come to light as early as 1144 or 1145.[40]

We must also approach with caution an account written around 1267 by Anselm of Alessandria, a Lombard inquisitor. He wrote that some "Franks" were converted to Catharism while on crusade (1147) in Constantinople, installed a "bishop of the Latins," and upon returning home promoted the spread of Catharism.[41] However, in 1144 in Cologne there already was a Western Cathar bishop, and the crusaders returning to France were by no means the sect's first missionaries. Anselm apparently wrote down what he considered a likely explanation, one that might perfectly well be rooted in fact, namely, that the Second Crusade was a contributing factor in the sect's spread.

The Cathars' spiritual roots indubitably lay in the Bogomil East. Yet, this observation does not suffice to answer a fundamental question: Why was the sect able to take root in the West? We may assume from the outset that in the case of such a complex phenomenon an overly simplistic explanation can only serve to lead us astray. Furthermore, we will not be able to provide absolute proof for our contentions; when it comes to this subject, our only possible course is to stick to probable causes and set aside those which are less likely.

According to Morghen, the eleventh century was marked by population growth, economic prosperity, new powers of human creativity, the rise of urban communes in Italy, and a new awareness of individual worth. "It is only natural that all this would be accompanied by a new religious awareness as well." Church reform was launched from the upper reaches of society, while a movement for the religious renewal of society "arose from the depths."[42] Russell contended that the rapid growth in heresy from the mid-eleventh century on was in part attributable to the following factors: "widening literacy, the growth of centers of learning in the cities, and the exchange of ideas through commercial intercourse."[43] Cinzio Violante discussed the spread of trade and cultural contact, and, as contributing factors, he identified increased mobility; the exchange of ideas along the trade and pilgrimage routes, in light of the growing popularity of making pilgrimages; the blurring of social distinctions through marriage; the strengthening of ties between urban and rural areas; and a new vitality in economic, social, and political matters.[44]

Such lists—and it would be easy to cite others—enumerate mainly prerequisites or favorable circumstances for the spread of heresy. They reflect aspects of what has been labeled a new "key to understanding the High Middle Ages,"[45] namely, a revolution, fundamental change, etc. It is rare nowadays to come across interpretations relating the rise in heresy to the corruption of the clergy, although such theories were once quite common.[46] Nevertheless, we should not disregard this factor, once it is stripped of all polemics.

The vast majority of scholars interpret these heresies as manifestations of a primarily religious phenomenon with links to phenomena in the areas of social relations, economics, politics, and spirituality in general. For that reason, a multitude of causes have been proposed. The only simple explanation is that based on the Marxist theory that socioeconomic relationships cause and drive all other developments: The heresies, then, are aspects of a revolutionary process through which the underclasses revolt against the feudal ruling class, the church being part of the latter group. Heresies thus come to be seen as covert attempts to overturn the social order.

In just a few key words Friedrich Engels sketched out this approach in 1850; it has since become the interpretative basis for Marxist historians, two of whom have been cited in these pages, Ernst Werner on Western heresies and Dimitur Angelov on the Bogomils.[47] And even outside orthodox Marxist circles, a modified form of this thesis has come to influence nonideological historians as well. Georges Duby, for example, wrote that heresy brought together the victims of feudal society.[48] And the Byzantine scholar Hans-Georg Beck formulated the opinion that the Cathar sect attempted "in metaphysical terms to substantiate or to provide justification after the fact for its rejection of contemporary society and of its ingrained stereotypes."[49]

No doubt having the reins tightened "from above" or being consigned to hopeless circumstances during difficult times might induce an individual to deem the world evil and to adopt Catharism. Let us recall that the first Cathar bishop in northern Italy had worked as a gravedigger among the citizens of Milan following the siege of the city and the expulsion of its populace.[50] That was not the situation, however, for non-Cathar sectarians like the clerics of Orléans or the people of Monforte and their countess. Engels's oft-quoted remark that people attempted "to free themselves from everything that served to keep them in their place in the established social order" is certainly not applicable to the middle and upper merchant classes.[51]

Even though erroneous, the Marxist theory had the advantage of injecting the socioeconomic perspective into the discussion. In the process, people have come to reject the view, traceable back to Engels, that all Western heresies were in their initial stages urban in nature.[52]

The "still" heresies of the eleventh century were not reliant on crowded conditions; "loud" itinerant preachers in the twelfth century, like Peter of Bruis and Henry the Monk, spent their careers partly wandering through the countryside, partly courting their urban audiences in full view of the very clergy against whom they inveighed. Cathars were to be found in urban areas and in the countryside, though in Toulouse relatively fewer lived in the city; their bishops preferred to locate their residences in small rural communities. Those residences served as the jumping-off points for the bishops' itinerant existence.

The Cathars were not evenly distributed across a region, and while some areas had large Cathar populations, others had very small ones. This may also be the result of the political situation. Thus, for example, there were no Cathars in the duchy of Aquitaine. In those areas, however, where there was no strict central authority in charge, where instead the minor nobility was left to its own resources or played off the higher powers against each other, the ground was fertile for the sects. It was common for noblemen—along with their dependents: family, servants, and vassals— to embrace the same religion as their lord. The peasant classes, on the other hand, played only a minor role in this process.

In the urban milieu there was tension between the patricians living in the heart of the city and the craftspeople and immigrants from the surrounding countryside, who inhabited the suburbs. Since the Cathar "believers" were not bound to embrace poverty, they could be rich merchants or in later times even bankers. We have already discussed the kinship linking sectarianism with commerce and the merchant trade. In speaking of "townspeople," some caution is in order. For example, in Toulouse many residents earned their livelihoods as craftspeople, yet moved to the countryside during the summer to tend the fields.[53] The close interrelationships between a northern Italian city and its surrounding countryside (contado) are well known. As the urban populations increased, portions of the surrounding countryside were absorbed into the city. Thus, lands outside the city gates settled by craftspeople were transformed into suburbs encircled by a new town wall, but these suburbs initially received only limited spiritual ministration—ideal conditions for the growth of sectarianism. The urban population bought from and sold to the rural population, which in turn might be subservient to lords who had moved to the city, as often happened in northern Italy. When the people of Monforte were brought to Milan to be dissuaded from their beliefs, they, "like good clerics," recited passages from the Bible "daily in private [*privatim*] for the peasants who assembled in the city to catch sight of them."[54]

In the former German Democratic Republic, Engels's thesis that the heresies of that time were urban in nature continued to be applied to northern France, Italy, and Germany, but no longer to southern France.[55] In fact, however, the evidence for Germany and northern France is too spotty to support such suppositions. As for Italy, it was once assumed that the cities, suburbs, and strongholds (*castella*) were teeming with heretics;[56] the word *castella* would encompass fortified villages as well. And in the north of France, Borst termed the small village of Mont-Aimé in Champagne a "principal Cathar residence."[57]

It seems that the clergy or semiclergy often promoted the heresies. Herbert Grundmann already proved this true for "religious movements" on the whole: Monks, hermits, and canons transmitted the heresies "to the laity while acting as itinerant preachers and not initially to the urban population, or primarily to the lower classes."[58] According to Peter the Venerable, Henry the Monk "had started out timorously whispering about in barren regions and small estates" and turned his steps toward the area around Toulouse only after he had assembled adherents and experience.[59] There he became a "loud" heretic.

Minor merchants and craftspeople are considered typical of the urban scene. They were, however, members of marginal classes subject to great fluctuations in status. The Cathars in Cologne assured Everwin of Steinfeld: "We are the Poor of Christ, of no fixed abode, fleeing from city to city."[60] In 1157 a synod in Rheims used almost the exact same words to describe the "reprobate weavers who often flee from one place to another and change their names."[61] In this context questions about the urban or rural nature of heresy lose all meaning. If anything, it might be more appropriate to use the terms "stable" and "mobile" (because of occupational circumstances) when referring to these heretical groups.

Since Grundmann, scholars have viewed similarly all those individuals at the margins of society, heterodox and orthodox. Individual monks (by definition prohibited from preaching), canons, and secular clergy discovered a purpose to their lives in itinerant preaching and then—with or without the assistance of the upper clergy—established strict, more or less stable communities. Setting the stage for this development were the efforts made in the second half of the eleventh century to reform the church. Of particular note in this respect are Robert of Arbrissel (d. 1117),

Bernard of Tiron (d. 1117), Vitalis of Savigny (d. 1122), and Norbert of Xanten (archbishop of Magdeburg, d. 1134).[62]

Eremitism, too, enjoyed a new rise in popularity from the eleventh century on into the twelfth. Since hermits might also be laymen, they often had no training in theology. Some of them traveled great distances, even the whole way from East to West or vice versa. For the most part they practiced an austerely ascetic way of life and were viewed as saints by the common people. Preaching was not their primary activity; nonetheless, the hermits seem to have been involved in the quiet spread of unorthodox tenets, even though that cannot be inferred from the Western sources. Cosmas was the only one to mention the wandering "false" hermits who propagated Bogomil tenets.[63] Bogomil missionaries admonished their adherents to be circumspect around the orthodox: "If people were to hear of our prayers and activities, all our work would come to naught."[64]

The battle against autonomous hermits had been concluded successfully in Carolingian times through the absorption of these individuals by monasteries; in the early eleventh century, these gains were often rolled back as "people lost their roots."[65] Some probably entered upon a path similar to the one taken by the Bogomil "false hermits." Generally speaking, hermits waged a personal battle, as it were, against the devil in much the same way as their Eastern models, the desert fathers, had before them. Their view of the world was frequently quite simplistic, molded by a belief in the dichotomy between the divine spirit and the recalcitrant "flesh." Someone as intelligent as Peter Damiani praised a certain Dominicus as a role model: His speech was crude, and for many years he wore an iron chain around his body in his battle against evil spirits; hardly a day went by without his reciting the whole Psalter twice, all the while wielding scourges in both hands for his self-castigation.[66] However, Peter did not approve of eremites' being found in cities as well, arousing amazement among the populace through the paleness of their visages and the draw of the ascetic life. "Worn in solitude, a hairshirt is a garment; worn in the city, it is an ostentation. Going about with one's arms and legs uncovered is fine for solitary places, but in the marketplace it is a tasteless form of license."[67]

In the eyes of churchgoers the hermits occupied a niche somewhere between the saints and public penitents. Coming into contact with one of them was an extraordinarily momentous occasion. The wise hermit, sought after by the populace, was a stock character in the nascent romance fiction of the time and still cropped up in Weber's nineteenth-century opera *Der Freischütz*. In some respects, the Cathar "perfects" corresponded to this well-known figure. Taking them for saintlike ascetics, people asked for their blessing whenever the perfects passed by in their dark robes. In times of persecution, however, they went about in disguise, and some of them moved to other regions, where they lived under assumed names.[68] Similar stories circulated about the Waldensians, who "attired themselves in the garb of various classes and crafts." Upon seizure, one Waldensian was found to have many such garments and insignia on his person.[69]

Urban and rural ways of life, stability and mobility—these are all facets of the external manifestations of heresies, not of their inner essence. The latter topic falls within the purview of the history of religion, or, more properly, the history of religiosity. For this problem, too, people have proposed simple solutions, general contentions that retain some influence even today.[70]

The Italian historian Raffaello Morghen took as his starting point, on the one hand, the work done at the beginning of this century by Gioacchino Volpe, who was influenced by the socioeconomic school of thought and viewed the heresies within a social and political framework.[71] In Volpe's view, after the end of the eleventh century a "new people" evidenced a new attitude to religion, which found expression in the heresies. On the other hand, Morghen himself was a participant in a dispute within the Catholic Church, the so-called Modernist controversy, which remained unresolved even with the movement's condemnation in 1907. Morghen felt that the movement's goals for the future were embodied by the heretics of the past: a plain form of evangelical Christianity molded exclusively on the Gospels and averse to the ecclesiastical hierarchy. "Common to all of the eleventh-century heretics was their condemnation of the corrupt church and their desire to establish a people's church more in line with the traditional apostolic way of life." In Morghen's view, this represented a rebellion against the feudal church, an uncompromising shift toward the law of the Gospels and the ideal of the apostolic church.[72] A new religious and civic consciousness was present among laypeople, "and among the new classes that appeared on the scene: Medieval heresy was for the most part the expression of a new religious consciousness among the laity."[73] "The majority of these heretics . . . belonged, generally speaking, to the lowest classes in medieval society; except for twelve or thirteen clergymen in Orléans sentenced to the stake and a few noblemen . . . from Monforte, all the rest . . . were from the countryside and uneducated."[74]

The study of systematic theology was "totally irrelevant" to such people—they held quite the opposite opinion, however, of criticism directed against dogma and the hierarchy, for such criticism was simply the product of common sense ("pure ragioni di buon senso").[75] Central to the thinking of church reformers and heretics alike was "the ideal of a moral renewal of the individual and the church."[76]

In formulating his theory on the role played by the New Testament in the inception of heresy, Morghen turned his attention to the Bogomils.[77] They also sought to base their interpretation of the New Testament on common sense, and it was thus unnecessary to look to earlier forms of heterodoxy in order to explain their way of thought.[78] According to Morghen, the same was true for the Cathars, who first came under "Manichaean" influences around 1190.[79] Thus, he considered the adherents of "radical dualism" from 1167 on to be part of the Christian people's church as well, even though the majority of scholars prefer to distinguish between Christian and non-Christian elements in their analysis of this movement.

The heretics relied almost exclusively upon the Gospels for their doctrine; that reliance "and the reversion to a literal interpretation of the Gospels are the basic premises and the absolutely predominant orientation of the sect." That was just as true for the Bogomils as for the Western heretics, who formulated their own—secondary—nuances.[80] Elsewhere Morghen referred to the "weighty literal interpretations of scriptural passages written as polemics against the hierarchy and official doctrine."[81] At the end of the twelfth century, moreover, "the revolt against Rome and the condemnation of the Roman Church" formed the crux of all heretical doctrines.[82]

In recent decades insufficient emphasis has probably been placed on two aspects of heresy, anticlerical emotionalism and alienation from the institutional church. Popular thought is also an important element in the history of sectarianism, although we must question whether truly "new classes" came on the scene, or whether the classes already in existence just kept on growing until groups broke off into separate units. The "new people" Volpe alluded to seem to be meant as a metaphor. Like Grundmann,[83] we must distinguish between "popular" and "scholarly heresies" without losing sight of the fact that individuals knowledgeable about the Bible always seem to figure in a heresy's inception.

Indeed, it is correct to stress the primarily religious roots of heretical phenomena. The driving force of experience, that accrual of the lessons one draws from life, also had an important role to play in the layperson's search for a new, truly Christian way of life. Formerly, the rise of heresy was ascribed to doctrinal conflicts, even though that approach presupposed a level of specialized training not found among the laity. For after all, there were heretics who put such a premium on their beliefs that they often died for them rather than recant. We must take this mind-set into consideration even in cases where it did not engender a consistent theological system and where individual members of the group might have held different beliefs.

The weakest link in Morghen's thesis is his contention that the most divergent doctrinal viewpoints derived from a perusal of the Bible by laypeople with "common sense." Heretics who interpreted biblical passages in this manner did not form consistent views on even the most basic rules of life (as, for example, the proper attitude to take toward work). Cosmas recounted that some Bogomils worked, while others, citing Matt. 6:25, were idle.[84] Cathars and Waldensians were still debating this point in the thirteenth century. This exegetical approach proved all the more problematic when applied to items of dogma, especially those based on the literal interpretation of particular texts, for it was often possible to counter with other scriptural passages open to seemingly contrary interpretation. That occurred time and time again in the course of doctrinal debates, even though "basic common sense" should have enabled the participants to view a particular biblical passage in light of the text as a whole—laypeople just could not perform this feat, even when they focused solely on the text of the New Testament.

In addition, heretics quite often resorted to the opposite approach of propounding an allegorical, rather than a literal, interpretation of a text. It was not just the educated clerics of Orléans who took this tack, but also the laypeople of Monforte, and the Bogomils and Cathars, both of whom, in fact, resorted to this approach quite often. Thus, for example, they held that the miracles of Christ did not connote actual healings at all, but the remission of sin, and that the miracle of the loaves and fishes referred to the composition of the four Gospels and the Acts of the Apostles. These interpretations served to preclude any contact between matter and Christ—in short, their fundamental doctrinal viewpoints were secondarily proved to be true on the basis of the Bible. The allegorical method they used was quite erudite; its roots can be found in Paul's writings, and beginning with Origen it was employed systematically by the Alexandrian school.

The view that the heretics relied "almost exclusively" on the New Testament for their doctrine can be ruled out, especially in light of their ethical concerns. The ascetic dietary and sexual practices of the Bogomils and Cathars have their roots not so much in the Bible as in the regimens of the Eastern hermits and monks. Common to the "perfects" and Eastern monasticism was a rigorous regimen of prayer alien to lay churchgoers. With difficulty the heretics attempted to substantiate this regimen by applying a metaphorical interpretation to scriptural passages stating that one should pray "at all times" or "constantly" (Luke 18:1 and 21:36; 1 Thess. 5:17). Additionally, in no instance was the hierarchy of the established church replaced by a "people's church" under the direction of laypeople. Among the Bogomils and Cathars the only individuals belonging to the "church" were former laypeople who had joined a sort of monastic class. We can hardly expect otherwise at a time when there was no Christian ethical system distinctly for laypeople. That was a product of the late Middle Ages, and until then "laypeople occupied positions of respect in Christian society only if they emulated the clergy and, above all, the monks."[85]

For Morghen the principal religious movements of the eleventh century were easily placed within the context of the great church reform at that time.[86] Jeffrey Burton Russell pursued this idea further in his book on dissent and reform.[87] Strictly defined, dissent denotes the refusal to profess the doctrines of the Church of England, while in a wider sense the word embraces all nonconformists and, applied most broadly, sectarians. Russell also employs the term "Reform dissidents"[88] to describe, for example, the Bogomils mentioned by Gerard of Csanád; all groups of heretics were thus reformers. Furthermore, their puritanism led them to exaggerate the dualistic components found even in Christianity.[89] According to Russell, Catharism in its strictest sense sparked a revival of dormant Western dualism; the adoption of the vibrant strain of dualistic thought from the Balkan countries prompted this process.[90] "The Gregorian papacy was, like the apostolically minded heretics, moving in the direction of reform."[91] "Robespierre, Lenin, Calvin, Hildebrand, Valdes, Tanchelm, Claudius of Turin—they were enthusiasts all, puritans all, fanatics all, and all revolutionaries and reformers."[92]

Many things can be held up for comparison, even the Investiture Contest and the Russian Revolution, but to do so means abandoning the conventions of scholarly discourse. It may very well be feasible to define two different concepts in such a way that they admit to reduction to some common denominator. This common denominator will be abstract in nature and more general than the two original concepts. The advantage to choosing a negative abstraction—like, for example, dissent—is that it easily lends itself to such methods. As modes of human behavior, revolution, reform, and dissent are by definition all characterized by a critical attitude toward established institutions and their agents. This deduction does not tell us very much, however. In terms of results, this behavior can lead to either a violent, complete, and permanent transformation or a peaceful, recurring approximation of an ideal.[93] Reform accomplishes the latter result, whereas revolution brings about the former. We should not automatically lump "dissenters" or "dissidents" in with reformers: Many dissenters considered themselves part of Christ's established church (in the sense of Christendom), while others did not. Conceptually, reform may begin with details, but it can address general issues as well—thus, the church as a whole.[94] Heretics were hence prone to renounce the established church and to label their own community "the church."

As a practical matter, the reform movement split into various components, for example, reform of the priesthood (canonical reform), monastic reform, and episcopal and papal reform; a distinction was also drawn between institutional reform and reforming one's private life. Attempts by individuals to imitate the apostolic way of life are manifestations of the latter. Here, and not in the institutional arena, heresy could also provide a constructive point of departure. Alternatively, individuals who opposed the misuse of the sacraments and unworthy priests might feel compelled to leave the established church and to erect in its stead a new edifice deemed the "proper" church. This was going beyond reform.

Russell's book underlines an affinity between the heretics' ideals and those of the monks, even though it is not possible to prove that the reformed monasteries exerted any influence in this regard.[95] Violante has lined up solid evidence that the heresies were not merely one expression of church reform.[96] The Patarenes in Milan formed the popular wing of a reform movement for the most part engaged with inner spirituality, but they did not proclaim any heretical viewpoints in the eleventh century. At that point no definitive answer was available to the question whether sacraments conveyed by unworthy priests, in particular by priests who had been ordained by unworthy bishops, were indeed valid. The members of the Gregorian party dragged their feet somewhat in deciding this issue, because it constituted a strong weapon against the clergy opposed to reform. Such clerics were branded heretics and indeed guilty of "simoniac heresy," a catch phrase predating Gregory the Great, who was able put it to good use. From this perspective, anyone seeking to purchase a church office in the manner of Simon Magus misconstrued the meaning of the Holy Spirit. Such issues had nothing to do with popular heresies, however.

The question of their ordination aside, starting in the eleventh century how clerics conducted their lives came under closer scrutiny than ever before. The tendency to associate the priesthood with the apostles and the apostolic way of life brought about this development—and the clergy was found wanting on both counts. The comparison rested of course on shaky ground: According to the official teachings of the church, only bishops were successors to the apostles, because they continued to exercise the apostles' authority and were able to administer the sacerdotal ordination to those who assumed the office of priest in imitation of Jesus' seventy-two disciples. Some masters at the University of Paris still advocated this exclusory viewpoint during the struggle against the mendicant orders.[97] Because of their mode of life, monks claimed that they approximated the apostles and asserted that their monastic rule was the rule followed by the apostles; one author, perhaps Rupert of Deutz, went so far as to aver that the church had its roots in the monastic life, for "all the apostles were in truth monks."[98] The regular canons advanced a similar claim on the basis of their communal life and sacerdotal nature.[99] Perhaps in part due to the currency of such notions, from the eleventh century on churches were frequently dedicated to an apostle. By the beginning of the eleventh century, the ideal of the sacerdotal life had already begun to approximate the apostolic model; in other words, it presupposed a life unencumbered as much as possible by worldly cares, spent in a communal setting and in the absence of individual property. Of course, something was missing from this picture: itinerancy and the obligation to preach.

These initial steps were not enough in the eyes of the many laypeople who wanted the clergy to revert completely to the apostolic way of life. Since the clergy seemed unable to fulfill this demand, many such laypeople felt called to imitate the apostles on their own and thus came into conflict with the ecclesiastical hierarchy. Whereas Henry the Monk justified his actions with the scriptural passage "make disciples of all nations" (Matt. 28:19), his opponent, William, pointed out the constraints on missionary activity: Christ had dispatched the apostles, who in turn created other missionaries by calling upon them and by a laying on of hands; anyone not commissioned by these two acts had no right to evangelize.[100] As long as laypeople did not take seriously the call to preach, their claim that they lived like the apostles served as a metaphor for their piety. Heeding the call to preach, however, brought them into conflict with canon law and exposed them to the charge of disobedience, even heresy, in the days before Innocent III offered laypeople a partial solution to this dilemma by permitting them to deliver moralizing sermons. Even in such cases, however, the layperson could not bypass the local bishop entirely and preach without a *missio* in the form of a license to preach.[101] Furthermore, evangelism beyond the hierarchy's reach was not deemed to be reform. Conversely, those monks and canons who appeared on the scene as preachers without a fixed abode stayed within the framework of reform. Peter Damiani had already cleared the way for them.[102]

In addition to the claim that they imitated the apostles, both reformers and sectarians expressed opposition to the abuses practiced by the clergy. These two positions were not inexorably linked. Thus, followers of the Patarenes opposed the marriage of priests, but did not aim to imitate the apostles, while the struggle against married clergymen played no or only a minor role for the heretics. Both reformers and sectarians focused on the problem of human sanctity, and the concept "sanctity of office" would have struck both groups as strange. They demanded personal sanctity of those who wished to redeem others and themselves. This was not mere rigorism, but rather a perception of civic and ecclesiastical authority that was deeply held at the time.

Unlike in classical times, in the early Middle Ages people were no longer able to conceptualize institutions as abstract yet real entities. The state, comprising institutions with tangible functions, came to be viewed as a community of individuals headed by a king, and the church was seen much the same way. People began to focus on the individual officeholder, not the office itself, and they often no longer grasped that an institution as an entity could act as the driving force behind sanctification. A tract attacking the heretics recounted that nonbelievers asked the Catholics in scorn: "Tell us, what is the church of God, where is it to be found, and what makes it God's church? We would like to become acquainted with this church. . . . We are searching for things that are perceptible, and it is our understanding that things that cannot be perceived are to be rejected."[103] The office became an expression of the individual officeholder, and its efficacy a reflection of the individual's competence. To govern properly a king hence needed God's grace, and for the sacraments to be efficacious the priest had to be a saint. An incompetent king or an unholy priest was to be removed from office, for he was not an officeholder in the true definition of the word. He may even have been installed by the devil.

In the twelfth century this mode of thinking enjoyed particular success in regions where relations among the secular authorities were in flux, as, for example, in southern France. In neighboring Aquitaine, on the other hand, where the Plantagenets ruled with an iron fist, the clergy remained unchallenged, and there were almost no heretics.[104] As for the spiritual realm, around this time the focus fell not on the church as the embodiment of Christendom, but on the church as embodied by a sacerdotal hierarchy that placed a strong emphasis on its driving force as an institution. This conceptual shift was bolstered by the propensity of certain reformers to push for a priesthood that personified individual holiness. Among churchgoers the church continued to be widely perceived as a community of individuals, pure and simple. As the Waldensians remarked, "The Church is always present wherever there is a gathering of believers who have faith and fulfill it by performing works."[105] Thus, the church consisted of a community of individual believers, not of a hierarchy based on church offices and officeholders. The Waldensians—and not just they alone—clung to this belief: "These particular heretics state . . . that the powers to ordain and bless, to bind and loosen, are effected more by merit than by [clerical] state or [ecclesiastical] office."[106] In line with this viewpoint, it became feasible to entrust these powers to pious individuals within the community.

As the sacerdotal church became centralized and more institutionalized, it also came to adopt a more "legalistic" approach; this functioned as the conceptual backbone, so to speak, for the centralization and general institutionalization of the church. Nevertheless, at least one jurist, Hugh Speroni in Piacenza, clung to the concept of a church of individuals. At the end of the twelfth century this founder of his own sect, whom we shall discuss in more detail later on, taught that one was a priest not by virtue of the *ordo* [order], but instead by virtue of the meritorious manner in which he lived: "If a person is a cleric, then he is undoubtedly holy as well."[107]

While serving as a consul in his native city, Hugh Speroni became entangled in disputes with the ecclesiastical authorities. This experience may have contributed to his sense of detachment from the clergy, but still it was not the reason underlying his convictions. In other cases, too, anticlericalism motivated by practical considerations was hardly ever the primary cause for the growth of a sect; very often, however, it did contribute to the spread of a sect. Many complaints about the clergy probably had their origin in such emotions. For example, in a letter addressed to Saint Bernard, Geoffrey of Auxerre reported from southern France: "We came across a few knights who were recalcitrant not so much due to error . . . as to avarice and maliciousness. They simply hated the clergy."[108] Under circumstances not marked by conflicting interests, people were often remarkably tolerant of the clergy's way of life and actions. Thus, it is reported that almost all the clerics living in Alsace around 1200 still kept concubines, "because the peasants generally encouraged them to"—thereby ensuring that their own wives would be spared the clergy's attentions.[109] Such tolerance is a sign of indifference toward the clergy and of inner detachment from priests. We shall see how this sense of detachment could also extend to religion as a whole.

5

The Religious and Political Environment

 Was there really such a thing as a "Christian Middle Ages," or is that concept no more than the brainchild of the romantics, subsequently adopted by certain scholars of our own era? Even during the Middle Ages, there were people indifferent to religion and nonbelievers side by side with the believers. Naturally, they kept their ideas to themselves, since they lived in a Christian society. Moreover, the chroniclers who were clergymen had little interest in recording the views of such people.

Heretics, on the other hand, were believers, and they often risked their lives for their religious convictions; they were believers who had successfully made the transition to a different religious plane without becoming irreligious. Since they were already heretics, they had the difficult phase behind them, of course, the stage during which they had grown to doubt all matters of faith. Some came away with views that, if they suited and supported subsequent heretical convictions, might then be all the more pronounced.

Alan of Lille recounted a certain line of reasoning employed by the heretics. Many things, they would assert, occur by chance and obviously not at God's behest. After their listeners granted that this was true, the heretics used this premise as the cornerstone for their proof that creation derived not from God but from the devil.[1] They apparently believed that whatever appeared so senseless or unjust that it could not possibly have proceeded from God was due to chance—and practically every person has had one such experience in their lives. At this juncture, the Cathars' missionary zeal came to the fore: Was it not more likely, they would contend, that these injustices were caused by some force comprehensible in personified form? And the figure they then proposed, the devil, was familiar to all Christians. Granted, according to the official teachings of the church, the devil could effect only what God sanctioned, but that view had never really gained acceptance. The extent of God's rule over the world was delimited by the mere fact that chance was ceded a role in his creation. Into the void stepped the evil principle, in the fullness of its own power, so to speak—to some, this explanation for the existence of evil in the world seemed plausible.

This process of reevaluation was not always provoked by the Cathars. While people may not have ascribed significant events to chance, they responded with anger, even quite publicly, against certain expressions of God's will. In 1133, for example, two kings, Lothar III and Conrad III, vied for hegemony over the Milanese, and two popes, Innocent II and Anacletus II, claimed the papal throne. The parish priests behaved scandalously; contrary to the political position taken by the archbishop of Milan, they derided Conrad's bid for the kingship and heaped scorn upon the antipope Anacletus. In a cathedral packed with people attending mass, the archbishop pronounced excommunication over those clergymen who had sabotaged the ceremonies to honor King Conrad. As a consequence of this excommunication, "the Jews have no interest in learning about Christ born of a Virgin, and the vast majority of the citizens and of the Lombards are enraged against the framer of spiritual and secular law."[2] People may have conceded that the archbishop had acted appropriately from his standpoint—it was God, however, who had made the political situation so terribly confusing.

If even respectable citizens were able to disassociate themselves from the worship of God, then it was all the easier for individuals of lesser rank, some of whom were unremittingly irreligious, even on professional grounds, so to speak. Not just criminals fell into this category, but also certain professional soldiers called routiers (*ruptarii*) or Brabançons.[3] These terms were used to signify the members of mercenary bands commanded by ringleaders often descended from the minor nobility. Since they were rarely paid, the mercenaries turned to pillage, and the best sources of booty were churches and cloisters. After deploying such individuals in 1174 in England, Henry II Plantegenet had to swear never to employ them again, yet he did so nonetheless when reasserting his hegemony over Aquitaine. His vassal Walter Map recounted: "Our King Henry II banished these new heretics, a sect that brought great harm, from all of the lands in his dominion. While with their mouths they profess the same things indeed as we do about Christ, . . . they still go about armed from head to toe in leather and iron, and wielding maces and swords they burn down cloisters, manors, and cities, violate women indiscriminately, and proclaim with all their heart, 'There is no God!' [Ps. 13:1]. . . . They have instituted their own law, which violates all law, and they are joined by fugitive insurgents, false clerics, renegade monks, and whoever else has abandoned God in any way."[4]

Herein lay a contradiction: The Brabançons professed "with their mouths" to believe in Christ, yet they were allegedly heretics and disavowers of God. We can only speculate that, as in the case of simony, their very way of life provided evidence for a "practical form of heresy." This perspective seemed to justify their wholesale condemnation. Prompted by Frederick Barbarossa's use of 1,500 Brabançons in his third march on Rome in 1166, Alexander III issued just such a condemnation in 1179. (Frederick had granted the mercenaries license to plunder the outskirts and environs of Rome.) Thus, canon 27 of the Third Lateran Council was directed not just against the Cathars, but also against the "Brabançons, Aragonese, Navarrese," and others who like heathens ruthlessly attacked cloisters, women, and children. People were urged to take up arms against them and confiscate their possessions (bona), a term not necessarily limited to immovable property. The canon appears to have been drafted by Henry of Clairvaux, who was the papal legate in Provence[5] and acquainted with the situation there. Whoever survived the dissolute and dangerous life of a brigand might very well retire to a small holding in the semianarchic south of France without fear of losing his spoils. To our knowledge no one took up arms against the Brabançons, and we shall even hear of an archbishop who entered into league with them.

This practical sort of skepticism, marked by little or no soul-searching, was certainly not found only among such outsiders. Marc Bloch made reference to the *scepticisme vulgaire* [common skepticism], translated somewhat inaccurately into German as "vulgar rationalism."[6] Rationalism is something more and other than an unreflective disassociation from phenomena related to the religious sphere. Instead, this dubiety was directed above all against particular aspects of hagiolatry and belief in miracles.[7] Moreover, there were certain individuals who had little grasp of the Christian faith altogether, owing to the circumstances of their life and personal experience, or simply to their limited religious sense. Nonetheless, they would hardly have given vent to these feelings in an age marked by an emphasis on conforming to the dictates of "good conduct." To avoid drawing attention to themselves, such individuals might participate in church rituals; if they declined to do so, canon law had not as yet promulgated sanctions against them. Such measures were held to be unnecessary as long as the moment for definitive legal action had not yet arrived and social pressure saw to it that laypeople behaved properly.

What was at a minimum required of the faithful was first codified in conjunction with canon laws aimed against the heretics: For example, the faithful were obliged to take communion at least once a year (Fourth Lateran Council, 1215, c. 21) and, in areas marked by heresy, to swear an oath of loyalty at least once a year, in addition to fulfilling their duty to perform penance and attend church on a regular basis (Synod of Toulouse, 1229). Thus, we see that the church resorted to legal measures only once (and where) there was a breakdown in "propriety" and communal oversight. During the entire Middle Ages there was no general obligation to attend Sunday mass.

On many occasions twelfth-century theologians attempted to draw a connection between an individual's inner attitude toward faith and his or her public profession. Thus, in a single breath Alan of Lille listed "not believing in God, not attending church, and the like" as examples of vice. It was through external actions, he maintained, that people revealed their psychological point of view, their contempt (*contemptus*) for goodness and their evil intention of renouncing good.[8] Those who had other reasons for not attending mass—because, for example, they did not approve of the officiating priest's conduct—were also lumped in with the godless.

Estrangement from the congregation was surely difficult for the lone individual; he would perforce seek out another community to bolster his resolve. He might turn to adherents of the Patarenes—or to heretics. Yet another alternative was open to intellectuals, that of seeking refuge in a spiritual camaraderie they felt with the authors whose books they had read. While the difficulty was thus relegated to a higher plane, the individual was still left wide-open to charges of godlessness—leveled not by a congregation but by one's colleagues. In remarks oversimplifying the Stoic elements expressed in the thinking of William of Conches, William of Saint-Thierry hence charged: "He seems to follow the teachings of ignorant philosophers who say that nothing exists beyond matter and material phenomena [*corporea*]. According to them, God is nothing more within the world than the confluence of elements and the consonance of nature." According to Stoic doctrine, God was the immanent principle behind the elemental qualities, their regulating principle (*temperatura*).[9] The ease with which a scholar might be branded a heretic is a subject we shall return to later.

In the course of the twelfth century, innovative ways of thought made their mark on individuals from various social classes, with various results. To the best of their knowledge and belief, the educated endeavored to master problems posed by classical scholarship; in some lands laypeople were compelled to take a position on heresy, though they often lacked the skills prerequisite to meeting this challenge. It was necessary to have a background not just in theological matters, but sometimes also in politics, for at the upper strata of society the threads of spiritual and secular life were tightly interwoven, and a change in faith could have concrete repercussions. In southern France, particularly, there were noblemen who sympathized with the Cathars and permitted the female members of their families to convert but who themselves remained formally Catholic. A similar situation existed in the cities, for example, in Toulouse: "The avowed heretics became the center of a 'neutral zone' composed of individuals whose emotional reactions [to the heretics] ranged from admiration to resignation. The broad range of emotional response sufficed to preclude any action against the heretics."[10] This neutrality born of practicality allowed people to have it both ways; it was in fact promoted by the Cathar custom of requiring individuals to profess their faith once and for all by receiving the laying on of hands only when on their deathbeds. This state of affairs was not fundamentally altered by the persecutions. Even in later periods there were people who made donations to both clergymen and perfects, because they did not know "'which of the two beliefs [was] the more valid.'" This approach was termed "fish[ing] from both banks" of the river.[11] In the duchy of Foix and probably elsewhere as well, it was indicative of good breeding for members of the upper classes to display a certain indifference toward matters of faith.[12]

In this state of flux the lowest forms of popular religion (or, if you will, superstition) assumed greater importance because people vulnerable to life's perils felt unable to place their trust wholeheartedly in either the saints or the perfects. In 1211 Count Raymond VI of Toulouse broke off his negotiations with papal legates and went off on his way because a particular sort of bird flew past him on his left, "which greatly alarmed him. For like the Saracens, he believed in augury based on the flight and singing of birds."[13] Elsewhere we learn about a count from Gascony who wished to become a vassal to Simon de Montfort. Just as he was about to perform homage, Simon de Montfort had to sneeze. The count thereupon refused to participate in the legal proceeding. "The very ignorant people of this region are so heedful of the significance of omens (*auguria*) that they firmly believe that if they should sneeze once or someone with whom [they are] doing business should sneeze once, then nothing they undertake on that day can meet with success."[14]

As for the Catholics, they feared the magical powers of the Cathars. For example, a nobleman hailing from the region around Vienne was said to carry consecrated salt at all times and to sprinkle it on foods given him by the Cathars; they were credited with the ability to deceive people into accepting their faith by means of such foods.[15] Furthermore, Heribert the

Monk asserted that the Cathars of Périgord performed wondrous acts. Upon being captured, some of them were put under guard in an upside-down wine barrel, with their hands and feet shackled; the next morning they were gone—the devil had set them free.[16]

In good times people commended themselves to God and the saints, but now many of them led a precarious existence fraught with exposure to evil. These circumstances proved fertile ground for the Cathar conviction that God was distant and the devil ever near. The popular tendency to mingle the corporeal and the spiritual spheres of existence also contributed to people's receptivity to Catharism. Traces of animism, by which inanimate things are imbued with life, were juxtaposed with a mythical mind-set by which moral concepts were framed in material terms,[17] for example, purity as cleanliness. There is evidence for this tendency among both heretics and simple churchgoers. Hugh of Amiens said that the heretics "and other impious individuals" did occasionally grasp difficult concepts, but then they transferred their conceptualization of corporeal objects onto incorporeal, divine ones;[18] in other words, they comprehended them in material terms. Moreover, as Abelard wrote, "[W]hat unlettered or simple man would bear to listen to you if you announce that God has no eyes or ears or the other parts which seem to us necessary members. Surely, he will immediately object that one without eyes can never see, likewise one can neither hear nor work who lacks ears and hands."[19] These words surely reflected his personal experience. During a disputation held in Verfeil (near Toulouse) in 1206, Diego of Osma asked some prominent Cathars to consider a biblical passage in which God says, "Heaven is my throne and the earth is my footstool" (Isa. 66:1). He then asked them if they thought God's legs reached all the way from heaven down to earth. "When they said that they did believe that, he proclaimed 'You are staunch heretics [grossi haeretici]!'"[20]

We encounter this sort of anthropomorphism time and time again, and not just among laypeople. Rather of Verona complained about clerics in the diocese of Vicenza whose spurious interpretations of the Bible led them to assign a corporeal existence to God.[21] The monk Odorannus of Sens, whom we have already encountered above in connection with the heretics of Orléans (1022), attacked the "false brothers" who waylaid him because he had asserted God did not possess hands or other limbs.[22] While the metaphors found in the Old Testament—in the older portions particularly—support such interpretations, the text itself hardly contains such statements in black and white. These metaphors are far more the product of a general human outlook on life common to many religions.

Believers who sought a new understanding of the Bible based on their "common sense" were not the first to view the mystery of the Eucharist in material terms. An ancient complaint underlying this view already had cropped up in the tract by Bishop Gerard of Cambrai-Arras attacking those heretics he had dealt with in 1025: How could it be that Christ's body, "which was received daily in so many pieces, at so many different times, by so many nations and individuals, is not diminished?"[23] Individual Cathars told Ekbert of Schönau: "I cannot believe what is said about Christ's body, because I in no way understand how it could be." To which Ekbert responded that God is able to do things that are beyond human understanding; that is the situation with all things related to faith. Once when Ekbert attempted to administer communion to a dying Cathar, the man voiced the old complaint with a local twist: Even if Christ's body had been as large as the Hermelstein (a massive outcropping of rock near Koblenz), it would still have been eaten up by now.[24] The device of comparing the host to a mountain or a tower was familiar to Berengar of Tours as well,[25] even though he had no dealings with Cathars.

Material images similarly influenced people's thoughts about the Resurrection of the Dead at the Last Judgment. "We see how sometimes human bodies are torn apart and scattered about, or dragged away and devoured by wild animals and birds. . . . There is no way to reassemble these bodies."[26] While it may have been the Cathars who expressed such views, they were certainly not alone in subscribing to them. Many people responded with silence to ideas that only the heretics dared to challenge openly. Thus, something identified as a common denominator between various forms of sectarianism may in fact have been rooted in the thinking patterns of the broader population. What is more, clergymen were not entirely exempt from the influence of such imaginings either. Even an archbishop, Leutrich of Sens, came under reproach for interpreting the mysteries of the Trinity, baptism, and Eucharist in an "exceedingly carnal" manner (*nimis carnaliter*).[27] According to an account by Helgald of Fleury, King Robert had asked the archbishop, "Why do you ascribe corporeal affliction to the divinity and associate the weaknesses of human suffering with the divine nature?"[28] Understood in a concrete sense, he seems to have been referring in particular to the concept that Christ in the form of the host suffered torments whenever an unworthy person received communion; later tales of bleeding hosts fall into the same category of thought.

Also characteristic of popular religiosity was the belief that an individual's religious striving was translatable into the measurable and quantifiable performance of devotional exercises. As we have already heard, the Bogomils and Cathars had quite detailed guidelines governing the number of prayers and the times they were to be recited, not to mention precepts about genuflections, food, and other regulated areas. These were analogous to the *consuetudines* [the rules and customs of an order] found in Catholic monasteries, particularly Cluniac houses, which governed daily life down to the smallest detail, including the continuous recitation of the Psalms. The aforementioned Helgard found it particularly praiseworthy that his king recited the Psalms frequently and took pains with the smallest details of the liturgy. An individual's piety was expected to be manifest in his or her actions, audible and measurable in prayer.[29] This sort of attitude encouraged people to set down guidelines for rules of conduct and to become reliant upon written texts. If there was no text to use as a crutch, literate individuals could search through the Gospels for a passage to cite in support of any action.

In formulating these guidelines, people did not draw upon the corpus of ecclesiastical literature composed after the Apostolic Age, and not just because of practical considerations. Even educated individuals possessed as yet only a dim sense of history; popular thinking was bereft of it altogether. People were not cognizant of the gradual evolution and increasing complexity of the Christian faith through the centuries; rather, they focused on the disjunction between Christianity's original and current forms. Thus, in addition to holding a negative opinion of the clerical way of life, they recognized that the clergy's teachings did not bear comparison with the Gospels either. Such was the intensity of their faith that people yearned for simplicity, indeed for a new fundamentalism.

It is not clear at what point this attitude came to represent the norm. All the same, the developments of the eleventh century were particularly important in its adoption. Some scholars have expressed the opinion that the popular religion of this period underwent a change, ostensibly in connection with these developments. Beforehand, in the words of Richard W. Southern, "the veneer of Christianity was still very thin," and it was replete with only partially suppressed pagan elements. "It is not until the eleventh century that we get the first convincing signs . . . that Christianity was becoming a popular religion."[30] While this judgment may strike us as harsh, it is probably justified if one defines being a Christian as entailing the involvement of one's entire person. It is in this sense that scholars have referred to a "new religiosity" in the period around 1000 and compared it to a similar phenomenon in late antiquity.[31]

It is difficult to provide concrete substantiation for such commonly held assertions when during the period we are studying the vast majority of individuals were never able to express themselves in writing and when what we know of these people is at best preserved in historical sources written by clerics. Nevertheless, one authority on the history of the early eleventh century has discerned "an awakening of conscience in the Christian people," marked by the growing appeal of personal prayer, examination of one's conscience, and criticism of mores. As part of this process, "[t]he material penances of the old penitential books, so vigorously denounced by Abelard, gave way to the considered judgment advocated in the *summae* of confession."[32]

Integral to this awakening of the conscience was a new attentiveness to doctrinal issues, as people became less inclined to do meekly as they were told. Thus, for example, Hugh of Amiens wrote: "Our people ask questions, not in an argumentative manner, as do the heretics, but filled with pious zeal as Catholics. They ask why the church exists. But no one can comprehend that unless he has received the Holy Spirit within the unity of the church." God's will was done in all things, "thus we should not ask why, with what, or when God created the world."[33] We can well imagine how much discomfort such questioning by the laity could cause the clergy and how gladly they retreated behind the cover of their own *ordo* granted them by the Holy Spirit.

In the eyes of ruminative individuals, such answers might cast a light on the clergy itself as the problem. Given that people found abstract thinking difficult and were accustomed to judging things by their outward appearance, whatever religious doubts they may have harbored grew all the more profound. "The soul perishes along with the body, or so say many false Christians, indeed, heretics of our age," reported Alan of Lille, who also noted the rationale offered for this belief: "Just as after the death of an animal no trace of its soul is visible, so after the death of a person no trace of the soul is left behind."[34] The use of reason to analyze matters of faith could lead to skepticism. Thus, Abelard, himself a thinker of the new school, remarked: "Among all people, the most unfortunate are those who, lacking faith and hope, neither believe like the pagans in the immortality of the soul nor hope for reward from God for doing good; like beasts they devote themselves entirely to the experiences of the senses [*sensuum experimentis*]. And like animals they are fated to perish along with the flesh."[35]

Are we mistaken in suspecting that Abelard, whose description seems so empathetic, was for a time visited by such thoughts himself? No one undertaking the journey from traditional ideas to a personal religious experience is likely to be spared such thoughts. Even the most conservative believers could be shadowed by doubt. A monk, Otloh of St. Emmeram (a monastery near Regensburg), wrote a treatise, *On His Temptations*, in which he described how he had entertained the idea that the Gospels had been fabricated.[36] And the nun Elizabeth of Schönau, a visionary venerated as a saint, recounted that she was induced to doubt her faith by the devil, who caused her to question Christ's true nature. "Could everything the Bible says about him really be true?" Finally, the devil whispered to her that she should put an end to her distress by committing suicide.[37] The mind suffused with doubt [*zwîvel*] also figured in Middle High German literature. In the so-called Millstätter Exodus "the repeated occurrence of this theme makes it clear that *zwîvel* was a problem to which the author attached considerable importance."[38] For Wolfram of Eschenbach, doubt, particularly religious doubt, was the "central theme" of his early-thirteenth-century poem *Parzival*.[39]

Otloh of St. Emmeram and Elizabeth of Schönau overcame their doubt. Others assailed by doubt, however, fell in with the heretics and put trust in their doctrines. There was also a no-man's-land in between, marked by endless vacillation and rumination. Peter the Venerable wrote that after their expulsion the followers of Peter of Bruis left in their wake a body of noxious ideas "in the secret thoughts of even good Catholics," who might come to harm because of (previously) "unheard-of questions."[40] In addition, people took to debating matters of faith: "The blind lead the blind, the one in error leads the heretic . . . possessing knowledge concocted in his own mind, dangerous because of his erroneous opinions. . . . '"Knowledge" puffs up, but love builds up.' [1 Cor. 8:1]"[41] This biblical passage was certainly inapplicable to those troubled individuals who were disillusioned by the clergy and at odds with the heretics' propositions and who sought their own path to God. By the thirteenth century there were true "freethinkers," who borrowed some heretical ideas without succumbing entirely to heresy.[42] In fact, already in the twelfth century individualists were to be found joining groups on the fringes of society; this phenomenon characterized the early Scholastic "schools," in whose proximity young scholars "stumbled about like vagabonds, . . . simultaneously rejecting, disdaining, and ridiculing all [teachers], as if they had nothing to impart that made sense."[43]

The practitioners of the new, "resurrected," and intensive lay piety often sought to institute stability and cohesiveness by means of the close adherence to sacred texts. Alternatively, illiterate individuals would commit such texts to memory with the same goal. Up to then, the most laypeople had been expected to commit to memory was the Lord's Prayer and the Creed. Now, however, they drew directly upon the Bible itself for the precepts guiding their daily existence and for the fundamental beliefs underlying their religious views. And the less receptive people were to the clergy's sermons and sacraments, the more central these precepts and beliefs became to their thinking. Those who adopted this new approach, and at first there were very few, had to apply a more intense mental awareness to the text, for now every word in the Bible assumed importance to one's very own existence.

Observations such as these formed the groundwork for Brian Stock's

theses. In his view, "heresy, reform, sacramental theology, and the philosophical attitudes towards texts" led to a change, to a rebirth of culture by
means of "literate ways of thinking."[44] We are indebted to Stock for
pointing out anew how heresy, theology, and philosophy, to which one
might add jurisprudence both inside and outside of the church reform
movement, developed along parallel tracks. Was all this triggered by a
shift in focus to texts on which people could pattern their lives? The
people of Arras, for example, lived in compliance with a collection of
passages derived from the Gospels and Acts of the Apostles by their
magister [master] Gundulf, and "they would accept no other text except
this one."[45] Gundulf's disciples had "attended" the master, and he presented them with a written compendium of the main points of his beliefs
for them to take along on their travels. The disciples had internalized the
text and now lived in conformance to it. According to Stock's thesis, the
group's members should as a result have become more rational or even
rationalistic. However, we have no information to that effect. On the other
hand, their "rule" surely served to preserve their cohesiveness as a group.

According to Stock, literacy leads to self-consciousness and the power
to perceive things critically. His observation is perhaps more applicable to
the early Scholastic schools than to heresy as a whole. We find also that a
charismatic master could indeed attract a circumscribed circle of heterodox followers—even without a textual framework. The illiterate Eon of
Stella and his bands of brigands, Peter of Bruis, and Henry the Monk all
come to mind, though Henry admittedly knew a few words in Latin and
transcriptions were made of his sermons. One can surely not reduce the
heretical Leutard, the clerics of Orléans, and the craftspeople of Arras to a
single common denominator, namely, a reliance on the written word that
led to the espousal of a "rationalistic ethic" in accordance with the
precepts of the New Testament. This view is predicated upon a quantitative approach by which each sect and each text is granted equal weight,
whether or not the text consisted of "a few maxims or an elaborate
programme." According to Stock, "written rules" determined individual
behavior and led to "interactions" within the group.[46]

Although the observations made by historians may indeed be enriched
by this sociolinguistic point of view, some modifications are in order.
Already at the dawn of monasticism people patterned their lives and
actions on a written text, which served not only as a rule for outward
comportment but also as a rudimentary guide to spiritual practice by, for
example, prescribing that monks internalize the passages they read and
recite the Psalms. The Cluniac order later added extensive regulations
covering monastic behavior and the daily regimen. As far as we know, the
Bogomils were not subject to such strict regulation, although they emu-

lated in part the lifestyle of the Basilian monks, whose founder, Basil, had authored several monastic rules. For the Bogomils and the Cathars, the whole of the Gospels constituted their "text." Ekbert of Schönau realized that the Cathars prided themselves on being the only ones to "know" and observe the Gospels.[47] Their opponents were compelled to adopt a similar sort of "textuality." The two manuscripts of the *Liber antihaeresis* by Durand of Huesca, written in a tiny hand on small parchment leaves, attest that it was necessary for a missionary to carry a compendium of biblical passages with him.[48] The coat of arms for the Dominican order, whose *raison d'etre* was the conversion of heretics, includes a book.

Of course, this intensive study of the texts, which entailed learning and not just reading, had its limits. The Bogomils came to reject the Old Testament and never made any headway into the writings of the Greek fathers of the church. They maintained no libraries, since "scholarly" works were written either in Greek or in an overly ornate, scarcely comprehensible Slavonic. As one scholar put it, "The Bogomils denied everything they did not comprehend."[49] In the West the situation was not much different. One need only recall that the Old Testament contains approximately thirty times more text than the Gospels. On the other hand, the Old Testament is quoted repeatedly in the New Testament; references to the Psalms alone cover eight full printed pages, while those to Isaiah cover nine.[50] Portions of the Old Testament were hence accepted by some heretics. Furthermore, they did not need to adopt the commentaries so crucial to an understanding of the Old Testament, because they sought to comprehend a text on a sentence-by-sentence basis rather than in terms of its overall structure. This was particularly true when the heretics also did not have the entire New Testament or a compendium of passages from the Gospels in front of them, but had to recite the text from memory, much like Moslems reciting the suras of the Koran. This fragmentation of knowledge stands in juxtaposition to its increasing sanctification. As we recall, the people of Monforte believed that Christ was born of the Holy Scriptures and that the Holy Spirit consisted in comprehending this text. This reflected an allegorical (or mythical), rather than a rational, interpretation of the holy text. Conversely, whatever material was rejected could be accounted the devil's work, and a figure like Moses deemed an evil magician.[51]

The heretics invoked the power of reason when inveighing against the authority and the mysteries of the postapostolic church. However, this approach should not be equated with "rationalism," because it did not result in the heretics' viewing the New Testament and various mythical ideas with a critical eye. That laypeople could train their memories, and with such remarkable success, was an innovation. In debates they always knew just when to insert a learned remark, which served to counterbalance any advantage their erudite opponents might possibly possess due to training in rhetoric and dialectic. The term "quasi-literate" has been used to describe such individuals,[52] and these laypeople were eager to share their knowledge. In a letter Peter Damiani recounted how, instead of tilling the fields or tending to their pigs, farmers publicly debated the meaning of the Scriptures before an audience of prostitutes and cattle drovers.[53] Disregarding the hyperbole of the passage, we see that religious issues might be the topic of the day at the marketplace, provided that the participants were familiar with the sacred texts, a proficiency not expected of the average layperson.

Furthermore, there is yet another side to "textuality": A book can serve as an "inspirated" object. Cathar perfects commonly carried a book containing the Gospels, which they placed on the heads of individuals receiving the baptism of the Holy Spirit. One such booklet survives; it is written in a Romance dialect, and only the prologue to the Gospel According to John is in Latin.[54]

We have attempted to summarize the religious and overall cultural milieu of heterodoxy. Now we must perform the same task vis-à-vis heresy's political and social environment—but merely in a rudimentary manner, based on a few examples from the region visited most by heresies. We will thus focus on a portion of southern France, namely Provence as it was delineated in the Middle Ages, not in its much more circumscribed modern guise. For the most part, we will disregard regional differences: Cathars were found in abundance within a north–south corridor of land about fifty kilometers wide; they were sparse east of the Rhône River, in Gascony, around Narbonne, etc.[55] This distribution reflected political and social conditions. We have already described how, with the Brabançons' assistance, the king of England purged his Aquitainian domain of every seemingly harmful influence.[56] Conversely, regions marked by political anarchy were so vulnerable to the heretics that in those areas Cathars could even help themselves to church property. Individual cases illustrate just how adversely affected were those regions where the ecclesiastical and secular districts did not coincide and no count was at hand to protect episcopal rights.[57] Furthermore, it was only in such areas that the two creeds, Catholic and Cathar, maintained something of an equal balance, whereas in the greater part of Provence the Cathars and their sympathizers constituted a minority. It has been estimated that they represented 5 to 10 percent of the total population in those areas,[58] although that estimate remains unsubstantiated given the condition of the sources.

The political history of southern France at this time is characterized by the lack of centralized authority and by confrontations between various powers, even "foreign" ones. Since 1032 the Roman-German ruler had been the king ("of Burgundy"). In the imperial lands east of the Rhône, however, his rule was for the most part merely nominal, until Frederick I attempted to assert his sovereign rights. In the process he met with opposition from the local magnates and King Alfonso II of Aragon, who claimed sovereignty over the county of Provence. Count Raymond V of Toulouse (1148–95) and his adversary, the Count of Barcelona, ruled in the southwestern region. The burden of supporting the military expeditions mounted by these magnates fell upon the minor vassals above all, and the excessive demands for feudal services engendered noncompliance. Political egotism knew no bounds.

The count of Toulouse owed fealty to the king of France, who eventually gained control of southern France following the death of King Peter II of Aragon on the battlefield in 1213. The crusade against the Cathars had rendered the countryside semidesolate, and France moved rather slowly to exercise its rule. It was not until Count Raymond VII of Toulouse arranged for the engagement of his only daughter to King Louis IX's brother (1229) that a greater part of the land fell under the king's sway.

The south of France thereby became a province, clearing the way for its return to the Catholic fold, with the assistance of the Inquisition. Although the complete extirpation of Catharism would take a century, the political situation had long before then ceased to provide fertile ground for the movement. The nobility of the region, all those counts and viscounts, lords and stewards of castles, had paid for their choice with their freedom. They knew which faith to profess if they wanted to retain and enlarge their holdings, and their kinsmen, servants, and peasants shared this knowledge. Very few could afford to be true to their religious convictions after so many had been made to atone for theirs. Yet even before the crusade had brought all this to pass, members of the nobility mainly had political considerations in mind.

In Termes (near Carcassonne), up on a high cliff, stood a stronghold deemed impregnable. "The lord of this stronghold was a knight named Raymond . . . who openly professed heresy . . . and feared neither God nor any man. He put so much trust in the strength of his fortress that he once revolted against the king of Aragon, another time against the count of Toulouse, and on yet another occasion against his feudal lord, the viscount of Béziers."[59] Opportunism was rampant. Many noblemen, for example, pledged their support to the crusaders' leader, Simon de Montfort; following the disbandment of the army, he was to administer the region, yet in 1209 "almost all the local nobles abandoned our count, because in a very short time he had lost more than forty strongholds."[60]

Their determination to resist a foreign occupying force and concerns about their own status became intertwined with their aversion to Catholicism. The nobility's opportunity to do as it pleased came to an end, however, with the announcement before the declaration of peace in 1215 that excommunicated knights were not permitted to enter cities, ride swift horses, bear arms, or wear more than one spur.[61] This was tantamount to debarring them from the practice of their profession; the nobles were also subjected to the dishonor of becoming objects of scorn to the "common people," to whom they had formerly been so very superior.

Excommunicated knights who owned or had co-ownership of landed property could still depend on those possessions for their basic sustenance; worse off were those knights whose ownership rights applied to property located in cities they were no longer permitted to enter. In Carcassonne, for example, those rights consisted of revenues from defense towers and taxes on the surrounding precinct.[62] Many knights were in service to a magnate or were military vassals like those, for example, in Verfeil, where "there were quarters [hospitia] for one hundred knights outfitted with horses bearing coats of arms [on their saddlecloths] and weapons, and who did not look to others to feed their horses, but had their own oats."[63] In other words, there were yet others who depended on the lord to feed them and their horses.

This brings us to the problem of the secular members of the upper classes in southern France, who contributed greatly to the political and religious destabilization of the region by virtue of their numbers, high sense of entitlement, and low sense of obligation. Even in the Carolingian period, the bond of feudalism was weak and sometimes nonexistent altogether in this region marked by a "written" law traceable back to a Provençal-Roman literary tradition. The customary bond between individuals, even between the ruler and his "retainers," consisted of a *convenientia*, or contract, rather than the deep commitment of a "man" to his "lord." Not all land was held in the form of fiefs; some members of the lower nobility held alodial lands and did not have to swear fealty, but only a general oath of loyalty, considered a mere formality and nonbinding.

In the eleventh century, feudalism in southern France had reached a crisis point; the rural and urban lower nobility successfully disencumbered themselves of their feudal obligations to the magnates, in what has been described as a "time of rapid decentralisation."[64] Of the approximately 500 strongholds belonging to the Trencavel family, the viscounts of Béziers, only one tenth were in their possession, while 100 had been granted as fiefs; 350 were in the hands of "retainers" or vassals who were for all practical purposes independent. Neither these vassals nor the ecclesiastical lords in the viscountcy could be prevailed upon to furnish a military force.[65] From the twelfth century on, the decline in the magnates' power gave rise to insecurity in the region, to its infiltration by external forces, and to the recruitment of "Brabançons, Aragonese, Navarrese,"[66] who grievously afflicted the land.

As for feudal services, in this region it was not axiomatic that the feoffee had to do his utmost to assist his lord; rather, the "duty of the fief" was defined by the provisions of the contract, and it was possible to commute that service through the payment of money. Where payments replaced service, the fief could be divided up, alienated, and exploited for real estate speculation.[67] However, even if the fief remained undivided and unalienated, and passed down to the heirs in the form of a joint inheritance or parcenary (paragium, pariage), it was ill suited to providing military support in the case of war. Since each of the heirs was equally duty-bound to provide the full military service, not one of them would respond individually; they all tended to stay home.[68]

Whereas in northern France the law of primogeniture hindered the dismantling of fiefs held by the lower nobility, in southern France all the members of one's immediate family, initially daughters as well, were recognized as coheirs holding equal rights. They might enter into a mutual agreement to hold the fief in common, which might be all right in the first generation but which in the second and third generations could produce bizarre situations. If a stronghold and its surrounding lands had many owners, each of them was entitled to a portion of the living quarters and revenues. This arrangement did not necessarily impoverish families, and we cannot furnish any concrete examples of that having occurred.[69] Even so, such circumstances must have been very stressful psychologically and surely contributed to the further destabilization of the situation. An individual could either opt to proffer his services to a member of the upper nobility (a class that had, by the way, avoided the pitfalls of divided property) or remain on the common property, with no hope of establishing a family of equal rank and perhaps brimming with a bitterness that would prove receptive to Catharism.

Perhaps it was only coincidence that the three strongholds with the greatest number of co-owners harbored Cathar communities: In 1165 a Cathar creed was drafted in Lombers (with fifty coheirs); six hundred Cathars assembled in the stronghold Mirepoix (thirty-six heirs) for a synod in 1206; and in 1209 Montréal (likewise thirty-six heirs) was the site of a religious conference.[70] It has been proposed that the one hundred knights in the stronghold of Verfeil were likewise coheirs.[71] While that is certainly not accurate, it does bring a related story to mind. Bernard of Clairvaux once tried to preach there, but the knights made such an uproar that he did not get a word in edgewise. Bernard put a curse on the place.

From that time on, it was supposedly visited by natural catastrophes, revolts, and feuds, bringing extreme poverty in their wake.[72] It is more likely that exorbitant demands were made on the demesne for revenues.

It was not always feasible to express one's beliefs so loudly. Some members of the aristocracy were caught between the two faiths, due in part to political, in part to familial considerations. A knight told Bishop Fulk of Toulouse that there was merit to the arguments put forward by the Roman Church. When asked why the heretics were not then driven out of the land, the man responded: "We cannot do that, because we have grown up [nutriti] with them and have kin among them, plus we see that they live honorably."[73] Members of the upper nobility, too, particularly those who had themselves remained Catholic purely for political reasons, were not overeager to exterminate the heretics. Count Raymond Roger of Foix was married to a woman known to all as a heretic, and one of his two sisters had received the baptism of the Holy Spirit in his presence, while the other sympathized with the Waldensians.[74] Even a bishop could come from a Cathar family. During the siege of a heretic stronghold in the see of Carcassonne, for example, the local bishop was among the besiegers, while his mother and brother were among the besieged; Bishop Bernard Raymond negotiated with his kin, but to no avail.[75] One bishop of Toulouse was named Raymond of Rabastens; all of the coheirs to that stronghold were Cathars. He himself was deposed because he sympathized with the opposition, and in 1211 the same fate was meted out to the aforementioned bishop of Carcassonne, who had been elected in 1207.[76]

The rupture of families along religious lines posed a grave problem. Count Raymond V of Toulouse complained that the bonds between husbands and wives, between sons and fathers, were dissolving.[77] This remark was uttered thirty-three years before the crusade; the confusion unleashed by that conflict reached such proportions that a count of Toulouse was driven to commit fratricide. Following his defeat in battle near Muret, Count Raymond VI of Toulouse ordered the hanging of his brother Baldwin, who had fought on the opposing side.[78] While he was allegedly extracting a blood vengeance for King Peter II of Aragon, who had been killed in battle near Muret, the issue of creed formed the backdrop: Baldwin was a pious Catholic, while Raymond VI was one of those members of the upper nobility "who predominately protected the heretics and gave them shelter, had great love for them, and defended them from God and the church."[79] In stark contrast to the situation in southern France, in northern Italy only a single feudal magnate can be shown to have sided with the heretics.[80]

The chivalric milieu of those days was marked by the creation in song and text of an imaginary landscape in which members of the nobility could escape their troubles. It is not true that the troubadours' poems were meant to be interpreted symbolically and were actually expressions of their Catharism[81]. In these circles one need hardly have disguised such ideas. Furthermore, the poets' idealization of the aristocratic lifestyle did not always reflect social developments, for example, the impoverishment of the knights. The earliest known troubadour was William IX, count of Poitiers and duke of Aquitaine. On the other hand, one poet was a merchant from Marseille, another was the son of a servant, and a third had been a foundling.[82] The troubadours' courtly game had nothing whatsoever to do with Christianity; it was played on a purely temporal field. The game was informed by the basic concepts of feudal law: Rather than choose a lord, one chose a lady love, to whom one owed obedience and faithfulness. The rules dictated that the love remain unrequited and completely discrete, although the lady's spouse often viewed the situation with tolerance; it was a means of attracting young men to his court without having to provide them with material recompense. Of course, the troubadours not only sang of their ladies, but also wove other wishes—for a swift horse and the like—into the texts of their songs.

Various factors may account for the absence of religious sentiment in these poems. Their young writers were predominantly poor and belonged to a social class preoccupied with making the best of one's lot on earth, not with attaining heaven—one could think about that later. At the end of their lives, some did indeed become monks or canons; one even became the bishop of Toulouse. It is also possible that in deference to courtly etiquette the troubadours sidestepped a topic on which there was no unanimity of opinion and which placed such a nervous strain on their contemporaries. Some troubadours surely opposed the clergy, and one or the other may have harbored Cathar sympathies. However, even the great magnates only seldom declared openly that they were Cathars, if for no other reason than that they held ecclesiastical fiefs and rights. The troubadour toiled to please his lady (and lord), and thus he strictly adhered to the social conventions of the day. He "sought to insinuate himself into the milieu of [noble] dominion and to blend in."[83] There is no agreement whether this phenomenon was "the beginning of a new chapter in Western culture," symptomatic of the decline of feudalism in southern France, or just one of the games played at court.[84] Moreover, there were other literary genres that also took love as their subject, though in a scholarly fashion and in Latin.

In times of war, this Mount Parnassus underwent a transformation. The word used to describe its denizens, *masenata* (*mainata, maisnie*), had three meanings: first, the members of the lord's household; second, his vassals in military service; and third, an armed band similar to the Brabançons.[85]

Of the poor knights who were vassals to a nobleman, some served him for limited periods of time, while others served as mercenaries on military expeditions. On such occasions they met up with Brabançons and often became their commanders.[86] Under certain conditions courtly life could turn quite barbaric; thus, the count of Foix, a Cathar supporter, took up lodgings in a monastery "in the company of Brabançons, jesters, and prostitutes."[87] Chroniclers and papal letters mentioned the Cathars and Brabançons (*haereticos et ruptarios*) in a single breath as enemies of the clergy. Of Count Raymond VI of Toulouse it was said: "He loved the Brabançons beyond all measure . . . and used them to rob churches, destroy monasteries, and, to the extent he was able, deprive all around him of their patrimony." He drove off two bishops, and caused two more to be stripped of their possessions, with the result that the episcopal revenues devolved to the counts.[88] Those knights who were later excommunicated and allowed to appear in public only if unarmed and mounted on slow horses had merely wound up on the wrong side of the fence.

The Cathars were not the only ones to employ mercenaries. In 1209, after the magnates had withdrawn with their contingents, Simon de Montfort wrote to Pope Innocent III: "I must hire mercenaries at a higher price than in other wars, for I can scarcely keep a few on my side unless I pay them double."[89] As long as money was forthcoming, that tack might work, but woe betide the land where troops lived on plunder instead of pay. When the count of Toulouse could no longer guarantee the bishop's safety or his own, "he summoned brigands from Spain and gave them permission to rove freely through the land," in other words, to help themselves to whatever they wanted.[90] Some fortified their villages against such brigandage; as early as 1184 a carpenter from Le Puy founded the Fellowship of the Hooded Ones, which spread quickly throughout southern France and put up stiff resistance to the marauding bands of mercenaries. Not just the nobility, who relied on such troops, but the prelates as well took to the field against the Hooded Ones, who were not able to stand up to both of these powers and were for the most part obliterated.[91]

The pope and councils may have cited and condemned the Brabançons in the same breath with the heretics, but Archbishop Berengar II of Narbonne managed to put them to good use. One of these brigands, by the name of Nicholas, had been excommunicated by Berengar's predecessor; for his part, Berengar appointed Nicholas as castellan (*villicus*) of two of his strongholds. This character was a "leader of the Aragonese, devastator of the land, avid destroyer of monasteries and churches." He levied unlawful tolls on the roads near both strongholds, and he hauled into one of them—in the bishop's presence no less!—the booty taken from a defeated "stronghold of the Catholics."[92] This caused such a scandal—

and Berengar had been so negligent in the performance of his episcopal duties—that the archbishop was finally removed from office. For example, even though Narbonne was the most important metropolitan see in southern France, Berengar had not visited it even once during his entire thirteen years as archbishop. As the half-brother of the king of Aragon and the illegitimate son of the count of Barcelona, he embraced the attitudes basic to the aristocracy, including the thoughtless accumulation of debt in the pursuit of political goals. He left ecclesiastical offices vacant so that he could pocket the revenues, demanded money to consecrate a bishop, and tolerated scandalous behavior by monks and canons.[93]

Innocent III wrote that the clergy in the ecclesiastical province of Narbonne "do everything for the sake of usury. All of them . . . from the mightiest to the lowest indulge in avarice. . . . They do not care about most of the churches and church offices, and bestow them on illiterate boys. . . . Hence comes the distrust, and, from the heretical camp, the malicious talk against God by magnates and common people, and the contempt for churches. This is how prelates become the laughingstock of the laypeople."[94] And the situation had not been very much better two generations earlier. In 1143, while Henry the Monk was still alive, Bernard of Clairvaux wrote that in the county of Toulouse "the churches have no congregations, the faithful have no priests, the priests are not revered [by the population], the Christians live without Christ"; people died without giving confession and taking communion, children were not baptized.[95]

Bernard and Innocent III were both highly gifted rhetoricians; it was only natural for them to portray the situation impressively in black-and-white terms. Just as heretics were not present everywhere, so such conditions did not prevail everywhere. However, wherever heretics were present, they put their stamp on the overall tenor of thought and affirmed the nobility's attitude that ecclesiastical property and tithes were there for the taking. At the very least, the members of the nobility took no notice when warned to desist from such activities, and thus disputes over the property rights to everything from small vineyards to priories dragged on for years. Only when the usurper was excommunicated or his territory placed under interdict did he capitulate—at least until, with the passage of time, the game began all over again.[96]

These were not the only reasons behind the clergy's impoverishment. During the age of church reform, members of the Provençal nobility were preoccupied with their own concerns and already disinclined to make donations. The up-and-coming townspeople, moreover, made only paltry donations, with the result that the steadily increasing drain on ecclesiastical resources was not balanced by a comparable growth in gifts from other sources. It thus becomes clear why in 1200 the bishop of Toulouse was reduced to dependence on the cathedral chapter for his food. The canons granted him one pound of bread and approximately one-half liter of wine each day, as well as twice as much meat, fish, eggs, and cheese as the ration granted to a cathedral canon.[97] Due to a dispute with a vassal, the bishop's successor was forced to mortgage houses and strongholds; he was removed from office, and the papal legate procured the episcopate for a Cistercian in 1205. This monk was named Fulk, who had at one time been a rich merchant in Marseille, then a troubadour at the court of the king of Aragon. When he moved into the bishop's residence, he brought his four mules with him, but could not take them down to the riverbank for a drink; creditors would torment the bishop, who had found only ninety-six gold pieces in the episcopal treasury.[98]

How could a bishop so maligned in his own city bring his influence to bear? In 1211 the papal legate pronounced an interdict over every locale visited by the count of Toulouse. Hence, Fulk approached the count with the request that he at least take a walk outside the city during celebrations of the mass in the cathedral. In response, the count expelled the bishop, who had no military force at his disposal. Whenever he visited outlying parishes, the bishop turned to the local noblemen for a military escort— which was provided for a price.[99]

In consequence of their economic difficulties, on the one hand, and their way of life and lack of education, on the other, clergymen were held in low esteem. Just how interconnected these factors were is clear from these observations by William of Puylaurens: Whenever clergymen went out, they would comb their hair so that their tonsures were covered. "For the knights rarely dedicated their children to the clerical life; they would present the children of their retainers [hominum] to the churches whose tithes they collected, and the bishops ordained anyone they could to the priesthood."[100] If a clergyman's source of support had been alienated, then either the church office remained vacant, or an unfree and ill-suited man unable to read and write was recruited to administer the sacraments. For example, in 1178 a Cathar bishop and his deputy were cross-examined in the vernacular because neither knew Latin. Three years later, one of them had become a cathedral canon, while the other was a canon at Saint-Sernin in Toulouse.[101] In the intervening period, their knowledge of Latin had certainly not improved. What mattered most at the time was not their preparation for office, but seeing to it that two officials "converted" from the opposing camp were provided for and under supervision.

In every debate the Cathars loved to make a point of the clergy's way of life. The Cistercians sent to southern France by Innocent III as legates wanted to abandon the undertaking "because they could accomplish little or nothing with their sermons. Every time they sought to preach to the heretics, the heretics reproached them for the terrible way the clergy lived. If they were to reform the clergy's conduct, they would have to lay aside their preaching."[102] To be sure, the sermons may not have been exactly polished works, either. In his *History of the Albigensians*, Peter of Vaux-de-Cernay, a Cistercian and missionary to the Cathars since 1206, inveighed against the Cathars at every opportunity. He lambasted them as the straw in the fire of hell, the limbs of the Antichrist, the devil's firstborn, wrongdoers, hypocrites, and liars, who led astray the hearts of the simple.[103]

When in a sermon Bishop Berengar I of Carcassonne threatened the Cathars with a crusade and the last judgment, they drove him out of the city and had the bailiff announce that anyone who did business or otherwise had dealings with the bishop and his retainers would be gravely punished.[104] This was the obverse of the *cordon sanitaire* that Innocent III hoped to erect against the heretics in Viterbo; his initial step was to issue a decretal in 1199, *Vergentis in senium*, which subsequently became quite celebrated. According to this decretal, whoever aided and abetted the heretics would be stripped of his rights as a citizen, or of his offices and benefices as a cleric.[105] At that point Innocent was still pursuing a cautious policy against the heretics outside imperial Italy, but in the following year the range of these sanctions was extended to include southern France. When the civil authorities refused to enforce this decretal, Innocent placed his hopes in military coercion. The dispute escalated into a furious battle fought with fire and sword. At the close of the hostilities, a bishop asked a Provençal nobleman whom he hated more, the clergy or the French. The clergy, the nobleman responded, for they were the ones who introduced the French into the region, and if it had not been for them, the "Gauls" would never have come.[106]

We have not yet discussed the urban milieu. It must be noted that in only a few instances has the local history of a city been investigated from a modern point of view. Toulouse, the capital of ancient Aquitaine and the former royal residence of the Western Goths, was the first city to be studied in this way. The nexus of political and religious relationships in this, the most important city in southern France,[107] exemplifies the way in which the rise of the middle class served to complicate inextricably the state of affairs in an urban area only partly given to Catharism.

That Bishop Fulk of Toulouse was totally powerless, as we saw above, cannot be laid to the heretics. Already in the eleventh century, members of the nobility controlled the clergy, and for all intents and purposes they regarded church property as their own or as a fief; the count of Toulouse was the bishop's lord, and hence he was the one to determine who would assume that office. In the wake of church reform, the count was stripped of this authority, yet the bishop was never able to wield any real power. The rapid ascendance of urban society in this center of commerce situated between the Atlantic and the Mediterranean passed the bishop by. He was unable to retain ecclesiastical jurisdiction over criminal cases involving laypeople; in the wake of reform, the cathedral chapter submitted directly to papal authority, while the Church of Saint-Sernin and its holdings became the property of St. Peter's. This represented the only episode of Cluniac influence here, while in the rest of the land the old Benedictine monasteries, along with the early Cistercian foundations dedicated to cultivating virgin lands, asserted and expanded their rights. Further strengthening the links between the city and countryside was the insatiable appetite of Toulousan patrician families—knights and urban dwellers—for real estate; already in possession of approximately three hundred defense towers, they bought up property near their strongholds, because almost the only way to invest one's wealth was to acquire landed property. Toulouse resembled some of the northern Italian city-states in another respect as well: The many military forays undertaken by the city succeeded in consolidating the surrounding countryside under the city's dominion.

Entrepreneurial city dwellers purchased or leased estates and whole domains; the buyer would purchase the land for a given price and then collect the revenues generated by the land until such time as the original owner repurchased it at the initial price. Business practices perceived as all too "creative" elicited countermeasures from those adversely affected by such dealings. In the old city of Toulouse a confraternity of the "Whites," made up of patricians as well as craftsmen, seized usurers and destroyed their homes; in the suburbs, the "Blacks" were in control, up-and-coming businessmen who defended the collection of interest. Cathar families backed the latter group because the sect did not prohibit earning interest on loans; furthermore, the usurers were often targeted by the episcopal tribunal for legal action. The only reason Toulouse did not become embroiled in civil war was that it had to represent a united front against the new, external threat against the city posed by the crusade against the heretics.

In the late twelfth century, before the advent of such straits, people already had recourse to a statute that granted to any "aggrieved" individual the right to declare a feud against his oppressor. If, in the course of an attack against the oppressor by the aggrieved party and his friends, one of the attackers was killed, the aggrieved party had the right to bring charges against the perpetrator(s). The magistrate adjudicated who qualified as oppressors. For the most part, they resided in areas adjacent to the city, and city militias were charged with executing the magistrate's verdict. The city's dream of exercising hegemony over the countryside was shattered in 1215, however, when Simon de Montfort, the city's new lord, ordered that the city walls be dismantled.[108] Most of the defense towers, however, were not torn down until 1226, upon the order of King Louis VIII of France.[109]

Providing more specific information on the role played by heresy in Toulouse is not a simple matter. The unraveling of old urban and ecclesiastical ties, and the rapid ascendance of new social groups, surely provided fertile ground for heresy. And as the members of one group pushed their way up the economic ladder, others lost their footing. The poor, craftspeople perhaps, fell prey to usurers; some patricians lost their social status and political influence. A few leading heretics belonged to this group. Conversely, the *nouveaux riches* and the prominent moneylenders were more likely to belong to the Catholic faction.[110] Nevertheless, the confraternity of the "Whites," founded by Bishop Fulk at the behest of the papal legate, was likewise in the same camp. While the sources provide insufficient material to demonstrate this statistically, the probable result of such an analysis would be that one's religious affiliation, Cathar or Catholic, was only minimally a function of one's social class.

Last, some remarks about the counts of Toulouse are in order here. At the time they abandoned the principle of coinheritance in favor of primogeniture in 1054, the counts were the most powerful lords in southern France and well-nigh unanointed kings. Their estates lay between the Garonne and the Rhône, and stretched beyond these rivers into (modern-day) Provence. This process of expansion commenced under Raymond IV and ended under Raymond VI (1194–1222), whose landed properties outranged even those of his ancestor. However, his position was weak due to the general disdain people had for fealty and the political disintegration of the ruling class. Already in 1181, the troubadour Bertrand de Borne counted among Count Raymond V's enemies his most important vassals: the Trencavels in Béziers, the counts of Foix and of Comminges. They favored the Cathars, while the count was Catholic.[111] Only rarely did the counts reside in the city of Toulouse, and on each occasion it soon slipped out of their grasp. In the 1180s there was an open revolt against Raymond V by a party of citizens who favored the exercise of Aquitanian influence over their city.[112]

Raymond V died in 1194; his son Raymond VI was inwardly sympathetic to Catharism, while he tried to sustain the outward appearance of Catholicism. He treated the clergy with respect, promoted the establishment of monasteries, and made donations to religious institutions; in private, however, he voiced his skepticism and sanctioned the conveyance of the baptism of the Holy Spirit to one of his four wives so that she might vanish into a Cathar convent. "Whenever one of his wives displeased him, he sent her away and married someone else," wrote Peter of Vaux-de-Cernay.[113] In actuality, matters were not quite that simple, for these were political marriages, two of which involved the sisters of kings. Raymond also refused to take up arms against the heretics. He met his fate in 1209, when he had to hand over seven strongholds to the crusaders and submit to a dishonorable punishment: The count was required to appear naked before the cathedral and an assembly of twenty-two bishops, and to swear an oath of obedience. The papal legate thereupon absolved him, placed a stole around his neck, and, while beating him, dragged him into the church.[114] To the populace this was high drama, but to the knightly class it was worse than an execution.

In just a few strokes we have sought to depict the political and social milieu of Catharism in Provence; we have not done so thinking that these circumstances might account for Catharism, but rather in hopes of showing how they provided a fertile ground for heterodoxy. Concomitant events may also have served to point heresy in a particular direction. Although groups like those of Orléans, Arras, Monforte, and even heretical preachers in the twelfth century relegated the devil to an insignificant role, both the Bogomils and Cathars imbued him with a real presence; indeed in their eyes he was the actual operative power on earth. We are probably justified in assuming that this belief was in some measure due to the repeated ravages of war and foreign rule in the Balkans and, likewise, to the political instability endemic to parts of the West. The mysteries of the Christian religion, proffered by a clergy deemed unholy, were eclipsed by a myth preached by the "perfects," who were living saints.

In their search beyond Christianity for the significance of this movement, nineteenth-century scholars in southern France abetted the mythologization of Catharism itself. From approximately 1840 on, southern France was glorified by the romantic movement as a land that spawned free spirits and poetry, more culturally advanced than northern France, which condemned this efflorescence to the bonfire's flames and war's destruction. In a touching tribute to the renewed enthusiasm for the old popular culture, Frédéric Mistral began writing poetry in Provençal and founded the Muséon Arlatén in Arles. Intellectuals made pilgrimages to the ruins of Montségur Castle, where Cathars had taken refuge as late as 1244. In 1925, under the leadership of Déodat Roché, some intellectuals founded a neo-Cathar movement propagated by a Society of the Friends of Montségur and published a periodical. They associated the castle with the legend of the Grail, alleging that this magical emerald had been the object of worship in Montségur following its arrival from the Orient; the crusade against the heretics was thus recast as a "battle against the Grail."[115]

Almost a half century later, in 1970, a book was published entitled *La pensée cathare au XXe siècle* [Cathar thought in the twentieth century]. Its author claimed that as far back as the first century after Christ, the downtrodden and debased masses had begun to rise up against the Roman nobility; Christianity had misrepresented this revolt, while the pure Christians, the Cathars, have preserved the true faith up until today. Among other things, they are credited with believing in metempsychosis and in a family structured around "living" the Gospels. "The Cathar family lives according to this motto: liberty, equality, [and] fraternity!"[116]

This is a twentieth-century myth, a myth composed on the typewriter. And this sort of thing can under certain circumstances have historical consequences. More germane to our discussion here, however, is the actual guise in which this mythical approach effected the beliefs and thought of the High Middle Ages.

Part Two

Myth and Mystery

6

The Religious Myth: Bogomils and Cathars

Alan of Lille, himself no stranger to thinking in mythical terms, reproached the Cathars for not being like the heretics of classical times, who hoped to conquer the Christian faith by citing rational arguments. Instead, they irrationally "fabricated outrageous things according to their will and whim."[1] Even today some believe that the Cathars made a conscious effort to manipulate the terms of the discourse, and they note, for example, "that the Cathar's prime goal was to substitute myth for history."[2] This view does not do justice to history.

Plato used the term "myth" to denote the manner in which he presented his ideas; in modern times, this term has assumed a broader, but not definitive, meaning.[3] The word signifies discourse, narrative, and fable, and the storytelling aspect remains central to the concept, even when it contains fabulous imagery (e.g., the cosmological man, the heavenly dragon), since indeed the imagery is always depicted verbally. It has been said that "[e]very myth tells a story."[4] So does every novel, and yet the two genres are quite different. The myth is more than mere fiction; a myth elicits an intense reaction, indeed it is experienced and internalized like reality. Of paramount importance is the "significance it possesses for human consciousness and the power it exerts on consciousness."[5]

In religious myth the narrative performs a doctrinal function. For example, according to the Bogomils of Byzantium, Christ did not come as the Redeemer, nor was there a Passion. In their stories Christ is an instructor showing people how to escape from their imprisonment by Satan.[6] The philosophical myth, on the other hand, is a pedagogical construct, a tale "spun" by the master imparting instruction; this is how Plato used myth. In modern times, various efforts have been made to synthesize a collective myth—one generally with a political bent—to function as a *Weltanschauung* [worldview], with or without scholarly pretensions. Over the course of time every myth is subject to such alteration that it may retain almost nothing of its initial form, but the religious myth is the most resilient to change. Nevertheless, the gods of classical mythology came to be interpreted in philosophical terms, while Platonism, conversely, almost became a religion.

Moving from one plane to another in this fashion is simplified by the fact that myth does not recognize any compartmentalization of our surroundings into various realms. On the contrary, all things are interrelated and can transmute from one manifestation to any other. In addition to such "mythical metamorphoses," mythical thinking involves equating two entities that share some qualities.[7] Such stuff is abhorrent to the logician, and even Plato tried his best to distance himself from it. The purpose of the philosophical myth is to make an intangible idea more accessible through stories and images without asserting that they exist in reality. From a stylistic standpoint, the philosophical myth employs the narrative technique associated with myth and is so like poetry that the romantics regarded poetry as the wellspring of mythical thought. Thus, both the philosophical myth and the religious myth are amenable to permutation and elaboration. There being no "canonical" or definitive text to uphold, the stories of the fall of the angels and the escape of the souls could be reworked again and again. Likewise, no one strove to preserve Plato's works in their "pure" form; on the contrary, Plato's commentators let their imaginations run free with the material, giving rise to a new Platonism.

From a strictly formal point of view, myth represents a unique genre incompatible with Aristotelian dialectic. Even so, that does not mean that this genre is rooted entirely in an affective, emotional, and irrational mind-set.

Mythical thinking does in fact involve rational thought processes, but with different starting points and goals. Ernst Cassirer referred to this as "mythical causality," a process by which one may "take every contact in time and space as an immediate relation of cause and effect."[8] When the things involved are also living forces, not merely inanimate objects, causality takes on a different cast. In contrast, the mystery of Christ or the miracles of the Bible are admissible only insofar as they can be made to conform with the religious myth. The myth is exclusory, and one's perceptions of God and the world must conform to the myth. Philosophical myths did not function in this manner, particularly not Plato's myths, which had already undergone modification at his hands.

As for the Bible, certain sections, like Genesis, are inherently mythical. Elsewhere the Bible does not purport to be a simple narrative, but a historical narrative recording the passing generations of mankind in a set text not subject to amplification. A great crack opened up between this type of text and the freewheeling, so to speak, myth of the Bogomils and Cathars, which the sectarians plastered over with reinterpretation, association, and omission—an arduous task bringing ever more doctrinal diversity in its wake. The historical sections of the Old Testament recounting the history and redemption of the Israelites were not amenable to exposition in terms of a myth, particularly not an "etiologic myth" tracing the current human condition back to a primordial event. From that perspective, even though it was written in a narrative form redolent of myth, Genesis was of no service to the Bogomils and Cathars, since it relegates the devil to a mere secondary role in the fairy-tale guise of a snake. In order to revitalize the concept of evil, they recast the God of the Old Testament as the god of evil or as the evil son of God. In the New Testament the battle between good and evil is waged almost exclusively within each person; such a conflict cannot be depicted in mythical terms. Hence, it was necessary to shift the emphasis to the dichotomy between pure and impure, spirit and matter, and the imprisonment of the soul versus its liberation by means of the proper doctrine.

The question whether such beliefs can still be called Christian has engendered various responses; they hinge for the most part on the distinction between moderate and radical dualism. Hence, by designating the devil as the son of God, the former would qualify as a Christian heresy, while the latter, with its belief in two gods, one good and one evil, would be categorized as paganism. This approach may appear sound from a doctrinal perspective, but still seems to overlook the crux of the issue. Christianity is a religion based on a mystery, regardless of the fact that some may unjustly count it among the religions rooted in myth. In contrast, Catharism seems to preclude any element of mystery, even though it makes use of biblical characters and stories. The mystery is subjected to mythical interpretation or to rationalization.

The kerygma, that is, the "message" that lends a myth its force, poses another problem. Since this message is neither demonstrable nor even inferable in any rational sense, its efficacy depends entirely on its "fit" into the mind-set and living conditions of the people who place their faith in that message, much like a key "fits" into a lock. This view is underscored by the fact that the message does not fill a vacuum, but must supplant or assimilate other religious conceptions bereft of their vitality. Of course, one may also contend that this process succeeds only if the previous system of beliefs was not very deep-seated.

The message of Catharism was that the devil ruled the world and that it was possible to escape his clutches by entering a sort of monastic order. God took a backseat, since he was not operative in this world and was enthroned far above in heaven. We may presume that the people most receptive to this message were themselves conscious of God's absence and the devil's rule, whether due to personal misfortune or a "negative attitude toward life." Such people may have felt that Christianity underestimated evil's real power. The reality was discernible in the wrack and ruin brought about by war and natural catastrophes, the rule of evil fellowmen and of evil authority. That God did not prevent such things from occurring probably indicated that he could not hinder them—but why? The Bogomils and Cathars had the answer; not only that, they were "good people," who could be trusted to see to a person's salvation.

In their view, the battle between good and evil was not waged within each individual, but rather—and this was much easier to grasp— between the hosts of heaven and the force of darkness; on a personal level, the good individual battled matter, which was associated with evil, achieving perfection thereby. Thus, the limelight was on the cosmogonic and cosmological dimension of the myth, while the psychological one remained in the shadows.[9] Questions about the origin of the spirit, or soul, were hardly at the root of a myth about the creation of the world and the fall of the angels. And this makes sense from a developmental perspective, for a person first apprehends the external world and then subsequently his or her individual identity; how each individual apprehends the world, however, is certainly affected by his or her personal character.

Personality may reflect a particular stage of human psychological development. In childhood one relies on the family for a sense of security, while in adolescence humans express their rebelliousness and volatility by distancing themselves from the pressures of the external world. The individual is confronted by the negative aspects of existence. For some individuals this stage of development is but a fleeting phase; others persist in renouncing their environment, while yet a third group comes to take a pragmatic approach to life uninformed by a general overview. The individual who views the world as a vale of tears must retain a firm trust in God if he is to remain a Christian; should he lack this trust, then he will search for a way to escape all the troubles of this world.

The place for the devil is in theology; philosophers and philosophically minded theologians, on the other hand, prefer to frame their discussion of "evil" in terms of ethics. Illuminated by reason, they demonstrate that evil has no real existence. Boethius had asserted that goodness is a transcendental quality, and thus anything that exists must be good; building upon that proposition, Gilbert of Poitiers contended that all things are good because the creator of all things is good.[10] This line of reasoning seemed to settle the question, and the positive outlook on life was given the scholarly stamp of approval. Just as evil was a negation of the divine essence, so the actions of humans could be evil if they involved the misapplication of God-given talents. This was as true, for example, of the practice of magical arts as of "the heretical sciences."[11] Seen from that perspective, sin is reduced to the act of not doing (something that should be done), thus nothingness.[12] Augustine placed great emphasis on this view as a rejoinder to Manichaeism. In words quoted by Abelard, he went even one step further and asserted "it is well that not only good but also evil should exist," at least it was "good" in the sense of being "useful," for it made us desire goodness.[13] Such notions would have provided scant consolation to the average layperson.

In Plato's view, a benign Demiurge molded matter according to his own image, and thus matter was itself worthy of veneration and study. Unformed primordial matter was something beyond the grasp of the human mind, to be sure, but for Platonists evil was above all integral to human nature. In late antiquity such tenets concerning matter may have proved efficacious in debates against Gnostics trained in philosophy and against the Manichaeans. They were of little effect, however, against the Cathars, who did not believe in the existence of evil per se, but rather in the existence of the evil fiend, who was either the son of God or a god himself. To be sure, in the New Testament the devil appears as an adversary, not as the architect and lord of the visible world; the Cathars consequently fell back on an unusual exegetical reading of the prologue to the Gospel According to John (John 1:3), which held that everything was created by God "and nothingness was created without him [*factum est nihil*]." This interpretation can be traced back to Origen and Jerome, who equated nothingness and sin—in their opinion sin could not have its origin in God. According to some Cathars this nothingness was the essence of the devil's nature: "By 'nothingness' some of them mean a corporeal substance, an incorporeal substance, and all visible creatures. That is how the Manichaeans and the modern Cathars in the dioceses of Albi, Toulouse, and Carcassonne think."[14]

In the past much ink was spilled without warrant over the question whether this substance represented an operative god;[15] today, it is generally answered in the affirmative. What is more, in their speculations concerning the condition of nothingness Cathar theologians also referred to the famous passage from 1 Cor. 13:2 in which Paul asserted that he was nothing if he had not love. The same was true, they contended, for all things that had not love. "If all the evil spirits and evil people, and all that is visible in this world, are nothing because they have not love, then they were made without God." For indeed John had said, "Without him [God] nothing [nothingness] is made."[16] We will return later to the subject of the Cathar's unique biblical exegesis.

This negative assessment of existent things finds repeated expression in the remnants of Cathar literature, among them a tract reviewing all the biblical passages from David through Paul held to support this view. Sorrow and darkness permeate everything, the world contains more evil than good, and hence it belongs to the devil rather than God. Since our days are also marked by fear, illness, hardship, and misfortune, things that we humans must suffer in this life, "We say that the days of this present world are evil."[17] Such statements confirmed what the believers knew from their experience; they needed no syllogisms, like the one cited above about love. Their major concern was that there be a way, shown them by the perfects, to escape earthly trials and tribulations.

Indeed, this religion was not concerned with redemption, but with liberation through knowledge and conduct in the form of gnosis. Gnosticism—in its various ramifications and manifestations—has been termed an "artificial myth."[18] That may be true; nonetheless gnosis still sprouted from fundamental existential questions. This observation is as valid for Manichaeism as it is for Bogomilism and Catharism, and what has been written about Manichaean gnosis could just as well be applied to those doctrines: It was born "of the fear, inherent to human nature," evoked by an "alien, intolerable, utterly evil situation."[19]

In light of the political and social conditions of late antiquity, Gnosticism has been described as "the apprehension of the world as [a] profane and hence impious coercive system."[20] The recurrence of Gnostic ideas in the Middle Ages has been cited in rebuttal to this contention.[21] To be sure, the political and social order found in late antiquity is not comparable to that encountered by the Bogomils and Cathars. However, that "fear inherent to human nature" can apparently reach such proportions due to all sorts of exigencies that—given a lack of spiritual guidance on the part of the duly responsible clergy—it opens the door to a myth characteristic of such circumstances. There is no warrant to speak of "medieval Gnosticism" in this context,[22] since the sources do not support the notion of a link between gnosis and Bogomilism. The similarities noted by scholars may, moreover, merely be instances of "parallel" beliefs cropping up spontaneously.

Whoever apprehends the world as a vale of tears must have a potential means of escape and of finding a new existence in the luminous heights. Whoever perceives the world as a maelstrom of incomprehensible phenomena will try to impose some order. The simplest mode of organization is a "binary" system that categorizes things as either "on" or "off," being or nonbeing, or in the dualistic terms common to the worldviews and religious concepts of the most diverse peoples.[23] As we have already noted, it appears that people first discerned this duality within the cosmic realm, and then secondarily applied it to the human and—more particularly—ethical domain. "The development of the mythical feeling of space always starts from the opposition of *day* and *night, light* and *darkness*. The dominant power which this antithesis exerts on the mythical consciousness can be followed down to the most highly developed religions."[24]

While this antithesis was not necessarily the product of the dichotomy between good and evil, an association was often drawn between them. Thus, commentators on Plato's *Timaeus* evaluated its dualism according to ethical criteria. Those criteria related first and foremost to human aspirations, which "lacked substance" in the Aristotelian sense of the word. The Gnostics, Bogomils, and Cathars went on to associate the human spirit with the luminous good principle, while the body, by virtue of its material aspect, was associated with the principle of evil (or, as some Gnostics would say, of "nonbeing"). In their hands dualism became the key to unlocking the meaning of the universe. It was said of the Cathars that "they . . . maintain . . . there are two ages of the world [*saecula*], a good one and an evil one; similarly, there are two worlds [*mundos*], two realms, two heavens, two earths, and in this way they maintain that there are two of everything."[25] While this remark is not strictly accurate, it still illustrates a fundamental tendency inherent to this ontology. And only a story that did not rest content with the Gnostic idea of an emanating good principle could measure up to this view. The prosaic Gnostic myth was supplanted by one that played upon human emotions to greater dramatic effect, involving as it did the fall of the angels, imprisonment, liberation, and reascendence.

The battle was fought on a cosmic scale, but also within the human breast. One Cathar tract asserted that "every day the evil god effects great evil against him [the good god] . . . and the latter god, our god, exercises great power in combating the former one."[26] This should not be mistaken for mere moral dualism, for the biblical passages cited by the Cathars reflect a mix of cosmological and moral concerns. When Paul spoke of the children of the devil and the children of light, he was addressing a community well versed in the use of hyperbole as a rhetorical device. In contrast, the only way the Cathars could understand such a passage was literally, just as they understood these words from Ecclesiasticus (42:25): "All things come in twos, one the obverse of the other, and [God] sees to it that nothing is missing"—even though this passage pertains to the works of God and the existence of two genders in nature.[27] To be sure, such quotes are derived from tracts written during a later period, but we have no indication that the Cathars thought any differently before 1167. The only difference was that they began systematically to assess the streams of dualistic thought coursing through the Judeo-Christian tradition.

This brings us to yet another problem. Was this mythical element to be found outside sectarian circles as well? Some theologians have referred to the Bible's "mythical nature," but this is surely an overstatement—even though portions of Genesis and the Revelation to John have mythical qualities. During the first centuries after Christ, however, people were so attuned to mythical modes of thought that it would be surprising if no echoes of myth reverberated in mainstream Christianity. For example, the aversion to the "flesh" (in the Pauline sense), to which monks were particularly sensitive, falls into this category; also, some monks, like the legendary John Colobos, devoted great effort to emulating angels.[28] Some of this seeped into Bogomilism and Catharism.

Another manifestation of this mode of thought was the doctrine, propounded by Pseudo-Dionysius the Areopagite, that there were nine heavenly hosts and nine corresponding orders of demons; in the West this teaching found expression in the works of John Scotus (Eriugena) and Alan of Lille.[29] And as far back as Gregory the Great, a tradition existed within the church—without reference to the Bible—that the creation of humans was sparked by the need to replenish the angelic ranks following the banishment of some of their number.[30]

Even a scholar like Hugh of Saint Victor (d. 1141) could write: "In the beginning God created the world, and from the beginning the devil possessed it. Thence, a dispute arose between God and the devil." The dispute, however, consisted of a verbal exchange, which Hugh went on to recreate.[31] This notion is related to one held by other noteworthy theologians, that the first man had accepted the devil's dominion and that mankind now belonged to the devil's kingdom, for God could not act contrary to the principle of law and justice. The devil nonetheless consigned the sinless Jesus Christ to the kingdom of death, hence violating this principle and forfeiting his claim. It was for this reason that Christ performed the act of redemption.[32] Some theologians contended that an angel or a human might also have performed the redemptive act, but neither would have been able to reinstate mankind to its former freedom. Since a slave can change hands only if a buyer redeems him, only Christ by means of the Incarnation could overcome this legalistic impediment in the case of mankind.[33] God and the devil are depicted here as two equal parties to a contract, and the mystery of the Redemption becomes a clever stratagem. To comprehend the incomprehensible, these thinkers chose to shift the issue to a different plane, that of common law.

As for the number and inhabitants of the heavenly spheres, those topics will be addressed later on, in a discussion of the cosmological narratives of the twelfth century. We should note here that the author of one such epic, Alan of Lille, associated the angelic choirs with professions practiced by humans, identifying the seraphim with monks, the cherubim with teachers of theology, and so forth, and in some instances he drew a moral lesson from the pairing. "Work hard, O human," he exhorted, "so that by virtue of your burning love you may be received into the order of seraphim!"[34] Human souls and angels meld into one single order, even if they are not identical in nature. It does not take a great leap in imagination to go from this to the supposition that human souls had already inhabited these spheres before the fall of the angels or that they had been created subsequently to replenish the number of angels in heaven. All in all, however, we find relatively few examples of such speculation on the part of orthodox Christians during the High Middle Ages; the Christian point of view had already been delineated in the early centuries after Christ through the disputes between Christianity and Gnosticism in its various manifestations.

The existence of such elements within orthodox circles should not be interpreted in purely negative terms, hence as indicative of a dearth of doctrinal definitions. Rather, it reflects that most human of tendencies to amplify an established belief, much as a storyteller never stops embellishing his story. Where orthodoxy and heterodoxy differed was in the lengths to which they could go.

Seen from this perspective, drawing the line between moderate or radical dualism becomes somewhat less important as well. One could either take a dogmatic approach, as exemplified by Nicetas in 1167, or a more flexible one, admitting a range of permissible variations on a single theme. What mattered most to the Cathars, from an existential point of view, was that the devil possessed power over the world, while God was relegated to a secondary position. It was not of paramount importance to them whether the devil practiced deception by calling himself god in the Old Testament or was truly a divinity.

Cosmas alleged that the Bogomils in the tenth century believed that the devil had created the world; he did not elucidate whether this devil was a god or a son of God. There is much debate among scholars whether the Bogomils were radical or moderate dualists, or even both, depending on the particular group under consideration. In a work written after 1150 Michael Psellos recounted that the "Enchites" (Bogomils) believed that "[o]nly ethereal things pertain to the father, and, of his sons, the younger rules over the heavenly spheres, the older over the visible world." The latter was named Satanael. Since the younger son sent natural catastrophes to humans, they cursed him—for his part, he was cross with them for worshiping Satanael.[35] Thus, the devil was a son of God who was himself worshiped like a god. According to Euthymios Zigabenos, the Byzantine Bogomils in the early twelfth century subscribed to a different account: Satanael was formerly an angel seated at God's right hand and had shown his disloyalty in governing the realm (cf. Luke 16:1–8). Following his banishment he created another heaven and the first two humans, encouraging them to worship him as a "second god." Logos, one of God's emanations, shackled and hurled him down into hell. "Afterward, however, he [Logos] joined together with the essence of the father, from whom he had emanated." However, in one variant Satanael is called Samael and identified as God's older son, whose right of primogeniture passed to Logos after his fall.[36]

We see here that the Bogomils did not espouse some "pure doctrine," but variations on a general theme. Thus, it is all the more surprising that in 1167 Nicetas, the putative or real bishop of Constantinople, obliged the Cathars of France and Italy to toe the line of radical dualism and ordained their bishops,[37] some of whom had already been consecrated. It is conceivable that due to their proximity to the orthodox hierarchy and its theologians, the Bogomils in Constantinople were able to solidify their doctrine and organization to such an extent that attention could be paid to things like "dogma." Additionally, it appears that Nicetas emphasized dualism in order to underscore his position as the herald of the true faith. In his performance of the role of standard-bearer from the East, he must have been very intelligent and moreover a persuasive speaker.

The process of mythmaking was reinvigorated toward the end of the twelfth century. Two texts that made their way to the West around 1190 served to spark people's imaginations: the *Interrogatio Iohannis* [Interrogation of John] and the *Visio Isaiae* [Vision of Isaiah]. Both tracts were examples of the biblically inspired apocryphal literature circulating in the East.[38] In addition, we possess evidence predating 1209 that the Cathars were familiar with the doctrine of metempsychosis,[39] which was known to have originated with the Pythagoreans. By means of the repeated appropriation of old "stories," the mythical narrative was expanded and, to some extent, emended. Thus, according to the *Vision of Isaiah*, a work dating back to the second century and preserved in a Bulgarian text, the prophet, while journeying through the seven heavens, saw "another earth," which had been created by God, not the devil. In that place the stones were made of sapphire, and the soil was gold; God's people resided there until the "Prince of this world" arrived with his armies and forced the children of God to descend to earth. Durand of Huesca, who had read this text, asked in typically medieval fashion: If the soil on this earth up in the heavens were made of gold, how would it have been possible to grow grain?[40]

Around 1190 Bishop Nazarius of Concorezzo, the one responsible for popularizing this tract in the West, was apparently the first to contend that Christ had not assumed a human nature, but an angelic nature "and a heavenly body," whereas the Virgin Mary was an angel.[41] We discern two antithetical tendencies at work here: first, a materialization of heaven concomitant with the heavenly city of the Apocalypse; second, an immaterialization of Mary and the human aspect of Christ. This should be viewed less as a pronouncement of dogma than as an effort to provide the faithful with answers to their questions through stories. The *Interrogatio*, too, was valued for its stories, even though the decrees of 1167 rendered its teachings obsolete. For example, it contains the following story supposedly recounted by Jesus at the Last Supper in response to questions from the apostle John:

Satan, a high functionary in God's service, incited a portion of the angels to revolt and was for that reason banished by God to a lower heavenly sphere. He was granted permission to do whatever he wished until the seventh cosmic day. And so, from the watery wastes he wrested out dry land; he made the sun and moon out of an angel's crown, and the stars out of its precious stones. Satan created (or, more properly, fashioned) man in his own image by investing an angel with a body made of dirt. Later on, he revealed his divinity to his servant Enoch and through him taught mankind to extol Satan as the only god. The good god dispatched Christ against him; Satan had one of his angels order his servant Moses to fetch the wood of three trees for Christ's crucifix. The tale continues in this vein until in the end the angelic souls, liberated from their bodies, revert back to heaven and reclaim the raiments and crowns they had left behind.[42]

Before the dissemination of the *Interrogatio*, the Italian Cathars had no explanation to offer for the banishment of Satan and his angels, or they gave this account: There existed besides God an evil spirit subject to neither time nor motion; this was Chaos (personified). It was he who advised Lucifer to revolt against God.[43] In effect, as long as the crux of the overall story was preserved, portions of the myth could be dropped in exchange for other, even unrelated, doctrines like the material about Chaos, derived from the realm of philosophy. In another twist, the son of the evil god was held responsible for the angels' revolt, which gave rise to this popular explanation: The son of the evil god disguised himself as the angel of light and ascended to heaven, where the angels (i.e., not the omniscient God) installed him as their ruler. He enticed them to sinfulness and dragged them down with him to the realm of the evil god.[44] Alternatively, the story was associated with the parable of the prodigal son (Luke 15:11–32): God's younger son, Adam, left heaven and squandered his wealth. Having learned his lesson, he returned home and reacquired his heavenly body (as ceremonial vestments) from God. Satan, God's older son, was incensed by this and rose in revolt.[45]

In addition to this primary myth with all its variants, the Cathars subscribed to yet another set of ideas concerning sexuality and the human diet, which served as the mythical underpinning to an ascetic rule of life. This rule of life could just as well have been compiled from biblical pronouncements; however, in this case, too, popular thought dictated that the rule be based on a myth, even one fabricated in an ad hoc fashion. Some said that eating meat was forbidden because Satan had placed a curse over the dry land, on which four-legged beasts grazed; whoever ate of their flesh became subject to this curse. This was allegedly the reason why Christ ate fish and not meat, not even the Easter lamb. Then again, some said that land animals—but not fish—contained the souls of humans and hence should not be killed.[46]

The commonly held view that the sin committed by the first two humans was of a sexual nature left its mark on Cathar versions of the story. "They say that the devil made Eve and slept with her, and the fruit of that union . . . was Abel, who, they say, murdered Cain [not the other way around!], and dogs were engendered from his blood and hence are so loyal to humans. They say that the unions between Eve's daughters and demons produced giants, who were told by their fathers, the demons, that the devil had created everything."[47] Here the legend of the giants is associated with one possible explanation for the strong bond between domestic animals and humans; everything is explained from a "genealogical" perspective and debased by its subsumption into the sexual realm. The expanded version of this text reads: "They believe that the devil is the sun and that he had sexual intercourse with Eve, the moon, on a monthly basis, like a man consorting with a prostitute."[48] This tale is an ancient Manichaean myth with thirteenth-century embellishments,[49] in which the biblical mother of the human race is transformed into a celestial deity.

The doctrine of metempsychosis also appears to have been appropriated from the stock of foreign myths, and the earliest evidence for its inclusion into Cathar beliefs dates to the early thirteenth century. The motif of reward and punishment for one's actions on earth—otherwise absent from Cathar doctrine—is here evident. Caesarius of Heisterbach recounted that a monk entered into conversation with a knight, who said that he gave alms so that his spirit might "live on honorably" after his death. The knight explained that if a person merited God's favor, his spirit would enter the body of a future prince, indeed of a future king. But were the opposite true, then his spirit would live as a poor or crippled person; he would wander through many bodies, even those of animals "and reptiles."[50] Only the perfects, the Cathars believed, were spared such wandering, though they, too, might have occupied an animal's body in the past. One of the perfects recounted that he had been a horse in a former life and had lost a shoe at a particular spot. The horseshoe was subsequently found by believers, "proof" that the doctrine was true.[51] The number of times one could be reincarnated was limited only by one's imagination; even Saint Paul was said to have gone through thirteen (or as many as thirty-two) lives before he reached perfection.[52] This doctrine was attributed to "Pythagoras" or the Pythagoreans; it is encountered among Manichaeans and certain adherents of non-Manichaean gnosis.[53]

Scholars have performed the daunting task of identifying and comparing the particular beliefs of various Cathar groups; the results of those studies will interest specialists in the subject. Most readers today do not feel comfortable with the myth and its many variations. This discomfort is a legacy of the Enlightenment; the romantics reveled in the diversity of mythical thought. Today we ask ourselves, how could people have been so gullible? Perhaps it was because they believed the pronouncements of preachers who came across as saints. People believed things from the mouth of a *perfectus* that they would hardly have believed from a village priest.

In addition, the myth recounts a dramatic sequence of external events that spur the imagination and heighten the believers' self-esteem. Who would not want to be an angel of light cast down to earth by an adverse twist of fate? In contrast, the parables in the New Testament have a very human setting, for they focus on the inner development of a religious identity.

On occasion Catholics themselves took pains to imitate this way of thinking. Thus, Alan of Lille, the Platonist and poet, included the following description in a sermon for Palm Sunday: The King of heaven and earth created the world on the model of a city. The stronghold protecting this city was manned by the army of angels, but units of this army mutinied against the King. They were hurled into an abyss, where they built themselves a second fortress, led Eve into sin, and initiated the procreation of the human race, which is why humans are counted among the devil's *familia* [domestics]. God and the loyalist angels launched a counterattack and constructed a second fortification on earth, namely

Mary, who was "fortified" by all the virtues. Christ descended to earth and raised yet another fortification, namely the Church.[54]

Since Alan's sermon was delivered in Latin, it was no doubt addressed primarily to clergymen and educated laymen. The text alone reflects the militant atmosphere in which the clergy and barons launched the violent conflict against the heretics in southern France. Indeed, in many respects that dispute qualified as a civil war. Alan of Lille had written a tract attacking the heretics, had dealt with the Cathars while a missionary, and had been influenced by their way of thought without succumbing to their beliefs. Recounting a cosmic epic to the faithful was called for in his view, if one wanted to stay in the "running" against the Cathars.

In terms of their missionary activity, the Cathars could not restrict themselves to impressing people with their personal appearance and their recitation of the myth. Christianity is a religion based on a text, and so to a limited extent the Cathars embraced this text as a source as well. Since it could not be emended to fit the myth, the myth was modified here and there in various ways to conform to the biblical text. This occurred through the appropriation of figures and a few tales from the Bible, partially or totally reinterpreted. We have already seen how this occurred with the parable of the prodigal son, and we have already referred to the improperly "installed" ruler, who, disguised as the angel of light, played a role in cosmological history. The man beset by robbers on the road to Jerusalem became the angel of light who was "most forcibly" squeezed into an earthly body by the devil.[55] The parable of the king who forgave the debt of one of his servants (Matt. 18:23–35) was also understood as signifying this incident. In that parable the same man said to one of his fellow servants, "Pay what you owe." That remark received the following interpretation: "In other words, submit to [envelopment in] human flesh. Yet Adam [!] fell to his knees and pleaded, 'Show me forbearance!' . . . Satan [!], however, would not let him be, but imprisoned him in a body of clay."[56]

The Cathars assimilated the most diverse biblical parables into their central myth. They did the same with isolated passages from the New Testament. Due in part to the illiteracy of many believers, a passage might come to be imbued with an almost indelible nature, as if it were an aphorism and not a statement that could be properly understood only in the narrative and didactic context of a Gospel or Epistle. Cosmas commented that the Bogomils' words did "not mesh together properly, but frayed apart like a worn-out scrap of cloth."[57] Nor were such tendencies unknown among Christians. The monk Otloh of St. Emmeram in Regensburg related how, on the basis of some biblical excerpts taken out of context, the devil wished to prove to him that prayer was useless. On the basis of just such piecemeal passages, God was able to prove the contrary. "In both instances, in keeping with a frequent medieval tendency, he [Otloh] gives absolute value to a few passages of the Bible without considering the rest."[58] From time immemorial the same had been true for the voluminous works of the church fathers; isolated passages were often quoted with no knowledge of their original context.[59]

Within the bounds of devotional literature, this tendency was for the most part benign, but in cases of controversy it could prove a potent weapon. Each side in a dispute was armed with a compendium of quotations in support of its position. Thus, how one deployed one's "ammunition" in disputations could be more decisive than one's view of the issues under contention. And should this ammunition fall short, the disputant might disregard the literal meaning of a biblical passage altogether in favor of the allegorical sense—an abuse assailed by, among others, both Pseudo-Dionysius and Thomas Aquinas, the latter with reference to the former.[60] While we will discuss allegorization as a tool later on, it should be noted here that delving into a biblical passage for deeper levels of meaning beyond the literal one was a form of creative activity associated with spiritual devotion—and one subject to all the pitfalls of subjectivity. For that reason alone it was important to preserve the overall context of the passage. In their exegesis, however, the Bogomils and Cathars paid no regard to context.

That they did not may be attributed, on the one hand, to their wish to cite the Bible in substantiation of their myth and, on the other, to their tendency to debase earthly reality, a practice prevalent among some monks as well. Whenever Rupert of Deutz discussed the literal meaning of a biblical passage, he did so with the caveat that temporal things, as opposed to eternal ones, were unreal in every respect. It was the allegorical meaning that embodied reality, in the same way as God, as opposed to the unreality of this world, embodied eternal truth.[61] Jerome had remarked that everything in the Bible—sentences, words, punctuation marks—was replete with (deeper) meaning.[62] And here the doubts expressed by Otloh of St. Emmeram again come to the fore: If everything is replete with spiritual meaning, how can we insist on interpreting biblical pronouncements literally? After all, as Paul wrote, the letter kills, the spirit—"and that is the [spiritual] meaning"—gives life (2 Cor. 3:6).[63]

The Bogomils and Cathars were not the only ones to avail themselves of allegorization to lend a biblical patina to their doctrines. According to Byzantine sources, the Paulicians contended that the heavenly Jerusalem, not Mary, was to be venerated as the mother of God; Christ's flesh and blood at the Last Supper consisted of the message of his discourse; and Christ's cross was the Lord himself.[64] We may recall that similar interpretations exercised a significant influence in Orléans (1022) and Monforte (1027/34). According to Cosmas, the Bogomils equated Christ's body with the four Gospels and his blood with the Acts of the Apostles,[65] even though both texts had not yet been written at the time of the Last Supper. This interpretation flew in the face of history. Cosmas, himself mindful of historical accuracy, exploited the inconsistency to refute this Bogomil belief by pointing out that Matthew wrote his gospel eight, Mark ten, Luke fifteen, and John thirty years after Christ's Ascension.[66]

Catholics did not submit the mysteries of their faith to any sort of allegorization. However, the mysteries did indirectly provide grist for that mill. For example, in compilations of possible allegorical interpretations for biblical terms we find bread equated with the Holy Scriptures. Thus, when the Bible says that the children begged for bread, that denotes the Holy Scriptures.[67] Indeed, Hildebert of Lavardin, a Catholic archbishop, introduced an interpretation even more redolent of the Eucharist: "The bread denotes the Holy Scriptures; breaking the bread means explaining the text. One thus comes to know Christ when the spiritual meaning [of the text] becomes clear."[68] This remark was in itself harmless, since Hildebert was referring to Christ's appearance to the two disciples at Emmaus (Luke 24:31) and not to the Last Supper. However, it does serve to illustrate to what extent orthodox exegesis skirted the very boundaries overstepped by Catharism. That the Cathars did so cannot be attributed to a "mania for innovation," as Durand of Huesca averred[69]—if anything, that passion was more pronounced among the Scholastics—but rather to the incongruity between matter (the bread) and spirit, in other words, Christ.

Eckbert of Schönau had already pointed out that the Cathars studied the Bible from an apologetical perspective: "They arm themselves with the words of the Holy Scriptures, which to some extent do seem to concur with their curious beliefs; and they know how to use those words in defense of their errors. . . . But they know much too little about the proper apprehension of the Bible, for that lies concealed beneath the holy words and can be perceived only by means of great discernment."[70] In this early period the Cathars may have appealed predominantly to the literal meaning of the Bible, with the result that in debates they found themselves subjected to lectures on the allegorical meaning, until they developed their own system of allegorization. Clergymen who had converted to Catharism may have facilitated this process, by which Catharism was transformed into a "science" in the traditional sense, all at a time when the concepts and methods of a modern theology were being developed.

Later on, important elements of their doctrine became overgrown with allegorization. Thus, Jesus' taking the bread connoted the sacred precepts and the law of the prophets (as opposed to the partially acknowledged Mosaic Law); his breaking of the bread signified his interpreting the text "in a spiritual manner" (*spiritualiter*). Jesus gave the bread to his disciples by teaching them, "This is my body." In other words: these spiritual precepts (of the ancients) are my body; I am in them (the disciples); I abide in them. The petition for bread in the oft-recited Lord's Prayer became a supplication for the strength to comply with Christ's law.[71] Due to their material aspect, Christ's miracles were given allegorical interpretations, as were biblical passages concerning marriage, which were said to refer to either Christ and the church, or the bishop and his flock, or the body and the soul.[72] How one chose to interpret marriage was not as important as one's renunciation of the institution in principle. No one even objected to contradictory interpretations as long as they served the proper ends. "On two consecutive pages the author [of the *Liber de duobus principiis*] offers antithetical interpretations for the same biblical passage, each time in substantiation of his theory."[73] What concerned these Cathars most of all was staying true to the myth and its "message," withdrawal from this evil world.

In the thirteenth century the allegorical method was already an obsolete "science," and there are isolated tracts that attempt to prove Cathar doctrine by means of dialectic. The results were pitiable[74] and saw the light of day only in regions where there were as yet no universities. Discussing theological matters in a sophisticated manner may have been important in terms of the perfects' reputation—it was not necessary for them or their flock. For the most part the perfects stood untouched on the sidelines as Scholasticism, along with its stress on method and systematization, gained in currency; to be sure, it would have been impossible for them to seek further training at a time of crisis and persecution. As for the common mass of believers, they seem to have been satisfied with their fragmentary knowledge of the Bible. Then again, a single source written in 1243 recounts that young Cathars were sent from northern Italy to Paris with the purpose of arming themselves, through the study of dialectic and theology, for the battle with Catholicism. The author of this work, a former cleric named Ivo of Narbonne, was not a stickler for the truth, however,[75] and thus we should not read into this report the existence of a systematic "missionary policy" on the part of the Cathars. On occasion they used rational arguments in their writings, but syllogisms are quite rare. No real attempt was made to bridge the gap between myth and reason.

7

The Philosophical Myth: Platonists

In Plato's dialogue *Phaedrus*, the soul is held to blame for being bound to the body; in the *Nomoi* [Laws], Plato alludes to the existence of both a good and an evil World-Soul. Yet, both of these notions represent the tentative constructs of a philosopher who was open to all points of view and who never systematized his thought. All in all, Plato had a positive view of this world and its creator (or, better, Demiurge). Nothing encountered in Plato's works is in fact truly analogous to the Cathar myth. Indeed, Plato's myth is quite different, since it is philosophical rather than primarily religious in nature. In his day, intellectuals no longer lent credence to the religious myths concerning the pagan gods; attempts were made to imbue them with allegorical and moral significance, but they proved of no avail with the more sophisticated thinker. What was needed was a new approach that provided an overview of the cosmos as a whole and attempted to apprehend its related elements.

"Primitive" thinkers identified such relationships pell-mell and assembled them into narrative myths, but that option was not open to erudite Greeks, who possessed a rational education and "enlightened" attitude that met gullibility with ridicule. This was true vis-à-vis both religion and philosophy. However, the repertory of purely rational propositions about the world is soon exhausted; one can either rest content with that body of thought or undertake to follow in Plato's footsteps, thus gaining a closer view of the fundamental nature of being, indeed of being itself, through the medium of metaphor.

This put a highly creative endeavor to philosophical use, against which not even the Sophists could raise objections. Plato pursued the truth by encircling his quarry. In his employ the myth did not convey a revelation, but expressed rather the provisory insights of its creator. At the same time, Plato used the myth as an artistic device to captivate his listeners and enlist them as disciples. The story about Atlantis in the *Timaeus*, for example, had served this very function, and to this day the educated and uneducated alike strive to fathom its meaning. Moreover, that dialogue was practically the only work by Plato known to twelfth-century thinkers, and, even so, all they possessed was a fragment of a fourth-century Latin translation with commentary by Chalcidius. Preserved were the anterior portions of the work dealing with cosmology; Plato's subsequent remarks about human beings were lost. His other works, written over the course of a long lifetime and proceeding from ever-changing intellectual points of departure, were known only second- or thirdhand, reflected through the prism of later Platonism. All in all, his Christian readers were quite comfortable with a pagan philosopher who believed in the immortality of the soul, in a unique creator of the world, and in a realm of Ideas, all while imperfection held sway in this world and matter, though not evil, had the effect of rendering humans "insipient."

Plato was an inspiration to the classical and the Western worlds, to the Middle Platonists and Neoplatonists, and again later to the early Scholastics, poised at a crossroads in intellectual development. During the thirteenth century his mantle passed to Aristotle, the systematizer of classical knowledge and a clear thinker who considered the myth a lesser construct of the human intellect.[1] An expository style born of an intuition reined only by reason yielded to a dry, empirical manner consonant with a systematization of knowledge. And yet, even though the Platonic doctrine of Ideas had outlived its usefulness, the Platonist body of ideas made its way back to Europe in a new form through the medium of Arabic commentaries and recensions of Aristotle's works.

Since the extant fragment of the *Timaeus* concerned the creation of the world, it was of particular value to those twelfth-century scholars who no longer focused exclusively on "God and the soul" in the Augustinian manner. Here was another way of apprehending God, through the medium of his creation. This side branch off the main trunk of contemporary knowledge would give rise to natural philosophy and later to the natural sciences. The *Timaeus*, which bears the name of one of Socrates' students participating in the dialogue, was written to depict the cosmological framework underlying the ethical and political reforms propounded by Plato. He believed that by meditating on the cosmos and its order, one would be purified and oriented toward the artificer of the world.[2] That divine master bestowed form upon matter; while he was not himself the creator, he came to be identified as such in the Middle Ages. This facilitated the "Christianization" of Plato's ideas; a stumbling block, however, was the proposition that matter had not been created by the artificer of the world. Moreover, Chalcidius himself had already diluted the mythical elements in the *Timaeus*.[3] A new process of "remythologization" from a Gnostic perspective would be initiated by later Platonists.

Plato's narrative concerning the emergence and essence of the world was not based on or drawn from an established tradition; it took a medieval mind to discern echoes of Genesis in its lines. This represented the convergence of a religious myth and a philosophical one. Both concur in affirming the very points repudiated by dualism: The world is good, which implied the existence of a good artificer. For the most part, Plato's discussion "of the celestial creatures," those "souls of the stars" contemplating nature from their sidereal perches, also aroused few qualms.[4] In this regard, extremely ancient notions left their mark on both the *Timaeus* and the Middle Ages.

Mythical images and narratives were intellectual constructs that invited amplification. In so doing, one was not bound strictly to a text, as were Christians grappling with the Bible. Thus there was no need to allegorize— though some attempted to do so. The text lent itself to being "elaborated" upon, as in fact it was at various times. In the eyes of Christians, particularly those in clerical orders, the works of the Platonists were the products of a type of poetical philosophy, not of religion, a view that served to mitigate their pagan nature. Just as Plato himself had experimented endlessly with new ideas revolving around a common theme, so could his successors engage in experimentation. These ideas were expressed metaphorically, in a style that better captured the nature of true being than did customary modes of expression.

Plato's method did not enjoy universal appeal, then or now. At the end of the eleventh century, Manegold of Lautenbach compiled a list of Plato's "definitions" of the soul, or, more properly put, of things to which Plato likened the soul, and he came up with twenty-three different similes.[5] When it came to paganism and innovative ideas, Manegold was a pedantic zealot who did not grasp any of Plato's remarks about the soul as an idea, a breath of spirit, or the twinkle of the stars. Yet, others were more receptive. Even Abelard, with his interest in linguistic logic, thought that images were a mirror of the divine. Speech was in his view less perfect than the contemplation of images.[6] It was admittedly dangerous to advance ever more daring analogies in the spirit of Plato. How might have Manegold reacted to this passage penned by Alan of Lille in the following century: "By means of reason the soul is transformed into spirit; by means of its participation in the [divine] intellect [*intellectualitas*], the human soul is transformed into God."[7] This remark did not place Alan of Lille in any danger, for taken in context it was credited with "edifying" significance. Only by disregarding the context could one mistake it for a tenet. Mystics, too, expressed similar ideas without being subjected to censure.

Down through the centuries, "Platonists" have felt free to amplify upon Plato's myths. Very few of Plato's actual works were available in the Middle Ages, and the corpus consisted for the most part of Neoplatonic texts, a voluminous assemblage of writings that encompassed every sort of contradictory doctrine. In addition, there were the works of the Latin writer Boethius, who had ties to the Alexandrine school and to the Athenian school of Pseudo-Dionysius the Areopagite.[8] An enduring legacy of Middle Platonism was a sort of philosophical trinity found in Chalcidius as well as in the Neoplatonists: first, the supreme and utterly transcendental God, whose essence was concealed from mankind; second, the mind of God, a separate entity encompassing the Ideas and providence; and last, the World-Soul,[9] related to individual human souls. This scheme seemed to solve the problem of reconciling the transcendence of God with his involvement in the world. Christian theologians were tempted to interpret this triad as a cryptic acknowledgment of the Father, the Logos of the prologue to the Gospel According to John, and the Holy Spirit. That the Ideas ("Forms") were contained in the mind of God and represented God's thoughts were notions introduced into Western thought by Augustine.[10]

As far back as the second century after Christ, the Middle Platonists had superimposed a religious veneer upon the philosophical elements in their teachings. Herein lay the seeds of a universal system advanced by Plotinus and the Neoplatonists from the third century on: The absolute and highest being has through emanations produced all things—the Mind containing the Ideas, the World-Soul, the corporeal world, and unformed matter. The Gnostics had identified this matter with evil, and evil was concretized in Platonism as well. Without transforming a generally optimistic view of the world into a pessimistic one, Chalcidius amplified what had been at most faint echoes of this in the *Timaeus*. According to the Neoplatonic system, concomitant to the descent from a transcendent god to insipient yet tempting matter was an ascendance to the luminous heights, a return home from foreign climes. What is divine in humans will return to the divine in the universe. Even in the Middle Ages, Platonism's inherent "optimism" served to differentiate it from the dualistic view to which the Manichaeans and later the Cathars subscribed. Moreover, Neoplatonism was an aggregate of the master's doctrines and ideas derived from the most varied—Aristotelian, Stoic, Pythagorean— sources, including some items apparently lifted from the mystery cults of the age. The contradictory stances taken by these authors and schools did not put off medieval thinkers, but rather served to stimulate their thinking; taken together, they had represented since patristic times a separate world of ideas existing side-by-side but nevertheless in contact with the Christian one. On occasion, this Neoplatonic corpus also provided polemical material against the Cathars. For example, a fourth-century work propounding emanationism entitled *The Book of First Principles* [*Liber de causis*] was cited again and again in attacks against the Cathars by authors from Alan of Lille on.[11] Platonism made its mark on the visual arts as well: Abbot Suger of Saint-Denis (1122–51) brought a "Neoplatonic set of ideas" to life in his monastery church. The background to that is worth considering, for it illustrates the various roundabout ways in which twelfth-century intellectuals fell under the influence of Platonism.

Dionysius was the name of an Athenian judge converted by Saint Paul. Nothing more is known about him. Around 500 an individual belonging to the Athenian school of Platonism assumed Dionysius as his nom de plume, and in 827 the Byzantine emperor Michael "the Stutterer" sent Louis the Pious a set of the works by this Pseudo-Dionysius the Areopagite. Louis forwarded the writings to the Abbey of Saint-Denis, which was thought to possess the relics of Saint Dionysius, its reputed founder. Abbot Hilduin was the first to undertake a translation of the Areopagite's works. John Scotus (Eriugena) subsequently produced a second, freer translation, which established the reputation of Pseudo-Dionysius in the West. Many years later, the monks of Saint-Denis would explode in anger when Abelard, having been transferred to their foundation, asserted that Dionysius had been a bishop of Corinth and in no way related to Saint-Denis.

John Scotus (Eriugena) was under the aegis of Emperor Charles the Bald (d. 877) and thus could afford to press against the limits of orthodoxy. His interest in Pseudo-Dionysius and his translations of mystical works brought him within a hairsbreadth of pantheism. Evil did not possess reality in his view, whereas God's light illuminated the world. It was not until the twelfth century that this "mysticism of light"[12] (or, more properly, "metaphysic of light") came to exert influence, for in the eleventh century John Scotus (Eriugena) and Dionysius were as good as forgotten. Suger's design for the church of Saint-Denis exemplified this principle by suffusing the structure with heavenly light; from then on, his design became the model for French cathedrals. Driven by the newly aroused interest in Platonism, individuals transcribed copies of texts relevant to this system of thought, occasionally adding the gloss that this or that statement was heretical.[13] However, it was not until 1225, thus 350 years after his death, that John's principal work was condemned by Pope Honorius III. By then, to be sure, the heyday of Platonism had already passed, although Platonism continued to have an impact, even on someone like Thomas Aquinas.[14]

Scholars have referred to the "Platonisms" of the twelfth century, and in fact any educated individual could dip into the abundant heritage of Platonism to appropriate and amplify upon whatever suited his needs. Such was the case with Abelard[15] and Gilbert of Poitiers, for example, but also with the scholars at Saint-Victor in Paris.[16] However, this practice was most pronounced at the school of Chartres—or so we may call it, although there is some doubt concerning the existence of an actual school[17] and although it was only one part of a greater whole. The school's inception may be traced back to Bernard of Chartres (d. 1124), whom John of Salisbury described as "the most accomplished Platonist of his century."[18] Even more noteworthy in the view of modern scholars was Thierry (Theodericus) of Chartres,[19] who was probably Bernard's brother and the chancellor at Chartres in the 1140s before his entry into a monastery. He endeavored to reconcile a literal (*ad litteram*) and nonallegorical interpretation of the biblical account of creation with the propositions in the *Timaeus*. In the process he could not refrain from resorting to mythical elements or a metaphorical style. Thierry was aware, however, of the intrinsically arbitrary nature of that stylistic mode. Thus, if we speak of God as the Father, the Son, and the Holy Spirit, why may we not in turn refer to God as the Mother, Daughter, and the Gift (*donatio*) as well? After all, the gifts of the Holy Spirit were signified by Latin nouns of feminine gender.[20] Such notions bear the mark of traditional Pseudo-Dionysian doctrines. All transitory things are but images, and consequently we must content ourselves with imagery when speaking of the eternal.

In the past Thierry has been accused of pantheism. While he did write, "Individual things derive their being from the divine," that assertion should be read in context. Specifically, it occurs in a passage concerning God's omnipresence.[21] That Thierry delineated the Persons of the Trinity in terms of their operative roles in the creation proved to be a greater source of consternation: The Father was the efficient cause, the Son the formal cause, and the Holy Spirit the final (or determinative) cause of matter.[22] Very little separates this "modalistic" view from an association of the Platonic Ideas (or "Forms") with the Second Person of the Trinity. Thierry's speculative theology retained its ties to Platonism despite its admixture of Pythagorean propositions with Trinitarian doctrines. Boethius had been the one to blaze that trail for Western theologians.[23]

Even before Thierry's sojourn in Chartres, the noteworthy thinker Gilbert of Poitiers had made his home there as a student, canon, and then chancellor. While we may lack firm evidence that both he and Thierry taught at Chartres, nonetheless they most surely participated in debates there with their colleagues and, by virtue of their strong personalities, exercised an influence upon them.[24] Gilbert was too independently minded to classify himself according to a school of thought. It was otherwise with Clarenbald of Arras, a little-known thinker who authored a commentary on Boethius and a tract appended to Thierry's works; as he himself said, Thierry was "his teacher."[25] Formerly attributed to Thierry, this *tractatulus* [little tract] contains Pythagorean material as well as Thierry's assertion that primordial matter "descended from God."[26] Another student, William of Conches, was, in contrast, among the more noteworthy scholars of the day, and it is likely that he also attended lectures there, since he practiced the same methodology as Bernard of Chartres.[27] Bernard Silvestris dedicated his cosmography to Thierry, recasting in poetical form a Platonic system similar to the one developed by his mentor.

The desire of these and other writers, indeed the calling of all Western intellectuals—for the first time since the days of the fathers of the church—was to come to terms intellectually with the Platonic legacy. Unlike the myth of the Cathars, this heritage proved to have an extraordinarily stimulating effect upon the thinking of the time. The religious myth invited belief or disbelief, while the philosophical myth involved experimentation with ideas and amplification upon Platonism. The struggle to Christianize Platonic thought was already underway in Augustine's day. In the *Confessiones* he recounted how someone had procured Latin translations of Plato's works for him and how upon reading them he had found passages that—if not literally, then in essence—resembled the opening passages of the prologue to the Gospel According to John.[28] At this point already "the Christian Plato" had assumed a place alongside "the Christian Virgil," whose fourth *Eclogue* seemed to foretell the coming of Christ. With the passing of centuries, such notions had lost their currency, but now people looked to reclaim them. One glossator on the *Timaeus* wrote, "We require that no one burst into laughter nor a listener express annoyance if we now and then in the course of our comments [about Plato] mention God the Father, God the Son, or the Holy Spirit."[29]

The Christianization of Plato had already led some of Augustine's contemporaries to contend that the master had known the works of the Jewish prophets, indeed had studied under them, perhaps in Egypt. Augustine rejected this contention: Plato and Jeremiah were not contemporaries; even if they had been, Plato would not have been able to read the prophets, for their works had not yet been translated into Greek.[30] Thus, the only alternative was to postulate that they were inherently connected: God inspired the classical philosophers to speak more truthfully than they knew or comprehended. Abelard gave a concrete interpretation to the biblical passage about the pagans' knowledge of God (Rom. 1:18–23):[31] "Besides the prophets, Plato, the greatest philosopher, and his followers . . . articulated the principal point [*summam*] of the whole doctrine of the Trinity when they described the Mind, which they termed *nous*, as born of God and eternal like God—in other words, the Son of God, whom we term the wisdom of God."[32] Abelard was not the only one to refer to the Son as the wisdom of God. William of Conches, for example, took that association one step further by equating the Second Person of the Trinity with God's Idea of the creation prior to its occurrence, a view that very clearly underscored his reliance upon the notions expressed in the *Timaeus*.[33] Of course, one had to be cautious; William of Saint-Thierry leveled the charge of heresy against those who wished to comprehend the Trinity in terms of the creation.

According to Christian doctrine, the Trinity was revealed in the New Testament and foreshadowed in the Old. Now, the doctrine of the Trinity was supported by two pillars, the New Testament and the classical philosophers, poets, and Sibyls. Abelard believed that the ancients had achieved greater clarity in these matters than the Jews, since the formulations of the Old Testament prophets concerning the Word (of God) were not as clear-cut as Plato's concerning reason (*mens*) born of God, the "Son of God." The philosophers were quite possibly not even cognizant of receiving a revelation.[34] Abelard, who was surely acquainted with Plato's methodology and prefaced the master's ideas with the qualifications "so to speak" and "in a way," succumbed here to the temptation to imbue philosophical concepts with a theological existence, thus to "ontologize" them. Since the Bible itself made reference to the revelation to the pagans, as did the fathers of the church, there did not appear to be a call for caution. Furthermore, the high ethical standards held by some of these pagans were commensurable with the individual "Christian" doctrines sprinkled among their beliefs.[35]

The divine Logos and the Platonic *nous*, that is, the Mind of God intent upon the creation of the world, could be seen as analogous, and the Logos correlated to the Idea of the creation. However, two other concepts, the Holy Spirit and the World-Soul, were less compatible. According to Plato's *Timaeus*, the deity created a visible Living Creature comprising within itself all other living creatures; due to God's providence, the world possessed a soul and reason.[36] Plato's notion was reinforced by his commentators, who transformed the World-Soul into a quasi-divine figure. Thus, the Greek fathers of the church had no misgivings about equating the Holy Spirit with the World-Soul. In the Latin West, however, people were more wary, and Augustine referred to this as a "great and obscure question."[37] Nevertheless, there is already in Genesis a reference to the spirit of God passing over the face of the waters. Macrobius, the commentator on Cicero, made a compilation of passages in which Virgil seemed to be alluding to the World-Soul as the spirit "that sustains the lands and seas and stars from within." That passage was quoted by Abelard;[38] without providing an explanation, he went on to aver that the World-Soul was equated here with the Holy Spirit.

In another passage, Abelard expressed his own opinion on the matter: References to the World-Soul were meant to be understood allegorically, and they could not signify the Holy Spirit, because the Holy Spirit was coeternal with the Father and not a creature of God. The Holy Spirit held sway over some believers, but not all individuals. Ever since the creation, Abelard continued, the Holy Spirit has also borne the name *anima* (soul) because he vivifies things (*animare* and *vivificare* being treated here as synonyms).[39] Yet in spite of these comments, at the Synod of Sens Abelard seems to have been brought up on charges of heresy for equating the Holy Spirit with the World-Soul.[40]

William of Conches was also for a time the target of such charges. He did in fact write: "The World-Soul is a force of nature. . . . It appears to me, however, that this force is the Holy Spirit."[41] Yet, in another passage he enumerated four different beliefs concerning the World-Soul and appended a fifth, described as his own: The World-Soul was the embodiment of divine providence or of fate based on divine wisdom.[42]

In this respect, hence, thinkers were unsuccessful in bridging the gap separating them from Plato. Toning down as ever any mythical elements, Aristotle replaced the mediating force between the Demiurge and creation with an unindividuated principle termed entelechy. This was the inner striving of organisms to achieve their divinely ordained form. Bernard Silvestris subscribed to a similar process, which in this context still entailed the Holy Spirit.[43] In the end, Aristotle's view prevailed, and the problem was relegated once and for all to the field of natural philosophy. Once removed from the theological realm, the remaining ambiguities lost their threat.

For his part, Hugh of Saint-Victor referred to "a hidden force of nature that is invisible yet nourishes and vivifies all things."[44] Alan of Lille imagined the World-Soul as a rotating sphere, yet one endowed with reason (*intelligibilis*);[45] to this entity he ascribed the functions of Natura,[46] a rational creature. Thus endowed, Natura was able to assume the role of a goddess in speculative poetry and play a central role in the tale about the cosmos and humankind.

The World-Soul was the stuff of theologians and practitioners of the nascent natural philosophy, thus, of a more specialized literature. Other ideas propounded by Plato stimulated more debate because they provided a philosophical underpinning to the study of grammar. We are referring here to the oft-discussed "question of universals."

The divine Demiurge, or Creator, was thought to possess "Ideas" of all the things to which he gave form; these Ideas were preexistent and different from the things themselves. This had to be true of words and the elements of speech as well. Whatever can be predicated of more than one particular thing resides, from our perspective, in the conceptual realm, or, as it was formerly called, the realm of universals. The difference is that for us ideas exist as cognitive phenomena, but universals were often regarded—in imitation of Plato—as metaphysical substances, as befitted the doctrine of Ideas. The *Timaeus* raised this problem as well. There the main focus was on the generative, artistic driving force possessed by the archetypes, not on their actual existence, whereas in the Middle Ages the latter was of central concern. Clearheaded thinker that he was, Aristotle did not hold with an otherworldly realm of ideas and in most of his works refrained from making more-specific assertions concerning the existence of idealike concepts.[47] His "new logic," which did contain more-specific material on the subject, was at that time still unknown to the West. Aristotle's "moderate realism" contrasted with the "radical realism" of the Neoplatonists and later with "nominalism," which posited that universals (*universalia*) possessed no real existence, but were merely "names" [*nomina*]. This dispute was not a quarrel initiated by the School-men of the twelfth century, but was the product of an ancient legacy: The topic was broached in the very opening pages of that popular textbook on dialectic by the Neoplatonist Porphyry, the *Isagoge* (Introduction) to Aristotle's works on logic.[48] In any case, all medieval thinkers, even nominalists, were realists in the sense that they believed in the reality and perceptibility of the external world.[49]

As early as the ninth century, Ratramnus of Corbie described the extremes to which radical Platonists had gone on this topic; a contemporary declared to him "that all people are a single person in terms of their substance, and that all souls endowed with reason were a single soul in terms of their substance."[50] Consonant with this formulation it was possible, for example, to explicate original sin as damage inflicted upon the substance of the collective soul.[51] According to Thierry of Chartres, the forms (ideas) and names (concepts) of things resided indivisibly within the mind of God. They achieved substantial existence in that God imbued them with names; when Adam later assigned names to the animals, etc., he acted under the influence of the Holy Spirit.[52] In this way, Platonic notions quite soon came to have an impact on theology. At the same time, these notions—along with the few controversial issues remaining in theology—served as points of departure for scholars seeking to sharpen their wits. This is illustrated by Abelard, for example, who as a young man used the question of universals to browbeat the famous Parisian teacher William of Champeaux into revising his theories. Abelard compelled William to concede that "the whole species" was not "essentially the same in each of its individuals," but the same "through nondifference."[53] This exchange redounded upon both participants: Among the students William's reputation plummeted, while Abelard's climbed.

Abelard made great strides in "demythologizing" the questions of universals and promoting a new philosophy of language. Differences of opinion exist about whether he should be labeled a nominalist; in all events, he was not a nominalist in the fourteenth-century sense of the term.[54] His assertion that the forms (ideas) were God's exemplars, but that the contents of words (i.e., the concepts) were not what existed in the mind of God, shows an abiding reliance on Plato. In Abelard's view, there were things, the mental images of things, and (divine) ideas. The latter two were not real things (res),[55] but they were also not arbitrarily ascribed to things: A real relationship existed between them and things. We would describe them as being a priori.

This approach also served to defuse a problem confronting the most daring of the realists: how to apply the philosophy of language to the concept of God. Plato had drawn a distinction between the absolutely transcendental divinity and the divine Demiurge absorbed with Ideas; this notion was not well received by Christians. However, by approaching the issue from the perspective of Platonism as well as linguistic logic, Gilbert of Poitiers focused on the distinction between God and the divine essence (essentia). When in 1148 the pope asked Gilbert in Rheims whether he could not after all accept that they were identical, he retorted, "No!" To his account of this exchange,[56] Otto of Freising appended the lengthy explanations Gilbert offered on the following day. Yet, a single sentence would have sufficed to clear him of the charge of heresy: The measure upon which the distinction was based was cognitive and not real in nature. But on this Gilbert persevered in his Platonism.

Plato's doctrine of Ideas had enriched people's thinking over the course of many centuries. In the twelfth century this effect was more pronounced vis-à-vis the philosophy of language than theology. Thus was the next leg taken in a journey already completed by Aristotle and Boethius, one culminating in the incorporation of myth into the realm of reason. People's thought processes were stimulated by the images painted by the Philosopher, which they modified into academic theories.

Although neither Plato nor the early Scholastics bequeathed a comprehensive system, they were all inflamed by the desire to trace the plethora of phenomena and events back to a few simple principles. It was for this reason as well that the *Timaeus* pointed out the parallels between the macrocosm and microcosm, not in an allegorical sense but in terms of their physical structure. Man was a microcosm endowed with a soul, and the same was true for the macrocosm; both, furthermore, consisted of the four elements. This did not represent that drawing of connections between all things that is indicative of a "primitive" mentality. In this case, thinkers tried to differentiate man from his environs and to comprehend both as composite units of a well-ordered cosmos.

Such views, propounded by Plato and others, were not only found in commentaries on the *Timaeus*; in the ninth century they found a proponent in John Scotus (Eriugena) and then, from the second quarter of the twelfth century on, enjoyed a rather sudden and broad resurgence.[57] A generation later, attempts were made—particularly at Prüfening, an abbey near Regensburg, and by Herrad of Landsberg—to delineate the "cosmic man" in a form redolent of its Byzantine origins.[58] For example, the flow of water could be likened to the circulation of blood, a parallel first remarked by Honorius Augustodunensis.[59] Taken to extremes, such comparisons became absurd. Hence, Hildegard of Bingen wrote that the skull represented the "upper bright fire" of heaven and the brain the "dark fire," while the facial region between the eye sockets and the tip of the nose corresponded to the ether together with the sun and the moon.[60] Here, the notion prevailed that the microcosmic "human" must mirror the macrocosm and that pointing out these parallels redounded to God's glory. Much like the "primitive" thought of earlier times, the search for correlations was boundless in range: "The human being encompasses all . . . and in him all is hidden."[61] Among other things, Hildegard drew a correspondence between the months and their attributes, and "the ages of man, and then [she] related them to the parts of the body, and, finally, [she] drew an analogy between the fruits of the earth and the works of the soul."[62]

In the twelfth century there were many well-meaning efforts to concretize Plato's analogies, even to relate them to the forms of government enumerated in Plato's *Republic*. The anonymous author of a gloss to the *Timaeus*, for example, wrote that Socrates beheld God and the planets at the pinnacle of the macrocosm, the spirits serving God midway, and in the lower spheres the demons. In analogous fashion, higher human faculties, like wisdom, are situated in the head; intermediate ones, like courage, in the heart; and lower ones, like greed, in the loins. "In line with this disposition," humans have set up high officials like senators, intermediate ones like, for example, officers, and lowly ones like craftsmen.[63] Juxtaposing the macrocosm and microcosm was quite often simply a way of distinguishing the supramundane and human spheres. Thus, for example,

Bernard Silvestris wrote about the world in his first book, entitled the *Megacosmus*, whereas he devoted his second book, the *Microcosmus*, to a discussion of man and how he was created.[64]

Plato's analogies contributed to the conceptualization of man as a natural being, whereas depicting the cosmos in human form led nowhere. God and man were not the only subjects for thought; people were also interested in the supramundane creation, and this topic became a focus of study, particularly at Chartres. To be sure, this study was not always carried out in the spirit of Plato and often strayed far from his thinking. Here the foundation, or at least the first building blocks, were laid for a Western natural philosophy that would transcend its classical counterpart.

We must still consider what the *Timaeus* taught about the stars: On each star there sits a soul contemplating (or monitoring) nature. Equal in number to the stars, these souls had received instruction from the Demiurge on the laws of everlasting order.[65] From time immemorial the movement of the heavenly bodies has fascinated humans, leading to the idea that the planets were inhabited by intelligent beings. Plato's World-Soul thus came to be relegated to the heavenly spheres as well, and the heavenly gods were granted intimate knowledge of people's destinies on earth. Chalcidius wrote that "the mathematician" was right to deduce on the basis of the stars whether a moment was auspicious.[66] In the Middle Ages reading the future in the stars was not considered unchristian, as long as one believed that the stars obeyed God and were not themselves gods.[67] People took this line of defense in the twelfth century when exposed to Arabic astronomy, with its strong astrological streak. They were no longer concerned with the souls of all the heavenly bodies, for at this point their interest was captured especially by the planets, with their strikingly eccentric movements.

Raymond of Marseille was of the opinion that the planets' ability to prophesy the future hearkened back to the Holy Spirit; just as there were seven planets, so people spoke of the "sevenfold" spirit of God[68]—a reference to the seven gifts of the Holy Spirit. This interpretation enabled one to meet the Platonists halfway. The same was true of the World-Soul, which, as noted above, William of Conches associated with the Holy Spirit.[69] Bernard of Chartres expressed the commonly held view when he wrote: "We do not believe that the stars or the planets are gods, and we do not pray to them; rather, we believe in their creator . . . and pray to him. We do believe, however, that the almighty gave the planets a force. As the ancients contended, it comes from the very stars." This force consisted in the planets' "ordaining by their very nature the destiny of all mortal things," should God not relent to prayer or "rise up in anger against an individual, dispensing bad instead of good."[70]

A backdoor was thus left open to reconcile fate writ in the stars with God's intervention. That mode of thought, however, made it more difficult to give free will its due. Augustine, Gregory the Great, and later Abelard as well recognized that the astrologists' tenets had to possess a deterministic bias, and John of Salisbury came to share this view.[71] In his commentary on the passage from the *Timaeus* cited above, William of Conches attempted to strike an accord: Only the physical world is subject to the stars. The planets imbue the earth and living things with warmth, cold, dryness, and wetness, even during their conception and birth, thence exerting an influence on humans. The assertion that the stars could guarantee riches and power is erroneous.[72] Nevertheless, one of William's enemies commented that reading the *Timaeus* and the philosophical works of William of Conches came down to much the same thing as believing that the stars were gods.[73]

Such efforts to Christianize Plato failed not just due to doctrinal discrepancies, but also due to a methodological misapprehension: They hinged upon the literal, rather than metaphorical, interpretation of Plato's impressive and pictorial language. At a time when biblical exegesis had reverted to the literal over the allegorical approach, it was difficult for a reader of Plato's works to bear in mind that he was an author of analogies. That some Platonists were successful at reviving this allegorical element and transplanting it into artistic soil is thus all the more significant. Naturally, they did not possess Plato's vigor and gift, and the fruits of their labors were tiresome academic verses.

An old literary tradition was thus reappropriated, as people reached for texts suitable for classroom use. Of these works, the most important was Martianus Capella's book *The Wedding of Philology and Mercury*, which incidentally contained more prose than poetry. In Martianus's early-fifth-century work, the heavenly spheres of antiquity, ascribed with allegorical import, are still the frame of reference for the journey. Besides the three Graces and the four cardinal virtues, the seven liberal arts put in an appearance here, depicted much as they would later be on the cathedral at Chartres. Twelfth-century Platonists did not revive this sort of motif because it could accommodate the breadth of ancient knowledge; rather, the genre of the poetical myth furnished them with the opportunity to rework and think through Platonic material without incurring censure. For example, the goddess Natura appears in Martianus Capella's work; Alan of Lille later assigned her a leading role in his poetry. Plotinus and his successors had already used the gods of antiquity to render abstract yet operative cosmological concepts into mythical terms. Now "the embodiment of the natural order" would come to preoccupy the Platonists as well.[74]

For a long time, any attention learned individuals may have paid to this world order was merely incidental. Monks had demonstrably turned their backs on the world, so to speak; nevertheless, they were not obligated to observe silence concerning the works of the creator. However, an external push was needed to open their eyes again to the cosmos. In the twelfth century that impetus came from reading Platonic works, which exposed monks to the "open-ended" method practiced by Plato and the philosophical poets. The poesy of yore was able to serve as the springboard to the new.

Bernard Silvestris (around 1085–1178) wrote a commentary on Martianus Capella's work, and in the 1140s he composed his principle work, the *Cosmographia*. It has been described as pagan or at least unchristian in nature; the text nevertheless contains a passage lauding Pope Eugene III, and an early thirteenth-century gloss maintained that the work was received favorably when read in the presence of that pope.[75]

A number of ladies make their appearance in this thoroughly unbiblical account of the creation; they are not the goddesses of antiquity, but personifications of ideas. The most important one is Natura. She implores Noys—divine providence—to imbue disordered matter with form. Noys separates the four elements, establishes the nine angelic orders in heaven, and affixes the stars in the firmament; thereupon follows a detailed description of the creation of the winds, animals, rivers, cereals, fish, birds, etc. In the second book of the work, Noys extols the beauty of the creation to Natura and vows to see it fulfilled with the creation of humans. Noys therefore dispatches Natura to Urania; Natura wanders through the heavens and is led by Urania to the uppermost reaches of heaven, where God assents to this plan. Natura then descends through the regions of the stars and moon. Drawing upon the rotation of the stars as a model, Noys conceives the idea of the human. Urania, Physis, and Natura bring the concept of the human to fruition, as described in the second portion of the work, the *Microcosmus*.

Replete as it is with characters drawn from classical mythology and, to a much lesser extent, Christianity, the treatment of that event pales in comparison to the *Megacosmus*. All the same, the nine choirs of angels, the archangel Michael, and the "triune majesty" of God do appear; Christ is the son of the Virgin, baptized in the waters of the Jordan River, and the true God. Thus, contrary to the opinions of R. L. Poole and E. R. Curtius, Bernard Silvestris should not be adjudged a pagan.[76] Neither was he a skeptic who placed as little stock in Christianity as in pagan religions. Citing a single clause—"if you were to formulate it theologically"—does not suffice to substantiate this contention. The remark itself is uttered about one small item, God's throne in the uppermost heaven,[77] upon which follows an uncritical reiteration of the doctrine of the angels. On the other hand, the work is unchristian in its emanationism and in its silence regarding the origin of matter. Yet, Bernard's purpose here was not to profess his religious faith, but rather to reduce the pagan and Christian apprehensions of God and the world to a common denominator by experimenting with the neutral medium of poetry. Much like Martianus Capella, Bernard took abstract concepts and imbued them with a personal life, all the while allegorizing the heavenly gods of the classical period.

Bernard's remarks concerning Gen. 1:6–7 shed significant light on his faith. In that passage, God is described as separating "the waters which were under the firmament from the waters which were above the firmament." This image served its purpose as long as people knew nothing about the circulation of water. Theologians were divided in their reactions to this image, and William of Conches repudiated it. Even so, Bernard renounced that view by citing the fathers of the church, particularly the Venerable Bede. Thus, when it came to questions of faith and ethics, one was not permitted to contradict patristic authors. Philosophy, he wrote, was another matter: The fathers of the church were greater than we, but human beings all the same.[78] In this respect, one enjoyed a sort of "academic freedom."

Thus, it is also incorrect to interpret the "two principles" Bernard mentioned at one point in his cosmography as theologically indicative of dualism.[79] The reference pertains to God and that which is other (*diversum*) than God; it is "of extreme antiquity," thus, not eternal. Before Plato's Demiurge imbued it with form, matter was, in the words of the *Timaeus*, "a formless potentiality"; as for its essence, matter occupies a position between substance and no substance.[80] It is also called *hyle* (forest). To a Greek, a woodland was a strange place, a disorderly clump of trees. In Chalcidius's commentary this *hyle* assumed sinister traits, but still it was not the principle of evil.

At the very beginning of Bernard Silvestris's poem, Natura deplores the disorder that is now to yield to agreeable order; indeed, the "forest" itself yearns for that state—the reference to the forest as "evil" is an amplification upon Chalcidius. Bernard Silvestris's view of the world is a positive one that grants the devil no quarter. Consonant with this philosophical mind-set, God is consigned to a far-off heaven above the heavens. Nevertheless, he expresses his concern about the world order through his agents. Who are these agents? Jesus, though here he is admittedly not God's only child; Bernard took the poetic license of granting the creator a firstborn (*prima*) daughter named Noys and a granddaughter, Natura.

Other than being a "mythical narrative" in the broadest sense, this poem shows no kinship with Catharism. The one thing common to both was a marked interest in cosmogony, yet—according to William of Conches—"almost all men nowadays [*moderni*]" shared that interest.[81]

In this work the author focused his thoughts on the macrocosm, but it was the microcosm, the human being, that would garner more interest toward the end of the century. Such was the case in two erudite compositions—intermingling poetry and prose—by Alan of Lille (Alanus ab Insulis), a teacher in Paris and member of the Cistercian order (since 1179). Alan was also the author of a tract attacking heretics, perhaps those he had met in southern France or, more likely, in Flanders.[82] He was a Platonist, yet he let his imagination run free only in reference to topics that seemed harmless from an orthodox point of view. Above all, Alan was a moralist; while his most interesting work, *The Plaint of Nature*, imitated Bernard Silvestris's composition in terms of style, in terms of content it addressed the ethical problem of homosexuality.

Natura, whose appearance is described in detail, has been commissioned by God, the heavenly emperor, to bring the creatures into being; man alone does not do as he is bid, turning away—just as the planets revolve counter to the stars—from universal order. Exemplary figures from antiquity make their appearance, and the ideas are sketched out by a "genius." Yet despite of this large cast of characters, the work is almost completely devoid of a real plot. The dramatic high point comes at the conclusion, when a curse is placed upon the sinners. According to an epilogue found in one manuscript, Alan wrote this attack in response to an abbot who "introduced many to this evil."[83]

While of little consequence in terms of its subject matter, the work has been cast as "an interesting attempt by a new myth to take root in Christian soil"; here "the breach with orthodox theology is no longer disregarded," for the poem "nowhere refers to Adam's Fall, man's original sin, and the redemption by Christ."[84] Could it be that Alan underwent such a change in focus during the period following the composition of his tract against the heretics? The Fall, original sin, and redemption concern all of Adam's descendants, while here the focus is on a specific problem. Borrowing the scholarly flourishes of Martianus Capella and Bernard Silvestris, Alan intended to invest the problem of deviant sexual behavior with cosmic significance.

Alan's second epic work, entitled the *Anticlaudianus de Antirufino*, resembles Bernard's *Cosmography* more closely in design. A poem by Claudian attacking Rufinus (d. 395), a minion of Emperor Theodosius I, served as the model for this work, which musters an extensive array of mythological and ethical material. Again, Natura takes center stage; she wishes to create a perfect human being, and with this in mind, she summons the virtues, her sisters, to a conference at her residence, which is decorated with the portraits of Plato, Aristotle, Virgil, and other worthies of antiquity. After some discussion, they agree to journey through the heavens, borne in a wagon fashioned by the seven liberal arts. It proceeds on its way past the angelic choirs and the Virgin Mary, upward until it reaches God's palace. God creates the soul through the agency of Noys, and then the return journey is undertaken, downward into the corporeal realm, where nature endows the human body with a form. This newly fashioned human has, to be sure, aroused the ire of the vices and the plagues, who now join ranks against him. However, the virtues come to his aid, and the nefarious fiends are driven back to the netherworld, with the result that good can reign over the earth in serene harmony.[85]

Who is this "perfect human," whom Natura could not create on her own, this "divine man" (divinus homo) whose creation ushers in a new age? In a political vein, he has been interpreted as the Capetian king who will reclaim western France from the Plantagenets, but this interpretation is not very plausible.[86] The figure has not been definitively identified; in some respects, he might connote Christ: "On earth he will be human, in heaven divine. . . . Thence he becomes human, thence a god."[87]

This particular question, however, is less important than the ambiguity surrounding the concept and figure of Natura. According to the biblical account of the creation, God acted alone, unassisted by agents or even intermediary forces. Augustine adamantly upheld the verity of this account, even in light of the problem of reconciling the hexaemeron with the continuous generation of ever more created things. As a way out of this quandary, he postulated that there existed in all things *rationes seminales* [seminal reasons], which do not all become real at the same time: The creation of these seeds of viability (or blueprints) seems to constitute the main focus of creation; thus, the hexaemeron was completed before individual things and organisms made their appearance. Abelard subscribed to this view, stating: "Nature as the creating principle [*Natura artifex*] is the same as God."[88]

This represented the total renunciation of views we have just encountered in the works of Bernard Silvestris and Alan of Lille. They depict God as creating single-handedly what he must, for example, the elements and the human soul; all else is relegated to his maidservants, whom Aristotle would have termed the *causae secundae* [secondary causes], alongside God, the *causa prima* [first cause, or prime mover]. In the preponderance of cases, God did not act as the proximate cause of all earthly phenomena, though he was always the final cause. By portraying God as the heavenly emperor, these poems turn him into a remote figure. Whoever was not able to comprehend the obscure *rationes seminales* was best off perceiving the intermediary causes and the whole chain of causality as personifications. While her range of action was still severely limited, Natura constituted the primary plot device in these poems. At home in poetry, Natura expanded her reach into natural philosophy as well. In the process, what we term "nature" came to signify the totality of the universe, what the term "cosmos" denoted to the ancients; the term "universe," which was used by John Scotus (Eriugena), assumed a specialized meaning.[89] Hence, Bernard Silvestris's work also bore the title *De universitate mundi* [On the universe]. Universe and nature were two words that gave entrée into an associative realm on a grand scale in an age when people used grand terms to comprehend grand and open-ended concepts.

The "reascendence of the idea of nature" has been termed "one of the fundamental characteristics of intellectual history in the twelfth century."[90] This process left its mark not just on the poetical works discussed above, but also on philosophical-theological writings. We find traces of this already in the eleventh century, for example, among the clerics of Orléans who in 1022 repudiated the Virgin Birth with these words: "What nature denies deviates always from [the will of] the Creator."[91] Here nature appears to be God's operative agent, subject to his will or to the natural law decreed by him. This law admits of no exceptions; God operates by means of general laws and not by impinging upon them through miracles.

Natura does not appear in the *Timaeus*; we do encounter her, however, in the works of classical Latin writers like Pliny the Younger. Thus, in this respect Bernard Silvestris and Alan of Lille have transcended Plato. Some scholars have averred that these two authors were here introducing the World-Soul in a Christian guise; this view is not very plausible.[92] It is true, however, that Natura assumed some of the functions ascribed to the World-Soul and also came to be equated with the divine *nous* (Noys) as the archetype of things existent in the mind of God.[93] In late antiquity the figure of "Mother Nature," drawn from various sources, was such a common one that the Christian apologist Lactantius went on the offensive against her: The pagans considered nature the mother of all things, yet without divine providence she was nothing. Hence, Lactantius contended, it was an error to term God "nature" in the pagan manner.[94]

Without nature, one could not undertake the formulation of a system on the basis of Plato's dialogues and contemporaneous religiosity. She figures in the commentaries by Chalcidius and Macrobius.[95] Chalcidius drew a distinction between the works of God, of nature, and of man, whose works imitated those of nature. Nature's works were the product of seeds (*semina*).[96] Hence, nature effectuated the *rationes seminales* without herself acting as an effective force. Bernard Silvestris and Alan of Lille restored to Natura her personal efficacy, aware that doing so opened the door to various interpretations: Alan wrote that unformed matter (*hyle*) could also be called nature or that God himself was identical to Natura.[97] The first view smacked of the stoa, the second of Abelard.

Since he was a member of the Cistercian order, Alan sought to dispel any doubts about his orthodoxy at the very outset of his poem about nature's complaint. In a prose passage Natura explains that she is God's humble disciple, and she gazes sighingly, so to speak, upon God's work from afar; she acknowledges that she is a creature and that her works are transient. "He creates from nothing, I beg the material for my work from someone [*ex aliquo*]. . . . I work in His name."[98] This last phrase was, of course, open to misinterpretation. Thereupon follows a metrical passage clearly glorifying Natura: "O child of God, mother of creation." She is God's "vicaress," and the laws that are not to be broken are "hers." To her, "as mistress of the universe, each and every thing pays tribute."[99] Thus, the poet—by employing what were in the final analysis noncommittal figures of speech—could indulge in panegyrics theologically unbecoming a monk.

Even if we were to discount classical poetry and the metaphors occasionally encountered in medieval works, this approach would not be entirely without precedent. Hildebert of Lavardin, who became the archbishop of Tours in 1125, depicted Natura as the begetter (*creatrix*) and defender of the (interior) law. It should be noted that the master Bernard Silvestris probably resided in Tours at that time.[100] We also find a reference to Natura as the "mother of procreation" (*mater generationis*) in an astronomical tract authored by an Arab and available in a Latin translation.[101] An as-yet-unpublished hermetic tract entitled *De VI principiis* (On the six principles) depicts Natura as an "artist" (*artifex*), and describes how she "fashioned man in detailed imitation of the world."[102]

Regardless of the precautions taken, any writer who cast off the poet's mantle had to steel himself against the accusations of heresy. Some individuals were so unreceptive to new points of view that they made no effort to comprehend them. For example, William of Conches had taught that God operated in the world partially on his own, partially by means of Natura; we have already heard that the creation of human souls fell into the former category, the formation of bodies into the latter. In an indictment listing "the errors of William of Conches," Abbot William of Saint-Thierry phrased it thus: "In describing the creation of the first man, he says that man's body was not made by God, but by nature." Taken out of context like that, the remark was ambiguous, but still not indictable. Abbot William therefore added this observation: "But then he says that

the bodies were made by spirits, which he calls demons, and by the stars."
Purporting to recount another doctrine propounded by the "insipient
philosophers" and upheld by William of Conches, the abbot then discussed Stoic beliefs concerning the corporeality of all existent things.
Finally, he returned to his initial assertion and charged that William was
"a patent [manifestus] Manichaean" in this respect, "for he says that the
human soul is created by the good god, while the body is created by the
prince of darkness."[103]

In such wise could a Platonist be branded a Manichaean (or Cathar).
Here, the intended recipient of the indictment was Bernard of Clairvaux.
William of Conches was in fact speculating about the role of the stars,
which God had set in motion to dispense heat and consequently life to the
elements; it was in this connection that he came to speak of the bodies of
the first two humans ("for the remark that God took a rib from the first
man cannot be understood literally").[104] In his principal work, William
offered a defense against the charge that Natura's role in forming the
bodies impaired God's power: On the contrary, he contended, the fact that
God "created the human body by means of Natura's efficacy" enhanced
his power. Subsequent thinkers would phrase it thus: God set the chain of
causality in motion, the end result being the human body.[105]

In the twelfth century, the purpose of Natura, the personification of the
effective force that participated in the creation, was to represent tangibly
the void between God, the final cause, and the individual phenomena in
the created world. Yet, if God was personally operative at all times and in
all places, then there was no such gulf, and there could consequently be no
"research into nature," for who might presume to fathom the works of
God? Even in speaking of Natura, one could only endeavor to relate how
she—ever the agent of God—bestowed form upon individual living
things. In the thirteenth century, after poetic natural philosophy had run
its course, Natura was relegated once again to the realm of nonphilosophi-
cal poetry, serving in the same capacity she had since classical times;
however, one also encounters her in the Roman de la rose and in the works
of Chaucer and others.[106] To the philosophers, the rationes seminales
mentioned above came to take precedence over Natura. This Aristotelian
concept had already garnered new respect at the school of Chartres.
Thierry of Chartres contended that following the creation of matter an
evolutionary process "based on certain God-given evolutionary principles
took place in the course of time." Of the four elements that were the
material causes underlying the evolutionary process, fire was the most
important because it provided the requisite warmth; it thus exercised an
effect upon the water and the earth, which thereby attained the power of
bringing forth life. The seminal causes represented by the elements thus

interacted. Under the direction of the divine Demiurge (*artifex*), fire acted as a "quasi-demiurge"[107]—even in this philosophical system stripped of personification it was not possible to dispense entirely with individual figures.

This evolutionary theory certainly did not originate with Thierry. As has been noted in somewhat overly modern terms, "What interested him was the newly discovered concept of an intramundane, self-driven evolution; his favorite topics were the generative power of primordial matter and the creative power of the elements."[108] At the very least, a challenge should be raised over the use of the word "self-driven." This process of generation was firmly predicated upon the existence of a God who was operative in the world; the only thing in dispute was the manner—direct or indirect—in which he operated. This view differed greatly from the stance of certain Cathars in a later period. According to one inquisitorial protocol (1280), they contended: "The crops do not grow because of God, but only because of the moisture in the ground. God has nothing to do with the things that are visited down upon us from heaven; rather, he allows them to take their course."[109] In addition to this example from northern Italy (Treviso), we can cite others from southern France (Montaillou): " 'The trees come from the nature of the earth and not from God.' " And: " 'The weather, following its course, causes cold and the flowers and the grain; and God can do absolutely nothing about it.' "[110] In 1326 one of the last Cathars in southern France professed a pantheistic creed that bordered on agnosticism: Nature herself was the good god, and the virginal elements of earth, water, and wind constituted the Trinity.[111]

There is nothing to indicate that the way of thought concomitant with natural philosophy produced such ideas among simple countryfolk. Interestingly, the devil was now no longer the ruler of the earth either. He stepped back into the shadows, where the good god had long abided. The triune elements were not symbolic of the Trinity; rather, the Trinity was a way of interpreting the elemental forces. Religiosity was abandoned as people focused on what they could see.

Among the educated as well, the groundwork was being laid, almost imperceptibly at first, for a transition to a nonreligious view of the world. In his work entitled the *Monologion*, Anselm of Canterbury had already referred to God as the "supreme nature" (*summa natura*).[112] As for the devil—a figure generally ignored by the philosophers—Abelard contended that the devil, in his dealings, availed himself exclusively of natural forces, and Abelard offered detailed proof for this view.[113] If even God's miracles were granted ever less scope, then there was certainly no room for marvels performed by the devil.

Beginning in the eleventh century, the concept of the "false miracle"[114] was subjected to stricter definition, and rational limits were set on the miraculous. According to a peasants' proverb, God was capable of making a calf out of a tree stump; still, William of Conches queried, had he ever done so? Even a miracle required a cause and purpose.[115] As was true in other cases, causality and finality served as the court of last resort, to which all existing things—except God—were accountable. Whereas in a prior age the rule of the miraculous held sway over the whole world, now a miraculous occurrence became the barely tolerated exception.

Alan of Lille recognized that the miracle—and hence God—stood in danger of being stripped of its role in worldly affairs. Due to his missionary work, he knew that the Cathars denied the existence of miracles in the "base" human world: "Some heretics believe that in the lower regions the only operative causality is that inherent to the nature of a thing. That is incorrect. In order to display his authority, God causes much to happen that is outside the usual course of nature."[116] Around 1200, the Paris master David of Dinant supposedly took a similar tack; influenced by the natural sciences of classical antiquity, he attributed the miracles of the Old Testament, as well as the star of Bethlehem and the earthquake at Christ's death, for example, to natural causes.[117] The church condemned David in 1210, although not for these remarks.

If God and his direct exercise of power on earth were no longer the focus of speculation, then the focus shifted to the cosmos. Manegold of Lautenbach had already complained that certain inquiring minds, driven by a "hunger for [knowing the] nature [of things]" (*naturali fame*) search (like Plato?) for the sun in caves.[118] There are those, Alan of Lille wrote, who spend their entire lives pursuing knowledge of the worldly sciences without ever advancing to theology: "I do not say this because God condemns the natural sciences [*naturales scientias*], which, after all, he himself devised." Yet, it was unseemly for someone to cling to the seven liberal arts as he got on in years. In doing so, the individual came to a standstill at the very spot where he ought instead to erect a bridge (to theology).[119] What is more, in the view of Hugh of Saint-Victor, the reason we engage in study was so that we might achieve cognizance of our own nature and learn that we should not search outside (*extra*) our nature for that which we can find within ourselves.[120] Thus, we can understand why William of Conches burst out in anger in reaction to the unremitting rebukes emanating from conservative circles: "Because they do not fathom the forces of nature, they wish to impede any research, so that [we may] all become their comrades in ignorance; they want us to have the faith of peasants and not question why. . . . When they know that someone is engaging in research, they shout that he is a heretic."[121]

The terms "research" and "engaging in research" are not to be understood in the modern sense as referring to the performance of scientific experiments; they are used to express a thirst for knowledge slaked solely at the well of pure thought. Already in the late eleventh century, individual thinkers began to sense this thirst; for example, Gilbert Crispin, a monastic theologian, wrote: "Much happens within us and around us, and yet we do not know how it happens. We experience the storm, yet as to what whips the air into motion . . . we know absolutely nothing."[122] Plato had taught that all things that exist can be traced back to a cause, and "modern" theologians were fascinated by the investigation into interrelated causes. What caused an earthquake? How was it that plants possessed medicinal powers? The science of the invisible causes for visible things was called "physics," and it had no truck with the direct intervention of God. "It is ordained by nature"; it occurs *secundum physicam*, by the laws of nature[123]—with such declarations thinkers answered the summons to give free rein to the laws of nature in their investigations. Much of what had formerly been interpreted allegorically, like Genesis, was now explicated in a "physical" manner. Consonant with his century's urge to synthesize everything, Abelard apprehended all the laws of nature as a whole comparable to the "written law" of the revelation: God did not reveal himself just in the Bible, but likewise in his creation, which is replete with rationality and perfection.[124]

Whoever rhapsodized about the beauty of the cosmos was in his element with Plato, but whoever pursued the natural sciences was not abetted by Plato's deductive method—investigating individual things by deriving them from the Ideas, or Forms. Even Aristotle did little to alter that, although he promoted a shift in focus to the discernment of facts and to their systematization within a larger context. Yet, they were still the objects of contemplation rather than observation. Philosophers continued to maintain that such observations could prove illusionary, as opposed to one's thoughts on the amassed facts. Admittedly, one can discern some stirrings, though they were very modest indeed, of experimental research. Thierry of Chartres observed a book through a piece of red glass—the parchment appeared to be red, and yet it was white. Conversely, he noted, air surely exists, and yet we cannot see it. The eye is just a coarse organ, for it does not register phenomena, or it allows itself to be deceived by them.[125]

Observations were integral to the study of medicine and astronomy, but even in those fields theoretical interpretations carried more weight.[126] Furthermore, we must also not forget that education remained the province of clergymen, who were enjoined from engaging in study with any view to practicality whatsoever. A system of secular patronage would have been needed to promote research in the natural sciences, and in contrast with modern times, one rarely encountered a Maecenas in the Middle Ages. Clerics were admonished that they had more essential things to do than be occupied with the world of externals. We must now turn our focus to this inner cosmos in relation to orthodoxy.

8

Religious Edification and Biblical Exegesis

 In the Epistle to the Romans (8:4), the apostle Paul drew a distinction between those individuals who live "according to the flesh" and those who live "according to the spirit." In Paul's writings the word "flesh" is occasionally imbued with a meaning not encountered elsewhere in the Bible; he closely related it to the concept of sin. The word "spirit" does not connote the Holy Spirit, yet whoever lives in the spirit is closely bound to God.

During the first centuries after Christ, the new religiosity entailed an attendant dilemma for many people: Did they desire citizenship in the city of God or in that of the devil? Were they to be children of darkness or of light? The individual who chose the way of salvation had to purge himself of sin and cleave to God, becoming a "spiritual person [*homo spiritualis, pneumatikos*]." The first one to popularize the word "spirituality" was Pelagius (d. between 423 and 429).[1] While it had much the same meaning as "piety," the term conjured up first and foremost the image of a religious professional at work, dedicating his life to God and availing himself of techniques consonant with this endeavor. Those might involve residing in a strictly disciplined community or living in solitude. Bernard of Clairvaux used to say that when he prayed and meditated in the woods, his only teachers were often the oak and beech trees. "The rocks," he advised, "will teach you things that you cannot learn from teachers."[2]

If we define the concept of spirituality broadly, then spirituality was to be found among secular individuals as well[3] and, of course, to varying degrees among nonmonastic clerics. Nevertheless, monasticism was the wellspring and hub of spiritual striving: In theory at least, monks had severed all their ties to the world and were totally free to devote themselves to God. Members of the secular clergy, on the other hand, were encumbered by worldly duties and remained at least partly bound to the world. It has been correctly noted "that the spirituality of the Western Church . . . in every domain of its activity, was completely impregnated with monastic doctrine."[4] This doctrine was not oriented toward speculation, but rather toward the pursuit of existential experience; in yearning to achieve and contemplate the highest good, monks sought to apprehend not so much knowledge about God as his love. All this was reflected in the monk's daily schedule, with its prescribed prayers and liturgical practices, and in the communal setting of his life, where the words "individual identity" had been struck from everyone's vocabulary.

The Psalms encountered in the prayers and liturgical practices associated with monasticism were a prime source of meditation (*meditatio*). Occasionally obscure but almost always poetical, the language of these verses lent itself better to portrayals of the state of one's soul than to rational pronouncements. Monks also received oral instruction, about which little is known, and engaged in formal and private readings. None of these activities was an end in itself, but rather marked the commencement of the community's involvement with its members. The practice of meditation was also referred to metaphorically as "rumination" [*ruminatio*]: "It means assimilating the content of a text by means of a kind of mastication."[5] Time was of no object; a long period might pass before the monk sensed the soul's flight to God or even a presentiment of paradise.

It is difficult for us today to enjoy the edifying literature of that age, given our wont to absorb and store intellectual texts with alacrity and precision. In those days, it often seemed superfluous to monks, perhaps even irritating, when a work was structured along logical lines or even when it progressed straightforwardly from one idea to the next. A work of meditative literature typically opened with a single idea or text around which the discussion revolved, before veering off into other areas and perhaps circling back to its original starting point. This discursive style is also encountered in works purporting to be commentaries—for example, in the commentaries on the Psalms, which so preponderated in this type of literature. Patristic works were towering examples of this approach and continued to serve as exemplars even in the twelfth century, when quite a different sort of literature was taking root in the same field. Clear thinking and provable propositions were integral to speculative theology; in contrast, the function of a spiritual text was to enhance one's experience by presenting, in language occasionally verging on the poetical, a series of images conducive to devotional practice. And Bernard of Clairvaux was

certainly the most accomplished master of this language forged in or
extracted from the Bible. His dazzling eloquence helped launch a crusade
and defined the spirituality of his order. Even so, he enjoyed only modest
success against heretics, who were not seeking religious exaltation.

Since devotional practice entailed a sort of emotional technique, one
was expected to abandon oneself to moderately emotional outpourings,
like joy in anticipation of the kingdom of heaven and sorrow for this
world, and to be filled with abhorrence for sin and with a growing
receptivity to divine love. For centuries one feature of this technique was
the monk's ability to control his physical state, so that he could, for
example, burst into tears at the appropriate moment.[6] Around 1152
Gerhoh of Reichersberg lent a friend a copy of his commentary on the
Psalms; upon returning the work, the friend showered it with praise and
apologized for staining with his tears those leaves of the manuscript
containing a passage comparing Christ to Odysseus. Peter Classen has in
fact found the traces of such stains on the manuscript, although, as a
product of the modern age, he went on to note that "Perhaps [a] forensic
examination could determine whether the liquid in question was truly
tears or some less sorrowful stuff."[7] Be that as it may, Gerhoh's text, which
holds scarce appeal for readers today, had fulfilled its purpose, given that
Gerhoh was the prior of a reformed cathedral chapter whose members
practiced monastic piety.

In the performance of their daily liturgical tasks, the members of the
monastic community worked together to attain a state of spirituality;
concurrently, individuals were granted the leeway to engage in private
contemplation based in particular on reading and reciting the Psalms. In
the twelfth century this leeway came to occupy a central position in
monastic life, and it was an important phenomenon of the "religious
movement" within the clergy. Whereas the members of heretical groups
practiced a suitably communal form of piety, members of the clergy received
a religious training that—undoubtedly influenced by eremitism—tended to
favor individuality. The soul took flight to God, God and man engaged in
a dialogue, and God entered into the soul. As early as the eleventh
century, this approach gave rise to such important literary achievements
as the *Meditations* by Abbot John of Fécamp, a work that was later
attributed to Saint Augustine himself and became one of the most widely
read texts of the Middle Ages.

God operated within the soul, and it was there that one might behold
him. This is the form of meditation that has earned the—much misused—
appellation of "mysticism." After arduously purging oneself of sin, the
individual could attain a personal closeness to God even in this life: "God
is at work in you, both to will and to work for his good pleasure" (Phil.

2:13), and he reveals his secrets to the soul. At this critical juncture a question arises: To what extent, if any, is the church in the position to pronounce judgment on a "private revelation," particularly if it is not in the form of a vision?

"We, however, have a law inscribed by the Holy Spirit in the innermost part of man," proclaimed the heretics of Orléans in 1022, and they then contrasted this revelation with the other "written on animal skins."[8] Rupert of Deutz asserted that he could not have kept silent about God's word, even if he had wanted to, stating: "I am confident that I have God in my soul as my witness."[9] While this approach did not preclude rational thought, it did exist in tandem with a propensity for ecstasy that could get out of hand. Alan of Lille referred to a "sober . . . intoxication," which attended the summoning of theological ideas from the highest level of reason.[10] Unlike the Platonists, mystics did not believe that there were any intermediate causes between God and the created world. Rather, they held that the world, with all of its particularized phenomena, came into existence as the direct expression of the divine will,[11] and that it possessed significance for humans solely because natural phenomena were symbolic of moral realities. For an individual to be concerned with the phenomena of the outer world, when it was possible to obtain (inwardly) a direct view of God, was but a sign of idle curiosity.[12] Even the sculptures and paintings found within the monastery walls were not related to the profane world outside, but served to promote inner attainments.

The true credit for "founding" the mysticism of the High Middle Ages belongs to Bernard of Clairvaux, who formulated a new mystical theology by attributing the emotive impetus behind monastic piety to God himself and by speaking of "God's yearning [deus desiderans]."[13] In Bernard's view, the apprehension of God was attainable through all manner of feelings, and consequently he distrusted those who sought closeness to God through the exercise of their reason. Individuals like Gilbert of Poitiers were totally beyond his ken, although he did not in principle reject scholarly activities.

For their part, Abelard, Gilbert, and others distrusted any sort of extreme emotionalism in theological matters, for it seemed to them that indeed the only way to scale the mystical heights was by means of a clear-cut method rooted in logic. In the prologue to his famous work Sic et non, Abelard made a remark that clearly indicates his skepticism about self-proclaimed divine illumination: "It has been proved that even the prophets sometimes lacked the gift of prophecy and proclaimed errone-ous things that were the products of their own minds, all the while believing that they possessed the prophetic spirit."[14]

One individual who might have aroused Abelard's skepticism, had the latter been aware of his existence at the time, was a mystic who would later be elevated to a prophet: Joachim of Fiore (d. 1203). When contemporaries asked him whence he had derived his prophecies identifying the third age of the world with the age of the Holy Spirit, he responded: "God, who in former times granted the prophets the spirit of prophecy, has granted me the spirit of intelligence [*intelligentia*], so that I, filled with God's spirit, may discern with the clearest vision all the mysteries of the Holy Scriptures, just as the holy prophets discerned them when long ago they, filled with God's spirit, wrote them down."[15] In this case, spirituality was reconstituted as a Christianity of the spirit peripheral to orthodoxy. In the thirteenth century individuals, including Joachim's followers, adopted various means to express their need for spiritual freedom within God. Most individuals moved by spiritual experiences did not have a high opinion of learning, since their life's focus was on forging a link to God in this world and in the next. Joachim declared that "reading" was a matter for the secular clergy, while psalmody and spiritual exaltation in the age of the Holy Spirit were proper to the monks.[16]

The less intellectual a mystically oriented devotional practice was, the more it found expression in visual and not verbal terms: Contemplation yielded to vision. Hildegard of Bingen (d. 1179) described how she experienced visions without going into ecstasy and with her eyes open, hence while awake. These visions occurred not in private, but in public places, "yet, only in my soul."[17] Their imagery bespeaks the influence of contemporary theologians like her teacher Rupert of Deutz, who had himself in turn been influenced by John Scotus (Eriugena).[18] Attempts were made, strangely enough, to put this gift to practical use, as during a discussion held at the Council of Rheims (1148) concerning a particularly obscure thesis propounded by Gilbert of Poitiers. At issue was whether "God" and "divinity [*divinitas*]," and "Father" and "paternity [*paternitas*]," were equivalent or not. The Parisian master Odo of Ourscamp referred this question to Hildegard, who wrote in reply: "In a genuine vision, . . . illuminated by the true light, I saw and learned, not by my own efforts or by delving into myself, that paternity and divinity are the same as God." Her substantiation for this contention, however, was the observation, anything but visionary, that humans were not to speak of God in the same way as they might about people. Particularizing God by means of words was tantamount to denying him.[19]

Later in his life, by the way, Odo shifted course and entered the Cistercian order. He deemed his subsequent appointment as cardinal to be God's punishment for his earlier life as a master and said: "I chose, despite Divine prohibition, to eat of the tree of knowledge of good and evil."[20]

Knowledge and learning, even in conjunction with theology, could prove dangerous if not held in moderation; insight must be bridled by temperance, wrote Manegold of Lautenbach—otherwise it will proliferate beyond control or suffer obfuscation in the shadows of absurdity.[21]

Hildegard was not one of those mystics who contemplated only God and the soul. She "saw" visions of the cosmos that encompassed mankind also, indeed concepts that did not normally lend themselves to visual representation. Her works reflect an interest in *physica*, the study of nature, as well as in therapeutics; from time to time she herself suffered psychosomatic episodes of paralysis. She was highly respected by her contemporaries and was never charged with *curiositas*, that useless form of curiosity Augustine had equated with the "knowledge of things," as opposed to wisdom, whose objective was the apprehension of God.[22] While Hildegard may have quoted Latin phrases and may have been familiar with the literature of her day, there is no discernible proof for the oft-repeated claim that she enjoyed an intellectual affinity with Bernard Silvestris and his cosmography.[23] She did not pursue "learning" as an edifying tool, but engaged in "cosmic contemplation," an activity familiar to her contemporaries from a tract attributed to "Asclepius."[24]

"There are those," Bernard of Clairvaux wrote, "who pursue knowledge for the purpose of edification, and that is [a manifestation of] love; others pursue knowledge for the purpose of acquiring an education, and that shows prudence." Whoever amasses knowledge for its own sake, however, behaves with contemptible curiosity; whoever seeks fame by such means behaves with contemptible vanity.[25] Looking back on the twelfth century, James of Vitry (d. 1240) echoed these sentiments and took aim against the contemporary state of academic studies at Paris: Few studied to be edified or to further their education.[26]

To engage in monastic contemplation, an individual required tranquillity and composure; he (or she) could not pursue many interests and become "distracted." This may appear to explain why intellectual curiosity born of mere inquisitiveness met with rejection; in fact that reaction was already evident during antiquity. Classical thinkers often viewed the desire for knowledge in a positive light up until a certain point, beyond which it became the subject of censure. As Seneca wrote, "The desire to amass more knowledge than is sufficient is a form of immoderation."[27]

Admittedly, one might ask, what is "sufficient"? During antiquity, many members of the upper classes were able over the course of their lifetimes to achieve mastery over just about all there was to know in that day and age. In the Middle Ages, it was not possible to lead such a life; everyone engaged in a particular profession. The old liberal arts curriculum seemed to satisfy the intellectual needs of the clergy, who in most cases received instruction only in its lower branches (the *trivium*). Influenced by eremitism, the monastic reform movement had such a narrow view of what constituted "sufficient" knowledge that it has been accused of "excessive anti-intellectualism."[28] While that may be something of an overstatement, the negative stance taken by the reform monks had the reverse effect of greatly promoting the growth of a new type of advanced schooling. From the early twelfth century on, with every passing generation ever more people had a need for learning, while at the very same time ever more classical scholarship became available. To little effect did Bernard of Clairvaux ask: "What did the apostles teach? . . . [It was] not to read Plato and obvert Aristotle's sophisms, or to undertake an interminable course of study that never leads to the apprehension of truth. What they taught us was how we should live."[29]

Nevertheless, in Bernard's view education did retain a practical purpose. He declared that he was well aware of the extent to which the church was indebted to educated individuals, and he noted two activities that had profited from their efforts: warding off heretics and providing elementary education. In any case, steps had to be taken to ensure that the education bore fruit (*fructus*) and possessed utility (*utilitas*).[30] For example, the first Dominicans later undertook to convert the heretics in southern France by means of intellectual arguments. Their "fruits" were meager. The courses offered in the monastic schools did not in any way bespeak the many possible educational opportunities appearing on the horizon. Seen from this perspective, traditional education and the new "academic" mode of scholarly activity were two totally alien systems, and the dichotomy between churchmen (*ecclesiastici*) and the Schoolmen (*scholastici*) could be writ in stone.[31]

Benedict of Nursia had exhorted his monks to read the Bible and the lives of the desert fathers.[32] Since there were no private cells or rooms for study, the monks were instructed to conduct their private readings in the cloister, chapter hall, dormitory, or church.[33] During the times set aside for private reading, the Cistercians found it necessary to dispatch lookouts, who walked around checking that no monk had dozed off in the shelter of his cowl.[34] The monks also participated in communal readings as part of the liturgical celebration, at chapter meetings, and at meals. The texts read in the dining hall were often drawn from a special collection, a sort of library for the refectory.[35] These works were truly used daily, and they constituted a minilibrary, compared to the monastery library, itself quite modest by today's standards. If, as Paul contended, "'knowledge' puffs up [people]," (1 Cor. 8:1), then most monks were not in any peril; the road to scholarship was not open to them. Their role was to practice "holy simplicity," a way of life already commended by Jerome, though it should of course be noted that this *sancta rusticitas* benefited only the individual practitioners themselves (and not others).[36]

Such assertions must be tempered somewhat, however. The passing centuries brought more and more priest-monks, who by this period constituted a majority of the monastic population. They had enjoyed a broader education than the monks, and in some instances were the cause of some concern to monastic reformers. Peter Damiani, for example, maintained, "As monks, we are not merely enjoined from pursuing our studies further, but we must trim whatever is superfluous from what we have previously learned."[37] Nonetheless, many Schoolmen were originally monks or took monastic vows in their later years, in particular as Cistercians. Even as masters entrusted with worldly matters, a few did not lose sight of the contemplative element underlying monasticism. Anselm of Canterbury, occasionally dubbed the "Father of Scholasticism," composed many devotional pieces, some written in a liturgical or poetic style. In the opening passage to his *Monologion*, so titled because it took the form of a monologue, Anselm recounted how his fellow monks had implored him to write down all he had told them about meditating on the divine being.[38] Time and time again, in speculative theology as well, this would be the topic thinkers were asked to address. In the monumental edition of his works, Anselm's meditative pieces fill an entire volume.

Once broached by Rupert of Deutz and others, the question whether monks could perform pastoral duties—in particular preaching—proved quite thorny. Saint Jerome had contended that it was the monk's charge to mourn, not to teach. He was to weep for himself and the world, and anxiously await the Lord's advent. In a letter addressed to Roscelin, his former teacher, Abelard cited Jerome's remarks and concluded with these words: "Notwithstanding your prior assumption of the monk's habit, you profess to be a teacher and teach lies; hence you have totally ceased being a monk."[39]

Even Joachim of Fiore considered preaching the province of the secular clergy, whereas maintaining a reverential silence befitted monks.[40] However, in light of the emphasis the religious reform movement placed on the apostolic life, that is, one devoted to itinerant preaching, there had long been disagreement within monastery walls over this issue. Monks who were itinerant preachers founded their own monasteries, indeed monastic orders; other monks, like the one named Henry whom we have encountered above, abandoned the cloister to preach sectarianism. Bernard of Clairvaux, who echoed Saint Jerome's sentiments, was the preeminent preacher of his age. At issue with heretics and preachers was not just their imitation of the apostolic life, but also their theology. There was in actuality such a diversity of lifestyles in the twelfth century that the patterns of the past could not be brought to bear on them. However, the dichotomy between these outlooks would still find expression in the two great mendicant orders: According to Francis of Assisi, his uneducated disciples were not to learn how to read, but rather were to strive to attain the spirit of the Lord. On the other hand, one had to study to become a Dominican.

The monk existed on two planes, the physical and the spiritual, bound by his daily routine, on the one hand, and by the mystery that transcended all earthly things, on the other. The concepts of myth and mystery should not, as is occasionally done, be equated: The religious myth concerns events, while the word "mystery" is used to signify the ineffable beyond reason, a "blank space" on the map of theology. The original Greek word for mystery is related to the idea of "closing the lips" and is defined as a secret or a secret teaching of a mystery cult. It does not focus on an event, assuming that one is even involved, but on the impenetrable quality of something that is nonetheless apprehended as having a real existence. One might attempt to approach this something in various ways, through the release of the soul upward in flight or through the apprehension of penetrating analogies—but no one could unravel the mystery. One of the charges leveled against Scholasticism was that its strategy for approaching this something lacked that awe for the numinous inherent to monasticism; what the monk beheld upon his knees, others sought to dictate from the lectern.

From time immemorial Latin translations of the Bible had rendered this concept with the word *sacramentum*. This term possessed a much broader meaning than it does nowadays in reference to the sacraments of the church; for example, it could refer to an oath or any other prescribed sacred formula, to the symbol for a holy object, or to "a holy secret." In the Old Testament there were *sacramenta* that were not sacred,[41] and so forth. Augustine's interpretation of the word *sacramentum* as a "holy symbol" (*sacrum signum*) conforms to traditional Platonism: The material thing was a *signum*, in contrast to the reality existent in the mind of God (the Idea). With the rediscovery of Aristotle in the twelfth century, things possessing material existence were increasingly perceived as "real," whereas "ideas" were increasingly viewed as "mere" symbols. These views assumed particular importance in light of the controversies over the nature of the Eucharist.

Such debates served to diminish the awe with which people viewed the divine sphere and to undercut, rather than encourage, piety. They were entirely off-limits to laypeople lacking the requisite education. Bernard of Clairvaux hence complained: "In the suburbs (*vicis*) and in the public squares, people discuss the Catholic faith, the Virgin Birth, the Eucharist, and the ineffable mystery of the Trinity."[42] Church assemblies, like the one held in Limoges in 1011, enjoined laypeople from engaging in debates about the Trinity; in 1199 Innocent III reiterated this stance in a letter addressed to the faithful of the diocese of Metz: "The secret mysteries of faith are not to be explained to all sorts of people everywhere, for they will not be understood everywhere and by all; rather, [they are to be explained] only to those who can embrace them with devout understanding. . . . In fact, the Holy Scriptures are so profound that plumbing them to their very depths is beyond the ability of not just simple and uneducated people, but also subtle and learned individuals."[43]

Profound mysteries lay concealed in the Bible. Since laypeople were illiterate or only semiliterate, they would perforce stumble into error were they to "research the Bible" without the guidance of experts. Lacking not just the educational background, but also the contemplative training, they were incapable of assuming the proper attitude toward the Bible. Clergymen, furthermore, did not necessarily have to study speculative theology in order to make valuable contributions to this field; some theological tenets were adopted from contemplative meditation, like those regarding the merits of the Virgin Mary.[44] The same purpose was served by the massive corpus of biblical literature accruing since late antiquity and promoting allegorization. Thus, all this work was not an end in itself, but served to benefit the spiritual life.

The text of the New Testament was inspired by the Holy Spirit, and hence from the very outset one might presume that hidden in its words lay much more meaning and signification than ordinary perusal might reveal. Jerome spoke for all biblical exegetes when he stated: "Each and every sentence, syllable, letter, and comma in God's writings is replete with meaning."[45] Origen, who championed the allegorical method, believed that it was extraordinarily difficult, if not impossible, to ascertain these meanings down to the last detail; Augustine referred to the Bible as the "book of mysteries."[46] Their search for meaning resembled that of the Gnostics and the Platonists. Sober and rational thinker that he was, Thomas Aquinas later noted: "Plato expresses things poorly. Namely, he teaches all things metaphorically [*figurate*] or by means of symbols [*per symbola*]."[47] Thomas had a low opinion of allegorization as well.

The intellectuals of ancient Rome were well versed in the art of imbuing pagan mythology with a deeper philosophical and ethical meaning. Jewish biblical scholars believed that the paradigms and factual material in the Old Testament were endowed with a deeper significance, and Paul imbued parts of Christ's recent passion and resurrection with a similar significance. This must not be seen as rhetorical hyperbole, but as the discovery of theological signification in simple testimony. In a pastoral letter to the Ephesians (5:31–32), Paul linked a biblical reference to marriage with notions about the Christian religion: In Genesis it says that man will leave his father and mother and cleave to his wife and become one flesh with her (Gen. 2:24). Paul continued: "This is a great mystery, and I take it to mean Christ and the church." In the preceding verses Paul had referred to the husband's role in nourishing the wife and their union, comparing this to Christ and the church. In Paul's hands this approach to a biblical text already served an edifying function.

It would be a mistake, to be sure, to think that the corpus of allegorical material—hence virtually all the theological scholarship produced before the twelfth century—was viewed as nothing more than a series of edifying analogies. If transient entities were no more than images of the eternal ideas and their creator, then the latter were the receptacles of spiritual reality. The Platonists were not the only ones who propounded this view; it became increasingly common for thinkers to apprehend the experiential world as unreal. At the catechetical school of Alexandria, the major center of Hellenistic learning, the Bible was not interpreted from a historical or grammatical perspective, as was the case, for example, at the school of Antioch. Did not the Bible itself indicate that the literal meaning of a word did not always represent its true meaning? For example, references to "the arm of God" were figurative of God's power. Were the words about the union of man and wife only to be understood in a physical sense (*physice*) and not in a much more lofty one? Whoever viewed the Bible as an ocean of secrets could set sail on voyages of discovery across its waters. "Allegorical" and "moral" biblical exegesis amounted to much the same thing, and their practice brought reward to a Christian.

In these waters lay a treasure trove of ideas to advance a monk's spiritual education. His very mode of existence epitomized the view that physical life was merely a necessary evil, and hence one should live spiritually. The monk started out with a coarse popular piety and was advised to approach the higher spheres gradually. As so often before, we can point to Abelard, who, though admittedly a cool-headed logician, also composed religious hymns for his monastery of the Paraclete. He divided these hymns into two books; one contained the hymns to be sung at night and was dedicated to the "darkness of the literal meaning," while the hymns for daytime services brought "the illumination of exegesis reserved to the day."[48] The Old Testament formed the basis for the first book, while the allegorical and moral interpretation of the New Testament underlay the second. Drawing upon the fathers of the church, Abelard stated in his *Dialogue of a* [pagan] *Philosopher with a Jew, and a Christian*, that descriptions of hell's torments and of paradise at the end of time were not to be understood in coarsely sensate terms, but spiritually, with a "mystical rather than corporeal" significance. For example, the Son of God does not actually sit at the right hand of the Father.[49] This metaphorical outlook also served Abelard and others well whenever they sought to reconcile the contradictions between Platonic or Platonist propositions and Christian thought. "Veiled" language was actually a Neoplatonist stylistic device, but Abelard took it a step further by attributing such contradictions time and time again to some secret teaching (*involucrum*) of the philosophers: Philosophy did not wish to divulge her secrets, particularly those about God and the soul, in plain language, so she shrouded them in stories (*fabulosa*).[50]

Allegory supplemented symbols; the liturgy in particular was replete with symbolism. Both allegory and symbol made it possible for an individual to "approximate" the mystery that eluded the crude grasp; both were closely related to an individual's existence and were not bloodless abstractions. Since Goethe and the romantic age, the word "allegory" has held negative connotations and raised associations with the tiresome allegorizations of Homer's epics and the pantheon of pagan gods. The imagery evoked by a symbol, in contrast, has an immediate, expressive power. In the monk's view, allegory and symbol provided equal access to one and the same goal: Both led him into the presence of the divine majesty while guarding its secrets.

The Catholic Church today subscribes to the Pauline mode of exegesis, but any further attempts at allegorization are endured rather than encouraged. The allegorical mode of perception is a form of primitive "precategorical thinking," by which interrelationships can be posited between all things and only a secondary role is accorded to causality; it often involves free association. Holy texts were known by heart, and in contemplating one passage, an individual could call to mind other sections, which were then tied in with the former. This process was not merely a feat of memory, but an accomplishment of the heart, thus producing in the monk that emotional surge constituting an essential part of his spiritual existence. The monk did not justify his pursuit of this activity by referring to his psychological needs, but rather acted out of the belief that he was discovering eternal truths. The infinite profusion of these truths betokened their divine origin. What difference did it make if there was no firm conceptual basis? One was lifted up into the realm of the suprarational, where logical considerations would be for naught in any case.

On the contrary, what mattered were the existential relationships deduced through allegory. For example, Jerusalem is, literally speaking, the name of a geographical location; for the monk, however, it is everywhere and anywhere. He seeks the heavenly Jerusalem in the next life and conducts his life here on earth as if he had already been vouchsafed this goal. After offering such traditional explanations, Bernard of Clairvaux provided his own amplification: "And if you must know, I am speaking of Clairvaux. There one can find a Jerusalem associated with the heavenly one through the heart's complete devotion."[51] The milieu and associated duties of monks did not, of course, always live up to Bernard's description of Clairvaux.

As a result of this word-by-word combing through the Bible, not a single location or person was beyond the reach of allegorization. It was quite commonly believed that a person's essence lay concealed in his or her name, and that one could—often through tenuous interpretations—throw light upon this essence. Reading about animals, plants, or gemstones, one might consult a bestiary, herbal, or lapidary. The information thus gathered about their appearance and effect upon humans could be interpreted from an edifying perspective, a process that often set off an interpretative chain reaction progressing from the stone to its color, from its color to its humors (with their associated colors), etc. Each detail took on a life of its own and revealed new perspectives. This was particularly true in the case of numerical symbolism, which Augustine had termed a "great mystery"; Pythagorean thought had exercised its influence on him and the entire culture of antiquity. People believed that the numbers in the Bible had meanings perceptible "only through the eyes of faith." Thus, the number one denoted perfection, and two impurity (Jerome); or the odd numbers were masculine, and the even were feminine (Macrobius); and so forth.[52] Three (the Trinity), five (books of Moses), seven (days of creation), and ten (commandments) were favored as "holy numbers," but the number four could also evoke various devotional associations: the Evangelists, the rivers of paradise, the four corners of the world—a list of such correspondences based on the number four covers five printed pages in Henri de Lubac's study on exegesis. There is even a comprehensive lexicon containing medieval interpretations of numbers.[53] Here we find echoes of something encountered also in the field of ethnology, the "mythical hypostatization" of numbers by which each integer is exalted to "its own individual nature and power."[54]

Since anyone could contribute to the established corpus of interpretations, the body of allegorical literature grew endlessly, and efforts were made to organize this mass of material, if only nominally, into some sort of order. There was the *sensus historicus* (the historical, or what we might call the factual, sense) and the allegorical one; additionally, the "moral" sense gained recognition as an independent level of meaning, as did the "anagogic" sense, which directed the monk to supranatural heights. Thus,

Jerusalem was (historically speaking) a city, (allegorically) the church, (morally) the soul, and (anagogically) heaven. According to Thomas Aquinas, the words "Let there be light!" referred to actual (historical) light, to the (allegorical) birth of Christ in the church, to the (moral) inspiration or enlightenment attained through Christ, as well as to the (anagogic) assumption into the heavenly kingdom.[55] These distinctions were not universally accepted; in the final analysis as many as seven levels of meaning might be proposed by some authors.[56] In such instances, we see how the Scholastic mode of thought was applied to an area that remained beyond its reach.

Over the course of many centuries the process and substance of allegorization had remained much the same. This approach now began to lose its luster, though to be sure it was not altogether abandoned. Biblical commentators increasingly declared that they did not intend to take the allegorical approach—in contrast to most of their predecessors—but to proceed *ad litteram*, that is to say, to ground their interpretation in the actual text and not take flight up to rarefied heights. This shift reflected a general tendency toward clearheaded rationality; it was also a consequence of a higher niveau of education, a newfound interest in nature, and perhaps also a change of heart prompted by missionary activity against the heretics. The latter brought home the inappropriateness of allegorical interpretations in religious disputations, particularly in light of the odd modes of allegorization found among the Cathars. In dealing with the heretics, one had to stick strictly to the Gospel texts. As Joachim of Fiore asserted, "They falsify [the text] by misunderstanding the meaning of the words."[57]

Taking a literal approach to biblical analysis was by this time long overdue, for little progress had been made in this area since Saint Jerome. People allowed the allegorical construct to grow taller and taller without ever bothering to test the weight-bearing capacity of its foundation. Once thinkers—in particular Hugh of Saint-Victor in Paris—reevaluated the importance of the literal sense, the potential existed for establishing a theology based on scholarship, one that would accord an appropriate place to allegory. There was now one body of theological literature for teachers and students, and another for monks and novices—one group striving to systematize exegesis and another attempting to explicate the Bible in terms of its most minute textual elements and relate them to biblical or nonbiblical matters. Both these activities were affected by contemporary opinions and objectives; allegorical exegesis could give rise to observations about church reform and church politics.[58]

Hugh of Saint-Victor wrote: "We read the Holy Scriptures but not the letters therein; we do not bother with the letters; rather, we give instruction in the allegories. If you were, however, to take away the letters, what would then remain of the Holy Scriptures?"[59] And this approach was truly risky, as Otloh of St. Emmeram in Regensburg had already perceived: Since biblical passages were imbued with a deeper meaning, could one even interpret them literally? Were these literal interpretations possibly fictions?[60] The individual who divested Christianity of its "Bible stories" did not merely strip religion of a place in history, but also exiled himself to a void outside Christianity. This void could admit any sort of gnosis and myth.

Conversely, there were risks associated with placing absolute faith in the literal meaning. For example, this approach might lead to an anthropomorphization of God or indeed hostility toward one's corporeal being. The Paris master Amalric of Bena (d. 1206) crossed over into heretical territory with his insistence that Saint Paul's remark "we are members of his body" (Eph. 5:30) be declared an article of faith.[61] He overlooked the fact that a metaphor does not have a literal meaning.

These observations apply primarily to literal exegesis. The Bible may have been replete with mystery, yet these mysteries were expressed as concepts and statements subject to the strictures of language. It would be surprising if the metaphoric element were not present in the biblical texts, alongside the conceptual and abstract one. Concepts often had to be expressed as (mental) images if they were to be understood at all. For example, the first thing that came into people's minds when they thought of the abstract "Church" was the physical church building containing the assembled congregation. Whoever possessed a particularly vivid visual imagination did not need to envisage the Church, but actually saw it. This ability to visualize things could be applied to completely abstract concepts, as we have seen with Hildegard of Bingen: She determined through a vision that God and *divinitas* were not two separate concepts.[62] Monkish spirituality was oriented toward the Bible, and that tradition had to be upheld. Nuns, however, were only minimally bound to that sort of tradition. Their contemplative gaze could transcend the Bible and fix itself upon the entire world.

Yet there were men, like Rupert of Deutz, who also sought to progress in this way from the word to the image—or to a mystical vision beyond exegesis, like Richard of Saint-Victor. For the latter thinker, rational meditation represented the second rung on the ladder of contemplation.[63] The higher one climbed on this ladder, the less important textual exegesis became, and the more receptive one's spirit was to images. This state of mind was granted uneducated nuns and canonesses already at a lower step. In this vein, the abbess Herrad of Landsberg (d. 1195) compiled the *Hortus deliciarum* (The garden of delights) for the devotional edification of her sister canonesses in Odilienberg (in Alsace); this encyclopedic work contained 336 illustrations and many quotes from the Bible and fathers of the church. Its symbolic figures as well as verbal allegories served to promote the reader's devotion. In the twelfth century the conversion of biblical, particularly eschatological, as well as philosophical motifs into graphic images enjoyed widespread popularity.

Hildegard of Bingen had received the same spiritual education as many other nuns. However, she alone possessed the gift of transforming even concepts into images: God's might she portrayed as a mountain, his providence as a mirror. "I write down what I see and hear in a vision. I do not alter the words that I hear; I just repeat them in unpolished Latin."[64] Unlike some learned exegetes, she was not conscious of the literary sources for her visions. Some were complicated utterances shrouded in more or less traditional garb, "configurations of many individual elements from the Bible."[65] For example, she envisaged the Church as a figure with its head ablaze in brilliant light; this denoted "the establishment of the sacerdotal order by the apostles." The chest and abdomen shimmered in a bright reddish light, which denoted the virginity of the monks and nuns. The bottom half of the figure was hidden in a white cloud, "to suggest that the end of the world was yet to come"; this part referred to the laity and procreation.[66] When it came to medical matters, Hildegard wrote frankly of forces and humors in the classical vein, but she always observed the boundaries associated with devotional pieces.

Nature could be depicted in the form of a goddess, as the Chartrians had, or viewed as an open book that invited decipherment, somewhat as the Bible was open to inquiry. Women like Hildegard of Bingen or Herrad of Landsberg did not, of course, conceive of themselves as researchers; rather, they dedicated their whole being to religious edification and discerning the glory of God manifest in his creation. The two activities were intrinsically connected, for the didactic poems infused with natural philosophy contained a measure of spiritual devotion, and Hildegard did engage in "research" when she gazed upon the cosmos and mankind. Many of her images express some of the visual power of the religious myth.

Catharism, Platonism, and religious spirituality were distinct phenomena. They did not define the twelfth century; indeed they are only associated with relatively small groups of individuals. That these modes of thought could coexist side by side, however, testifies to the unique niche occupied by this century in European history. Here are the first rumblings of a sea change to come; they were inwardly oriented and would in times to come reverberate in the external world as well. We have yet to treat of the most important of these changes, the shift to a more rigorous rationality.

Part Three

The Realm of Reason

9

Ratio and *Auctoritas*

We are like "dwarfs perched on the shoulders of giants. . . . We see more and farther than our predecessors, not because we have keener vision or greater height, but because we are lifted up and borne aloft on their gigantic stature."[1] Thus did Bernard of Chartres (d. 1124), himself a proponent of Platonism and future teacher of Gilbert of Poitiers, describe the accomplishments of contemporary thought. William of Conches was acquainted with this expression and cited it in connection with an observation by the grammarian Priscian about the practitioners of his art: "The younger they are, the more perspicacious."[2] Alexander Neckam (d. 1217) noted the similarity between this simile and the fable of the sparrow that is lifted into the air, clinging to the feathers of the eagle, and then, letting go, soars aloft to even greater heights.[3]

Various interpretations have been proposed for these statements, for example, that they were avowals of modernity or homages to an illustrious past, proud expressions of modesty and proofs of humility.[4] Above all, these statements reflect the view people had of the external world, a view encompassing far-off objects that the ancients could not yet perceive. Bernard of Chartres made his remark during the 1120s, at a point when the direction in which scholarship would take off in subsequent generations could hardly have been foreseen. What he did anticipate was that learning would take flight, propelled not by the denigration of the philosophers of yore, but rather by a respect for one's lofty predecessors, without whom scholarship would never have gotten off the ground.

Who were these "giants" of the past? Certainly Plato, perhaps Aristotle, most probably Augustine and other fathers of the church as well. Indeed, even later on, few perceived the gulf between patristic thought and modern Platonism, between tradition and renewal. What distinguished the "dwarfs" from the ancients was not the breadth of their knowledge, but rather their "perspicacity." This ushered in the age of Scholasticism.

William of Conches opened his reference to the simile with these words: "We do not, then, know more than the ancients, but we perceive [*perspicimus*] more. We possess their works plus a natural acumen that allows us to recognize new things."[5] The words *naturale ingenium* [natural acumen] do not refer to ingeniousness, but primarily only to one's "inborn nature," and then secondarily to the natural acumen of an individual. While William's remarks should not be overly interpreted, they do spell out Scholasticism's true underpinning: not an amalgamation of techniques, drawn for the most part from dialectic, but rather the requisite intellectual ability to employ those techniques effectively.

In 1113 the young Abelard, who was most likely a contemporary of Bernard of Chartres, came to Laon seeking instruction from a teacher whom he subsequently compared to a desiccated tree. Abelard's colleagues challenged him to do better, and so he decided to prepare a theology lecture for a select audience. They tried to dissuade him from scheduling the lecture for the next day; Abelard retorted angrily that he did not customarily meet with success by practicing (*per usum*), but rather by relying on his *ingenium*,[6] which in this case might be translated as "intelligence." And in fact, he won his bet.

A young student had to be exceedingly self-confident to wager that he could force his way into the ranks of the theology faculty with such alacrity. It was even more audacious, in light of the accomplishments of Plato and the fathers of the church, to intimate that one could achieve even more than they, as Bernard of Chartres did only a short time later. He was not proposing that something entirely new supersede what had up until then been generally regarded as a sacred legacy of the past, but he nevertheless desired to scrutinize and revise that inheritance.

In the work *On the Errors of William of Conches*, William of Saint-Thierry declared himself guided by the following principle: "Whatsoever we may say, we wish to say in conformance with the fathers of the church [*ex Patribus*], our teachers and guides, following in their footsteps and not pressing ahead on our own." When it came to matters of faith, it was appropriate to "disregard human reason or to force it like a captive to serve faith, to acknowledge the boundaries of faith drawn by our fathers and not to overstep them in any way."[7] Elsewhere, William drew the following distinction between knowledge and faith: The former is gathered by means of the intellect, while the latter rests exclusively on authority.[8] There was no middle ground here, and William did not delineate further what he meant by authority. It referred not so much to the authority vested in church teachings as to an aggregate of written authorities: the Bible and the fathers of the church.

Strict adherence to this principle precluded the expression of one's personal opinion, or meant that it had to be veiled in authoritative quotations. Like the disputations with the Cathars, theological debates were reduced to contests over who could cite more authorities in support of one's thesis. Thus, at the consistory held in Rheims in 1148, Gilbert of Poitiers was obliged to defend himself against adversaries who had brought before the assembly a single vellum sheet with *auctoritates* [authorities] contradicting his theses. Gilbert's clerical supporters, however—as both Otto of Freising and Geoffrey of Auxerre observed—dragged out massive volumes from which they proceeded to recite *auctoritates* supportive of their views.[9] In terms of methodology, that was surely the correct tack to take; however, it scarcely suited their practical objective. As the day wore on, the bored pope suspended the reading and addressed himself directly to Gilbert.

Therefore, one had to search through the very extensive biblical and patristic literature for material consonant with one's own opinion and contrary to the theses of one's opponent. With luck, help could be garnered from florilegia, collections of *sententiae* (sentences or opinions), and other similar works. Since it was impossible to prevent contradictions from cropping up when drawing propositions out of context, the foundation was laid for endless debates. Later on, we will discuss the attempts made by Abelard and others to devise a methodology for eliminating contradictions.

The works deemed authoritative were not catalogued; very broadly speaking, the works of the apostles and the prophets would be foremost in rank and then secondarily all the works "recognized" by the church, irrespective of their authorship—as, for example, in the case of the so-called Book of Job.[10] This represented quite an extensive range of works with which to expand one's horizons. Most of the works by the Greek fathers of the church that were available in translation tended to be devotional in nature. Some were biblical commentaries and historical overviews, whereas Greek polemical writings against heresy were only rarely copied and thus rarely translated as well.[11] In their disputes, the students of Gilbert of Poitiers availed themselves of a massive body of authoritative material hitherto unknown in the West. Hugh of Honau employed the same phraseology to describe these quarrels as that used by Gregory of Nazianzus against the Arians—hence, people envisioned themselves as the latest representatives of the infallible church, upholding the faith against adversaries who did not have all the theologians' tools at their disposal.

Texts that served as study aids, like the increasingly numerous glosses, were not considered authoritative. From a practical point of view, these auxiliary texts soon became indispensable, particularly those that were compilations of excerpts organized in some fashion by categories, a format that facilitated the user's access to the material. Arranging the excerpts in this way stripped them of their contextual significance, and hence much of what had lent the source its authoritative character. Abelard thus wrote: "It is often easy to resolve points of controversy when we can demonstrate that the same words have been used by various authors with various meanings."[12] Given his interest in linguistic logic, Abelard had a broader perspective than others. The texts authored by the "giants" of the past were not reiterated out of timorous reverence, but rather subjected to scrutiny according to the rules of scholarship.

It has been shown that during the tenth, eleventh, and twelfth centuries the holdings of Western libraries were "overwhelmingly patristic in nature"; by the end of this period, however, a sea change had taken place, and copies of patristic writings were rarely made anymore.[13] While the age of the *auctoritates* had not yet run its course, they now nowhere dominated the field. Authors like Manegold of Lautenbach and Rupert of Deutz cited the Bible almost exclusively, without any reference to the fathers of the church.[14] Alongside such rigorists, there were modernists, who had little interest in the literature of the past and preferred to consult the works of contemporaries. Writers in Germany still produced commentaries on entire ancient texts,[15] while in the West—reflecting the influence of the advanced schools—the preponderance of authors were already compiling collections of *sententiae* with analytical commentaries.

Thomas Aquinas finally verbalized an idea that must long since have occurred to many: "Authority is the weakest source of proof." If a teacher resolves a question by citing "authorities only" without providing his own commentary, then "the student will be convinced that the thing is so, but he will have acquired no knowledge or understanding and he will go away with an empty mind."[16] This remark gave full vent to the inward detachment from the illustrious past and to a new self-assurance born of scholarly activity. Now thinkers acknowledged the existence of two equally worthy domains: the *authentica* (the Bible, the fathers) and the *magistralia* (works of contemporary scholars).[17]

Anselm of Laon appears to have been the first to quote both types of evidence concurrently and indeed in a reference work, the *Glossa ordinaria*.[18] He was the teacher whom Abelard had described so disparagingly, yet all the same he was one of the most respected men of his times, a former student of Anselm of Canterbury. That teacher, in turn, had presumed to author two important works, the *Monologion* and the *Proslogion*, without citing authorities; only in the prologue to the former did he note briefly that his views (about the Trinity and Christology) coincided with those of Augustine. All of his other remarks, he wrote, were necessitated by reason (*rationis necessitas*).[19] His use of the word *ratio* in contradistinction to making a case on the basis of past authorities was still quite striking in 1076, all the more so since this work was in all respects the product of a monastic and contemplative environment. He had written the work, Anselm explained, because his students wished to have available as reading material the remarks that he had made about the Trinity during their periods of meditation.

Even at a time when monastic spirituality played such a great role above all on a personal level, one had to be careful about expressing subjective opinions. It was necessary to take refuge in a higher power, be it an authoritative work, reason, or even divine inspiration. Thus, Rupert of Deutz lent authority to his commentary on the Song of Songs by referring to his visions.[20] Even a man such as he, however, could in other circumstances place his trust in personal acumen—within the framework of unerring reason, of course—as in the case of his commentary on the Apocalypse, which he cultivated "using the plowshare of my own acumen [*proprii ingenii vomere*]."[21]

In addition to the growing self-assurance felt by scholars, another factor that contributed to the declining respect for the Christian authorities was the broadening of intellectual horizons brought about by the growing familiarity with the ancient philosophers. Hugh of Honau, a laudable builder of bridges between the West and East, pointed out that all areas of learning (*disciplinae*) known to the Latin West were derived from Greek sources; he sought to "resolve our disagreements . . . by consulting the irrefutable authorities of the Greek sages."[22] He was referring above all to Christian authors like Cyril of Alexandria and John Damascene.[23] Other disputants, however, had no scruples about using the opinions of pagan philosophers as *auctoritates*.[24]

Bernard Silvestris even included poets—pagan and ancient Christians— among the *auctores*, those men possessing authority, since "the poets are the ones who introduce us to philosophy."[25] No one raised an eyebrow at this, for people already imputed to Virgil's works a deeper, Christian meaning and had a penchant for quoting Ovid out of a high regard for the moralistic content of his poems.[26] Of course, there were those who heartily despised the pagan poets and philosophers.

As for the philosophers, in people's view their forte consisted in their use of reason as the guiding principle of knowledge. Abelard attacked certain unsophisticated individuals who wished to declare "us enemies of the holy faith immediately upon seeing us borrow examples or analogies from philosophical works for the purpose of clarifying what we ourselves have in mind."[27] Faith was a matter of the heart and was to remain so even in light of the new appreciation for reason and rational methodology. According to Peter the Venerable, authority was fine for the devout (or monks, the *religiosi*), while reason was for the curious (*curiosi*).[28] It cannot be denied that those dwarfs gazing out into the distance from their perches on the giants' shoulders were motivated by a thirst for knowledge and hence by a form of curiosity.

Abelard vehemently protested against using *auctoritates* exclusively: That was appropriate only vis-à-vis individuals who lacked reason and were therefore not susceptible to rational arguments.[29] If we were to rely primarily on authorities, whose propositions were at some remove from reality and based on opinion rather than truth, then we would no longer be philosophers[30]—a remark bound to raise eyebrows, and accordingly placed by Abelard in the mouth of a non-Christian. Moreover, did not the method of quoting authorities lead to error? If all scholars would quote the same authors, then there might not be so many different doctrinal views (*fidei secte*). However, each scholar selected the authors he would trust as his guides. Ergo, the speaker concluded, "Rational arguments take precedence over authorities!"[31]

Those are the words of a pagan philosopher. What Abelard had in mind here was a diminution of the role accorded *auctoritates* in disputes, not the establishment of a rational Christianity beyond the reach of the Greek and Latin creeds, whose proponents had indeed locked horns over the authority of synodal decrees. During the course of the twelfth century, people attacked the *auctoritates* in even stronger words. Alan of Lille, for example, made that famous comment that the authorities had noses made of wax: Since they could be twisted this way and that to accommodate any view, it was better to hearken back to rational arguments.[32] As a precaution, he used the device of attributing this view to a pagan philosopher; it is quite likely, however, that in the course of writing his work against the heretics, Alan was reminded of the manner in which they interpreted biblical texts. Martin Grabmann contended that in this passage Alan was taking aim not at the *auctoritates* themselves, but merely at the way in which they were employed.[33] Were that the case, Alan would surely have said so more clearly. As a Platonist he sided with the philosophers and may have derived the idea for that image from a passage by "Plato" (Chalcidius). In Chalcidius's rendering of the *Timaeus*, primordial matter is likened to pliable wax, which can be molded into various shapes.[34] A simile like that was more likely to strike students as an academic witticism than to make them think of primordial matter, a circumstance that hardly bolstered respect for the authorities. Adelard of Bath even referred to them as "a trap."[35]

Conservative thinkers were of the opinion that the traps had been set by the dialecticians, by those modern theologians who pioneered, along with rationality, the dialectical method of drawing conclusions. As a consequence, individuals like Manegold of Lautenbach have been termed "antidialecticians," which does not address the real issue. They were conservatives, unsuccessful in their efforts to change theological learning back into a devout study of the Bible. However, at the end of the twelfth century there were still individuals like Garnier of Rochefort, who complained that the people he dealt with were (pagan) philosophers rather than theologians, "for if they were truly theologians, then they would agree with the evidence proffered by saints rather than by human reason, and they would comprehend that faith based on human reason is without merit."[36] This latter contention dates back to Gregory the Great.

Since *ratio* and *auctoritates* had to coexist, in the long run the rivalry between them boiled down to a question of standing. For example, a writer drawing upon the fathers of the church might take the position that those authorities had precedence over reason, even though both served to corroborate an opinion.[37] By citing Augustine's contention that "Authority is to take precedence over reason," even Abelard nominally acknowledged that to be true. He wrote that rational arguments that required amplification by authoritative sources were weak.[38] "In any disputation the giving of a reason is firmer than a display of authority"[39]—Abelard was not the only one to subscribe to this maxim. Stepping out of the giants' shadows, people began to think for themselves, rather than reiterate someone else's thoughts.

Still, conservative thinkers of this era availed themselves of the classical methodology, for the ensuing conclusions seemed sounder than those obtained empirically: They placed their trust in venerable axioms held to be self-evident, rather than in what were mere opinions derived from the observation of one's surroundings.[40] Their traditional view of the world of course delimited this approach. Furthermore, since revelation also had to be taken into account, "a systematic belief in reason as the sole method for uncovering the truth" could not take root.[41] Explanations adduced by human reason (*rationes humanae*) paled beside mysteries. And we have already noted the comment by Gregory the Great that faith based on human reason lacked religious merit.[42]

It was not possible for Abelard to dispute that pronouncement. He therefore questioned the motives of those who were in the habit of quoting it: They did so, he maintained, because they were incapable of discussing matters of faith. However, the placement of a ban on discussion would enable an idolater to contend that a piece of wood or a stone was his god.[43] Abelard put these words into the mouth of a pagan philosopher and thus stopped short of propounding a view that even Bernard of Clairvaux upheld: Rational doubts about Christian doctrine, like those stirred up by the Cathars, were to be met with rational arguments.

Riding at faith's anchor, so to speak, made it possible to net rational insights—therein lay the meaning of the phrase *credo, ut intelligam* [I believe so that I may understand]. Anselm of Canterbury made this statement not to counter theologians like Abelard, who upheld the coexistence of faith and learning, but rather to "counter those who do not wish to believe whatever they do not understand and who ridicule believers."[44] And such individuals did exist. Abelard himself had encountered students who said that "nothing could be believed unless it was first understood, and that it was absurd for anyone to preach to others what neither he nor those he taught could grasp with the understanding: The Lord himself had criticized such 'blind guides of blind men.'"[45] This contention was born of outright skepticism, and was not the product of some rationalistic system, or even of efforts by men like Abelard to limit the number of mysteries to an essential few. Occasionally, such men were thrown into the same pot as the skeptics. Thus, William of Saint-Thierry was attacking both sorts when he wrote: "Whosoever wishes to know everything and to believe nothing destroys . . . faith."[46] Anselm of Canterbury advocated a moderate stance in this respect; he wanted his *Proslogion* to bear the title "Faith Seeking Understanding." His *Monologion* had already been intended as "an example of a meditation on the [rational] grounds of faith."[47]

Here, faith and learning represented two harmonious spheres. The early Scholastics, who used rational methods to study theology, were suffused by a spirit of optimism born of the conviction that nothing was able to shake faith—a fundamental stance that differs markedly from true rationalism, which seeks a rational substantiation for everything. Anselm's faith quested after an understanding illuminated by God and trained in the contemplation of divine things, and even Abelard emphasized that reason had a divine origin in the "highest wisdom," the Logos.[48] The spirituality cultivated over the course of many centuries furnished the bridge to a knowledge consonant with reason. According to Hugh of Saint-Victor, "Whenever a creature attains knowledge, that knowing [occurs] within God, [and it represents] a participation in the wisdom of the eternal Logos." Or, "God is God in that he is knowing"—an audacious remark.[49]

Thus, it was possible to speak of a *fides rationabilis* [faith accessible to reason] without its being *rationalis* [subjugated to reason].[50] According to William of Conches, theology was *ratio de divinis*, the explanation of divine things, for *"theos* means God [and] *logos* reason [*ratio*]"—Augustine had already referred to God as the principle of reason and the source of all rational thought.[51] One could always cite the Epistle to the Romans, which contains a reference to *ratio fidei* (Rom. 12:6–7), although there the words originally had a different meaning: The passage refers to the multifarious gifts of God, as, for example, "prophecy, in proportion (*secundum rationem*) to our faith." This biblical phrase was already a favorite with Berengar of Tours and his contemporaries.[52]

This ratiocinative mode of thought emerged slowly from the shadows of spirituality. There now arose a speculative theology, at home ever less in the monastic community and ever more in the academic one. Speculative theology could, to be sure, continue to serve spiritual ends. The same applied to ethics, which was now also construed as an academic subject. However, the literary output in both those areas often lacked that sublimity of expression which lent edifying texts their true efficacy. Linguistic logic prevailed when the written word was put to the service of rationality. Probing for causal connections increasingly superseded symbolism and allegorization. Man is "to probe into the reason for his creation, and he will see how deserving of love his creator is."[53]

In the *Timaeus* (28 A), Plato wrote that nothing occurred without a cause. And apprehending causes, Chalcidius added, was the task of reason.[54] To a substantial degree, it was the study of classical philosophers that promoted this shift in interest to issues of causality and finality vis-à-vis earthly phenomena. However, this way of thinking seems to have had its actual roots in a new attitude that acceded more than before to the claims of reason. Whoever did not make this intellectual transition completely was open to vehement censure by the innovators. Overcome by emotion, William of Conches railed against his traditionalistic colleagues: "Wretches! Could anything be more wretched than saying that something exists because God *can* make [or effectuate] it, and yet not . . . having any reason why it should exist, or showing the usefulness for which it would exist?"[55] In accordance with the contemporaneous scholarly standards, a cause had to be "necessary," in other words, valid at all times and in all instances. Moreover, each chain of causality was thought to lead back to God. As a consequence, nothing could occur by chance. Abelard pointed this out,[56] and reason became the keystone of his school of thought. It was said that God could not act and had no potency without reason.[57] Alan of Lille depicted reason as a goddess; she possessed a mirror in which she beheld the chain of causal connections and peered into the "fount of things."[58]

The high value placed on reason as the fundamental principle underlying the cosmos enabled thinkers to integrate a plethora of phenomena
and, as one might say, "strip" them of their numinous quality. Whereas the
primitive mind considered the miracle to be a commonplace occurrence,
in a world governed by reason the miracle was granted at most a
peripheral role. In that framework, God was the first cause of all things;
the intermediate causes (*causae secundae*) were linked together into a chain
in compliance with the rules of reason. As a result, direct intervention by
God could now only be warranted in the rarest of instances. The Jews,
Abelard hence wrote, had needed to see Christ's miracles, but ever since
then there had for the most part been a dearth of miraculous signs, and
words must be used to persuade people—with rational individuals
conceding that words were more powerful than miracles, which might
moreover be the devil's handiwork.[59] Even this subject was now "ratio-
nalized": Demons, it was said, harnessed the natural forces possessed by
stones, plants, etc., and they knew just as much about the operation of
these forces as they did about that of spiritual ones.[60]

The central role now played by reason served above all to transform its
relationship to the *auctoritates*. It was not possible, of course, simply to
exclude the latter, for the concerns and gist of Christian doctrine were
contained in these texts, in spite of the methodological weaknesses to
which they were subject and of which rational theologians were ever more
keenly aware: This corpus contained discordant propositions that scholars
sought to reduce to some common denominator by means of a new
methodology. Taking a historical perspective, the practitioners of the new
method attempted to gain an understanding of a text in terms of its milieu.
However, it was philology that above all provided the means for textual
interpretation. This was true even for the Bible. Syllogisms lurk in that
text, Honorius Augustodunensis wrote, like fish in water.[61] The Holy
Scriptures no longer enjoyed a God-given immunity, and they became
subject to scrutiny. Auxiliary tracts were soon available: Alan of Lille
authored the *Regulae theologicae* [The principles of theology], a compendium of grammatical, arithmetical, and dialectical axioms transmuted
into maxims applicable to the field of theology.[62] In their scrutiny, however, scholars did not lose sight of the fact that the concepts and methods
devised for the "liberal arts" were not applicable to propositions about
God; nevertheless, they harbored the hope that in light of its rational
quality, this mode of thinking was not too far off the mark vis-à-vis those
aspects of the divine secret expressible in words. Above all, it enabled
them to juxtapose things of this world with those of the divine one.[63]

Seen from a modern perspective, it may appear that little was to be
gained from such biblical research; yet while some findings may seem

obvious to us, thinkers in those days derived pleasure from the fact that the obvious was substantiated by scholarship: that the words "the Holy Spirit," for example, constituted a descriptive phrase known rhetorically as a *circumlocutio*; that mathematical theorems more than other sorts of concepts were transferable to God; that this translation could take place only in the abstract and not in actuality; etc. This sort of thing puts into stark relief the fatal flaw of scholarly activity, the perception that it was an end in itself.

This rather rough-and-ready attack on authority *in toto* did not succeed in elevating theology to a higher scholarly niveau. That achievement was more closely tied to something not originally associated with theology, even though it would later achieve renown as the *"sic-et-non* [pro-and-con] method"*: It was a methodology designed to forge compromises between seemingly antithetical propositions. The appellation is taken from the title of one of Abelard's books, but he did not in any way formulate the methodology, which hailed from far outside theology.

Given the profusion of biblical, patristic, and canonical works, people inevitably stumbled across contradictions in the sources. During periods of piety and self-assurance, those were noted with complete equanimity. In a work written at the beginning of the twelfth century, Gilbert Crispin has a Christian speaker point out that in Gen. 1:29 God freely bestowed the fruits of the trees upon humans for food, while in Gen. 2:17 he revoked this sanction for the tree standing at the center of paradise. "One can accept this only [by deeming it] as a mystery," the Christian contended. For his part, the Jew did not feel driven to give this any thought: God has commanded and man must obey.[64] When confronted by such discrepancies, Christians also customarily fell back on God's will. Contrariwise, a jurist would have been equipped to settle the inconsistency by pointing out that it was possible to issue first a broad authorization and then an exemption thereto—hence, that the *praeceptio generalis* [general rule] did not logically contradict the *praeceptio particularis* [particular rule].

Dialectic was known as the art of disputation; here, it became the art of reconciliation. Questions of canon law in particular called out for resolutions promoting accord. Canonical determinations varied greatly in age and origin; one merely extracted those texts that corresponded to one's own standpoint. As individuals plumbed this corpus with ever greater frequency, they became increasingly dissatisfied with the poor manuscript tradition. This gave rise to methods that would set the standard for the field of rational theology as well.

When it came to propositions expressed in pictorial terms and imbued with symbolic meaning, the tools of dialectic were of little use; however, when it came to clearly elucidated concepts, preferably those expressed in binary terms—pro (*sic*) and con (*non*)—they proved very beneficial. Platonists accordingly had less truck with dialectic than did Aristotelians. Congruent with the intellectual needs of the age, a new group of relevant works by Aristotle (from his *Organon*) became available in the late twelfth century, greatly enriching proficiency in dialectic. Arab writers also played an influential, if long underestimated, role in this process. Islamic dialectic began to flourish in the ninth century, and "the *sic-et-non* method has its natural habitat in Muslim religious law."[65] One might contend that in both cultural milieux, similar conditions traceable back to their common classical heritage gave rise to similar intellectual constructs. Islamic jurists might very well have been capable of tapping that heritage sooner than the Western canonists.[66]

Every step forward may also be viewed as a step backward, and hence Martin Grabmann deplored the fact that "linguistic logic and hairsplitting were admitted to the shrine of theological learning." Furthermore, he contended, "The submergence of the self within the great nexus of religious mysteries, as loved and practiced by Anselm [of Canterbury], was incompatible with quarrels based on dialectics."[67] Yet already in Anselm's day, people had concerns besides spiritual meditation, like church politics and other pressing matters upon which dialectic had a reconciliatory and not factious effect. That the disputing parties often resorted to issuing reciprocal excommunications had especially served to complicate the situation. Against this backdrop, a work written after 1084 tackled the problem by proposing "rules of reconciliation," which augured the future. These rules used rational and historical tools to reconcile contradictory canonical determinations and patristic citations.[68]

For example, if two canonical decrees seemed irreconcilable, then it was important to fathom not merely the individual texts, but also their historical background and the circumstances behind their composition. To gain this understanding, it might be necessary to consider who had been involved in drafting the relevant passages, as well as when and where they had been issued. For what reason and under what circumstances was the determination made? How long was it to be in force, provisionally or permanently? There was a catalogue of issues to consider, akin to those commonly posed by historians in later centuries. If the contradictions were irreconcilable, then the authenticity of the texts had to be questioned, since, for example, they may have been imperfectly transcribed. And so, scholars embarked upon the difficult task of comprehending the "proper text."

In its essential features, this methodology had been employed for quite some time. It had proved indispensable to authors like Augustine, who desired to scrutinize controversial issues thoroughly without falling back on God's will. Even before the Investiture Contest, this methodology informed the compilation of canon laws by Burchard of Worms.[69] As the church became an increasingly legalistic institution, the need for an authoritative text became all the more pronounced, just as had once been true for the Bible. With so much in flux, people craved a secure harbor.

A firm methodological underpinning was also requisite to tackling controversial theological tenets. In addition to the Trinity, Christology, and Mariology, another major area of controversy was Eucharistic doctrine, which concerned each and every Christian. Gerbert of Aurillac had already undertaken a comparison of disputed teachings regarding the presence or nonpresence of Christ's real body in the Eucharist and had declared the contradictions between them an illusory problem.[70] The whole issue hinged on one's interpretation of a few words spoken by Christ; merely engaging in interpretation implied reliance on a general theory of meaning and imagery, and on dialectic again, of course. Often regarded as dead weight in monastic education, the classical liberal arts gained unexpected currency.

As had proved true with canon law, so too with theology: People did not use their scholarly activity as a battering ram against established thought, but rather as a beneficial tool, and consequently learning was accorded greater respect. Abelard played a central role in this area, too, by writing a book on logic for beginners (*Logica "Ingredientibus"*) and his most famous work, *Sic et non*.[71] In the latter, Abelard juxtaposed 158 contradictory viewpoints, the majority of which hailed from the fathers of the church, though a limited number came from legal sources, including Justinian. While Abelard was able to build upon prior works of this ilk, his composition ranks as a great accomplishment. He may not have held the authorities in high regard, yet he did not wish to subject them to ridicule when pointing out their weaknesses. He did not voice his own opinions, but in the famous prologue to the work he did offer hints on how one might resolve such contradictions. Those hints resemble the "rules of reconciliation" formulated by the jurists.

This compendium was meant to serve as an exercise book for young students and thus dispensed with any organizational principle. The entries were quite diverse: "That Adam and Eve were created mortal, and that they were not" (no. 51); that one was permitted to tell a lie, "and that one was not" (no. 154); "that one should not celebrate mass before the third hour of the day [approximately 9:00 A.M.], except on Christmas, and the contrary opinion [*et contra*]" (no. 121). The discrepancies found among biblical texts were more worrisome, but in these cases one's scope was strictly limited: The author, Abelard wrote, was infallible, but the codex from which the biblical quotations were taken might very well contain errors, or the translator of the text (from Hebrew or Greek) might have made a mistake, "or you do not grasp the material." In the case of more recent texts, the reader should examine whether the pronouncements are substantiated by canonical writings; otherwise, the reader may draw his own conclusions: "Should he not like [the remark] or not wish to lend it credence, he will not be subject to reproach." Should discrepancies persist, one will of course cede to the more eminent authority, without consequently labeling the fathers of the church prevaricators. For even the prophets and apostles were not entirely free of error—an attention-grabbing remark for which Abelard might, however, have provided evidence.

Abelard was not opening a crucial new chapter to the conflict between *auctoritas* and *ratio* here, for he did not challenge the essential function of the authorities. All the same, it was permissible to disagree with them. His conservative contemporaries reacted with outrage. William of Saint-Thierry viewed this stance as a threat to the very crux of Christianity: Abelard, he charged, was taking the same innovative approach to the field of scriptural exegesis as he was accustomed to taking vis-à-vis dialectic, behaving like a critic, not a student of faith; an emendator, not an imitator (of Christ).[72] Abelard's insistence that a text's *auctoritas* was related to how accurately it had been transmitted contrasted with the approach commonly taken since late antiquity toward compendia of passages from ecclesiastical authors.[73] In disputes the "emendators" could always accuse their opponents of employing quotes in an unscholarly manner. Whoever did not comply with the new rules could be charged with irrational or—what is deemed most horrible in learned circles—unscholarly behavior.

10

The Intellectual Pursuits of the Early Scholastics

 Following his death at Cîteaux in 1202, Alan of Lille was memorialized there with these words: "Alan suffered from goiter and was short of stature, but he knew everything a person could know." A second epitaph also emphasized that he "knew all that there was to know."[1] Even as the age we have labeled early Scholasticism drew to a close, there were monks who did not perceive a gap between the education of the day and its possible scope, between explored knowledge and knowledge open to exploration, and who were satisfied with the instruction they had received in school. This may have been a function of their opinion that man's cognitive abilities had been undermined by the original sin, for Adam had sought to know what he was not vouchsafed to know.[2] On the contrary, Hugh of Honau contended, the sin lay in his disobedience; ever since then, humans have had to struggle to recover the knowledge they lost in punishment. Of course, there existed feebleminded individuals and those born with physical handicaps, like the insane, the blind, etc. According to Hugh, such people were as insuperably ignorant as small children, and there also were elderly individuals who suffered from senility: One scholar named Simon of Tournai had lost his memory entirely; others no longer even recognized the letters of the alphabet.

Whoever lacks reason, Hugh maintained, is not compelled to know. He may be ignorant, but he is not an ignoramus. Others do not know what they ought; they have negligently forsaken their duty to know—as, for example, in the case of drunkards—or they suffer from an "error of human weakness," either hating to study, or finding it boring, or preferring to do other things. In short, whoever falls into this category, thus opposing or shunning study, is a wicked person.[3]

Since time immemorial, Christians have purported to know what was good and what was evil. Around 1180 Hugh of Honau undertook to expand the list of vices in the course of a polemical attack against ignorant clergymen who held themselves aloof from the modern educational system. The positive aspect to Hugh's viewpoint had already been noted two generations earlier by Hugh of Saint-Victor: "Striving after knowledge is truly a good of the soul. By nature it is inherent to every soul."[4] These words open one of the canon's lectures on theology. The observation was not self-evident, and its significance heralded future developments. Beginning with Augustine, the fathers of the church had drawn a distinction between *scientia*—knowledge, or learning—and *sapientia*, or wisdom. *Scientia* denoted the comprehension of corporeal and other transient, mutable things inherent to earthly life. *Sapientia* signified the apprehension or contemplation of eternal truths. It focused on the One, whereas learning involved analyzing the temporal objects under investigation.[5]

Knowledge was therefore a matter of secondary importance, a stance adopted by Hugh of Saint-Victor. The school of thought associated with Gilbert of Poitiers, on the other hand, subscribed to a different view: Knowledge (or learning) apprehends objects by means of reason, while wisdom is nonrational divine love. "What we apprehend by the latter we call 'believing,' not 'knowing.'"[6] Thus, it was possible to apprehend theological matters rationally, and there was a "learning" about God.

Assigning wisdom to the sphere of faith flew in the face of the classical views that Thierry of Chartres encountered in Boethius's works: "Philosophy is . . . the love of wisdom; wisdom is the consummate apprehension of the true nature of existent objects. . . . Thus, no one other than the philosopher possesses wisdom."[7] The word *scientia* had not yet assumed the full range of meanings associated with the concept of "learning" today. Philosophy reigned as the queen of "truth consummately apprehended"; indeed her very name meant "love of wisdom." From the ninth century onward, she again took on the trappings furnished her by Boethius. In one hand she grasped a scepter, in the other a book or books; her accouterments later came to include a crown.[8] Philosophy was the queen not just of knowledge, but of the Christian virtues as well. As Cyprian had written: "We [Christians] are philosophers by means of deeds, not words!"[9] But this did not offset the lady's pagan origin. According to Otto of Freising, Bernard of Clairvaux abhorred those masters (*magistri*) who placed all too much trust in "worldly wisdom."[10]

Vis-à-vis the love of wisdom, this newly awakened love of learning made only gradual headway. One proponent made the point that humans strove innately to apprehend and that God himself apportioned apprehension, since he was after all the "spirit of learning" (*spiritus scientiae*).[11] Even profane knowledge had theological relevance. In amassing knowledge, it made no difference whether one expropriated the insights of an earlier time or exerted oneself to elaborate upon them, hence, to engage in research. Such efforts had always been made, but they now acquired justification. Admittedly, up until now people had had no pressing need to justify their research, for in most cases what they had produced was in response to particular issues of their day, relating above all to controversial theological doctrines; engaging in research had not been the expression of a fundamental attitude. From the close of the eleventh century on, however, individuals began to take a broader view of that legacy, and "innovators"[12] assumed their place alongside the upholders of traditional thought. What we must not lose sight of, however, is that up into the third decade of the twelfth century these innovators constituted a minority in conjunction with the traditionalists. The term "early Scholasticism" is meaningful only if we keep this qualification in mind.

We can grasp only imperfectly the inner attitude that led to the important intellectual strides made by the early Scholastics and the favorable external circumstances that contributed thereto. Among the latter was an increased exposure to Greek patristic sources and to classical philosophy, which was fostered by the Western orientation evidenced during the reign of Emperor Manuel I Comnenos (1143–80). The religious schism between the Eastern and Western churches had no effect upon the study of the Greek *auctores* of yore; individuals continued to translate those portions of the corpus relevant to their own speculative theology and to use them as a springboard for their own original notions.

One such transmitter was Hugh of Honau, deacon palatine to Frederick Barbarossa and a student of Gilbert of Poitiers. Twice he visited Constantinople, where he expressed his opposition to those in the West who viewed his activities with suspicion: "We do not adjudge anyone a heretic for propounding something new in his writings or teachings, but rather for deviating from the proper way to comprehend the meaning of something."[13] William of Saint-Thierry, who denounced proponents of innovation to Bernard of Clairvaux, also admitted as much,[14] yet he concluded with this quote from Saint Paul (Gal. 1:8): "But even if we, or an angel from heaven, should preach to you a gospel contrary to that which we preached to you, let him be accursed." Admittedly, not even William could have had a true return to biblical fundamentalism in mind here. Like most conservatives, he expressed views on matters of speculative theology, particularly the doctrine on the Trinity, that Paul had not at all addressed in his writings.

During previous ages, like the ninth century, selected doctrinal issues would be debated within a small circle of theologians who did not in the process attract a flock of students. Now such disputations reverberated more widely, and divine matters were held in even less reverence. Peter Cantor complained that people dealt with the text of the Bible as if one of the liberal arts or a craft were involved.[15] Students had little experience with spiritual life, and there was often a dearth of such experience among teachers as well. On the other hand, they believed they possessed an eternally valid, highly objective methodology that was now to be applied to divine matters.

Engaging in methodological disputations and scrutinizing individual topics by means of the *quaestio* are the hallmarks most often noted of Scholasticism. Just as important from our perspective was the determined effort by Scholastic thinkers to delineate and define the notions they used, a practice rarely followed during antiquity and for the most part abandoned during subsequent epochs. In this respect, the pedagogical dimension of Scholasticism proved very beneficial; the extreme formalism proved detrimental, however, because it posited that all issues associated with verbal expression had been solved or were solvable by formal means. Today, we know otherwise. Furthermore, the formation of concepts left much to be desired. One and the same word had to denote various concepts: The word *ratio*, for example, meant "calculation, account," as well as "reason."[16]

In his tract *On the Difference Between Nature and Person* (in the Trinity), the above-mentioned Hugh of Honau noted which words would play an important role in his essay: "persona, natura, substantia, essentia." He noted these words, "so that when we discuss something, we do not remain ignorant of the things covered by the word used for it [*res verborum*]."[17] This did not take the place of having a concept of a logical "term," which people still lacked; nevertheless, thinkers strove to reach that point. Equally important were their efforts to simplify "popular" notions burdened with all too many meanings. The process of differentiation associated with Scholastic thinking now gave rise, in the words of John of Salisbury, to a logically sound way of "distinguishing things that are imbued with diverse meanings."[18] What is a person, Hugh of Honau asked, and then he enumerated the possible responses: In the narrowest sense, a *persona* is a mask worn by an actor; second, it is an individual of standing (senators, lay and ecclesiastical dignitaries); and third—now in a figurative sense—every human; it was in this last sense that the word "person" also applied to "the theological persons,"[19] hence to the Persons of the Trinity.

Philosophy was thus no longer regarded merely as the love of wisdom, but evolved into the "science of drawing distinctions" (*discernendi scientia*).[20] This sort of process was characterized by expressive clarity and subtlety, both of which yielded extraordinarily positive, as well as a few negative, results: The affective and animated imagery, the shadowy figures rendered in a symbolic and allegorical style—all were routed by a clearheaded approach averse to the ineffable. Solutions to disputes—or the semblance of solutions—seem quite often to rest on terminological distinctions, without assuming a real-life quality. In terms of nomenclature alone, the doctrine of the Trinity became in the specialists' hands ever more complicated and thus ever less intelligible; the same thing occurred with other topics as well. As important as it was to heed the dictates of formalism, that element began to take on a ghostly life of its own in the classroom, and the mysteries of faith became the material of seminarians' exercises. On the other hand, theology for the first time became a science in the narrower sense of the word, thanks to the efforts of noteworthy scholars; that they occasionally succumbed to heresy in the process is a subject we shall address separately later on.

Were it not for a more pronounced belief in the potential of human reason and the attendant self-confidence among researchers, this upturn would not have been possible. In the process, use was made of Boethius's fourfold classification of the faculties of the human soul: sense perception, imagination, reason (*ratio*) defined as the ability to distinguish items and form judgments, and, finally, *intelligentia* [intelligence], which transcends worldly concerns and points the way to the realm of eternal forms. This scheme was exceedingly abstract, and hence, when Alan of Lille sought to depict it allegorically, he reverted to images found in late classical and early Christian poetry: The soul endowed with reason travels in a wagon whose four wheels signify the aforementioned faculties. They are far superior to the faculties encountered among animals: These also possess powers of perception and imagination, but humans are distinguished by their reason and ability to exercise *intelligentia*.[21] The new learning rested on two pillars, so to speak, the Christian and the pagan traditions, or revelation and reason.

Scholars strove to approach concepts and the distinctions among them from a lexical standpoint. This effort was complicated by the fact that allegorization had imbued the concepts encountered in the Bible with multifarious meanings. Theologians still had to contend with these meanings, and here too the Scholastic sense of order rose to the occasion. During the late twelfth century, five massive compilations became available; these contained a profusion of words, chiefly from the Bible, and their definitions, arranged alphabetically, often supplemented with references—a tremendous undertaking that in this hybrid format, however, could be of use only to the authors of devotional literature. Even Alan of Lille composed such a lexicon, *The Book for Distinguishing Theological Terms*. We discover there, for example, that the word wormwood (*absinthium*) could connote a bitter religious doctrine, the devil, or any one of a host of other meanings.[22] We would do well not to lose sight of the fact that in those times, too, theology had a practical function and that new ideas did not completely supplant old ones. They coexisted.

The actual work performed by the researcher observed the rules of logic, or dialectic, established during antiquity. Abelard equated research with "discriminating between arguments" (*discretio argumentorum*). Hence, he placed particular emphasis on the process of differentiation, much as Cicero and Boethius had in the past.[23] It was not just that definitions pointed the way to logical conclusions; it was also a matter of carving out a broad domain for linguistic logic, which was an offshoot of the discipline of grammar and to which, as it happens, Abelard himself had made great contributions. We will address the subjects of grammar and dialectic, two of the "liberal arts," in their proper context. It is important to note here, however, the blanket manner and the boldness with which the dialectical method was applied to theology. Intellectual speculation was no longer delimited to a few controversial theological issues; rather, it was reconfiguring itself as a system. Although this systematization came to fruition in the thirteenth century, theological *summae* [summary treatises] already existed in the late twelfth century.

Dialectic is the art of discourse between individuals proposing arguments and counterarguments. The individual working on his own did not need to forswear the invigoration sparked by such a debate; he used a fictional character to make the statements that he then disproved. For young scholars, the lecture hall served as a sort of tourney field for the intellect; they could challenge each other or even their teachers. In cities like Paris, which hosted competing masters heading their own schools, the rivalries took on an even more interesting aspect. Here there was a concentration of intellectual energy quite beyond that to be found in quieter places with only a single teacher.[24] Of course, in such surroundings debates often led to polemical battles, with each side vying to attain victory and to enhance its reputation. Even so, the debates drew upon the intellectual training of the participants and the listeners, and they shaped a new mentality.

The disputatious theologian possessed of a keener intellect was a figure already encountered in the early days of the church; later on, he would subsequently surface only sporadically. The general atmosphere of change in the eleventh century seems to have breathed new life into this figure. For example, legal and social conditions were undergoing rapid transformation or compartmentalization,[25] while the institutions of "state" and "church" assumed new definitions. However, the root causes of innovation cannot be found in phenomena like the rise of the cities. Urban life may have been conducive to a new intellectualism; when all is said and done, however, intellectualism is a phenomenon unto itself.

The liberal arts—at least those pertaining to verbal communication—had always been taught in schools; people had shown scant interest, however, in applying them to *philosophia* [philosophy], understood in the Boethian sense of a "comprehensive apprehension of existent things."[26] That now changed somewhat. In the disputes of the masters, a new theological scholarship began to take shape, one that could not afford to forgo grammar and dialectic. Of the seven liberal arts, these two above all experienced a florescence, while rhetoric declined in importance, and the upper branches of the *quadrivium*—arithmetic, geometry, astronomy, and music (theory)—continued to be consigned to the educational hinterlands until Arab treatises revived the interest in astronomy.

At one time, they were considered "liberal" insofar as one could not earn any money employing these—as opposed to the "practical"—arts, and thus they were deemed appropriate for freeborn [*liberales*] men. The sevenfold division declined in importance at a time when the old categorization of knowledge hardly sufficed. Some added ethics, physics, and mechanics to the *artes liberales*, others theology, ethics, and physics. Rhetoric was stripped of its role in the political arena and granted a new one on the pulpit, consequently becoming associated with (practical) theology; or, in light of the role it played in classical legal oratory, rhetoric was reckoned part of jurisprudence, itself a homeless discipline.[27] Jurisprudence would gain solid admittance into the university in the thirteenth century, as would "physics," narrowly defined as the art of medicine, for the natural sciences had yet to attain academic recognition. Even so, physicians and jurists were deemed desirous of earning money. The various practical professions and technologies (*artes mechanicae*) continued to be excluded from the classroom. And so it remained, in spite of efforts to amend the situation on the part of men like Hugh of Saint-Victor (in his *Didascalicon*). He contended that these activities were also governed by reason, which was the conduit to God. Success, however, eluded Hugh; even his own students considered commerce, agriculture, and the like, to be occupations beneath a philosopher's dignity.[28]

Grammar and logic (dialectic) were considered preparatory to the study of theology, yet both evolved into highly comprehensive and specialized

fields vital to the new educational system. It was said that it took six to
eight years for a student to achieve mastery of these areas. As a result,
students were no longer young boys but adults. Attaining a secure living
was the goal of many, and they hoped to find it thanks to their studies.
Nonetheless, some remained loyal disciples of grammar and dialectic, be
it as perpetual students in these fields, as young lecturers, or even as
wandering quasi-intellectuals. There was at this time a market for educated individuals and for those who gave the appearance of being
educated. Earlier, it had been otherwise; as Guibert of Nogent (1053–1124)
wrote: "In the recent past, and even partly during my childhood, there
had been such a shortage of teachers that you could hardly find any in the
towns [oppida], and rarely any in the cities. When one did happen to find
some, they knew so little that they couldn't even be compared to the
wandering scholars of the present day."[29]

Guibert did not even mention the cloisters here; it is highly unlikely that
all of them had access to capable teachers. To some extent, higher-ranking
laypeople also needed to know Latin, as is evident from Abelard and his
father before him, who had tutors at their castle near Nantes in Brittany.
Whoever desired to continue his education had to travel elsewhere, and at
a very young age Abelard was among those to do so.

Instruction in the liberal arts continued to be offered in Latin—which
was already at that time a foreign tongue even in areas where the
Romance languages were spoken—chiefly because the vernacular languages were extremely deficient in the vocabulary needed to express
abstract concepts. The nomenclatures of grammar and logic had been
available in Latin ever since late antiquity, but still people needed to learn
how to think abstractly, and the monastic schools were hardly up to that
task. Whoever did not devote years to such studies would never gain
entry into this intellectual realm.

Thus, some cloister students would have fared much the same as
Hildegard of Bingen: She could express herself in "unpolished Latin," but
did not have a firm command of grammar.[30] The Latin that served as the
vehicle for communication and the medium for devotional literature
differed from the scholarly Latin that was geared toward expressing ideas
precisely and differentiating the meanings of words. Theologians had to
lend focus to the vocabulary of the classical philosophers and indeed the
fathers of the church. Linguistic boundaries were intellectual boundaries,
and they were to be dismantled.

What remained was the intrinsic disparity between each thing and the
word used to denote it, or as Hilary of Poitiers had already phrased it:
"Speech is inferior to nature, and words cannot capture a thing as it really
is." He went on to explain, in much the same vein as the fathers of the

church, that heresies were the outgrowth, not of the words themselves, but of the variant intention or interpretation given to the meanings of words.[31] Gilbert of Poitiers, in particular, revived the theory that the grammatical meaning of a word might differ from the author's intended meaning. Thus, for example, Boethius sometimes wrote "divinity" (*divinitas*) rather than "God" (*Deus*), and "human" (*homo*) rather than "humanness" (*humanitas*).[32] In order to engage in biblical exegesis, an individual had to master biblical metaphors and figures of speech, and was likewise required to trace the allegorical expressions back to the actual scriptural text. By the way, one conclusion to be drawn from this is that the lexicons mentioned above were not worthless even vis-à-vis scholastic pursuits.

"What we comprehend is inferior to the thing itself; what we propound is inferior to our comprehension."[33] This lament is heard even today. The predicament had a particularly negative impact on speculative theology, especially when it came to highly technical issues like the doctrine of the Eucharist, as in the works by Berengar of Tours.[34] Again and again, humans show that they are incapable of capturing God's nature in words: We frail mortals, Hugh of Honau contended, cannot find words worthy and appropriate to this task. "What should we hence do? We cannot be silent, yet we are not capable of saying anything worthy of and appropriate to the subject. Thus, we wish to speak as he [God] inspires us to [*inspiraverit*], and proclaim what he himself has permitted us to know about him in as worthy a way as we are able."[35] The urge to engage in research was not quashed by the knowledge that its subject was unfathomable. In this respect humans are optimistic: God will sustain the researcher, indeed even "inspire" him. Spoken by one of Gilbert's adherents, this word did not sound as suspect as it might have coming from someone less rationally inclined. Incidentally, that assertion is based on an ancient tradition termed "grammatical Platonism," which teaches that things and the words (concepts) for them already coexisted in God's mind prior to the creation of the world. Adam did not assign names to the things around him out of his own accord, but was inspired by the Holy Spirit. God's wisdom is called the "word" on account of this connection between concepts and things.[36]

These individuals engaged in grammatical "research"—if we may use the term—had a fervent interest in the semantic underpinnings of language, and in this respect they performed a task neglected by Aristotle.[37] During the first half of the twelfth century, the theory of meaning engendered more detailed discussion than did the syntactic function of words. The meanings of words, Abelard averred, preceded the structure of a sentence.[38] This perspective has even been identified as the point of departure and foundation for Abelard's philosophy.[39]

Whereas other thinkers, Anselm of Canterbury among them, never broke free of a theology of language, Abelard went beyond the theory to scrutinize texts in terms of their mode of expression and use of individual words; indeed, he even presumed to revise Augustine's propositions, because in Abelard's view that author had not attached sufficient importance to expressing himself precisely. Thus, for example, when speaking of sin, the ambiguous word "will" should be replaced with the word "consent."[40] Abelard's philosophy of language never severed its close association with textual interpretation, the study of which had led him to develop some fundamental viewpoints. Hence, casuistry was the first means available for resolving problems posed by ambiguous wording. If a word's significance was unclear in a particular instance, then one would refer back to the author's intent. Taking this approach could prove tantamount to practicing psychology.

Whoever wished to avoid ambiguous and vague terminology had either to strike upon the correct phrase or, if there was none, to come up with the wording himself. In ancient times people had already resorted to coining neologisms when translating Hebrew or Greek texts. From the twelfth century onward, this technique proved extremely popular; in the practical realm, it was the urban way of life that called for a new terminology; in the scholarly one, it was theology above all. Again, Abelard applied himself to the task, and John of Salisbury wrote of him: "Still another takes refuge in a new tongue, since he does not have sufficient command of Latin."[41]

The more meticulous modern editions of works dating from this and the following eras include lists of the newly coined terms, which show that the Latin language commanded a growing vocabulary, particularly in the form of substantive nouns—with a predominance of words denoting abstract concepts.[42] We need not belabor the point that this process was fundamentally rational and often purely formal in nature. As a result, Scholasticism came to possess a professional terminology; whoever mastered this nomenclature and the Scholastic method by which it was formulated fancied himself a model of learning.

Since grammar was originally employed in a purely secular context, the relationship between this discipline and scholarly biblical exegesis had been somewhat strained since patristic times. Gregory the Great found it disgraceful that some wished to subordinate the heavenly message to the grammatical rules of Donatus's schoolbook; this sentiment was echoed often enough in the twelfth century.[43] In contrast, the Scholastics believed that God's word as contained in the Bible was fundamentally and utterly consonant with reason; as such, it should also bear comparison with the universally valid rules of grammar without suffering harm. To effect such

a comparison, they now undertook to broaden the speculative underpinnings of classical grammar, which posited that there was a universal
language based upon a universal grammar. Thinkers searched for ways to
link this approach to theology; as we have already noted, Thierry of
Chartres surmised that rather than refer to God the Father, God the Son,
and the Holy Spirit, one could just as well refer to the "Mother, Daughter,
Donatio [present, gift]," since God was indeed not of the masculine
gender.[44] "Grammatical anthropomorphism" had existed formerly, stemming from the desire to apply grammatical rules to theological concepts
like God's justice, wisdom, and power.[45] While later thinkers were more
circumspect, they often resorted to grammar when addressing theological
issues.

In the eleventh century, people had already begun studying the "scholarly" work of the grammarian Priscian (fl. around 500), as well as the more
practical schoolbook by Donatus. Priscian was now no longer just one
among many authors, but *the* grammarian, whose work eclipsed that of
Donatus—even in the unabridged edition. Unfortunately, the extant
manuscripts of Priscian's text in no way measured up to the standards of
scholars, for they were encumbered with interminable glosses; that was
the situation until, near the end of the twelfth century, the work's essential
elements were collected into a sort of *summa* stripped of the tedious
material inserted by the author and glossators.

In spite of these difficulties, so many students took to the subject of
grammar that Peter Damiani forcefully denounced those monks who,
after taking their vows, "take up with the common crowd [*vulgus*] of
grammarians, occupy themselves with this superficial and stupid skill,"
and, "puffed up with arrogance, insinuate themselves into the theatrical
gymnastics of the grammarians."[46] Apparently, students had already
begun thronging to the advocates of this "exact," albeit not universally
applicable, discipline. Around 1100 there were teachers who opened their
course of lectures by discussing the grammatical features of the text they
proposed to interpret. It could take quite some time before they came to
address the moral and philosophical aspects of the text.[47]

The shift to grammar promoted a renewed interest in studying the
literal meanings of the previously allegorized biblical texts. In order to
perform this philological task, it was necessary, insofar as possible, to refer
back to the original text. This was not difficult for the New Testament, in
contrast to the much more extensive Old Testament. Hugh of Saint-Victor
was said to have "ascertained" the literal meaning of the Pentateuch from
some Jews, and Richard of Saint-Victor, too, consulted Jewish scholars.
Such studies may have broadened somewhat the outlook of scholars, but
translating the important works by the Greek fathers of the church had a

much greater effect. This task fell in part to disciples of Gilbert of Poitiers, who himself knew no Greek.[48]

Most of the texts employed in the teaching of grammar even within the monasteries were of profane, predominantly classical origin. During the thirteenth century this continued to be the case in the "countryside," hence in Chartres and Orléans, while at the faculty of arts in Paris the works of philosophers, predominantly those of Aristotle (in Latin), were already being read; among the materials used in exercises, however, were also translations of Islamic and Jewish authors.[49]

The direction that research would take in the future was indicated not only by this interest in philosophy, but even more so by the new regard for logic (or dialectic). Just before the middle of the twelfth century, Peter Helias introduced the use of logical concepts in grammatical propositions, although he firmly maintained the distinction between the two disciplines.[50] This measure brought to light a mind-set that was already exemplified by the markedly rational tack taken in grammatical works at that time and that also underlay the theory that all languages shared a common origin. During the course of the century, grammar came more and more under the influence of dialectic. Young intellectuals were attracted to linguistic logic, while the pure grammarians were more and more taken up with developing a theory of meaning. What function, they asked, do nouns, pronouns, verbs, adjectives, etc., serve when an abstraction is designated by a term? The study of this rather turgid subspecialty, the *modi significandi* [modes of signifying things], was still gathering steam in the thirteenth century, and its proponents were called *modistae*. From the early thirteenth century on, linguistics and logic came to play a shared role in the systematic works composed in the spirit of the new speculative grammar. Linguistic theory lost its relevance to the practical curriculum and hence its natural roots.

In essence, grammar remained the study of signification and of proper sentence structure; determining the accuracy of a statement did not at all come under its purview, for the task of passing judgment on the formal premises underlying a proposition was the stuff of dialectic. As seen from actual written works, the two disciplines had always coexisted peacefully in practice and preserved their distinct nomenclatures. Both areas of study focused on verbal statements because the stuff of Boethian logic was not concepts and their evaluation, but words and sentences, and thinkers were only now engaged in the taxing job of developing the concept of the logical "term."[51] Linguistic logic was designed to address problems of signification; thus it also came to be associated with the semantic aspect of grammar; later, "terministic logic" would constitute a separate specialty. In the past, thinkers had lacked sufficient means for dealing with certain fundamental questions, for example, those concerning general terms (*universalia*). Now, drawing on grammar and logic jointly, they raised such problems to a higher plane.

Considering how closely associated these two "arts" were, there was remarkably little competition between them, or at least the evidence for it is rather late. Grammarians who did not embrace logic were considered reactionaries. This view was embodied in a poem composed by the troubadour Henry d'Andeli around 1250: Sir Grammar of Orléans takes to the field against Sir Logic of Paris and is defeated in battle.[52]

In turning their backs on classical authors, scholars were evidencing some of their newfound self-awareness and a yearning for spiritual adventure. "[A]ll literature [is] derided: logic wins the approbation of all," John of Salisbury complained. "He who studies the arts and the written texts [i.e., the authorities] is thought a poor debater, for an ally of the past cannot be a logician." Only logic counts.[53] Debates were mock battles in which young men could give vent to their ambition and self-assurance. What mattered was their ability to appear in public and prevail over others, not so much their command of the written word. In Bologna people took a different, more professionally oriented tack: Buoncampagno, a famous professor of grammar, put his art to good use teaching practical writing for real-life purposes, the *ars dictandi* [art of letter writing]. Mastering this art was one of the prerequisites for a legal career.

Young Abelard offers the best example of the bellicosity underlying this new technique for gaining the upper hand. In his autobiography he describes his noble background, his renunciation of the worldly prestige associated with his rank (*militaris glorie pompam*), and his preference for "the weapons of dialectic"; engaging in warlike debates appealed to him more than achieving military renown. "I began to travel about in several provinces disputing, like a true peripatetic philosopher, wherever . . . there was a keen interest in the art of dialectic." While still a very young man (*adulescentulus*), Abelard already wished to head his own school. In a dispute over the questions of universals some years later, he prevailed over his teacher in Paris, as a result of which the man lost many of his students and Abelard was established in his academic career. In the end, Abelard "set up camp there [outside the city of Paris] in order to lay siege to my usurper," namely, his former teacher's successor, who "had filled my [rightful] place." The former teacher returned, however, "apparently to deliver from my siege the soldier whom he had abandoned [in Paris]." With pride Abelard quoted Ovid: "'If you demand the issue of this fight, I was not vanquished by my enemy.'"[54]

During the early heyday of dialectic, ambitious young intellectuals like Abelard were constrained by neither ecclesiastical vows, which for the most part they would not have taken, nor by firm ties to an institution. Later on, circumstances changed, and Abelard himself matured. Private rivalries continued to exist between colleagues, and they were not always conducted on purely intellectual grounds. The dialectical method prevailed in the academic works written throughout the Scholastic period: A thesis was proposed, followed by the words "sed contra" [but conversely] marking the counterarguments, which were then disproved. Naturally, the author's *conclusio* [conclusion] was always correct. Such was the refined academic approach; there was a less civilized one, too, characterized by mutual invective. Roscelin, Abelard's former teacher, wrote him that now that he had been castrated, he should have his tongue cut out as well.[55]

Conservative scholars did not renounce disputation, but its abuse: "Discussing the proper meaning of something is the province of men; engaging in verbal arguments is a thing for boys, who have a poor grasp of the things they hear or say."[56] The scholarly debate was a venerable tradition, from the mock debates of the medieval schools all the way back to Neoplatonism and Greek philosophy. For example, in 980 at Ravenna, in the presence of Emperor Otto II, Gerbert of Aurillac engaged in a debate with the resident scholar of the Magdeburg cathedral on the branches of learning.[57]

Dialectic has been termed "the art of debating well."[58] Credit for this somewhat one-sided definition goes to Aristotle. In book 8 of the *Topics* he established rules for debating,[59] though it was not until the thirteenth century that people began to observe them more strictly. In the *Metalogicon* (1160), John of Salisbury promoted the so-called new Aristotelian logic, which was derived from newly translated works of Aristotle discussing the distinct forms of the conclusion. They encompassed the simple (syllogism), demonstrative, and plausible conclusions, the fallacy, and above all, of course, the intentional fallacies of the Sophists; there were, for example, thirteen different types of fallacies. These were to be avoided like the plague, and yet they proved intriguing. The examples found in these works were not taken from real life, but rather were meant to instill in the reader a sense of how to use words in a precise and discriminating fashion, as, for example, in cases where a word changed its meaning with the context.[60]

John of Salisbury advocated studying logic without regard for practical application, since it was the art of thinking and drawing conclusions. Even the dialectical acrobatics of the Sophists, which might set the heads of the uninitiated spinning, were not to be regarded as spectacles at some Vanity Fair, but they were examples of inaccurate thinking fabricated out of necessity.[61] Naturally, there was no way to bar people entirely from indulging their "creative impulses"—to use a modern term—and hence no means of obviating the risk that the gap between this learning and reality would yawn ever wider due to the use of formal subtleties. Aware of this hazard, Peter of Poitiers, later the first chancellor at the university at Paris, chose in his collection of sentences (1175) to limit the examples of conclusions to those drawn from actual (mostly theological) debates—nothing else was in his view proper material for disputation. At the same time, he was able to infuse his work with some professional humor and liven up the dull material; the debate on God's omnipotence, for example, contains the entertaining query whether God could have turned Socrates into a donkey.[62]

Some years later, Walter of Saint-Victor reviled Peter of Poitiers as one of the "four labyrinthine thinkers of France" and offered parodies of two syllogisms as part of his attack. The first opens with a major premise (*propositio*) in the spirit of Gilbert of Poitiers and then presents an allusion to the doctrine of sensate universals, whose proponent (Abelard?) is portrayed as a heretic (in the minor premise, *assumptio*). The devil infers the conclusion (*conclusio*). Here is the text of that syllogism:

> The dialectician proposes this premise: Every human is human by virtue of his humanity (*humanitate*).
> The heretic proceeds: But humanity is nothing.
> The devil draws the conclusion: Every human is thus nothing. If he is human by virtue of his humanity, and every human and humanity are nothing, then no human is a human. What a monstrosity![63]

Walter considered Gilbert to be one of the "labyrinthine thinkers" as well. One of the themes running through Gilbert's works was that a thing (*id quod*) and its cause (*id quo*) were entirely distinct, at least in terms of the formal causes, which were what interested the logician. Walter, on the other hand, was a believer in fundamentals: "They say that the human is human by virtue of his humanity. . . . That is not true. It is not owing to himself or to his humanity that he is anything, but it is owing to God. . . . The truth of the matter reproves the false rules of the philosophers."[64] A logician might have answered that his learning was concerned only secondarily with such matters, namely, only insofar as they were expressed in words. By its very nature as a "verbal art" (*ars sermocinalis*), dialectic was far removed from the natural sciences, or, as it was then called, from "physics."

The position taken by Walter of Saint-Victor vis-à-vis the proponents of dialectic may be attributed in part to the outlook customarily associated with the canons of his church even in the days of Hugh of Saint-Victor (d. 1141). Here dialectic was viewed with reservations.[65] Furthermore, Walter appears to have hearkened to those scholars who lacked an aptitude for the subtleties of logic; in one of his letters, Abelard confirmed the existence of such *doctores* [learned men] and slipped in a reference to the fable of the foxes and the sour grapes.[66] Walter's tract was not very polished or particularly influential. It was but a faint echo of the warning bells the "antidialecticians" had already set ringing in the eleventh century.

Of course, it is important to note that for the most part these individuals repudiated the new, unbridled version of dialectic and not the moderate form employed on occasion ever since the patristic age. The rigorist Peter Damiani fulminated against monks who spent their time on philosophical studies, and he tossed the "liberal arts" into the same pot with those practiced by poets, magicians, and astrologers; philosophy should serve as a handmaiden of theology and not usurp the right to offer independent instruction (*ius magisterii*).[67] What raised his hackles in particular was the discovery of some dialecticians "who were so simple-minded that they wished to see all the phrases in the Holy Scriptures subjected to the authority of dialectic";[68] that is, they scrutinized the Bible for its logical content. For all that, Peter himself sometimes stooped to engage in an adversarial dispute and even refuted one contention about God's omnipotence by availing himself of dialectical methodology, indeed by enlisting a reverse conclusion.[69] While Manegold of Lautenbach did not employ any dialectical arguments in a theological tract, he did not refrain from doing so in a political one.[70] In that respect, he was putting dialectic and rhetoric to their time-honored uses of molding political or legal opinions. Otloh of St. Emmeram in Regensburg was an "antidialectician" only when warning of the hazards inherent to this discipline: Dialectic was to serve the defense of the faith,[71] as shown by examples dating back to ancient times. In most other cases also, dialectic was not viewed as intrinsically evil; rather, it was the use to which it was put that engendered criticism.

In this context we have referred to two monks. As such, their concern was to preserve the simplicity of one's heart and fend off an inroad by the "world" into a sphere where it had no place. Generally speaking, dialecticians might be reproached for placing all too much confidence in their discipline and for viewing it as an end in itself. After an absence of ten years, John of Salisbury returned to find his former Parisian colleagues debating the same old questions; he concluded that while dialectic might be a useful tool in other disciplines, it was in and of itself bloodless and sterile.[72] John cited the words of Saint Paul: They are always studying and "never arrive at a knowledge of the truth." They speak nonsense and wish to be scholars.[73] Some of the "modern" dialecticians favored subtleties over reality, offered proofs for foregone conclusions, and in many instances possessed no sense of what was essential. The field was overwhelmed by innumerable specialized questions, and "the students spent their time solving riddles."[74] This was particularly true during the second half of the twelfth century, following the peak in the discipline's revival.

As Abelard came to disassociate himself from the superficialities of the academic life, even he leavened his high praise of dialectic with criticism. At that time, he attacked the "avowers [*professores*] of dialectic," who believed that armed with reason they could understand and delineate everything; they boasted that they believed only in themselves and scoffed at all authorities (teachers of the church). It was one thing to study the truth for devotional purposes, quite another to hold debates in the service of pride and the quest for glory. Abelard then offered a rationale for his own use of dialectic, writing that he had had recourse to this technique only to ward off attacks—that was certainly not true.[75] When he made this assertion, Abelard had already become a monk, and he wrote in a way befitting a monk.

In this very same work, however, Abelard praised the accomplishments of the *professores dialecticae* [avowers of dialectic]: "To a greater extent than all of Christ's enemies—the heretics, Jews, and heathens—and with greater subtlety, they scrutinize the doctrinal truth of the Trinity and uphold that truth with arguments of greater profundity"[76]—as he himself had or believed he had. In one work, Abelard derived the word logic from *logos*, thus Christ, and made reference to Christ's promise (Luke 21:15): "I will give you a mouth and wisdom, which none of your adversaries will be able to withstand or contradict." With these words Christ charged his followers to "gird themselves with reason," Abelard explained, "by which means they will become the best [*summi*] logicians in disputes."[77] In the same letter Abelard quoted Augustine's remarks about the "discipline of disciplines, which is called dialectic. It teaches [us] how to teach, it teaches [us] how to learn. . . . It is the only [discipline] with any knowledge; it does not merely lay out the path to knowledge, but can actually lead [you] there." Augustine's words "make it seem as if it [logic] was the only [discipline] worthy of being called scholarship."[78] This had not been Augustine's meaning, yet in response to rigorists and in strong language he had defended dialectic as a useful tool for Christians. Since dialectic determined the—albeit only formal—validity of a sentence, almost everyone viewed this discipline as a sort of requisite for engaging in scholarship.

Aristotle was the father of the scholarly discipline of logic, Boethius the guardian and herald of Aristotelian dialectic in the Christian West. For almost five hundred years, the latter's works enjoyed only limited influence. The time was perhaps not yet ripe for rationality to assume a dominant role in how people thought. Heralding this innovation was the appearance of individualists who possessed a strong intellectual bent: Gerbert of Aurillac, Fulbert of Chartres, and Berengar of Tours. A new golden age in the study of logic commenced with the close of their era, ushered in by the appearance of a handbook attributed to a certain Garlandus (before 1076); this handbook did not merely reiterate the standard material, but also contained original contributions to the field.[79]

At the beginning of the twelfth century, logic enjoyed a peak in popularity unrivaled before or after in the Middle Ages.[80] Its true success, however, was in conjunction with other branches of learning, for as an end in itself dialectic proved sterile. It continued to play an extremely important role in the academic enterprise; rather than concern themselves with grammar and rhetoric, many students devoted themselves to dialectic "as quickly as possible," "seeking the garrulous loquocity that will make them seem clever and keen."[81] That this phenomenon was also something of a fad became evident in the early thirteenth century with the shift in interest to Aristotle, whose philosophical works offered so much more substantive and topical material than the dialectic he had founded.

In the twelfth century logic made significant contributions to spiritual training and provided points of departure for a new speculative theology. Boethius, the author of five short theological tracts, had associated the two fields and introduced the speculative element characteristic of the Platonists into the discussion.[82] We have noted above that already in late antiquity use had occasionally been made of dialectic in discussions of specialized theological issues. That occurred to an even greater extent during the Eucharistic controversies between Lanfranc of Bec and Berengar of Tours in the eleventh century. From then on, an ever broader range of problems was handled from a dialectical perspective, until finally all of theology fell under its purview. Anselm of Canterbury had already endeavored to demonstrate God's existence using logic: God was the greatest being conceivable; such a being could not exist merely in the thoughts of humans, but must actually exist. In rebuttal it was rightly pointed out that the existence of a mental image did not prove that the thing hypothesized had existence; the largest island conceivable did not necessarily exist. Anselm was objective enough to have these criticisms, along with his responses to the points made by his antagonist, appended to his *Proslogion*.[83]

Certain difficulties stood in the way of applying this logical, academic mode of thought to theology. The relationship between a concept and reality, between signifier and signified, was not sufficiently clear; nor was the distinction between natural and supranatural being, between the bases of philosophy and of theology. Hence, thinkers could only endeavor to apply conclusions drawn from the earthly sphere to the heavenly one by analogy; the results were plausible, but not incontrovertible. With some qualms, one might cite Gilbert of Poitiers and his grammatical theology: "Therefore, we take the risk of speaking contrary to the rules of philosophical disputation when we discuss God [and] advance the following," namely, Gilbert's speculative thought about the Trinity.[84]

In its heyday, dialectic did not merely squelch interest in the field of grammar, but almost overwhelmed rhetoric as well, although the old saying that "Grammar is the introduction to eloquence, dialectic its cultivation, rhetoric its culmination" still held true.[85] Thierry of Chartres attacked the contention that rhetoric was the same as or one aspect of logic. In his view, logic dealt with generalities and rhetoric with specific, controversial *causae* [questions]: Was Orestes, for example, justified in killing his mother or not?[86] This case illustrates how akin rhetoric was to the legal oratory of antiquity, upon which the examples used in the schools were modeled. Eloquence consisted of assembling unproved statements and employing dialectic "to prove them true or false by means of plausible arguments."[87]

In those days there was only scant interest in the juridical as well as the political applications of rhetoric, even on the part of clergymen who spoke Latin, or were at least supposed to understand it. Spoken eloquence languished, while a mannered form of written prose continued in use; it was fostered by the reading of ancient texts and played a role in the art of composing letters and legal briefs. This practical branch of rhetoric came into its own as the *ars dictandi* [art of letter writing]. Cassiodorus had taught the West the organizational principles of classical oratory, and these rules were even reflected in the structure of medieval documents. In the eleventh century people began to rediscover and compose commentaries on Cicero's rhetorical works. A curious work by Anselm of Besate entitled the *Rhetorimachia* (1046/48), gave a practical twist to Cicero's *De inventione* and *Ad Herennium*.[88] Anselm was a cleric from a respectable Milanese family, who had studied dialectic in Parma and rhetoric in Reggio and was known as Anselmus peripateticus [Anselm the itinerant]. For a time he had even served as notary to Emperor Henry III. Composed in the form of a debate with an adversary, most probably fictional, the *Rhetorimachia* was intended to win the court's attention and admiration for its author, in spite or because of the fact that the work was shot through with obscene jokes and anecdotes. The job of the rhetorician, even in antiquity, was first and foremost to win over his audience to a viewpoint. Consequently, this discipline—as practiced by Cicero and others—served moral ends as well. In this period that feature fell by the wayside; rhetoric was more akin to the goliard poetry of young students, while ethics was left to more mature writers. Thus, the young Abelard sang his beloved's praises,[89] and then in his later years produced a work entitled *Ethics*.

It comes as no surprise that rigorists found as much at fault with rhetoric as they did with dialectic. Robert of Melun, who had taught John of Salisbury, attacked the practice of embellishing statements rhetorically and the whole academic enterprise that fostered it: The Old Testament was not informed by rhetoric, and even the New Testament used simple and plain diction. Whoever went in for such things controverted the Evangelists and especially Paul.[90] That last observation is incorrect; Paul possessed a classical education and a gift for great eloquence—and he justifiably employed hyperbole in his letters to the different communities. The authors of edifying texts rarely eschewed this tool, with the afore-mentioned result that the old oratorical art was transmuted into a literary one. Augustine inveighed at great length against the rigorist tendencies of his contemporaries and contended that Christians were not to forgo the use of rhetorical devices: Just as in times of yore the Jews took golden and silver vessels with them out of Egypt, so is there now justification for making practical use of the pagans' arts. Augustine's retort was also aimed at non-Christians who "scoffed" at the Bible because of its artless-ness: It too contained rhetorical devices, but without succumbing to ostentation.[91] From that time on, rhetorical devices formed a natural stylistic ingredient in many texts. Rhetoric itself continued to be taught, to be sure, but little cultivated as a discipline; the field splintered into specialized branches like "the art of preaching," the art of letter writing (*ars dictandi*), "the notarial art," and so forth. Among Italian notaries this last "art" increasingly became a practical component of jurisprudence. There are isolated cases of twelfth-century juridical summations com-posed in accordance with the rules of the discipline, but they owe more to the ecclesiastical law of Gratian than to the works of Cicero and Quintil-ian.[92]

Languages other than Latin also possessed oratorical traditions with the same roots as classical rhetoric: the verbal ability to express oneself well, intelligence, and a facility for judging the relative merits of various methods and stratagems. The two forms of oratory—Latin and vernacular—could come into confrontation, as evidenced by one author's remarks about the city of Bruges in the year 1123. The count had prohibited all feuding there, and adversaries consequently aired their disagreements before judicial sessions. "In those days rhetoric was practiced by those who had received instruction in it and those who possessed it naturally; many were in truth illiterate . . . but the ones who had received instruction in rhetoric could in no way hold their own against them." God, who had bestowed this eloquence upon the uneducated, did not wish them to prevail because of trickery (*fallaciis*), however, and hence visited a famine upon the city.[93]

Citing the existence of natural eloquence, students tried to get out of taking courses in grammar and rhetoric. John of Salisbury named this sort of student "Cornificius," after a literary opponent of Virgil. In his words, these individuals full of shameless ignorance took up the study of rhetoric with the sole purpose of bringing their studies to a quick end. They contended that it was superfluous to study the verbal disciplines and all their rules, because speech was a gift of nature, and consequently these rules did not need to be the focus of study.[94]

John's reaction to such views might be termed overly dramatic, were we not aware that it was itself a rhetorical device. He proceeded to brand "Cornificius" a public enemy (*hostis publicus*), for the very foundations of (civil) society were, according to Cicero, at stake here![95] Such declarations could scarcely have been received with complete seriousness. This was part of the "witty" side to rhetoric, employed in hopes of retaining one's audience. The polemical outburst by John of Salisbury against "Cornificius" and his followers was not perceived as inconsistent with his serious, pedagogical goal.

Unlike the lower division of the "liberal arts," or *trivium*, the disciplines constituting the upper division can be reviewed much more briefly, for they were, to begin with, quite often omitted from monastic training. Most monasteries lacked the qualified teachers, and sometimes a young monk would be assigned to a very distant cloister so that he could study at least some of the disciplines there. The caliber of instruction in mathematics at the newer advanced schools was also not truly equal to that in the verbal or the practical disciplines. Evidence for this comes, for example, from a manuscript containing the educational curriculum used by Thierry of Chartres: Of the 595 folios in the manuscript, only 161 are devoted to the disciplines of the *quadrivium*.[96] All the same, a theology student was expected to have some command of arithmetic, geometry, astronomy, and music theory—not because these subjects represented the wave of the future in the formal and natural sciences, but rather for theological purposes. They were the paving stones on the path leading to God, the highest reason.

Platonism had, by the way, already taken this very same tack. It was said that Plato did not admit anyone ignorant of mathematics into his academy; Platonism and Pythagoreanism shared a belief in a "world harmony" embodied by numbers, a belief that continued to exercise influence in the Middle Ages and was indeed still a motivating force behind Galileo Galilei and Kepler. The *Timaeus* was based on numerical speculation, and in other instances as well, numbers exhibited a capacity for clarifying divine matters. This capacity was as likely to be expressed within the framework of allegory as it was within a rational speculative process, here one akin to mathematics.

In this respect as well, medieval thinkers were not as prone as we are today to distinguish between concepts and objects. According to Thierry of Chartres, the number one generates all the other numbers, just as the One (God) begets all things. Thus, it is possible to speak of the number one as omnipotent in the sense that it creates an infinity of numbers. From here, Thierry launched into a sort of theology of numbers.[97] The Trinity also figured in this discussion, although Thierry more plausibly compared it to a geometric shape, the equilateral triangle.[98] Such speculation crops up again and again, as, for example, in two tracts written by Garnier of Rochefort at the beginning of the thirteenth century.[99] In his view, the mystery (*sacramentum*) of the equilateral triangle lay in the uniqueness of its nature: Nothing could be added to or subtracted from this shape without distorting the circle by which it could be circumscribed. It was a triad unbroken by unity, a unit unbroken by triplicity, and so forth. Therefore, geometry also served a purpose, although its practical application in surveying land had long since faded from memory.

People continued to enjoy studying the stars, which were so obviously associated with the heavenly sphere. Astronomers and manuscripts about astronomy were, to be sure, rarely encountered in the West. Adelard of Bath (d. around 1130) recounted one case of an individual steeped in astronomical lore, Duke Henry of Normandy, who had read about the revolution of the stars in Latin works and "sentences" by Arabs. It was his contention that whoever does not know what materials and plan served in the construction of his dwelling is not worthy of living there—the same thing applies to whoever is born and raised in the palace of this world. Whoever, upon reaching a reasonable age, shows no interest in the world's composition is not worthy (of the princely office) and should be removed if possible.[100] In the main this was surely Adelard's opinion; what is more, it calls to mind a contemporary saying already found in a work by John of Salisbury, that an uneducated king is an ass with a crown.[101]

The common people were wary of Gerbert of Aurillac, not least because of his nocturnal activities with astronomical devices, and they considered him in general to be a magician. As a young woman, Heloise must also have been greatly impressed by an armillary sphere; where she might have seen one is not clear, but in any event Abelard had not pursued the study of astronomy. Since the days of Ptolemy, that device for depicting the heavenly orbits had been known as an *astrolabium* [astrolabe], and

"Petrus Astrolabius" was the name that Heloise gave her infant son. Is it possible that it was merely the word with which she was familiar and that she "wished merely to convey that the child was descended from the heavens"? In that case, "Astrolabius" was to be understood as *astrolapsus* [descended from the stars],[102] a mediocre pun and hardly indicative of an interest in astronomy.

William of Hirsau, a contentious proponent of Gregorian reform who died in 1091 and had been a monk at St. Emmeram in Regensburg before 1069, may be credited with a scholarly interest in astronomy. He and Otloh had struck up a friendship there, and together they undertook the compilation of an astronomy "course in dialogue form": William dictated, while Otloh wrote down the tract to which, unfortunately, only the preface survives.[103] In that text, William justified his undertaking to those critics who contended that it was unsuitable for monks to study the liberal arts when they were meant rather to intone the Psalms. Yet, William averred, all educated believers (*catholicis inidiotis*) clearly recognized that an individual should endeavor—insofar as he possessed the aptitude—to retrieve something of the knowledge of physical things Adam had lost by committing the original sin.

To a great extent William's *Astronomy* was no doubt a rehashing of old school material; were we to believe the introduction, however, it also contained "marvelous discoveries," things God had revealed to William— which out of monkish modesty he attributed to Otloh. Even if they were no more than minor reinterpretations, the work would be interesting if only because of its forward-looking approach. William also wrote a tract on music, which contained borrowings from works by Boethius and medieval authors and superseded those sources in one respect: In it he postulated the existence of three additional musical intervals. Otloh had supposedly beseeched him to elaborate upon the theories of earlier scholars with some of his own corollaries.[104]

This desire to rise above the old material did not engender any important original astronomical achievements in the twelfth century. With the reconquest of Spain from the Moors, however, people could potentially gain access to Arabic scholarship on astronomy. Arabic scholarship typically consisted of elaborations upon the Aristotelian and Ptolemaic image of the world: To them, the universe was like an onion, whose concentric spheres were nested one within the other around the earth in the center. How was it that the spheres, particularly those of the planets, had such different rotations against the background of fixed stars? That feature might be laid to the World-Soul, which sustained the structure and movement of the whole system, or to the actions of celestial divinities, as was contended by astrologers. Following in the steps of classical thinkers,

Arab scholars proposed a mechanistic solution to the problem: The universe was like a clockwork that, once set in motion by God, continued to run. While the stellar spheres rotated, the terrestrial spheres and the souls of humans, all bound with them in world harmony, "vibrated." Whenever humans played music, it was thanks to their participation in this cosmic harmony.

Hermann of Carinthia propounded these teachings in his principal work on the fundamental elements of astronomy, *De essentiis*, which has only within recent decades gained the recognition it deserves.[105] On account of his life history alone, Hermann is a noteworthy figure. Who sent this Carinthian to northern France, where he would come to claim Thierry of Chartres as his teacher and himself come to call Rudolf of Bruges a student? How was it that he left northern France for Toulouse, and where did he gain the knowledge needed to translate Ptolemy and Arabic authors from Arabic into Latin? The account that maintains that the abbot of Cluny charged Hermann with gathering information about Muhammad and Islam during his sojourn "by the banks of the Ebro" offers some hints. This all transpired at a time when parts of Spain, and hence the libraries of Spain as well, were being thrown open to the Christian West.

Ptolemy and the Arabs divided the universe into the celestial spheres and the terrestrial world under their influence. The former were governed by mathematical laws, the latter by the axioms of "physics" discerned by means of sensate observations. These propositions may strike us as quite modern, an impression dispelled by the speculative element common to both fields at the time. Even among the Arabs, theology played a part in astronomy, which occupied a position between mathematics and theology. Hermann concluded that the terrestrial world and the heavenly spheres were linked due to the relationship between the numbers eight (the heavenly spheres) and four (elements), and to the fact that the earth was the geometric epicenter of the universe.

All this is too much for modern readers. In emulation of the Greeks and Arabs, Hermann at least wished to draw conclusions on the basis of observations as well; furthermore, he introduced the mathematical element into Western cosmology.[106] In his desire to calculate the distances between the sun, moon, and earth, Hermann naturally became caught up in classical music theory. That system furnished concrete numbers for describing the relationships between notes, and it was those relationships that were thought to underlie the whole universe.

Yet, given the mode of thought and tools of his age, even this cosmopolitan gentleman, whose gaze extended beyond the old horizons of scholarship, was unable to set foot upon those new shores that Copernicus and Kepler would reach much later. His speculations were essentially Platonic in nature; his knowledge of Aristotle and Avicenna was at most indirect. In his field, however, Hermann initiated the intellectual exchange with the Arabs that at the beginning of the following century would constitute a major bone of doctrinal contention at the recently established University of Paris.

A review of the extent to which each of the "liberal arts" was studied in the twelfth century indicates that if dialectic enjoyed the greatest resurgence in popularity, then the least was experienced by musicology, a subject about which little was to be gained from the Arabs. Alongside the traditional rationale for studying the *artes* as preparatory to monastic spirituality, people now expressed an ever-growing interest in scholarly subjects for their own sake, sparked indeed by an inner drive. Thus, for example, William of Hirsau wrote that "obliged by a signal from God," he was possessed by a love for the *quadrivium*, and for astronomy in particular, that was stronger than all the passions.[107]

In earlier centuries, this sort of scholar had been a rare and isolated phenomenon. Now such teachers and students still constituted a minority, to be sure, but as their numbers increased, they gained a new awareness of representing a distinct group with transnational connections. What distinguished them from the multitude of their fellow monks was their sweeping identification of rationality as the guiding principle behind their propositions, even those relating to a field beyond reason, theology. They placed absolute confidence in methods devised by pagans and could adopt them because both paganism and Christianity affirmed the rational nature of the cosmic order. Some scholars incorporated this affirmation into their religious thinking. Long before he fell into disrepute, John Scotus (Eriugena) had already alluded to two Gospels, one the Holy Scriptures and the other a "corporeal, visible Gospel," the created world.[108] Emulating Boethius, Thierry of Chartres categorized theology as one of the subdivisions of philosophy, along with logic, ethics, mathematics, and "physics."[109]

This was possible because philosophy tackled not just the world, but God as well. In Latin, the meaning of the word "philosophy" was analogous to the concept of *sapientia* [wisdom], which Boethius had defined as understanding of realities in "immutable form,"[110] hence in the form of Platonic Ideas residing in the mind of God. Upon entering the monastery of Saint-Denis, Abelard expressed the wish to become "a true philosopher not of the world, but of God," and to devote himself exclusively to "holy reading." Nevertheless, he did proceed to offer instruction in the liberal arts in order to deepen young people's interest in theology.[111]

Insofar as such "reading" could at least peripherally involve dealing with speculative or practical theological problems, a transitional step separated the old biblical research (*sacra pagina, sacra lectio*) from "modern" theology. We have made repeated reference to Abelard and must do so yet again vis-à-vis the formulation of theological scholarship. He was the first[112] or among the first to employ the word "theology," quite prominently in fact as the title to his principal work, *Theologia christiana*. Abelard had a very specific understanding of the word's meaning, but had not coined it: He might have come across it in his readings of Boethius and other authors. As for Bernard of Clairvaux, the new term subsumed Abelard's name, and he derisively labeled him "our theologian" or the "new theologian."[113]

The noun *theologia* was paired with the attribute *speculativa*. This latter term had been employed occasionally in prior centuries as well; now it assumed a new and important function. The Zwettl *Summa*, a product of the school of Gilbert of Poitiers, used it thus in a passage on theology: "The mutable nature of the human spirit rises upward in order to spy out (*speculari*) the divine power that transcends all."[114] To spy out, or, to put it more properly, investigate the divine sphere, one cannot employ the bodily senses, but rather must use the rational methodology perpetuated by philosophy.

Ecclesiastical scholars like Augustine and Hilary of Poitiers had already engaged in speculative theology with respect to isolated controversial issues. Questions about the Trinity and Christology were now again at the forefront, but over the course of the twelfth century the new discipline suffused the entire field of theology. As a result, people hit upon questions that were scrutinized more for taxonomic reasons than for their urgency.[115] The schools' continual need for new exercise material had the same effect.

For the time being, practical theology took a backseat to speculative theology. At the same time, and in response to the influence of classical ethics, it likewise came to constitute a separate field of study, although, if anything, this pastoral theology was the product of conservative forces. Neither branch of theology outgrew the old constructs altogether. Moreover, biblical exegesis often provided the framework within which the new scholarship took shape. Abelard had started out as a biblical exegete; he had intended to write a commentary on the book of Ezekiel in order to make his mark as a scholar, but he encountered opposition to that plan in Laon and moved to Paris, where he continued his exegetical studies. Instruction at the advanced schools proceeded in the same manner as at a monastery: A spiritual text was read aloud and then elucidated by either the superior or the master. The listeners were to "meditate" on the material. In a monastery this practice called for hardly any written material, but individuals studying at the schools probably needed a copy of the text underlying the lecture. Spiritual meditation was replaced by intellectual interpretation; often, specialized questions arose that could be tackled only by consulting ecclesiastical or philosophical authorities, in other words, by operating within a literary framework. The students would advance theses and antitheses, discussing each in detail. In the end, the teacher proposed a "sentence," which rendered the final judgment, and its grounds. Such sentences were compiled into books; hence, the scholarly corpus of *libri sententiarum* came to encompass more than textual exegesis and to embrace a format that came to be more widely read than others.

Studying God's word was thus no longer an isolated undertaking; it was augmented in ways that appealed to students as vehicles for stimulating one's intellectual abilities and distinguishing oneself in disputations. In the thirteenth century, the situation had reached such straits in Paris that the field of biblical exegesis was greatly compromised, and the reins were pulled in on debating: Disputations were now permitted only in lecture courses on the sentences. Nonetheless, these disputations took up such a large portion of the curriculum that biblical exegetes had to beg for "open" time on the lecture schedule.[116]

We have already heard that traditional biblical research focused primarily on deciphering the various levels of allegorical meaning. Now more and more attention was paid to a text's literal meaning explicated by means of grammatical, dialectical, and factual approaches. People chose above all to study those books of the of Bible that promised to yield a rich trove of theological material. This was the juncture at which biblical research began to cross over into theology. Concurrently, serious efforts were being made, particularly at the school in Laon, to develop an independent scholarly methodology. Anselm of Laon taught nothing other than how to comment upon the text in this manner—reaping, perhaps not quite deservedly, Abelard's vituperation in return.

The scholar who undertook a phrase-by-phrase elucidation of the Bible soon found himself confronted by questions of a specialized nature. He could gloss over them or address them in depth, as was more in keeping with his aspiration to scholarship. Some authors distinguished such digressions graphically from the rest of the text in the form of *quaestiones*. These passages might be segregated completely from the biblical text, and this trend gave rise to a new format. For the most part, the *quaestiones* opened with a brief formulation of the question ("quaeritur, utrum . . ." ["It is asked whether . . ."]). Thereupon followed opinions and contrary opinions, the sources for which might or might not be noted, and the solution to the problem, arrived at in most cases by citing rational arguments in the dialectical manner. Quite often, the *sic-et-non* [pro-and-con] mode of dialectic was employed, which had, if anything, a harmonizing effect. For the most part, it involved demonstrating that the arguments proposed by one side harbored an error or an ambiguity that was then clarified by drawing a distinction (*distinctio*) between significations. This constituted the *solutio*, a solution often auxiliary to a greater whole, an entire system. Even the great summae of the thirteenth century were constructed of innumerable *quaestiones*. They had already been preceded by many tracts composed in this recently developed format, by an entire corpus of *quaestiones*.

This interrogatory method has been traced back to the dialogues of Plato and his students. The established literary style of the disputation played as great a role among Alexandrine scholars as it did among the fathers of the church,[117] and in the ninth century people engaged in disputations termed *quaestiones*. From the eleventh century on, the genre of *quaestiones disputatae* came to enjoy growing popularity, for even students could participate, indeed could themselves propose questions for debate. Young students could sustain the discussion, even without a master to ensure that the proceedings followed the rules. For example, Anselm of Besate, author of the *Rhetorimachia*, sent his teacher the text of a disputation that he and his friends supposedly held at the imperial court.[118] In a (fictitious) *Disputation Between a Christian and a Heathen*, Gilbert Crispin (d. around 1117) recounted how he arrived at an inn and encountered a few educated men, students of logic, sitting at the front doors, engaged in a debate over a *quaestio* based on one of Aristotle's propositions. Inside the dwelling, a discussion was underway between a Christian and a heathen. They were "two philosophers of great renown, but from different schools."[119]

The Christian and heathen were not quarreling with each other; rather, they struggled together to achieve factual knowledge. Abelard took this contemporary form of dialogue and expanded the scope of the (fictive) disputation to give a Jew his say along with the Christian and the heathen.[120] This genre constituted the literary manifestation of Scholastic inquiry, and it was increasingly devoid of the ornamentation and drama associated with the rhetorical debate. At the same time, renderings of actual discussions, like the four-part summa by Alan of Lille, *On Faith*, might also be included in this category.[121] Alan had dealt with Cathars and, as he noted in the prologue, now undertook "to render an account of the rational faith using reasonable arguments." He presented his opponents' views, taken from written works as well as rationally deduced, and then refuted them according to the rules of grammar and dialectic.

The bitter truth was that the heretics did not constitute the proper audience for such accounts, and even their opponents often lacked the requisite educational background. Be that as it may, formal disputations were held with both Cathars and Waldensians. The sides would agree upon a venue, choose arbiters, and undertake to abide by their decision. For example, in a disputation with Waldensians initiated by the archbishop of Laon (1189 or 1190), the "charges" were brought by ecclesiastical and lay Catholics and rebutted point by point by the Waldensians in a lively exchange that went on for quite some time; both sides produced many *auctoritates*. Finally, the arbiter, a highly respected priest, proclaimed his "definitive sentence" in writing—the Waldensians were found guilty on all charges. The verdict had no practical repercussions. The discussion itself was reworked into a written tract.[122]

Many similar discussions were held with the Cathars in southern France before the outbreak of religious war. The most impressive was a two-week-long disputation held in Montréal (1207). On one side was Diego of Osma, the spirit behind the establishment of the Dominican order; on the other, a number of prominent Cathars. The two sides agreed to recognize two noblemen and two townsmen as arbiters and to limit their arguments to the New Testament. Every single proposition was submitted in writing for consideration. Overwhelmed by their task, the arbiters declined to reach a verdict.[123]

The disputations within the province of the *artes* that actually took place—as opposed to those held on paper—were often exhibition matches in which the prestige of a school or a scholar was at stake. When theological matters were at issue, laypeople were hard-pressed to follow the arguments; when there were consequent conversions, as was allegedly the case in Montréal, they were not so much due to the force of the arguments as to the persuasive manner in which they were presented. If clerics were pitted against clerics in a theological discussion, then they were sometimes known to avail themselves of venerable rhetorical practices as well. Thus, when Gilbert of Poitiers had to answer the charges against him in the presence of the pope in Rheims (1148), he banked on a strategy of outlasting the pope: For hour after hour, he had patristic passages that supposedly concurred with his teachings read out loud. Finally, the pope, "as though affected by weariness," interrupted the recitation: "Brother, you say much, you have caused to be read much— and things which perhaps we do not understand." The discussion revolved around the Persons of the Trinity; upon being backed into a corner, Gilbert recouped his position by—inaccurately—deriving the word *persona* from *per se una*, or "a priori a single (thing)." "And to the great astonishment of many present, the assembly recessed for the day," recounted Otto of Freising.[124]

This was a rhetorical device with no bearing on the issue at hand, but it proved quite effective nevertheless. The older modes of biblical exegesis marked by allegorization had always attached great importance to the explication of biblical names; beginning with Plato, it was assumed that the essence of a thing must be hidden in its name—therefore no one ventured to accuse Gilbert of a play on words. He may himself have believed that his etymology was correct, although at the time it was already known that, strictly speaking, *persona* referred to the *persona theatralis*,[125] hence to a classical actor reciting his part from behind a mask.

As far as Gilbert was concerned, at stake was the strict application of a grammatical and logical theory of meaning to the language of theology. Those who had never heard his lectures might have been put off by his deductions. Otto of Freising complained that young students found Gilbert's propositions incomprehensible, and that even scholarly and educated individuals could barely extract their meaning.[126] This excessive linguistic rigorism represented a backlash against the somewhat inexact and confusing note creeping into theological formulations, to which the availability of translations of Greek texts also contributed. Around 1076, for example, the eminent Anselm of Canterbury wrote: "In stating that the supreme Trinity may be said to consist of three substances, I have followed the Greeks, who acknowledge three substances [*substantias*] in one Essence, in the same faith wherein we acknowledge three Persons in one Substance. For they designate by the word *substance* that attribute of God which we designate by the word *person*."[127]

In addition to specific lexical problems, theologians had to grapple with the above-mentioned difficulty that our speech was formulated to deal with the natural realm and only by analogy could be applied to the supranatural one: God is not foremost the Father or Son, but rather is so only in our imagination and mode of expression. God is a unity in three Persons, but the names and number of the Persons cannot be grasped in words or conceptualized by our understanding.[128] Pursuing this line of reasoning, the Gilbertine school of thought wound up espousing a negative theology: One cannot know what God is, rather only state what he is not.[129] This approach was not a novel one and would crop up again later. Nevertheless, Gilbert and his students took great pains to articulate the relationship between substance and the Persons in God. God's secrets, one student contended, are not to be grasped sensually or intellectually, but they are "scrutable" (*scrutabilia*) rationally; one might be able to gain a limited "glimpse," provided one was conscious of the fact that *intelligentia* was less than *intellectus*, complete insight.[130]

Since human speech cannot describe God, there can be no definition of God—and thus no explanation of his essence. In this respect and others as well, the realm of mystery almost always remains inviolate. According to Gilbert of Poitiers, heretics fall into error when they apply rational arguments to the divine sphere without qualification. The Father, the Son, and the Holy Spirit are together one God; however, one cannot say that Plato is a human being, Cicero is a human being, Aristotle is a human being as well, and hence all three are a single human being.[131]

The new theology did not propose replacing mystery with reason, but it did favor seeking out rational solutions, insofar as linguistic logic seemed applicable to this field. At stake in the disputes between the new theologians and the conservatives was the extent to which it was, as well as the latter's lack of understanding for the subtleties associated with speculative investigations. No attempt had yet been made to comprehend and "survey" the entire field of religious mystery; for the most part, thinkers were satisfied to approach the subject equipped with the fundamental tools of grammar and linguistic logic. For example, one rarely encounters a pronouncement about original sin. Abelard wished to consign that topic to the field of ethics and "rationalize" the issue. Proceeding cautiously, he came close to hypothesizing that Christ's preaching and love, thus not Christ's expiatory death, might have served to lift mankind out of its sinful state.[132]

It was thanks to Abelard that speculative theology was propelled in certain directions. He also made contributions to the course of practical theology in that he composed a book on ethics while living among Cluniac monks at the end of his life.[133] Manuscripts of the work bear the title *Know Thyself* (*Scito teipsum*), and the text places great emphasis on psychological motivation vis-à-vis the doctrine of sin. In what was probably the product of his retrospective self-analysis, Abelard theorized that evil does not lie in the act; rather, consideration must be given to the intention [underlying the act]; the only sins are those committed in violation of one's conscience.[134] In his dialogue contrasting the three worldviews of the philosopher, the Jew, and the Christian, Abelard had already termed ethics the culmination and consummation of all the disciplines; however, we should no longer call this discipline ethics or morals, as the pagans did, but rather *divinitas* [divinity], since it leads to God. All other fields perforce pale in comparison,[135] hence even speculative theology.

With such words an older but wiser Abelard devoted himself to the simple ideal of the monastic education—with one difference: As never before, ethics was now viewed as a distinct discipline. During antiquity, one received instruction in ethics in the course of reading the classical authors and as an integral part of rhetoric, and so it remained far into the Middle Ages. During the second half of the twelfth century, people began to draw a distinction between philosophical ethics and Christian moral theology. Theology, Alan of Lille remarked, contains a rational and a moral sphere; the latter addresses human morality and its instillment.[136]

Speculative theology was and remained the province of relatively few masters and their students; contrariwise, moral theology, the most important aspect of practical (or pastoral) theology, touched all individuals, cleric and lay. The virtues and vices, the problem of free will, sexuality, matrimonial issues, and much more lay within its scope; it provided the guiding principle for life on this earth. Biblical passages and patristic texts formed the stuff of moral theology, often derived from handy compendia in which *sententiae* [sentences] were organized by topic. Men like Bernard of Clairvaux and Peter the Venerable kept their distance from speculative theology, and yet did their utmost to promote practical theology within the old framework of "monastic theology"; others, like Peter Lombard, combined the two. On account of his collection of sentences, Peter Lombard was branded one of the "four labyrinths of France," and yet in his biblical commentaries, he had concurrently provided allegorical exegesis and contemplative training.[137] Even Gilbert, that most radical advocate of speculative theology, had as bishop of Poitiers to deliver sermons; to be sure, on just such an occasion he was also not able to refrain from speaking about the Trinity, and these remarks prompted two archdeacons present at the sermon to bring a complaint against him before the pope in Rome.[138]

From then on, theology was and remains divided into two major areas, one marked by theory and speculation, the other by practical and moral concerns; up to that point the former had often been categorized as philosophy, the latter even as poetry.[139] This distinction, which now made it possible to draw a line between doctrinal and moralizing sermons, had a significant impact on the church's relationship with religious fringe groups. Indeed, lay religious communities, like the Waldensians and the Humiliati, who felt called to preach, had been rebuffed time and time again by the church, until at the beginning of his pontificate Pope Innocent III formally recognized this distinction and in 1201 granted the Humiliati permission to deliver moralizing sermons. This represented a turning point, which to be sure came a generation too late for the majority of the Waldensians.

Moral theology did not burn all of its bridges to the philosophical ethics of antiquity, which was undergoing a resurgence due to the study of Platonistic works. In the *Timaeus*, "natural justice" figures as the foundation of the positive justice of the moral and political orders, which are analogous to the cosmic one. William of Conches and John of Salisbury would again embrace these notions: The political system is based upon natural law, which operates much like the effective force does in the soul and the cosmos.[140] In order to provide a foundation for positive law, jurists also had to posit the existence of natural law. In this respect, they concurred with theologians of both stripes. According to Abelard, natural law was intrinsic to each individual by virtue of his or her nature as a rational being, and it constituted the medium by which humans gained a certain cognizance of God, indeed of the Trinity; at the same time, the moralistic streaks in natural law had promoted irreproachable behavior on the part of pagans. Philosophers and patriarchs had lived according to the rule of natural law, for it indeed antedated the Mosaic Law. The pagan in Abelard's dialogue equated natural law and ethics.[141]

This brings us to the field of jurisprudence, which enjoyed a new resurgence consonant with its strong dependence upon and interaction with theology. The revival encompassed both the "scholarly," or canon, law of the church and the civil system of law. In the schools and the later universities north of the Alps, instruction was offered solely in those areas; only in northern Italy, particularly in Pavia, were there individuals who taught the "Lombard" law and a rudimentary form of Roman law. These "schools" were not formal institutions. All the same, a written vestige of their activities contains material about feudal and urban laws. In London, on the other hand, the Inns of Court were the repository of the common law.[142] Thus, there were only a few islands of legal literacy in that vast sea of predominantly unwritten customary law and all its multitudinous manifestations.

New ideas took shape wherever the sacerdotal church evolved into a rigidly structured organization and the "modern" state quashed the traditional structures of civil society. In the latter arena, people availed themselves of the old Roman imperial law, which had first to be painstakingly reconstructed and adapted. It seems that this effort did not represent the continuation of an ongoing process, but rather a truly new start. The situation was quite different for canon law, which covered an extensive corpus of ecclesiastical determinations formulated over the course of many centuries. In this case, a new, rational methodology was needed if all the material was to be mastered and systematized.

Such matters engendered very little interest in the tenth century; the period has been described as marked by a declining familiarity with canon law.[143] No extant work of a higher caliber on canon law was produced between the time Regino of Prüm (d. 915) composed his handbook and the time Bishop Burchard of Worms (d. 1025) compiled his Decretum. In the introduction to his collection, Burchard complained that priests were ignorant of this field and that a "dissonance" marked the extant authorities on canon law. However, there was no means yet at hand to systematize this material. All the same, the texts recorded in collections had long been organized, not chronologically, but instead topically, with admittedly no feasible means for truly distinguishing items of canon law from those of theology. This was particularly true of moral theology, but also of dogma, like the sacraments. For the most part, practical consider-ations greatly outweighed theoretical ones, then as well as later on. Thus, for example, we possess a work by Burchard entitled the *Corrector*, which addresses a broad range of confessional issues, as well as the types and degrees of penance. There was an ancient tradition of such handbooks.

A new wind began to blow after the mid-eleventh century. At the time, the church was becoming increasingly "legalistic" and centralized; due somewhat to the influence of Gregory VII, his pontificate was marked by a greater attention to detail, as was that of Urban II (1088–99). Writers sought to harmonize the material at hand and to establish the prerogatives of the papacy. In addition to "Gregorian" compilations, there were those of Lothringian and French origin.[144] With the rediscovery in the West of the Code of Justinian, a new world of juridical thought was revealed, and people began studying the digests even with the initial prospect of little practical gain. Nevertheless, scholars like Ivo of Chartres were able to obtain some benefit from the exercise.

Ivo (d. 1117), the expert in canon law, and Irnerius (d. 1130), the founder of a school of Roman law in Bologna, ushered in for both fields a new age marked by a critical and systematic approach. Both writers maintained an affinity for theology: For example, in his *Decretum* Ivo discussed in detail the doctrine of the Eucharist and adopted the official creed of Berengar of Tours; Irnerius produced a compendium of theological sentences.[145] Dur-ing an era of shifting norms, Irnerius discovered as a jurist a new legal footing in the rational, universally applicable Roman law; the purely practical activities of the northern Italian judges and lawyers were now joined by those of the "school," later the university, in Bologna. One of the instructors there was a Master Roland, who was for a long time identified with Roland Bandinelli, the future Pope Alexander III (1159–81) and most significant adversary of Frederick Barbarossa. That emperor was in con-tact with the Bolognese jurists engaged in reviving the old imperial law.

The compilation by Ivo of Chartres represented the first systematic, if not yet standardized, overview of the entire body of canon law. At the time the work was written, around the end of the eleventh century, a focus of concern, in light of the life-and-death problems stirred up by the so-called Investiture Contest, was the development of a methodology for critiquing texts in terms of their factual, logical, and historical facets. At first, this occurred in works of limited scope: Bernold of Constance addressed the ostracism of excommunicates (*De excommunicatis vitandis*), and Alger of Liége composed a tract on mercy and justice. Both works contained rules for reconciling texts.[146] They were written after 1084 and 1095, respectively, hence long before Abelard wrote his introduction to *Sic et non*.[147]

The question has consequently been raised whether the seeds of the Scholastic method were planted by jurists rather than theologians. Be that as it may, it seems more important to note that working hand in hand both disciplines underwent "rationalization," an imposition of order upon their textual bases, which soon gave rise to a beneficial new construct. As objective as the criteria underlying the rules for reconciliation may in themselves have been, they were still often applied in support of a system of beliefs that the results were constrained to uphold. Just as with theology, there existed in this case as well a vast array of works addressing specialized issues (*quaestiones*), some involving linguistic logic.[148]

Around 1140 in Bologna the Camaldolese monk Gratian capped the work of the canonists by issuing his great collection of canon law, which was famous for centuries as the *Decretum Gratiani*. It was from this title that the word "decretist" was derived to designate those who commented on the work. Gratian drew upon the many preceding collections and upon the methodology of Roman law. The innovative cast of the work could already be gleaned from its original title: *Concord(ant)ia discordantium canonum*, a concordance of the seemingly discordant precepts of canon law. Gratian has been called the founder of the science of canon law. First and foremost, he was a clear-thinking technician who placed practical considerations above all else. The anterior portion of the work consisted of systematized texts and was followed by a section on casuistry, in which issues of a legal nature (*quaestiones*) drawn from individual cases were discussed and resolved by citing authorities. The bond to theology remained inviolate, indeed was reinforced.

Certain subjects were the province of both canon law and moral theology, like the system of penance and questions concerning simony; however, speculative theology was also represented in the collections of canon law, as in the material on the doctrine of the Eucharist. In addition, each field would from time to time borrow from the other. Jurists uncovered material in collections of theological sentences, while theologians mined the collections of canon law for serviceable patristic pronouncements, as evidenced by the actions of Gilbert of Poitiers in Rheims (1148).

It was in this respect that the rules applied by both disciplines in reconciling texts proved of limited value. People neglected to put passages taken from patristic works into context; they engaged in disputes over the orthodoxy of this or that proposition, drawing upon excerpts, not upon the entire text. Simple Catholics and sectarians did this, as did masters appearing before an ecclesiastical forum. Since verifying the citations was unfeasible, the more eloquent adversary prevailed. Whereas omitting the sources of one's documentary evidence would today be considered unscholarly, in those days scholars thought otherwise. A student of Gilbert of Poitiers gave this account of such an individual: "He provided no record of the authorities he had cited; he ceded to the skillful reader the credit due for identifying passages from the Holy Scriptures. . . . In the prologue to his work [on Boethius's *De Trinitate*], he avers that zealous researchers would be able to discern that whatever he says is lifted from others [*furta*], rather than his own invention."[149] In this case, tracing the quotations back to their source would be particularly difficult, since they were drawn primarily from works by the Greek fathers of the church.

Both theologians and jurists produced compilations of significant pronouncements, or "sentences," in book form. Just as Gratian's *Decretum* was integral to the jurists' practice, so too these collections of theological sentences became indispensable in the classroom. Nevertheless, at the end of the twelfth century jurisprudence still set the standard in this area for theologians. Sometime after 1179, a student of Gilbert of Poitiers wrote this comment apropos his collection of sources concerning Trinitarian issues: "Since it is not easy to read or even to put one's hands on the great number of books from which the authorities cited here were excerpted, . . . a compendium of the individual authorities, . . . in the manner of the books used by jurists, is welcome."[150]

Ranging beyond northern Italy, legal studies found a home at the schools in Valence and Die in southern France. Collections of excerpts were produced at those schools around 1130—hence antedating those produced in northern France—and they were disseminated as far as Austria even before 1160.[151] From approximately 1150 on, there were to our knowledge canonists in Paris who practiced as lawyers.[152] Even so, as early as 1130 monks and canons were precluded from studying law by conciliar decrees, which were renewed by subsequent popes. In certain cases, practicing law or medicine could prove quite lucrative; individuals who chose these professions commonly forsook the spiritual life. Nevertheless, adherents of the new science of legal studies were to be found among monks and canons. Much like the academic theologians, they communicated with one another over vast distances. This has been proved for northern France, the Rhineland, and Austria by tracing the transmission of manuscripts.[153] In an analogous fashion, the school of speculative theology identified with Gilbert of Poitiers had an advocate at the Babenberg court in Vienna, the chaplain Peter. A theological *summa* preserved at the Austrian cloister of Zwettl has been attributed to him.[154]

There now existed among the clergy a class of intellectuals who were few in number yet spread throughout Europe and who were interested in researching a circumscribed topic. Also, jurists now achieved the very thing that had been a matter of course for the theologians, namely, recognition that their activities constituted a separate profession.[155] Roman law assumed its place alongside canon law, though it was accorded a subsidiary role in legal practice. Roman law excelled over prior juridical practices because it was inherently rational and potentially valid in all regions. Particularly in northern Italy, this universality made it feasible to cast aside the many disparities between the Frankish and Lombard law codes. As the cities experienced growth, so did the number of legists in their service, and the progressively legalistic nature of religious institutions made canonists indispensable to their administration. In this manner, the canonists were presented with career opportunities that could lead to extremely prestigious positions. Of the twelve individuals first to write commentaries on Gratian's *Decretum*, two eventually became cardinals, and five, bishops.[156]

Theology and jurisprudence were associated predominantly on a methodological level; in terms of content, the increased emphasis on rationality triggered, if anything, a decline in the juridical element customarily associated with theological thought. The mystery of the Redemption had been framed in terms of the Roman imperial and successive legal codes: In committing the original sin, Adam became Satan's property; to remedy this legal predicament, Christ descended to earth and, himself immaculate, suffered an expiatory death for the human race—in consequence of which the devil lost his rights over humans.[157] Anselm of Canterbury opposed this view, yet it continued to be upheld at the school in Laon and even by Bernard of Clairvaux. Indeed, people considered it a matter of course that the legal and social circumstances characteristic of their own age would be universally valid and theologically applicable. For example, in repudiating certain Christological theses, Gerhoh of Reichersberg based his argument on Christ's nobility (*nobilitas*) and on his status as the legitimate heir to the Father. Gerhoh enumerated six false doctrines that depicted Christ as lacking nobility or being less noble than the Father or Christ's mother, Mary.[158]

In the minds of the early Scholastics, too, there lingered traces of the somewhat coarse and simplistic attitude of previous generations. Yet, that attitude could no longer dominate the field as formerly. A figure like Gerhoh of Reichersberg, along with his clan of relatives and friends, was branded "provincial" when he opposed the "new and scandalous doctrines" of Gilbert of Poitiers and his school. Admittedly, those pursuing this new knowledge tended to formalize a great deal and hence to wind up building castles in the air, all while their adversaries kept both feet firmly on the ground. Yet, this revamping of the customary mode of

thought brought lasting rewards—in terms of language, to begin with—
and imbued individuals with a new ability to form abstract conclusions.
Facility and subtlety in thought and speech were now, for the first time,
positive attributes, whereas previously they had been all too often associated with frivolity and sophistry.

11

The New Schools

 "Flee the heart of Babylon; flee and save your souls! Hasten to the places that offer refuge!"[1] Thus did Bernard of Clairvaux cry out to the secular clergy and advocate entering his order as preferable to living in the "world" with its dangers. His student David of Himmerod (d. 1179) exemplified Bernard's message: David left Italy to study in France, heard about the Cistercian order, and "[g]iving up the studies he had already begun, he chose in preference to be instructed in the disciplines of the *Rule*; he would rather be ignorant of certain things in complete security, than learn them at the risk of his soul."[2] The Cistercians were not the only ones to fear the risks associated with learning and the academic life; they did, however, reinforce the reservations harbored by monks since time immemorial and by reformers in particular.

At the same time, the great masters were reaping praise in student circles; one panegyric closed with a curse upon monks who feigned religiosity but were infused with superstition: "Flee these people and avoid them! . . . The herd of cowled monks is to be disdained and driven from the schools of philosophy. Amen!" What is more, the poem charged, the foremost (*primas*) monk has had master Abelard (*Palatinus*) muzzled.[3] This is a reference to Bernard of Clairvaux and the events of 1141 in Sens. How Abelard himself felt about the traditional system of monastic education may be gleaned from the rule he wrote for the nuns in the cloister of the Paraclete: "But those who are educated in monasteries today are so persistent in their stupidity that they are content merely with the sound of letters, pay no attention to understanding them, and care only to instruct the tongue, not the heart. . . . Such men are the less able to love God and be filled with ardor for him, the further they keep themselves from understanding him and appreciating the Scripture that teaches us about him."[4]

One may argue that a scholarly education is not a prerequisite for monastic spirituality. Abelard's criticism was more applicable to the quality of many monastic schools. Very few of them met the standards of the day; the vast majority were so bad that monks themselves attended "open" schools, even though they were not made welcome, according to the *Metamorphosis Golyae*. The paucity of good schools was attributed to various causes; the most significant one was in all probability so obvious that it was scarcely mentioned: People's expectations had risen greatly from the days when all a school needed to impart was a passing familiarity with the Latin language and formal writing. This elementary form of education, the *trivium*, had sprouted branches of knowledge to which some masters devoted their whole lives.

The students were also of a different stripe. For many centuries, the monastic ranks were for the most part filled with former *pueri oblati*, children who had been dedicated to the religious life by their families and who grew up within a monastery, where they almost always stayed on as monks. Both parties benefited from this symbiosis: The monastery received donations from the secular members of the children's families, and the donors expected a secure place in heaven, given that their children as well as entire monasteries were praying for them. Moreover, this represented one way of disencumbering oneself of surplus sons and daughters, and retaining the right to reclaim them as needed for the secular world. Finally, monasticism was a particularly good option for children with any sort of disability. When the newly elected abbot of Andernes assumed office in 1161, he noted with alarm that most of the monks possessed physical deformities. There were monks who limped, who were crippled, one-eyed, and even blind. "Almost all of them came from noble families."[5]

Corporeal disfigurements obviously had no bearing on an individual's intellectual abilities—Hermann the Lame (d. 1054), of the monastery at Reichenau, was a son of a count and *puer oblatus* with some important achievements to his name. The reformers, however, were not pleased with the status quo; they loosened the ties to noble families and opposed raising children in the cloister. Thus, for example, Cluny did not maintain an "external school"; in other words, the monastery did not offer instruction to secular clerics or laymen. Naturally, admitting novices from the age of approximately fifteen and up, young people who already knew what they were committing themselves to, was preferable. These individuals might be illiterate, as in the case of lay brothers, or—as they were known in the Cistercian order—*conversi*; alternatively, they might be young adults who already possessed a rudimentary education upon which they might base their studies preparatory to ordination. There were now such young people, for at this time the lower nobility seem to have pursued private instruction in the Latin language, an advantage once reserved to the upper nobility. This practice was present even in Brittany, where a member of the lower nobility arranged for his sons to receive instruction in Latin before their training in arms. Drawing upon what he had learned at his father's castle, one of them, Abelard, was able to embark upon advanced studies.

While the monastic schools were no longer the normal stepping-stone to an advanced education, the regular clergy did not by any means disassociate itself completely from this system of instruction.[6] Thus, some individuals took lessons from a chaplain or from a priest in the immediate area, or perhaps from a wandering cleric who was a product of one of the schools; the details remain sketchy, for the sources are all too often inadequate. Information has come down to us of cases in which an abbot of a monastery sent a young monk to one of the new schools to have him trained for the priesthood. We have already heard how the "cowled monks" elicited ridicule and annoyance there.

External schools continued to exist in isolated instances, supervised for the most part by a cleric unaffiliated with the monastery.[7] The abbey of Saint-Victor in Paris maintained an "open" school[8] and propelled it to great prominence. Here, Augustinian canons and not monks were involved; the institution was founded by a teacher, William of Champeaux, and his students. Abelard studied there and quickly became William's rival.

Canons, even those subject to the Augustinian rule, maintained closer ties to the "world" than did monks, and they were less anxious about preserving their spirituality in light of the ascendance of the new learning. By order of Pope Gregory VII (1079), cathedral canons in episcopal cities were obligated to establish schools.[9] To some extent at least, the cathedral schools compensated for the deterioration of the monastic educational system and contributed to the shift in the locus of education to urban settings. There, though the schools were affiliated with institutions, the instructors retained total academic freedom: A teacher could gather his pupils anywhere they were prepared to follow him, even outdoors on a meadow. The cathedral schools prepared individuals for careers as secular priests, whose calling was to tackle the skeptical questions of laypeople. Anselm of Laon summed it up in these words: "The secular clergy are to preach and instruct those in their charge; the monks are to pray."[10] Offering instruction verged on scholarship. Since they were priests, cathedral canons had to be free of physical defects and were expected in their appearance and conduct to redound to the reputation of the bishopric.

External factors favored the new schools. The political climate in northern France had improved; the power of the king was being consolidated; and the peace that had settled over the land promoted intellectual exchange and individual travel. Urban settlements, even Paris, were still small and were yet to put their stamp on the elite. There were also no town schools,[11] and attempts to prove the existence of a characteristically urban mode of thought in the new schools would surely be of no avail.[12] In northern Italy, however, the law schools were more closely associated with the cities in whose service their graduates might earn a living.

Cathedrals often maintained their traditional ties to the circle of families whose members made donations to the chapter and occupied most of the cathedral's prebends. The students drawn from those families remained in their social grouping.[13] Things were different for individuals with other origins: They were outsiders, and that is how it remained for foreign students at the university as long as it was organized into corporations. A letter to Pope Urban III (1185–87) recounted how, when a monk fell sick, two brothers prepared his bed, gave him food and drink, watched over him, and, when the time came, administered extreme unction. "When a student [*scholaris*] falls sick, however, who helps him unless he is very rich? . . . A single servant or some serving girl or other closes the dying man's eyes; two or three clerics are present. Who is there to sing the Psalms? Woe betide the person who is alone!"[14]

The students were regarded as clerics even if they had not yet received any ordination. They were tonsured and wore clerical garb, though there were no strict regulations concerning its appearance. They had pledged celibacy; however, it was scarcely feasible to supervise their behavior. In most cases, a student's living expenses would be covered by his family, which perhaps hoped that the course of study would lead to a solid profession. Alternatively, the young man was provided with an ecclesiastical benefice that could support him at school. A substitute would perform the ecclesiastical functions—usually for a pittance—that the benefice was endowed to support.

In those days, living on one's own, outside one's accustomed social surroundings, was deemed a distressful state of affairs. Hence, young people sought out new associations, and, if things went favorably, found them in the company of pupils attached to a gifted teacher. People tended to speak of "sects" named after their teachers; Anselm of Besate considered himself a member of "Drogo's sect," Drogo having been his teacher in Parma,[15] and even later on people used the term in a neutral sense to signify a "school [of thought]."[16] Hugh of Honau, himself one of

Abelard's former students, recounted of his own pupils: "There are some who grow up in our school, are bound to us in a friendly manner, and hence may be termed 'our' students. They apply themselves zealously to our disciplines and accept with due respect the things they hear from us." There were, to be sure, other students who were foolish and incompetent, and in their presence Hugh kept silent "concerning that which it would be wicked to conceal from the accomplished."[17] This sounds somewhat like a secret teaching, and the practice probably also served to safeguard the teachers against accusations, a position in which the Gilbertines had often found themselves. "There is," Hugh of Honau continued, "yet another sort of student . . . : A few do not commit themselves entirely to any institution; rather, they wander like vagabonds among the schools of all [teachers]. They 'submit themselves to all teachers' [a quote from Gregory of Nazianzus], as if they wanted to select the best offered by each; but after switching [teachers] often, they reject all of them and scorn them, indeed ridicule them, as if their teachings made no sense."[18]

Various reasons could be proposed why students did not show their teachers "due respect" but rather deserted them in disappointment: youthful *Sturm und Drang*, the extreme formalism of the teachings, the vanity of the professors, and even the desire to find a place of study where one need not expend too much time and effort to complete the courses. There might also be financial reasons. Not every student had access to a guaranteed income that could defray his living expenses over the course of many years and perhaps cover his share of those incurred by the teacher as well. To be sure, the normal road to a clerical career was the study of theology, for which a firm grasp of the *artes* was a prerequisite. Due to the inordinately protracted study of grammar and dialectic, and the need to master the methodology for debating narrow questions, the formerly preparatory course of study was transformed into a hurdle that was difficult to clear. William of Conches pointed out that Pythagoras's students had to "listen and have faith" for seven years, for not until the eighth were they themselves permitted to ask questions. Now, however, "upon entering the course of study they already ask questions; indeed— which is even worse—even before they have taken their seats they form judgments [about issues]. Students disdainfully think that within a single year all knowledge will fall into their laps; they pluck off small wisps, chatter stuff of no consequence, and go out into the world, full of arrogance and devoid of solid information."[19]

At the other extreme stood teachers who spent ten years or more, indeed their entire academic careers, fabricating ever new *quaestiones* and formulating responses consonant with all the rules of the art, without ever finishing the course and synthesizing the material. If things went well, a small number of students completed their training and would themselves go on to become teachers in the schools. If things did not, nothing bridged the gap between the teacher's subtlety and the listeners' lack of understanding. John of Salisbury recounted that "when professors of the arts [*artes*] were promising to impart the whole of philosophy in less than three or even two years," William of Conches and a colleague quit teaching, "overwhelmed by the onslaught of the ignorant mob. . . . Since then, less time and attention have been given to the study of grammar."[20]

Here we see a foreshadowing of the problem with a mega-university—and in the following century Paris would be host to at least several thousand students—and with the withdrawal of learning behind the walls of the scholar's chambers. We have already commented that John of Salisbury dubbed those who sought practical gain from their studies Cornificiani,[21] meaning disciples of a "Cornificius" satirically memorialized by Virgil. Fruitless attempts have been made to identify this figure with one of John's anonymous contemporaries,[22] and it would be an exaggeration to speak of a Cornifician "movement."[23] A pragmatic mentality alien to scholarship was more likely the issue here. John might have made a study of this type at the English royal court, where, surrounded by clerical careerists, he would have been the odd man out.

Whoever abandoned the long road of the *artes* and theology in order to earn his keep somewhere else might entertain vague hopes of profiting by his studies. He could enter a monastery with the aim of eventually becoming an abbot or at least a prior—although more and more the higher monastic officers were selected from the ranks of priest-monks. As a *clericus* who knew how to write, he could, if fortune smiled upon him, be called upon to carry out various tasks at a prince's court or in a nobleman's household, in the hope that he would later be rewarded with a benefice or even a position at court. He might apply himself to studying the *artes lucrativae*, thus law or medicine, which were best studied in Bologna or Salerno.

Walter of Châtillon (d. 1203),[24] who had probably served at the court of Henry II of England and had been forced to leave the country as a consequence of Becket's fall from favor (1164), was the author of satirical poems in which he also addressed the decline of the *artes*. They would have flourished for a long time, he complained, but ever since the legal profession gained predominance, they were useless; proponents of the law were hypocrites, avaricious and simoniac men. They were able to realize their goals of becoming abbots or bishops because they paid for those offices, whereas a poor man like Walter could offer only his knowledge of the *artes* and theology. Other subjects he held in low regard. On one occasion, when preaching to an audience of lawyers in Bologna,

Walter explained that a command of the law and even of the entire Code of Justinian was no more conducive to leading a righteous life than the learning of doctors about the human body. Nevertheless, Walter continued, many young people desirous of becoming rich pursued the study of one of these two fields. Studying the law impeded the search for wisdom and could pose a risk to society: When masters of the *artes* engaged in disputes about universals and such stuff, the outcome was worthless, but not dangerous. A dispute between lawyers, however, could, according to Walter, lead to a great miscarriage of justice.

Even Walter was not a scholar merely for the sake of scholarship. Speaking as an impoverished poet, he affirmed that a life without money was just as miserable as death. Unless he were to find himself a patron, a Maecenas, it would be foolish for him to continue with his studies. Sleeping in a soft bed with someone at one's side was more pleasant than spending whole nights in a cold room alone at one's studies. Students should quit studying and while away the time in eating and drinking— but who would foot the bill?

This sentiment was common in the goliard poetry that provided upstart intellectuals with a release from material cares. Walter knew that fewer people were devoting themselves to studying the *artes*, but he saw that mainly as a reflection of the times, which was true, but in a different way than he thought: Ever more doors were open to those with academic training, and ever more students looked to pass through those portals. Pursuing an education became like an adventure that could bring great honor or entrée into the new class of the academic proletariat.

Attempting to explain the growth in the student population exclusively in terms of supply and demand, as if it were some economic phenomenon, would certainly be mistaken. The personal charisma of the teachers who undertook to make their scholarship interesting to their pupils played a great role in this regard. By Southern's estimate, a few hundred students flocked to Anselm of Laon (d. 1117) in a small town of perhaps three thousand inhabitants, "a floating population held together only by the presence of master Anselm."[25] As the first or one of the first to teach by means of *quaestiones*, Anselm certainly did not make things easy for his students. Abelard, following his departure from Saint-Denis, would experience the lengths to which inspired students would go to follow their master. He was permitted to leave on the condition that he not enter another community, but dwell in the wilderness, which he did. His account reads: "No sooner was this known than the students began to gather there from all parts, hurrying from cities and towns to inhabit the wilderness, leaving large mansions to build themselves little huts, eating wild herbs and coarse bread . . . , spreading reeds and straw."[26]

When speaking of the studies they had undertaken, people often made reference to their teachers but not to the places where they had studied; thus, an individual who had received instruction from Robert of Melun called himself "a Meluner" (*Melidunensis*)—even though Robert had taught in Paris! The students of Gilbert of Poitiers [*Porretanus*] were called *Porretani*; those of Adam of Petit-Pont in Paris were the *Parvipontani*; and so on.[27] The personal element compensated for institutional inadequacies. This practice favored the formation of conventicles, though at this time no fights seem to have broken out between the members of different "sects."

The resurgence of dialectic, even more than that of speculative theology, had about it an aura of setting sail for distant shores of knowledge. In a "sermon about clergymen who do not advance to theology," Alan of Lille contended that such individuals pursued the study of trivial and transient philosophy, and that they neglected theology for "frivolous investigations." At the same time, Alan attacked all those who performed "worldly tasks" and were hence apostates[28]—most likely a reference to the activities of some students forced to earn their own livelihood. Material that one person found frivolous might engage the fervent interest of another, because the insights it provided lifted him above the common crowd. In this regard, Thierry of Chartres cited Chalcidius, Plato's commentator, on insight (*intelligentia*): It was vouchsafed to God and for the time being to only a few humans. Those individuals able to understand (*intelligere*) things in their pure form, Thierry continued, are to be regarded among men as gods.[29] What serious student would not want to belong to this elite? One's career was not at stake here, for no one expected a priest or even a bishop to engage in speculative theology. People considered it important for the practitioners of this field to be unencumbered by worldly matters and cares, content with their lot, at utter spiritual peace.[30] This suggests monastic contemplation taken to a new, rational plane. Monasticism, particularly as practiced by the Cistercians, was no longer such a far cry from this: Bernard of Clairvaux recruited monks also from among the students in Paris; his secretary Geoffrey of Auxerre was one of Abelard's former students.

Only rarely did instruction in actual practice live up to the ideal. Thierry of Chartres derided those teachers who had to perform stunts to keep their pupils from straying off, lest they be deserted in the lecture room. Some masters took the view, "If I want to be heard, then I will buy off pupils."[31] But not Thierry, who prided himself on routinely barring unworthy individuals from participating in his course.[32] Whoever was permitted to remain could think of himself as a superior individual, one of those receptive to reason and the search for the truth, in contrast to the "members of the vulgar populace, who in the manner of beasts know nothing beyond what they experience with their senses."[33] These words were uttered by a man who was descended "from one of the most noble families of Normandy"—pride in one's aristocratic lineage ran in his blood and the blood of so many others, and here this sentiment was transformed into pride in one's descent from a religious elite. Thierry's grandfather had founded the monastery of Bec, the culturally preeminent institution of its time, from whose school issued future archbishops and bishops.

A similar frame of mind marked that scion of the Breton nobility Abelard, who was not loyal to any teacher, for he "was so conceited and had such confidence in his own intellectual power that he would scarcely so demean himself as to descend from the heights of his own mind to listen to his teachers."[34] This portrayal was written by Otto of Freising, who did not need to strike such a pose, given that he was the son of a margrave and stepbrother to King Conrad III. In his later years, Abelard himself alluded to his former pride, "which had grown in me through my learning—for in the words of the Apostle, 'Knowledge breeds conceit' ['scientia inflat,' 1 Cor. 8:1]."[35] We have already touched upon the young Abelard's bellicose manner, evident even in his choice of metaphors drawn from the world of combat.[36] Lacking somewhat in self-confidence, young people sought to prove themselves in the least demanding way: through the mastery, not of subject matter, but of people, thus of one's teacher and fellow students, whom one could outdo in acumen and in the art of debate. The verbal *artes* particularly invited this sort of practice. In a sermon attacking the "artists" who did not wish to study theology, Alan spoke of two sorts of students, those "who intend to get [others] to pay them through the nose [*emungere*], like the jurists and the doctors," and those who intend "to procure meaningless fame, like the grammarians and the dialecticians."[37]

At first, this fame was in regard to a very circumscribed group consisting of one's fellow students; it brought personal gratification, but no material reward. The student who successfully assembled his own group of students, however, whether as a teacher's successor or competitor, became a master. Otto of Freising noted sardonically that Abelard had "cloaked himself in the [position of] master (*induens magistrum*)."[38] Given his extraordinary talent, Abelard certainly qualified for the title, but others did not: Many, wrote William of Conches, usurped the title of master without knowing philosophy, and they were ashamed to acknowledge that anything was beyond their ken. "They lecture unwary students on things about which they possess no knowledge."[39] Only later did ecclesiastical licenses to teach gain partial acceptance. Running a school could be lucrative; Abelard noted self-critically later on that he had lectured on philosophy and theology in Paris out of the "desire for wealth and fame."[40]

Often, even individuals who did not teach were termed masters; this was similar to the custom of terming a literate layperson a *clericus* "because he did what is associated with a cleric."[41] The master has been termed a "status-holder in an ill-defined social setting";[42] besides "unaffiliated" teachers, teachers at cathedral schools and religious institutions were referred to in this manner, as were individuals who had once attended an advanced school.[43] Almost all of these were individuals named in charters and belonging to that class of clerks involved in the drafting of documents, mostly in service to great magnates. Much like academic titles today, the honorific of "master" was apparently meant to stress one's membership in not just a profession but a social class as well. The appellation is also encountered in documents drafted in almost all areas where there were no advanced schools. During the course of the twelfth century, the number of individuals bearing the title of master grew dramatically.[44]

The standing associated with the title was modeled on that held by the cathedral schoolmaster, who was normally a member of the chapter and entrusted with exercising the church's educational authority within the entire see.[45] At the cathedral church in Paris and elsewhere in France, the office of cathedral schoolmaster was tied to that of the cantor, likewise a position held in high regard; as a consequence, the title of cantor often supplanted that of the schoolmaster. As for educational jurisdiction, the individual bearing this authority in Paris, William of Champeaux, had to suffer the defiance of Abelard, who eluded his grasp and opened his own school in Melun. William's injunctions came to naught, for the noble family controlling Melun approved of the matter.[46] Later on, Abelard was able to do the same thing in Laon and even in Paris itself, albeit within monastery walls. Things took a similar turn elsewhere, in Rheims, for example.[47] That the scholars situated on the left bank of the Seine fell under the jurisdiction of the abbot of the monastery of Sainte-Geneviève-sur-Mont worked to Abelard's benefit.[48] Even when a very high official of the chapter of Notre-Dame, the chancellor, assumed responsibility for the educational system within the diocese, he was unable to revoke this exemption and close the flourishing school at Sainte-Geneviève.

Under Pope Alexander III new regulations governing the authority to grant the license to teach (*licentia docendi*) were issued, with the aim also of impeding the sale of this license to lecturers. In Paris the regulatory action did not entirely achieve its purpose; it would still take some time before a solid institution, the university, emerged from the profusion of schools. Until then, apart from those who held benefices—for example, canons—

the individuals offering instruction were a migratory and quite fluid group of teachers who came from various regions and were to a great extent dependent upon the money they received from students. There is no discernible evidence that these masters endeavored to establish a corporate identity in the sense of the later university. In their sermons they excoriated the excesses of the established educational system, without addressing organizational problems. The academic teachers themselves came under similar criticism from the rigorists. In his enumeration of the various sorts of masters, Bernard of Clairvaux distinguished between those who lived for the sake of knowledge and those "who desired knowledge so that they might peddle their learning in exchange for money or high office—what an ignominious business!" In Bernard's view, learning had only one allowable function, to serve devotion, "not vainglory or intellectual curiosity or anything similar."[49]

Monks and canons did not need to teach for money, as Abelard had had to do for a time. Even when he was older, Abelard, in his work on *Ethics*, still drew a distinction between living and teaching: "So the teaching of such men is not to be held in contempt; they preach well although they live badly, and they instruct in the word although they do not edify in example, . . . they should be condemned less for the blindness of ignorance than for the fault of negligence."[50] Hence, one could impart intellectual knowledge even if one lived the easygoing life of a bohemian.[51]

Such "negligence" was in all events not as reprehensible as unscholarly thinking. When Bernard of Clairvaux challenged Gilbert of Poitiers to an exchange of views following the proceedings in Rheims, Gilbert retorted that Bernard should make a better study of the *artes* beforehand.[52] In a similar vein, a member of Gilbert's school made this comment concerning Bernard: He had received a paltry education in the liberal arts, none at all in the handling of theological issues. Bernard was an expert, not at argumentation, but at eloquent persuasion (*ornata persuasio*). Much of what he said concerning moral and practical theology (*moralis facultas*), however, was to be believed.[53] Bernard's strengths lay in his high morals, firm grasp of the Bible, and oratorical talent. These qualities were of little value to an elite group of speculative theologians, given the training they had received from Gilbert.

A justifiable pride in one's accomplishments became arrogance in the case of a less gifted individual who was nonetheless intent upon playing the part of a master. "The title of master [*nomen magisterii*] is a splendid thing—people crave it greatly—and under its spell some seize upon a profession for which they have no understanding or ability; that is why they chase after the glory of applause above all and derive greater pleasure from being preeminent than from being productive [for others]."[54] These words, written by a Gilbertine, alluded to the Rule of St. Benedict, which had set the standard for social conduct in a religious community.

Criticism was also voiced from within the ranks and not just by those who completely repudiated the "schools." For example, the words "Scholastic" and "ecclesiastical" held antithetical meanings for Gerhoh of Reichersberg, and he viewed "the schools of France" and "the Roman Church" as irreconcilable entities. The "undisciplined questioning" practiced in the schools was in his view the source of false doctrines. [55]

Gerhoh was the provost of a small foundation of canons on the Inn River, and he had personal connections in Rome, but he did not wield any great influence over his contemporaries. We do not know how many clerics shared his opinion of the schools. If we are to believe William of Conches, the views of the French bishops had more detrimental consequences: "Most of our prelates scour the whole world for tailors and cooks who skillfully [docte] prepare meals seasoned with pepper and other things that delight the palate, . . . [T]hey avoid those striving after knowledge [studentes sapientiae], however, as if they were lepers; in order to disguise their own wickedness, they reproach them [the students] for poisonous arrogance or abusiveness or some other offense."[56]

The members of the upper clergy in France were well aware of the difficulties that might impede the incorporation of scholars or masters into an ecclesiastical organization. William had probably encountered rejection whenever he wanted to board students with the church. On the other hand, one should not draw generalizations from his experience. Of the masters teaching in Paris between 1179 and 1215, 38–46 percent rose to be prelates (including four cardinals and twelve bishops or archbishops), 35–36 percent came to hold high offices in college chapters, and 18–27 percent became canons or monks without further opportunity for preferment. The validity of these statistics is undercut by the fact that they are based on a sample group of only 47 individuals, of whom 24 were theologians, 11 "artists," 10 jurists, and 2 medical doctors.[57] Quantitative data for the period covering the lifetime of William of Conches (d. 1154) are even less reliable.[58]

Due to the sharp growth in the number of students during the last two decades of the century, for every teacher there were certainly more than twenty pupils. One of them might harbor hopes of qualifying to teach as a master, and the others were left with such prospects as were open to individuals who had completed the study of theology and with the renown of having pursued an advanced education. Of course, for many individuals, that merely sufficed to procure a position as a parish priest. Whoever wound up in those circumstances vanished for the most part from the purview of the historical researcher. In only one instance have the lots that befell the students of a Parisian master received systematic study, and that was due to their arrest as heretics. This occurred in either 1202 or 1203, in connection with an affair involving the predeceased master Amalric of Bena; we will speak of him later. Almost all of the former pupils were country priests living in the immediate or greater vicinity of Paris.

Even though many of the former students may have slipped back into provincialism, there still extended over parts of Europe a network—albeit still a loose one—of personal relationships among men educated in the schools, analogous to the one linking the secular magnates. Already in the eleventh century, individuals searching for suitable teachers might cover great distances, a circumstance leading one modern scholar to write: "A kind of bush-telegraph rapidly developed to signal the masters who were worth finding and the places where they were to be found."[59] In those days, even before the Ile de France was to emerge as the meeting place for young intellectuals, noble scions were already making the journey westward. The Piedmontese Anselm (of Canterbury) received instruction at the monastery of Bec in Normandy from Lanfranc, who hailed from Pavia; in spite of his noble lineage, the latter scholar spent his entire life as an itinerant teacher of dialectic. Lanfranc and Anselm rose successively to the office of archbishop, holding the title Primate of England.[60]

Both men had many students. They were probably the reason why the English held scholars in such high regard at the close of the twelfth and beginning of the thirteenth centuries: The king and bishops in England employed at least twice as many masters as did their counterparts in France, where a much greater number of students were to be found.[61] There is surely some truth to the observations that one need not have actively pursued the study of theology in order to become a priest and bishop, and that linguistic logic and late classical grammar were certainly not prerequisites for drawing up charters and drafting letters.[62] For all that, people perhaps placed a premium on the disciplined and precise mode of thought associated with studying. Above all, however, it appears that when it came to impressing the uneducated, the "splendid title of master" (*splendidum magisterii nomen*)[63] did not miss the mark. We may also presume that in aristocratic circles, letting one's sons study was believed to increase the family's prestige. Margrave Leopold III of Austria sent his sons Conrad and Otto off to Paris; Otto became the bishop of Freising, while Conrad became the bishop of Passau and, subsequently, the archbishop of Salzburg, "certainly not on account of his scholarly education,"[64] but probably because he was a member of a princely family eschewing provincialism. Viewed within this context, it was most likely the margrave who, at the advice of Otto of Freising, invited the chaplain Peter, a proponent of the "modern" theology of Gilbert of Poitiers, to Vienna.[65] From there, Peter corresponded with theologians in Constantinople. The Babenberg duke and his Byzantine wife were certainly not averse to such contact, thanks to the policies of Emperor Manuel I. Comnenus toward the West.

Gilbertine writings and, to a lesser extent, the works of Abelard are to be found in Austrian and Bavarian libraries.[66] The personal relationships between scholars probably played a role in their dissemination. Abelard is also well represented in the German libraries found beyond Bavaria,[67] which indicates the presence of theologians who paid assiduous attention to the new developments in the Western schools. We have already alluded to the involvement of *magistri* [masters] in the preparation of written documents, particularly charters, in this region. In all likelihood, most of these individuals had studied—at least for some length of time—in France; indeed, Germany had no schools of the new sort. The data generated by a statistical survey due to be completed a few years hence will for the first time allow us to evaluate the drawing power of the French schools.[68]

One probably cannot speak of an "academic class" of the twelfth century. Nevertheless, a small segment of the population was now composed of young people with intellectual training; as a mark of their background, these individuals were permitted to use a dignified title, even if they were not actively engaged as teachers. An aura of cultivation and intelligence surrounded the master, and by drawing upon both of these qualities, he bolstered the standing of the man whom he served. In the midst of power and authority, an emissary from the sublime realm of reason was now to be found.

12

Early Scholasticism and Heresy

In prior chapters of this book, we have dealt with various expressions of heterodoxy; still awaiting our consideration is one different from all the rest. It involved theologians who, much like those from Orléans, had completed their studies but, employing the new scholarly methods, pried into particular areas of the Christian mysteries and thereby aroused the animosity of their colleagues. Apart from the odd noble sympathizer, their adherents were not to be found among common parishioners. Only a few specialists were qualified to evaluate their subtle theories concerning Eucharistic and Trinitarian doctrines; bishops were compelled to turn to such individuals or to forward the case to the papacy. Even popes reached their decisions at a consistory or a synod on the basis of expert testimony. In the process, the upper clergy shunned extreme measures; hence, such proceedings did not produce any martyrs for their beliefs during the eleventh and twelfth centuries. For a scholar, being forced to recant or even to toss his book into the flames with his own hands was probably worse than being burned at the stake.

In the tenth century, a word from a bishop might still have sufficed to silence a brazen questioner. In his biography of Saint Wolfgang, Otloh of St. Emmeram recounted—admittedly much after the fact—how Emperor Otto II had commanded that bishop to respond to a "heretic" who had offered the following commentary to the verse "And the Word became flesh" [John 1:14]: "If this pertains to the Word [as used in the prologue to the Gospel according to John], then it did not become [flesh]; if it did, then this does not pertain to the Word."[1] The learned bishop thereupon examined the man on the—Aristotelian—distinction between substance and accident, and resolved the problem: God's humanity was an accident that did not affect his divine substance. This response would not have pleased theologians in the future, but it satisfied this brazen "son of the devil" (*filius Belial*).

The situation was different in Paris at the end of the twelfth century. "Contrary to the sacred precepts, people engage in disputes about the ineffable divinity; flesh and blood [that is, humans] quarrel about the incarnation of the Word in a prolix and irreverent manner. They divide the indivisible Trinity and point out disparities between its Persons. There are as many errors as there are learned men [*doctores*], as many objectionable doctrines as there are circles of students [*auditoria*], as many blasphemies as there are public squares."[2] This complaint came from the abbot of Sainte-Geneviève-sur-Mont in Paris, the site of a school of theology. He was not the only one with these concerns.

According to Otloh's account, Wolfgang had placed the "heretic" under an order of silence; in 1177 a papal order enjoined the schoolmasters of Paris and Rheims "and the surrounding cities" to observe silence in reference to a Christological thesis, upon threat of excommunication.[3] The papacy was not proactive in these matters, reacting instead to reports submitted to the curia by theologians residing in affected regions. It was difficult for the curia to get a clear picture of the situation and determine whether it did not involve personal animosities between theologians or even politics with a theological twist. The latter could be taken to such extremes that a military venture on the part of King Henry I of France against the count of Anjou was to take the form of a crusade against heresy because the count's "court theologian," Berengar of Tours, had disseminated Eucharistic theses that had been condemned by the pope in Vercelli in 1050 (as the doctrines of "John Scotus"). The private war never took place; a peace was concluded in 1052, and nothing more was heard of the sanctions—recant or be sentenced to death—promulgated by a synod in Paris against Berengar's adherents.[4] A quarter of a century later, Berengar still feared that, upon stubbornly defending his doctrine before the pope, he would be consigned to anathema and, "as a necessary consequence, so to speak," to mob justice.[5] At the time, such practices did not normally occur; that sort of thing would have also contravened papal intentions.

Whoever wanted to proceed against the proponents of the new learning could draw sustenance from the distrust expressed by individuals who were not pleased with the new, open educational system and who derived just as little pleasure from the fact that it made reference to the tenets of pagan philosophers. "The philosophers are the patriarchs of the heretics," Tertullian had declared, and, in this vein, Honorius Augustodunensis enumerated seventy-five heresies that traced their lineage to "the philoso-phers."[6] The very idea of engaging in research concerning doctrinal matters could trigger the suspicion of heresy.[7] Masters and their adherents were sometimes dreadfully elitist. We have already heard how Thierry of Chartres prided himself on barring the "common people" (profanum vulgus, a phrase borrowed from Horace) from participating in his course,[8] as well as how teachers and their students sometimes formed exclusion-ary societies termed sectae [sects]. The word secta could denote either a group of adherents or a community of coreligionists.[9] It did not take much to suspect such groups of espousing secret doctrines of a dubious nature. The followers of Berengar of Tours had already been accused of engaging in "secret disputations";[10] Abelard mounted a spirited defense against the charge that he had concealed some of his doctrines from the public.[11] Geoffrey of Auxerre reported that Gilbert of Poitiers taught his students novel ideas in secret and that "among these like-minded individuals the new dogmas were kept secret; however, they did nevertheless come to light on one occasion."[12]

In this instance the charge does not appear to have been totally unwarranted. Citing Gregory of Nazianzus, Hugh of Honau wrote that "our secrets" were not to be spread among malevolent listeners, for such people would distort one's propositions. Divine mysteries should be revealed to benevolent individuals, Hugh contended, whereas they should be conveyed to others only in the form of analogies: Even the doctores, hence the fathers of the Church, did not prostitute the truth, but rather they explicated it to the foolish by means of analogies in such a way that those individuals understood the truth and yet did not understand.[13] Hugh may here have been reiterating the opinion of his master Gilbert. Among those who "understood . . . and yet did not understand" Gil-bert's theses were perhaps these two respected figures: Master Adam of Petit-Pont, one of Gilbert's colleagues and a canon in Paris, and Hugh of Champfleury, the royal chancellor. At a consistory in Paris attended by Pope Eugene III (1147), they testified, in lieu of an oath, that they had heard from Gilbert's own mouth some of the items underlying the charge of heresy against him.[14]

Gilbert and his students undertook to coin a new rational and subtle terminology for the field of speculative theology, and it was inevitable that its modes of expression would become a stumbling block for "traditional" theologians. In this respect, his "minor school," as it was termed, was confronted by a "superpower" directed by Bernard of Clairvaux. In his biography of Bernard, Gutolf of Heiligenkreuz later sketched a picture of this dispute as it might have appeared in the eyes of the public: Abelard and Gilbert of Poitiers were monsters whom the saint had successfully combated.[15] Here, the focus was no longer on theses, but on producing a black-and-white portrait characteristic of hagiography. At the time this work was written, in the latter part of the thirteenth century, the tumultuous days of early Scholasticism and of holding it at bay were long past.

   The successes Bernard achieved at the latter undertaking were due to his personal prominence and popularity. He also resorted to historical arguments in the form of allegedly analogous cases dating from the early centuries of church history. Citing analogous cases seemed to have obviated the need to deal with the new heresies more closely. Equating the Bogomils and Cathars with the Manichaeans meant that uneducated heretics and their learned counterparts were treated similarly. As an initial approach to such phenomena, this may have sufficed; when it came to fathoming them, it was, to be sure, an impediment. In the presence of the papal legate at a synod in Soissons (1121), Abelard was condemned as a *Sabellianus haereticus* [Sabellian heretic],[16] hence as an adherent of the third-century thinker Sabellius, who had believed that God was a single person with three aspects—creator, savior, and Holy Spirit. In rebuttal, Abelard employed analogies drawn from dialectic (syllogistic logic) for unity in three Persons; as Otto of Freising put it, and probably with justification, "The analogies he used were not good." Only in a remote sense was Sabellius associated with these matters. Conversely, Gilbert of Poitiers, in defending himself against the condemnation of his view that God and godliness (or divinity, *divinitas*) were distinct entities, labeled the assumption that they were identical "Sabellianism."[17]

   In such instances, taking this tack might still be sufferable, because it served to promote understanding between experts. It was more troubling when it cropped up in a letter from Pope Innocent II to the bishops of France and to Bernard of Clairvaux in which are listed heresiarchs condemned by councils for their Christological errors: Arius, Mani, Nestorius, Eutyches, and Dioscurus. (Eutyches is primarily known for his opposition to the Nestorians.) "Moreover, we grieve that . . . because of the pernicious doctrine of Master P. Abelard, the heresies of those whom we have mentioned and other perverse dogmas have begun to spring up."[18] Walter of Saint-Victor cited this papal correspondence in a yet further simplified abridgment. If in Rome itself churchmen expended so little effort, then why should anyone do otherwise elsewhere?

   The battle against innovative speculative theologians was fought on various fronts, but predominantly on the field of letters. The arguments involved in waging this war revolved around grammatical and dialectical issues, and in this regard the conservative scholars were only rarely matches for the opponents whom they suspected of heresy. This was true even of Bernard of Clairvaux. In fact, only Berengar of Tours had a rival who was his equal, namely, Lanfranc of Bec. An example of the polemical works by conservative thinkers is the tract by Walter of Saint-Victor entitled *Against the Four Labyrinths of France*. We have already spoken of this author in connection with his satire on syllogisms.[19]

At their school and in their writings, the canons of Saint-Victor in Paris had sought to maintain a middle course between the old and the new; Walter, the weakest of these thinkers in terms of learning, was the first to engage in narrow-minded polemics, attacking four eminent theologians of his age whom he termed "labyrinths": Abelard, Gilbert, Peter Lombard, and Peter of Poitiers. All of them, he contended, were possessed by the spirit of Aristotle and believed that they were able to resolve issues concerning the Trinity and Incarnation by means of "Scholastic nonsense."[20] Walter called upon "Saint Bernard" as his witness against them; the tract was hence composed after Bernard had been canonized (1174).

In Walter's view, the four theologians merely exemplified a tendency he opposed. These individuals wished to investigate the mysteries of the faith, although it had been well established "that nothing is more foolish than wishing to understand something beyond the grasp of created beings."[21] The classical philosophers seemed to furnish the tools for such investigations, but "all heretics are engendered by philosophers and dialecticians."[22] Walter named "the heretics and the grammarians, who argue childishly," in the same breadth.[23] It was easy to learn how properly to draw conclusions at the schools, "which exist outside of the church," but it was in the Holy Scriptures that one found something about the truth of a statement.[24] "If only the new doctors, or, to put it better, the new heretics who are descended from the old sectarians and not from dialecticians, would finally cease uttering these novel, secular pronouncements, which were hitherto part of neither the teaching of the Holy Scriptures nor the beliefs of the church!"[25] They were erudite performers (*doctores theatrales*), William continued, and they should follow the divine, rather than the liberal, arts, the apostles and not the philosophers.[26]

In terms of methodology, we are dealing here with the long-standing technique of summoning authorities, thus first and foremost the Bible and the fathers of the church, against the new theses, which were geared predominantly toward rational arguments and linguistic logic. In searching for such arguments, Walter of Saint-Victor took the easy way out: The first book of his tract is "nothing more than an uninterrupted plagiarism of an anonymous work on Christ's incarnation."[27] Other material was borrowed from yet other sources, even from the four authors whom Walter opposed. He had succeeded Richard of Saint-Victor as prior upon the latter's death (1173)—but how they differed! Richard had been a prolific author on the subject of the speculative doctrine of the Trinity and, in this respect, an intellectual partner to the early Scholastics, with their dialectical orientation. Walter, on the other hand, could come up with no ideas of his own; under his priorate Saint-Victor lost touch with this epoch-making movement. The polemicists could neither revoke nor mediate the innovations of the age. The latter action necessitated a new spirituality, which was beginning to arise within the nascent mendicant orders.

Thus ends the general section of our chapter on early scholasticism and heresy. For more detailed information, we now turn to individual case histories, the majority of which concern scholars whom we have already mentioned above. A man with a well-known name and large circle of students was the most likely to utter bold statements and to be threatened by denouncement. But there were other thinkers as well, less effusive personalities who developed a single thesis and then defended it for the rest of their lives. The earliest member of this group, Berengar of Tours, may have drawn upon a pre-Scholastic, the monk Ratramnus of Corbie (d. after 868), but he primarily employed linguistic logic against his opponent, Lanfranc of Bec, since Lanfranc was one of the early dialecticians.

Berengar was born in the first decade of the eleventh century. He came from a very well-to-do family, received a prebend as a cathedral canon in Tours, and became the archdeacon of Angers; he was a generous benefactor of the poor, and his enemies complained that Berengar had provided financial support to his poorer students so that they would propagandize on his behalf.[28] Berengar's teacher had been Bishop Fulbert of Chartres, who was more of an ecclesiastical politician than theologian; he has already been mentioned in our review of the background to the scandal in Orléans (1022).[29] It was during this period that Berengar was indelibly impressed, in a way that may even have had a decisive effect upon his doctrine, not by the bishop himself, but by the inscription on his chalice, which included the words *transitorium sacramentum*—Berengar interpreted this to mean "a transitory sign," and he traced the citation back to Augustine.[30]

The so-called first Eucharist controversy had occurred in the ninth century. Paschasius Radbertus, a monk at the monastery of Corbie, wrote the tract *On the Body and Blood of the Lord* (831); Ratramnus of Corbie composed a rejoinder bearing the same title, which was later attributed to John Scotus (Eriugena). After reading both tracts, Berengar embraced Ratramnus's viewpoint. This presented him with an opportunity to prove his erudition as the schoolmaster of Tours vis-à-vis the up-and-coming, recently established school at the cloister of Bec. He challenged his counterpart Lanfranc of Bec to a public debate over the two works and declared that he would uphold the viewpoint of "John Scotus."

This was quite imprudent on Berengar's part, for in John's own day his doctrines had been condemned at two synods, and Lanfranc, a scion of the northern Italian nobility, presented the matter in Rome rather than debate. There, people knew or learned that Berengar was a member of the circle associated with Count Geoffrey of Anjou, who was just at that time engaged in a serious conflict with Pope Leo IX. Geoffrey had imprisoned a bishop and as a result brought a papal ban upon himself and an interdict upon his domain.[31] Under these circumstances, it was not hard for Lanfranc to secure a renewal of the papal sentence against the work of John Scotus and hence against Berengar's views as well (at Rome and Vercelli, 1050). As we have already noted above, this all transpired at the same time as King Henry I of France was making preparations for a sort of crusade against heretics. In the process Berengar was even briefly taken into custody.

The rest of Berengar's life was marked by efforts to justify his doctrine, summons to synods, formal submissions to their findings, and the search for ever new arguments in favor of his thesis. At a synod in Poitiers (1075) "about the Body and Blood of the Lord," held under the auspices of the papal legate Gerald of Ostia, Berengar very nearly lost his life; we lack detailed information concerning the incident.[32] Lanfranc was already the archbishop of Canterbury at the time, but "Berengar's heresy" continued to occupy the curia until 1079, when Berengar prostrated himself at the Lenten synod in Rome and confessed that he had hitherto been in error. He received the pardon he had sought in return for renewing a solemn vow to remain silent about the doctrine under contention,[33] a vow he honored. Archbishop Lanfranc wrote him at the time: "Humbled in body but not humiliated in heart, in the presence of the holy council you lit a fire and tossed in the books containing the perverse doctrines while swearing . . . to preserve the sacred faith transmitted [to us] by the fathers present at the council."[34] Lanfranc was well enough acquainted with his foe to know that inwardly Berengar persevered in his thesis. Furthermore, Gregory VII considered the matter so important that he had made this doctrinal issue the first order of business at the Lenten synod of 1079; only afterward did the council address the second item on its agenda, "drawing the Apostolic sword out of its sheath" against Henry IV and his supporters. Berengar died at a ripe old age in 1088, and Lanfranc outlived him by one year.

Berengar had the backing of Count Geoffrey Martell of Anjou, who died in 1060, however, and of Bruno Eusebius of Angers, the diocesan bishop for the county of Anjou. As we have noted, Berengar was the archdeacon of Angers, yet after 1060 the new count of Anjou sought to oust him from that office. In any case, it took a few years until that course met with success. Berengar's adherents were not to be found among the "common people," but probably within the ranks of the clergy. He himself did not make an appearance at the synod in Vercelli, "but some of his well-wishers [*fautores*] came, saying that they were his legates and wished to defend him"—at which they failed in any case.[35] In his recapitulation of the synod in Rome (1078), Berengar listed the members of the upper clergy "who sympathized with him," among whom were four cardinals, the archbishop of Milan, and "the [papal] chancellor Peter."[36] As we shall still hear, Berengar was not always scrupulous about the truth when it came to such matters. On the other hand, according to the minutes for the Lenten synod of 1079, "some" individuals there did not share the opinion of the majority (*multi, maxima pars*) concerning the doctrine of the Eucharist but, having been "struck by an all too profound and protracted blindness," defended Berengar's thesis.[37]

What mattered to Berengar was that whoever was pope at the time pronounce in his favor. To accomplish this, he did not shrink from employing underhand methods. Berengar wrote to Cardinal Stephen, whom he had met during the latter's legation to France, that he needed a papal letter of safe-conduct against persecution by the count of Anjou; the cardinal was to attend to this matter and not to be put off by any expenses he might thereby incur: "I will reimburse you for your expenses, no matter how high they may be, and—should you wish—at quadruple their rate."[38] At stake was the archdeaconate, a source of income that Berengar tried in vain to retain. Nevertheless, he attempted to acquire papal letters of safe-conduct through forgery; involved were four *litterae* [letters] from Pope Alexander II dating to the same period (around 1062–64).[39] During the pontificate of Gregory VII, Berengar kept up this activity,[40] but he had already cultivated the impression of enjoying particular favor with Hilde-brand. A letter addressed to Hildebrand in the name of Count Geoffrey Martell of Anjou contained the assertion that Hildebrand had recognized the erroneous nature of the heresy charge against Berengar, yet had remained silent concerning the matter out of fear.[41] With regard to the proceedings in 1079, Berengar related that Gregory VII had confirmed the accuracy of his opinion in the presence of a cardinal and had substantiated this stance with a favorable comment from the Holy Virgin Mary fur-nished in a vision to one of his familiars.[42]

In those days such methods could scarcely have had influence on public opinion; only with the advent of printing did they achieve that effect, with scholars—in a steady stream up until today—coming to regard Gregory VII as one of Berengar's sympathizers. Perhaps Berengar solaced his adherents with the forgeries, for Count Geoffrey's letter indicates that they felt disappointed in Hildebrand.[43] An insulting reference to the pope as "a former student of the heretic Berengar," which was made at a synod held in Brixen by Henry IV (1080), has contributed to the confusion among modern scholars[44]—the comment was, however, a figment of the imagination fabricated by some propagandist involved in church politics. Of note is a story, recounted in this camp, that Gregory had asked two cardinals to pray for a sign from God indicating which side in the Eucharist controversy was right, but that such a sign had not been forthcoming.[45] If this rumor made the rounds at the papal court, then Berengar may have employed the members of his camp to give it an advantageous twist.

Ascertaining the number of people who lent Berengar their support has proved elusive. As schoolmaster in Tours, he would at least have had the opportunity to recruit students, and Bishop Bruno of Angers was surely not the sole eminent French theologian to sympathize with Berengar's doctrine. His teaching concerned a very specialized subject and did not spawn true sectarianism; that Berengar's supporters regarded themselves as the real church and all those who thought differently as unchristian was a polemical and objectively untenable assertion on Lanfranc's part.[46] When silence was imposed upon Berengar in Rome, he was granted an exception were he to reform his adherents. Berengar himself testified that he had observed this order; his opponents, however, charged that "even after so many condemnations at synods and after renouncing his heresy so often, he continued to spread it everywhere in secret."[47] This remark should be taken with a grain of salt, for in the same passage the author asserted that Berengar had insultingly referred to the papacy as the seat of Satan, "both in his speeches and in his writings," and had called the church a church of miscreants. If Berengar had been of this opinion, then he would hardly have striven to obtain official approval of his thesis.

Charges that Berengar and Bruno of Angers rejected infant baptism and "legitimate" (ecclesiastical) marriage are similarly to be taken with a grain of salt. It has been averred that they arrived at this stance because both rites have a material basis and were being treated analogously to the Eucharist.[48] However, Berengar always dissociated himself emphatically from Docetism: In his view, the Eucharistic Christ "is the real body of the Lord, not the semblance of one [*phantasticum*], as the Manichaeans [aver]; rather, it is real and human."[49] Moreover, sacramental marriage does not have a material basis. These charges occur in a previously discussed letter written around 1050 to King Henry I of France from the imperial bishop Theodoin of Liège.[50]

Common beliefs, recurring even among heretics, held that marriage was a matter involving only the bridal pair and their families, and that baptism had meaning only if the individual to be baptized participated volitionally. They are not encountered anywhere, however, in either Berengar's works or the ecclesiastical indictments against him. In this case, the bishop of Liège must have associated Bruno of Angers and Berengar with other individuals, perhaps with those heretics who were the subject of a synod in Rheims in 1049.

Berengar's main work was a rebuttal to Lanfranc's tract *On the Body and Blood of the Lord*. Written before 1070, the treatise was apparently not disseminated, probably owing to the order of silence that was already in effect at that time.[51] The sole surviving manuscript, in Wolfenbüttel, was published by the eminent author and critic Gotthold Ephraim Lessing (d. 1781), who served as librarian there. Berengar was not, to be sure, a man of the Enlightenment and a rationalist in the modern sense of the word.[52] He propped up a dated theory with passages taken from the works of a father of the church, yet he interpreted the quotations using dialectical methods tailored to this theory.

As has already been noted, the word *mysterium* was customarily rendered with the Latin *sacramentum*, which Augustine had equated with a "holy sign" (*sacrum signum*). This phrase was not a definition and was supposed to be understood in the context of the passages where it appeared. Berengar diligently compiled these passages and even slightly amended some of them.[53] If the Eucharist involved a sign, then, in the view of scholars with a dialectical bent, there was also a thing being signified (*res sacramenti*), and that was the body of Christ. Were one to apply Christ's words to the bread and wine as well as to the Eucharist, the former *grammaticus* [grammarian] of Tours continued, then either the subject or the predicate of the sentence would be nullified, and something else would take its place. However, substituting a new subject or predicate rendered a true sentence untrue in the logician's view.[54] Furthermore, the transfigured body of Christ was in heaven, for the Son sits to the right of the Father. If that is where he is, then what exists on earth can only be a sign of that body, not the body itself.[55]

Nonetheless, Augustine had said that the *sacramentum* of the Lord's body was "in a way" this body itself, and Berengar steadfastly adhered to this assertion.[56] In a higher sense—as seen by the eye of the spirit and not the corporeal eye—the "sign" is the "thing being signified." Hence, Berengar could admit that the bread and wine became the Body and Blood of Christ after the consecration, provided that this did not connote a material change. It should be noted here that thinkers at the time commonly subscribed to "ultrarealism," with the result that Berengar had to endorse the belief that the Body and Blood of the Lord were "administered and broken" by the priest and "chewed by the teeth of the faithful."[57] An enraged Berengar recounted that in Poitiers he had conversed with a clergyman who delineated the subsequent course taken by the Eucharistic elements.[58] Later generations would modify such notions.

In the view of Lanfranc and many others, characterizing the Eucharist as a sign diminished its meaning. Bernold of Constance wrote that, according to this thesis, bread and wine were "not really and essentially changed into the flesh and blood of the Lord, but rather just metaphorically."[59] One of Berengar's most prominent contemporaries, Cardinal Humbert of Silva Candida, also took this to be his meaning and had him swear at the Easter synod of 1059 that in no way was it a matter "of just a sign and not the real body and real blood" of Christ.[60]

The quotations from Augustine in Berengar's work are indicative of a different perspective, that of a Christian Platonism: God is real being, the single actual reality; all else is of a lesser nature; the material world can never be more than a shadow, a sign of the divine. Everything transient is merely an image of the single and true reality; the inscription on Bishop Fulbert's chalice did refer to a "transitory sign" (*transitorium sacramentum*), and words found in one of Berengar's letters expound upon this fragment best: "The sign is transitory to be sure, yet the power effectuated by the sign and its suffusing grace are eternal."[61] Augustine had not thought to define the *mysterium* as a mere sign, but rather had elected to avail himself of paraphrases for the ineffable, much as other fathers of the church did and even Paul had already done. The first ones to look for definitions were the dialecticians; we have already mentioned how they played Platonism and dialectic off against each other. Manegold of Lautenbach disapprovingly enumerated twenty-three "definitions" of the soul in Plato.[62]

Why Berengar assumed that the sign of the Lord's body was "in a way" that body itself becomes clear in the context of patristic pronouncements. On this point, a modern author would be tempted to say that he was engaging in a "metaphorical use" of the word.[63] However, in the eleventh century it was quite commonly believed that a word or a thing could have a higher meaning, and that this meaning was just as "real" as, indeed even "more real" than, its original one. These ideas reflect the "precategorical" characteristics of allegorical thinking.[64] The "eye of the spirit" saw reality, the corporeal eye only bread and wine.

Berengar's opponents enlisted another concept of reality that was philosophical to be sure, but areligious: Aristotle did not proceed from divinity in his reasoning, but from the phenomena of this world. Here, he at times uncovered the essence, the gist of a thing, and a number of attendant characteristics or modes of existence. These basic concepts of substance and accidents were known from Boethius. Now, it appeared that this concept of substance—matter-of-fact and based in reality— offered a fitting antithesis to the "signs" of Berengar's proponents. At the Lenten synod of 1079, Berengar had to attest that the body of the Lord was present *substantialiter* [in substance] upon the altar, "not merely by means of the sign [*signum*] and the power of the sacrament, but in actual nature and true substance."[65]

Previously, the concept of substance had been employed infrequently and in passing, if at all. From this point on, the idea increasingly regained the significance it had possessed in Aristotle's works; this represented a "Christian Aristotelianism," which superseded "Christian Platonism." In adopting a philosophy with an altogether worldly orientation, individuals came up with clear concepts, which to be sure required radical modification when applied in the religious realm. A substance undergoing a transformation while its accidents remained the same was not a notion familiar to Aristotle. As is made clear by the use of the words *substantialiter converti* [changed in substance] in 1079 and the pronouncement of the doctrine of the transubstantiation by the Fourth Lateran Council in 1215,[66] mystery retained its position and did not lend itself to rational solution.

Berengar may be seen as a precursor to the eminent dialecticians of the twelfth century. He did endeavor to cite authorities from prior epochs, to be sure, yet in doing so he relied almost exclusively on Augustine, refining the profusion of ideas found in the latter's works down to a single proposition. Berengar omitted other interpretations of the concept *sacramentum* recognized by Augustine; he was himself aware that such alternatives existed. The weakness in his arguments comes to the fore in his quoting Eph. 5:32 ("sacramentum hoc magnum est") and remarking that "the mystery of the allegory is encompassed in the word *sacramentum*."[67] In this passage, Paul interpreted the (spiritual) relationship between husband and wife as symbolic of the one between Christ and the Church.

Those who attempted to use Christ's own words to deduce the accuracy of Berengar's view of the Eucharist fell prey to a second methodological fallacy. Amending the subject or predicate of a statement affected its grammar and (philosophical) logic, but not necessarily a (theological) reality, a being. In other instances, too, as in the debate about universals or in proofs of God's existence, no notice was taken of the leap that was made from the semantics of linguistic logic to ontology. At this time language was still believed to present a complete and accurate likeness of things. Later on, Abelard in particular recognized that things were unapproachable through verbal expression and that a chasm yawned between mental and real objects.[68]

Lanfranc had accused his adversary Berengar of disregarding the church authorities and of seeking "refuge in dialectic." Berengar retorted that he did not repent of this, for he saw that God's wisdom and power in no way conflicted with dialectic.[69] Berengar thus shifted the debate to a different footing, and Lanfranc followed suit only reluctantly, in order to refute him. Their exchange represented the first great dispute using the intellectual tools of the Scholastics, and it inaugurated the epoch of early Scholasticism. We must point out once again that the old ways endured alongside the new, and that reason did not by any means dominate the field in place of the authorities. This is also demonstrated in the subsequent course of the doctrine of the Eucharist.

Two generations after Berengar, it was the turn of Rupert of Deutz (born around 1070) to latch onto Augustine. In the latter's works, he read that the Eucharist consisted of two aspects, just as there were two natures in Christ. Out of this analogy Rupert fashioned a proposition rooted in philosophical realism: In the same way as there is an incarnation (*incarnatio*) of Christ, so there is an "impanation" (*inpanatio*) of Christ, or real presence of Christ in the bread. Rupert's adversary, Alger of Liège, termed this "a novel and absurd heresy."[70] An investigation was launched against Rupert in 1116; he only narrowly escaped conviction.[71]

The dialectician Roscelin, who was a canon in Compiègne (born around 1050) and became one of Abelard's teachers, belonged to the generation flanked by those of Berengar and Rupert; except for a rude letter to his former student, none of his works has survived. Some of his teachings were professed by contemporaries. In 1092 he was compelled in Soissons to recant his views on the Trinity, the topic of foremost interest to theologians, in terms of their speculative work, during this as well as the following century. There is initially no discernible connection between Roscelin's thesis and dialectics. He contended that the Father, Son, and Holy Spirit were three distinct substances sharing the same will, knowledge, and capability; they could be compared to three human souls. One of his learned colleagues noted that the matter reflected a problem with translation: Whereas Western theologians attributed a single substance and three Persons to God, the Greeks spoke of three hypostases, translated as *substantiae* [substances], and a single essence (*essentia*). Roscelin should thus refer not to three substances, his contemporary indicated, but to three hypostases.[72]

That is not what he did, however, and soon afterward he had to answer for his thesis. Roscelin's obstinacy has been attributed to his position on the aforementioned question of universals. As we have noted, this concerned the nature of general concepts, a difficult topic because at that time the word "concept" was not yet understood in its modern sense. In Platonism, the "general essences" were envisioned as higher realities,

Ideas in the Mind of the world's artificer. Roscelin opposed "ultrarealism," perhaps because he was a "nominalist," but at any event because he was an innovator. Anselm of Canterbury contended that heretics considered the universal Forms, hence the Ideas, the equivalent of a sequence of sounds made by the human voice.[73] This remark was directed at Roscelin and suggested that he had repudiated Platonic viewpoints, but not necessarily that he had rejected the possibility of rational apprehension. For the sounds of the spoken word do convey a meaning that perhaps encompasses the existence of general concepts; these, then, existed in human thought. Roscelin perhaps felt called upon, for the benefit of the triune God, to resolve God's "general substance" from three [Persons] into one [Person] composed of the most intimately interrelated individual substances. Subjected to gross oversimplification, this thesis propounded the existence of three gods instead of the one, Trinitarian God.

This "tritheism" was also—unjustly—imputed to Abelard. The occasion was an ecclesiastical assembly in Soissons (1121) and in the presence of the papal legate. Otto of Freising recounted that Abelard was not given the opportunity to comment on the charge, because people feared his disputative skill. He was forced to throw one of his own books, the first redaction of his *Theologia summi boni*, into a fire.[74] In the process, an example was set for other excessively modern theologians and freethinkers, one of whom had not long ago (around 1114) caused a stir in Soissons: At that time, it was said that Count John of Soissons "loved the heretics" and had made remarks contrary to faith.[75]

Unlike Berengar, Abelard did not devote decades to the defense of a single thesis; he was by temperament a wide-ranging thinker, and, consonant with the dictates of his research, he repeatedly ventured to the very bounds of its potential range. Hence, on various occasions he also came into conflict with conservatives who contended he had overstepped these bounds. In this connection, there exist whole lists of his infractions, as, for example, a catalogue of fourteen offending points, about which its most recent editor has remarked: "In an age with a penchant for condemning thoroughly debatable theological differences of opinion as heresies, the doctrinal views contained in the *capitula heresum* [chapters of heresies] probably sounded like 'profane novelties' to some ears, but later on they no longer inspired wonderment."[76] Another modern expert posed the rhetorical question whether, in the cases of Abelard and Gilbert of Poitiers, Bernard of Clairvaux had not in fact taken for heresies things that were no more than the products of "bold research," along "with all the attendant novelties and items that ran the chance of error without, however, endangering the faith."[77]

In Soissons, Abelard did not yet have Bernard as his opponent; he was denounced to the archbishop there by two of his colleagues from Rheims. Abelard later contended that the two had so aroused the populace against him and his students that they were almost stoned upon their arrival. Abelard had brought along his book and wished to present it to the papal legate attending the synod in Soissons for review. However, the legate refused to read it and ordered that the book be handed over to the archbishop and Abelard's opponents. "As the legate was less of a scholar than he should have been, he relied largely on the advice of the archbishop, who in turn relied on theirs [that of Abelard's enemies]."[78]

This caustic statement communicates basically the same information as the account of the affair by Otto of Freising: The members of the upper clergy were not equipped to serve as judges in Scholastic disputations. Berengar defended a single thesis for decades and found his match in his adversary Lanfranc; Abelard, on the other hand, erected a system that would have taken years to critique, and he was a master of debate—as he proved to his opponents in the course of the synod in Soissons. They took refuge in formalities: To condemn the (unread) book, it sufficed that the author had lectured on it without waiting for permission from the pope or from authorized members of the clergy. An example had to be set here in order to hinder others from acting with similar boldness.[79]

As long as the course of study was not institutional in nature and the bishops possessed only little or no training in Scholasticism, academic oversight and censorship could exist only in theory. The exercise of these functions was contingent upon the filing of charges by individuals not always acting out of concern for the faith. This state of affairs proved more conducive to the development of speculative theology than a tight rein would have.

First and foremost, scholars faced the task of applying the tools of grammar and dialectic to the new scholarship; only once the meanings of the relevant concepts were clarified was the stage set for forming rational judgments about theological matters. The grammatical and logical specu-lation about the mysteries of faith attendant upon this ongoing process was not always viewed in a favorable light. For example, Abelard in particular seems to have pursued such a course in his early years. Otto of Freising offered the not-quite-accurate report that Abelard had been condemned in Soissons in 1121 for having established a parallel between the Persons of the Trinity and the parts of the syllogism—major premise, minor premise, and conclusion.[80] In the last quarter of the century, the disciples of Gilbert of Poitiers still recalled Abelard's thought experiment about the Trinity: "Another master, a man whose manner of thinking was very subtle, embarked unguided upon a path into the unknown; ex-hausted by his walk, he fell asleep in the wilderness. . . . He dreamed that God the Father was as subsumed in the Son of God as a genus is in its species." On that account, the passage continues, he was condemned to perpetual silence.[81] Bernard of Clairvaux took the analogy so seriously that he polemicized against it, "using the tools of Abelard's dialectic."[82]

Bernard and his friend William, at one time the abbot of Saint-Thierry, near Rheims, and subsequently a Cistercian, launched their attack against Abelard when, in the wake of terrible setbacks, the latter resumed teaching in Paris and gained an ever greater following. He "had attracted a very great throng of pupils to him," wrote Otto of Freising.[83] Abelard was summoned to a synod in Sens (1140), which was also attended by the king of France, many noblemen, "and countless numbers of the people." In the course of their debate over Abelard's beliefs, "fearing an uprising of the people, he [Abelard] asked that he might appear before the Roman see."[84] Abelard thus sidestepped condemnation as a heretic by a court that offered him only formal prospects for a fair trial. To be sure, Bernard was in extremely good standing with Pope Innocent II, whose side he had decisively favored during the schism. Bernard dispatched a treatise to Rome discussing Abelard's heresies, as well as a letter to the bishops of northern France, and he had a hand in the above-mentioned compilation of questionable passages.[85] The papal decision was much as one might have expected: Abelard's "perverse teachings" were condemned wholesale. As a heretic, he was to remain permanently silent, while his defenders and followers were to suffer excommunication.[86] This occurred in 1141. Abelard had no time to recover from the blow; he died within the year.

Bernard and the bishops had accused Abelard of wanting, "by means of human reason, to comprehend in its totality what God is." As for the book that had been burned in Soissons (1121), they reported that it had "risen up from the dead and with it the dormant heresies of many." This book was apparently the second redaction of the *Theologia summi boni*. The letter to the pope also accused him of reviving old heresies. Bernard contended that "when he [Abelard] speaks of the Trinity, it smacks of Arius; when he talks about grace, it smacks of Pelagius; what he says about the Person of Christ smacks of Nestorius."[87]

In the tract he sent to Pope Innocent II, Bernard concentrated on repudiating fewer points than appeared on the list of Abelard's heresies. First and foremost, the dispute revolved around Abelard's attempt to attribute distinct characteristics to each Person of the Trinity: omnipotence to the Father, wisdom to the Son, and kindness (or generosity, *benignitas*) to the Holy Spirit. In the edifying literature of earlier centuries, such material would hardly have raised any hackles; in the work of an author intent on rational definitions and distinctions rooted in logic, it was sure to come across as suspicious. For Abelard had offered this analogy in support of his thesis: The species of a bronze seal is shown in its matter, the genus in its engraving—in the same way, wisdom is a subcategory of power, which was the general conception.[88] Here again Abelard's train of thought focused on applying the distinction between species and genus to the Trinity. "Since . . . the genus . . . is inferior to and has less precedence than the species," Bernard rebutted Abelard, "be it far from us to apply this distinction to God the Father and the Son of God."[89]

Bernard expressed his views on two additional points more briefly. According to Abelard, faith is an opinion (aestimatio)—to the contrary, Bernard declared, faith is absolute knowledge.[90] In the view of the logician Abelard, all things that lacked proofs were assumptions, while in Bernard's view what counted was inner certainty, a quality that even his adversary did not undertake to repudiate, but assigned to practical and not speculative theology. Furthermore, once again the dispute involved the World-Soul and an attempt to equate it with the Holy Spirit. "Here, he strains to turn Plato into a Christian and, in doing so, proves that he himself is a heathen."[91]

Bernard devoted the most space to defending a view that we have already mentioned.[92] Due to his Fall, Adam had become a servus (servant) of the devil, and Christ nullified this legal arrangement by means of his voluntary expiatory death; it would not have been possible to free humankind from that onus by any other means. Abelard rejected this categorical validation of the classical and medieval social order and its application to theology, albeit on different grounds. In his works a moralistic and mystical explanation for the Redemption took the place of a juridical one: Through his sacrifice Christ taught humans how, enflamed by his labor of love, to endure all trouble for his sake.[93] "I heed prophets and apostles," Bernard replied heatedly; "I obey the Gospels, but not the gospel according to Peter [Abelard]. Have you invented a new gospel?"[94]

Bernard of Clairvaux restored to monasticism that confidence in its course and goals which stood in danger of being swept away by the torrent of new scholarship. Victory was his in the battle against the most interesting and most resolute proponent of innovation, but the schools remained and became ever more popular. Abelard was revered by his students and his students' students, one of whom applied John's words about Christ's passion to the master. Berengar of Poitiers wrote an *Apology Against [Saint] Bernard* in the aftermath of the synod in Sens, in which he stated: "The high priests and Pharisees convened an assembly and said: What should we do, since this man speaks of many wonderful things? If we let him go on like this, all will believe him. One of them, named Abbot Bernard, the leader of this assembly, prophesied and said, 'It is to our benefit that a single man of the people lose his life and the entire people not be ruined.' From that day on, they had in mind to condemn him."[95]

William of Conches was a member of Abelard's generation and akin to him intellectually. He was a Norman who studied medicine, engaged in natural philosophy, came under suspicion of heresy, and, under the protection of Count Geoffrey of Anjou, became the tutor to the future king Henry II of England; he died in 1154, the same year Henry assumed the throne. In the immediate wake of the synod in Sens, William of Saint-Thierry, who had assisted Bernard of Clairvaux, addressed this comment to his master in a work entitled *On the Errors of William of Conches*: "This man . . . and Peter Abelard are, insofar as one can judge from their writings, of the same spirit in the way they express themselves and in the way they go astray. . . . With the spirit of this world they research the most sublime matters of God. They know the same things, they speak the same things."[96]

The main charge leveled against William of Conches was that he engaged in what would later have been described as "modalistic" speculation about the Trinity. He was one of those theologians who considered the use of concepts associated with family life—like father and son—to be a stopgap measure vis-à-vis the Persons of the Trinity, and who looked for ways to supplement or even replace these adopted terms. For his part, William of Saint-Thierry denied that the biblical designations for the Persons of the Trinity were to be understood solely in a nominal sense (*nuncupative*) and that they admitted of substitution by other words. Much like Peter Abelard, William of Conches had proposed designating God the Father as the effective force (*potentia*), the Son as wisdom (*sapientia*), and the Holy Spirit as the will (*voluntas*). The effective creative force brings forth the wisdom disposing it to created things, and both bring forth the will to create the things themselves.[97]

In this sphere, the imperfect nature of human speech became particularly manifest, and thought experiments that drew attention to this circumstance were probably sufferable. It became troubling, however, whenever these intellectual constructs were considered—as was only natural—theological theses. In such instances, William of Saint-Thierry was correct in pointing out that these ideas were untenable: God had still other qualities that could be listed, yet none of them could be attributed to only one of his Persons. Indeed, there existed the wisdom of the Father, the effective force of the Son, etc. However, he was not correct in branding his adversaries as "Sabellians." The presuppositions underlying early Scholastic speculation were entirely different from those of the third century, even if the "modern" pronouncements seemed akin to the earlier ones. That they did seem so was linked to the fact that there was a relatively limited number of ways in which one could think about this subject, the Trinity.

A second accusation concerned an opinion alleged to William of Conches, that Adam's body was not created by God, but rather by nature—or, as was his thesis later on, "by spirits, which he called demons, and by the stars." According to this view, only the human soul came from God.[98] This was probably an intentional oversimplification of views held by William of Conches, who in no way wished to call God's creation of the human body into question: God is the first cause, he contended, to which all the forces of nature are joined as secondary causes.[99] William of Saint-Thierry was drawing upon this material when he asserted: "In his second interpretation, he [William of Conches] is a patent Manichaean, for he says that the human soul is created by the good god, while the body is created by the prince of darkness."[100] This was an unfair and not very deft instance of chicanery. In the view of William of Conches, personifying the forces of nature in the Platonistic manner was an intellectual tool of which he occasionally availed himself, and it did not represent a belief in any sort of dualism.

Yet a third eminent scholar belonged to the same generation as Abelard and William of Conches. He was Gilbert of Poitiers (or *Porretanus*, "of the leek field"?), the most complex thinker of the three, even in the eyes of contemporaries, and the founder of a school of thought that continued to exert influence following his death (1154) until almost the end of the century. We have referred to this "minor school" and its master on several occasions already. The state of research on both these topics has benefited from the extraordinary efforts of Nikolaus Haring, who placed Gilbert head and shoulders above Abelard and on a par with Thomas Aquinas in stature. However, Abelard was surely more than a "clever compilator and textual analyst." And Thomas, who has been termed the prince of Scholasticism, overshadows Gilbert certainly not due solely to the "historical advantages which were denied to the former."[101] Rather, we are dealing with two different types of scholars here, the "generalist" Thomas and the specialist Gilbert, who wrestled to apply a severe linguistic logic to his Trinitarian speculation.

According to Otto of Freising, Gilbert was born in Poitiers, where from 1142 on he was engaged in teaching and subsequently served as bishop. He had previously been a canon in Chartres and studied logic and theology in Paris. In 1146, while bishop, Gilbert came under suspicion of heresy: Two of his archdeacons filed a complaint with Pope Eugene III concerning a sermon delivered by their superior. In two consistories held in Paris (1147) and in the aftermath of the Council of Rheims in 1148, the matter was addressed by the pope and bishops. We have already related how the pope had declared that he scarcely understood Gilbert's scholarly explications.[102] Pope Eugene had been a student of Bernard of Clairvaux, and the latter's assistant Geoffrey compiled a tract containing material countering Gilbert.[103] Nevertheless, the cardinals at the council were not well disposed toward Bernard; they feared his excessive influence, and hence Gilbert found support among the participants.[104] He was compelled to retract his controversial book, a commentary on Boethius, and submit to some corrections,[105] but Gilbert retained his bishopric. Bernard of Clairvaux later invited him to a personal exchange of views, but was rebuffed.

Banning books only serves to arouse curiosity. Geoffrey of Auxerre reported that Gilbert's students "did not halt their continued reading of the forbidden pages, which was all the more injurious to them, the more secretly they did so."[106] Hugh of Honau, and probably other students of Gilbert as well, did not customarily communicate all he had taught to all of their listeners, but only to selected, "consummate" students.[107] An elitist tendency marked those Gilbertines who knew that due to their subtle quality and severely abstract nature, the master's doctrine and the subsequent elaborations upon it by many theologians would not be understood. Even Otto of Freising, who had an affinity for this school, complained that Gilbert "said many things that were not consonant with the conventional manner of using language."[108]

In theological works written in bygone centuries for predominantly edifying purposes, the fathers of the church had employed turns of phrase more in keeping with the rhetorical use of words than with dialectical precision. For example, Augustine had said: "The form of God took on the form of a person, and the deity became flesh." Gilbert corrected him: A nature (form) cannot take on the form of another nature; a person cannot become another person.[109] Gilbert undertook to draw such a strict distinction between godhood (or divinity, *divinitas*) and God that he was suspected of wanting to invent a fourth divine Person. He postulated that the language of theology would, through its subordination to the rules of classical grammar and dialectic, be raised up to a new standard, one revealing new perspectives. In the process, however, a thousand-year-old verbal tradition fell by the wayside.

Gilbert performed this experiment in terms of the very topic that theologians found most difficult and to be sure most interesting, the doctrine of the Trinity. In the process, he perforce aroused the resolute opposition of thinkers in conservative circles, who deployed against him a profusion of authorities from centuries past or even simply declared: "This explanation is over our heads [supra nos est]."[110] The balance between *auctoritas* and *ratio* seemed to have been tipped; the language that was rich in imagery and tugged at the heartstrings, that imparted the secrets of God, was supposed to yield to something new contrived by a scholar. Even when this new language was not objectionable, it could still trigger misunderstandings. Bernard of Clairvaux oversimplified theses propounded by Gilbert and then repudiated them in their modified form. In one case, he remarked while doing so that he was not attacking Gilbert, but rather those who read and copied the thinker's works.[111]

Gilbert assumed that the predicate of a sentence expresses how the sentence's subject, which was thought of as a kind of substance, participates in universal forms—we would call them universals. For example, the sentence "Socrates is a human" means that this person [Socrates, the subject] is assigned a quality of a universal nature, namely, that of being a human, or humanity (*humanitas*). Socrates is an individual [substance] (*id quod*), and humanity is one universal in which he participates (*id quo*). So that theology might benefit from these determinations, Gilbert now turned his attention to God. He did not believe that God, like Socrates, was composed of substance and qualities, but that in God's case *id quod* and *id quo* coincided.[112] Nevertheless, it was possible for humans to draw an analogy here with the created world and to draw conclusions that were not definitive, to be sure, but analogous in nature. Hence, Gilbert stated, one might say that "God the Father is [by means of his divinity] God," not, however, that "God is God the Father, God the Son, and the Holy Spirit," for Persons could not be predicates. In rebuttal, Geoffrey of Auxerre of course cited a statement by Saint Augustine: "We believe that the one God is the Father, the Son, and the Holy Spirit."[113] The rules of academic logic, which were now to govern every theological proposition, were not always observed in patristic works. Consequently, such writings were also more interesting than Scholastic tracts tended to be.

Gilbert contended that the dichotomy between substance and qualities, or properties (*proprietates*), was a human construct.[114] When humans apply human speech to God, then this dichotomy also exists—for us humans—in God. He is God by means of his divinity, Father by means of his paternity. At this juncture already, other theologians parted company with Gilbert: No such diversity (*diversitas*) exists in God. Bernard of Clairvaux steadfastly contended in Rheims (1148) that the properties of the divine Persons were one and the same as they.[115] An explicit statement on Gilbert's part that his contention pertained to conceptual constructs, existent solely in the minds of theologians, would have cleared up the situation. Geoffrey of Auxerre asserted that Gilbert regarded the *proprietates* as "eternal things" (*res eterne*), and in fact a statement to this effect does occur in Gilbert's tract on the Trinity.[116] He took concepts and transported them into the realm of reality.

Hence, God's essence (*essentia*) could exist side by side with God. In Rheims, Pope Eugene III inquired of Gilbert "whether you believe that the highest essence [*essentia*], wherein you declare the three persons are one God, is God." According to the account of the interrogation by Otto of Freising, the exhausted Gilbert responded, "No!" whereupon the secretary of the synod immediately noted in his report: "The bishop of Poitiers has written and declared that the divine essence is not God."[117] This yielded a quaternity, the assumption that there was a fourth divine person; thus oversimplified, the remark was patently heretical.

Scholastic subtlety and a propensity to differentiate concepts were not the only forces at work here. Nor can everything be laid to Aristotle's doctrine of categories; Gilbert, though the most consistent, was not the first thinker to apply them to God. The material he possessed, however, did not represent the "pure" thought of Aristotle, with its thoroughly temporal orientation, but rather the Boethian version, with its interspersion of Platonistic thought. "Who is a man or God," Boethius had written, "relates to the substance wherein [or out of which] something is, that is, man or God." Gilbert quoted this remark and explained: "to the substance, not which he is, but rather wherein he is."[118] At issue here were the *res eterne*, eternal and real ideas that existed beyond the Persons. In this way, it was possible to draw a distinction between God and the reality of his essence without undertaking to elevate the latter to a divinity.

Gilbert was compelled to recite a creed drafted by Bernard containing a retraction of the view that there were in God "other things at all, whether they be called relations or properties . . . that are from eternity and are not God."[119] Insofar as he himself had emphasized God's singleness— the various "forms" in God were different in name, but the same in substance—Gilbert would have concurred with that statement.[120] This was true of God, but not of the manner in which humans understood God. Thus, in this instance, Gilbert might have considered a "realistic" solution to the problem of universals correct. After all, he had been a cathedral canon during the chancellorship of Bernard of Chartres, the most important Platonist of his time. His acquaintance with the works of Boethius most likely dated from that period as well.[121] It was during this time, too, that Thierry of Chartres, who was probably Bernard's brother, founded "grammatical Platonism."[122] With reference to the general concepts, the universals, this thinking taught that the "universal forms" existed as metaphysical essences.[123] A more modern approach was taken by Abelard, whose teacher, Roscelin, had not been a realist, and who achieved the first success of his career arguing against the realistic thesis of William of Champeaux.[124] In Abelard's view, the general forms existed in the spirit of God and in the human spirit, without being things (*res*).

Gilbert of Poitiers was a bold thinker of unimpeachable morals. He considered himself a researcher, not an "artiste" in the modern sense of the word, even when called upon to perform breathtaking balancing acts with Aristotle, Plato, and the teachings of the church. The difficulty, indeed the unintelligibility, of some of his explications did not deter his students; on the contrary, no twelfth-century master had such loyal followers. They continued to perform research in his spirit, for example, on nature and person as they pertain to the Trinity. We have already mentioned how they introduced hitherto unknown Greek authors to the West and established a network of far-flung contacts across Europe. The Gilbertines also ran schools themselves, as evidenced by their modest outpost in Vienna, of all places.[125]

Around 1200 the "minor school" associated with Gilbert of Poitiers vanishes from the sources. The last written reference to this school of thought derives from a former teacher of canon law, Everard of Ypres, who became a Cistercian and in the 1190s wrote a dialogue between the "Athenian" Ratius and a man named Everard.[126] Ratius, whose name is reminiscent of *ratio*, was a Gilbertine, and his counterpart in the discussion was the author. As a Cistercian, Everard had distanced himself from Gilbert's teachings, yet preserved very warm memories of him as a person. At approximately fifteen years of age, Everard was one of four individuals who studied the *artes* with the almost sixty-year-old teacher in Chartres, and he accompanied Gilbert to Paris in 1141. There he attended the master's lectures in the company of three hundred students; soon afterward, Gilbert became bishop and had to abandon teaching. Everard later composed an epitaph for Gilbert and, as a fitting monument, the dialogue. In that work, Ratius remarks that Gilbert is thought to be close to God's secrets, now that he is in the heavenly palace.[127]

As a Cistercian Everard felt duty-bound by his heightened sense of right and wrong to draw the attention of the new pope Urban III (1185–87) to the errors of unnamed lecturers and students in Paris and elsewhere. "Father, you heard these errors in the schools, and you had associations with the errant ones." In those days, the future pope had not possessed the authority to intervene; now, however, he should initiate a debate in Paris concerning these individuals.[128] At issue here were the Trinity and, of primary concern to Gilbert's students, the relationship between the nature and Person (or the natures and Person) of Christ. The pope had other worries, to be sure, in view of his encirclement by Hohenstaufen forces and the jockeying for position in northern Italy.

In the course of his work, Everard touched upon the problem of the relationship between God and divinity; it was Gilbert's handling of this topic in Rheims (1148) that had sparked the scandal. Taking a moderate course here, Everard traced it back to an axiom of linguistic logic. One should not say, he stated, that God is the truth, but rather that God is true. Carthage was not destroyed by Scipio's wisdom, but rather by the wise Scipio. In theology the figurative language of rhetoric should be replaced by a terminology that is logically precise.[129] Thus it follows vis-à-vis the issue under dispute: God is divine—which, to be sure, provided no grist for the mills of the speculative theologians. As we have already noted, this Trinitarian speculation was ultimately of little consequence, but it did serve to render the technical language of theology objective and to some extent logical, and this mode of expression spread to other areas as well. Scholastic Latin expanded the frontiers of the intellectual world, yet it was matter-of-fact and plainspoken in comparison with the Latin employed by the fathers of the church and Bernard of Clairvaux.

Everard of Ypres also expressed an opinion on Bernard's opposition to Gilbert, though he placed the criticism in Ratius's mouth: Bernard knew something only of practical theology and could not entirely follow Gilbert's explanations. One should not hold it against Bernard himself that he had a negative viewpoint, but rather against those haughty and arrogant individuals who presumed they did have that sort of understanding. Bernard believed them out of that love which "believes all things" (1 Cor. 13:7).[130] In the most famous passage from the Pauline epistles, the hymn to Christian love, Everard found a conciliatory note on which to bring to a close the conflict that so long had divided the Gilbertines and Cistercians.

One of the theologians invited to Rheims in 1148 in order to hear Gilbert's case was Peter Lombard. He agreed with—or provided the proof for—Bernard's opinion that something heretical was at issue here.[131] No one knew at this point that Peter Lombard himself would later be reckoned one of the "four labyrinths of France," along with Gilbert, Abelard, and Peter of Poitiers.[132] Yet, Peter Lombard (born around 1095) was surely more of a compiler than a quarreler by nature. His book of sentences is a treasure trove of diverse opinions and pertinent quotations from the Bible, fathers of the church, canon-law sources, and works on speculative and practical theology. The book's usefulness as an instructional tool began to be evident around the time Peter, by then bishop of Paris, died (1160). In the thirteenth century, the work became a popular handbook, though not, as it has been dubbed, a "textbook of religious dogma."[133] Based on the material it contains, the reader is able to form his own opinion on points of controversy. Walter of Saint-Victor gave this description of how the material was presented: Peter would advance three theses, a heretical, a Catholic, and a third theorem that was neither one nor the other; as the universal teacher (*magister universalis*), Peter would attempt to substantiate all three viewpoints with citations from patristic authorities. He claimed not to know which view was doctrinally correct, leaving it up to the reader to delve further into the literature. "An entirely new doctrine by which no one stays Catholic! At any rate, a heresy that supports all heresies equally!"[134]

Peter Lombard's work dates from approximately the mid-twelfth century, a period during which the turbulence attending the onset of a new speculative theology was already beginning to give way to a more reflective, less rousing pursuit of knowledge. However many quotations a person might memorize, they no longer sufficed to prove one's thesis. There were always yet other quotations based on other authorities, and Peter Lombard gave all their due. In view of the ever greater subtlety and complexity of theological speculations, he had trained his students to be objective and cautious. Not until the thirteenth century did a generation come of age that would, with complete dispassion, establish a new, universal system on this basis.

The first wave of speculative thinking had not yet entirely ebbed, however, and the material found in the collection of sentences inspired new lines of thought. One such line of thought, presented as pure opinion (*opinio*) by Peter Lombard, has been termed Christological nihilism (or nihilianism). Operating within the framework of "nature and person," some theologians came to the conclusion that Christ had separately assumed the body and the soul of a human, and hence did not become human in the full sense of the word, but rather remained God. Alexander III remonstrated against this doctrine in Paris (1170) and at a consistory in Rome (1177).[135] In the period following Peter Lombard's death, the principal proponent of this view seems to have been his student, Peter of Poitiers, who taught at the cathedral school in Paris and later became cathedral chancellor (1193) and subsequently the first chancellor of the university as well. After presenting excerpts from Peter's discussions of this subject on many pages of his work, Walter of Saint-Victor pronounced him damned: "Your work does not need to be revised, but rather it belongs in Hell—no Catholic who reads it doubts that!"[136]

Before turning to the period around 1200, we should take one last look at Italy. Besides the popular heresies, there were hardly any incidents involving controvertible theses of the "academic" sort. One exception concerns the jurist Hugh Speroni, who had studied in Bologna before 1145, together with the later glossator Vacarius. A native of Piacenza, Hugh went on to serve as a counsel there for many years. In that capacity, he brought a lawsuit against a cloister, which filed an appeal with the pope but lost the case nonetheless; in 1189 a dispute flared up between

Piacenza and its bishop, but since Hugh had already been termed a heretic around 1185,[137] his stance was hardly affected by external events.

Hugh Speroni accused ecclesiastical teachers of writing things about the Eucharist that were not to be found in either the Old or the New Testament.[138] He apparently regarded the Bible as law and church doctrine as a loose legal construct, hence as something at which jurists customarily looked askance. Seen from this perspective, there was no basis for the existence and power of the clergy, and religion boiled down to the depth of one's feelings, the spirit of Jesus, and wisdom. Speroni's adherents did not lead an apostolic life and did not practice asceticism. The sect was still active in Piacenza in 1235.[139]

Of greater interest is the last figure in this series of twelfth-century French masters who were accused of heresy; we know the least about his teachings, perhaps because they were cloaked in silence. The individual involved was the tutor to the heir apparent, the future Louis VIII (1223–26). Named Amalric, he was a native of Bena (Bène), in the diocese of Chartres, and he may have attended the famous cathedral school; there are insufficient grounds, however, for imputing to him the "Platonism" practiced there.[140] Chroniclers named Amalric among the instructors in Paris: "He was experienced in the art of logic, and for a long period he taught logic and the other liberal arts at the school; then he turned to research on the Bible [sacram paginam]. Based on that work, he used to declaim stubbornly even about theology itself, asserting that every Christian was obliged to believe that he was a member of Christ's body."[141]

Amalric seems to have made the transition from dialectic to theology otherwise than Abelard. His theses did not involve the application of logical and grammatical methods to theological speculation, but rather were a product of the biblical exegesis practiced down through many centuries before and, to a modest extent, concurrently with the new style of theology. Paul had emphasized that the Church is analogous to the mystical body of Christ "because we are members of his body," of his flesh and bone (Eph. 5:30), and he "is the head of the body, the church" (Col. 1:18). The passage was meant to be understood allegorically, as was often the case with Paul. Amalric must have known this and had his reasons for giving a literal interpretation to an allegorical text. The matter appears to have been so significant to him that he showed a willingness to meet objection head on by turning to the pope. The pope's verdict proved unfavorable to Amalric, who was compelled to declare the antithesis of his previous teachings in the presence of the Parisian theologians—"with his mouth, not with his heart," for he persevered in his thesis until his death soon thereafter (1206).[142]

At the order of an ecclesiastical assembly in 1210, Amalric was posthumously excommunicated, condemned, and exhumed; his remains were scattered to the winds. He was regarded as the founder of a heretical sect. In fact, a group of his students had developed his teachings further and recruited believers. At a synod in Paris, charges were filed against fourteen clergymen, of whom all were educated and a few bore the title of master; ten were burned to death, and four were imprisoned for life. We will return presently to one member of the group who "took fright and became a monk."[143] His name was Peter of Saint-Cloud.[144] As in Orléans (1022), the sect was exposed with the help of two undercover agents, but with greater difficulty because some of the suspects were engaged as parish priests in northern French dioceses. The official findings of the archbishop of Sens concerning the incident do not inform us about the nature of the charges.

The Fourth Lateran Council (1215) took a similar tack, reissuing a condemnation of the "very perverse dogma of Amalric" without detailed substantiation. The decretalist Henry of Susa later explained that this occurred out of consideration for Amalric's surviving students.[145] Most important among them was in all likelihood Louis VIII, who was still heir to the throne in 1215. As king, he proved his loyalty to Catholicism by instituting death at the stake as the punishment for heresy in France (1226). In taking this measure Louis was playing catch-up, so to speak, with the southern portion of the country, where it had long been the practice, and with his father, Philip II Augustus, who had sanctioned this punishment in 1210 for the Amalricians.[146]

The fact that Peter of Saint-Cloud afterward took refuge in the "royal cloister" of Saint-Denis in order to become a monk may indicate a certain closeness between the royal house and this group.[147] It is quite striking that the Amalricians' prophesied the subjection of all kingdoms to the king of France and his son; the son would "'live under the dispensation of the Holy Spirit and . . . never die; and there will be given to the king of France twelve loaves, i.e. the knowledge and power of the [Holy] Scriptures.'"[148] The age of the Holy Spirit was derived from the doctrine of Joachim of Fiore concerning the three ages of the world, which in particular "William, a goldsmith [or alchemist], who was their prophet," disseminated among the Amalricians.[149]

Herbert Grundmann, who pointed out that this represented the earliest instance in which Joachimite historical thought was applied to politics, voiced skepticism for the long-prevailing opinion that Amalric's views could be reconstructed from those held by the Amalricians, "since we have nothing of [Amalric's] own thoughts."[150] It all depends on whether we view the statement that all baptized individuals must believe themselves to be members of Christ as an isolated observation or as part of a larger whole. In fact, the remark is mentioned in the sole systematic rejoinder to the Amalricians, which is attributed to Garnier of Rochefort. The tractate's composition, probably sometime soon after 1210, was apparently triggered by the appearance of Amalricians in Amiens under a Master Godinus.[151]

"They say that no one can attain salvation unless he believes that he is a member of Christ." The rejoinder voiced the objection that a human had the ability to sin and would thereby be a "member of the devil." In this case, the statement was interpreted metaphorically, but that was certainly not what Amalric intended—if it had been, then he would not have aroused outrage. The believers "are" the transfigured Christ; Marie-Dominique Chenu coined the term "panchristism" to denote this view and recalled the grammatical-logical verbalism of the Parisian master Adam of Petit-Pont.[152]

Christ is sinless, and a member of Christ cannot commit a sin. Amalric would have drawn this logical conclusion himself, without teaching it publicly. "They so exalted the power of love," related one chronicler about the Amalricians, "that they said that it was not a sin when a person empowered by love did something that would otherwise be a sin." Another writer expressed it more simplistically: "They said that if anyone were in the Spirit, and even if he were to commit fornication, . . . yet there would be no sin in him, because that Spirit, who is God, . . . cannot sin."[153] This doctrine does not appear in the works of John Scotus (Eriugena), a finding altogether consistent with more recent research, which no longer regards him as a source for the sect's thinking.[154] The belief that John Scotus (Eriugena) was the spiritual father of this heresy first gained currency during the thirteenth century, at the same time as Thomas Aquinas and others were defining the fundamental concepts of Platonism. Whether Amalric, who came from Chartres, was a Platonist must, as we have already noted, remain an open question.[155]

It was but a short step from Amalric's "panchristism" to his students' proven pantheism. How this step came to be taken may be deduced from a statement referring to the heretics' conviction "that each of one them was both Christ and the Holy Spirit."[156] Whoever is a member of Christ is Christ; whoever is Christ is also the Holy Spirit (and the Father). The remarks concerning the body and members of Christ in the first epistle to the Corinthians (1 Cor. 12:12) come right after the principal passage associated with the Amalricians' pantheism: "[T]here are varieties of working, but it is the same God who inspires them all in every one" ["qui operatur omnia in omnibus," that is, who works all things in every one] (1 Cor. 12:6). It is from this passage that the notion of immunity from sin was derived: "God works all things in every one. They [the Amalricians] interject: hence, both the good and the bad. It follows from this that the individual who knows that God works in him cannot sin."[157]

The shift to pantheism could not have been accomplished in the few years between Amalric's death and the discovery of this sect. At the time of their exposure, his "listeners" were for the most part parish priests in the dioceses of Paris, Troyes, and Langres, disseminating the heretical teachings in those areas. In the wake of his capture, one of them, the priest of Ursines (in the vicinity of Versailles), bid his parishioners farewell with the words that they should not believe anyone who taught otherwise than he.[158] All indications point to a secret doctrine that went back to Amalric's time and probably had been formulated by him in conjunction with his students. One of those under arrest had attended Amalric's lectures on theology for ten years; another "was more than sixty years old and had been a student of theology for a long time"; and the priest from Saint-Cloud, near Paris, who would take refuge at Saint-Denis was also a "sexagenarian."[159] Hence, this matter did not involve a circle of exuberant schoolboys. However, it is quite possible that one or another of them interpolated additional teachings, just as within this circle of sectarians "their prophet" William came forward with a Western version of the legend of the "last emperor." This tale complemented the extremely energetic efforts of the royal court at just that time to associate itself with the reign of Charlemagne.[160]

A fairly large amount of material exists regarding the Amalricians' teachings, with those of a negative cast striking contemporaries as particularly important: repudiation of the sacraments, of Christ's resurrection, and of hell and heaven in the traditional sense. Under interrogation these individuals themselves repeatedly referred to the cornerstone of their suppositions, which was less a thesis than an experience of identification with Christ, or with God. At the end of the twelfth century, even among theologians certain ideas took shape that were related to the simplistic mysticism of nuns and laypeople: "They say that whoever experiences God residing in him should not lament, but laugh."[161] "Experience" (*cognitio*) is a key word here; it corresponds to the concept of "gnosis" and exempts those who know from the gamut of religious practice. "If a Jew knows the truth that we possess, then it is not necessary for him to be baptized."[162] "Hell is nothing more than ignorance, and paradise nothing more than the knowledge of truth, which they claim to possess."[163]

John Scotus (Eriugena) had indeed stated that the eternal life was the knowledge of truth; there was no misery other than incomprehension.[164] Nevertheless, the Amalricians had not necessarily read his work, which first appeared on the intellectual horizon at the University of Paris in 1225 and was banned. Spiritualizing heaven and hell was the prerogative of every philosopher, particularly one who propounded the Neoplatonic philosophy of identity, which had never been quite forgotten. As for Amalric's identifying every existent being with one another, this has been traced back to the pre-Socratics and to Plato,[165] who even figured in the work *Against the Amalricians* [*Contra Amaurianos*]: Some of them distinguished between the real body of Christ and his "inward body," that divine power which Plato had termed the Ideas.[166] Hence, they believed in a duality between the sensually perceptible substance—the "visible and tangible body that was nailed to the cross"—and the body that embodied the Idea. They moreover contended that the body of the Lord was omnipresent and that ordinary bread was on that account to be shown the same veneration as the consecrated wafer.[167] True pantheism—or panchristism—was here at work. Such inconsistencies demonstrate that the Amalricians were not constructing a doctrinal system, and that for them religious doctrine took a backseat to experiencing God.

Contrariwise, there is no mention anywhere of experiencing the evil principle, which was such a factor in the Cathars' beliefs. Much like the former heretics of Orléans, the Amalricians were all clergymen. The former had believed that the Holy Spirit resided in them; the latter went them one better by apotheosizing the members of their sect. It was left to the least educated member of this group, a subdeacon named Bernard, to draw some practical inferences from this: Since he was God, he asserted, no one could torture him or burn him at the stake.[168]

This sect was the product of the open educational system in Paris, which was evolving into a university, and thus of a dialectical environment. However, the concern of earlier theologians to come up with speculative findings, based on logic and grammar, about the mysteries of the faith meant little to these individuals. Once Amalric had found the key to the sum of all knowledge in the first epistle to the Corinthians, his adherents no longer engaged in research. Theology became the outer vessel of a mystical experience, and the mysteries were no longer mysteries in light of a new gnosis akin to Platonism. We can no longer determine how much of this had historical antecedents and how much was a unique construct involving "spontaneously" arising parallel beliefs. Amalric wrote hardly anything down, and even in 1210 there was no reference to works by him, although at the time works by Aristotle and David of Dinant came under prohibition. These latter bans were reissued in 1215 by the cardinal-legate Robert of Courson, and to them was appended one concerning "the books . . . of the heretic Amalric."[169] This may only have represented a precautionary measure without any concrete basis. In the same year, the Fourth Lateran Council condemned the "not so much heretical as unsound [*insana*] doctrine" of Amalric, but no written works by him. These references were the last signs of life from the sect.

A distant echo of this incident registered at the Scottish cloister of Melrose. In an entry for 1210, a chronicler there recounted that heretics visited widows in their homes and secretly led them astray by means of perverse misinterpretations of the Holy Scriptures.[170] This corresponds with a report that in 1210 the judges "spared the women and other simple souls [*simplices*] whom these ones had deceived," hence, took no action against them.[171] The tractate *Against the Amalricians* alleged that the doctrine of sinlessness was exploited to make "reprobate wenches more disposed to sin."[172] However, no one dredged up against heretics that ancient allegation that they organized secret orgies.

The Amalrician sect is also noteworthy for molding the new academic system into a vessel for an irrational viewpoint that might have developed into a popular heresy. The later Middle Ages did not prove a fertile soil for these first seeds of a new myth, even though mysticism probably enjoyed its greatest period of growth at the time. In the thirteenth century the "novel learning" of Scholasticism took on a new character; the rapid torrent became a broad current whose shallow waters could pose a new danger.

A Look Ahead

 Heresy and early Scholasticism are two separate phenomena that shared a number of similarities. It should be noted, however, that this observation does not apply to the measures taken against those who challenged orthodoxy. The proceedings were by definition different for laypeople and theologians, and did not have a substantial effect on the new learning. What is meant, rather, is the manner in which individuals emerged from the security of a primitive trust, forsook a simple faith without taking up contemplation, and refused merely to accept incomprehensible phenomena and to place their confidence in the explanations advanced since time immemorial. When we consider the new attitude that superseded the traditional one in each case, then the parallel no longer seems to hold: Here myth is the defining factor, there dispassionate rationality. But the situation was not quite that simple. The new learning evolved in tandem with the myth of Plato and the Platonists; yet the mode of thought marking the latter construct threw up cognitive impediments to exceedingly important ideas proceeding from the former mode of thought. As for the heretics, they did not live by mythical notions alone. Some of them also undertook to "rationalize" Christian doctrines that did not fit in with their creed. The theological innovators and heretics both represented very small minorities existing side by side with a majority bound to the traditional system. The boundaries between them and the traditionalists were not always clear-cut and might shift: Individuals changed their minds, and besides converted heretics, there were dialecticians who entered monastic orders.

As for the rational aspect of the heretics' thought, it was said of the Cathars, "They do not rely solely on scriptural passages . . . , but also on rational arguments that strike them as natural [*naturales*] or logical."[1] In the early thirteenth century, the Cathars fashioned syllogisms out of biblical passages to substantiate their doctrines.[2] However, rationality was not as great a concern in their milieu as it was in that of the advanced schools; to the Cathars it was a tool for smoothing the way for the myth, much as allegory was employed by some to explain away Christ's miracles, because those often involved material objects. For example, the five loaves of bread in the miracle of the loaves and fishes were said to represent the Gospels and the Acts of the Apostles.[3]

Among the heretics as among the early Scholastics, the teeming religious cosmos was reduced to the essentials. The heretics had no saints; the theologians continued to believe in their existence, but one could search high and low in these theologians' technical works, at least the speculative ones, and find barely a trace of their veneration. This parallel also has its limits when one examines its background. The heretics possessed an intense experience of the human condition that almost always served to accentuate the dichotomy between their prior beliefs and a new faith with fundamentalist characteristics. The proponents of the new learning had an affinity for the god of the philosophers, who suffered no popular cults beside him. In their "private" lives, the Scholastics may very well have continued to pray to the saints, but in their works space was granted these figures only if—and this did occur—the saint served an edifying purpose. The view that the figure of evil had barely any substance, in other words, had no real existence, was of a piece with the god of the philosophers. The devil rarely appears in the theological works of the early Scholastics, nor was he, by the way, of any discernible importance to the clerics of Orléans (1022). In contrast, the Bogomils and the Cathars considered him the lord of the world. Here, the line of demarcation was apparently not drawn between orthodoxy and heterodoxy, but rather between intellectual and popular religiosity.

Much the same may be said of the relationship to literacy. As a religion based on a scripture, Christianity always has to be preached with reference to the texts; these texts are first of all the province of the clergy. When people lose their faith in the clergy, they may endeavor to "learn" the texts according to which they wish to conduct their lives. In the process, they drastically winnow down the material to be learned, with possible implications for their faith. "The Bogomils denied everything they did not comprehend," particularly the quite voluminous Old Testament, which required a reading knowledge of Greek.[4] At least there was a dual-language text of the Gospels, although, as we have heard, the heretics of

Arras were satisfied with a compilation of biblical passages written down by their master, Gundulf.[5]

Orthodox Christians also "internalized" texts and attempted to live by them. The proper place for this practice was the monastery, where even so it might involve a small selection of works from the gigantic patristic corpus. The attitude of the teachers and students at the advanced schools was quite different, however: There, the whole enterprise revolved around gaining new knowledge, hence around engaging in research on a rational basis; one was supposed to be familiar with the authorities of yore, but these were instead treated like a quarry supplying the building blocks for a new edifice of specialized knowledge. In the process, something transpired that countervailed the new methodology[6] and repeated on a higher plane a practice of the heretics. Scholastics extracted whatever suited their own thesis from the works of other authors and even from simple compilations of biblical passages. Whereas for the heretics one's faith was at stake, in scholarly disputes such methods were even put to the service of personal ambition. It was said of the scholars in Paris that there were as many errors (errores) as teachers (doctores).[7]

Speculative theology continued to make progress in the thirteenth century, but it was no longer the area of greatest innovation or currency. When the bishops passed judgment on the Amalricians in 1210, they also decreed that "the booklets [quaternuli] by the master David of Dinant be brought to the bishop of Paris before Christmas and there consigned to flames," and, furthermore, that "Aristotle's books on natural philosophy and the commentaries [on Aristotle] not be read in Paris either in public or in private," in other words, not serve as the basis for lectures. At the same time, all theological works in the vernacular were to be surrendered, "as well as the credo and Lord's Prayer in the Romance tongue." Violators were to be deemed heretics.[8] Vernacular translations of sacred texts were viewed with suspicion; they might be of Waldensian or Albigensian derivation, and we know of an Amalrician Lord's Prayer in French.[9]

Whoever "read" [i.e., lectured on] Aristotle's works on natural philosophy or one of the—predominantly Arabic—commentaries on Aristotle did not thereby become a heretic, yet he was to be excommunicated. That was a disciplinary measure reserved to the bishops. They foresaw what might be termed an "Aristotelian shift" in the history of knowledge. The body of knowledge associated with Aristotle had triggered the first great transformation in twelfth-century theology by training people to think logically. Now, with the second reception of Aristotle's works, many diverted their attention from speculative theology to another sphere that promised profuse, indeed almost immeasurable, knowledge. That was the world, the cosmos with all of its interrelations. The master had constructed a "universal science" truly of this world, and for the most part he took a dim view of Plato's propositions, at least those found in the *Timaeus*.

Older studies of this period justified the prohibitions against Aristotle by observing that the Aristotelian works available at the time inextricably intermingled material from the original Greek text with that from Arabic commentaries, and that "pure" redactions of Aristotle's writings first became available through the efforts of Dominicans at the University of Paris. The previous texts were adulterated by the presence of Neoplatonic material inclined to pantheism and even to areligiosity, thereby rendering them repugnant to the theologians. The Dominicans did achieve a great deal by keeping Arab philosophy at arm's length, incorporating Aristotle into the course of study, and thereby fending off the condemnation of "modern" scholarship. However, there were "pure" Latin redactions of the philosopher's texts as early as the mid-twelfth century and, to be sure, not just of his works on logic. A Venetian named James who resided in Constantinople was probably the first to prepare translations of the eight books on physics, the short works on science, and the tract on metaphysics.[10] The last work, concerning the universal principles, was based on Aristotle's scientific system and hence took an inductive approach.

Such translations were not unknown in the West, although initially they exercised little influence. The works on logic, too, were for the most part read in later adaptations. Produced in late antiquity, these were commentaries informed by Neoplatonism with sprinklings of Stoicism.[11] People probably preferred being able to study, in addition to Aristotle, the findings of later periods and hence material absent from the works of the master himself—for example, the doctrine of the probable causes or hypothetical syllogisms, which could only be found in Boethius's works.[12] Even in the area of logic, the full brunt of Aristotle's influence was first felt in the thirteenth century, and opening the door to future research were hypothetical conclusions that were based on premises deemed correct by some or all individuals.[13] Practical reason came to share the stage with pure reason, and the investigation of mutable phenomena—carried out by individuals who were themselves subject to change—gained a place alongside the desire to apprehend the immutable.

The new studies focused on animate and inanimate nature, as outlined and defined by Aristotle in his universal work. This corpus offered a profusion of facts and a methodology that the masters would have been incapable of devising. Aristotle did not supplant theology, but he was now a more attractive topic of study. It had reached the point in the thirteenth century where theological scholarship embodied the traditional past,

while the Aristotelian brand of worldly knowledge was excitingly novel—
people could have availed themselves of it earlier, but they had placed too
low a value on it at the time.

When the prohibition against reading Aristotle's scientific works was
issued in 1210, it also applied to the "booklets" of the master David of
Dinant; by that we mean notebooks containing for the most part excerpts
from Aristotle. These concerned water circulation, the composition of
clouds out of water droplets, the wind, the causes of earthquakes, and the
Pythagorean hypothesis that the earth was nothing more than a star[14]—
the entire thing was a jumble, but a treasure trove for inquisitive minds.
The notebooks made the rounds at the formative University of Paris, but
their author resided at the papal curia, where he received his first
appointment in 1206 as a member of the papal chapel.[15] He had attended
a Greek school, and he apparently discovered and translated a copy of
Aristotle's tract *On Philosophical Problems*. David drew upon this work in
his "booklets," of which unfortunately only fragments have been preserved, which were first published in 1963.

David's scientific interests did sidetrack him from theology, yet they
were not the reason that the notebooks were declared heretical, despite
their author's position at the curia. David did in fact slip the odd item into
his Aristotelian texts, but rather sporadically, as a afterthought. For
example, the World-Soul crops up, and there is a questionable affinity
between God and the world due to a uniquely developed theory of
being.[16] In contrast to the bodies and souls of humans, primordial matter
and the World-Soul consist of substance without accidents. This sort of
substance can only exist uniquely; thus primordial matter was equated
with the World-Soul, and the latter was equated with God.[17] Here,
Aristotle's teaching about categories was applied to Platonism in circum-
vention of the no longer "modern" doctrine of ideas. Even if this was
pantheism, it was still unrelated to that of the Amalricians; in the latter
case, we are dealing with the central proposition of their doctrine on life,
while in the former, with one passage in notebooks replete with entirely
different material. Furthermore, the fact that David was the author of the
(lost) book *On the Anatomy of Veins, Arteries, and Nerves of the Entire Body*
indicated just how broad his interests were.[18] Drawing a connection
between him and the Cathars is untenable,[19] for the latter were unfamiliar
with the notion of primordial matter and probably had only a passing
familiarity with Aristotle, perhaps from authors who quoted him.[20] His
name did appear once in the writings of Cathars, where he is confused,
however, with the Jewish scholar Avicebron (d. around 1070).[21]

In contrast with Amalric of Bena, David was not mentioned again in the
canon on heretics issued by the Fourth Lateran Council (1215). His case is

unimportant in and of itself, but it does provide an example of how the reception accorded Aristotle's works in the thirteenth century shocked the church. Not only did the reception entail the assimilation of Aristotle's "universal science," extricating it thereby from the milieu of the "liberal arts" and Christian theology—not only were dubious doctrines like that of the eternal nature of the world to be found in David's works—but the philosophical myth of the Platonists retained such potency that in this author's hands Aristotle's ideas assumed Platonistic characteristics. He thus accomplished the same thing as the Arabic commentators before him. Perhaps it was in response to a more basic need that David decked out tedious scholarship about this world in mythical elements and thereby made it more palatable.

Epochs in which the traditional form of religion is met with disinterest or less interest than formerly seem predisposed to this approach. Arabic philosophers from Samarkand to Toledo were regarded as free spirits by the Islamic clergy that renounced them, even though the latter adopted much that the former had proposed. With their free-floating religiosity coupled with Neoplatonism, Avicenna (ibn-Sina), al-Kindi, al-Farabi, and al-Ghazali all imbued their commentaries on Aristotle with a penchant for pantheism and mysticism. Missing from this list of Arab scholars was an individual who would later hold the greatest importance for the University of Paris but who was in 1210 as yet unknown there: Averroës (ibn-Rushd, d. 1198).[22] Most of the other Arabic commentaries were already available, at least in Catalonia, at the time Hermann of Carinthia was "on the banks of the Ebro" compiling accounts about Islam.[23]

By the thirteenth century, the heyday of the secular cleric as master had passed. The majority confined themselves to teaching, and few were dynamic enough to come up with new theses. To offset their intellectual aimlessness and propensity for heresy, representatives of the mendicant orders, Dominicans and Franciscans, were installed at the University of Paris, though the latter were themselves open to criticism on account of the split between Conventuals and Spirituals. The Spirituals sympathized with the thought of Joachim of Fiore, whose works some of them termed "the eternal Gospel" of the approaching world age—ammunition for the leader of the secular clergymen among the masters, William of Saint-Amour, in the battle against the new competitors. The secular clergy itself was divided. Many drew on Averroës' works, in which the World-Soul resurfaced in a moderated form as the *intellectus agens*, the universal spirit of all humans, accordingly eliminating the possibility of individual immortality and, naturally, free will.

With a shrug of his shoulders, so to speak, Averroës had placed his Aristotelianism side by side with the traditional teachings of Islam, which he did not look to abrogate: By means of the former, the philosopher gained a clear understanding of what the prophet was compelled to clothe in imagery for the sake of the common people. Some Parisian theologians reiterated a doctrine originally proposed by the Jewish scholar Moses Maimonides in defense of the belief that God created the world: namely, that something might be impossible in the realm of nature and yet possible in the supranatural one. The bishop of Paris perceived this as heretical, as an expression of the doctrine of the double truth,[24] and issued a condemnation. He was mistaken; yet the Parisian Averroists did, to be sure, tend to focus their thought on Aristotle and consign Christianity to the sidelines.

Averroës had been banished to Morocco, and his works and those of Aristotle were banned by the caliphs. However, in neither Cordoba nor Paris did such tactics daunt the students of philosophy. In conservative circles, it appeared that the only way to remedy the situation was to retreat into a Christian fundamentalism, faith versus reason, the Bible versus the *summae* of "modern" academic works. That would have meant the end of the University of Paris, or at the very least would have changed its course entirely. We can at best only surmise to what extent this step, taken at that early juncture, would have advanced the secularization of Western thought.

Such a withdrawal would also have deprived the young Dominican order of its intellectual foundation. The Dominican coat of arms depicts a book, for the order was established to bring about the conversion of the Cathars by intellectual means, namely, preaching and study. The Dominicans did not meet with success, and they were soon ordered to assist in the Inquisition. Hence, they sought out a new intellectual field of endeavor. Paris became the chief proving grounds, as the Order of Preachers became an order of professors and instructors, authoring more works than all of the Latin fathers of the church combined. Here, high Scholasticism found a home.

Under the leadership of Albert the Great and his student Thomas Aquinas, the Dominicans performed the significant task of closing the gap between Aristotelian philosophy and Christianity. Franciscans were also represented at Paris, and in a moderating fashion they reconciled Scholastic learning with the patristic legacy. Thus, there were three groups in Paris: conservatives, Christian Aristotelians, and Averroists. The last group lost ground only by degrees; in spite of the papal prohibitions, they were still to be found in Paris in the fourteenth century and in Italy until the end of the Middle Ages.

Having made its peace with Christianity, Aristotelianism maintained its position of dominance far into modern times. Platonistic elements have concurrently survived, transmitted for the most part by patristic works, particularly those by Augustine. In the revival of Aristotle's universal science, it was the grounding in grammar and dialectic that made it possible to construct monumental *summae* with precision. Like the annual rings of a tree, these works were assemblages of material that had shaped people's view of the world in various epochs. In the *summae* the abstract element almost always predominated, and herein lay the limits to Scholastic research. In contrast, facts and data about the external world are central to most investigations today. Reason, once the mistress, is here relegated to the role of handmaiden.

Notes

Abbreviations

CC cont. med.	Corpus Christianorum, Continuatio Mediaevalis
CSEL	Corpus Scriptorum Ecclesiasticorum Latinorum
Mansi	J. D. Mansi, *Sacrorum Consiliorum Nova et Amplissima Collectio*
MGH	Monumenta Germaniae Historica
MPL	J. P. Migne, *Patrologiae Cursus Completus, Series Latina*
SS	Scriptores

Notes to the Introduction

1. Radulfus Ardens, *Homiliae*, II, 1, MPL 155, 1947. The *sententia* was given apropos a question about the doctrine of the Trinity; the reference goes unnoted by Suitbert Gammersbach, *Gilbert von Poitiers und seine Prozesse im Urteil der Zeitgenossen*, Neue Münstersche Beiträge zur Geschichtsforschung, 5 (Cologne, 1959), 144.

2. Jerome, *Contra Vigilantium*, c. 15, as cited by Gilles Gerard Meersseman, "Teologia monastica e riforma ecclesiastica da Leone IX a Callisto II," in *Il monachesimo e la Riforma ecclesiastica: Atti della quarta settimana . . . Mendola . . . 1968*, Pubblicazioni dell'Università cattolica (Milan, 1971), 267.

3. Rupert of Deutz, *De omnipotentia Dei*, c. 27, MPL 170, 477. Marie-Dominique Chenu, *Nature, Man, and Society in the Twelfth Century*, trans. J. Taylor and L. Little (Chicago, 1968), 272.

4. William of Conches, *De philosophia mundi*, I, 22, MPL 172, 56 (attributed there to "Honorius Augustodunensis"); see page 194 and note 121 to Chapter 7. Chenu, *Nature, Man, and Society*, 11 and n. 21. John Newell, "Rationalism at the School of Chartres," *Vivarium* 21 (1983): 125.

5. Peter Abelard, in the prologue to *Sic et non*, MPL 178, 1349; edited of late by Blanche B. Boyer and Richard McKeon (Chicago, 1976). Wilfried Hartmann, "Manegold von Lautenbach und die Anfänge der Frühscholastik," *Deutsches Archiv* 26 (1970): 143.

6. Heinrich Fichtenau, *Living in the Tenth Century: Mentalities and Social Orders*, trans. Patrick J. Geary (Chicago, 1991), 435ff.

7. Otloh of St. Emmeram, *Liber de temptationibus suis*, I, MPL 146, 32f.; Fichtenau, *Living in the Tenth Century*, 400. Elizabeth of Schönau, *Vita*, c. 14, MPL 195, 128.

8. Peter of Vaux-de-Cernay, *Petri Vallium Sarnaii Monachi Hystoria Albigensis*, II, 32, ed. P. Guébin and E. Lyon (Paris, 1926), 1:33f. Jean Duvernoy, *Le catharisme*, vol. 1, *La religion des Cathares* (Toulouse, 1976, 1979, and 1989), 52.

9. Duvernoy, *La religion*, 90 (based on *Le registre d'inquisition de Jacques Fournier, évêque de Pamiers [1318–1325]*).

10. Tertullian, *De praescriptione haereticorum*, c. VII/5, CC ser. lat. I, 192f. Gerhard Rotten-wöhrer, *Unde malum? Herkunft und Gestalt des Bösen nach heterodoxer Lehre von Markion bis zu den Katharern* (Honnef, 1986).

11. Cosmas the Priest, *Le traité contre les Bogomiles de Cosmas le Prêtre*, c. 13, ed. Henri-Charles Puech and André Vaillant, Travaux publiés par l'Institut d'études slaves, 21 (Paris, 1945), 75.

12. Ibid., c. 13, 74. The latter allusion is to Luke 16:1–8.

13. Jean Bollack, at the roundtable portion of the conference "Terror und Spiel," published in *Terror und Spiel: Probleme der Mythenrezeption*, ed. M. Fuhrmann, Poetik und Hermeneutik, 4 (Munich, 1971), 588.

14. Herbert Grundmann, *Neue Forschungen über Joachim von Fiore*, Münstersche Forschungen, 1 (Marburg, 1950), 67.

15. Anselm of Liège, *Gesta episcoporum Leodiensium*, c. 63, MGH SS 7, 228.

16. Othmar Hageneder, "Der Häresiebegriff bei den Juristen des 12. und 13. Jahrhunderts," in *The Concept of Heresy in the Middle Ages (11th–13th Centuries): Proceedings of the International Conference Louvain, 1973*, ed. W. Lourdaux and D. Verhelst, Mediaevalia Lovaniensia ser. I, studia 4 (Louvain and The Hague, 1976), 42ff. Peter Classen, "Der Häresie-Begriff bei Gerhoch von Reichersberg und in seinem Umkreis," in ibid., 27ff.; rpt. in Peter Classen, *Ausgewählte Aufsätze*, Vorträge und Forschungen, 28 (Sigmaringen, 1983), 461ff.

17. Mariano d'Alatri, "'Eresie' perseguite dall'inquisizione in Italia nel corso del duecento," in *The Concept of Heresy*, ed. Lourdaux and Verhelst, 222f.

18. Peter Abelard, *Theologia christiana*, III, 17, CC cont. med., 12 (1969), 202.

19. As quoted by Jean Leclercq, "L'hérésie d'après les écrits de S. Bernard de Clairvaux," in *The Concept of Heresy*, ed. Lourdaux and Verhelst, 20.

20. William of Conches, *De philosophia mundi*, I, 14, MPL 172, 46, and Eugenio Garin, *Studi sul platonismo medievale* (Florence, 1958), 67.

21. *Chartularium Universitatis Parisiensis*, no. 1, ed. H. Denifle and E. Châtelain (Paris, 1899; Brussels, 1964), 1:59–61. Last evaluated by Werner Maleczek, "Das Papsttum und die Anfänge der Universität im Mittelalter," *Römische Historische Mitteilungen* 27 (1985): 97.

22. Cf. pages 306–11 above on Amalric of Bena and the Amalricians.

Notes to Chapter 1

1. Georges Duby, *L'an mil* (Paris, 1967), 33.

2. Rodulfus Glaber, *Rodulfi Glabri Historiarum Libri Quinque*, II, 12 (23), ed. and trans. J. France (Oxford, 1989), 92 and 93 (hereafter J. France), and idem, *Les cinq livres de ses histoires (900–1044)*, ed. M. Prou, Collection de textes, 1 (Paris, 1886), 50 (hereafter Prou). The remarks concerning additional heretics in Italy, Sardinia, and Spain are no longer given credence by, for example, Malcolm D. Lambert, *Medieval Heresy*, rev. 2d ed. (London, 1992), 29: "This seems improbable." The quotation draws on Rev. 20:2f. On the following material, cf. Heinrich Fichtenau, "Zur Geschichte der Häresien Italiens im 11. Jahrhundert," in *Società, Istituzioni, Spiritualità nell'Europa medioevale: Studi in onore di Cinzio Violante* (Spoleto, 1994), 1:332–36.

3. Rodulfus Glaber, *Historiarum libri quinque*, II, 12 (23), in J. France, 92 and 93, and Prou, 50. France, 92 n. 1, considers it likely that Rodulfus heard the report about Vilgard from Abbot William in Dijon. The abbot had brought many Italians to Dijon, among them two monks from Ravenna.

4. Arno Borst, *Lebensformen im Mittelalter* (Frankfurt and Berlin, 1973), 592.

5. See pages 29–30 and note 87 below.

6. Huguette Taviani, "Naissance d'une hérésie en Italie du Nord au XIe siècle," *Annales ESC* 29 (1974): 1242. Robert J. Moore, *The Origins of European Dissent* (London, 1977; Oxford and New York, 1985), 23, believes that educational systems supported by towns did exist.

7. Domenico Comparetti, *Virgilio nel medio evo* (rev. ed., 1937), 1:113, and Lupus of Ferrières in *Loup de Ferrières*, no. 8 (837), ed. L. Levillain, Les classiques de l'histoire de France, 20 (Paris, 1964), 1:70.

8. Caesarius of Heisterbach, *Caesarii Heisterbacensis Dialogus Miraculorum*, V, 22, ed. J. Strange (Cologne, Bonn, and Brussels, 1851; Cologne, 1922), 1:304; trans. H. von E. Scott and C. C. Swinton Bland, *The Dialogue of Miracles* (London, 1929), 1:348.

9. Henri de Lubac, *Exegèse médiévale*, vol. 4, II/2, Études . . . Lyon-Fourvière, Théologie, 59 (Paris, 1964), 247.

10. Abelard, *Theologia christiana*, I, 128, 127.

11. Peter Abelard, *Theologia "Summi Boni,"* c. 38, ed. E. M. Buytaert and C. J. Mews, CC cont. med., 13/3 (1987), 99.

12. De Lubac, *Exegèse médiévale*, vol. 4, II/2, 236.

13. Rodulfus Glaber, *Historiarum libri quinque*, II, 11 (22), in J. France, 88ff. and 89ff., and Prou, 49f.

14. It is assumed that the French Cathar bishop had his final residence there; according to Arno Borst, *Die Katharer*, Schriften der MGH, 12 (Stuttgart, 1953), 93 and n. 15. Jean Duvernoy, *Le catharisme*, vol. 2, *L'histoire des Cathares* (Toulouse, 1979 and 1989), 127, doubts this assumption.

15. According to an "ancient chronicle" mentioned in an unprinted history of the diocese. Duvernoy, *L'histoire*, 94f. For complete details, see Renate Gorre, *Die Ketzer im 11. Jahrhundert* (Ph.D. diss., Constance, 1981), 253 n. 120.

16. Gorre, *Die Ketzer*, 242 n. 16.

17. Abbo of Fleury, *Apologeticus*, MPL, 139, 462f. See Herbert Grundmann, *Ketzergeschichte des Mittelalters*, Die Kirche in ihrer Geschichte, II, G 1 (Göttingen, 1963, 1967, and 1978), 8 and n. 20.

18. Other than this instance, there is only one firmly documented suicide during the seventh through eleventh centuries. See Fritz Peter Knapp, *Der Selbstmord in der abendländischen Epik des Hochmittelalters*, German. Bibliothek, 3d ser. (Heidelberg, 1979), 75 and n. 38. The instance recounted by Ekkehard IV of St. Gall is questionable; see Heinrich Fichtenau, *Lebensordnungen des 10. Jahrhunderts*, Monographien zur Geschichte des Mittelalters, 30/II (Stuttgart, 1984), 521 n. 85.

19. According to Cinzio Violante, *La società milanese nell'età precomunale* (Bari, 1953 and 1974), 220, the asexual propagation of bees was a theme in classical literature, the Catholic liturgy, and also for the heretics of Monforte (see pages 41–46 above).

20. Gregory of Tours, *Historia Francorum*, X, 25, MGH SS rer. Merov. (1875), 1:437.

21. Henri-Charles Puech, in Cosmas, *Le traité*, 170.

22. Bonaccursus, *Manifestatio haeresis Catharorum*, c. 10, ed. R. Manselli, *Bullettino dell'Istituto Storico Italiano per il Medio Evo* 67 (1955): 208.

23. Moore, *European Dissent*, 152, and Steven Runciman, *The Medieval Manichee* (Cambridge, 1947 and 1955), 74.

24. James Fearns, "Peter von Bruis und die religiöse Bewegung des 12. Jahrhunderts," *Archiv für Kulturgeschichte* 48 (1966): 318 and 331.

25. Euthymios of the Peribleptos monastery (around 1050) stated in the most extreme terms that the repudiation of one's wife was prerequisite for salvation; see Puech, in Cosmas, *Le traité*, 266: "Hostis ouk aphesei ten gynaika autou, ou sozetai." (Whoever does not repudiate his wife will not be saved.)

26. Cinzio Violante, "La povertà nelle eresie del secolo XI in occidente," in *Studi sulla cristianità medioevale*, Cultura e storia, 8 (Milan, 1972), 93.

27. Robert-Henri Bautier, "Les foires de Champagne," in *La foire*, Recueils de la Société J. Bodin, 5 (Brussels, 1953), 104. For a description of the area, see Elizabeth Chapin, *Les villes de foires de Champagne des origines au début du XIVe siècle*, Bibl. de l'École des Hautes Études, sc. hist. et philol., 268 (Paris, 1937), 3.

28. Chapin, *Les villes*, 233.

29. See Jean Favier's article in *Handbuch der europäischen Wirtschafts- und Sozialgeschichte*, ed. Hermann Kellenbenz (Stuttgart, 1980), 2:318, and Karl Ferdinand Werner, *Vom Frankenreich zur Entfaltung Deutschlands und Frankreichs* (Sigmaringen, 1984), 261: "the fairs for which we begin to have tangible proof at the end of the tenth century."

30. Bautier, "Les foires," 98f. John Gilissen, "The Notion of the Fair in the Light of the Comparative Method," in *La foire*, Recueils de la Société J. Bodin, 5 (Brussels, 1953), 334, defines the fairs as "large organized gatherings at regularly spaced intervals of merchants coming from distant regions." The terms of this definition were certainly not yet fulfilled around the year 1000.

31. See page 16 and note 15 above.

32. Mansi, 19:423, based on Luc d'Achery, *Spicilegium* (Paris, 1677), 1:606. At that time, the word *supplicium* [punishment] did not yet refer to torture.

33. For a review of research on this subject up to 1954, see Jeanne-Marie Noiroux, "Les deux premiers documents concernant l'hérésie aux Pays-Bas," *Revue d'histoire ecclésiastique* 49 (1954): 843. More recently, Jeffrey Burton Russell, "À propos du synode d'Arras de 1025," *Revue d'histoire ecclésiastique* 57 (1962): 66–87, identifies Reginard as the recipient of the letter. Violante, "La povertà," 89 n. 26, agrees with Russell. Moore, *European Dissent*, 36, finds for Roger. Duvernoy, *L'histoire*, 93, is undecided. Erik Van Mingroot, "Acta synodi Atrebatensis (1025): Problèmes de critique de provenance," *Studia Gratiana* 20 (1976, Mélanges G. Fransen): 203–30, presents a detailed case for Roger.

34. Noiroux, "Les deux premiers documents," 855. A letter from the church in Liège complaining about heretics does not date back to 1048–54, but to 1144/45; see Hubert Silvestre, *Revue d'histoire ecclésiastique* 58 (1963): 979f., and Paul Bonenfant, "Un clerc cathare en Lotharingie au milieu du XIIe siècle," *Le Moyen Âge* 69 (1963): 278.

35. Egbert of Liège, *Fecunda ratis*, ed. Ernst Voigt (Halle, 1889), 205.

36. Emile Lesne, *Histoire de la propriété ecclésiastique en France* (Lille, 1940), 5:351.

37. "Synodus Atrebatensis," in Mansi, 19:424–60; the letter appears as the "Praefatio," in ibid., 423.

38. On Gerard, cf. Theodor Schieffer, "Ein deutscher Bischof des 11. Jahrhunderts," *Deutsches Archiv* 1 (1937): 323–60; Heinrich Sproemberg, "Gerhard I. Bischof von Cambrai," in *Mittelalter und demokratische Geschichtsschreibung*, Ausgewählte Abhandlungen (Berlin, 1971), 103–18; and Josef Fleckenstein, *Die Hofkapelle der deutschen Könige*, Schriften der MGH, 16/2 (Stuttgart, 1966), 186.

39. Hartmut Hoffmann, *Gottesfrieden und Treuga Dei*, Schriften der MGH, 20 (Stuttgart, 1964), 58f. For the ideological underpinnings to Gerard's actions, see Fichtenau, *Living in the Tenth Century*, 383.

40. J. F. Böhmer, *Regesta Imperii*, vol. 3, I/1, *Die Regesten des Kaiserreiches unter Konrad II.*, no. 22 b, ed. Heinrich Appelt (Graz, 1951), 21. On the following, see Fichtenau, "Zur Geschichte der Häresien Italiens," 342–43.

41. Mansi, c. 17, 19:460 D.

42. Georges Duby, *The Knight, the Lady, and the Priest*, trans. Barbara Bray (New York, 1983), 112; for a similar view, see Moore, *European Dissent*, 288.

43. Mansi, c. 2, 19:430.

44. Ibid., c. 1, 19:424 D.

45. A letter to the French bishops from Pope Gregory VII containing complaints against the "pillage" (through the levy of tolls) of Italian merchants "who traveled to a fair in Francia." *Das Register Gregors VII.*, II, 5, ed. Erich Caspar, MGH Epistolae Selectae II/1 (Berlin, 1920), 130–35; cf. ibid., II, 18, 150f.

46. Mansi, c. 1, 19:425 D: "de laboribus manuum suarum victum parare." Werner's interpretation, that they were merchants who "wished to earn their living through manual labor" — "in other words, they rejected the beneficed clergy" — is untenable. Ernst Werner, *Häresie und Gesellschaft im 11. Jahrhundert*, Sitzungsberichte der Sächsischen Akademie, philologische-historische Klasse, 117/5 (1975), 49.

47. For a list, see K. F. Werner, *Vom Frankenreich*, 261.

48. Paul Bonenfant, "L'épisode de la nef des tisserands de 1135," in *Études sur l'histoire du Pays mosan au Moyen Âge: Mélanges Félix Rousseau* (Brussels, 1958), 104. *Gesta abbatum Trudonensium*, XII, 12, MGH SS 10, 310.

49. Mansi, c. 1, 19:425 B. On the relationship between word and text, see pages 136–39 above.

50. Ibid., 425 D.

51. J. F. Niermeyer, *Mediae Latinitatis Lexicon Minus* (Leiden, 1976), 862.

52. Violante, "La povertà," 88. In support, see also Georges Duby, *The Three Orders: Feudal Society Imagined*, trans. Arthur Goldhammer (Chicago, 1980), 36. Brian Stock, *The Implications of Literacy* (Princeton, 1983), 121, talks of an "alleged interrogation." From the perspective of Stock's book, the people of Arras may be termed a "textual community," albeit they represent a borderline case. Huguette Taviani, "Le mariage dans l'hérésie de l'an mil," *Annales ESC* 32, (1977): 1084, thinks they used the apocryphal Acts of Andrew; this is untenable. Rather, it was the bishop who did. In order to place the heretics in context, he notes that Andrew was one of the apostles whom they considered role models. Mansi, c. 2, 19:433 C.

53. Mansi, c. 6, 19:457 B.

54. Ibid., c. 2, 433 B; c. 1, 425 D–E; c. 2, 436 A; and c. 8, 448 A.

55. Gorre, *Die Ketzer*, 162.

56. Mansi, c. 1, 19:430 C.

57. Ibid., c. 1, 427 E.

58. Ibid., c. 5, 444 D-E.

59. Ibid., c. 1, 430 C.

60. Ibid., c. 10, 449 A: "De connubiis vero, quae vos [. . .] abominanda iudicatis, dicentes coniugatos in sortem fidelium nequaquam computandos." [Truly, the things you declare about marriage are abominable, for you say that those who have married will in no way be counted among the faithful.] This tenet is disproved in detail. Cf. Duby, *The Knight*, 112–16.

61. See note 25 above.

62. Mansi, c. 17, 19:459 D: "[haeresis] quae legitima connubia devitat" [heresy that avoids lawful marriages]. If one places the accent on *legitima*, then Duby, *The Knight*, 121, may be correct: "priests should have nothing to do with the ceremonies that took place in the vicinity of the marriage bed" (marriage as a matter for the secular authority, not for the clergy).

63. Mansi, c. 13, 19:453 C–D.

64. Ibid., c. 7, 445 A.

65. As noted by Violante, "La povertà," 85.

66. Anselm of Liège, *Gesta episcoporum Leodiensium*, c. 62, MGH SS 7, 226f.

67. Ibid., c. 63, 227f. Rpt. in *Ketzer und Ketzerbekämpfung im Hochmittelalter*, no. 17, ed. J. Fearns, Historische Texte, Mittelalter, 8 (Göttingen, 1968), 52–54.

68. Raoul Manselli, *L'eresia del male*, Collana di storia . . . , 1 (Naples, 1963 and 1980), 141f. n. 45.

69. Antoine Dondaine, "L'origine de l'hérésie médiévale," *Rivista di storia della Chiesa in Italia* 6 (1952): 66 and n. 39.

70. Acts 6:5f., 8:17, and 13:2f. On the expression "baptism in the Holy Spirit," see John 1:33.

71. Augustine, *De civitate Dei*, c. 20, ed. E. Hofmann, CSEL 40/1 (Vienna, 1899), 38. Wazo attributed this view to the Arians, even though Augustine spoke of the Manichaeans.

72. See pages 29–30 above.

73. Mansi, 19:742; *Ketzer und Ketzerbekämpfung*, no. 18, 54.

74. Ovidio Capitani, "Studi per Berengario di Tours, II," *Bullettino dell'Istituto Storico Italiano per il Medio Evo* 69 (1957): 125f., argues against the proximity of the *novi haeretici* [new heretics] to Berengar.

75. *Corpus Documentorum Inquisitionis Haereticae Pravitatis Neerlandicae*, ed. P. Fredericq, no. 30 (Ghent and The Hague, 1889), 1:31f. On the identification of the place, see Borst, *Die Katharer*, 91f. and n. 11.

76. Entry for the year 1053 in *Lamperti monachi Hersfeldensis opera*, ed. O. Holder-Egger, MGH SS rerum Germanicarum, 38 (1894), 63. Gerhard Rottenwöhrer, *Der Katharismus* (Honnef, 1990), 3:219–22.

77. Entry for the year 1052 in *Herimanni Augiensis Chronicon*, MGH SS 5, 130.

78. Manegold of Lautenbach, *Liber ad Gebehardum*, MGH Libelli de lite, vol. 1 (1891), 378, lines 38ff.

79. Anselm of Liège, *Gesta*, c. 63f., 228.

80. See note 71 above and Epistle 236 to Bishop Deuterius, MPL 33, 1033: "Animas non solum hominum, sed etiam pecorum de Dei esse substantia" [The souls not just of humans, but even of beasts (are held) to be of the (same) substance as (the substance of) God].

81. Last discussed by Borst, *Die Katharer*, 80 n. 23. Borst, 79, however, recognizes the connection with Châlons: "Their belief was probably a true reflection of the heresy of Châlons."

82. Adémar of Chabannes, *Chronicon*, III, 69, ed. J. Chavanon, Collection de textes, 20 (Paris, 1897), 194.

83. Ibid., appendix, 210, taken from Ms. Bibl. Nat. Lat. 6290. Cf. ibid., III, 49, 173: baptism, the crucifix, abstinence, and chastity "in the manner of monks."

84. Mansi, c. 13, 19:849, and *Ketzer und Ketzerbekämpfung*, no. 18 B, 54. Adémar of Chabannes, *Chronicon*, III, 59, 185. For a review of the manuscripts, see Chavanon, in the introduction to Adémar of Chabannes, *Chronicon*, vii, and Monica Blöcker, "Ein Zauber-prozeß im Jahre 1024," *Schweizerische Zeitschrift für Geschichte* 29 (1979): 535–42.

85. Theodoin of Liège, *Contra Brunonem et Berengarium epistola*, MPL 146, 1439–42. On Berengar, cf. pages 286–93 above.

86. Jeffrey Burton Russell, "Les Cathares de 1048–1054 à Liège," *Bulletin de la Société d'art et d'histoire du diocèse de Liège* 148 (1961): 6–8, offers a different viewpoint.

87. Corrected text in Lambert, *Medieval Heresy* (1977), 347. The sentence omitted here was corrected in a second hand and concerns France. Most recent edition by G. Silagi, CC Cont. med. 49 (1978), 51.

88. Colomannus Juhász, "Gerhard der Heilige, Bischof von Maroschburg," *Studien und Mitteilungen zur Geschichte des Benediktiner-Ordens* 48 (1930): 23 n. 11. On this, cf. Fichtenau, "Häresien Italiens," 331f.

89. Lambert, *Medieval Heresy* (1977), 347.

90. Milan Loos, *Dualist Heresy in the Middle Ages* (Prague, 1974), 157f.

91. *Cartulaire de l'abbaye de Saint-Père de Chartres*, c. 3, ed. M. Guérard, Collection des cartulaires de France, vol. 1 (Paris, 1840), 109–15. MPL 155, 263–68.

92. Monica Blöcker, "Zur Häresie im 11. Jahrhundert," *Zeitschrift für Schweizerische Kirchengeschichte* 73 (1979): 220 n. 122, presents a summary of the evidence.

93. The year in which this Norman duke died. Robert-Henri Bautier, "L'hérésie d'Orléans et le mouvement intellectuel au début du XIe siècle," in *Actes du 95e Congrès national des sociétés savantes, Reims 1970*, Sect. philol. et hist., I (Paris, 1975), 67, dates it "before 1026."

94. Ibid., 77–88, reviews in detail the political context of the incident. More recently, cf. Michel Bur, *La formation du comté de Champagne, v. 950–v. 1150* (Nancy, 1977), 158; Thomas Head, *Hagiography and the Cult of Saints: The Diocese of Orléans, 800–1200*, Cambridge Studies in Medieval Life and Thought, 4th ser., 14 (Cambridge, 1990), 265–67 and 270; and Heinrich Fichtenau, "Die Ketzer von Orléans (1022)," in *Ex ipsis rerum documentis: Festschrift Harald Zimmermann* (Sigmaringen, 1991), 417–27.

95. Adémar of Chabannes, *Chronicon*, III, 59, 184. Only the letter from the monk John referred to laypeople: "de melioribus clericis sive de nobilioribus laicis prope XIIII eiusdem civitatis" [around fourteen people from the higher clergy or from the more noble laymen of this city]. Andreas of Fleury, *Vie de Gauzlin abbé de Fleury*, ed. Robert-Henri Bautier and G. Labory, Sources d'histoire médiévale, 2 (Paris, 1969), 180. Jean-Pierre Poly and Eric Bournazel, *The Feudal Transformation: 900–1200*, trans. Caroline Higgitt (New York, 1991), 274, probably had this in mind when they spoke of "two lay nobles." Still, as the other sources report, only clergymen of different orders of ordination were likely involved. Rodulfus Glaber said they totaled thirteen; *Historiarum libri quinque*, III, 8 (31), in J. France, 150 and 151, and Prou, 80.

96. Blöcker, "Zur Häresie," 198.

97. Rodulfus Glaber, *Historiarum libri quinque*, III, 8 (31), in J. France, 150 and 151, and Prou, 81.

98. See page 14 and note 3 above.

99. Monica Blöcker, "Volkszorn im Mittelalter," *Francia* 13 (1985): 131, ascribes to King Robert the intention of "consigning the heretics immediately to hell."

100. Adémar of Chabannes, *Chronicon*, III, 59, 185.

101. Entry for the year 1023 in Odorannus of Sens, *Opera omnia* , ed. Robert-Henri Bautier and M. Gilles, Sources d'histoire médiévale, 4 (Paris, 1972), 11, 14, and 100. Bautier, "L'hérésie d'Orléans," 82. See page 132 and note 22 to Chapter 5.

102. Rodulfus Glaber, *Historiarum libri quinque*, III, 8 (31), in J. France, 150 and 151, and Prou, 81.

103. Cf. page 133 above, and Helgald of Fleury, *Vie de Robert le Pieux*, 6, ed. Robert-Henri Bautier and G. Labory, Sources d'histoire médiévale, 1 (Paris, 1965), 64 and 66.

104. Adalbero of Laon, *Les poèmes satiriques d'Adalbéron*, ed. G.-A. Hückel (Paris, 1901), 176, lines 308–26. Last discussed by Poly and Bournazel, *The Feudal Transformation*, 275.

105. In Andreas of Fleury, *Vie de Robert le Pieux*, no. 4, 180 and 182. Bautier, "L'hérésie d'Orléans," 65. The alleged letter from Bishop Baldwin of Thérouanne warning of heretics in Orléans is a forgery combining texts from Rodulfus Glaber and Adémar of Chabannes. Jeffrey Burton Russell, *Dissent and Reform in the Early Middle Ages* (Berkeley and Los Angeles, 1965), 28 and 276f. n. 24; Lambert, *Medieval Heresy* (1977), 346, was correct.

106. Adalbero of Laon, *Poème au roi Robert*, ed. C. Carozzi (Paris, 1979), 4–6, lines 56f.; Blöcker, "Zur Häresie," 216 n. 103.

107. This topic was last discussed by Jean-François Lemarignier, *Le gouvernement royal aux premiers temps capétiens* (Paris, 1965), 80 n. 53. Bautier, "L'hérésie d'Orléans," 76.

108. Rodulfus Glaber, *Historiarum libri quinque*, III, 8 (26), in J. France, 138 and 139, and Prou, 74.

109. Adémar of Chabannes, *Chronicon*, III, 58, 184, in conjunction with Borst, *Die Katharer*, 75 n. 10. For a different view, see Blöcker, "Zur Häresie," 204 n. 40: "probably added by Adémar himself."

110. Rodulfus Glaber: "[mulier], ut erat diabolo plena" ([a woman] being possessed of the devil); Adémar: "Adorant diabolum" [they worship the devil]. Cf. also André Vauchez, "Diables et hérétiques," in *Santi e demoni, Settimane . . . Spoleto, 36, 1988* (Spoleto, 1989), 2:574ff.

111. Adémar of Chabannes, *Chronicon*, III, 59, 184f.

112. *Cartulaire de Saint-Père*, 112. Alexander Patschovsky, "Der Ketzer als Teufelsdiener," in *Papsttum, Kirche und Recht: Festschrift Horst Fuhrmann* (Tübingen, 1991), 320–22, stresses the apologetic nature of the account.

113. Guibert of Nogent, *Autobiographie*, III, 17, ed. E.-R. Labande, Les classiques de l'histoire de France au Moyen Âge, 34 (Paris, 1981), 430; trans. Paul J. Archambault, *A Monk's Confession* (University Park, Pa., 1996), 196. Patschovsky, "Der Ketzer," 322f.

114. Blöcker, "Zur Häresie," 204 n. 44. Gerhoh of Reichersberg repeated an account of a black mass supposedly celebrated in the Old Chapel in Regensburg by Henry IV and his court, an account he had heard from the people of Regensburg. Karl Heisig, "Eine gnostische Sekte im abendländischen Mittelalter," *Zeitschrift für Religions- und Geistesgeschichte* 16 (1964): 271–74, took this politically motivated slander seriously. Discounted also by Lambert, *Medieval Heresy* (rev. 2d ed.), 60 n. 67.

115. Herbert Grundmann, "Der Typus des Ketzers in mittelalterlicher Anschauung," in *Ausgewählte Aufsätze*, Schriften der MGH, 25 (Stuttgart, 1976), 1:324f. n. 37.

116. Tertullian, *Apologeticum*, VII, 1, ed. H. Hoppe, CSEL, 69 (1939), 18, with variants at VIII, 1–9, 21f., and IX, 1–20, 23–27. Cf. Duvernoy, *L'histoire*, 34 n. 38 and 87. Patschovsky, "Der Ketzer," 318, also refers to Justin Martyr and Minutius Felix in this connection.

117. Robert J. Moore, "The Origins of Medieval Heresy," *History* 55 (1970): 27 and 33.

118. Andreas of Fleury, *Vie de Gauzlin*, c. 56 a, 98. Bautier, "L'hérésie d'Orléans," 66.

119. See page 39 above and note 128 below.

120. See note 105 above.

121. Rodulfus Glaber, *Historiarum libri quinque*, III, 8 (27), in J. France, 142 and 143, and Prou, 76.

122. Gorre, *Die Ketzer*, 89f. and 268 n. 79, cites a statement by John Scotus (Eriugena) concerning the identification of substances (Ideas) with God "antequem in formam essendi veniant" [before they come into existence], which is a different proposition.

123. Borst, *Die Katharer*, 75 n. 11, discerns "early Bogomil dualism" at work here. Dondaine, "L'origine," 75, had already recognized the contradiction between the proposition in the cartulary ("a Deo omnium creatore" [by God, the Creator of all things]) and the belief that the world was eternal. His attempt at solving the question (n. 59) is quite improbable. Correct in Rottenwöhrer, *Der Katharismus*, 3:169.

124. According to Blöcker, "Zur Häresie," 217 n. 106, with reference to a possible example from Augustine, *De civitate Dei*, XI, 4.

125. *Cartulaire de Saint-Père*, 111. Source for the following information also.

126. Ibid., 114. On the proposition concerning the Virgin Birth, cf. page 190 above.

127. In Dondaine, "L'origine," 69, presented in support of a Bogomil origin of the heresy.

128. Andreas of Fleury, *Vie de Gauzlin*, c. 56 a, 98: "Filii Dei genitricem se habere similem et per omnia iactabant, cum nec similis visa sit nec habere sequentem" (They boasted they had a mother like unto the Mother of God [Mary] indeed in every essential respect, even though nothing else like her [Mary] had ever been seen, and she did not have a successor.) Lambert, *Medieval Heresy* (1977), 343, and idem, review of *Ketzer und Professoren*, by Heinrich

Fichtenau, *Deutsches Archiv* 49 (1993): 338, states that there was probably a liturgical origin for the proposition.

129. Cited by Runciman, *The Medieval Manichee*, 78. Cf. page 75 and note 32 to Chapter 3.

130. Augustine, "Epistula 147," CSEL 40/3, 278–80. Quoted in this connection by Blöcker, "Zur Häresie," 225 and n. 143f.

131. See page 38 above. Fichtenau, "Die Ketzer von Orléans," 426 and n. 53.

132. *Cartulaire de Saint-Père*, 111.

133. Horst Kusch, "Studien über Augustinus," in *Festschrift F. Dornseiff* (Leipzig, 1953), 200.

134. Ibid., 181 (*Confessiones*, 13, 22, and 32).

135. Etienne Delaruelle, *La piété populaire au Moyen Âge* (Turin, 1975), 152 (91).

136. Gerard Verbeke, "Philosophy and Heresy," in *The Concept of Heresy*, ed. Lourdaux and Verhelst, 192f. *Chartularium Universitatis Parisiensis*, no. 12, 1:71: "Spiritus sanctus in eis incarnatus, ut dixerunt, eis omnia revelabat." [The Holy Spirit, having been incarnated in them, as they said, has revealed all things to them.] Cf. page 308 and note 156 to Chapter 12 (Caesarius of Heisterbach).

137. See page 38 above; concerning the idea of nature, see page 189 above.

138. Peter Abelard, *Expositio in Hexaemeron*, MPL, 178, 746 C, and David Edward Luscombe, "Nature in the Thought of Peter Abelard," in *La filosofia della natura nel medioevo: Atti del III Congresso . . . Mendola, 1964* (Milan, 1966), 315.

139. According to Moore, "The Origins of Medieval Heresy," 26.

140. Mansi, c. 3, 19:438, quoted by Blöcker, "Zur Häresie," 212 n. 80; see Blöcker, "Zur Häresie," 211, for the reference to Augustine, *De civitate Dei*, VII, 5, CSEL, 40/1, 308f.

141. Andreas of Fleury, *Vie de Gauzlin*, c. 56 a, 98. According to Andreas, the heretics rejected the idea of a church entirely ("non credebant Ecclesiam esse" [they did not believe there was a church]).

142. "Modo quodam locutionis ostenditur, quo significatur per id quod continetur, illud, quod continet, sicut [. . .] appellamus ecclesiam basilicam, qua continetur populus qui vere appellatur Ecclesia." [A certain mode of speech illustrates that a thing containing something is signified by the name of the thing that it contains, for example (. . .) we signify as "church" the basilica that contains the people who are in truth the "church."] In "Epistula 190," c. 19, ed. A. Goldbacher, CSEL, 57, *Epistulae* (Vienna, 1911), 4:154.

143. Gerhoh of Reichersberg, "Epistola 21," MPL 193, 585 A, a letter to the cardinals containing a text for Pope Innocent II.

144. According to the generally accepted theory of Ilarino da Milano, "Le eresie popolari del secolo XI nell'Europa occidentale," *Studi Gregoriani* 2 (1947): 68 n. 35. "Cannot be determined for sure," according to Taviani, "Naissance," 1224.

145. Landulf the Elder of Milan, *Historia Mediolanensis*, c. 27, MGH SS 8, 65, and *Landulphi Senioris Mediolanensis Historiae Libri Quattuor*, ed. A. Cutolo, Rerum Italicarum Scriptores, new ed., IV/2 (Bologna, 1942), 67. Violante, "La povertà," 98–102.

146. Rodulfus Glaber, *Historiarum libri quinque*, IV, 2 (5), in J. France, 176 and 177, and Prou, 94. Borst, *Die Katharer*, 77, speaks of "approximately thirty members of the nobility."

147. Taviani, "Naissance," 1246f. Monforte was a region of more interest to the margrave of Turin, who had much land in the area. Cf. Gorre, *Die Ketzer*, 219.

148. Taviani, "Naissance," 1225, considers this likely.

149. Rodulfus Glaber, *Historiarum libri quinque*, IV, 2 (5), in J. France, 178 and 179, and Prou, 94f., preceded (IV, 1) by a passage on his reservations about Conrad II. See France, in the introduction to J. France, 1.

150. Arno Borst in "Discussione," in *Atti del X Congresso internazionale di Scienze Storiche, Roma 1955* (Florence, 1957), 350, unfortunately without a reference.

151. See page 50 above and Gilles Gerard Meersseman and E. Adda, "Pénitents ruraux communautaires en Italie au XIIe siècle," *Revue d'histoire ecclésiastique* 49 (1954): 343–90.

152. Landulf, *Historia*, MGH SS 8, 66. Here we find the surely incorrect reading "misterium." Same in Landulf, ed. Cutolo, 69.

153. On the *endura*, see Manselli, *L'eresia del male*, 239 (evidence for the practice since ca. 1240). Borst, *Die Katharer*, 197f. and n. 22; Jean Duvernoy, *La religion*, 165 n. 89 (*endura* as a fast, not suicide), and 166 n. 93 (no connection between the deaths in Monforte and Catharism); and Rottenwöhrer, *Der Katharismus*, vol. 2/2, 600. Raoul Manselli, "Per la storia dell'eresia nel secolo XII," *Bullettino dell'Istituto Storico Italiano per il Medio Evo e Arch. Mur.* 67 (1955): 225–31, links *endura* with the word *martirium* in an oath of abjuration from Moissac (twelfth century); see also 234.

154. Violante, *La società*, 221, correctly emends the reading from "qui omnia ut ab initio" [who all things as from the beginning] to "qui omnia est ab initio" [who is all things from the beginning].

155. Taviani, "Naissance," 1236.

156. Ibid., 1236 n. 66. "Animus itaque, id est intellectus omnium, Dei filius est. Ipse est enim, ut ait sanctus Augustinus, intellectus omnium, immo omnia." [Thus, the spirit, that is, the intellect of all things, is the son of God. Indeed he is, as Saint Augustine says, the intelligence of all things, indeed all things himself.]

157. Taviani's explanation, ibid., 1238 (*sensus interior* [inner sense]), is unconvincing. The word *sensualiter* played a part in the controversy over the Eucharist in 1059, where it denoted the concrete reality of Christ's Body in the Host. Berengar of Tours preferred the word *intellectualiter* [intellectually].

158. *Annales Nivernenses*, MGH SS 13, 90. Russell, *Dissent*, 182 and n. 66, adds this source to the *corpus* on heresy.

159. *Corpus Documentorum*, I, no. 5, 8f. Cf. note 34 above.

160. MPL 143, 1346f. Ilarino, "Le eresie," 78, believes he has discovered in this instance a beachhead by a non-European heresy. Russell, *Dissent*, 182, maintains that the warning would not have been issued "had there not been heretics in Provence." He sees no evidence here for the existence of Cathars: "[it] can be rapidly dismissed," 198.

161. Manegold of Lautenbach, *Liber contra Wolfelmum*, ed. Wilfried Hartmann, MGH Quellen zur Geistesgeschichte des Mittelalters, 8 (Cologne, 1972). Hartmann poses this question and then provides evidence for his answer, 84f.

162. Max Manitius, *Geschichte der lateinischen Literatur des Mittelalters*, Handbuch der Altertumswissenschaft, IX/2/3 (Munich, 1931), 3:176.

163. Borst, *Die Katharer*, 80.

164. Entry for the year 1091 in Bernold of Constance (St. Blasien), *Chronicon*, MGH SS 5, 451f. and 462, and Grundmann, *Ketzergeschichte*, 15 and n. 11.

165. *Das Register Gregors VII.*, IV, 10, II/1, 309, and VII, 16, II/2, 490.

166. Vacarius, I, 2, ed. Ilarino da Milano, *L'eresia di Ugo Speroni nella confutazione del Maestro Vacario*, Studi e testi, 115 (Vatican City, 1945), 485. See pages 305–6 above.

167. *Chron. s. Andreae castri Cameracensis*, III, 3, MGH SS 7, 540, written in 1135 by a monk of the monastery.

168. According to *Corpus Documentorum*, 1:11 n. 1.

169. *Das Register Gregors VII.*, IV, 20 (March 25, 1077), 1:328f.

170. Ibid., IV, 22 (May 12, 1077), 332.

171. Borst, *Die Katharer*, 82.

172. *Liber de unitate Ecclesiae conservanda*, c. 38, MGH Libelli de lite, 2:266.

173. Entry for the year 1075 in the *Annales Augustani*, MGH SS 3, 128.

174. See page 43 and note 151 above. Entry for the year 1091 in Bernold of Constance (St. Blasien), *Chronicon*, 452f.

175. Ibid., 453.

Notes to Chapter 2

1. Grundmann, *Ketzergeschichte*, 16.

2. Most recently published by Fearns in *Ketzer und Ketzerbekämpfung*, no. 3, 15–18; previously published by Fredericq in *Corpus Documentorum*, no. 11, 1:15–18. Russell, *Dissent*, appendix B, 265–69, provides a review of the sources and literature; cf. Grundmann, *Ketzergeschichte*, 16 n. 2. On the chronology of the trip to Rome, see Russell, *Dissent*, 65 and 282 n. 9.

3. *Vita Norberti archiepiscopi Magdeburgensis* (first version), c. 16, MGH SS 12, 690f., and *Corpus Documentorum*, no. 14, 1:23. Lambert, *Medieval Heresy* (rev. 2d ed.), 51, cites a modern analogy: "Garibaldi's servant found a good sale, all unknown to his master, for his bathwater."

4. *Vita Norberti* (second version), MGH SS 12, 690n, and *Corpus Documentorum*, no. 15, 1:24. Both versions are based on the letter from the Utrecht clergy and are thus not reliable sources.

5. *Corpus Documentorum*, no. 17, 1:26; now also available in CC. cont. med., 13/3.

6. Edouard de Moreau, *Histoire de l'Église en Belgique* (Brussels, 1940), 2:312. Moreau wrote that the majority of the canons were not priests, and that they "devaient uniquement s'acquitter de la récitation de l'office divin" [only had to see to it that the divine office was recited].

7. William of Newburgh, *Historia rerum Anglicarum*, I, 19, ed. R. Howlett, Rerum Britannicarum Scriptores, 82/1 (London, 1884 and 1964), 60f.; source also for the following material.

8. Entry for the year 1148 in *Continuatio Praemonstratensis des Sigebert von Gembloux*, MGH SS 6, 454; entry for the year 1146 in *Cont. Gemblacensis*, MGH SS 6, 389.

9. Otto of Freising, *Ottonis et Rahewini Gesta Friderici I. imperatoris*, I, 56, ed. G. Waitz and B. de Simson, MGH SS rerum Germanicarum, 46 (Hannover and Leipzig, 1912), 81; trans. Charles Mierow, with Richard Emery, *The Deeds of Frederick Barbarossa* (New York, 1953; 1966), 94–95.

10. On Peter of Bruis, cf., i.a., Borst, *Die Katharer*, 83; Duvernoy, *L'histoire*, 200f.; Fearns, "Peter von Bruis," 311–35; Raoul Manselli, *Studi sulle eresie del secolo XII*, Istituto Storico Italiano per il Medio Evo, Studi storici, 5 (Rome, 1953), 25–43; Russell, *Dissent*, 74f.; and Grado G. Merlo, *Eretici ed eresie medievali* (Bologna, 1989), 21–26.

11. Peter the Venerable, *Petri Venerabilis Contra Petrobrusianos Hereticos*, ed. J. Fearns, CC cont. med., 10 (1968); the dedicatory letter addressed to the clergy of Dauphiné appears on 3–6 and in *Ketzer und Ketzerbekämpfung*, no. 4, 18–21.

12. Borst, *Die Katharer*, 83 n. 10. Fearns dates the onset of Peter's activities to this year and his death to 1139 or 1140; on the other hand, Borst, *Die Katharer*, 83, proposes the period from 1105 to 1126. The background cited here is based on Manselli, *Studi*, 29; detailed counterarguments in Fearns, "Peter von Bruis," 313–17.

13. Peter the Venerable, *Contra Petrobrusianos*, c. 4, 9f., and c. 274, 162.

14. Fearns, "Peter von Bruis," 323. Lambert, *Medieval Heresy*, 53 (1977) and 49 (rev. 2d ed.), concurs with this explanation.

15. Peter the Venerable, *Contra Petrobrusianos*, c. 4, 9: "populi rebaptizati" [people were

rebaptized]. Manselli, *Studi*, 25 n. 1, was the one to draw attention to the passage by Peter Abelard, *Introductio ad theologiam* (= *Theologia "Scholarium"*), II, 4.

16. Fearns, "Peter von Bruis," 321, reaches this conclusion because of the use of the term *lavantur* [*peccata*] [sins are washed away] in reference to adult baptism.

17. Ibid., 330 and n. 98.

18. Ibid., 326. Fearns concludes that the heretics of Orléans rejected the Old Testament because they "did not believe in the Incarnation." On Arras, see ibid., 325.

19. Ibid., 329.

20. Concerning Henry, see in particular Manselli, *Studi*, 45–67, and the original version of the article "Il monaco Enrico e la sua eresia," *Bullettino dell'Istituto Storico Italiano* 65 (1953), which includes an edition of a *disputatio* [debate] between Henry and a monk named William on 36–63.

21. Bernard of Clairvaux, *Sämtliche Werke lateinisch-deutsch*, "Ep. 241," ed. G. B. Winkler et al. (Innsbruck, 1992), 3:292. Alberic of Trois-Fontaines, *Chronicon*, ed. P. Scheffer-Boichorst, MGH SS 23, 839, termed him a former "black monk" (Benedictine) from the area around Albi; the latter may not be correct.

22. *Gesta Pontificum Cenomannensium*, Recueil des historiens des Gaules et de la France, 12 (Paris, 1875), 550 C, and 547–50 for the following material.

23. In other words, he only drank wine. A second member of the delegation was called "Alderic the heathen" (*paganus Aldricus*); the third was called Hugh "de Osello," which, translated literally, means "of the little bones" (dice?). Ibid., 548 E.

24. "[I]pse, cuius divinitati non desinis contraire" [He, whose divinity you do not cease to deny], and cf. a previous passage, "multa contra fidem catholicam, quae fidelis Christianus retractare exhorrescit [. . .] protulisti" [you assert many things contrary to the Catholic faith, things that a pious Christian dreads to go over again]. Ibid., 549 AB.

25. Peter the Venerable, in the dedicatory letter to *Contra Petrobrusianos*, c. 10, 5; *Ketzer und Ketzerbekämpfung*, no. 4, 20f.

26. See note 20 above.

27. Manselli, *Studi*, 58, and idem, "Il monaco Enrico," 19.

28. Mansi, c. 3, 21:226f.

29. Ibid., c. 23, 21:532f.

30. *Gesta Treverorum, continuatio I*, MGH SS 8, 193ff. This pertains to Ivois, canton Carignan, arrondissement Sedan, in the diocese of Trier. On the incident in 1122, see Duvernoy, *L'histoire*, 107.

31. See page 46 and note 159 to Chapter 1.

32. Manselli, "Il monaco Enrico," 48: "parvulos, quod verum est, originale peccatum contrahere asseris, sed sine baptismi lavarro salvos esse deliras" [you claim to apply original sin to small children, as is true, but you rave that they are saved without the cleansing of baptism]; and 47: "in qua sententia originale peccatum destruis, in Pelagianam haeresin incidisti" [by which opinion you undermine original sin, and you have fallen into the heresy of Pelagianism].

33. *Annales Rodenses*, MGH SS 16, 711; cf. *Annales Aquenses*, MGH SS 16, 685. At Bucy-le-Long near Soissons in 1115 heretics were accused of rejecting, i.a., the Eucharist, infant baptism, and marriage (*coniugia*). Cf. page 77 above and note 42 below.

34. Everwin of Steinfeld, MPL 182, 676–80; partial edition (only passages about the Cathars) in *Ketzer und Ketzerbekämpfung*, no. 6 (entry for 1143), 24–26. On these Cathars, see page 79 above.

35. Everwin of Steinfeld, MPL 182, c. 4, 678; source also for the following material.

36. Ibid., c. 6, 679.

37. Otto of Freising, *Gesta Friderici*, II, 28, 133; trans. Mierow, *The Deeds of Frederick Barbarossa*, 143.

38. Jacques Verger, "Abélard et les milieux sociaux de son temps," in *Abélard en son temps: Actes du Colloque . . . IXe centenaire de la naissance de Pierre Abélard* (Paris, 1981), 118.

39. Arsenio Frugoni, "Filii Arnaldi," *Bullettino dell'Istituto Storico Italiano* 70 (1958): 521–24.

40. Ekbert of Schönau, "Sermo V," c. 11, MPL 195, 34.

41. See page 63 above.

42. Raoul Manselli, "Ecberto di Schönau e l'eresia catara in Germania alla metà del secolo XII," in *Arte e Storia, Studi L. Vincenti* (Turin, 1965), 331 n. 45. This corresponds in certain aspects with the testimony by Guibert of Nogent, *Autobiographie*, III, 17, 430, concerning heretics in Bucy-le-Long near Soissons: "ita ut vir cum femina, singulus cum singula, non moretur, sed viri cum viris, feminae cum feminis cubitare noscantur, nam viri apud eos in foeminam coitus nefas est." [Trans. Archambault, *A Monk's Confession*, 196: "Nor do men and women confine themselves to the same partner: men are known to sleep with other men, women with women, for they hold the intercourse of man and woman to be a crime."] This group, however, much like the Cathars, rejected marriage altogether. Cf. note 33 above and page 77.

43. Entry for the year 1183 in Sigebert of Gembloux, *Chronographia, cont. Aquicinctina*, MGH SS 6, 421. *Corpus Documentorum*, no. 48, 1:48. In spite of the discrepancy in dates, the Flemish group involved here must be the same as that which complained to Pope Alexander III in 1162 about charges made against them by the archbishop of Rheims. *Corpus Documentorum*, no. 37, 1:37, and no. 38, 1:38f. This would explain how Alexander came to hold his own opinion on the heretics, while Louis VII considered them Manichaeans or "Populicani" (Cathars) in his letter to the pope. *Corpus Documentorum*, no. 37, 1:37; Herbert Grundmann, *Religious Movements in the Middle Ages*, trans. Steven Rowan (Notre Dame, Ind., 1995), 24–25. Cathars from Flanders were burned in Cologne in 1163; see page 84 above.

44. Raoul Manselli, "I Passagini," *Bullettino dell'Istituto Storico Italiano* 75 (1963): 189–210. Rpt. in Raoul Manselli, *Il secolo XII* (Rome, 1983), 295–310. Further literature in Borst, *Die Katharer*, 112 n. 11.

45. See page 50 above.

46. Meersseman and Adda, "Pénitents ruraux," 350–90.

47. Grundmann, *Religious Movements*, 32–40; on social rankings, see 69–71.

48. Gottfried Koch, "Neue Quellen und Forschungen über die Anfänge der Waldenser," *Forschungen und Fortschritte* 32 (1958): 147. Fearns, "Peter von Bruis," 334, is more circumspect.

49. Grundmann, *Religious Movements*, 192ff.

50. According to a monk named William (versus Henry the Monk), text in Manselli, "Il monaco Enrico," 46.

51. Kurt-Victor Selge, *Die ersten Waldenser*, Arbeiten zur Kirchengeschichte, 37 (Berlin, 1967), 1:250ff., particularly 251 n. 60. Walter Map, *De nugis curialium*, I, 31, ed. M. R. James, L. Brooke, and R.A.B. Mynors (Oxford, 1983), 126.

52. Of the extensive literature on the subject, Giovanni Gonnet, "Le cheminement des vaudois vers le schisme et l'hérésie (1174–1218)," *Cahiers de civilisation médiévale* 19 (1976): 309–45, particularly 333, is worthy of note. On Waldensians and Cathars in the duchy of Austria, see Peter Segl, "Häresie und Inquisition im Bistum Passau im 13. und beginnenden 14. Jahrhundert," *Ostbairische Grenzmarken* (1981): 45–65, and idem, *Ketzer in Österreich*, Quellen und Forschungen aus dem Gebiet der Geschichte, n.s., 5 (Paderborn, 1984).

Notes to Chapter 3

1. Cosmas, *Le traité*, did not yet use the term "Bogomils."
2. Ernst Werner, "Bogomil eine literarische Fiktion?" *Forschungen und Fortschritte* 33 (1959): 24–28, in opposition to V. S. Kiselkov, rejects this interpretation. Vaillant, in Cosmas, *Le traité*, 27, considers it a pseudonym.
3. Vaillant, in Cosmas, *Le traité*, 27 n. 2, rejects the translation "cher à Dieu" (loved of God), which is found in many works, i.a., Runciman, *The Medieval Manichee*, 67.
4. Puech, in Cosmas, *Le traité*, 132f. and n. 6; cf. 289.
5. Cosmas, *Le traité*, c. 2, 57.
6. Ibid., c. 11, 71, and c. 2, 55.
7. Ibid., c. 19, 86.
8. Dimitur Angelov, "Aperçu sur la nature et l'histoire du bogomilisme en Bulgarie," in *Hérésies et sociétés dans l'Europe pré-industrielle, 11e–18e siècles*, Civilisations et sociétés, 10 (Paris and The Hague, 1968), 79.
9. As noted correctly by Manselli, *L'eresia del male*, 88f.
10. Cosmas, *Le traité*, c. 19, 85, as well as Puech, in ibid., 277.
11. Dmitri Obolensky, at the roundtable portion of the conference on heresies and societies in preindustrial Europe, 1000–1800, in *Hérésies et sociétés*, 144f.
12. Cosmas, *Le traité*, c. 17, 83, as well as Puech, in ibid., 273.
13. Ibid., c. 15, 81.
14. Ibid., c. 30, 120f.
15. Ibid., c. 30, 121.
16. Ibid., c. 30, 121f.
17. Ibid., c. 13, 76. In Byzantium the Bogomils were reproached for their "pseudomonastic" dress. Paolo Eleuteri and Antonio Rigo, *Eretici, dissidenti . . . a Bizanzio*, c. 17 (Venice, 1993), 144.
18. Cosmas, *Le traité*, c. 18, 85.
19. Ibid., c. 14, 77, and Loos, *Dualist Heresy*, 58.
20. Cosmas, *Le traité*, c. 15, 81f.
21. Ibid., c. 3, 58; c. 5, 59; and c. 16, 82f.
22. Ibid., c. 3, 58.
23. Ibid., c. 17, 83.
24. Ibid.
25. Ibid., c. 7, and cf. c. 6, 63.
26. Puech, in ibid., 242f.
27. Euthymios Zigabenos, *Panoplía dogmatiké*, in Migne, *Patrologia Graeca*, 130. Puech, in Cosmas, *Le traité*, 142.
28. Runciman, *The Medieval Manichee*, 80. Puech, in Cosmas, *Le traité*, 140f.
29. Puech, in Cosmas, *Le traité*, 254f.
30. See Dondaine, "L'origine," 66, for further details.
31. Moore, *European Dissent*, 148.
32. Puech, in Cosmas, *Le traité*, 258f. See page 39 and note 129 to Chapter 1 for a similar assertion by the heretics of Orléans.
33. See Franjo Šanjek, "Le rassemblement hérétique de Saint-Félix-de-Caraman (1167) et les Églises cathares au XIIe siècle," *Revue d'histoire ecclésiastique* 67 (1972): 789–91, for a review of the research on this topic; see also Bernard Hamilton, "The Origins of the Dualist Church of Drugunthia," in *Monastic Reform, Catharism, and the Crusades* (London, 1979), 7:115–24.

34. Dmitri Obolensky, *The Bogomils* (Cambridge, 1948), 133.

35. On their location, see, i.a., Hans Söderberg, *La religion des Cathares: Études sur le gnosticisme de la basse antiquité et du Moyen Âge* (Ph.D. thesis, Uppsala, 1949), 34f., and Hamilton, "The Origins," 115f.

36. Obolensky, *The Bogomils*, 127–29. It seems that this story may be traced back in part to Cosmas, *Le traité*, c. 14, 77: The devil had tempted humans to eat meat, drink wine, and have sexual relations.

37. As noted correctly by Manselli, *L'eresia del male*, 94, and Hamilton, "The Origins," 121.

38. Euthymios of the Peribleptos monastery, cited by Puech, in Cosmas, *Le traité*, 180 and n. 4; alternatively, they discerned a trinity consisting of God the Father, Satan, and Christ, ibid., 181.

39. Cosmas, *Le traité*, c. 13, 75.

40. This is an abbreviated version; see Runciman, *The Medieval Manichee*, 75–77, for the detailed account given by Euthymios Zigabenos.

41. Borst, *Die Katharer*, 175.

42. See pages 17–18 and note 23 to Chapter 1.

43. Guibert of Nogent, *Autobiographie*, III, 17, 428–34, trans. Archambault, *A Monk's Confession*, 195–98; source also for the following material. Rottenwöhrer, *Der Katharismus*, 3:227ff.

44. See page 35 and note 113 to Chapter 1.

45. As in Manselli, *L'eresia del male*, 146.

46. Guibert of Nogent, *Autobiographie*, III, 17, 428, and III, 16, 424–28; trans. Archambault, *A Monk's Confession*, 197 and 193–95. *Tractatus de incarnatione contra Iudeos*, MPL 156, 489–98, especially 490f.

47. *Tractatus de incarnatione*, I, 2, MPL 156, 492.

48. Ibid., 493.

49. Borst, *Die Katharer*, 95 n. 21. On the letter's contents, see Elisabeth Größmann, "Der Brief Hildegards von Bingen an den Kölner Klerus zum Problem der Katharer," in *Die Kölner Universität im Mittelalter*, Miscellanea mediaevalia, 20 (Berlin and New York, 1989), 312–20.

50. Moore, *European Dissent*, 173. M. Brandt in Ernst Werner, *Die Bogomilen in Bulgarien*, Studi medievali ser. III, 3 (1962), 270 and n. 68, proposes a different date (1182/83).

51. Runciman, *The Medieval Manichee*, 72.

52. Everwin of Steinfeld, MPL 182, 679; *Ketzer und Ketzerbekämpfung*, no. 6, 26; and Merlo, *Eretici*, 39. Duvernoy, *L'histoire*, 110, translates "tempore martyrum" [in the time of the martyrs] as "depuis les temps des apôtres" [since the time of the apostles]. On their historical consciousness, see also Ekbert of Schönau, "Sermo I," MPL 195, 13: "per multa tempora latuerunt [. . .] per omnes terras multiplicati sunt" [they have lasted for a long time . . . they have spread over all lands]; and 16: "Talia iam longo tempore susurraverunt" [they have whispered such things now for a long time].

53. See pages 63–64 and notes 34–36 to Chapter 2. Various dates have been proposed for the letter: 1143 in *Ketzer und Ketzerbekämpfung*; between 1143 and 1144 in Borst, *Die Katharer*, 4; not 1144 in Manselli, *L'eresia del male*, 92; and around 1145 in Rottenwöhrer, *Der Katharismus*, vol. 1/1, 155.

54. *Annales Brunwilarenses*, MGH SS 16, 727.

55. Manselli, "Ecberto," 315f. and n. 11.

56. Borst, *Die Katharer*, 201 n. 31, draws attention to this analogy.

57. Ibid., 210, speaks of the "bid for a Cathar pontificate" (as an honorific).

58. Ibid., 211 and n. 29.

59. *Corpus Documentorum*, no. 30, 1:32f. Georges Despy, "Hérétiques ou anticléricaux? Les 'Cathares' dans nos régions avant 1300," in *Aspects de l'anticléricalisme du Moyen Âge à nos*

jours: Hommage à Robert Joly (Brussels, 1988), 23–33, considers this a reform movement unrelated to Catharism. Alessandra Mascalchi, review of "Hérétiques ou anticléricaux? . . ." by Georges Despy, *Medioevo latino* 12 (1991): 850, concurs with this view. See M. Sutor, "Le Triumphus sancti Lamberti et le catharisme à Liège," *Le Moyen Âge* 91 (1985): 241–49, for the last discussion of the dating (1144/45).

60. See pages 26–27 and note 75 to Chapter 1.

61. Borst, *Die Katharer*, 176.

62. Heribert the Monk, "Epistola de haereticis Petragoricis," MPL 181, 1721f.; last edited (in three redactions) by Guy Lobrichon, "Le clair-obscur de l'hérésie au début du XIe siècle en Aquitaine: Une lettre d'Auxerre," in *Historical Reflections/Réflexions historiques*, 14 (Waterloo, Ontario, 1987), 441f., 443f., and 444 (the last one dated 1163). Lobrichon refers to Vauchez, "Diables et hérétiques," 578f. See Borst, *Die Katharer*, 4 and n. 8, on the dating of the letter (before 1147). Five copies date to the twelfth century; Lobrichon found a sixth in a Parisian manuscript of miscellaneous works from the ninth through eleventh centuries. It is likely that the letter dates to the latter century and was written between 1020 and 1030. In Lobrichon's view it is not an objective report about the heretics, but instead a "pamphlet" attacking the Cluniacs' adversaries, the bishops, or competing reformers. Since this interpretation is based upon the paleographical dating of the text, the dating needs to be confirmed.

63. Bernard of Clairvaux, "Sermo in Cantica 65," c. 2, MPL 183, 1088f.

64. Ibid., c. 12, 1100.

65. Ibid., c. 5, 1092.

66. *Corpus Documentorum*, no. 31, 1:33.

67. See note 62 above. Only *laicus* (layman) appears in recension A by Lobrichon, while the sentence is entirely missing from recension C (dating to the late twelfth century).

68. Borst, *Die Katharer*, 92.

69. Mansi, c. 1, 21:843.

70. On this topic, see Borst, *Die Katharer*, 248 and n. 3.

71. See page 79 and note 55 above. See Manselli, "Ecberto," and Borst, *Die Katharer*, 6f., on the following material.

72. Ekbert of Schönau, *Sermones contra Catharos*, MPL 195, 11–102. (Pages 97–102 contain excerpts from Augustine.)

73. Borst, *Die Katharer*, 93f. and n. 18; Duvernoy, *L'histoire*, 112; and Russell, *European Dissent*, 224ff. (on 1166). Rottenwöhrer, *Der Katharismus*, 3:330–38.

74. *Chronica regia Coloniensis*, ed. G. Waitz, MGH SS rerum Germanicarum, 18 (1880; 1978), 114. Manselli, "Ecberto," 317 n. 14. Cf. Caesarius of Heisterbach, *Dialogus miraculorum*, V, 19, 1:298; trans. Scott and Bland, *The Dialogue of Miracles*, 1:341–42.

75. Bonenfant, "Un clerc cathare," 271–80.

76. Rottenwöhrer, *Der Katharismus*, no. 4f., vol. 1/2, 450.

77. Listed in Borst, *Die Katharer*, 103 n. 18f.

78. Loos, *Dualist Heresy*, 147f.

79. Wanda Cherubini, "Movimenti patarinici in Orvieto," *Bullettino dell'Istituto Storico Artistico Orvietano* 15 (1959): 13. On the following material, see also Manselli, *L'eresia del male*, 276f. and 185f., and Duvernoy, *L'histoire*, 170f. Gabriele Zanella, *Itinerari ereticali: Patari e catari tra Rimini e Verona*, Studi storici, 153 (Rome, 1986), cautions that disobeying ecclesiastical directives was often termed heresy and that the term *patari* does not mean adherents of Catharism. Conversely, John H. Mundy, review of *Ketzer und Professoren*, by Heinrich Fichtenau, *Catholic Historical Review* (1993): 518–19, offers a very high estimate for the proportion of Cathars in Italy.

80. Borst, *Die Katharer*, 93, 96, and 235. Duvernoy, *L'histoire*, 167.

81. See pages 29–30 and note 87 to Chapter 1.

82. Hamilton, "The Cathar Council of Saint-Félix Reconsidered," in *Monastic Reform*, 9:23–53, argues for a later date (between 1174 and 1177).

83. Manselli, *L'eresia del male*, 198.

84. Borst, *Die Katharer*, 244.

85. Ibid., 100.

86. Ibid., 240–53 (appendix II), for details; in addition, Bonenfant, "Un clerc cathare," 276; Söderberg, *La religion*, 7 n. 1 (Novatianists); and Duvernoy, *La religion*, 303–11. On equating Albigensianism with radical dualism (beginning with Dondaine in 1946): Manselli, *L'eresia del male*, 170, and Duvernoy, *La religion*, 8. James W. Marchand, "On the Origins of the Term Popelican(t)," *Medieval Studies* 38 (1976): 496–98, and Moore, *European Dissent*, 182f. and 185. "Patarenes": Grundmann, *Ketzergeschichte*, 24 n. 8. "Arians" (equated with moderate dualists): Raoul Manselli, "Una designazione dell'eresia Catara: 'Arriana Haeresis,'" *Bullettino dell'Istituto Storico Italiano per il Medio Evo e Archivo Muratoriano* 68 (1956): 233–46.

87. Ekbert of Schönau, "Sermo II," c. 2, MPL 195, 19.

88. Tract about the Cathars in Durand of Huesca, *Une somme anti-cathare: Le Liber contra Manicheos de Durand de Huesca*, c. 14, ed. Christine Thouzellier, Université catholique de Louvain, Études et documents, 32 (Louvain, 1964), 227: "Sed quid ego vos hereticos ammonendo diucius laboro?" [But why do I bother admonishing you heretics any longer?]

89. See page 53 and note 2 to Chapter 2.

90. See page 79 and note 52 above.

91. *Ecritures cathares*, ed. R. Nelli (Paris, 1959; 1968), 220.

92. Duvernoy, *La religion*, 227f., and Georg Schmitz-Valckenberg, *Grundlehren der katharischen Sekten des 13. Jahrhunderts*, Münchener Universitätsschriften, 11 (Munich, 1971), 50f. (based on Moneta of Cremona, *Adversus Catharos et Waldenses*, written in 1241).

93. Borst, *Die Katharer*, 198, and Rottenwöhrer, *Der Katharismus*, vol. 2/1, 35f.

94. Manselli, "Ecberto," 336, and Ekbert of Schönau, "Sermo VIII," c. 3, MPL 195, 52.

95. Duvernoy, *La religion*, 236.

96. Rottenwöhrer, *Der Katharismus*, vol. 2/1, 345, disputes the existence of a separate ordination rite for bishops.

97. Text of the "council" in Šanjek, "Le rassemblement," 773f.: "N. episcopus Ecclesiae N. venit cum consilio suo" [Bishop (name) of (name of church) came with his council, or: counsel]. For more on this topic, see Duvernoy, *L'histoire*, 216–18, and Hamilton, "The Cathar Council," 51–53.

98. Last published in *Ketzer und Ketzerbekämpfung*, no. 6, 24. Duvernoy, *La religion*, 238, hypothesizes that the arrangement originated in Lombardy ca. 1200, yet in *L'histoire*, 225, he refers (probably in connection with 1178) to a bishop of Toulouse "and his second-in-command."

99. Duvernoy, *La religion*, 206f.

100. In the acts of the council, it is termed "coepit consolare" [he began the consolation]; in other words, he was the first to lay his hand on the head of the bishop in question, and the others then followed suit.

101. Manselli, *L'eresia del male*, 194.

102. Hugh of Amiens (Rouen; d. 1164), *Contra haereticos sui temporis . . . libri tres*, II, 1, MPL 192, 1273.

103. Peter of Vaux-de-Cernay, *Hystoria*, II, 28, 1:32.

104. Hamilton, "The Origins," 118.

105. For example, compare the detailed charts on the administration of the baptism of the Holy Spirit in Rottenwöhrer, *Der Katharismus*, vol. 2/1, 214ff., 230ff., and 259ff.

106. Ibid., vol. 2/2, 458.

107. Borst, *Die Katharer*, 191.

108. Grundmann, *Religious Movements*, 35. Borst, *Die Katharer*, 191 n. 5: "It was not unusual for the Waldensians and the mendicants of the thirteenth century to recite the Lord's Prayer one hundred times a day."

109. Manselli, "Ecberto," 333, and Duvernoy, *La religion*, 147. Borst, *Die Katharer*, 192, refers to a "pre-*consolamentum*." On the division of the consolamentum, see also Rottenwö-hrer, *Der Katharismus*, vol. 2/1, 143.

110. Raffaello Morghen, "L'eresia nel medioevo," in *Medioevo cristiano* (Bari, 1951, 1962, and 1968), 269f. (based on the Cathar ritual book) and 270 n. 1. Rottenwöhrer, *Der Katharismus*, vol. 2/1, 59. Manselli, *L'eresia del male*, 233, was referring to the interpretation of the bread as the word of God.

111. Arno Borst, "Abälard und Bernhard," *Historische Zeitschrift* 186 (1958): 504.

112. Borst, *Die Katharer*, 192.

113. Peter of Vaux-de-Cernay, *Hystoria*, II, 13, 1:15. John Hine Mundy, *Men and Women at Toulouse in the Age of the Cathars*, Studies and Texts, 101 (Toronto, 1990), 3, correctly recognizes that for the same reason no social or political directives could be issued to the believers.

114. Manselli, "Ecberto," 327 and n. 35.

115. Ekbert of Schönau, "Sermo I," MPL 195, 31: "qui perfecte sectam illorum ingressi sunt" [who have completely entered into their sect]; on Alan of Lille and Everard of Béthune: Duvernoy, *La religion*, 235. See Ekbert of Schönau, "Sermo V," c. 5, MPL 195, 31, on the perfects' terming themselves *perfecti*.

116. De Lubac, *Exegèse médiévale*, vol. 2, I/2, 578.

117. Ekbert of Schönau, "Sermo IV," c. 1, MPL 195, 25.

118. Borst, *Die Katharer*, 101.

119. William of Puylaurens, in the prologue to his *Chronique*, ed. Jean Duvernoy, Sources d'histoire médiévale (Paris, 1976), 26, and Christine Thouzellier, *Catharisme et Valdéisme en Languedoc à la fin du XIIe siècle* (Louvain and Paris, 1966, 1969, and 1982), 15 n. 9.

120. Jean Duvernoy, "L'acception de *haereticus* (*iretge*) = 'parfait cathare' en Languedoc au XIIIe siècle," in *The Concept of Heresy*, ed. Lourdaux and Verhelst, 204.

121. Peter of Vaux-de-Cernay, *Hystoria*, II, 17, 1:18.

122. Duvernoy, *La religion*, 154.

123. Peter of Vaux-de-Cernay, *Hystoria*, II, 33, 1:34.

124. Rottenwöhrer, *Der Katharismus*, vol. 2/2, 558.

125. Duvernoy, *La religion*, 176, and Rottenwöhrer, *Der Katharismus*, vol. 2/2, 690.

126. Everard of Béthune, cited by Duvernoy, *La religion*, 300 n. 26: "Praetendentes faciei pallorem, intonsi cum capillorum prolixitate incedentes et barbati, o barbata barbaries!" [Showing pallid faces, walking unshorn and bearded with overgrown hair, oh what bearded barbarism!]

127. For translations of the bestowal of the Lord's Prayer and the *consolamentum*, see "Rituel occitan," in *Ecritures cathares*, 215–17 and 218–22, respectively.

128. Bernard of Clairvaux, "Sermo 65," c. 6 and c. 4, MPL 183, 1092 and 1091. Addressing the same subject, the first canon of the Council of Rheims (1157) seems to have been drafted in the aftermath of Bernard's attack: Mansi, 21:843.

129. William of Puylaurens, *Chronique*, c. 8 (entry for the year 1207), 48; see, in addition, Mundy, *Men and Women*, 23 n. 5, and Gottfried Koch, *Frauenfrage und Ketzertum im Mittelalter*, Forschungen zur mittelalterlichen Geschichte, 9 (Berlin, 1962), 52.

130. "L'us teis e l'autra fila, l'autra fa so sermo, cossi à fag diable tota creatio." Duvernoy, *La religion*, 219 and 265 n. 103, based on "Le débat d'Izarn et de Sicart de Figueiras."

131. Same as note 128 above.

132. Richard Abels and Ellen Harrison, "The Participation of Women in Languedocian

Catharism," *Medieval Studies* 41 (1979): 226 (based on Rainer Sacconi, *De Catharis et Pauperibus de Lugduno*). Duvernoy, *La religion*, 265; on 264f., Duvernoy enumerates the few Cathar theological views favoring women.

133. Koch, *Frauenfrage*, 55f., and Abels and Harrison, "Participation," 226. Eleanor McLaughlin, "Die Frau und die mittelalterliche Häresie," *Concilium* 12 (1976): 34–44. Peter Segl, "Die religiöse Frauenbewegung in Südfrankreich im 12. und 13. Jahrhundert zwischen Häresie und Orthodoxie," in *Religiöse Frauenbewegung und mystische Frömmigkeit im Mittelalter*, ed. P. Dinzelbacher and D. Bauer (Cologne and Vienna, 1988), 100 and 105.

134. Koch, *Frauenfrage*, 51, and Ernst Werner and Martin Erbstösser, *Ketzer und Heilige* (Vienna, Cologne, and Graz, 1986), 345f.

135. Koch, *Frauenfrage*, 57, and Abels and Harrison, "Participation," 231f.

136. Koch, *Frauenfrage*, 56f., and Werner and Erbstösser, *Ketzer und Heilige*, 336.

137. Jordan of Saxony, *Libellus de principiis Ordinis Praedicatorum*, Monumenta Ordinis Praedicatorum Historica, 16 (1935), 39; Koch, *Frauenfrage*, 28; M.-H. Vicaire, "La naissance de Sainte-Marie de Prouille," in Pierre Mandonnet, *St. Dominique* (Paris, n.d.), 1:102; and Duvernoy, *L'histoire*, 249.

138. Lambert, *Medieval Heresy* (1977), 117. Borst, *Die Katharer*, 125, enumerates the various professions practiced in the thirteenth century.

139. Duvernoy, *La religion*, 253.

140. J. Lestocquoy, "Inhonesta Mercimonia," in *Mélanges Louis Halphen* (Paris, 1951), 413f., with reference to synodal statutes from 1275 and the expansion of a list of "disreputable" occupations (executioner, horse trader, etc.) to include textile work.

141. *Gesta abbatum Trudonensium*, c. 12, MGH SS 10, 310. See also Bonenfant, "L'épisode," 104.

142. Borst, *Die Katharer*, 248: "an insult." Loos, *Dualist Heresy*, 125 n. 93, agrees with Borst.

143. Ekbert of Schönau, "Sermo I," MPL 195, 14. Cf. Bernard of Clairvaux, "Sermo 65," c. 4, MPL 183, 1091: "vos in tenebris et subterraneis domibus delitescitis." [You hide in the shadows and in underground dwellings.]

144. Everwin of Steinfeld, in *Ketzer und Ketzerbekämpfung*, no. 6, 24.

145. Heribert the Monk, "Epistola de haereticis Petragoricis." See pages 81–82 and note 62 above for dating and editions. Observation not found in recension C edited by Lobrichon.

146. From the vernacular ritual book *Ecritures cathares*, 224.

147. William of Puylaurens, in the prologue to his *Chronique*, 22.

148. Durand of Huesca, *Liber antihaeresis*, ed. Kurt-Victor Selge, in *Die ersten Waldenser*, vol. 2, *Edition des Liber antihaeresis des Durandus von Osca*, 72; and Duvernoy, *La religion*, 197.

149. Duvernoy, *L'histoire*, 204f.; and William of Puylaurens, *Chronique*, 43 n. 1.

150. Everwin of Steinfeld, MPL 182, 679. (These words are not found in *Ketzer und Ketzerbekämpfung*, no. 6, 26, because Fearns apparently thought they applied to another group of heretics found in Cologne in 1143.)

151. See note 62 above.

152. Bonaccursus, *Manifestatio*, 207–11.

153. Peter of Vaux-de-Cernay, *Hystoria*, II, 22, 1:24f., and Duvernoy, *La religion*, 15.

154. Thouzellier, *Catharisme*, 38–40, and cf. 21–23. See page xx above.

155. Peter of Vaux-de-Cernay, *Hystoria*, II, 54, 1:47f., and William of Puylaurens, *Chronique*, c. 9, 50 and 52.

156. Borst, *Die Katharer*, 12 and n. 28: "volumen magnum decem quaternorum" [a great book consisting of ten quires]. Rottenwöhrer, *Der Katharismus*, vol. 4/1, 277f., expresses doubts concerning its authorship by John of Lugio. A second tract, extant only in fragments and compiled around 1220, contained more than thirty chapters and thus may have been even larger. See Rottenwöhrer, *Der Katharismus*, 4/2, 17–66, concerning this other work.

157. *Liber de duobus principiis*, in *Ecritures cathares*, 161.
158. References in Duvernoy, *La religion*, 29.
159. Manselli, *L'eresia del male*, 207.
160. Duvernoy, *La religion*, 71, based on the minutes of an inquisition.
161. Ibid., 103, based on Moneta of Cremona and Rainer Sacconi. Manselli, *L'eresia del male*, 207.
162. Cathar tract in Durand of Huesca, *Une somme anti-cathare*, c. 5, 168.
163. Schmitz-Valckenberg, *Grundlehren*, 53.
164. Loos, *Dualist Heresy*, 140.
165. Russell, *European Dissent*, 203.
166. Loos, *Dualist Heresy*, 140. See Borst, *Die Katharer*, 155 and nn. 16 and 18, for variants on the doctrine, and n. 17, concerning later, partial acknowledgment of Christ's divinity. Duvernoy, *La religion*, 80.
167. Peter of Vaux-de-Cernay, *Hystoria*, I, 11, 1:11. Cf. Gal. 2:20: Paul himself no longer lives, Christ lives in him.
168. Duvernoy, *La religion*, 85 (based on Moneta of Cremona) and 86.

Notes to Chapter 4

1. Caesarius of Heisterbach, *Dialogus miraculorum*, V, 21, 1:300; trans. Scott and Bland, *The Dialogue of Miracles*, 1:343.
2. Duvernoy, *La religion*, 366–77 and 387f.: "essentiellement origéniste" [essentially Origenist], "origénisme indubitable" [undoubtably Origenism]; and Taviani, "Naissance," 1244.
3. Duvernoy, *La religion*, 366. See Borst, *Die Katharer*, 61, on Greek precursors.
4. Söderberg, *La religion*, 267f.
5. Ibid., 268.
6. Ibid., 7.
7. Ekbert of Schönau, "Sermo I," c. 5, MPL 195, 18; see 97–102 for the excerpts from Augustine's works.
8. Söderberg, *La religion*, 266. Cf. Henri-Charles Puech, *Le manichéisme*, Musée Guimet, Bibliothèque de diffusion, 56 (Paris, 1949 and 1967), 69–72, on Manichaeism as a form of Gnosticism.
9. See pages 27–28 and notes 79 and 80 to Chapter 1.
10. "Nos et patres nostri generati apostoli" [we and our forefathers, apostles by descent], *Ketzer und Ketzerbekämpfung*, no. 6, 25.
11. Obolensky, *The Bogomils*, 20.
12. Dondaine, "L'origine," 72f. and n. 57. Puech, *Le manichéisme*, 181f. n. 364, disputed the existence of a Manichaean baptism.
13. Introduction to *Ecritures cathares*, 10. Alberic of Trois-Fontaines, *Chronicon*, MGH SS 23, 945.
14. Ilarino, "Le eresie," 44f., and Borst, *Die Katharer*, 73 n. 3.
15. In a lecture delivered in 1952 entitled "Die Entstehung des Manichäismus im Abendland," published in Heinrich Sproemberg, *Mittelalter und demokratische Geschichts-schreibung*, Ausgewählte Abhandlungen (Berlin, 1971), 85–102.
16. Armand Abel, "Aspects sociologiques des religions 'manichéennes,'" in *Mélanges René Crozet* (Poitiers, 1966), 1:33–46. Puech, *Le manichéisme*, 64, was rather skeptical of this idea.
17. Runciman, *The Medieval Manichee*, vii.

18. Dondaine, "L'origine," 64. Cf. in particular the reviews by Jeffrey Burton Russell, "Interpretations of the Origins of Medieval Heresy," *Medieval Studies* 25 (1963): 36f., and Loos, *Dualist Heresy*, 118f. n. 1.

19. Dondaine, "L'origine," 75. See page 37 and notes 123 and 124 to Chapter 1 for discussion.

20. Dondaine, "L'origine," 75 n. 59.

21. Morghen, "L'eresia nel medioevo," 212–86, and idem, "Il cosidetto neomanicheismo occidentale del secolo XI," in *Oriente e occidente nel medio evo*, Accademia Nazionale dei Lincei, XII convegno Volta (Rome, 1957), 84–160. See Heinrich Fichtenau, "Zur Erforschung der Häresien des 11. und 12. Jahrhunderts," *Römische Historische Mitteilungen* 31 (1989): 75–86, for more on Morghen's works and his ecclesiastico-historical approach. See also pages 164–65 above.

22. Moore, *European Dissent*, 295 n. 27.

23. Moore, "The Origins of Medieval Heresy," 35. See Puech, "Catharisme médiéval et Bogomilisme," in *Oriente e occidente*, 56–84, for a similar stance. Cf. Russell, "Interpretations," 37f.

24. Arno Borst, *Medieval Worlds: Barbarians, Heretics, and Artists*, trans. Eric Hansen (Chicago, 1992), 115, and Lambert, *Medieval Heresy*, 32f. (1977) and xiif. (rev. 2d ed.).

25. See pages 17–18 and note 23 to Chapter 1, and page 73 above.

26. See page 59 above.

27. Fearns, "Peter von Bruis," 325.

28. Ibid., 320–22.

29. Jean Musy, "Mouvements populaires et hérésies au XIe siècle en France," *Revue historique* 99, no. 253 (1975): 52.

30. Adémar of Chabannes, *Chronicon*, III, 59, 184.

31. Rodulfus Glaber, *Historiarum libri quinque*, III, 8 (26), in J. France, 138 and 139, and Prou, 74. See page 34 and note 108 to Chapter 1.

32. Puech, "Catharisme," 81, argues that it is not possible to prove that the Bogomils practiced the laying on of hands.

33. Cosmas, *Le traité*, II, c. 22, 93.

34. Heinrich Fichtenau, "Gentiler und europäischer Horizont," in *Beiträge zur Mediävistik* (Stuttgart, 1986), 3:85.

35. See page 30 and note 87 to Chapter 1.

36. Werner and Erbstösser, *Ketzer und Heilige*, 82, unfortunately without documentation. There may be a mix up with Monforte in the reference.

37. Puech, in Cosmas, *Le traité*, 166 and 140.

38. See pages 64 and 79 above. "Greece" probably meant Byzantium.

39. Lambert, *Medieval Heresy* (1977), 63, interprets the account by Ekbert of Schönau in this manner. See Manselli, "Ecberto," 331 and n. 45, for a different interpretation.

40. See page 81 above. On the various routes to the West, see Puech, "Catharisme," 62.

41. Anselm of Alessandria, *Tractatus de haereticis*, ed. Antoine Dondaine, *Archivum fratrum Praedicatorum* 20 (1953): 308–24. Christine Thouzellier, "Hérésie et croisade," *Revue d'histoire ecclésiastique* 49 (1954): 855–72, rev. rpt. in her *Hérésie et hérétiques*, Storia e letteratura, 116 (Rome, 1969), 17–37, is overly enthusiastic in her estimation of the account's importance. Cf. Arno Borst in *Deutsches Archiv* 11 (1954/55), 617f., and Russell, "Interpretations," 49. Puech, "Catharisme," 64f., interprets the word "Franks" in the narrowest sense, thus as denoting the northern French.

42. Raffaello Morghen, "Movimenti religiosi popolari nel periodo della Riforma della Chiesa," in *X Congresso internazionale di Scienze Storiche, Roma 1995*, Relazioni, vol. 3 (Florence, n.d.), 354.

43. Jeffrey Burton Russell, *Lucifer* (Ithaca and London, 1984), 184.

44. Violante, *La società*, 230.

45. According to Johannes Fried, in a review in *Historische Zeitschrift* 245 (1987): 644f.; see 646–51 for valid criticism (with warmest thanks to Othmar Hageneder, Vienna, for the reference).

46. Russell, "Interpretations," 53.

47. The passage by Engels was last discussed by Musy, "Mouvements," 37, and Segl, *Ketzer*, 240 n. 623. Werner and Angelov have published so extensively that it is not possible to cite all their works here.

48. Duby, *The Three Orders*, 132–33. Cf. Gorre, *Die Ketzer*, 235 n. 11. As similarly observed by Duby, *The Knight*, 107.

49. Hans-Georg Beck, *Actus fidei: Wege zum Autodafé*, Sitzungsberichte der Bayerischen Akademie der Wissenschaften, philosophische-historische Klasse, 3 (1987), 58.

50. See page 86 and note 80 to Chapter 3.

51. As quoted in Ernst Werner, *Die gesellschaftlichen Grundlagen der Klosterreform im 11. Jahrhundert* (Berlin, 1953), 71.

52. Cinzio Violante, "Eresie nelle città e nel contado in Italia dall'XI al XIII secolo," in *Studi*, 349f. and 379. (First published in French in *Hérésies et sociétés*, 171f. and 201.)

53. Philippe Wolff, *Histoire de Toulouse* (Toulouse, 1958), 67.

54. Landulf, *Historia*, II, 27, MGH SS 8, 66; Violante, "Eresie," 356 (in *Hérésies et sociétés*, 176f.); and Landulf, II, 27, ed. Cutolo, 69.

55. Werner and Erbstösser, *Ketzer und Heilige*, 334.

56. Bonaccursus, *Manifestatio*, MPL 204, 778; passage not found in Manselli's edition.

57. Borst, *Die Katharer*, 231 n. 1a. See page 81 and note 59 to Chapter 3.

58. Herbert Grundmann, "Neue Beiträge zur Geschichte der religiösen Bewegungen im Mittelalter," in *Ausgewählte Aufsätze*, 1:74.

59. Peter the Venerable, *Contra Petrobrusianos*, c. 6, 10.

60. Everwin of Steinfeld, in a letter to Bernard of Clairvaux, *Ketzer und Ketzerbekämpfung*, no. 6, 24; and c. 3, MPL 182, 677 D. See page 99 and note 144 to Chapter 3.

61. Mansi, c. 1, 21:843; and see pages 83–84 and note 69 to Chapter 3.

62. Grundmann, *Religious Movements*, 263f. n. 57.

63. J. Becquet, in remarks made at the conference on heresies and societies in preindustrial Europe, 1000–1800, in *Hérésies et sociétés*, 140 and 144, and Obolensky, in ibid., 144f.

64. Loos, *Dualist Heresy*, 57.

65. Violante, "L'eremitismo," in *Studi*, 139f.

66. Peter Damiani, "Ep. 44," in *Die Briefe des Petrus Damiani*, ed. K. Reindel, MGH Die Briefe der deutschen Kaiserzeit, vol. 4/2 (Munich, 1988), 21.

67. Ibid., no. 44, 14.

68. See page 100 and note 153 to Chapter 3 for an account by Peter of Vaux-de-Cernay of one such instance (1207).

69. Selge, *Die ersten Waldenser*, 1:305.

70. Cf. Fichtenau, "Zur Erforschung der Häresien," 75–86, on the following material.

71. Gioacchino Volpe, "Eretici e moti ereticali dall'XI al XIV secolo, nei loro motivi e riferimenti sociali." Rpt. in idem, *Movimenti religiosi e sette ereticali nella società italiani* (Florence, 1922). For the work's influence on Ernst Troeltsch, cf. Stock, *The Implications of Literacy*, 94f.

72. Morghen, "Il cosidetto neomanicheismo," 101, and idem, "Movimenti," 352.

73. Morghen, "L'eresia nel medioevo," 278.

74. Morghen, "Movimenti," 337.

75. Ibid., 340.

76. Morghen, "L'eresia nel medioevo," 244.

77. Ibid., 271.

78. Morghen, "Il cosidetto neomanicheismo," 93, and idem, "Problèmes sur l'origine de l'hérésie au Moyen-Âge," in *Hérésies et sociétés*, 125f.

79. Morghen, "L'eresia nel medioevo," 274–76.

80. Ibid., 276 n. 1.

81. Morghen, "Movimenti," 343.

82. Morghen, "L'eresia nel medioevo," 280.

83. Herbert Grundmann, "Hérésies savantes et hérésies populaires au Moyen Âge," in *Hérésies et sociétés*, 209–14 (discussion on 215–18). Rpt. in idem, *Ausgewählte Aufsätze*, 1:417–22. In the discussion, omitted from the reprint, Grundmann states, "Dans sa génèse, l'hérésie n'est pas le fait d'illettrés." [At its inception, heresy is not the product of illiterate individuals.] *Hérésies et sociétés*, 218.

84. As noted by Duvernoy, *L'histoire*, 17f.

85. Delaruelle, *La piété populaire*, 160 (99).

86. Morghen, "Movimenti," 351f.

87. Russell, *Dissent* (1965), and in his prior work, "Interpretations" (1963).

88. Russell, *Dissent*, 6f., 38, etc.

89. Ibid., 191f.

90. Russell, "Interpretations," 41, based on Söderberg.

91. Ibid., 44.

92. Russell, *Dissent*, 5f.

93. Gerhart B. Ladner, *The Idea of Reform* (Cambridge, Mass., 1959), 30f.

94. Ibid., 61.

95. Moore, *European Dissent*, 41; Lambert, *Medieval Heresy* (1977), 29f.; and Borst, *Medieval Worlds*, 115.

96. In *Hérésies et sociétés*, 118. Stock, *The Implications of Literacy*, 88, remarks that the heretics and reformed monks shared a preference for the written word.

97. For example, William of Saint-Amour. Grundmann, *Religious Movements*, 27–28.

98. Chenu, *Nature, Man, and Society*, 206 and n. 6. On the authorship of the tract containing this quote, see ibid., 205 n. 2.

99. Stanislaw Trawkowski, "Entre l'orthodoxie et l'hérésie: *Vita apostolica* et le problème de la désobéissance," in *The Concept of Heresy*, ed. Lourdaux and Verhelst, 159.

100. Text rpt. in Manselli, "Il monaco Enrico," 46.

101. See pages 66–68 above.

102. Chenu, *Nature, Man, and Society*, 215.

103. Hugh of Amiens (Rouen), *Contra haereticos*, c. 7, MPL 192, 1294.

104. Beryl Smalley, review of *The Origins of European Dissent*, by Robert Moore, *English Historical Review* 93 (1978): 855. Cf. the work cited in note 58 to Chapter 5.

105. Durand of Huesca, *Liber antiheresis*, in Selge, *Die ersten Waldenser*, 2:95.

106. Alan of Lille in Ms. Vat. Lat. 903, cited by Thouzellier, *Le Catharisme*, 96 n. 92. Cf. also Grundmann, *Religious Movements*, 42, and idem, *Religiöse Bewegungen*, 95 n. 46.

107. According to a polemical work by Hugh's adversary, Master Vacarius, in Ilarino, *L'eresia di Ugo Speroni*, XXVIII, II, 559. Vacarius refuted this statement by turning around the wording (III): "Si laicus, procul dubio est immundus." [If a person is a layman, then he is undoubtedly unholy.]

108. Cited in the *Vita prima* of Bernard of Clairvaux, c. 5, MPL 185, 412. Koch, *Frauenfrage*, 27 n. 86.

109. *Kolmarer Chronik*, MGH SS 17, 232, and Grundmann, *Religious Movements*, 159.

Notes to Chapter 5

1. Alan of Lille, *De fide catholica contra haereticos sui temporis praesertim Albigenses*, I, 3, MPL 210, 309.

2. Landulf the Younger of Milan, *Historia Mediolanensis*, c. 57, MGH SS 20, 45; and Rerum Italicarum Scriptores, new ed., V/3, 35. This passage was noted by Manselli, "I Passagini," 210 n. 1. Landulf phrases it euphemistically ("ignorant, minime amant" [they do not know, and hardly have love for]).

3. On the following material, cf. Herbert Grundmann, "Rotten und Brabanzonen," *Deutsches Archiv* 5 (1942): 419–92, and Jacques Boussard, "Les mercennaires au XIIe siècle," *Bibliothèque de l'École des Chartres* 106 (1945/46): 189–224.

4. Walter Map, *De nugis curialium*, I, 29, 118. Grundmann, "Rotten," 427 n. 1.

5. Thouzellier, *Catharisme*, 24.

6. Marc Van Uytfanghe, "Scepticisme doctrinal au seuil du Moyen Âge," in *Grégoire le Grand: Colloques internationaux du CNRS, Chantilly 1982* (Paris, 1986), 317; cf. 323 n. 16.

7. František Graus, *Volk, Herrscher und Heilige im Reich der Merowinger* (Prague, 1965), 451–55.

8. Alan of Lille, *De virtutibus et de vitiis et de donis Spiritus Sancti*, c. 2, art. 1, ed. O. Lottin, *Medieval Studies* 12 (1950): 40.

9. Tullio Gregory, *Anima Mundi*, Pubblicazioni dell'Istituto di Filosofia dell'Università di Roma, 3 (Florence, 1955), 151.

10. Wolff, *Histoire de Toulouse*, 89.

11. Emmanuel Le Roy Ladurie, *Montaillou: The Promised Land of Error*, trans. Barbara Bray (New York, 1978), 324 and n. 1.

12. Duvernoy, *La religion*, 270.

13. Peter of Vaux-de-Cernay, *Hystoria*, III, c. 212, 1:211.

14. Ibid., III, c. 228, 1:228f.

15. Walter Map, *De nugis curialium*, I, 30, 120.

16. Heribert the Monk, "Epistola de haereticis Petragoricis," MPL 181, 1722. Lobrichon, "Le clair-obscur," includes all the redactions. On the dating of the letter, see note 62 to Chapter 3.

17. Ernst Cassirer, *The Philosophy of Symbolic Forms*, vol. 2, *Mythical Thought*, trans. Ralph Manheim (New Haven, 1955), 58.

18. Hugh of Amiens (Rouen), *Contra haereticos*, I, 9, MPL 192, 1263.

19. Peter Abelard, *Dialogus inter philosophum, Judaeum et Christianum*, ed. R. Thomas (Stuttgart, Bad Cannstatt, 1970), 147; trans. Pierre J. Payer, *A Dialogue of a Philosopher with a Jew, and a Christian* (Toronto, 1979), 144.

20. William of Puylaurens, *Chronique*, c. 8, 46 and 48.

21. Rather of Verona, "Sermo II de quadragesima," c. 29, MPL 136, 705ff., and Ilarino, "Le eresie," 51 n. 22.

22. Odorannus of Sens, *Opera omnia*, 11, 14, 100, and c. 13, 264. See page 33 and note 101 to Chapter 1.

23. Mansi, c. 2, 19:433 B. See pages 23–24 above.

24. Ekbert of Schönau, "Sermo XI," c. 15, MPL 195, 93, and c. 14, 92.

25. Duvernoy, *La religion*, 214.

26. Hugh of Amiens (Rouen), *Contra haereticos*, III, 3, MPL 192, 1288.

27. Giorgio Cracco, "Spunti storici e storiografici in Elgaudo di Fleury," *Rivista storica italiana* 81 (1969): 125–32, esp. 126.

28. Helgald of Fleury, *Vie de Robert le Pieux*, c. 6, 66. Cf. page 33 above.

29. Delaruelle, *La piété populaire*, 12f. (318f.).

30. Richard W. Southern, *Saint Anselm and His Biographer*, Birkbeck Lectures, 1959 (Cambridge, 1963), 351.

31. Mandrou, at the roundtable portion of the conference on heresies and societies in preindustrial Europe, 1000–1800, in *Hérésies et sociétés*, 136.

32. Chenu, *Nature, Man, and Society*, 285.

33. Hugh of Amiens (Rouen), *Contra haereticos*, III, 9, MPL 192, 1297.

34. Alan of Lille, *De fide catholica*, I, 27, MPL 210, 328f.

35. Peter Abelard, *Theologia christiana*, III, 42, 211.

36. Otloh of St. Emmeram, *Liber de temptationibus suis*, I, MPL 146, 32f., and Fichtenau, *Living in the Tenth Century*, 400.

37. Elizabeth of Schönau, *Vita*, c. 14, MPL 195, 128, and Fichtenau, *Living in the Tenth Century*, 400.

38. Dennis Howard Green, *The Millstätter Exodus* (Cambridge, 1966), 353; see 354 for additional references on *zwîvel*.

39. Christopher N. L. Brooke, "Heresy and Religious Sentiment," *Bulletin of the Institute of Historical Research*, 41, no. 104 (1968): 123.

40. Peter the Venerable, *Contra Petrobrusianos*, c. 278, 165.

41. Hugh of Amiens (Rouen), *Contra haereticos*, I, 9, MPL 192, 1264.

42. Cinzio Violante, at the roundtable portion of the conference on heresies and societies in preindustrial Europe, 1000–1800, in *Hérésies et sociétés*, 205.

43. Hugh of Honau, *Liber de diversitate naturae et personae*, VIII, 1, ed. Nikolaus M. Haring, in "The *Liber de Diversitate Naturae et Personae* by Hugh of Honau," *Archives d'histoire doctrinale et littéraire du Moyen Âge* 29 (1962): 132.

44. Stock, *The Implications of Literacy*, 455.

45. See page 22 and note 49 to Chapter 1.

46. Stock, *The Implications of Literacy*, 150 and 90f.

47. Ekbert of Schönau, "Sermo XII," c. 1, MPL 195, 94.

48. Selge, *Die ersten Waldenser*, 2:xii. See Delaruelle, *La piété populaire*, 217 (159), for further information on pocketbooks (in the collection of the Bibliothèque Nationale in Paris).

49. Vaillant, in Cosmas, *Le traité*, 33.

50. Wilhelm Dittmar, *Vetus Testamentum in Novo* (Göttingen, 1903), 331–40 and 311–21.

51. Borst, *Die Katharer*, 157. See Emmanuel Le Roy Ladurie, *Montaillou, village occitan, de 1294 à 1324* (Paris, 1975), 454f., for a detailed discussion.

52. Franz H. Bäuml, "Varieties and Consequences of Medieval Literacy and Illiteracy," *Speculum* 55 (1980): 246.

53. Peter Damiani, "Ep. 121," in *Die Briefe*, vol. 4/3 (1989), 393. Cf. note 2 to Chapter 12.

54. Duvernoy, *La religion*, 32f.

55. Duvernoy, *L'histoire*, 196 and the map on 233.

56. See page 125 and note 104 to Chapter 4.

57. Duvernoy, *L'histoire*, 197.

58. B. Guillemain, "Le duché d'Aquitaine hors du Catharisme," in *Effacement du catharisme?* Cahiers de Fanjeaux, 20 (1985); cf. the review by Giulia Barone in *Studi medievali*, ser. III, 29 (1988), 470f.

59. Peter of Vaux-de-Cernay, *Hystoria*, III, c. 172, 1:174.

60. Ibid., III, c. 136, 1:139.

61. William of Puylaurens, *Chronique*, c. 23, 90.

62. Pierre Belperron, *La croisade contre les Albigeois et l'union du Languedoc à la France* (Paris, 1942, 1946; rpt. Paris, 1967, with amended pagination and no index), 30 (58).

63. William of Puylaurens, *Chronique*, c. 1, 26.

64. John Hine Mundy, *Liberty and Political Power in Toulouse, 1050–1230* (New York, 1954), 21 and 23.

65. Belperron, *La croisade*, 20 (48) and note 4 (3).

66. See pages 128–29 above.

67. Wolff, *Histoire de Toulouse*, 70.

68. Belperron, *La croisade*, 20 (47f.).

69. John Hine Mundy, "Urban Society and Culture: Toulouse and Its Region," in *Renaissance and Renewal in the Twelfth Century*, ed. Robert L. Benson and Giles Constable, with C. D. Lanham (Oxford, 1982), 240.

70. Belperron, *La croisade*, 19f. (47), for the numbers of coheirs. Cf. Thouzellier, *Catharisme*, 244f., on the importance of strongholds to Catharism.

71. See page 141 and note 63 above. Duvernoy, *L'histoire*, 205 n. 38.

72. William of Puylaurens, *Chronique*, c. 1, 26 and 28.

73. Ibid., c. 8, 48 and 50. Sources dating to the thirteenth century provide us with the earliest evidence for Cathar missionary activity among the nobles. For example, Archbishop Frederick Visconti of Pisa (1254–77) recounted in a sermon that the Cathars attacked the *avaritia* [cupidity] and *luxuria* [concupiscence] of the "nobles living in certain strongholds," who expropriated pack animals loaded with bolts of cloth that belonged to Pisan merchants traveling through their domain. Text reprinted by André Vauchez, "Les origines de l'hérésie cathare en Languedoc," in *Società, Istituzioni, Spiritualità nell'Europa medievale: Studi in onore di Cinzio Violante* (Spoleto, 1994), 2:1024f.

74. Peter of Vaux-de-Cernay, *Hystoria*, II, c. 48, 1:44. Loos, *Dualist Heresy*, 172.

75. Peter of Vaux-de-Cernay, *Hystoria*, III, c. 185, 1:188f.

76. Belperron, *La croisade*, 102 (128).

77. Ibid., 111f.

78. William of Puylaurens, *Chronique*, c. 22, 86 and 88.

79. Peter of Vaux-de-Cernay, *Hystoria*, I, c. 9, 1:9.

80. Manselli in "Discussione," in *Atti del X Congresso*, 349.

81. Denis de Rougemont, *L'amour et l'Occident* (Paris, 1937). See Belperron, *La croisade*, 48 (76), for counterarguments.

82. Belperron, *La croisade*, 43f., 102f. n. 1, and 49 (72, 128 n. 1, and 77).

83. Ariane Loeb, "La définition et l'affirmation du groupe noble comme enjeu de la poésie courtoise?" *Cahiers de civilisation médiévale* 30 (1987): 307.

84. Colin Morris, *The Discovery of the Individual, 1050–1200* (Toronto, 1972 and 1987), 109 and 111.

85. *Mediae Latinitatis Lexicon Minus*, ed. J. F. Niermeyer and C. Van de Kieft (Leiden, 1976), 658.

86. Belperron, *La croisade*, 20 and 25 (48 and 52).

87. Peter of Vaux-de-Cernay, *Hystoria*, III, c. 200, 1:201.

88. Ibid., II, c. 42, 1:38f. and n. 3, and 40.

89. No. 109, MPL 216, 141f.

90. William of Puylaurens, *Chronique*, c. 6, 42.

91. Belperron, *La croisade*, 25 n. 1 (52 n. 1).

92. Letter from Innocent III to the abbot of Cîteaux and papal legates, year VII, no. 75, MPL 215, 355f. (with warmest thanks to Othmar Hageneder for the reference).

93. Belperron, *La croisade*, 102 (128).

94. Letter from Innocent III, year III, no. 24, MPL 214, 905.

95. Bernard of Clairvaux, "Ep. 241," in *Sämtliche Werke*, 3:125. *Ketzer und Ketzerbekämpfung*, no. 5, 21.

96. Michel Parisse, "La conscience chrétienne des nobles aux XIe et XIIe siècles," in *La*

cristianità dei secoli XI e XII in occidente, Mendola 1980, Miscellanea del Centro di Studi medievali, 10 (1983), 271f.

97. Mundy, *Liberty and Political Power in Toulouse,* 81–82.

98. William of Puylaurens, *Chronique,* c. 6f., 40–44.

99. Peter of Vaux-de-Cernay, *Hystoria,* III, c. 221, 1:221f. William of Puylaurens, *Chronique,* c. 6, 42.

100. William of Puylaurens, in the prologue to his *Chronique,* 24.

101. Thouzellier, *Catharisme,* 21f. and 40.

102. Peter of Vaux-de-Cernay, *Hystoria,* II, c. 20, 1:22f.

103. Ibid., II, 22, 1:25; I, 12, 1:12, etc.

104. Ibid., III, 99, 1:100.

105. Innocent III, *Die Register Innocenz' III.: 2. Pontifikatsjahr,* ed. O. Hageneder, W. Maleczek, and A. Strnad, Publikationen des Historischen Instituts beim österr. Kulturinstitut in Rom, pt. 2, ser. 1, vol. 2 (Rome and Vienna, 1979), 4.

106. Duvernoy, "L'acception," 208 n. 52.

107. Mundy, *Liberty and Political Power in Toulouse,* and Wolff, *Histoire de Toulouse,* for the following material.

108. William of Puylaurens, *Chronique,* c. 24, 92.

109. Belperron, *La croisade,* 30 n. 1 (58 n. 1).

110. Mundy, *Liberty and Political Power in Toulouse,* 78f.

111. Belperron, *La croisade,* 15 (42f.).

112. Ibid., 27 (55).

113. Peter of Vaux-de-Cernay, *Hystoria,* II, c. 38, 1:35.

114. Ibid., III, c. 77, 1:77f. and 78 n. 1.

115. Belperron, in the introduction to *La croisade,* xiv (20); Borst, *Die Katharer,* 49f.; and Runciman, *The Medieval Manichee,* 187.

116. Jean Pierre Dubuc, *La pensée cathare au XXe siècle* (Narbonne, 1970), 8f., 134, and 251.

Notes to Chapter 6

1. Verbeke, "Philosophy and Heresy," 180 n. 44, and Alan of Lille, in the prologue to *De fide catholica,* MPL 210, 307.

2. Schmitz-Valckenberg, *Grundlehren,* 7.

3. Merkelbach, at the roundtable portion of the conference "Terror und Spiel," published in *Terror und Spiel,* 589.

4. Claude Lévi-Strauss, *La pensée sauvage* (Paris, 1962), 38. Herzog, at the roundtable portion of the conference "Terror und Spiel," published in *Terror und Spiel,* 610 n. 24.

5. Cassirer, *Mythical Thought,* 5.

6. Borst, *Die Katharer,* 165–67.

7. Cassirer, *Mythical Thought,* 47 and 250f.

8. Ibid., 45.

9. See Borst, *Die Katharer,* 144, for a different explanation.

10. John Marenbon, "Gilbert of Poitiers," in *A History of Twelfth-Century Western Philosophy,* ed. Peter Dronke (Cambridge, 1988), 338.

11. Alan of Lille, *Regulae theologicae,* no. 68, MPL 210, 654f.

12. Jean Jolivet and Maurice de Gandillac, at the roundtable portion of the conference on Peter Abelard, in *Pierre Abélard, Pierre le Vénérable,* Colloques internationaux du Centre National de la recherche scientifique, 546 (Paris, 1975), 609.

13. Abelard, *Dialogus,* 168f.; trans. Payer, *A Dialogue,* 166f.

14. Durand of Huesca, as quoted by Thouzellier, *Catharisme*, 340.

15. René Nelli, *Le phénomène cathare*, Nouvelle Recherche, 21 (Paris, 1964), 20f.

16. Cathar tract in Durand of Huesca, *Une somme anti-cathare*, c. 13, 217f.

17. Ibid., c. 9, 175, and Durand's response, 176 f; and c. 15, 244.

18. Loos, *Dualist Heresy*, 22.

19. Puech, *Le manichéisme*, 69.

20. H. Jonas, *Gnosis und spätantiker Geist*, Forschungen zur Religion und Literatur des Alten und Neuen Testaments, n.s., 33 (1934), 47, as quoted by Söderberg, *La religion*, 39 n. 1.

21. Söderberg, *La religion*, 39.

22. Ibid., 8.

23. Lambert, *Medieval Heresy* (1977), 7, and Borst, *Die Katharer*, 59–61.

24. Cassirer, *Mythical Thought*, 96.

25. Durand of Huesca, *Une somme anti-cathare*, c. 2, 105.

26. *Liber de duobus principiis*, in *Ecritures cathares*, 151.

27. Schmitz-Valckenberg, *Grundlehren*, 88. See 88–92 for a list of "dualistic" passages from the Bible according to Moneta of Cremona.

28. See, i.a., Fichtenau, *Living in the Tenth Century*, 250, for more information on this type of asceticism.

29. Fichtenau, "Zur Erforschung der Häresien," 90.

30. Marie-Dominique Chenu, "L'homme et la nature," *Archives d'histoire doctrinale et littéraire du Moyen Âge* 19 (1952): 58.

31. Hugh of Saint Victor, *Adnotatio in quosdam psalmos*, MPL 177, 596.

32. Southern, *Saint Anselm*, 94.

33. Gilbert Crispin, "Sermo in Ramis Palmarum," c. 13, in *The Works of Gilbert Crispin, Abbot of Westminster*, ed. A. Sapir Abulafia and G. R. Evans, Auctores Britannici medii aevi, 8 (London, 1986), 174.

34. Alan of Lille, "Sermo in die s. Michaelis," ed. Marie-Thérèse d'Alverny, in *Alain de Lille*, Études de philosophie médiévale, 52 (Paris, 1965), 251.

35. Milan Loos, "Satan als Erstgeborener Gottes," *Byzantino-Bulgarica* 3 (1969): 23.

36. Ibid., 25f.

37. See page 76 above.

38. See Edina Bozóky, "Les apocryphes bibliques," in *Le Moyen Âge et la Bible*, ed. Pierre Riché and Guy Lobrichon, Bible de tous les temps, 4 (Paris, 1984), 429–48, esp. 430 and 432, and Rottenwöhrer, *Der Katharismus*, vol. 4/3, 239–76, for discussions of these works.

39. Duvernoy, *La religion*, 93.

40. Durand of Huesca, *Une somme anti-cathare*, c. 16, 256–59.

41. See Morghen, "L'eresia nel medioevo," 276, for the quote (from Rainer Sacconi) and its dating.

42. There are numerous redactions of the Latin translation of the tract, for example, R. Reitzenstein, *Die Vorgeschichte der christlichen Taufe* (Leipzig and Berlin, 1929; 1967), 297–311; *Ecritures cathares*, 34–51; Söderberg, *La religion*, 96–100; and Edina Bozóky, *Le livre secret des Cathares* (Paris, 1980). The Bulgarian text survives in a manuscript compiled at the latest in the twelfth century.

43. Manselli, *L'eresia del male*, 202, based on the anonymous text *De heresi Catharorum*.

44. Schmitz-Valckenberg, *Grundlehren*, 76, and Duvernoy, *La religion*, 59 (based on Moneta of Cremona).

45. Schmitz-Valckenberg, *Grundlehren*, 77f.

46. Rottenwöhrer, *Der Katharismus*, vol. 2/2, 531f., 541, and 543.

47. *De confessione hereticorum et de fide eorum*, c. 3f., ed. Manselli, in "Per la storia dell'eresia nel secolo XII," 206.

48. Bonaccursus, *Manifestatio*, c. 25, 210.

49. Morghen, "L'eresia nel medioevo," 271–73.

50. Caesarius of Heisterbach, *Dialogus miraculorum*, V, 21, 1:301; trans. Scott and Bland, *The Dialogue of Miracles*, 1:344–45.

51. Borst, *Die Katharer*, 169. The text of this story (just one version of many) may be found in Le Roy Ladurie, *Montaillou*, trans. Bray, 292.

52. Duvernoy, *La religion*, 96.

53. Manegold of Lautenbach, *Liber contra Wolfelmum*, c. 1, 45; Morghen, "L'eresia nel medioevo," 234 (based on Moneta of Cremona); and Söderberg, *La religion*, 153.

54. D'Alverny, *Alain de Lille*, 141f.

55. Bonaccursus, *Manifestatio*, c. 2, 207.

56. Moneta of Cremona, as quoted in Morghen, "L'eresia nel medioevo," 272.

57. Loos, *Dualist Heresy*, 58.

58. Jean Leclercq, "Modern Psychology and the Interpretation of Medieval Texts," *Speculum* 48 (1973): 478.

59. Artur Michael Landgraf, *Einführung in die Geschichte der theologischen Literatur der Frühscholastik unter dem Gesichtspunkt der Schulenbildung* (Regensburg, 1948), 29.

60. According to Thomas Aquinas, "Symbolica theologia non est argumentativa" [Symbolic theology is not admissible as proof]. Quotation in de Lubac, *Exegèse médiévale*, vol. 4, II/2, 277.

61. Marie-Dominique Chenu, "La décadence de l'allégorisation, in *L'homme devant Dieu: Mélanges H. de Lubac*, Théologie, 57 (Paris, 1964), 2:134.

62. Quotation in de Lubac, *Exegèse médiévale*, vol. 4, II/2, 61 n. 11.

63. Otloh of St. Emmeram, *Liber de temptationibus suis*, MPL 146, 32f. Fichtenau, *Living in the Tenth Century*, 400.

64. Runciman, *The Medieval Manichee*, 51.

65. Cosmas, *Le traité*, I, 6, 62; the miracle of the loaves was interpreted similarly, I, 16, 83.

66. Ibid., I, 6, 63.

67. Alan of Lille, *Liber de distinctiones dictionum theologicalium*, MPL 210, 890. The reference is to Lam. 4:4.

68. As quoted in de Lubac, *Exegèse médiévale*, 2:407. Hildebert of Lavardin, *Locorum Scripturae moralis applicatio*, MPL 171, 1278.

69. Durand of Huesca, *Manifestatio*, as quoted by Duvernoy, *La religion*, 50.

70. Eckbert of Schönau, in the preface to the *Sermones*, MPL 195, 13f.

71. *Rituale latinum* in *Ecritures cathares*, 230 n. 4. See Rottenwöhrer, *Der Katharismus*, vol. 2/2, 784f., for further material.

72. Söderberg, *La religion*, 245, taken from the *Liber Supra Stella* by Salvo Burci.

73. Borst, *Die Katharer*, 267.

74. Cf., for example, the unsuccessful syllogism (in proof of dualism) in Garnier of Rochefort, *Isagogae theophaniarum symbolicae*, I, c. 1, cited in [Garnier of Rochefort], *Contra Amaurianos*, ed. C. Baeumker, Beiträge zur Geschichte der Philosophie des Mittelalters, 24, pt. 5/6 (Münster, 1926), 28 n. 2; also the attempt at interpreting John 1:3 in the *Liber de duobus principiis*, in *Ecritures cathares*, 120, 134f., 143, etc. Schmitz-Valckenberg, *Grundlehren*, 105f., and Duvernoy, *La religion*, 53. Cf. note 2 to "A Look Ahead," below.

75. In a letter from Ivo of Narbonne to Archbishop Gerald of Bordeaux preserved only by Matthew Paris, *Chronica maior*, MGH SS 28, 230–33. For an assessment of this letter, see Fichtenau, *Beiträge*, 1:204–6, and Segl, *Ketzer*, 76–111, particularly 88 concerning this account.

Notes to Chapter 7

1. Bollack, at the roundtable portion of the conference "Terror und Spiel," published in *Terror und Spiel*, 67.

2. Tullio Gregory, "The Platonic Inheritance," in *A History of Twelfth-Century Western Philosophy*, ed. Dronke, 54.

3. Brian Stock, *Myth and Science in the Twelfth Century* (Princeton, 1972), 19.

4. Plato, *Timaeus a Calcidio translatus*, ed. P. J. Jensen and J. H. Waszink, Corpus Platonicum medii aevi, II, 1, 4 (London, 1962), 41 DE.

5. Manegold of Lautenbach, *Liber contra Wolfelmum*, c. 3, 49f.

6. Peter Dronke, *Fabula*, Mittellateinische Studien und Texte, ed. K. Langosch, 9 (Leiden and Cologne, 1974), 66.

7. Alan of Lille, "Sermo de sphaera intellegibili," ed. d'Alverny, in *Alain de Lille*, 303.

8. Stephen Gersh, "Platonism—Neoplatonism—Aristotelianism," in *Renaissance and Renewal*, ed. Benson and Constable, 512.

9. Gregory, "The Platonic Inheritance," 55.

10. Gersh, "Platonism" 530f.

11. Borst, *Die Katharer*, 273.

12. Hans Sedlmayr, *Die Entstehung der Kathedrale* (Zurich, 1950), 314 and elsewhere.

13. Edouard Jeauneau, "Le renouveau érigenien du XIIe siècle," in *Eriugena Redivivus*, Abhandlungen der Heidelberger Akademie der Wissenschaften, philosophische-historische Klasse, 1987, 1. Abhandlung, 44.

14. Garin, *Studi sul platonismo medievale*, 2.

15. Cf., for example, Hartmann, "Manegold von Lautenbach," 78–81, and Gregory, "The Platonic Inheritance," 60.

16. An unpublished tract identified by Marie-Thérèse d'Alverny, "Achard of Saint-Victor, *De Trinitate, de unitate et pluralitate creaturarum*," *Recherches de théologie ancienne et médiévale* 21 (1954): 299–306; cf. d'Alverny, *Alain de Lille*, 168 n. 26.

17. For the literature on Chartres, see Winthrop Wetherbee, "Philosophy, Cosmology, and the Twelfth-Century Renaissance," in *A History of Twelfth-Century Western Philosophy*, ed. Dronke, 21 n. 1.

18. Garin, *Studi sul platonismo medievale*, 50.

19. Peter Dronke, "Thierry of Chartres," in *A History of Twelfth-Century Western Philosophy*, ed. Dronke, 358–85.

20. Ibid., 365 and n. 28. See page 239 and note 44 to Chapter 10.

21. Gregory, *Anima Mundi*, 80.

22. Theodore Silverstein, "The Fabulous Cosmogony of Bernardus Silvestris," *Modern Philology* 46 (1948): 113 and n. 144.

23. Edouard Jeauneau, "Note sur l'École de Chartres," *Studi medievali*, ser. IIIa, 5/2 (1964): 826.

24. Peter Dronke, "New Approaches to the School of Chartres," *Anuario de Estudios Medievales* 6 (1969): 119.

25. Nikolaus M. Häring, "Die Erschaffung der Welt und ihr Schöpfer nach Thierry von Chartres und Clarenbaldus von Arras," in *Platonismus in der Philosophie des Mittelalters* (Darmstadt, 1969), 164f.

26. Ibid., 257f. and n. 44.

27. Dronke, "New Approaches to the School of Chartres," 121.

28. Augustine, *Confessiones*, VII, 29, CSEL, 33 (Vienna, 1896), 144.

29. Glosses in Ms. Lat. 8624, Bibliothèque Nationale, Paris, as noted by Tullio Gregory,

Platonismo medievale, Istituto Storico Italiano per il Medio Evo, Studi storici 26/27 (Rome, 1958), 125.

30. Augustine, *De civitate Dei*, VIII, 11, as quoted by Abelard, *Theologia christiana*, I, 118, 122. Gregory, *Anima Mundi*, 45 and n. 1.

31. Wetherbee, "Philosophy," 38, and Jean Jolivet, "Doctrines et figures de philosophes chez Abélard," in *Petrus Abaelardus*, ed. R. Thomas and Jean Jolivet, Trierer theologische Studien, 38 (Trier, 1980), 105.

32. Abelard, *Theologia christiana*, I, 68, 100.

33. Gregory, *Anima Mundi*, 68f.

34. Jolivet, "Doctrines," 107f.

35. Abelard, *Theologia christiana*, I, 54–60, 94f., and II, 14–58, 139–56.

36. Plato, *Timaeus*, 30 B, and George D. Economou, *The Goddess Natura in Medieval Literature* (Cambridge, Mass., 1972), 72f.

37. Gregory, *Anima Mundi*, 125 and 127.

38. Abelard, *Theologia christiana*, I, 111, 118; cf. I, 68, 100.

39. As found in Abelard's *Dialectic*, thus before the composition of the *Theologia christiana*. Cf. Alexander Victor Murray, *Abelard and St. Bernard* (Manchester and New York, 1967), 80 n. 2; Jean Jolivet, *Abélard ou la philosophie dans le langage*, Philosophes de tous les temps (Paris, 1969), 162f.; and Gregory, *Anima Mundi*, 147.

40. See page 297 above. *Capitula heresum Petri Abelardi*, ed. Constant J. Mews, in "The Lists of Heresies Imputed to Peter Abelard," *Revue bénédictine* 95 (1985): 108, no. 3. Otto of Freising, *Gesta Friderici*, I, 51, 74; trans. Mierow, *The Deeds of Frederick Barbarossa*, 88.

41. William of Conches, *Comm. in Boethium*, manuscript cited by Silverstein, "The Fabulous Cosmogony of Bernardus Silvestris," 114 n. 160.

42. Silverstein, "The Fabulous Cosmogony of Bernardus Silvestris," 114f.

43. Ibid., 115f.

44. Chenu, "L'homme et la nature," 55f. and n. 4.

45. Alan of Lille, "Sermo de sphaera intelligibili," ed. d'Alverny, in *Alain de Lille*, 299.

46. Gregory, *Anima Mundi*, 153.

47. Martin M. Tweedale, *Abailard on Universals* (Amsterdam, 1976), 307.

48. Stephen C. Ferruolo, *The Origins of the University* (Stanford, 1985), 149.

49. Tweedale, *Abailard on Universals*, 9.

50. Letter from Ratramnus of Corbie to Oddo of Beauvais, MGH Epistolae VI, no. 11, 153f., and Garin, *Studi sul platonismo medievale*, 26.

51. Martin M. Tweedale, "Logic (I): From the Late Eleventh Century to the Time of Abelard," in *A History of Twelfth-Century Western Philosophy*, ed. Dronke, 210.

52. Dronke, "Thierry of Chartres," 372f.

53. Peter Abelard, *Historia calamitatum*, ed. J. Monfrin, Bibliothèque de textes philosophiques (Paris, 1959, 1962, and 1978), 65, lines 85ff.; trans. Betty Radice, *The Story of His Misfortunes*, in *The Letters of Abelard and Heloise* (New York, 1974; 1978), 60.

54. Tweedale, *Abailard on Universals*, 8.

55. David Edward Luscombe, "Peter Abelard," in *A History of Twelfth-Century Western Philosophy*, ed. Dronke, 291. Tweedale, "Logic (I)," 217.

56. Otto of Freising, *Gesta Friderici*, I, 58, 82f.; trans. Mierow, *The Deeds of Frederick Barbarossa*, 96f. Cf. page 302 above.

57. Chenu, "L'homme et la nature," 39.

58. Hans Liebeschütz, *Das allegorische Weltbild der hl. Hildegard von Bingen*, Studien der Bibliothek Warburg, 16 (Leipzig, 1930; Darmstadt, 1964), 105.

59. Ibid., 91.

60. Ibid., 86.

61. Heinrich Schipperges, *Das Menschenbild Hildegards von Bingen*, Erfurter theologische Schriften, 5 (Leipzig, 1962), 15.

62. Ibid., 17.

63. Gregory, "The Platonic Inheritance," 62.

64. Bernard Silvestris, *Cosmographia*, ed. Peter Dronke, Textus minores, 53 (Leiden, 1978), 97 and 121; trans. Winthrop Wetherbee, *The Cosmographia of Bernardus Silvestris*, (New York, 1973; 1990), 67 and 91.

65. See page 174 and note 4 above.

66. As quoted by Barbara Helbling-Gloor, *Natur und Aberglaube im "Policraticus" des Johannes von Salisbury* (Ph.D. diss., Zurich, Einsiedeln, 1956), 26 n. 65.

67. Ibid., 14.

68. Marie-Thérèse d'Alverny, "Abélard et l'astrologie," in *Pierre Abélard, Pierre le Vénérable*, 619 n. 28.

69. See page 180 and note 41 above.

70. Tullio Gregory, "L'idea di natura prima dell'ingresso della fisica di Aristotele," in *La filosofia della natura*, 53.

71. Helbling-Gloor, *Natur und Aberglaube*, 96f.

72. Ibid., 27.

73. Walter of Saint-Victor, *Contra IV labyrinthos Franciae*, IV, 6, ed. P. Glorieux, *Archives d'histoire doctrinale et littéraire du Moyen Âge* 19 (1952): 273.

74. Wetherbee, "Philosophy," 44.

75. Bernard Silvestris, *Cosmographia*, III, 55 (*Megacosmus*), 105, and, on the gloss, 2 and n. 3 (for dating); trans. Wetherbee, *The Cosmographia of Bernardus Silvestris*, 20 and n. 85, and 76 and n. 63.

76. Etienne Gilson, "La 'cosmogonie' de Bernardus Silvestris," *Archives d'histoire doctrinale et littéraire du Moyen Âge* 3 (1928): 8, 12, and 20.

77. Bernard Silvestris, *Cosmographia*, V, 1 (*Microcosmus*), 128; trans. Wetherbee, *The Cosmographia of Bernardus Silvestris*, 98.

78. Jeauneau, "Note sur l'École de Chartres," 848f.

79. Bernard Silvestris, *Cosmographia*, XIII, 1 (*Microcosmus*), 146.

80. Plato, *Timaeus*, 51 B.

81. Stock, *Myth and Science in the Twelfth Century*, 228.

82. Alan of Lille, *De fide catholica*, and d'Alverny, *Alain de Lille*, 158.

83. D'Alverny, *Alain de Lille*, 43 and n. 53. The text of *De planctu Naturae* has been edited by Nikolaus M. Haring, "Alan of Lille *De planctu Naturae*," *Studi medievali*, IIIa, ser. 19 (1978), 806–79, and translated by James J. Sheridan, *The Plaint of Nature* (Toronto, 1980).

84. Hans Robert Jauss, "Allegorese, Remythisierung und neuer Mythos," in *Terror und Spiel*, 205.

85. The text of the *Anticlaudianus* has been edited by R. Bossuat, *Anticlaudianus*, Textes philosophiques du Moyen Âge, I (Paris, 1955), and translated by James J. Sheridan, *Anticlaudianus or The Good and Perfect Man* (Toronto, 1973).

86. Linda E. Marshall, "The Identity of the 'New Man' in the *Anticlaudianus* of Alan of Lille," *Viator* 10 (1979): 77–94.

87. Alan of Lille, *Anticlaudianus*, I, 236, 64; trans. Sheridan, 55.

88. Tullio Gregory, "Considérations sur *ratio et natura* chez Abélard," in *Pierre Abélard, Pierre le Vénérable*, 569–84, esp. 575f.

89. Chenu, "L'homme et la nature," 48.

90. Philippe Delhaye, "La nature dans l'œuvre de Hugues de St.-Victor," in *La filosofia della natura*, 272.

91. See page 38 above.

92. D'Alverny, *Alain de Lille*, 35 and 169.

93. According to one of the three definitions Hugh of Saint-Victor gave for Natura, as noted by Silverstein, "The Fabulous Cosmogony of Bernardus Silvestris," 104 and 105 (no. 1).

94. Economou, *The Goddess Natura*, 55.

95. Ibid., 19f.

96. As quoted by Silverstein, "The Fabulous Cosmogony of Bernardus Silvestris," 109. This passage was cited by Hugh of Saint-Victor and William of Conches.

97. Santo Arcoleo, "La filosofia della natura nella problematica di Alano di Lilla," in *La filosofia della natura*, 256, based on Alan of Lille, *Liber de distinctionibus dictionum theologicalium*, MPL 210, 871.

98. Alan of Lille, *De planctu Naturae*, 829; trans. Sheridan, *The Plaint of Nature*, 124.

99. Ibid., c. 7, 831; trans. Sheridan, 128f.; cf. 805: Her *subvicaria* [subvicaress] is Venus.

100. Dronke, in his introduction to Bernard Silvestris, *Cosmographia*, 7.

101. Stock, *Myth and Science in the Twelfth Century*, 65 and n. 7.

102. As quoted by Silverstein, "The Fabulous Cosmogony of Bernardus Silvestris," 106.

103. William of Saint-Thierry, *De erroribus Guilelmi de Conchis ad sanctum Bernardum*, c. 8, ed. Jean Leclercq, in "Les lettres de Guillaume de Saint-Thierry à Saint Bernard," *Revue bénédictine* 79 (1969): 389f. On William and his contributions to medieval mysticism, see Kurt Ruh, *Geschichte der abendländischen Mystik* (Munich, 1990), 1:276–319.

104. Gregory "L'idea di natura," 46.

105. William of Conches, *De philosophia mundi*, I, 22, MPL 172, 56, and Marie-Dominique Chenu, "Nature ou histoire?" *Archives d'histoire doctrinale et littéraire du Moyen Âge* 20 (1953): 29.

106. Economou, *The Goddess Natura*, 104–50, for a detailed discussion.

107. Häring, "Die Erschaffung," 189–91.

108. Berthe Widmer, "Thierry von Chartres, ein Gelehtenschicksal des 12. Jahrhunderts," *Historische Zeitschrift* 200 (1965): 560.

109. Borst, *Die Katharer*, 148 n. 19; cf. 153f.

110. Le Roy Ladurie, *Montaillou*, trans. Bray, 322.

111. Borst, *Die Katharer*, 156.

112. Dronke, "Thierry of Chartres," 375. Bernard Silvestris, *Cosmographia*, III, 12 (*Megacosmus*), 104: "Extramundanus creditur esse Deus" [God is believed to be supramundane]. Anselm of Canterbury, *Monologion*, c. 13, c. 14, c. 17, and so on, in *Opera omnia*, ed. F. S. Schmitt (Seckau, 1938; Edinburgh, 1946; and Stuttgart, 1968), 1:27, 29, 31, and elsewhere; trans. S. N. Deane, *Monologium*, in *Basic Writings* (Chicago, 1962; 1996), 106f.

113. Maurice de Gandillac, at the roundtable portion of the conference on Peter Abelard, in *Pierre Abélard, Pierre le Vénérable*, 630. For the proof, see also Peter Abelard, *Ethics*, ed. and trans. David Edward Luscombe (Oxford, 1971), 36 and 37.

114. Le Goff, at the roundtable portion of the conference on heresies and societies in preindustrial Europe, 1000–1800, in *Hérésies et sociétés*, 102.

115. William of Conches, *De philosophia mundi*, II, 3, 58. Tina Stiefel, *The Intellectual Revolution in Twelfth-Century Europe* (London and Sydney, 1985), 75 n. 35.

116. Alan of Lille, "Expositio prosae de angelis," ed. d'Alverny, in *Alain de Lille*, 209.

117. Marian Kurdzialek, "David von Dinant als Ausleger der Aristotelischen Naturphilosophie," in *Auseinandersetzungen an der Pariser Universität im 13. Jahrhundert*, ed. A. Zimmermann, Miscellanea mediaevalia, 10 (Berlin and New York, 1976), 191; and see page 316 above.

118. Manegold of Lautenbach, *Liber contra Wolfelmum*, c. 8, 58f. Gregory, *Platonismo medievale*, 23.

119. Alan of Lille, "Sermo de clericis ad theologiam non accedentibus," ed. d'Alverny, in *Alain de Lille*, 275.

120. Hugh of Saint-Victor, *Didascalicon*, I, 1, MPL 176, 742. (I was not able to procure the 1939 edition by C. H. Buttimer.)

121. William of Conches, *De philosophia mundi*, I, 22, MPL 172, 56; Chenu, "L'homme et la nature," 52 and n. 2; and Alexander Murray, *Reason and Society in the Middle Ages* (Oxford, 1978; 1985), 238.

122. Gilbert Crispin, *De anima*, c. 23f., in *The Works of Gilbert Crispin*, 160f.

123. Dronke, "New Approaches to the School of Chartres," 133, based on Thierry of Chartres. Charles Burnett, "Scientific Speculations," in *A History of Twelfth-Century Western Philosophy*, ed. Dronke, 166f.

124. Luscombe, "Nature in the Thought of Peter Abelard," 318f.

125. Thierry of Chartres, *Commentum super Boethium De Trinitate*, II, 2f., ed. Nikolaus M. Haring, in "Two Commentaries on Boethius (*De Trinitate et De Hebdomadibus*), by Thierry of Chartres," *Archives d'histoire doctrinale et littéraire du Moyen Âge* 27 (1960): 91.

126. Burnett, "Scientific Speculations," 152–54.

Notes to Chapter 8

1. Jean Leclercq, *Spiritualitas*, Studi medievali, IIIa, ser. 3 (1962), 280.

2. Murray, *Abelard*, 20f.

3. Hence, Delaruelle, *La piété populaire*, 142ff., devotes a chapter to the discussion of "spiritualité populaire" in the eleventh century and contends (on 188) that a "véritable revolution" occurred in the second half of the twelfth century due to laic influence on spirituality.

4. Jean Leclercq, *The Love of Learning and the Desire for God*, trans. Catharine Misrahi (New York, 1961; 3d ed., 1991), 193.

5. Ibid., 73f.

6. Fichtenau, *Living in the Tenth Century*, 253.

7. Peter Classen, "Aus der Werkstatt Gerhochs von Reichersberg," 391.

8. See page 38 above.

9. Friedrich Ohly, *Hohelied-Studien*, Schriften der wissenschaftlichen Gesellschaft an der J. W. Goethe-Universität Frankfurt, Geisteswissenschaftliche Reihe, 1 (Wiesbaden, 1958), 122f.

10. Alan of Lille, *Anticlaudianus*, V, 169f., 128; trans. Sheridan, 143.

11. Gregory, *Anima Mundi*, 138f.

12. Ibid., 176.

13. Martin Grabmann, *Geschichte der scholastischen Methode* (Freiburg, 1911; Graz, 1953), 2:104. Ohly, *Hohelied-Studien*, 138f., based on Etienne Gilson, *La théologie mystique de Saint Bernard* (Paris, 1934). Ruh, *Geschichte der abendländischen Mystik*, 1:230 and 259.

14. Abelard, in the prologue to *Sic et non*, MPL 178, 1345.

15. Radulphus of Cogeshall, *Chronicon Anglicanum*, last quoted by Grundmann, "Dante und Joachim von Fiore," in *Ausgewählte Aufsätze*, 2:201; cf. 324.

16. Joachim of Fiore, *Vita s. Benedicti*, as quoted by Thouzellier, *Catharisme*, 123 n. 77.

17. As quoted by Liebeschütz, *Das allegorische Weltbild der hl. Hildegard von Bingen*, 43n and 168 n. 2.

18. Christel Meier, "Eriugena im Nonnenkloster?" *Frühmittelalterliche Studien* 19 (1985): 495.

19. Gammersbach, *Gilbert von Poitiers*, 41f. Letter from Hildegard of Bingen to "V," no. 127, MPL 197, 352f.

20. Leclercq, *The Love of Learning*, 196–97.

21. Manegold of Lautenbach, *Liber contra Wolfelmum*, c. 5, 53, based on Rom. 12:3.

22. Augustine, *Confessiones*, 21, 38. Kusch, "Studien," 133. Cf. page 230 and note 5 to Chapter 10.

23. Dronke, in the introduction to his edition of Bernard Silvestris, *Cosmographia*, 11.

24. Wetherbee, "Philosophy," 26.

25. As quoted by Grabmann, *Geschichte der scholastischen Methode*, 2:106. Bernard of Clairvaux, "In Canticum sermo 36," MPL 183, 968.

26. As quoted by Abel, "Aspects sociologiques," 44.

27. Seneca, *Ep. LXXXVIII*, 36. Richard Newhauser, "Towards a History of Human Curiosity," *Deutsche Vierteljahresschrift für Literaturwissenschaft und Geistesgeschichte* 56 (1982): 572.

28. Meersseman, "Teologia monastica e riforma ecclesiastica," 266.

29. Bernard of Clairvaux, "Sermo in festo ss. Petri et Pauli," I, 3, MPL 183, 407.

30. Bernard of Clairvaux, "Sermo 36," as quoted by Joachim Ehlers, "Monastische Theologie, historischer Sinn und Dialektik," in *Antiqui und Moderni*, ed. A. Zimmermann, Miscellanea mediaevalia, 9 (Berlin and New York, 1974), 62 and n. 22.

31. As in the view of Gerhoh of Reichersberg; see Peter Johanek, "Klosterstudien im 12. Jahrhundert," in *Schulen und Studium im sozialen Wandel des hohen und späten Mittelalters*, ed. Johannes Fried, Vorträge und Forschungen, 30 (Sigmaringen, 1986), 43.

32. Benedict of Nursia, *Regula*, c. 73, discussed by Donatella Nebbiai-Dalla Guarda, "Les listes médiévales de lecture monastiques," *Revue bénédictine* 96 (1986): 272.

33. Nebbiai-Dalla Guarda, "Les listes," 272 (based on the *Consuetudines*).

34. Text in Pl. Lefèvre, "À propos de la *lectio divina* . . . ," *Revue d'histoire ecclésiastique* 67 (1972): 802 and 805.

35. Nebbiai-Dalla Guarda, "Les listes," 317.

36. Leclercq, *The Love of Learning*, 232 n. 82.

37. Peter Damiani, *De profectione monachorum*, MPL 145, 307, as quoted by Hartmann, "Manegold von Lautenbach," 114 n. 301.

38. Anselm of Canterbury, *Monologion*, in *Opera omnia*, 1:7; trans. Deane, *Monologium*, 81–82.

39. Edited by Joseph Reiners, *Der Nominalismus in der Frühscholastik*, Beiträge zur Geschichte der Philosophie des Mittelalters, VIII/5 (Münster, 1910), 80.

40. As quoted by Thouzellier, *Catharisme*, 123 n. 82.

41. Cf. the detailed discussion in [Garnier of Rochefort], *Contra Amaurianos*, c. 12, 48ff.

42. Bernard of Clairvaux, "Ep. 332," in *Sämtliche Werke*, 3:568. Cf. page 282 and note 2 to Chapter 12, and Murray, *Abelard*, 7.

43. Innocent III, *Die Register*, no. II/132, 2:272f.

44. Leclercq, *The Love of Learning*, 220.

45. As quoted by de Lubac, *Exegèse médiévale*, vol. 4, II/2, 61 n. 11.

46. Ibid., 85 and 87f.

47. As quoted by F.J.E. Raby, "*Nuda Natura* and Twelfth-Century Cosmology," *Speculum* 43 (1968): 74.

48. David Edward Luscombe, "From Paris to the Paraclete: The Correspondence of Abelard and Heloise," *Proceedings of the British Academy* 74 (1988): 269 n. 112.

49. Abelard, *Dialogus*, as quoted by de Lubac, *Exegèse médiévale*, vol. 4, II/2, 153; relevant passages trans. Payer, *A Dialogue*, 143–57.

50. Chenu, *Nature, Man, and Society*, 70–71 and nn. 40 and 42.

51. Leclercq, *The Love of Learning*, 55.

52. De Lubac, *Exegèse médiévale*, vol. 4, II/2, 7–15.

53. Ibid., 36–40. Cf. Heinz Meyer and Rudolf Suntrup, *Lexikon der mittelalterlichen Zahlenbedeutungen*, Münstersche Mittelalterschriften, 56 (Munich, 1984).

54. Cassirer, *Mythical Thought*, 142f.

55. Thomas Aquinas, "In Gal. c. V, lect. 7," as quoted by de Lubac, *Exegèse médiévale*, 2:644.

56. Chenu, "La décadence de l'allégorisation," 130.

57. As quoted by Thouzellier, *Catharisme*, 117 n. 44.

58. Peter Classen, *Gerhoch von Reichersberg* (Weisbaden, 1960), 141.

59. Marie-Dominique Chenu, "Les deux âges de l'allégorisme scripturaire au Moyen Âge," *Recherches de théologie ancienne et médiévale* 18 (1951): 25 n. 22. Hugh of Saint-Victor, *De scripturis et scriptoribus sacris . . .* , c. 5, MPL 175, 13. See Patrice Sicard, *Hugues de Saint-Victor et son école* (Turnhout, 1991), 22f., concerning a remark by Hugh that the literal meaning serves as the basis for allegory.

60. Otloh of St. Emmeram, *Liber de temptationibus suis*, MPL 146, 32f. Fichtenau, *Living in the Tenth Century*, 400.

61. Cf. 1 Cor. 6:15 and 12:27. See page 306 above.

62. See page 200 above.

63. Richard of Saint-Victor, *Beniamin maior*, I, 6, MPL 196, 70. Ruh, *Geschichte der abendländlischen Mystik*, 1:401.

64. Liebeschütz, *Das allegorische Weltbild der hl. Hildegard von Bingen*, 6 n. 1.

65. Christel Meier, "Scientia Divinorum Operum," in *Eriugena Redivivus*, 94f. For a rebuttal of the contention that an affinity existed between Hildegard and the works of John Scotus (Eriugena), see Ruh, *Geschichte der abendländlischen Mystik*, 1:14 n. 3.

66. Liebeschütz, *Das allegorische Weltbild der hl. Hildegard von Bingen*, 21.

Notes to Chapter 9

1. John of Salisbury, *Metalogicon*, III, 4, ed. C.C.J. Webb (Oxford, 1929), 136; trans. Daniel D. McGarry, *The Metalogicon of John of Salisbury* (Berkeley and Los Angeles, 1955; 1962), 167.

2. Edouard Jeauneau, "Nani Gigantum Humeris Insidentes," *Vivarium* 5 (1967): 84 (Florentine manuscript containing glosses on Priscian by William of Conches) and 86 (manuscript in Copenhagen): "Antiqui multo meliores fuerunt modernis." [The ancients were much more accomplished than men nowadays.]

3. Gerhart B. Ladner, "Terms and Ideas of Renewal," in *Renaissance and Renewal*, ed. Benson and Constable, 8 n. 41.

4. Jeauneau, "Nani Gigantum Humeris Insidentes," 80–82.

5. Ladner, "Terms and Ideas of Renewal," 8 n. 41.

6. Abelard, *Historia calamitatum*, 69, lines 208f.; trans. Radice, *The Story of His Misfortunes*, 63.

7. William of Saint-Thierry, *De erroribus Guilelmi de Conchis*, c. 2, 384.

8. William of Saint-Thierry, *Liber de corpore et sanguine Domini*, MPL 180, 345.

9. Otto of Freising, *Gesta Friderici*, I, 58, 82; trans. Mierow, *The Deeds of Frederick Barbarossa*, 96. Letter from Geoffrey of Auxerre to Albinus (the papal legate), c. 4, MPL 185, 589f. For more on the recipient, see Nikolaus M. Haring, "The Porretans and the Greek Fathers," *Medieval Studies* 24 (1962): 182 n. 13. In his letter Geoffrey went on to report: "The next day we brought so many codices with us that the advocates for the bishop [Gilbert] were stunned" (c. 6, MPL 185, 590).

10. In the view of Robert of Melun; Grabmann, *Geschichte der scholastischen Methode*, 2:346f.

11. Leclercq, *The Love of Learning*, 91f.

12. Abelard, in the prologue to *Sic et non*, MPL 178, 1344. Marie-Dominique Chenu, *La théologie au douzième siècle*, Études de philosophie médiévale, 45 (1957; 3d ed., Paris, 1976), 362–65.

13. Grabmann, *Geschichte der scholastischen Methode*, 2:87.

14. Hartmann, "Manegold von Lautenbach," 109.

15. Peter Classen, "Zur Geschichte der Frühscholastik in Österreich und Bayern," in *Ausgewählte Aufsätze*, 302.

16. Thomas Aquinas, *Summa theol.*, Ia p.1 a. 2, ad 2; Quodl. IV, a. 18. As quoted by Chenu, *Man, Nature, and Society*, 77 and 292 n. 50.

17. John W. Baldwin, "Masters at Paris, 1179–1215," in *Renaissance and Renewal*, ed. Benson and Constable, 161.

18. Gammersbach, *Gilbert von Poitiers*, 5.

19. Anselm of Canterbury, *Monologion*, in *Opera omnia*, 1:7; trans. Deane, *Monologium*, 82–83.

20. Ohly, *Hohelied-Studien*, 124.

21. Peter Classen, "Die hohen Schulen und die Gesellschaft im 12. Jahrhundert," in *Studium und Gesellschaft im Mittelalter*, Schriften der MGH, 29 (Stuttgart, 1983), 24.

22. Hugh of Honau, *Liber de diversitate*, I, 4, 121.

23. Ibid., I, 9, 123.

24. For example, Alan of Lille, *De fide catholica*, I, 7, MPL 210, 314. See Chenu, *La théologie au douzième siècle*, 316, on the use of "pagan" definitions concerning matters of faith.

25. J. Reginald O'Donnell, "The Sources and Meaning of Bernard Silvester's Commentary on the *Aeneid*," *Medieval Studies* 24 (1962): 247.

26. See page 15 above concerning Virgil, and Philippe Delhaye, "*Grammatica* et *Ethica* au douzième siècle," in *Enseignement et morale au XIIe siècle*, Vestigia, 1 (Fribourg and Paris, 1988), 98, regarding Ovid.

27. Abelard, *Theologia christiana*, III, 8 b, 198.

28. Peter the Venerable, *Contra Petrobrusianos*, c. 278, 164.

29. Abelard, *Letters IX–XIV*, no. 13, ed. E. R. Smits (Groningen, 1983), 271.

30. Abelard, *Dialogus*, 91; trans. Payer, *A Dialogue*, 79.

31. Ibid., 94; trans. Payer, 82.

32. Alan of Lille, *De fide catholica*, I, 30, MPL 210, 333.

33. Grabmann, *Geschichte der scholastischen Methode*, 2:467.

34. Dronke, introduction to *A History of Twelfth-Century Western Philosophy*, ed. Dronke, 7f.

35. Maria Teresa Fumagalli Beonio Brocchieri, "*Ratio, sensus* e *auctoritas* nelle opere di Adelardo di Bath," in *Pierre Abélard, Pierre le Vénérable*, 631.

36. [Garnier of Rochefort], *Contra Amaurianos*, c. 10, 32. Gregory the Great, *Homil. 26 in Evangelia*, MPL 76, 1197.

37. William of Champeaux, in Grabmann, *Geschichte der scholastischen Methode*, 2:156.

38. Abelard, *Theologia christiana*, III, 1, 194.

39. Abelard, *Dialogus*, 97; trans. Payer, *A Dialogue*, 86.

40. See Burnett, "Scientific Speculations," 154, for a more detailed discussion.

41. Murray, *Reason and Society*, 8.

42. See note 36 above.

43. Abelard, *Dialogus*, 93; trans. Payer, *A Dialogue*, 81.

44. Verbeke, "Philosophy and Heresy," 76f. and 177 n. 28.

45. Abelard, *Historia calamitatum*, 83, lines 696–701; trans. Radice, *The Story of His Misfortunes*, 78. The reference is to Matt. 15:14.

46. See note 8 above.

47. Anselm of Canterbury, in the prologue to *Proslogion,* in *Opera omnia,* 1:94; trans. Deane, *Proslogium,* 48.

48. Jolivet, *Abélard,* 92. On Anselm, see Gammersbach, *Gilbert von Poitiers,* 2 and n. 10. Meersseman, "Teologia monastica e riforma ecclesiastica," 261.

49. "Deus est eo, quod est sciens, Deus." As quoted by Artur Michael Landgraf, *Dogmengeschichte der Frühscholastik,* pt. 2 (Regensburg, 1954), 2:69f.

50. "[D]isertis rationibus de fide rationabili reddere rationem" [by eloquent reasons to adduce the reason underlying reasonable faith], a phrase that illustrates the broad meaning of *ratio;* excerpted from an unpublished Ms. Vat. Lat. 903, Alan of Lille, *Summa quadripartita,* as quoted by Thouzellier, *Catharisme,* 82 n. 9.

51. Gillian Rosemary Evans, *Old Arts and New Theology* (Oxford, 1980), 34 and 36.

52. Margaret Gibson, *Lanfranc of Bec* (Oxford, 1978), 88 n. 3.

53. Gilbert Crispin, *Disputatio Christiani cum Gentili,* c. 6, in *The Works of Gilbert Crispin,* 63.

54. Burnett, "Scientific Speculations," 169.

55. William of Conches, *De philosophia mundi,* II, c. 3, as quoted by Chenu, *Man, Nature, and Society,* 12 n. 22.

56. Stiefel, *The Intellectual Revolution,* 30 n. 37.

57. David Edward Luscombe, *The School of Peter Abelard,* Cambridge Studies in Medieval Life and Thought, 14 (Cambridge, 1969), 155.

58. Alan of Lille, *Anticlaudianus,* I, 70f., lines 455ff.; trans. Sheridan, 63f.

59. Abelard, *Letters IX–XIV,* no. 13, 276. Abelard, *Dialogus,* 90; trans. Payer, *A Dialogue,* 78.

60. M. de Gandillac, at the roundtable portion of the conference on Peter Abelard, in *Pierre Abélard, Pierre le Vénérable,* 630.

61. Jean Châtillon, "La Bible dans les écoles du XIIe siècle," in *Le Moyen Âge et la Bible,* ed. Riché and Lobrichon, 186.

62. Evans, *Old Arts and New Theology,* 112f. Alan of Lille, *Regulae theologicae,* MPL 210, 621–84.

63. Evans, *Old Arts and New Theology,* 116. On the following, see Alan of Lille, *Regulae theologicae,* Reg. 53, MPL 210, 646, and Reg. 31, 636.

64. Gilbert Crispin, *Disputatio Iudei et Christiani,* c. 20 and c. 33f., in *The Works of Gilbert Crispin,* 12 and 15.

65. George Makdisi, "The Scholastic Method in Medieval Education," *Speculum* 49 (1974): 648f.

66. Ibid., 649.

67. Grabmann, *Geschichte der scholastischen Methode,* 2:212.

68. Cf., i.a., Hartmann, "Manegold von Lautenbach," 139; and Grabmann, *Geschichte der scholastischen Methode,* 2:237, on the following material as well.

69. Oskar Greulich, "Die kirchenpolitische Stellung Bernolds von Konstanz," *Historisches Jahrbuch* 55 (1935): 12.

70. Gerbert of Aurillac, *De corpore et sanguine Domini,* MPL 139, 180–82.

71. Peter Abelard, *Sic et non,* MPL 178, 1339–610; and ibid., ed. B. Boyer and R. McKeon (Chicago, 1976).

72. As quoted by Verbeke, "Philosophy and Heresy," 178 n. 37.

73. Stock, *The Implications of Literacy,* 364.

Notes to Chapter 10

1. D'Alverny, *Alain de Lille,* 24. The second version probably represented the "official" text of the epitaph; Bossuat, in his introduction to *Anticlaudianus,* 10.

2. Hugh of Honau, *Liber de ignorantia*, VII, 20–VIII, 23, ed. Nikolaus M. Haring, in "Hugh of Honau and the *Liber de ignorantia*," *Medieval Studies* 25 (1963): 218, in reference to Gen. 3:5: "Eritis sicut dii, scientes bonum et malum" [You will be like God, knowing good and evil].

3. Hugh of Honau, *Liber de ignorantia*, IX, 24ff., 219.

4. Bernhard Bischoff, "Aus der Schule Hugos von St. Viktor," in *Mittelalterliche Studien* (Stuttgart, 1967), 2:184.

5. Augustine, *De trinitate*, 12, 15, and 25, according to Kusch, *Studien*, 144f.

6. *Summa Zwetlensis*, in *Die Zwettler Summe*, I, 4, ed. Nikolaus M. Häring, Beiträge zur Geschichte der Philosophie und Theologie des Mittelalters, n.s., 15 (Münster, 1977), 25f.

7. Thierry of Chartres, *Prologus in Eptatheucon*, ed. Edouard Jeauneau, in "Note sur l'École de Chartres," 854. Dronke, "Thierry of Chartres," 361.

8. Marie-Thérèse d'Alverny, "Alain de Lille et la *Theologia*," in *L'homme devant Dieu: Mélanges H. de Lubac*, Théologie, 57 (Paris, 1964), 2:112.

9. Joseph de Ghellinck, *Le mouvement théologique du XIIe siècle* (Bruges, Brussels, and Paris, 1948), 93.

10. Otto of Freising, *Gesta Friderici*, I, 49, 68; trans. Mierow, *The Deeds of Frederick Barbarossa*, 82.

11. Abelard, *Theologia christiana*, III, 6, 196.

12. Landgraf, *Einführung*, 13.

13. Hugh of Honau, *Liber de diversitate*, II, 1, 124.

14. William of Saint-Thierry, *De erroribus*, c. 2, 384.

15. Leclercq, *The Love of Learning*, 203.

16. See pages 222–23 and note 50 to Chapter 9.

17. Hugh of Honau, *Liber de diversitate*, XII, 8, 138.

18. "Distinctio eorum, quae multipliciter proferuntur." John of Salisbury, *Metalogicon*, as quoted by Grabmann, *Geschichte der scholastischen Methode*, 2:450 n. 1.

19. Hugh of Honau, *Liber de diversitate*, XIII, 1–XV, 1, 138ff.

20. Luscombe, "Peter Abelard," 298.

21. Boethius, *De consolatione philosophiae*, V, 4f., and d'Alverny, *Alain de Lille*, 170 and 182.

22. Alan of Lille, *Liber in distinctionibus dictionum theologicalium*, MPL 210, 689.

23. Luscombe, "Peter Abelard," 283 and n. 15. Cf. Abelard, *Letters IX–XIV*, no. 13, 272f.

24. Peter Classen, "Die hohen Schulen," 23.

25. Violante, at the roundtable portion of the conference on heresies and societies in preindustrial Europe, 1000–1800, in *Hérésies et sociétés*, 205.

26. As adopted by Thierry of Chartres. See note 7 above.

27. Delhaye, "*Grammatica et Ethica*," 86 and 89–93.

28. Wetherbee, "Philosophy," 23. Ferruolo, *The Origins of the University*, 35.

29. Guibert of Nogent, *Autobiographie*, I, 4, 26; trans. Archambault, *A Monk's Confession*, 14–15.

30. Hildegard of Bingen, in the preface to *Scivias*, as quoted by Liebeschütz, *Das allegorische Weltbild der hl. Hildegard von Bingen*, 161 n. 1; cf. 162.

31. Nikolaus M. Häring, "Commentary and Hermeneutics," in *Renaissance and Renewal*, ed. Benson and Constable, 196, and idem, "A Treatise on the Trinity by Gilbert of Poitiers," *Recherches de théologie ancienne et médiévale* 39 (1972): 30.

32. Häring, "Commentary and Hermeneutics," 196f.

33. Gilbert of Poitiers on the Trinity, as quoted by Häring, "A Treatise on the Trinity by Gilbert of Poitiers," no. 62, 47. See also 30.

34. See page 292 and note 68 to Chapter 12.

35. Hugh of Honau, *Liber de diversitate*, IV, 2, 126.

36. Jean Jolivet, "Quelques cas de 'platonisme grammatical' du VIIe au XIIe siècle," in *Mélanges R. Crozet* (Poitiers, 1966), 1:99, apropos Thierry of Chartres.

37. Jan Pinborg, *Logik und Semantik im Mittelalter*, Problemata, 10 (Stuttgart, 1972), 11f.

38. Karen Margareta Fredborg, "Speculative Grammar," in *A History of Twelfth-Century Western Philosophy*, ed. Dronke, 181.

39. Jolivet, *Abélard*, 90.

40. Luscombe, in the introduction to his edition of Abelard, *Ethics*, xxxiv.

41. John of Salisbury, *Metalogicon*, II, 17, 95, as quoted by Jean Jolivet, "Notes de lexicographie Abélardienne," in *Pierre Abélard, Pierre le Vénérable*, 531; trans. McGarry, 116.

42. As, for example, in the introduction to Bernard Silvestris, *Cosmographia*, ed. Dronke, 51–53.

43. Evans, *Old Arts and New Theology*, 117; Häring, "Commentary and Hermeneutics," 195.

44. Thierry of Chartres, *Glosa super Boethii librum de Trinitate*, V, 22, as quoted by Dronke, "Thierry of Chartres," 365. See page 177 and note 20 to Chapter 7.

45. As done by Ulger of Angers. Chenu, *La théologie au douzième siècle*, 101 and 104.

46. Peter Damiani, "Ep. 153," in *Die Briefe*, vol. 4/4 (1993), 37. Leclercq, *The Love of Learning*, 230 n. 44.

47. Morris, *The Discovery of the Individual*, 55.

48. Häring, "Commentary and Hermeneutics," 197.

49. Martin Grabmann, "Die Entwicklung der mittelalterlichen Sprachlogik," in *Mittelalterliches Geistesleben* (Munich, 1926), 1:114.

50. Jan Pinborg, *Die Entwicklung der Sprachtheorie im Mittelalter*, Beiträge zur Geschichte der Philosophie und Theologie des Mittelalters, 42/2 (Münster, 1967), 23.

51. Reiners, *Der Nominalismus*, 14, cf. 61.

52. Grabmann, "Die Entwicklung der mittelalterlichen Sprachlogik," 115.

53. Leclercq, *The Love of Learning*, 200.

54. Abelard, *Historia calamitatum*, 63ff.; trans. Radice, *The Story of His Misfortunes*, 57ff.

55. Printed in Reiners, *Der Nominalismus*, 64.

56. Anselm of Laon to Abbot "H.," MPL 162, 1587, cited by Grabmann, *Geschichte der scholastischen Methode*, 2:154 n. 1.

57. Richer of Rheims has the emperor making the opening remarks; *Historiarum libri IV*, III, 58, ed. R. Latouche (2d ed., Paris, 1964), 2:68 and 70.

58. Jean Châtillon, "Abélard et les écoles," in *Abélard en son temps*, 135f.

59. Grabmann, *Geschichte der scholastischen Methode*, 2:18.

60. Klaus Jacobi, "Logic (II): The Later Twelfth Century," in *A History of Twelfth-Century Western Philosophy*, ed. Dronke, 238–40.

61. Ibid., 250 and 243.

62. Grabmann, *Geschichte der scholastischen Methode*, 2:510.

63. Walter of Saint-Victor, *Contra IV labyrinthos*, II, 2, 223. Gammersbach, *Gilbert von Poitiers*, 117.

64. Walter of Saint-Victor, *Contra IV labyrinthos*, II, 2, 223.

65. Joachim Ehlers, *Hugo von St. Victor*, Frankfurter historische Abhandlungen, 7 (Wiesbaden, 1973), 46.

66. Abelard, *Letters IX–XIV*, no. 13.

67. Verbeke, "Philosophy and Heresy," 175 n. 16. Gerhart B. Ladner, *Theologie und Politik vor dem Investiturstreit*, Veröffentlichungen des österreichischen Instituts für Geschichtsforschung, 2 (Baden bei Wien, 1936; Darmstadt, 1968), 32 and 115 n. 122.

68. Verbeke, "Philosophy and Heresy," 175 n. 20.

69. Hartmann, *Manegold von Lautenbach*, 117.

70. Ibid., 110.

71. Irven M. Resnick, "*Scientia Liberalis*, Dialectics and Otloh of St. Emmeram," *Revue bénédictine* 97 (1987): 252.

72. John of Salisbury, *Metalogicon*, II, 10, 79f., cited by Phillippe Delhaye, "L'organisation scolaire au XIIe siècle," *Traditio* 5 (1967): 262 n. 40; trans. McGarry, 100.

73. 2 Tim. 3:7; 1 Tim 1:6–7. John of Salisbury, *Metalogicon*, II, 7, 72f.; trans. McGarry, 89; and the citation in Jacobi, "Logic (II)," 231, which pertains to the following material as well.

74. Jacobi, "Logic (II)," 235.

75. Abelard, *Theologia christiana*, III, 20, 203; III, 15, 202; and IV, 161, 346.

76. Ibid., III, 4, 195.

77. Abelard, *Letters IX–XIV*, no. 13, 275.

78. Ibid., 271f. Grabmann, *Geschichte der scholastischen Methode*, 2:183.

79. See Tweedale, "Logic (I)," 198–204, for a detailed review of the handbook's contents.

80. Ibid., 196.

81. Gerald of Wales, *Speculum ecclesiae* (1220), as quoted by Ferruolo, *The Origins of the University*, 181.

82. Tweedale, "Logic (I)," 197.

83. Cf., of late, Michael Haren, *Medieval Thought*, New Studies in Medieval History (London, 1985), 101f., on Anselm's proof for the existence of God.

84. Nikolaus M. Häring, "Saint Bernard and the '*Litterati*' of His Day," *Cîteaux, Commentarii Cistercienses* 3 (1974): 209; Hugh of Amiens (Rouen), *De fide catholica*, MPL 192, 1327.

85. From a tenth/eleventh-century scholium to the *Ars poetica* by Horace. O'Donnell, "The Sources and Meaning," 245. On rhetoric in the High Middle Ages, see, of late, Rolf Köhn, "Schulbildung und Trivium im lateinischen Hochmittelalter und ihr möglicher praktischer Nutzen," in *Schulen und Studium*, ed. Fried, 265–81.

86. From a commentary on Cicero's *De inventione* by Thierry of Chartres, c. 6 and 8, in Nikolaus M. Häring, "Thierry of Chartres and Dominicus Gundissalinus," *Medieval Studies* 26 (1964): 282f.

87. Häring, "Thierry of Chartres and Dominicus Gundissalinus," 283.

88. Anselm of Besate, *Rhetorimachia*, ed. K. Manitius, MGH Quellen zur Geistesgeschichte des Mittelalters, 2 (Weimar, 1958). Cf. the introduction, 61ff., and Gibson, *Lanfranc*, 13.

89. Abelard, *Historia calamitatum*, 73; trans. Radice, *The Story of His Misfortunes*, 66.

90. Grabmann, *Geschichte der scholastischen Methode*, 2:351f.

91. Augustine, *De doctrina christiana*, IV, ed. G. Green, CSEL 80 (Vienna, 1963), 118ff.

92. Hubert Silvestre, "Dix plaidoiries inédites du XIIe siècle," *Traditio* 10 (1954): 373–97. Delhaye, "*Grammatica* et *Ethica*," 93. They were in all probability academic exercises; cf. Silvestre, "Dix plaidoiries inédites," 375.

93. Galbert of Bruges, *Passio Karoli comitis Flandrensis*, c. 1, MGH SS 10, 562.

94. Ferruolo, *The Origins of the University*, 141. See also pages 271–72 above.

95. Ernst Robert Curtius, *European Literature and the Latin Middle Ages*, trans. Willard R. Trask (New York, 1953), 77. John of Salisbury, in the prologue to *Metalogicon*, 7 and I, 1, 13ff.; trans. McGarry, 5 and 9ff.

96. Widmer, "Thierry von Chartres," 558f.

97. Discussed in detail by Häring, "Die Erschaffung," 194ff.

98. Thierry of Chartres, *Commentum super Boethium De Trinitate*, II, 35, 101.

99. [Garnier of Rochefort], *Contra Amaurianos*, 33, and Garnier's tract *Isagogae theophaniarum symbolicae* (cod. Troyes), cited in ibid., 33n.

100. As quoted by Gregory, *Anima Mundi*, 8n.

101. John of Salisbury, *Policraticus*, IV, 6, ed. C.C.J. Webb (Oxford, 1909), I, 254, as quoted by Herbert Grundmann, "Litteratus—illitteratus," *Ausgewählte Aufsätze*, 3:52 n. 33.

102. D'Alverny, "Abélard et l'astrologie," 611 and n. 2. Arno Borst, *Astrolab und Kloster-reform an der Jahrtausendwende*, Sitzungsberichte der Heidelberger Akademie der Wissen-schaften, philosophische-historische Klasse, 1989, 1:85, offers some different thoughts on the matter.

103. William of Hirsau, *Astronomica*, MPL 150, 1639–42.

104. Manitius, *Geschichte der lateinischen Literatur*, 3:221–23.

105. Hermann of Carinthia, *De essentiis*, ed. Charles Burnett (Leiden and Cologne, 1982). For more information on this point and on the following material, see Charles Burnett, "Hermann of Carinthia," in *A History of Twelfth-Century Western Philosophy*, ed. Dronke, 386–404.

106. Burnett, "Hermann of Carinthia," 396. Concerning practical arithmetic and the growing importance of numbers, cf. Murray, *Reason and Society*, 157–87.

107. William of Hirsau, in the preface to *Astronomica*, MPL 150, 1639.

108. De Lubac, *Exégèse médiévale*, 1:124.

109. Thierry of Chartres, *Commentum super Boethium De Trinitate*, II, 8, 93.

110. Ibid., II, 7, 93, and II, 2, 91.

111. Abelard, *Historia calamitatum*, 82; trans. Radice, *The Story of His Misfortunes*, 77.

112. D'Alverny, "Alain de Lille et la *Theologia*," 113.

113. Evans, *Old Arts and New Theology*, 31. Bernard used the words *theologia* and *theologus* (with negative overtones) exclusively in reference to Abelard and his work; the term *schola* referred solely to the training instilled in a cloister. Jacques Verger, "Le cloître et les Écoles," in *Bernard de Clairvaux: Oeuvres complètes*, Sources chrétiennes, 380 (Paris, 1992), 1:468.

114. *Summa Zwetlensis*, I, 18, 30.

115. Landgraf, *Dogmengeschichte*, pt. 2, 1:172.

116. De Lubac, *Exégèse médiévale*, 1:117. *Chartularium Universitatis Parisiensis*, no. 419, 1:473. On the following, see Châtillon, *La Bible*, 176 and 186.

117. De Lubac, *Exégèse médiévale*, 1:95.

118. Published as an appendix, 181–83, to the edition cited in note 88 above. At issue was the premise that it was logically possible for there to be no resolution to controversial issues.

119. Gilbert Crispin, *Disputatio Christiani cum Gentili*, c. 1 and 4, 62. See page 270 and note 16 to Chapter 11.

120. Abelard, *Dialogus*; trans. Payer, *A Dialogue*.

121. Alan of Lille, *De fide catholica*, MPL 210, 305–430, and on that work, Thouzellier, *Catharisme*, 81–106.

122. Bernard of Fontchaude (Fonte Calida), *Contra Valdenses et contra Arianos*, MPL 204, 793–810. Thouzellier, *Catharisme*, 50f.

123. Thouzellier, *Catharisme*, 198.

124. Otto of Freising, *Gesta Friderici*, I, 58, 82, and I, 54, 76; trans. Mierow, *The Deeds of Frederick Barbarossa*, 96 and 90. According to Everard of Ypres, *Dialogus Ratii et Eberhardi*, ed. Nikolaus M. Haring, in "A Latin Dialogue on the Doctrine of Gilbert of Poitiers," *Medieval Studies* 15 (1953): 274, Pope Eugene III said the following about Gilbert: "How are we to reach a judgment about something we do not understand? Indeed, this man does not speak to humans, but to God."

125. See pages 232–33 and note 19 above.

126. Otto of Freising, *Gesta Friderici*, I, 52, 75, and cf. I, 48, 67f.; trans. Mierow, *The Deeds of Frederick Barbarossa*, 88, and cf. 82.

127. Anselm of Canterbury, in the prologue to *Monologion*, in *Opera omnia*, 1:8; trans. Deane, *Monologium*, 83. Cf. page 293 above.

128. Nikolaus M. Haring, "The Case of Gilbert de la Porrée, Bishop of Poitiers (1142–1154)," *Medieval Studies* 13 (1951): 23.

129. *Summa Zwetlensis*, I, 9, 27.

130. Hugh of Honau, *Liber de ignorantia*, IV, 10, and V, 12, 216.

131. Marenbon, "Gilbert of Poitiers," 335.

132. Luscombe, "Peter Abelard," 306.

133. Abelard, *Ethica seu Scito teipsum*; ed. and trans. Luscombe, *Ethics*.

134. Jolivet, *Abélard*, 87f.

135. Abelard, *Dialogus*, c. 1265, 1275, and 1285, 88f.; trans. Payer, *A Dialogue*, 76.

136. Alan of Lille, in the prologue to *De virtutibus*, 25.

137. Philippe Delhaye, *Pierre Lombard* (Montreal and Paris, 1961), 19.

138. Otto of Freising, *Gesta Friderici*, I, 48, 68; trans. Mierow, *The Deeds of Frederick Barbarossa*, 82.

139. Delhaye, "*Grammatica et Ethica*," 91.

140. Wetherbee, "Philosophy," 25 and 42.

141. Luscombe, "Peter Abelard," 299 and 303.

142. Charles M. Radding, *The Origins of Medieval Jurisprudence* (New Haven and London, 1988), 97 and 158. Charles Homer Haskins, *The Renaissance of the Twelfth Century* (New York, 1960), 218 and 220.

143. Horst Fuhrmann, *Einfluß und Verbreitung der pseudoisidorischen Fälschungen*, Schriften der MGH, 24/2 (Stuttgart, 1973), 2:309; see 442 on the following material.

144. For a review, see de Ghellinck, *Le mouvement théologique*, 423–45.

145. This work has again come to light thanks to Martin Grabmann; Grabmann, *Geschichte der scholastischen Methode*, 2:131.

146. See page 226 and note 68 to Chapter 9.

147. See page 227 above.

148. Landgraf, *Einführung*, 12. He surmises that the method of using *quaestiones* "was cultivated more in canon law than in theology." Ibid., 40.

149. Hugh of Honau, *Liber de diversitate*, I, 10, 123.

150. *Liber de vera philosophia*, ed. P. Fournier, in "Un adversaire inconnu de S. Bernard et de Pierre Lombard," *Bibliothèque de l'École des Chartes* 47 (1886): 402.

151. Winfried Stelzer, *Gelehrtes Recht in Österreich*, Mitteilungen des Instituts für "österreichische Geschichtsforschung, suppl. vol. 26 (1982), 32f. and 190.

152. Baldwin, "Masters at Paris," 146.

153. Stelzer, *Gelehrtes Recht in Österreich*, 190–93.

154. Heinrich Fichtenau, "Magister Petrus von Wien," in *Beiträge zur Mediävistik*, 1:218–38, and *Summa Zwetlensis*, 131.

155. Johannes Fried, *Die Entstehung des Juristenstandes im 12. Jahrhundert*, Forschungen zur neueren Privatrechtsgeschichte, 21 (Cologne and Vienna, 1974), esp. 249.

156. De Ghellinck, *Le mouvement théologique*, 211 n. 3.

157. Haren, *Medieval Thought*, 103. Luscombe, *The School of Peter Abelard*, 174f. Origen had already voiced this notion. Cf. also pages 162–63 and 297 above.

158. Classen, *Gerhoch von Reichersberg*, 97 and n. 27.

Notes to Chapter 11

1. Bernard of Clairvaux, *De conversione ad clericos*, c. 21, as quoted by Delhaye, "L'organisation," 227 n. 14.

2. David's *Vita*, as quoted by Leclercq, *The Love of Learning*, 197.

3. *Metamorphosis Golyae episcopi*, ed. R.B.C. Huygens, in *Mitteilungen aus Handschriften*, Studi medievali, ser. IIIa, 3 (1962), 3:771f. For an assessment of this work, see John F. Benton,

"Philology's Search for Abelard in the *Metamorphosis Goliae*," *Speculum* 50 (1975): 215f. Wetherbee, "Philosophy," 40f.

4. "Abelard's Rule for Religious Women," ed. T. P. McLaughlin, *Medieval Studies* 18 (1956): 290; "Letter 7: Abelard to Heloise," in *The Letters of Abelard and Heloise*, trans. Radice, 265.

5. *Chronicon Andrensis monasterii*, as quoted by Delhaye, "L'organisation," 230.

6. As correctly emphasized by Johanek, "Klosterstudien," 62.

7. Delhaye, "L'organisation," 229.

8. Dronke, introduction to *A History of Twelfth-Century Western Philosophy*, ed. Dronke, 12, and Haren, *Medieval Thought*, 87.

9. Ehlers, "Monastische Theologie," 72.

10. Ibid., 72 n. 69.

11. By the terms "town schools" and "urban schools," Leclercq, *The Love of Learning*, 193, 195, etc., meant the schools located in cities.

12. Hence bearing out Jean Leclercq, "The Renewal of Theology," in *Renaissance and Renewal*, ed. Benson and Constable, 74.

13. Johanek, "Klosterstudien," 65f.

14. Everard of Ypres to Urban III; text published by Jean Leclercq, "Textes sur Saint Bernard et Gilbert de la Porrée," *Medieval Studies* 14 (1952): 126, and Everard of Ypres, *Dialogus*, 288. Peter von Moos, "Literatur- und bildungsgeschichtliche Aspekte der Dialogform im lateinischen Mittelalter," in *Tradition und Wertung, Festschrift F. Brunhölzl* (Sigmaringen, 1989), 203.

15. Anselm of Besate, in a letter to Drogo, in *Rhetorimachia*, 181.

16. Gilbert Crispin, *Disputatio Christiani cum Gentili*, c. 4, 62: "duos magne fame sed diverse secte philosophos" [two philosophers of great renown, but from different schools]. See page 256 and note 119 to Chapter 10.

17. Hugh of Honau, *Liber de diversitate*, V, 1 and 4, 127f. Cf. IX, 2, 132f., and page 283 and note 13 to Chapter 12.

18. Hugh of Honau, *Liber de diversitate*, VIII, 1, 132.

19. William of Conches, *Dragmaticon*, as quoted by Gregory, *Anima Mundi*, 265.

20. John of Salisbury, *Metalogicon*, I, 24, 57f.; trans. McGarry, 71. Classen, "Die hohen Schulen," 21 and n. 65.

21. See page 249 and note 94 to Chapter 10.

22. John O. Ward, "The Date of the Commentary on Cicero's *De Inventione* by Thierry of Chartres and the Cornifician Attack on the Liberal Arts," *Viator* 3 (1972): 223 n. 3.

23. Ibid., where reference is made to a "Cornifician crisis" and "Cornifician movement."

24. The following material is based on Ferruolo, *The Origins of the University*, 98ff.

25. Richard W. Southern, "The Schools of Paris and the School of Chartres," in *Renaissance and Renewal*, ed. Benson and Constable, 116f.

26. Abelard, *Historia calamitatum*, 92; trans. Radice, *The Story of His Misfortunes*, 88.

27. Southern, "The Schools," 114.

28. Alan of Lille, "Sermo de clericis ad theologiam non accedentibus," ed. d'Alverny, in *Alain de Lille*, 274. See page 194 and note 119 to Chapter 7.

29. Thierry of Chartres, *Commentum super Boethium De Trinitate*, II, 6, 92.

30. Hugh of Honau, *Liber de diversitate*, X, 1, 133, based on Gregory of Nazianzus.

31. Lesne, *Histoire de la propriété ecclésiastique en France*, 5:488 n. 5.

32. Haring, "Thierry of Chartres," 277 n. 52.

33. Gilbert Crispin, *Disputatio Christiani cum Gentili*, c. 5, 62f. Gilbert spoke of the *vulgus* [crowd], Thierry (note 32 above) of the *vulgus profanum* [common crowd], borrowing from Horace. The quote may also be found in Classen, "Die hohen Schulen," 21 n. 66.

34. Otto of Freising, *Gesta Friderici*, I, 49, 69; trans. Mierow, *The Deeds of Frederick Barbarossa*, 83.

35. Abelard, *Historia calamitatum*, 71, line 267; trans. Radice, *The Story of His Misfortunes*, 65.

36. See page 241 above.

37. See note 28 above.

38. See note 34 above.

39. William of Conches, in the prologue to *De philosophia mundi*, MPL 172, 43.

40. Abelard, *Historia calamitatum*, 81; trans. Radice, *The Story of His Misfortunes*, 77. Classen, "Die hohen Schulen," 7 n. 15.

41. Philip of Harvengt, abbot of Bonne-Espérance, *De institutione clericorum*, c. 110, MPL 203, 816, as quoted by Delhaye, "L'organisation," 211: "Loquendi usus obtinuit, ut, quem viderimus litteratum, statim clericum nominemus, [. . .] quoniam agit quod clerici est." [A manner of speaking gained currency by which whoever struck us as literate, we at once termed a "cleric," [. . .] because he did what is associated with a cleric.]

42. Southern, "The Schools," 134f. (appendix II).

43. Rainer Maria Herkenrath, "Studien zum Magistertitel in der frühen Stauferzeit," *Mitteilungen des Instituts für österreichische Geschichtsforschung* 88 (1980): 34. Manfred Groten, "Der Magistertitel und seine Verbreitung im deutschen Reich des 12. Jahrhunderts," *Historisches Jahrbuch* 113 (1993): 21–40, took a different view: "Within the German empire, the title of master preceding an individual's name, first encountered sporadically from 1150 on and then more frequently from around 1170, normally signified that a degree had been conferred on the individual, who had completed the course of study at an advanced school in France." An individual could, of course, bear the title whether or not he had been in France and completed his studies there, since it was unlikely that someone would check up on him. Even today, we can only rarely check up on its use.

44. Herkenrath, "Studien zum Magistertitel," 34.

45. Lesne, *Histoire de la propriété ecclésiastique en France*, 5:472.

46. Abelard, *Historia calamitatum*, 64; trans. Radice, *The Story of His Misfortunes*, 59.

47. Lesne, *Histoire de la propriété ecclésiastique en France*, 5:473.

48. Ferruolo, *The Origins of the University*, 189.

49. Bernard of Clairvaux, "Sermo 36," c. 3, MPL 183, 968. Maleczek, "Das Papsttum," 94.

50. Abelard, *Ethics*, 106 and 107.

51. Abelard, *Historia calamitatum*, 73; trans. Radice, *The Story of His Misfortunes*, 66–67.

52. As quoted by Gammersbach, *Gilbert von Poitiers*, 105 n. 10, taken from John of Salisbury, *Historia pontificalis*, c. 12, ed. R. L. Poole (Oxford, 1927), 27.

53. Everard of Ypres, as cited by Gammersbach, *Gilbert von Poitiers*, 122f.

54. Hugh of Honau, *Liber de diversitate*, III, 1, 125. The play on the words *praeesse* and *prodesse* had already occurred in the *Regula s. Benedicti*, c. 64.

55. Classen, "Der Häresie-Begriff," 471.

56. William of Conches, *Dragmaticon*, 157, as quoted (from the 1567 edition) by Gregory, *Anima Mundi*, 266n.

57. Baldwin, "Masters at Paris," 144ff. Cf. Maleczek, "Das Papsttum," 86f.

58. According to Joachim Ehlers, "Deutsche Scholaren in Frankreich während des 12. Jahrhunderts," in *Schulen und Studium*, ed. Fried, 114, five *scholares* were elevated directly to the office of bishop during the reign of Philip I (1060–1108), and ten during that of Louis VI (1108–37), "but many achieved the office of archdeacon or chancellor at their cathedrals." During the reign of Louis VII (1137–80), 3 percent of the teachers (*magistri regentes*) became bishops, and during that of his successor, Philip II Augustus, the proportion was 13–16 percent. Baldwin, "Masters at Paris," 154.

59. Southern, "The Schools," 115.

60. Manitius, *Geschichte der lateinischen Literatur*, 3:88.

61. Köhn, "Schulbildung und Trivium," 284 (based on Baldwin). Murray's remark, in *Reason and Society*, 220, that the twelfth century marked the beginning of the "golden age of careerism via the schools" is still most applicable to England.

62. Köhn, "Schulbildung und Trivium," esp. 283, emphasizes this point, counter to the thesis Classen propounds in "Die hohen Schulen."

63. See pages 277–78 and note 54 above.

64. Ehlers, "Deutsche Scholaren in Frankreich," 111.

65. See page 264 and note 154 to Chapter 10.

66. Catalogued by Classen, "Zur Geschichte der Frühscholastik," 290ff.

67. Ibid., 287f.

68. Ehlers, "Deutsche Scholaren in Frankreich," 99.

Notes to Chapter 12

1. Otloh of St. Emmeram, *Vita s. Wolfgangi episcopi*, c. 28, MGH SS IV, 537f. Köhn, "Schulbildung und Trivium," 257f.

2. Stephan of Tournai, in a letter to Pope Celestine III or Innocent III (written before 1203), *Chartularium Universitatis Parisiensis*, no. 48, 1:48. Remarks cited above by Peter Damiani (page 139 and note 53 to Chapter 5) and Bernard of Clairvaux (pages 205–6 and note 42 to Chapter 8) attest to the topical nature of the passage.

3. Jaffé-Löwenfeld, *Regesta pontificum Romanorum* (Leipzig, 1885–88), no. 12785; cited by Walter of Saint-Victor, in the prologue to *Contra IV labryrinthos*, 202. Ibid., c. 3, 195: "De novis hereticis qui dicunt Christum non esse aliquid in eo quod est homo" [On the new heretics who say that Christ, in his human nature, is nothing]. This Christological proposition has been termed "nihilianism"; see page 305 above. Palémon Glorieux, "Mauvaise action et mauvais travail," *Recherches de théologie ancienne et médiévale* 21 (1954): 180.

4. Carl Erdmann, "Gregor VII. und Berengar von Tours," *Quellen und Forschungen aus italienischen Archiven und Bibliotheken* 28 (1937/38): 64f. According to Durandus of Troarn, who provided an account of these events, Berengar's followers would have recanted before a council a short time later; *Liber de corpore et sanguine Christi*, c. 33, MPL 149, 1424.

5. Berengar of Tours, *Iuramentum Berengarii*, ed. R.B.C. Huygens, in "Bérenger de Tours, Lanfranc et Bernold de Constance," *Sacris erudiri* 16 (1965): 402 (on the occasion of a Lenten synod at Rome in 1079).

6. Verbeke, "Philosophy and Heresy," 172, and Evans, *Old Arts and New Theology*, 147.

7. Cf. the remark by William of Conches, page xx and note 121 to Chapter 7.

8. See pages 274–75 and note 32 to Chapter 11.

9. The wording used by Bernold of Constance with reference to Berengar illustrates both meanings: "cum ipse sectam suam catholicae fidei contrariam denegare non posset" [since he was not able to repudiate (the charge) that his sect was hostile to the Catholic faith]. From his *De Berengario*, last printed in Huygens, "Bérenger de Tours," 382f.

10. Evans, *Old Arts and New Theology*, 147.

11. Peter Abelard, *Confessio fidei*, ed. Charles S. Burnett, *Medieval Studies* 48 (1986): 132.

12. Geoffrey of Auxerre, *Libellus contra capitula Gilberti*, c. 1, MPL 185, 595. Gammersbach, *Gilbert von Poitiers*, 110 n. 9.

13. Hugh of Honau, *Liber de diversitate*, VI, 5, 129, and XI, 5f., 135.

14. Otto of Freising, *Gesta Friderici*, I, 53, 75; trans. Mierow, *The Deeds of Frederick Barbarossa*, 89.

15. Nikolaus Haering, "Abélard und Gilbert nach der Darstellung des Dichters Gutolf von Heiligenkreuz," *Cîteaux, Commentarii Cistercienses* 4 (1968): 265–83.

16. Otto of Freising, *Gesta Friderici*, I, 49, 69; trans. Mierow, *The Deeds of Frederick Barbarossa*, 84.

17. Ibid., I, 58, 83; trans. Mierow, 98. Cf. also page 182 above.

18. Jaffé-Löwenfeld, *Regesta pontificum Romanorum*, 8148 (July 16, 1141); also in Bernard's letters, c. 3, no. 194, MPL 182, 360f. See Walter of Saint-Victor, *Contra IV labyrinthos*, 309 (*additamenta*), for an abbreviated version. The complete text appears in Otto of Freising, *Gesta Friderici*, 71–73; trans. Mierow, *The Deeds of Frederick Barbarossa*, 86–87, from which the passage quoted here has been taken. Cf. page 296 and note 86 below.

19. See page 243 and notes 63 and 64 to Chapter 10.

20. Walter of Saint-Victor, in the prologue to *Contra IV labyrinthos*, 201.

21. Ibid., 197 (concerning III, 7).

22. Ibid., 197 (concerning IV, 8).

23. Ibid., III, 1, 246.

24. Ibid., III, 8, 257.

25. Ibid., III, 15, 268.

26. Ibid., IV, 1, 270.

27. *Apologia de Verbo incarnato* (incorrectly attributed to John of Cornwall). Glorieux, "Mauvaise action et mauvais travail," 187, and the references in Walter of Saint-Victor, *Contra IV labyrinthos*.

28. According to Gutmund of Aversa, as quoted by Jean de Montclos, *Lanfranc et Bérenger*, Études et documents, 37, Spicilegium sacrum Lovaniense (Louvain, 1971), 30 n. 4.

29. See page 31f. above.

30. *Briefsammlungen der Zeit Heinrichs IV.*, no. 88, ed. C. Erdmann and N. Fickermann, MGH Die Briefe der deutschen Kaiserzeit, vol. 5 (Weimar, 1950), 153. It has not been possible to discover the original passage in Augustine's works. The postscript may represent the complete text of the inscription; ibid., 154.

31. On the latter incident, see Erdmann, "Gregor VII. und Berengar von Tours," 63 and n. 4.

32. Entry for the year 1075 in the chronicle of Saint-Maixent, *Recueil des Historiens des Gaules et de la France*, Nouv. ed. by L. Delisle (Paris, 1877), 12:401. The confession Berengar was compelled to recite in Poitiers has been uncovered by Robert Somerville, "The Case Against Berengar of Tours: A New Text," *Studi Gregoriani* 9 (Rome, 1972): 55–75 (68f.). Rpt. in Robert Somerville, *Papacy, Councils, and Canon Law in the 11th–12th Centuries* (Aldershot, 1990), no. 1.

33. *Das Register Gregors VII.*, VI, 17a, 2:425–27. Berengar, *Iuramentum*, 402: "prostratus [. . .] me errasse confessus sum."

34. Letter from Lanfranc to Berengar, in Huygens, "Béranger de Tours," 371.

35. According to Bernold of Constance, ibid., 379.

36. Berengar, *Iuramentum*, 390f.

37. *Das Register Gregors VII.*, VI, 17a, 2:425f.

38. *Briefsammlungen der Zeit Heinrichs IV.*, no. 100, 168.

39. Jaffé-Löwenfeld, *Regesta pontificum Romanorum*, 4546, 4547, 4588, and 4601; published by Edmund Bishop, "Unedirte Briefe zur Geschichte Berengars von Tours," *Historisches Jahrbuch* 1 (1880): 273–75. Concerning the forgery, see Erdmann, "Gregor VII. und Berengar von Tours," 52–55. Montclos, *Lanfranc et Bérenger*, 20, offers additional arguments for attributing the forgeries to Berengar. However, Ovidio Capitani has offered many counterarguments; see, of late, his "Status quaestionis dei falsi berengariani," in *Fälschungen im*

Mittelalter, MGH Schriften 33, pt. 2 (Hannover, 1988), 191-215. Ibid., 191 n. 1, contains a bibliography on the issue.

40. Jaffé-Löwenfeld, *Regesta pontificum Romanorum*, 5103 and 5197. Erdmann, "Gregor VII. und Berengar von Tours," 50 and 54f.

41. *Briefsammlungen der Zeit Heinrichs IV.*, no. 87, 148ff. According to Erdmann, this letter was forged after 1079; Capitani and Montclos date its composition to 1059.

42. Berengar, *Iuramentum*, 401.

43. *Briefsammlungen der Zeit Heinrichs IV.*, no. 87, 151.

44. *Decretum synodi*, no. 70, MGH Constitutiones, 1:119.

45. Beno, *Gesta Romanae Ecclesiae contra Hildebrandum*, I, c. 4, MGH Libelli de lite, 2:370f.; Ladner, *Theologie und Politik*, 122–22 nn. 153 and 157; and Jürgen Miethke, "Theologieprozesse in der ersten Phase ihrer institutionellen Ausbildung: Die Verfahren gegen Peter Abaelard und Gilbert von Poitiers," *Viator* 6 (1975): 90.

46. Gibson, *Lanfranc of Bec*, 82.

47. According to Bernold of Constance, in Huygens, "Bérenger de Tours," 382.

48. Gibson, *Lanfranc of Bec*, 65 and 78, contends that Berengar's starting point had been the general doctrine of the sacraments.

49. Berengar, *Iuramentum*, 399. Berengar made a similar statement in a letter to Adelman of Liège, "Epistola contra Altmannum," ed. Montclos, in *Lanfranc et Bérenger*, 531.

50. Theodoin of Liège, *Contra Brunonem*; see pages 29 and 46 and notes 85 and 159 to Chapter 1. Ilarino, "Le eresie," 78f.

51. Cited in most instances as *De sacra coena*, in the new edition as *Rescriptum contra Lanfrancum*, ed. R.B.C. Huygens, CC cont. med., 84 and 84 A (rpt. 1988).

52. Montclos, *Lanfranc et Bérenger*, 442.

53. Ibid., 133.

54. Berengar, *Iuramentum*, 396 and 398,

55. Berengar, "Epistola contra Altmannum," ed. Montclos, in *Lanfranc et Bérenger*, 531.

56. Ibid., 533 and n. 4.

57. At the synod of Tours (1054). Text in Bernold of Constance, ed. Huygens, in "Bérenger de Tours," 381.

58. *Briefsammlungen der Zeit Heinrichs IV.*, no. 88, 153.

59. According to Bernold of Constance, in Huygens, "Bérenger de Tours," 378.

60. The complete text of the oath is found only in Lanfranc's tract; see Ladner, *Theologie und Politik*, 90–91 n. 8.

61. *Briefsammlungen der Zeit Heinrichs IV.*, no. 88, 154. Cf. note 30 above.

62. See page 174 above. Manegold was considered an "antidialectician" and may have been a "converted" dialectician.

63. Montclos, *Lanfranc et Bérenger*, 147 and 589.

64. See page 208 above.

65. Protocol to the Lenten synod in *Das Register Gregors VII.*, VI, 17a, 2:426f.

66. In the credo countering the Cathars. The phrase *substantialiter converti* was employed often (as a substantive or a verb) from the beginning of the twelfth century onward. According to oral tradition, Gilbert's followers credited the formulation of this concept to a Master Robertus Pullus, who taught around 1130/40. Joseph Goering, "The Invention of the Transubstantiation," *Traditio* 44 (1991): 147–70. On this point, cf. Innocent III, *Die Register*, no. 120, 5:237f.

67. Berengar, "Epistola contra Altmannum," ed. Montclos, in *Lanfranc et Bérenger*, 536.

68. L. M. de Rijk, "The Semantical Impact of Abailard's Solution of the Problem of Universals," in *Petrus Abaelardus*, ed. Thomas and Jolivet, 132f. Stock, *The Implications of Literacy*, 278.

69. Berengar, *Rescriptum*, II, 1756f. and 1789–91, 84f.

70. Alger of Liège, *De sacramento corporis et sanguinis Dominici*, I, 6, MPL 180, 754.

71. John Van Engen, "Rupert of Deutz and William of Saint-Thierry," *Revue bénédictine* 93 (1983): 328.

72. Letter from Walter of Honnecourt to Roscelin, ed. Germain Morin, in "Un écrivain inconnu du XIe siècle: Walter, moine de Honnecourt, puis de Vézelay," *Revue bénédictine* 22 (1905): 173–75. On this point, see page 258 above.

73. Reiners, *Der Nominalismus*, 29f. (also on the following material). On Garlandus Computista, one of Roscelin's precursors, cf. Tweedale, "Logic (I)," 198–204, and page 246 above.

74. Otto of Freising, *Gesta Friderici*, I, 49, 69; trans. Mierow, *The Deeds of Frederick Barbarossa*, 84. Abelard, *Historia calamitatum*, 82 and 87; trans. Radice, *The Story of His Misfortunes*, 79 and 83. Miethke, "Theologieprozesse," 91–95.

75. See page 78 above; John characterized the leader of the heretics of Bucy-le-Long near Soissons (page 77 above) as the wisest person he had ever seen. Guibert of Nogent, *Autobiographie*, III, 17, 428; trans. Archambault, *A Monk's Confession*, 195–96.

76. Nikolaus M. Häring, "Die vierzehn capitula heresum Petri Abaelardi," *Cîteaux, Commentarii Cistercienses* 1 (1980): 43. A list containing nineteen points has been published of late by Mews, "The Lists," 108–10. A third list, drafted by William of Saint-Thierry, can be found in Leclercq, "Les lettres de Guillaume de Saint-Thierry à Saint Bernard," 377f. The formulation of some points was influenced by Bernard of Clairvaux, who apparently directed the editing of the text at the synod of Sens; Mews, "The Lists," 96f.

77. Leclercq, "L'hérésie," 26.

78. Abelard, *Historia calamitatum*, 87; trans. Radice, *The Story of His Misfortunes*, 82.

79. Ibid.

80. Otto of Freising, *Gesta Friderici*, I, 49, 69; trans. Mierow, *The Deeds of Frederick Barbarossa*, 83. See page 284 above.

81. *Liber de vera philosophia*, 408. Concerning the authorship of this tract, see Gammersbach, *Gilbert von Poitiers*, 61.

82. Bernard of Clairvaux, "Ep. 190," c. 7, in *Sämtliche Werke*, 3:86.

83. Otto of Freising, *Gesta Friderici*, I, 50, 69; trans. Mierow, *The Deeds of Frederick Barbarossa*, 84.

84. Ibid., I, 50, 70; trans. Mierow, 84. Lothar Kolmer, "Abaelard und Bernhard von Clairvaux in Sens," *Zeitschrift für Rechtsgeschichte, Kanonistische Abteilung* 67 (1981): 136ff., delineates the significantly more complicated course of events.

85. Bernard of Clairvaux, "Ep. 190," in *Sämtliche Werke*, 3:74–121; letter to the bishops quoted by Otto of Freising, *Gesta Friderici*, I, 50, 70f.; trans. Mierow, *The Deeds of Frederick Barbarossa*, 84–85; *Capitula*, ed. Häring or (preferably) Mews, see note 76 above.

86. Jaffé-Löwenfeld, *Regesta pontificum Romanorum*, 8148 (July 16, 1141). Reproduced by Otto of Freising, *Gesta Friderici*, I, 50, 71–73; trans. Mierow, *The Deeds of Frederick Barbarossa*, 86–87. Cf. page 284 and note 18 above. For a detailed discussion of the synod at Sens, see Miethke, "Theologieprozesse," 96–102; for the literature, see 96 n. 46, as well as the more recent essay by Kolmer, "Abaelard und Bernhard von Clairvaux in Sens," 121–47.

87. Bernard of Clairvaux, "Ep. 192," in *Sämtliche Werke*, 3:44, as quoted by Häring, "Saint Bernard and the 'Litterati' of His Day," 217, with the remark "His basic and standardized accusation."

88. *Capitula*, no. 1, ed. Häring, "Die vierzehn capitula heresum Petri Abaelardi," 43f.

89. Bernard of Clairvaux, "Ep. 190," c. 7 and c. 4, in *Sämtliche Werke*, 3:86 and 80.

90. Ibid., c. 9, 88.

91. Ibid.

92. See page 265 and note 157 to Chapter 10.

93. *Capitula*, IV, 4, ed. Häring, "Die vierzehn capitula heresum Petri Abaelardi," 46.

94. Bernard of Clairvaux, "Ep. 190," c. 12, in *Sämtliche Werke*, 3:94.

95. Cf. John 11:47–51. Berengar of Poitiers, *Apologia contra sanctum Bernardum [. . .] et alios qui condemnaverunt Petrum Abaelardum*, ed. R. M. Thomson, in "The Satirical Works of Berengar of Poitiers," *Medieval Studies* 42 (1980): 115.

96. William of Saint-Thierry, *De erroribus*, c. 2, 384.

97. Ibid. Concerning similar attempts by Thierry of Chartres, see page 177 above, and in Abelard's works, see pages 296–97 above.

98. William of Saint-Thierry, *De erroribus*, c. 8, 389f. See page xx above.

99. As last discussed by Dorothy Elford, "William of Conches," in *A History of Twelfth-Century Western Philosophy*, ed. Dronke, 317f.

100. William of Saint-Thierry, *De erroribus*, c. 8, 390. See page 192 above.

101. Haring, "The Case of Gilbert de la Porrée," 2.

102. See page 257 and note 124 to Chapter 10. On Gilbert in Paris (1147) and Rheims (1148), see Miethke, "Theologieprozesse," 104–10.

103. Geoffrey of Auxerre, *Libellus contra capitula Gisleberti episcopi Pictavensis*, ed. Nikolaus M. Haring, in "The Writings Against Gilbert of Poitiers by Geoffrey of Auxerre," *Analecta Cisterciensia* 22 (1966): 3–83. Previously published in MPL 185, 595–618.

104. Gammersbach, *Gilbert von Poitiers*, 87. For a detailed discussion of the proceedings and of the following material, see Häring, "Saint Bernard and the '*Litterati*' of His Day," 219ff. Cf. page 277 and note 52 to Chapter 11.

105. Mansi, 21:713.

106. Geoffrey of Auxerre, *Libellus contra capitula Gisleberti*, MPL 185, 597.

107. See page 271 and note 17 to Chapter 11.

108. See page 258 and note 126 to Chapter 10.

109. As quoted by Walter of Saint-Victor, *Contra IV labryrinthos*, II, 3, 226.

110. For example, Geoffrey of Auxerre; Häring, "A Treatise on the Trinity," 33.

111. Haring, "The Case of Gilbert de la Porrée," 13.

112. Ibid., 8, and Häring, "A Treatise on the Trinity," 21.

113. Geoffrey of Auxerre, *Libellus contra capitula Gisleberti*, c. 31, MPL 185, 606.

114. This reflected the Gilbertine teaching according to his student Hugh of Honau, *Liber de diversitate*, XVIII, 11, 146f., where this proposition concerning Aristotle's theory of categories is substantiated with passages from the Greek fathers of the church.

115. Häring, "A Treatise on the Trinity," 18f. and 21.

116. Ibid., 19 and n. 37, and 21 and n. 46.

117. Otto of Freising, *Gesta Friderici*, I, 58, 82; trans. Mierow, *The Deeds of Frederick Barbarossa*, 96. Cf. also page 182 above.

118. Haring, "The Case of Gilbert de la Porrée," 12.

119. Otto of Freising, *Gesta Friderici*, I, 59, 85; trans. Mierow, *The Deeds of Frederick Barbarossa*, 98.

120. Haring, "The Case of Gilbert de la Porrée," 18.

121. Gammersbach, *Gilbert von Poitiers*, 13. Concerning Bernard and Thierry, cf. pages 177–78 above.

122. See page 237 and note 36 to Chapter 10.

123. See pages 181 and 293–94 above.

124. See page 182 above.

125. "Caute in scolis tuis doceas" [You should exercise caution when teaching in your schools], Gerhoh of Reichersberg warned Peter of Vienna, Gilbert's student; in Gerhoh's

view, Peter disseminated "doctrinas novas" [novel doctrines] to his students, who concurred in all he said. Fichtenau, "Magister Petrus von Wien," 229f.

126. The following material is based on Moos, "Literatur- und bildungsgeschichtliche Aspekte der Dialogform," 169 and 172. Everard of Ypres, *Dialogus*, 252.

127. Everard of Ypres, *Dialogus*, 252. Nikolaus M. Haring, "The Cistercian Everard of Ypres and His Appraisal of the Conflict Between St. Bernard and Gilbert of Poitiers," *Medieval Studies* 17 (1955): 152.

128. Everard of Ypres, "Epistola [. . .] ad Urbanum papam III," ed. Haring, in "The Cistercian Everard of Ypres," c. 3, 162, and c. 19, 167.

129. Moos, "Literatur- und bildungsgeschichtliche Aspekte der Dialogform," 192f.

130. Everard of Ypres, *Dialogus*, 272.

131. On Peter Lombard's viewpoint, cf. Nikolaus M. Haring, "The Porretani and the Greek Fathers," *Medieval Studies* 24 (1962): 190.

132. According to Walter of Saint-Victor; see page 285 above.

133. Grundmann, *Ketzergeschichte*, 22.

134. Walter of Saint-Victor, in the prologue to *Contra IV labyrinthos*, 201; cf. II, 3, 225, and II, 5, 246f.

135. Ibid., 201. Cf. page 282 and note 3 above. Jaffé-Löwenfeld, *Regesta pontificum Romanorum*, 12785.

136. Walter of Saint-Victor, *Contra IV labyrinthos*, 304 (*additamenta priora*).

137. Ilarino, *L'eresia di Ugo Speroni*, 42ff., and Merlo, *Eretici*, 63ff.

138. Ilarino, *L'eresia di Ugo Speroni*, 66.

139. Lambert, *Medieval Heresy*, 81f. (1977), and 77f. (rev. 2d ed.).

140. Marie-Thérèse d'Alverny, "Un fragment du procés des Amauriciens," *Archives d'histoire doctrinale et littéraire du Moyen Âge 18* (1950/51), 326 n. 3.

141. Alberic of Trois-Fontaines, *Chronica*, MGH SS 23, 890, citing William the Breton. J.M.M.H. Thijssen, "Master Amalric and the Amalricians," *Speculum 71* (1996): 43–46, has compiled an overview of the literature on Amalric's teachings; see 47–65 for the canonical grounds to the legal proceedings taken against this group.

142. Alberic of Trois-Fontaines, *Chronica*, MGH SS 23, 890. The year in which he died (1206) is derived from Alberic's entry for 1210: "post quatuor annos sue tumulationis" [after he had been buried for four years]. On the following, cf. Gary Dickson, "The Burning of the Amalricians," *Journal of Ecclesiastical History* 40 (1989): 347–69.

143. Caesarius of Heisterbach, *Dialogus miraculorum*, V, 22, 1:304 and 307; trans. Scott and Bland, *The Dialogue of Miracles*, 1:347–48 and 351—who named only thirteen of the individuals.

144. *Chartularium Universitatis Parisiensis*, no. 11, 1:70. The appellation *aurifaber* [gold-smith], which also appears there, is hardly to be understood as a professional designation; it pertained to a cleric who had been stripped of his holy orders.

145. Paolo Lucentini, "L'eresia di Amalrico," in *Eriugena Redivivus*, 185 and the citation in 175 n. 2.

146. Caesarius of Heisterbach, *Dialogus miraculorum*, V, 22, 1:307: "in adventu regis, qui tunc praesens non erat, exusti"; trans. Scott and Bland, *The Dialogue of Miracles*, 1:350: "on the return of the king, for he happened to be absent at that time, they were burned at the stake."

147. *Chartularium Universitatis Parisiensis*, no. 11, 1:70, and note 143 above.

148. Caesarius of Heisterbach, *Dialogus miraculorum*, V, 22, 1:305f.; trans. Scott and Bland, *The Dialogue of Miracles*, 1:349.

149. Ibid., 304f.; trans. Scott and Bland, 1:348f.; cf. note 144 above.

150. Grundmann, *Religious Movements*, 358f. n. 13.

151. [Garnier of Rochefort], *Contra Amaurianos*, c. 8, 24. D'Alverny, "Un fragment," 328f.

Godinus is mentioned in *Contra Amaurianos*, c. 9, 24, and c. 10, 30, and ridiculed as "God" and the "incarnation of Christ."

152. Chenu, *La théologie au douzième siècle*, 319.

153. William the Breton, *Gesta Philippi Augusti*, ed. F. Delaborde, Ouvres de Rigord et de Guillaume le Breton, vol. 1 (1882), 232, as quoted by Lucentini, "L'eresia di Amalrico," 175f. n. 3, and Grundmann, *Religiöse Bewegungen*, 373 n. 40. Caesarius of Heisterbach, *Dialogus miraculorum*, V, 22, 1:304f.; trans. Scott and Bland, *The Dialogue of Miracles*, 1:348.

154. According to Lucentini, "L'eresia di Amalrico," 185, superseding, for example, Grundmann, *Religious Movements*, 155, etc. From 1271 on, heresies associated with John Scotus (Eriugena), who had by then been condemned, were imputed to Amalric.

155. See note 140 above.

156. Caesarius of Heisterbach, *Dialogus miraculorum*, V, 22, 1:305; trans. Scott and Bland, *The Dialogue of Miracles*, 1:348.

157. [Garnier of Rochefort], *Contra Amaurianos*, 2, 9.

158. Fragment of a court proceeding in d'Alverny, "Un fragment," 332.

159. Caesarius of Heisterbach, *Dialogus miraculorum*, V, 22, 1:304; trans. Scott and Bland, *The Dialogue of Miracles*, 1:348.

160. Robert Folz, *Le souvenir et la légende de Charlemagne dans l'Empire germanique médiéval*, Publications de l'Université de Dijon, 7 (Paris, 1950), 277–79.

161. [Garnier of Rochefort], *Contra Amaurianos*, c. 6, 19.

162. Ibid., c. 5, 17.

163. Ibid., c. 3, 13.

164. As quoted by d'Alverny, "Un fragment," 333 n. 2.

165. Karl Albert, "Amalrich von Bena und der mittelalterliche Pantheismus," in *Die Auseinandersetzungen an der Pariser Universität im XIII. Jahrhundert*, Miscellanea mediaevalia, 10 (1976), 211.

166. [Garnier of Rochefort], *Contra Amaurianos*, c. 11, 46.

167. Ibid., c. 12, 47.

168. *Chartularium Universitatis Parisiensis*, no. 12, 1:71; see, in addition, Caesarius of Heisterbach, *Dialogus miraculorum*, V, 22, 1:304; trans. Scott and Bland, *The Dialogue of Miracles*, 1:348.

169. *Chartularium Universitatis Parisiensis*, no. 20, 1:78f., and d'Alverny, "Un fragment," 325.

170. As quoted by Grundmann, *Religiöse Bewegungen*, 357 n. 4.

171. See note 141 above.

172. [Garnier of Rochefort], *Contra Amaurianos*, c. 2, 9.

Notes to "A Look Ahead"

1. Moneta of Cremona, *Adversus Catharos et Valdenses*, taken from the edition by Ricchini (Rome, 1743), 23, as quoted by Morghen, "L'eresia nel medioevo," 253.

2. Examples (taken from Everard of Béthune and Moneta) in Duvernoy, *La religion*, 48, 81, and 181. Cf. note 74 to Chapter 6.

3. Cf. page 170 and note 65 to Chapter 6.

4. See page 138 and note 49 to Chapter 5. Vaillant, in Cosmas, *Le traité*, 33, also makes mention of the fathers of the church: "la science religieuse était toute grecque" [religious knowledge was entirely Greek].

5. See page 22 and note 49 to Chapter 1.

6. See page 218 and note 12 to Chapter 9.

7. *Chartularium Universitatis Parisiensis*, no. 48, 1:48; see page 282 and note 2 to Chapter 12.

8. *Chartularium Universitatis Parisiensis*, no. 11, 1:70.

9. Published by d'Alverny, "Un fragment," 330, no. 1.

10. L. Minio-Paluello, "Iacobus Veneticus Grecus, Canonist and Translator of Aristotle," *Traditio 8* (1952): 265–304.

11. Pinborg, *Logik*, 16.

12. Jolivet, *Abélard*, 105, and Grabmann, *Geschichte der scholastischen Methode*, 2:443.

13. Grabmann, *Geschichte der scholastischen Methode*, 2:443.

14. David of Dinant, *Davidis de Dinanto Quaternulorum fragmenta*, ed. Marian Kurdzialek, Studia Mediewistyczne, 3 (Warsaw, 1963). On his attribution of biblical miracles to natural causes, cf. Kurdzialek, "David von Dinant," and page 194 and note 117 to Chapter 7.

15. Innocent III to the abbot and chapter of the Church of Dinant (in the diocese of Liège), June 6, 1206. Potthast, *Reg. Pont.* (Rome), 2790. Enzo Maccagnolo, "David of Dinant and the Beginnings of Aristotelianism in Paris," in *A History of Twelfth-Century Western Philosophy*, ed. Dronke, 431, including additional accounts about David and references.

16. Marian Kurdzialek, "David von Dinant und die Anfänge der Aristotelischen Naturphilosophie," in *La filosofia della natura*, 413.

17. David of Dinant, *Quaternulorum fragmenta*, 70f.; Maccagnolo, "David of Dinant," 440. The work of this researcher remained unfinished upon his death, and as a consequence the grounds for his theory that David was not a heretic remain unclarified.

18. Mentioned in his *Quaternulorum fragmenta*, 38.

19. Robert Kalivoda, "Zur Genesis der natürlichen Naturphilosophie im Mittelalter," in *La filosofia della natura*, 402–4.

20. Duvernoy, *La religion*, 42.

21. Johannes de Lugio, *Liber de duobus principiis*: "sicut probat Aristoteles in tertio phisicorum" [as Aristotle proved in the third part of the Physics]; as quoted by Verbeke, "Philosophy and Heresy," 185 n. 82. In her edition of the *Liber*, Thouzellier notes: "Non inveni; revera Avicebron, Fons vitae" [I did not find (it there); actually in Avicebron, *Fons vitae*].

22. According to Maccagnolo, "David of Dinant," 429 n. 4, the prohibited *commenta* pertained to Averroës; cf., however, the editorial comment, ibid.

23. See page 252 above.

24. The doctrine of the double truth was never defined as a thesis; nevertheless, it was condemned in Paris in 1277. On this topic, see, of late, Richard C. Dales, "The Origin of the Doctrine of the Double Truth," *Viator* 15 (1984): 169–79. According to Ludwig Hödl, "they spoke as if there were two contrary truths"; in *Philosophie im Mittelalter*, ed. J. P. Beckmann et al. (Hamburg, 1987), 225–43.

Select Bibliography

Primary Sources

Abelard, Peter. *A Dialogue of a Philosopher with a Jew, and a Christian*. Trans. Pierre J. Payer. Toronto, 1979.

———. *Dialogus inter philosophum, Judaeum et Christianum*. Ed. R. Thomas. Stuttgart, Bad Cannstatt, 1970.

———. *Historia calamitatum*. Ed. J. Monfrin. Bibliothèque de textes philosophiques. Paris, 1959, 1962, and 1978.

———. *Letters IX–XIV*. Ed. E. R. Smits. Groningen, 1983.

———. *Peter Abelard's Ethics*. Ed. and trans. D. E. Luscombe. Oxford, 1971.

———. *Sic et non*. Ed. Blanche B. Boyer and Richard McKeon. Chicago, 1976.

———. *Sic et non*. MPL 178, 1339–610.

———. *The Story of His Misfortunes*. In *The Letters of Abelard and Heloise*, trans. Betty Radice. New York, 1974 and 1978.

———. *Theologia christiana*. CC cont. med. 12. 1969.

Adémar of Chabannes. *Chronicon*. Ed. J. Chavanon. Collection de textes, 20. Paris, 1897.

Alan of Lille (Alanus ab Insulis). *Anticlaudianus*. Ed. R. Bossuat. Textes philosophiques du Moyen Âge, I. Paris, 1955.

———. *Anticlaudianus or The Good and Perfect Man*. Trans. James J. Sheridan. Toronto, 1973.

———. *De fide catholica contra haereticos sui temporis praesertim Albigenses*. MPL 210, 306–430.

———. *De planctu Naturae*. Ed. Nikolaus M. Haring. In "Alan of Lille *De planctu Naturae*." *Studi medievali*, IIIa, serie 19 (1978), 797 (ed. 806)–879.

———. *De virtutibus et de vitiis et de donis Spiritus Sancti*. Ed. O. Lottin, *Medieval Studies* 12 (1950): 25–56.

———. *The Plaint of Nature*. Trans. James J. Sheridan. Toronto, 1980.

———. *Regulae theologicae*. Ed. Nikolaus M. Häring. *Archives d'histoire doctrinale et littéraire du Moyen Âge* 48 (1981): 197–226.

———. *Regulae theologicae*. MPL 210, 617–86.

———. "Textes inédits." Ed. Marie-Thérèse d'Alverny. In *Alain de Lille*, 185f. (See Secondary Sources below.)

Alberic of Trois-Fontaines. *Chronicon*. Ed. P. Scheffer-Boichorst. MGH SS 23, 631–950.

Andreas of Fleury. *Vie de Gauzlin abbé de Fleury.* Ed. Robert-Henri Bautier and G. Labory. Sources d'histoire médiévale, 2. Paris, 1969.

Anselm of Besate. *Gunzo, Epistola ad Augienses,* and *Rhetorimachia.* Ed. K. Manitius. MGH Quellen zur Geistesgeschichte des Mittelalters, 2. Weimar, 1958.

Anselm of Canterbury. *Basic Writings.* Trans. S. N. Deane. Chicago, 1962, 1996.

———. *Opera omnia.* Ed. F. S. Schmitt. Vol. 1. Seckau, 1938; Edinburgh, 1946; Stuttgart, 1968.

Berengar of Tours. *Iuramentum Berengarii.* Ed. R.B.C. Huygens. In "Bérenger de Tours," 388–403. (See Secondary Sources below.)

———. *Rescriptum contra Lanfrancum.* Ed. R.B.C. Huygens. CC cont. med. 84 and 84 A. Rpt. 1988.

Bernard of Clairvaux. *Sämtliche Werke lateinisch-deutsch.* Ed. G. B. Winkler et al. Vols. 2 and 3. Innsbruck, 1992 and 1993.

Bernard Silvestris. *Cosmographia.* Ed. Peter Dronke. Textus minores, 53. Leiden, 1978.

———. *The Cosmographia of Bernardus Silvestris.* Trans. Winthrop Wetherbee. New York, 1973; 1990.

Bernold of Constance (St. Blasien). *Chronicon.* MGH SS 5, 385–467.

———. *Die Chroniken Bertholds von Reichenau und Bernolds von St. Blasien.* Ed. I. S. Robinson. MGH SS Rerum Germanicarum, n.s., 14. Munich, 1992.

Bonaccursus. *Manifestatio haeresis Catharorum.* Ed. R. Manselli. *Bullettino dell'Istituto Storico Italiano per il Medio Evo* 67 (1955): 207–11.

Briefsammlungen der Zeit Heinrichs IV. Ed. C. Erdmann and N. Fickermann. MGH Die Briefe der deutschen Kaiserzeit, vol. 5. Weimar, 1950.

Caesarius of Heisterbach. *Caesarii Heisterbacensis Dialogus Miraculorum.* Ed. J. Strange. Vol. 1. Cologne, Bonn, and Brussels, 1851; Cologne, 1922.

———. *The Dialogue of Miracles.* Trans. H. von E. Scott and C. C. Swinton Bland. Vol. 1. London, 1929.

Capitula heresum Petri Abaelardi. In "Anonymi Capitula heresum Petri Abaelardi." Ed. E. Buytaert. CC cont. med. 12, 473–80. 1969.

———. In "Die vierzehn capitula heresum Petri Abaelardi." Ed. Nikolaus M. Häring. *Cîteaux, Commentarii Cistercienses* 1 (1980): 34 (ed. 43)–52.

———. In "The Lists of Heresies Imputed to Peter Abelard." Ed. Constant J. Mews. (See Secondary Sources below.)

Cartulaire de l'abbaye de Saint-Père de Chartres. Ed. M. Guérard. Collection des cartulaires de France, 1:109–15. Paris, 1840.

Chartularium Universitatis Parisiensis. Vol. 1. Ed. H. Denifle and E. Châtelain. Paris, 1899; Brussels, 1964.

Contra Amaurianos. (See Garnier of Rochefort below.)

Corpus Documentorum Inquisitionis Haereticae Pravitatis Neerlandicae. Ed. P. Fredericq. Vol. 1. Ghent and The Hague, 1889.

Cosmas the Priest. *Le traité contre les Bogomiles de Cosmas de Prêtre.* Ed. Henri-Charles Puech and André Vaillant. Travaux publiés par l'Institut d'études slaves, 21. Paris, 1945.

Das Register Gregors VII. Ed. Erich Caspar. MGH Epistolae Selectae, II/1 and II/2. Berlin, 1920 and 1923.

David of Dinant. *Davidis de Dinanto Quaternulorum fragmenta*. Ed. Marian Kurd-zialek. Studia Mediewistyczne, 3. Warsaw, 1963.

Die Zwettler Summe. (See *Summa Zwetlensis* below.)

Durand of Huesca. *Une somme anti-cathare: Le Liber contra Manicheos de Durand de Huesca*. Ed. Christine Thouzellier. Université catholique de Louvain. Études et documents, 32. Louvain, 1964.

————. *Liber antihaeresis*. Ed. Kurt-Victor Selge. In *Edition des Liber antihaeresis des Durandus von Osca*, vol. 2 of *Die ersten Waldenser*. (See Secondary Sources below.)

Ecritures cathares. Ed. R. Nelli. Paris, 1959; 1968.

Ekbert of Schönau. *Sermones contra Catharos*. MPL 195, 11–102.

Everard of Ypres. *Dialogus Ratii et Eberhardi*. Ed. Nikolaus M. Haring. In "A Latin Dialogue on the Doctrine of Gilbert of Poitiers." *Medieval Studies* 15 (1953): 243 (ed. 245)–289.

[Garnier of Rochefort]. *Contra Amaurianos*. Ed. C. Baeumker. Beiträge zur Geschichte der Philosophie des Mittelalters, 24, pt. 5/6. Münster, 1926.

Geoffrey of Auxerre. *Libellus contra capitula Gisleberti episcopi Pictavensis*. Ed. Nikolaus M. Haring. In "The Writings Against Gilbert of Poitiers by Geoffrey of Auxerre." *Analecta Cisterciensia* 22 (1966): 3–83.

————. *Libellus contra capitula Gisleberti episcopi Pictavensis*. MPL 185, 595–618.

Gerard, Bishop of Cambrai-Arras. (See Synodus Atrebatensis below.)

Gilbert Crispin. *The Works of Gilbert Crispin, Abbot of Westminster*. Ed. A. Sapir Abulafia and G. R. Evans. Auctores Britannici medii aevi, 8. London, 1986.

Gilbert of Poitiers. *De Trinitate*. Ed. Nikolaus M. Haring. In "A Treatise on the Trinity," 34–50. (See Secondary Sources below.)

Guibert of Nogent. *Autobiographie*. Ed. E.-R. Labande. Les classiques de l'histoire de France au Moyen Âge, 34. Paris, 1981.

————. *A Monk's Confession*. Trans. Paul J. Archambault. University Park, Pa., 1996.

Helgald of Fleury. *Vie de Robert le Pieux*. Ed. Robert-Henri Bautier and G. Labory. Sources d'histoire médiévale, 1. Paris, 1965.

Heribert the Monk. "Epistola de haereticis Petragoricis." In Guy Lobrichon, "Le clair-obscur de l'hérésie," 441–44. (See Secondary Sources below.)

————. "Epistola de haereticis Petragoricis." MPL 181, 1721f.

Hugh of Amiens (Rouen). *Contra haereticos sui temporis . . . libri tres*. MPL 192, 1253–98.

Hugh of Honau. *Liber de diversitate naturae et personae*. Ed. Nikolaus M. Haring. In "The *Liber de Diversitate Naturae et Personae* by Hugh of Honau." *Archives d'histoire doctrinale et littéraire du Moyen Âge* 29 (1962): 103 (ed. 120)–216.

————. *Liber de ignorantia*. Ed. Nikolaus M. Haring. In "Hugh of Honau and the *Liber de Ignorantia*." *Medieval Studies* 25 (1963): 209 (ed. 214)–230.

Innocent III. Letters. MPL 214–17.

————. *Die Register Innocenz' III.: 2. Pontifikatsjahr*. Ed. O. Hageneder, W. Maleczek, and A. Strnad. Publikationen des Historischen Instituts beim österr. Kulturinstitut in Rom. Pt. 2, ser. 1., vol. 2. Rome and Vienna, 1979.

————. *Die Register Innocenz' III.: 5. Pontifikatsjahr*. Ed. O. Hageneder, W. Maleczek, and A. Strnad. Publikationen des Historischen Instituts beim österr. Kulturinstitut in Rom. Pt. 2, ser. 1., vol. 5. Vienna, 1993.

John of Salisbury. *Metalogicon.* Ed. C. C. J. Webb. Oxford, 1929.

———. *The Metalogicon of John of Salisbury.* Trans. Daniel D. McGarry. Berkeley and Los Angeles, 1955 and 1962.

Ketzer und Ketzerbekämpfung im Hochmittelalter. Ed. J. Fearns. Historische Texte, Mittelalter, 8. Göttingen, 1968.

Landulf the Elder of Milan. *Historia Mediolanensis.* MGH SS 8, 37–100.

———. *Landulphi Senioris Mediolanensis Historiae Libri Quattuor.* Ed. A. Cutolo. Rerum Italicarum Scriptores, new ed., IV/2. Bologna, 1942.

Liber de vera philosophia. Ed. P. Fournier. In "Un adversaire inconnu de S. Bernard et de Pierre Lombard." *Bibliothèque de l'École des Chartes* 47 (1886): 394–417.

Manegold of Lautenbach. *Liber contra Wolfelmum.* Ed. Wilfried Hartmann. MGH Quellen zur Geistesgeschichte des Mittelalters, 8. Cologne, 1972.

Odorannus of Sens. *Opera omnia.* Ed. Robert-Henri Bautier and M. Gilles. Sources d'histoire médiévale, 4. Paris, 1972.

Otloh of St. Emmeram in Regensberg. *Liber de temptationibus suis.* MPL 146, 27–58.

Otto of Freising. *The Deeds of Frederick Barbarossa.* Trans. Charles C. Mierow, with Richard Emery. New York, 1953 and 1966.

———. *Ottonis et Rahewini Gesta Friderici I. imperatoris.* Ed. G. Waitz and B. de Simson. MGH SS rerum Germanicarum, 46. Hannover and Leipzig, 1912.

Paul of Chartres. (See *Cartulaire* above.)

Peter Damiani. *Die Briefe des Petrus Damiani.* Ed. K. Reindel. MGH Die Briefe der deutschen Kaiserzeit, vol. 4, pt. 2. Munich, 1988; pt. 3, 1989; and pt. 4, 1993.

Peter of Vaux-de-Cernay. *Petri Vallium Sarnaii Monachi Hystoria Albigensis.* Ed. P. Guébin and E. Lyon. 3 vols. Paris, 1926, 1930, and 1939.

Peter the Venerable. Letter of dedication for *Contra Petrobrusianos Hereticos,* in *Ketzer und Ketzerbekämpfung,* no. 4, 18–21. (See above.)

———. *Petri Venerabilis Contra Petrobrusianos Hereticos.* Ed. J. Fearns. CC cont. med. 10. 1968.

Plato. *Timaeus a Calcidio translatus.* Ed. P. J. Jensen and J. H. Waszink. Corpus Platonicum medii aevi, II, 1, 4. London, 1962.

Puylaurens. (See William of Puylaurens below.)

Rodulfus Glaber. *Cronache dell'anno mille.* Ed. G. Cavallo and G. Orlandi. Milan, 1989.

———. *Les cinq livres de ses histoires (900–1044).* Ed. M. Prou. Collection de textes, 1. Paris, 1886.

———. *Rodulfi Glabri Historiarum Libri Quinque: The Five Books of the Histories.* Ed. and trans. J. France. Oxford, 1989.

Summa Zwetlensis. In *Die Zwettler Summe,* ed. Nikolaus M. Häring. Beiträge zur Geschichte der Philosophie und Theologie des Mittelalters, n.s., 15. Münster, 1977.

"Synodus Atrebatensis" (Arras 1025). Mansi, 19:424–60.

——— (abridged). In *Ketzer und Ketzerbekämpfung,* no. 2, 12–15. (See above.)

Theodericus. (See Thierry below.)

Theodoin of Liège. *Contra Brunonem et Berengarium epistola.* MPL 146, 1439–42.

Thierry of Chartres. *Commentum super Boethium De Trinitate*. Ed. Nikolaus M. Haring. In "Two Commentaries on Boethius (*De Trinitate et De Hebdomadibus*), by Thierry of Chartres." *Archives d'histoire doctrinale et littéraire du Moyen Âge* 27 (1960): 80–136.

Walter Map. *De nugis curialium*. Ed. M. R. James, L. Brooke, and R.A.B. Mynors. Oxford, 1983.

Walter of Saint-Victor. *Contra IV labyrinthos Franciae*. Ed. P. Glorieux. *Archives d'histoire doctrinale et littéraire du Moyen Âge* 19 (1952): 195–334.

William of Conches. *De philosophia mundi*. MPL 172, 39–102 (attributed to "Honorius Augustodunensis").

William of Hirsau. *Astronomica*. MPL 150, 1639–42.

William of Puylaurens. *Chronique*. Ed. Jean Duvernoy. Sources d'histoire médiévale. Paris, 1976.

William of Saint-Thierry. *De erroribus Guilelmi de Conchis ad sanctum Bernardum*. Ed. Jean Leclercq. In "Les lettres de Guillaume de Saint-Thierry à Saint Bernard." *Revue bénédictine* 79 (1969): 375 (ed. 382)–391.

Secondary Sources

Abel, Armand. "Aspects sociologiques des religions 'manichéennes.'" In *Mélanges René Crozet*, 1:33–46. Poitiers, 1966.

Abélard en son temps: Actes du Colloque . . . IXe centenaire de la naissance de Pierre Abélard. Paris, 1981.

Abels, Richard, and Ellen Harrison. "The Participation of Women in Languedocian Catharism." *Medieval Studies* 41 (1979): 215–51.

Atti del X Congresso internazionale di Scienze Storiche, Roma 1955. Florence, 1957.

Baldwin, John W. "Masters at Paris, 1179–1215." In *Renaissance and Renewal*, ed. Benson and Constable, 138–72. (See below.)

Bautier, Robert-Henri. "Les foires de Champagne." In *La Foire*, Recueils de la Société J. Bodin, 5:97–147. Brussels, 1953.

———. "L'hérésie d'Orléans et le mouvement intellectuel au début du XIe siècle." In *Actes du 95e Congrès national des sociétés savantes, Reims 1970*. Sect. philol. et hist., I:63–88. Paris, 1975.

Belperron, Pierre. *La croisade contre des Albigeois et l'union du Languedoc à la France*. Paris, 1942 and 1946. Rpt. with amended pagination and no index, Paris, 1967.

Benson, Robert L., and Giles Constable, eds. (with C. D. Lanham). *Renaissance and Renewal in the Twelfth Century*. Oxford, 1982.

Benton, John F. "Philology's Search for Abelard in the *Metamorphosis Goliae*." *Speculum* 50 (1975): 199–217.

Blöcker, Monica. "Zur Häresie im 11. Jahrhundert." *Zeitschrift für Schweizerische Kirchengeschichte* 73 (1979): 193–234.

Bonenfant, Paul. "L'épisode de la nef des tisserands de 1135." In *Études sur l'histoire du Pays mosan au Moyen Âge: Mélanges Félix Rousseau*, 99–109. Brussels, 1958.

————. "Un clerc cathare en Lotharingie au milieu du XIIe siècle." *Le Moyen Âge* 69 (1963): 271–80.

Borst, Arno. *Barbaren, Ketzer und Artisten.* Munich and Zurich, 1988.

————. *Die Katharer.* Schriften der MGH, 12. Stuttgart, 1953.

————. *Medieval Worlds: Barbarians, Heretics, and Artists in the Middle Ages.* Trans. Eric Hansen. Chicago, 1992.

Burnett, Charles. "Hermann of Carinthia." In *A History of Twelfth-Century Western Philosophy,* ed. Dronke, 386–404. (See below.)

————. "Scientific Speculations." In *A History of Twelfth-Century Western Philosophy,* ed. Dronke, 151–76. (See below.)

Cassirer, Ernst. *Philosophie der symbolischen Formen.* Vol. 2, *Das mythische Denken.* Oxford, 1954; Darmstadt, 1977.

————. *The Philosophy of Symbolic Forms.* Vol. 2, *Mythical Thought.* Trans. Ralph Manheim. New Haven, 1955.

Châtillon, Jean. "La Bible dans les écoles du XIIe siècle." In *Le Moyen Âge et la Bible,* ed. Riché and Lobrichon, 163–97. (See below.)

Chenu, Marie-Dominique. "La décadence de l'allégorisation." In *L'homme devant Dieu: Mélanges H. de Lubac,* Théologie, 57, 2:129–35. Paris, 1964.

————. *La théologie au douzième siècle.* Études de philosophie médiévale, 45, 1957; 3d ed., Paris, 1976.

————. "L'homme et la nature." *Archives d'histoire doctrinale et littéraire du Moyen Âge* 19 (1952): 39–66.

————. *Nature, Man, and Society in the Twelfth Century.* Trans. J. Taylor and L. Little. Chicago, 1968.

Classen, Peter. *Ausgewählte Aufsätze.* Vorträge und Forschungen, 28. Sigmaringen, 1983.

————. "Der Häresie-Begriff bei Gerhoch von Reichersberg und in seinem Umkreis." In *The Concept of Heresy,* ed. Lourdaux and Verhelst, 27–41. (See below.) Rpt. in *Ausgewählte Aufsätze,* 461–73. (See above.)

————. "Die hohen Schulen und die Gesellschaft im 12. Jahrhundert." In *Studium und Gesellschaft im Mittelalter,* Schriften der MGH, 29:1–26. Stuttgart, 1983.

————. *Gerhoch von Reichersberg.* Wiesbaden, 1960.

————. "Zur Geschichte der Frühscholastik in Österreich und Bayern." In *Ausgewählte Aufsätze,* 279–306. (See above.)

d'Alverny, Marie-Thérèse. "Abélard et l'astrologie." In *Pierre Abélard, Pierre le Vénérable,* 611–28. (See below.)

————. *Alain de Lille.* Études de philosophie médiévale, 52. Paris, 1965.

————. "Alain de Lille et la *Theologia.*" In *L'homme devant Dieu: Mélanges H. de Lubac,* Théologie, 57, 2:111–28. Paris, 1964.

————. "Un fragment du procès des Amauriciens." *Archives d'histoire doctrinale et littéraire du Moyen Âge* 18 (1950/51): 325–36.

de Ghellinck, Joseph. *Le mouvement théologique du XIIe siècle.* Bruges, Brussels, and Paris, 1948.

Delaruelle, Etienne. *La piété populaire au Moyen Âge.* Turin, 1975.

Delhaye, Philippe. *Enseignement et morale au XIIe siècle.* Vestigia, 1. Fribourg and Paris, 1988.

―――. "*Grammatica et Ethica* au douzième siècle." In *Enseignement*, 83–134. (See above.)

―――. "L'organisation scolaire au XIIe siècle." *Traditio* 5 (1967): 211–68. Rpt. in *Enseignement*, 1–58. (See above.)

de Lubac, Henri. *Exegèse médiévale*. 4 vols. Études . . . Lyon-Fourvière, Théologie, 41, 42, 59. Paris, 1959–64.

Dondaine, Antoine. "L'origine de l'hérésie médiévale." *Rivista di storia della Chiesa in Italia* 6 (1952): 47–78.

Dronke, Peter. Introduction to *A History of Twelfth-Century Western Philosophy*, ed. Dronke, 1–18. (See below.)

―――. "New Approaches to the School of Chartres." *Anuario de Estudios Medievales* 6 (1969): 117–40.

―――. "Thierry of Chartres." In *A History of Twelfth-Century Western Philosophy*, ed. Dronke, 358–85. (See below.)

―――, ed. *A History of Twelfth-Century Western Philosophy*. Cambridge, 1988.

Duby, Georges. *The Knight, the Lady, and the Priest*. Trans. Barbara Bray. New York, 1983.

―――. *Le chevalier, la femme et le prêtre*. Paris, 1981.

―――. *Les trois ordres ou l'imaginaire du féodalisme*. Paris, 1978.

―――. *The Three Orders: Feudal Society Imagined*. Trans. Arthur Goldhammer. Chicago, 1980.

Duvernoy, Jean. "L'acception de *haereticus* (*iretge*) = 'parfait cathare' en Languedoc au XIIIe siècle." In *The Concept of Heresy*, ed. Lourdaux and Verhelst, 198–210. (See below.)

―――. *La religion des Cathares*. Vol. 1 of *La catharisme*. Toulouse, 1976, 1979, and 1989.

―――. *L'histoire des Cathares*. Vol. 2 of *La catharisme*. Toulouse, 1979 and 1989.

Economou, George D. *The Goddess Natura in Medieval Literature*. Cambridge, Mass., 1972.

Ehlers, Joachim. "Deutsche Scholaren in Frankreich während des 12. Jahrhunderts." In *Schulen und Studium*, ed. Fried, 97–120. (See below.)

―――. "Monastische Theologie, historischer Sinn und Dialektik." In *Antiqui und Moderni*, ed. A. Zimmermann, Miscellanea mediaevalia, 9:58–79. Berlin and New York, 1974.

Erdmann, Carl. "Gregor VII. und Berengar von Tours." *Quellen und Forschungen aus italienischen Archiven und Bibliotheken* 28 (1937/38): 48–74.

Eriugena Redivivus. Abhandlungen der Heidelberger Akademie der Wissenschaften, philosophische-historische Klasse, 1987. 1. Abhandlung.

Evans, Gillian Rosemary. *Old Arts and New Theology*. Oxford, 1980.

Fearns, James. "Peter von Bruis und die religiöse Bewegung des 12. Jahrhunderts." *Archiv für Kulturgeschichte* 48 (1966): 311–35.

―――, ed. *Ketzer und Ketzerbekämpfung*. (See Primary Sources above.)

Ferruolo, Stephen C. *The Origins of the University*. Stanford, 1985.

Fichtenau, Heinrich. *Beiträge zur Mediävistik*. Vols. 1 and 3. Stuttgart, 1975 and 1986.

———. "Die Ketzer von Orléans (1022)." In *Ex ipsis rerum documentis: Festschrift Harald Zimmermann*, 417–27. Sigmaringen, 1991.

———. *Lebensordnungen des 10. Jahrhunderts*. Monographien zur Geschichte des Mittelalters, 30/I and 30/II. Stuttgart, 1984.

———. *Living in the Tenth Century: Mentalities and Social Orders*. Trans. Patrick J. Geary. Chicago, 1991.

———. "Magister Petrus von Wien." In *Beiträge zur Mediävistik*, 1:218–38. (See above.)

———. "Zur Erforschung der Häresien Italiens des 11. und 12. Jahrhunderts." *Römische Historische Mitteilungen* 31 (1989): 75–91.

———. "Zur Geschichte der Häresien Italiens im 11. Jahrhundert." In *Società, Istituzioni, Spiritualità nell'Europa medioevale: Studi in onore di Cinzio Violante*, 1:331–43. Spoleto, 1994.

Fried, Johannes, ed. *Schulen und Studium im sozialen Wandel des hohen und späten Mittelalters*. Vorträge und Forschungen, 30. Sigmaringen, 1986.

Fuhrmann, M., ed. *Terror und Spiel: Probleme der Mythenrezeption*. Poetik und Hermeneutik, 4. Munich, 1971.

Gammersbach, Suitbert. *Gilbert von Poitiers und seine Prozesse im Urteil der Zeitgenossen*. Neue Münstersche Beiträge zur Geschichtsforschung, 5. Cologne, 1959.

Garin, Eugenio. *Studi sul platonismo medievale*. Florence, 1958.

Gersh, Stephen. "Platonism—Neoplatonism—Aristotelianism." In *Renaissance and Renewal*, ed. Benson and Constable, 512–34. (See above.)

Gibson, Margaret. *Lanfranc of Bec*. Oxford, 1978.

Glorieux, Palémon. "Mauvaise action et mauvais travail." *Recherches de théologie ancienne et médiévale* 21 (1954): 179–93.

Gorre, Renate. *Die Ketzer im 11. Jahrhundert*. Ph.D. diss., Constance, 1981.

Grabmann, Martin. "Die Entwicklung der mittelalterlichen Sprachlogik." In *Mittelalterliches Geistesleben*, 1:104–46. Munich, 1926.

———. *Geschichte der scholastischen Methode*. 2 vols. Freiburg, 1909, 1911; Graz, 1953.

Gregory, Tullio. *Anima Mundi*. Pubblicazioni dell'Istituto di Filosofia dell'Università di Roma, 3. Florence, 1955.

———. "L'idea di natura prima dell'ingresso della fisica di Aristotele." In *La filosofia della natura*, 27–65. (See below.)

———. "The Platonic Inheritance." In *A History of Twelfth-Century Western Philosophy*, ed. Dronke, 54–80. (See above.)

———. *Platonismo medievale*. Istituto Storico Italiano per il Medio Evo, Studi storici 26/27. Rome, 1958.

Grundmann, Herbert. *Ausgewählte Aufsätze*. Schriften der MGH, 25. 3 vols. Stuttgart, 1976, 1977, and 1978.

———. *Ketzergeschichte des Mittelalters*. Die Kirche in ihrer Geschichte, II, G 1. Göttingen, 1963, 1967, and 1978.

———. *Religiöse Bewegungen im Mittelalter*. Historische Studien, 267. Berlin, 1935; Darmstadt, 1961 and 1970.

——. *Religious Movements in the Middle Ages.* Trans. Steven Rowan. Notre Dame, Ind., 1995.

Hamilton, Bernard. "The Cathar Council of Saint-Félix Reconsidered." In *Monastic Reform*, 9:23–53. (See below.)

——. *Monastic Reform, Catharism, and the Crusades.* Reprints. London, 1979.

——. "The Origins of the Dualist Church of Drugunthia." In *Monastic Reform*, 7:115–24. (See above.)

Haren, Michael. *Medieval Thought.* New Studies in Medieval History. London, 1985.

Haring (Häring, Haering), Nikolaus M. "Alan of Lille *De planctu Naturae.*" (See Alan of Lille in Primary Sources above.)

——. "The Case of Gilbert de la Porrée, Bishop of Poitiers (1142–1154)." *Medieval Studies* 13 (1951): 1–40.

——. "The Cistercian Everard of Ypres and His Appraisal of the Conflict Between St. Bernard and Gilbert of Poitiers." *Medieval Studies* 17 (1955): 143–72.

——. "Commentary and Hermeneutics." In *Renaissance and Renewal*, ed. Benson and Constable, 173–200. (See above.)

——. "Die Erschaffung der Welt und ihr Schöpfer nach Thierry von Chartres und Clarenbaldus von Arras." In *Platonismus in der Philosophie des Mittelalters*, 161–267. Darmstadt, 1969. (Rev. of "The Creation and Creator of the World According to Thierry of Chartres and Clarenbald of Arras." *Archives d'histoire doctrinale et littéraire du Moyen Âge* 22 [1955]: 137–216.)

——. "Die vierzehn capitula heresum." (See *Capitula heresum Petri Abaelardi* in Primary Sources above.)

——. "Hugh of Honau and the *Liber de ignorantia.*" (See Hugh of Honau in Primary Sources above.)

——. "A Latin Dialogue on the Doctrine of Gilbert of Poitiers." (See Everard of Ypres in Primary Sources above.)

——. "The *Liber de Diversitate Naturae et Personae* by Hugh of Honau." (See Hugh of Honau in Primary Sources above.)

——. "Saint Bernard and the 'Litterati' of His Day." *Cîteaux, Commentarii Cistercienses* 3 (1974): 199–222.

——. "Thierry of Chartres and Dominicus Gundissalinus." *Medieval Studies* 26 (1964): 271–86.

——. "A Treatise on the Trinity by Gilbert of Poitiers." *Recherches de théologie ancienne et médiévale* 39 (1972): 14 (ed. 34)–50.

——. "Two Commentaries on Boethius (*De Trinitate et De Hebdomadibus*), by Thierry of Chartres." *Archives d'histoire doctrinale et littéraire du Moyen Âge* 27 (1960): 65–136.

——. "The Writings Against Gilbert of Poitiers." (See Geoffrey of Auxerre in Primary Sources above.)

——, ed. *Die Zwettler Summe.* (See *Summa Zwetlensis* in Primary Sources above.)

Hartmann, Wilfried. "Manegold von Lautenbach und die Anfänge der Frühscholastik." *Deutsches Archiv* 26 (1970): 47–149.

Helbling-Gloor, Barbara. *Natur und Aberglaube im "Policraticus" des Johannes von Salisbury.* Ph.D. diss., Zurich. Einsiedeln, 1956.

Hérésies et sociétés dans l'Europe pré-industrielle, 11e–18e siècles. Civilisations et sociétés, 10. Paris and The Hague, 1968.

Herkenrath, Rainer Maria. "Studien zum Magistertitel in der frühen Stauferzeit." *Mitteilungen des Instituts für österreichische Geschichtsforschung* 88 (1980): 3–35.

Huygens, R.B.C. "Bérenger de Tours, Lanfranc et Bernold de Constance." *Sacris erudiri* 16 (1965): 355–403.

Ilarino da Milano. "Le eresie popolari del secolo XI nell'Europa occidentale." *Studi Gregoriani* 2 (1947): 43–88.

———. *L'eresia di Ugo Speroni nella confutazione del Maestro Vacario.* Studi e testi, 115. Vatican City, 1945.

Jacobi, Klaus. "Logic (II): The Later Twelfth Century." In *A History of Twelfth-Century Western Philosophy,* ed. Dronke, 227–51. (See above.)

Jeauneau, Edouard. "Nani Gigantum Humeris Insidentes." *Vivarium* 5 (1967): 79–99.

———. "Note sur l'École de Chartres." *Studi medievali,* ser. IIIa., 5/2 (1964): 821–65.

Johanek, Peter. "Klosterstudien im 12. Jahrhundert." In *Schulen und Studium,* ed. Fried, 35–68. (See above.)

Jolivet, Jean. *Abélard ou la philosophie dans le langage.* Philosophes de tous les temps. Paris, 1969.

———. "Doctrines et figures de philosophes chez Abélard." In *Petrus Abaelardus,* ed. Thomas and Jolivet, 103–20. (See below.)

Koch, Gottfried. *Frauenfrage und Ketzertum im Mittelalter.* Forschungen zur mittelalterlichen Geschichte, 9. Berlin, 1962.

Köhn, Rolf. "Schulbildung und Trivium im lateinischen Hochmittelalter und ihr möglicher praktischer Nutzen." In *Schulen und Studium,* ed. Fried, 203–84. (See above.)

Kolmer, Lothar. "Abaelard und Bernhard von Clairvaux in Sens." *Zeitschrift für Rechtsgeschichte, Kanonistische Abteilung* 67 (1981): 121–47.

Kurdzialek, Marian. "David von Dinant als Ausleger der Aristotelischen Naturphilosophie." In *Auseinandersetzungen an der Pariser Universität im 13. Jahrhundert,* ed. A. Zimmermann, Miscellanea Mediaevalia, 10:181–92. Berlin and New York, 1976.

Kusch, Horst. "Studien über Augustinus." In *Festschrift F. Dornseiff,* 124–200. Leipzig, 1953.

Ladner, Gerhart B. *The Idea of Reform.* Cambridge, Mass., 1959.

———. "Terms and Ideas of Renewal." In *Renaissance and Renewal,* ed. Benson and Constable, 1–33. (See above.)

———. *Theologie und Politik vor dem Investiturstreit.* Veröffentlichungen des österreichischen Instituts für Geschichtsforschung, 2. Baden bei Wien, 1936; Darmstadt, 1968.

La filosofia della natura nel medioevo: Atti del III Congresso . . . Mendola, 1964. Milan, 1966.

Lambert, Malcolm D. *Medieval Heresy*. London, 1977; rev. 2d ed., Oxford, 1992.

Landgraf, Artur Michael. *Dogmengeschichte der Frühscholastik*. Pt. 2, 2 vols. Regensburg, 1953 and 1954.

———. *Einführung in die Geschichte der theologischen Literatur der Frühscholastik unter dem Gesichtspunkt der Schulenbildung*. Regensburg, 1948.

Leclercq, Jean. *L'amour des lettres et le désir de Dieu*. Paris, 1957.

———. "Les lettres de Guillaume de Saint-Thierry à Saint Bernard." (See William of Saint-Thierry in Primary Sources above.)

———. "L'hérésie d'après les écrits de S. Bernard de Clairvaux." In *The Concept of Heresy*, ed. Lourdaux and Verhelst, 12–26. (See below.)

———. *The Love of Learning and the Desire for God*. Trans. Catharine Misrahi. New York, 1961; 3d ed., 1991.

Le Roy Ladurie, Emmanuel. *Montaillou: The Promised Land of Error*. Rev. trans. Barbara Bray. New York, 1978.

———. *Montaillou, village occitan, de 1294 à 1324*. Paris, 1975.

Lesne, Emile. *Histoire de la propriété ecclésiastique en France*. Vol. 5. Lille, 1940.

Liebeschütz, Hans. *Das allegorische Weltbild der hl. Hildegard von Bingen*. Studien der Bibliothek Warburg, 16. Leipzig, 1930; Darmstadt, 1964.

Lobrichon, Guy. "Le clair-obscur de l'hérésie au début du XIe siècle en Aquitaine: Une lettre d'Auxerre." In *Historical Reflections/Réflexions historiques*, 14:423–44. Waterloo, Ontario, 1987.

Loos, Milan. *Dualist Heresy in the Middle Ages*. Prague, 1974.

———. "Satan als Erstgeborener Gottes." *Byzantino-Bulgarica* 3 (1969): 23–35.

Lourdaux, W., and D. Verhelst, eds. *The Concept of Heresy in the Middle Ages (11th–13th Centuries): Proceedings of the International Conference Louvain, 1973*. Mediaevalia Lovaniensia ser. I, studia 4. Louvain and The Hague, 1976.

Lucentini, Paolo. "L'eresia di Amalrico." In *Eriugena Redivivus*, 174–91. (See above.)

Luscombe, David Edward. "Nature in the Thought of Peter Abelard." In *La filosofia della natura*, 314–19. (See above.)

———. "Peter Abelard." In *A History of Twelfth-Century Western Philosophy*, ed. Dronke, 279–307. (See above.)

———. *The School of Peter Abelard*. Cambridge Studies in Medieval Life and Thought, 14. Cambridge, 1969.

Maccagnolo, Enzo. "David of Dinant and the Beginnings of Aristotelianism in Paris." In *A History of Twelfth-Century Western Philosophy*, ed. Dronke, 429–42. (See above.)

Makdisi, George. "The Scholastic Method in Medieval Education." *Speculum* 49 (1974): 640–61.

Maleczek, Werner. "Das Papsttum und die Anfänge der Universität im Mittelalter." *Römische Historische Mitteilungen* 27 (1985): 85–143.

Manitius, Max. *Geschichte der lateinischen Literatur des Mittelalters*. Vol. 3. Handbuch der Altertumswissenschaft IX/2/3. Munich, 1931.

Manselli, Raoul. "Ecberto di Schönau e l'eresia catara in Germania alla metà del secolo XII." In *Arte e Storia, Studi L. Vincenti*, 311–38. Turin, 1965. Rpt. in *Il secolo XII*, 227–50. (See below.)

———. "Il monaco Enrico e la sua eresia." *Bullettino dell'Istituto Storico Italiano* 65 (1953): 1–63. Rev. in *Studi sulle eresie del secolo XII*, 45–67. (See below.) Rpt. in *Il secolo XII*, 101–18. (See below.)

———. *Il secolo XII*. Rome, 1983.

———. "I Passagini." *Bullettino dell'Istituto Storico Italiano* 75 (1963): 189–210. Rpt. in *Il secolo XII*, 295–310. (See above.)

———. *L'eresia del male*. Collana di storia . . . , 1. Naples, 1963 and 1980.

———. "Per la storia dell'eresia nel secolo XII." *Bullettino dell'Istituto Storico Italiano per il Medio Evo e Archivo Muratoriano* 67 (1955): 189–264.

———. *Studi sulle eresie del secolo XII*. Istituto Storico Italiano per il Medio Evo, Studi storici, 5. Rome, 1953.

Marenbon, John. "Gilbert of Poitiers." In *A History of Twelfth-Century Western Philosophy*, ed. Dronke, 328–51. (See above.)

Meersseman, Gilles Gerard. "Teologia monastica e riforma ecclesiastica da Leone IX a Callisto II." In *Il monachesimo e la Riforma ecclesiastica: Atti della quarta settimana . . . Mendola . . . 1968*, Pubblicazioni dell'Università cattolica, 256–70. Milan, 1971.

Meersseman, Gilles Gerard, and E. Adda. "Pénitents ruraux communautaires en Italie au XIIe siècle." *Revue d'histoire ecclésiastique* 49 (1954): 343–90.

Merlo, Grado G. *Eretici ed eresie medievali*. Bologna, 1989.

Mews, Constant J. "The Lists of Heresies Imputed to Peter Abelard." *Revue bénédictine* 95 (1985): 73–110.

Miethke, Jürgen. "Theologieprozesse in der ersten Phase ihrer institutionellen Ausbildung: Die Verfahren gegen Peter Abaelard und Gilbert von Poitiers." *Viator* 6 (1975): 87–116.

Montclos, Jean de. *Lanfranc et Bérenger. Études et documents*, 37. Spicilegium sacrum Lovaniense. Louvain, 1971.

Moore, Robert J. *The Origins of European Dissent*. London, 1977; Oxford and New York, 1985.

———. "The Origins of Medieval Heresy." *History* 55 (1970): 21–36.

Moos, Peter von. "Literatur- und bildungsgeschichtliche Aspekte der Dialogform im lateinischen Mittelalter." In *Tradition und Wertung, Festschrift F. Brunhölzl*, 165–209. Sigmaringen, 1989.

Morghen, Raffaello. "Il cosidetto neomanicheismo occidentale del secolo XI." In *Oriente e occidente*, 84–160. (See below.)

———. "L'eresia nel medioevo." In *Medioevo cristiano*, 212–86. Bari, 1951, 1962, and 1968.

———. "Movimenti religiosi popolari nel periodo della Riforma della Chiesa." In *X Congresso internazionale di Scienze Storiche, Roma 1955*, Relazioni, 3:333–56. Florence, n.d.

Morris, Colin. *The Discovery of the Individual, 1050–1200*. Toronto, 1972 and 1987.

Mundy, John Hine. *Liberty and Political Power in Toulouse, 1050–1230*. New York, 1954.

————. *Men and Women at Toulouse in the Age of the Cathars*. Studies and Texts, 101. Toronto, 1990.

Murray, Alexander. *Reason and Society in the Middle Ages*. Oxford, 1978 and 1985.

Murray, Alexander Victor. *Abelard and St. Bernard*. Manchester and New York, 1967.

Musy, Jean. "Mouvements populaires et hérésies au XIe siècle en France." *Revue historique* 99, no. 253 (1975): 33–76.

Nebbiai-Dalla Guarda, Donatella. "Les listes médiévales de lecture monastiques." *Revue bénédictine* 96 (1986): 271–326.

Noiroux, Jeanne-Marie. "Les deux premiers documents concernant l'hérésie aux Pays-Bas." *Revue d'histoire ecclésiastique* 49 (1954): 842–55.

Obolensky, Dmitri. *The Bogomils*. Cambridge, 1948.

O'Donnell, J. Reginald. "The Sources and Meaning of Bernard Silvester's Commentary on the *Aeneid*." *Medieval Studies* 24 (1962): 233–49.

Ohly, Friedrich. *Hohelied-Studien*. Schriften der wissenschaftlichen Gesellschaft an der J. W. Goethe-Universität Frankfurt, Geisteswissenschaftliche Reihe, no. 1. Wiesbaden, 1958.

Oriente e occidente nel medio evo. Accademia Nazionale dei Lincei, XII convegno Volta. Rome, 1957.

Patschovsky, Alexander. "Der Ketzer als Teufelsdiener." In *Papsttum, Kirche und Recht: Festschrift Horst Fuhrmann*, 317–34. Tübingen, 1991.

Pierre Abélard, Pierre le Vénérable. Colloques internationaux du Centre National de la recherche scientifique, 546. Paris, 1975.

Pinborg, Jan. *Logik und Semantik im Mittelalter*. Problemata, 10. Stuttgart, 1972.

Poly, Jean-Pierre, and Eric Bournazel. *The Feudal Transformation: 900–1200*. Trans. Caroline Higgit. New York, 1991.

————. *La mutation féodale, Xe–XIIe siècles*. Nouvelle Clio, 16. Paris, 1980.

Puech, Henri-Charles. "Catharisme médiéval et Bogomilisme." In *Oriente e occidente*, 56–84. (See above.)

————. *Le manichéisme*. Musée Guimet, Bibliothèque de diffusion, 56. Paris, 1949 and 1967.

Puech, Henri-Charles, and André Vaillant, eds. *Le traité contre les Bogomiles de Cosmas de Prêtre*. (See Cosmas the Priest in Primary Sources above.)

Reiners, Joseph. *Der Nominalismus in der Frühscholastik*. Beiträge zur Geschichte der Philosophie des Mittelalters, VIII/5. Münster, 1910.

Riché, Pierre, and Guy Lobrichon, eds. *Le Moyen Âge et la Bible*. Bible de tous les temps, 4. Paris, 1984.

Rottenwöhrer, Gerhard. *Der Katharismus*. 4 vols. Honnef, 1982, 1990, and 1993.

Ruh, Kurt. *Geschichte der abendländischen Mystik*. Vol. 1. Munich, 1990.

Runciman, Steven. *The Medieval Manichee*. Cambridge, 1947 and 1955.

Russell, Jeffrey Burton. *Dissent and Reform in the Early Middle Ages*. Berkeley and Los Angeles, 1965.

————. "Interpretations of the Origins of Medieval Heresy." *Medieval Studies* 25 (1963): 26–53.

Šanjek, Franjo. "Le rassemblement hérétique de Saint-Félix-de-Caraman (1167) et les Églises cathares au XIIe siècle." *Revue d'histoire ecclésiastique* 67 (1972): 767–99.

Schipperges, Heinrich. *Das Menschenbild Hildegards von Bingen.* Erfurter theologische Schriften, 5. Leipzig, 1962.

Schmitz-Valckenberg, Georg. *Grundlehren der katharischen Sekten des 13. Jahrhunderts.* Münchener Universitätsschriften, 11. Munich, 1971.

Segl, Peter. *Ketzer in Österreich.* Quellen und Forschungen aus dem Gebiet der Geschichte, n.s., 5. Paderborn, 1984.

Selge, Kurt-Victor. *Die ersten Waldenser.* Arbeiten zur Kirchengeschichte, 37. 2 vols. Berlin, 1967.

Silverstein, Theodore. "The Fabulous Cosmogony of Bernardus Silvestris." *Modern Philology* 46 (1948): 92–116.

Söderberg, Hans. *La religion des Cathares: Études sur le gnosticisme de la basse antiquité et du Moyen Âge.* Ph.D. thesis, Uppsala, 1949.

Southern, Richard W. "The Schools of Paris and the School of Chartres." In *Renaissance and Renewal,* ed. Benson and Constable, 113–37. (See above.)

———. *Saint Anselm and His Biographer.* Birkbeck Lectures, 1959. Cambridge, 1963.

Stelzer, Winfried. *Gelehrtes Recht in Österreich.* Mitteilungen des Instituts für österreichische Geschichtsforschung, suppl. vol. 26. 1982.

Stiefel, Tina. *The Intellectual Revolution in Twelfth-Century Europe.* London and Sydney, 1985.

Stock, Brian. *The Implications of Literacy.* Princeton, 1983.

———. *Myth and Science in the Twelfth Century.* Princeton, 1972.

Taviani, Huguette. "Le mariage dans l'hérésie de l'an mil." *Annales ESC* 32 (1977): 1074–89.

———. "Naissance d'une hérésie en Italie du Nord au XIe siècle." *Annales ESC* 29 (1974): 1224–52.

Thomas, R., and Jean Jolivet, eds. *Petrus Abaelardus.* Trierer theologische Studien, 38. Trier, 1980.

Thouzellier, Christine. *Catharisme et Valdéisme en Languedoc à la fin du XIIe siècle.* Louvain and Paris, 1966, 1969, and 1982.

Tweedale, Martin M. *Abailard on Universals.* Amsterdam, 1976.

———. "Logic (I): From the Late Eleventh Century to the Time of Abelard." In *A History of Twelfth-Century Western Philosophy,* ed. Dronke, 196–226. (See above.)

Vaillant, André. (See Cosmas the Priest in Primary Sources above.)

Vauchez, André. "Diables et hérétiques." In *Santi e demoni, Settimane . . .* Spoleto, 36, 1988, 2:573–607. Spoleto, 1989.

Verbeke, Gerard. "Philosophy and Heresy." In *The Concept of Heresy,* ed. Lourdaux and Verhelst, 172–97. (See above.)

Violante, Cinzio. "La povertà nelle eresie del secolo XI in occidente." In *Studi,* 69–107. (See below.)

———. *La società milanese nell'età precomunale.* Bari, 1953 and 1974.

———. *Studi sulla cristianità medioevale.* Cultura e storia, 8. Milan, 1972.

Ward, John O. "The Date of the Commentary on Cicero's *De Inventione* by Thierry of Chartres and the Cornifician Attack on the Liberal Arts." *Viator* 3 (1972): 219–73.

Werner, Ernst, and Martin Erbstösser. *Ketzer und Heilige.* Vienna, Cologne, and Graz, 1986.

Werner, Karl Ferdinand. *Vom Frankenreich zur Entfaltung Deutschlands und Frankreichs.* Sigmaringen, 1984.

Wetherbee, Winthrop. "Philosophy, Cosmology, and the Twelfth-Century Renaissance." In *A History of Twelfth-Century Western Philosophy,* ed. Dronke, 21–53. (See above.)

Widmer, Berthe. "Thierry von Chartres, ein Gelehrtenschicksal des 12. Jahrhunderts." *Historische Zeitschrift* 200 (1965): 552–71.

Wolff, Philippe. *Histoire de Toulouse.* Toulouse, 1958.

Index